Readings in American
Political History

Readings in American Political History

A Modern Reader

edited by Frank Otto Gatell, Paul Goodman, and Allen Weinstein

New York · OXFORD UNIVERSITY PRESS
London 1972 *Toronto*

Contents

Introduction   viii

1 The Power of Colonial Assemblies
   *The Role of the Lower Houses of Assembly in
   Eighteenth-Century Politics*
      JACK P. GREENE   3

2 Foundations of the American Republic
   The American Science of Politics
      GORDON S. WOOD   29

3 The Emergence of Political Parties
   The First American Party System
      PAUL GOODMAN   55

4 The New Politics and Political Innovation
   Changing Concepts of Party in the United States
      MICHAEL WALLACE   82

5 Nationalizing the Presidential Vote
   New Perspectives on Jacksonian Politics
      RICHARD P. MCCORMICK   104

6 Rich Men and Politics
   Money and Party in Jacksonian America
      FRANK OTTO GATELL   122

7 The Politics of Compromise
   *Democratic Senate Leadership and the
   Compromise of 1850*
      HOLMAN HAMILTON   141

8 Free Labor and Slavery in Republican Ideology
   Free Soil, Free Labor, Free Men
      ERIC FONER   158

9 The Uses of Politics
   *Party Politics and the Union and Confederate
   War Efforts*
      ERIC L. MCKITRICK   182

10 Reconstruction: A National View
    Negro Suffrage and Republican Politics
       LAWANDA AND JOHN H. COX   203

11 Reconstruction, a Local View
    The South Carolina Politicos
       JOEL WILLIAMSON   234

12 The Business of Politics
    National Party Structure in the Gilded Age
       ROBERT D. MARCUS   260

13 Voters and Their Roots
    The Politics of Rejection
       PAUL KLEPPNER   277

14 Progressives and the Issues
    Social Tensions and the Origins of Progressivism
       DAVID P. THELEN   303

15 A Giant Step Backward
    The Negro and Disfranchisement
       SHELDON HACKNEY   324

16 The Urban Thrust
    American Political Parties and the Rise of the City
       CARL N. DEGLER   346

Contents

17 WASP America's Pyrrhic Victory
Folklore of the Campaign of 1928
PAUL A. CARTER   368

18 FDR In the Saddle
The Roosevelt Reconstruction
WILLIAM E. LEUCHTENBURG   383

19 From FDR to Truman
Congress and the Fair Deal
RICHARD E. NEUSTADT   406

20 The Politics of Stasis
A Word on Eisenhower
EMMET JOHN HUGHES   438

21 Reaffirming the Stalemate
Stability and Change in 1960
PHILIP E. CONVERSE ET AL.   463

22 Lonesome Lyndon
*The Wrong Man from the Wrong Place
at the Wrong Time*
ERIC F. GOLDMAN   492

23 Intimations of Mortality
The End of American Party Politics
WALTER DEAN BURNHAM   513

A Selected Modern Bibliography   535

Introduction

Toward a New Political History

The student of politics has traditionally divided his attention between the art of gaining power and the craft of retaining it. Any dictionary definition of the term "politics" will recognize these dual functions: on the one hand, "policies or affairs of a government"; on the other, "the conducting of or engaging in political affairs, often professionally." When examined in tandem, they should provide a thorough understanding both of the way political power operates within a society, and some of its uses. Americans have been far from unique in asking questions of their political history that might help explain their contemporary society. In recent years, however, we have experienced a heightened sense of confusion concerning the directions of present-day America, and this lends special urgency to our desire for additional perspective through an understanding of our political past.

A century ago, even as recently as fifty years ago, United States political history seemed to most Americans (and to the country's historians) a refreshing and epic drama of expanding liberty and declining tyranny. This morality tale, pounded home in countless orations and sermons delivered on the Fourth of July and just about every other day, survived with hardly a phrase altered in the lectures of American history teachers from one-room grade schools to the universities. The United States, the story ran, had been founded in crisis by seventeenth-century North Europeans searching for religious and political freedom, created in revolution by eighteenth-century colonials struggling against imperial despotism, and consecrated in civil war by nineteenth-century

Unionists vindicating the national commitment to freedom by fighting against an aggressive slave power. Even in the nineteenth century, of course, there were dissents from this candy-coated version of political history. American Negroes (*after* Reconstruction), Socialists, utopian reformers, non-English-speaking immigrants, and Indians might be forgiven a dash of pardonable skepticism concerning the universality of America's reputed Mission to extend equally the boundaries of freedom. Nonetheless, for a majority of Americans, the prevailing image of libertarian nationalism, an "empire for liberty," seemed a reasonably adequate approximation of the realities of political life.

Growing doubts concerning the merits of this largely mythical and uncritical view of the American past emerged around 1900 as certain new perspectives began to take shape. Late nineteenth-century science had helped transform the way in which American history, along with other non-scientific disciplines, was studied in the universities. History became a profession, and historians became more exacting in their research techniques and increasingly more critical in their interpretations of the American past. When the historians of the first half of the nineteenth century did their work the American Revolution remained a still-vivid experience for many of their countrymen. Similarly, scholars in the latter half of the nineteenth century, both North and South, wrote under the lengthening and inhibiting shadow of a Civil War mythology. Historians who pioneered in critical assessments of their national past early in the twentieth century lived in a country fresh from easy yet disquieting imperial adventures and, moreover, touched everywhere by the ferment of a new reform wave.

The Progressive Era provided additional impetus, if any were needed, for historians to engage in a critical appraisal of the American past, if only to understand why industrialism and urbanization had brought in their wake so much political corruption, economic exploitation, and social misery. The hallmark of "Progressive history," as it came to be called, was a searching and present-minded view of contending forces within society. The American past seemed no longer the simple tale of freedom's triumph over oppression, but, instead, another simple tale—this one recounting a constant moral struggle of democratic against privileged elements. For Frederick Jackson Turner and others who saw the westward movement as the central interpretive clue to American development, conflicts between an expanding egalitarian frontier and stratified, older regions supplied the unifying theme. Shortly after Turner developed the frontier interpretation, another scholar, Charles A. Beard, presented another theory: he described American political history as a struggle among rival economic interest groups, a view that has remained powerful and influential among historians to this day. In Beard's analysis, class interests rather than sectional ties determined the fundamental lines of political cleavage in American history: farmers opposing merchants, workers opposing factory owners, Southern planters opposing Northern industrialists.

Progressivism had reflected the prevailing anxiety among Americans of most classes over "plutocracy," or unrestrained economic power, the threat posed to a democratic society by unsupervised business enterprise. Beard and his followers discovered similar threats at each stage in American political growth, which they interpreted as a constant struggle between competing economic classes for eontrol of the government. Although these conflicts had sometimes produced positive advances in democratic government, such as the abolition of slavery, suffrage extension, and government regulation of business, Progressive historians still worried over what lay ahead. The past had been a struggle; the future would inevitably be shaped by struggle as well. Whether twentieth-century American democracy could survive such violent clashes in an era of giant cities, conglomerate industries, massive concentrations of economic power, and new techniques for manipulating the public will remained questionable. Largely due to the work of scholars such as Turner and Beard, American political history no longer seemed a providential story of liberty's demanding yet unstoppable triumph over tyranny. If anything, the Progressive historians made the outcome of the imminent struggle appear to be a fifty-fifty proposition.

Before Beard died in 1948, the United States had become engulfed in global conflicts, first with German and Japanese fascism in the early 1940's, and then, since 1945, with Russian and Chinese communism—foreign conflicts which forced serious reappraisals of the American past by political historians.

Increased attention to a comparison of American political history with the experiences of European and Asian nations led a number of younger scholars, in the wake of World War II, to challenge the assumption of Progressive historiography that conflict had been *the* dominant aspect of United States history. Both Beard's stress on class antagonisms and Turner's model of sectional hostility evoked growing, sometimes massive skepticism among historians who saw that, when compared with social struggles in other countries, American disputes appeared milder, less internecine, and more capable of compromise through existing institutional channels. Historians during the 1950's also stressed the comparatively high degree of individual freedom and material prosperity enjoyed in the United States, and for the first time since the turn of the century, most of the major innovative studies of American history bypassed the assumptions and visions of angry reformism.

Many factors helped produce this new burst of historical *un*criticism, or "consensus" history—among them the stress on comparative history, the anxieties over national survival in an atomic age, and the growing body of scholarship which questioned numerous errors or oversimplifications in the work of the early masters such as Beard and Turner. For whatever reasons, the 1950's witnessed the brief heyday of consensus history, a bland yet often eloquent rewriting of American political history that accentuated the positive features while muting the importance of past conflicts.

An abrupt reversal of this "consensus" among American historians accompanied the growing economic, generational, and racial conflicts, in the 1960's. With the increase of social tension during the 1960's came a revival of the reform impulse among younger historians, a neo-Beardianism that owes far more to its originator's historical premises than its practitioners often recognize or care to admit. "New Left" akademicians, stressing class struggles as the determining factor in American political history, have yet to produce their own Beard or even a synthesis

of our past equivalent to his. Yet they have voiced the disen-
chantment of liberal scholars, as well as radicals, with a political
history based on "consensus" assumptions which, all too often,
either whitewashed or neglected the ample record of political op-
presion and social injustice in America.

Yet changes in American historiography do not result simply
from altered climates of opinion, but often proceed from new
methodology and new research within the historical profession
itself. Thus, a procession of historians had scrutinized the Progressive historians' arguments for several decades, beginning long
before World War II, and rejected many of them not because
of changing values but because of conflicting evidence. Historians
were trained and continue to be trained to examine new data and
to question received explanations in an effort to achieve deeper
understanding of the past. Thus, in analyzing frontier society in
specific areas much more systematically than Turner alone was
able to do, several historians discerned a highly stratified or, at
the very least, contradictory social structure rather than the democratic fluidity which Turner theorized. Similarly, recent scholarship has exploded Beard's portrait of Confederation era politics
as a clear-cut struggle between the mass of anti-Federalist farmers against a coalition of merchants, planters, and bondholders
who favored the new frame of government. Later historians,
studying a myriad of local economic and political groupings, ex-
humed a complex set of responses toward the Constitution absent
from Beard's simple economic demonology. Beard's world portrayed a constant procession of clashing economic interests;
Turner's, a welter of contending sectional interests. While not rejecting entirely either view of the American past, contemporary
historians have shown greater interest than their major predecessors in evaluating other keys to American political history. Such
factors as ethnic and religious ties, ideological commitments, and
irrational drives have been isolated as powerful determinants of
American political behavior by historians using a variety of new
techniques borrowed from the social sciences.

Much of this scholarship—"the new political history" as some
of its votaries dub it—cannot be explained merely through the

recovery of vast bodies of data previously untapped by indolent historians, although new historical evidence has indeed proliferated of late. The primary influence behind recent major reinterpretations of American political history lies in the profound impact of the social sciences upon historians over the past several generations. The discipline of history has traditionally straddled the humanities and social sciences, pivoting toward the former in that it sometimes enjoys status as a literary art, yet eyeing enviously the claims for certitude and predictability made by the latter. Having grown restless with this half-caste intellectual classification, a growing number of scholars have struggled to introduce a more precise technical analysis of available data than has previously characterized historical generalizations. The "new political history" has attempted to apply methods of analysis perfected by the various social sciences—political science, psychology, sociology, economics, and anthropology—to the search for a more accurate rendering of America's political past.

Although influenced just as heavily by today's social climate of opinion as were their scholarly, "non-scientific" predecessors of previous eras, much of the best new work in political history at least makes an attempt to counter inevitable present-mindedness by rigorous, and hopefully fair-minded, application of techniques such as the systematic quantification of political data, the analysis of group ideology, and multivariate analysis of political behavior.

In the selections that follow, students will find samples of the older as well as of the new political history, sometimes blended in the same selection. Traditionally, political historians have formulated hypotheses to account for a historical development and then tested their theories against the available evidence through a wide-ranging yet frequently impressionistic and unsystematic examination of relevant data. The impressionistic method, and the intuition upon which it relies so heavily, will always remain among the historian's principal tools, if only because in most cases the data needed to answer with certainty many of the most significant historical questions are lacking, and will remain so.

But quantification, though no panacea, offers a valuable additional method, a precision tool for writing political history. Techniques of quantitative analysis have allowed for more accurate measurement of voting patterns among important groups in American life, both at the national and local levels. They have also allowed inept practitioners, those with a tendency to quantificate, to publish numerical gibberish; but then no methodology, traditional or super-modern, is any better than the people who apply it. Yet quantification permits historians to speculate more securely on the motivations behind group political attitudes and behavior. We can learn more easily, for example, what kinds of people voted for William Jennings Bryan or supported William McKinley in 1896; we can determine which groups were most likely to support the Democrat Andrew Jackson against his Whig opponents in the 1830's; we can guage the composition of the "ethnic vote" in 1860 (or in 1960); or evaluate similar voting behavior at other critical points in the American past.

Recent quantitative analysis of American political behavior has shown, for example, that United States politics cannot be understood solely in terms of economic class categories, although in their time such Beardian explanations represented a considerable advance in American historical writing. Today's historians must take into account equally powerful influences on political behavior, such as race, religion, ethnic background, cultural milieu, and ideology. Those who assume that people invariably vote their pocketbooks will find that a systematic culling of voting data does not always bear out that assumption. Variables other than economic class shape the complex manner in which people perceive and respond to political events. No discussion of the origins of the Civil War that fails to include the pathological elements in Southerners' fears over slavery, or the similarly irrational components in the anxieties of antebellum Northerners, can hope to explain that war's background adequately.

All of which is yet another way of saying that political history is more than the study of past politics. Recognizing the axiom that political behavior cannot be comprehended in isolation from other patterns of human behavior, political history has broadened its range. Such factors as group psychology, racism, ethnicity, economic development, immigration, nativism, and urban-rural

conflicts have all become critically important (indeed, essential),
to the study of American political history in recent years.

The analysis of American politics within broader social and
cultural contexts has alerted historians to the influence of ideology, which is sometimes decisive for political action. The ideas
and values which men believe in and sometimes die for are
rarely accidental, and the forms they assume at any given time
and place reflect the delicate adjustments made by individuals
between their cultural beliefs and group interests. Yet ideas can
become so powerful at critical moments in the history of a society
as almost to assume a life of their own, exerting influences beyond the intellectual vanguard, often few in number, who transmit them. Thus the proto-revolutionaries of the 1760's and the
Republicans of the 1850's both constructed ideologies that helped
prepare their fellow countrymen for the impending realities of
civil conflict. The natural rights doctrines of colonial dissidents
during the Revolutionary era and the Republican party's free
labor ideology nearly a century later both produced consequences
that far exceeded their narrow class or group origins: American
independence in the first instance, and the abolition of slavery in
the second.

The newer political methodology, with its social analysis of
politics and quantification of political behavior, along with the
inconoclastic dismantling of the Progressive synthesis in recent decades, has left American political history in a state of confusion
and disarray. Since World War II revisionist historians, using both
new and traditional analytical techniques, have relentlessly and
persuasively modified traditional views on almost every major
question, often causing them to be discarded altogether. No alternative synthesis has yet emerged, however, to provide a coherent and systematic account of the growth of American politics.
The story itself, an embarrassment of riches, was slighted by Progressive historians, and we are left with the difficulty of assimilat-
ing leads offered by the social sciences. Our bequest is a historical
Tower of Babel that thus far defies synthetic reinterpretation.

Scholars also confront the compounding difficulties of the rapidly changing attitudes within the United States during the past

decade—a growing loss of faith in progress, a profound skepticism over the worth of intellect, a reluctant recognition of the irrational and uncontrollable aspects of human behavior, and a fundamental loss of confidence in America's national destiny—all of which have denied to political historians a firm ground of current and universally accepted beliefs from which they could base a systematic treatment of the past.

In time, if our society can survive its present crises, a new overview of American political growth will emerge. We hope that at least some of the selections represented in this anthology will contribute to that synthesis. Certainly it is too soon to chart the exact contours of this new political history, but it will most likely rest on a more sophisticated understanding of the complexities of individual and social psychology than its predecessors did. It will also probably devote greater attention than did earlier twentieth-century political syntheses to explaining how geographic and vocational mobility, ethno-cultural and religious diversity, racial hostilities, and regional diversity have kept Americans from dividing along clear-cut economic class lines. It may examine in greater depth the manner in which American voters and their politicians have responded to constantly-changing urban and industrial patterns from the mid-nineteenth century to the present, and it may make more effective use of the quantitative method to sharpen our knowledge of how specific groups organize and act politically. The following selections should serve the student as a reliable and stimulating introduction to some of the work already done and to other larger projects yet in progress.

It is fairly safe to predict that no new synthesis can hope either to be accepted or long-lived unless it grapples with the past in all its puzzling complexity. That complexity, and the existing gaps in our knowledge which historians have recently become sensitized to, stand as formidable obstacles in the path of providing a revised, modern interpretation of the growth of American politics. But without such an interpretation, we shall not know where we came from—and in that blissful state of ignorance, we can hardly expect to know where we are headed.

Readings in American
Political History

The Power of Colonial Assemblies

The Role of the Lower Houses of Assembly in Eighteenth-Century Politics

by Jack P. Greene

When American Revolutionaries took their stand against Parliament on the principle of "no taxation without representation," they were defending the authority of colonial legislative bodies, the principal instruments of self-government in America. Jack P. Greene here describes how the Southern assemblies exercised extensive power and became almost sovereign, with the powers, among others, to tax and to appoint local officials.

It had taken generations for these bodies to accumulate the authority that by the eighteenth century made them the most important centers of authority in the colonies. Representative government was not even planned for by the founders of Virginia or Massachusetts. American conditions and the English parliamentary tradition forced concessions in the direction of a more broadly based government. Although early assemblies, designed to act as advisory bodies rather than legislative centers, had limited roles, by the time the colonists challenged the parliamentary right of taxation in the 1760's they insisted that only their own assemblies could tax. The colonial assemblies, argued the British, derived their authority from the king and Parliament, and therefore were subordinate to those higher authorities. For over a century, however,

London had allowed the power of the colonial assemblies to grow. It was easier and cheaper to permit the Americans to govern themselves than to impose on them a complex and expensive bureaucracy.

Taking advantage of the superficiality of royal rule—the absence of a British army in America in peacetime, and the venality of crown officials—colonial politicians steadily eroded the authority of the Crown. Royal officials, especially the governors, learned that if they wanted co-operation from the assemblies they would have to go along with the colonials who controlled them. The British executive, the king, controlled an enormous patronage list, and he could ordinarily count on support from the largest parliamentary bloc, the independent country gentlemen. The colonial governor, on the other hand, had neither adequate patronage nor the prestige and mystique surrounding the throne in England. Moreover, he had no solidly reliable group in the colonial assemblies on whom he could count. Support had be to earned or purchased from the assemblies, and when received it was often at the expense of imperial authority.

The rise of the representative assemblies was perhaps the most significant political and constitutional development in the history of Britain's overseas empire before the American Revolution. Crown and proprietary authorities had obviously intended the governor to be the focal point of colonial government with the lower houses merely subordinate bodies called together when necessary to levy taxes and ratify local ordinances proposed by the executive. Consequently, except in the New England charter colonies, where the representative bodies early assumed a leading role, they were dominated by the governors and councils for most of the period down to 1689. But beginning with the Restoration and intensifying their efforts during the years following the Glorious

From *The Journal of Southern History*, XXVII (November 1961), 451–74. Copyright 1961 by the Southern Historical Association. Reprinted by permission of the Managing Editor; footnotes omitted. (This version has been revised by the author.)

Revolution, the lower houses engaged in a successful quest for power as they set about to restrict the authority of the executive, undermine the system of colonial administration laid down by imperial and proprietary authorities, and make themselves paramount in the affairs of their respective colonies.

Historians have been fascinated by this phenomenon. For nearly a century after 1776 they interpreted it as a prelude to the American Revolution. In the 1780's the pro-British historian George Chalmers saw it as the early manifestation of a latent desire for independence, an undutiful reaction to the mild policies of the Mother Country. In the middle of the nineteenth century the American nationalist George Bancroft, although more interested in other aspects of colonial history, looked upon it as the natural expression of American democratic principles, simply another chapter in the progress of mankind. The reaction to these sweeping interpretations set in during the last decades of the nineteenth century, when Charles M. Andrews, Edward Channing, Herbert L. Osgood, and others began to investigate in detail and to study in context developments from the Restoration to the end of the Seven Years' War. Osgood put a whole squadron of Columbia students to work examining colonial political institutions, and they produced a series of institutional studies in which the evolution of the lower houses was a central feature. These studies clarified the story of legislative development in each colony, but this necessarily piecemeal approach, as well as the excessive fragmentation that characterized the more general narratives of Osgood and Channing, tended to emphasize the differences rather than the similarities in the rise of the lower houses and failed to produce a general analysis of the common features of their quest for power. Among later scholars, Leonard W. Labaree in his excellent monograph *Royal Government in America* presented a comprehensive survey of the institutional development of the lower houses in the royal colonies and of the specific issues involved in their struggles with the royal governors, but he did not offer any systematic interpretation of the general process and pattern of legislative development. Charles Andrews promised to tackle this problem and provide a synthesis in the later volumes of his magnum opus, *The Colonial Period of American History*, but he died before completing that part of the project.

As a result, some fundamental questions have never been fully answered, and no one has produced a comprehensive synthesis. No one has satisfactorily worked out the basic pattern of the quest; analyzed the reasons for and the significance of its development; explored its underlying assumptions and theoretical foundations; or assessed the consequences of the success of the lower houses, particularly the relationship between their rise to power and the coming of the American Revolution. This essay is intended to suggest some tentative conclusions about these problems, not to present ultimate solutions. My basic research on the lower houses has been in the Southern royal colonies and in Nova Scotia. One of the present purposes is to test the generalizations I have arrived at about the Southern colonies by applying them to what scholars have learned of the legislatures in the other colonies. This procedure has the advantage of providing perspective on the story of Southern developments. At the same time, it may serve as one guidepost for a general synthesis in the future.

Any student of the eighteenth-century political process will sooner or later be struck by the fact that, although each of the lower houses developed independently and differently, their stories were similar. The elimination of individual variants, which tend to cancel out each other, discloses certain basic regularities, a clearly discernible pattern—or what the late Sir Lewis Namier called a morphology—common to all of them. They all moved along like paths in their drives for increased authority, and although their success on specific issues differed from colony to colony and the rate of their rise varied from time to time, they all ended up at approximately the same destination. They passed successively through certain vaguely defined phases of political development. Through most of the seventeenth century the lower houses were still in a position of subordination, slowly groping for the power to tax and the right to sit separately from the council and initiate laws. Sometime during the early eighteenth century most of them advanced to a second stage at which they could battle on equal terms with the governors and councils and challenge even the powers in London if necessary. At that point the lower houses began their bid for political supremacy. The violent eruptions that followed usually ended in an accommodation with the governors and councils which paved the way for the ascendancy of the lower houses and saw the virtual eclipse of the colonial executive. By the end of the Seven Years' War, and in some instances considerably earlier, the lower houses had reached the third and final phase of political dominance and were in a position to speak for the colonies in the conflict with the imperial government which ensued after 1763.

By 1763, with the exception of the lower houses in the corporate colonies of Rhode Island and Connecticut, which had virtually complete authority, the Pennsylvania and Massachusetts houses of representatives were probably most powerful. Having succeeded in placing its election on a statutory basis and depriving the Council of direct legislative authority in the Charter of Privileges in 1701, the Pennsylvania House under the astute guidance of David Lloyd secured broad financial and appointive powers during the administrations of Daniel Gookin and Sir William Keith. Building on these foundations, it gained almost complete dominance in the 1730's and 1740's despite the opposition of the governors, whose power and prestige along with that of the Council declined rapidly. The Massachusetts House, having been accorded the unique privilege of sharing in the selection of the Council by the royal charter of 1691, already had a strong tradition of legislative supremacy inherited from a half-century of corporate experience. During the first thirty years under the new charter first the benevolent policies of Sir William Phips and William Stoughton and then wartime conditions during the tenures of Joseph Dudley and Samuel Shute enabled the House, led by Elisha Cooke, Jr., to extend its authority greatly. It emerged from the conflicts over the salary question during the 1720's with firm control over finance, and the Crown's abandonment of its demand for a permanent revenue in the early 1730's paved the way for an accommodation with subsequent governors and the eventual dominance of the House under Governor William Shirley after 1740.

The South Carolina Commons and New York House of Assembly were only slightly less powerful. Beginning in the first decade of the eighteenth century, the South Carolina lower house gradually assumed an ironclad control over all aspects of South Carolina government, extending its supervision to the minutest details of local administration after 1730 as a succession of governors, including Francis Nicholson, Robert Johnson, Thomas Broughton, the elder William Bull, and James Glen offered little determined opposition. The Commons continued to grow in stature after 1750 while the Council's standing declined because of the Crown policy of filling it with placemen from England and the Common's successful attacks upon its authority. The New York House of Assembly began to demand greater authority in reaction to the mismanagement of Edward Hyde, Viscount Cornbury, during the first decade of the eighteenth century. Governor Robert Hunter met the challenge squarely during his ten-year administration beginning in 1710, but he and his successors could not check the rising power of the House. During the seven-year tenure of George Clarke beginning in 1736, the House advanced into the final stage of development. Following Clarke, George Clinton made a vigorous effort to reassert the authority of the executive, but neither he nor any of his successors was able to challenge the power of the House.

The lower houses of North Carolina, New Jersey, and Virginia developed more slowly. The North Carolina lower house was fully capable of protecting its powers and privileges and competing on equal terms with the executive during the last years of proprietary rule and under the early royal governors, George Burrington and Gabriel Johnston. But it was not until Arthur Dobbs's tenure in the 1750's and 1760's that, meeting more regularly, it assumed the upper hand in North Carolina politics under the astute guid-

ance of Speaker Samuel Swann and treasurers John Starkey and
Thomas Barker. In New Jersey the lower house was partially
thwarted in its spirited bid for power during the 1740's under the
leadership of John Kinsey and Samuel Nevill by the determined
opposition of Governor Lewis Morris, and it did not gain superiority until the administrations of Jonathan Belcher, Thomas Pow-
nall, Francis Bernard, and Thomas Boone during the Seven Years'
War. Similarly, the Virginia Burgesses vigorously sought to establish its control in the second decade of the century under Alexander Spotswood, but not until the administrations of Sir William Gooch and Robert Dinwiddie, when first the expansion of
the colony and then the Seven Years' War required more regular
sessions, did the Burgesses finally gain the upper hand under the
effective leadership of Speaker John Robinson.

Among the lower houses in the older colonies, only the Maryland House of Delegates and the New Hampshire House of Assembly failed to reach the final level of development in the period
before 1763. The Maryland body made important advances early
in the eighteenth century while under the control of the Crown
and aggressively sought to extend its authority in the 1720's under
the leadership of the older Daniel Dulany and again in the late
1730's and early 1740's under Dr. Charles Carroll. But the proprietors were usually able to thwart these attempts, and the
Delegates failed to pull ahead of the executive despite a concerted
effort during the last intercolonial war under the administration
of Horatio Sharpe. In New Hampshire, the House had exercised
considerable power through the early decades of the eighteenth
century, but Governor Benning Wentworth effectively challenged
its authority after 1740 and prevented it from attaining the extensive power exercised by its counterparts in other colonies. It should
be emphasized, however, that neither the Maryland nor the New
Hampshire lower house was in any sense impotent and along with
their more youthful equivalent in Georgia gained dominance during the decade of debate with Britain after 1763. Of the lower
houses in the continental colonies with pre-1763 political ex-

perience, only the Nova Scotia Assembly had not reached the final phase of political dominance by 1776.

The similarities in the process and pattern of legislative development from colony to colony were not entirely accidental. The lower houses faced like problems and drew upon common traditions and imperial precedents for solutions. They all operated in the same broad imperial context and were affected by common historical forces. Moreover, family, cultural, and commercial ties often extended across colony lines, and newspapers and other printed materials, as well as individuals, often found their way from one colony to another. The result was at least a general awareness of issues and practices in neighboring colonies, and occasionally there was even a conscious borrowing of precedents and traditions. Younger bodies such as the Georgia Commons and Nova Scotia Assembly were particularly indebted to their more mature counterparts in South Carolina and Massachusetts Bay. On the executive side, the similarity in attitudes, assumptions, and policies among the governors can be traced in large measure to the fact that they were all subordinate to the same central authority in London, which pursued a common policy in all the colonies.

Before the Seven Years' War the quest was characterized by a considerable degree of spontaneity, by a lack of awareness that activities of the moment were part of any broad struggle for power. Rather than consciously working out the details of some master plan designed to bring them liberty or self-government, the lower houses moved along from issue to issue and from situation to situation, primarily concerning themselves with the problems at hand and displaying a remarkable capacity for spontaneous action, for seizing any and every opportunity to enlarge their own influence at the executive's expense and for holding tenaciously to powers they had already secured. Conscious of the issues involved in each specific conflict, they were for the most part unaware of and uninterested in the long-range implications of their actions. Virginia Governor Francis Fauquier correctly judged the matter in 1760. "Whoever charges them with acting upon a premeditated concerted plan, don't know them," he wrote of the Virginia Burgesses, "for they mean honestly, but are Expedient Mongers in the highest Degree." Still, in retrospect it is obvious that throughout the eighteenth century the lower houses were engaged in a continuous movement to enlarge their sphere of influence. To ignore that continuity would be to miss the meaning of eighteenth-century colonial political development.

One is impressed with the rather prosaic manner in which the lower houses went about the task of extending their authority, with the infrequency of dramatic conflict. They gained much of their power in the course of routine business, quietly and simply extending and consolidating their authority of passing laws and establishing practices the implications of which escaped both colonial executives and imperial authorities and were not always fully recognized even by the lower houses themselves. In this way they gradually extended their financial authority to include the powers to audit accounts of all public officers, to share in disbursing public funds, and eventually even to appoint officials concerned in collecting and handling local revenues. Precedents thus established soon hardened into fixed principles, "undoubted rights" or "inherent powers," changing the very fabric of their respective constitutions. The notable absence of conflict is perhaps best illustrated by the none too surprising fact that the lower houses made some of their greatest gains under those governors with whom they enjoyed the most harmony, in particular Keith in Pennsylvania, Shirley in Massachusetts, Hunter in New York, and the elder and younger Bull in South Carolina. In Virginia the House of Burgesses made rapid strides during the 1730's and 1740's under the benevolent government of Gooch, who discovered early in his administration that the secret of political success for a Virginia governor was to reach an accord with the plantation gentry.

One should not conclude that the colonies had no exciting legislative–executive conflicts, however. Attempts through the middle decades of the eighteenth century by Clinton to weaken the financial powers of the New York House, Massachusetts governors

Samuel Shute and William Burnet to gain a permanent civil list, Benning Wentworth to extend unilaterally the privilege of representation to new districts in New Hampshire, Johnston to break the extensive power of the Albemarle Counties in the North Carolina lower house, Dinwiddie to establish a fee for issuing land patents without the consent of the Virginia Burgesses, and Boone to reform South Carolina's election laws each provided a storm of controversy that brought local politics to a fever pitch. But such conflicts were the exception and usually arose not out of the lower houses' seeking more authority but from the executives' attempts to restrict powers already won. Impatient of restraint and jealous of their rights and privileges, the lower houses responded forcefully and sometimes violently when executive action threatened to deprive them of those rights. Only a few governors, men of the caliber of Henry Ellis in Georgia and to a lesser extent William Henry Lyttelton in South Carolina and Bernard in New Jersey, had the skill to challenge established rights successfully without raising the wrath of the lower houses. Clumsier tacticians—Pennsylvania's William Denny, New York's Clinton, Virginia's Dinwiddie, North Carolina's Dobbs, South Carolina's Boone, Georgia's John Reynolds—failed when pursuing similar goals.

Fundamentally, the quest for power in both the royal and the proprietary colonies was a struggle for political identity, the manifestation of the political ambitions of the leaders of emerging societies within each colony. There is a marked correlation between the appearance of economic and social elites produced by the growth in colonial wealth and population on the one hand and the lower houses' demand for increased authority, dignity, and prestige on the other. In the eighteenth century a group of planters, merchants, and professional men had attained or were rapidly acquiring within the colonies wealth and social position. The lower houses' aggressive drive for power reflects the determination of this new elite to attain through the representative assemblies political influence as well. In another but related sense, the lower houses' efforts represented a movement for autonomy in local affairs, although it is doubtful that many of the members recognized them as such. The lower houses wished to strengthen their authority within the colonies and to reduce to a minimum the amount of supervision, with the uncertainties it involved, that royal or proprietary authorities could exercise. Continuously nourished by the growing desire of American legislators to be masters of their own political fortunes and by the development of a vigorous tradition of legislative superiority in imitation of the imperial House of Commons, this basic principle of local control over local affairs in some cases got part of its impetus from an unsatisfactory experience early in the lower houses' development with a despotic, inefficient, or corrupt governor such as Thomas, Lord Culpeper, or Francis, Lord Howard or Effingham, in Virginia, Lionel Copley in Maryland, Sir Edmund Andros in Massachusetts, Seth Sothell in North Carolina, or the infamous Cornbury in New York and New Jersey.

With most of their contemporaries in Great Britain, colonial Americans were convinced that men were imperfect creatures, perpetually self-deluded, enslaved by their passions, vanities, and interests, confined in their vision and understanding, and incapable of exercising power over each other without abusing it. This cluster of assumptions with the associated ideals of a government of laws rather than of men and of a political structure that restrained the vicious tendencies of man by checking them against each other was at the heart of English constitutionalism. In Britain and in the colonies, wherever Englishmen encountered a seeming abuse of power, they could be expected to insist that it be placed under legal and constitutional restraints. Because the monarchy had been the chief offender in seventeenth-century England, it became conventional for the representative branch to keep an especially wary eye on the executive, and the Glorious Revolution tended to institutionalize this pattern of behavior. The necessity to justify the Revolution ensured both that the specter of Stuart despotism would continue to haunt English political arenas throughout the eighteenth century and that representative bodies and representatives would be expected—indeed obliged—to be constantly on the lookout for any signs of that excess of gubernatorial power that would perforce result in executive tyranny. When colonial lower houses demanded checks on the prerogative and sought to undermine executive authority, they were, then, to some extent, playing out roles created for them by their predecessors in the seventeenth-century English House of Commons and using a rhetoric and a set of ground rules that grew out of the revolutionary conditions of Stuart England. In every debate, and in every political contest, each American legislator was a potential Coke, Pym, or Hampden, and each governor, at least in legislators' minds, a potential Charles I or James II.

But the lower houses' quest for power involved more than the extension of legislative authority within the colonies at the expense of the colonial executives. After their initial stage of evolution, the lower houses learned that their real antagonists were not the governors but the proprietors or Crown officials in London. Few governors proved to be a match for the representatives. A governor was almost helpless to prevent a lower house from exercising powers secured under his predecessors, and even the most discerning governor could fall into the trap of assenting to an apparently innocent law that would later prove damaging to the royal or proprietary prerogative. Some governors, for the sake of preserving amicable relations with the representatives or because they thought certain legislation to be in the best interest of a colony, actually conspired with legislative leaders to present the actions of the lower houses in a favorable light in London. Thus, Jonathan Belcher worked with Massachusetts leaders to parry the Crown's demand for a permanent revenue in the 1730's, and Fauquier joined with Speaker John Robinson in Virginia to prevent the separation of the offices of speaker and treasurer during the closing years of the Seven Years' War.

Nor could imperial authorities depend upon the colonial councils to furnish an effective check upon the representatives' advancing influence. Most councilors were drawn from the rising social and economic elites in the colonies. The duality of their role is obvious. Bound by oath to uphold the interests of the Crown or the proprietors, they were also driven by ambition and a variety of local pressures to maintain the status and power of the councils as well as to protect and advance their own individual interests and those of their group within the colonies. These two objectives were not always in harmony, and the councils frequently sided with the lower houses rather than with the governors. With a weakened governor and an unreliable council, the task of restraining the representative assemblies ultimately devolved upon the home government. Probably as much of the struggle for power was played out in Whitehall as in Williamsburg, Charleston, New York, Boston, or Philadelphia.

Behind the struggle between colonial lower houses and the imperial authorities were two divergent, though on the colonial side not wholly articulated, concepts of the constitutions of the colonies and in particular of the status of the lower houses. To the very end of the colonial period, imperial authorities persisted in the views that colonial constitutions were static and that the lower houses were subordinate governmental agencies with only temporary and limited lawmaking powers—in the words of one imperial official, merely "so many Corporations at a distance, invested with an Ability to make Temporary By Laws for themselves, agreeable to their respective Situations and Climates." In working out a political system for the colonies in the later seventeenth century, imperial officials had institutionalized these views in the royal commissions and instructions. Despite the fact that the lower houses were yearly making important changes in their respective constitutions, the Crown never altered either the commissions or instructions to conform with realities of the colonial political situation and continued to maintain throughout the eighteenth century that they were the most vital part of the constitutional structure of the royal colonies. The Pennsylvania and to a lesser extent the

Maryland proprietors were less rigid, although they also insisted upon their theoretical constitutional and political supremacy over the lower houses.

Colonial lower houses had little respect for and even less patience with such a doctrinaire position, and whether or not royal and proprietary instructions were absolutely binding upon the colonies was the leading constitutional issue in the period before 1763. As the political instruments of what was probably the most pragmatic society in the eighteenth-century Western World, colonial legislators would not likely be restrained by dogma divorced from reality. They had no fear of innovations and welcomed the chance to experiment with new forms and ideas. All they asked was that a thing work. When the lower houses found that instructions from imperial authorities did not work in the best interests of the colonies, that they were, in fact, antithetic to the very measures they as legislatures were trying to effect, they openly refused to submit to them. Instructions, they argued, applied only to officials appointed by the Crown.

Instructions from his majesty, to his governor, or the council, are binding to them, and esteemed as laws or rules; because if either should disregard them, they might immediately be displaced,

declared a South Carolina writer in 1756 while denying the validity of an instruction that stipulated colonial councils should have equal rights with the lower houses in framing money bills. "But, if instructions should be laws and rules to the people of this province, then there would be no need of assemblies, and all our laws and taxes might be made and levied by an instruction." Clearly, then, instructions might bind governors, but never the elected branch of the legislature.

Even though the lower houses, filled with intensely practical politicians, were concerned largely with practical political considerations, they found it necessary to develop a body of theory with which to oppose unpopular instructions from Britain and to support their claims to greater political power. In those few colonies that had charters, the lower houses relied upon the guarantees in them as their first line of defense, taking the position that the stipulations of the charters were inviolate, despite the fact that some had been invalidated by English courts, and could not be altered by executive order. A more basic premise which was equally applicable to all colonies was that the constituents of the lower houses, as inhabitants of British colonies, were entitled to all the traditional rights of Englishmen. On this foundation the colonial legislatures built their ideological structure. In the early charters the Crown had guaranteed the colonists "all privileges, franchises and liberties of this our kingdom of England . . . any Statute, act, ordinance, or provision to the contrary thereof, notwithstanding." Such guarantees, colonials assumed, merely constituted recognition that their privileges as Englishmen were inherent and unalterable and that it mattered not whether they stayed on the home islands or migrated to the colonies. "His Majesty's Subjects coming over to America," the South Carolina Commons argued in 1739 while asserting its exclusive right to formulate tax laws, "have no more forfeited this their most valuable Inheritance than they have withdrawn their Allegiance." No "Royal Order," the Commons declared, could "qualify or any wise alter a fundamental Right from the Shape in which it was handed down to us from our Ancestors."

One of the most important of these rights was the privilege of representation, on which, of course, depended the very existence of the lower houses. Imperial authorities always maintained that the lower houses existed only through the consent of the Crown, but the houses insisted that an elected assembly was a fundamental right of a colony arising out of an Englishman's privilege to be represented and that they did not owe their existence merely to the king's pleasure.

Our representatives, agreeably to the general sense of their constituents [wrote New York lawyer William Smith in the 1750's] are tenacious in their opinion, that the inhabitants of this colony are entitled to all the privileges of Englishmen; that they have a right to participate in the legislative power, and that the session of assemblies here, is wisely substituted instead of a representation in parliament, which, all things considered, would, at this remote distance, be extremely inconvenient and dangerous.

The logical corollary to this argument was that the lower houses were equivalents of the House of Commons and must perforce in their limited spheres be entitled to all the privileges possessd by that body in Great Britain. Hence, in cases where an invocation of fundamental rights was not appropriate, the lower houses frequently defended their actions on the grounds that they were agreeable to the practice of the House of Commons. Thus in 1775 the North Carolina Lower House denied the right of the Council to amend tax bills on the grounds that it was "contrary to Custom and Usage of Parliament." Unintentionally, Crown officials encouraged the lower houses to make this analogy by forbidding them in the instructions to exercise "any power or privilege whatsoever which is not allowed by us to the House of Commons . . . in Great Britain."

Because neither fundamental rights nor imperial precedents could be used to defend practices that were contrary to customs of the mother country or to the British constitution, the lower houses found it necessary to develop still another argument: that local precedents, habits, traditions, and statutes were important parts of their particular constitutions and could not be abridged by a royal or proprietary order. The assumptions were that the legislatures could alter colonial constitutions by their own actions without the active consent of imperial officials and that once the alterations were confirmed by usage they could not be countermanded by the British government. They did not deny the power of the governor to veto or of the Privy Council to disallow their laws but argued that imperial acquiescence over a long period of time was tantamount to consent and that precedents thus established could not be undone without their approval. The implication was that the American colonists saw their constitutions as living, growing, and constantly changing organisms, a theory which was directly opposite to the imperial view. To be sure, precedent had always been an important element in shaping the British constitution, but Crown officials were unwilling to concede that it was equally so in determining the fundamental law of the colonies. They willingly granted that colonial statutes, once formally approved by the Privy Council, automatically became part of the constitutions of the colonies, but they officially took the position that both royal instructions and commissions, as well as constitutional traditions of the mother country, took precedence over local practice or unconfirmed statutes. This conflict of views persisted throughout the period after 1689, becoming more and more of an issue in the decades immediately preceding the American Revolution.

In the last analysis it was the imperial denial of the validity of the constitutional defenses of the lower houses that drove colonial lawmakers to seek to extend the power of the lower houses at the very time they were insisting—and, in fact, deeply believed—that no one individual or institution should have a superiority of power in any government. No matter what kind of workable balance of power might be attained within the colonies, there was always the possibility that the home government might unleash the unlimited might of the parent state against the colonies. The chief fear of colonial legislators, then, was not the power of the governors, which they could control, but that of the imperial government, which in the circumstances they could never hope to control, and the whole movement for legislative authority in the colonies can be interpreted as a search for a viable constitutional arrangement in which the rights of the colonists would be secured against the preponderant power of the mother country. The failure of imperial authorities to provide such an arrangement or even to formalize what small concessions they did make, meant, of course, that the search could never be fulfilled, and the resulting anxiety, only partly conscious and finding expression through the classic arguments and ringing phrases of English political struggles of the seventeenth century, impelled the lower houses and the men who composed them relentlessly through the colonial period and was perhaps the most important single factor in the demand of patriot leaders for explicit, written constitutions after the Declaration of Independence.

It is nonetheless true that, if imperial authorities did not grant the validity of the theoretical arguments of the lower houses, neither did they make any systematic or concerted effort to force a rigid compliance with official policies for most of the period after 1689. Repressive measures, at least before 1763, rarely went beyond the occasional disallowance of an offending statute or the official reprimand of a rambunctious lower house. General lack of interest in the routine business of colonial affairs and failure to recognize the potential seriousness of the situation may in part account for this leniency, but it is also true that official policy under both Walpole and the Pelhams called for a light rein on the colonies on the assumption that contented colonies created fewer problems for the administration. "One would not Strain any point," Charles Delafaye, secretary to the lords justices, cautioned South Carolina's Governor Francis Nicholson in 1722, "where it can be of no Service to our King or Country." "In the Plantations," he added, "the Government should be as Easy and Mild as possible to invite people to Settle under it." Three times between 1734 and 1749 the ministry failed to give enthusiastic support to measures introduced into Parliament to ensure the supremacy of instructions over colonial laws. Though the Calverts were somewhat more insistent upon preserving their proprietary prerogatives, in general the proprietors were equally lax as long as there was no encroachment upon their land rights or proprietary dues.

Imperial organs of administration were in fact inadequate to deal effectively with all the problems of the empire. Since no special governmental bodies were created in England to deal exclusively with colonial affairs, they were handled through the regular machinery of government—a maze of boards and officials whose main interests and responsibilities were not the supervision of overseas colonies. The only body sufficiently informed and interested to deal competently with colonial matters was the Board of Trade, and it had little authority, except for the brief period from 1748 to 1761 under the presidency of George Dunk, Earl of Halifax. The most useful device for restraining the lower houses was the Privy Council's right to review colonial laws, but even that was only partly effective, because the mass of colonial statutes annually coming before the Board of Trade made a thorough scrutiny impossible. Under such arrangements no vigorous colonial policy was likely. The combination of imperial lethargy and colonial aggression virtually guaranteed the success of the lower houses' quest for power. An indication of a growing awareness in imperial circles of the seriousness of the situation was Halifax's spirited, if piecemeal, effort to restrain the growth of the lower houses in the early 1750's. Symptomatic of these efforts was the attempt to make Georgia and Nova Scotia model royal colonies at the institution of royal government by writing into the instructions to their governors provisions designed to insure the continued supremacy of the executive and to prevent the lower houses from going the way of their counterparts in the older colonies. However, the outbreak of the Seven Years' War forced Halifax to suspend his activities and prevented any further reformation until the cessation of hostilities.

Indeed, the war saw a drastic acceleration in the lower houses' bid for authority, and its conclusion found them in possession of many of the powers held less than a century before by the executive. In the realm of finance they had imposed their authority over every phase of raising and distributing public revenue. They had acquired a large measure of independence by winning control over their compositions and proceedings and obtaining guarantees of basic English parliamentary privileges. Finally, they had pushed their power even beyond that of the English House of Commons by gaining extensive authority in handling executive affairs, including the right to appoint executive officers and to share in formulating executive policy. These specific gains were symptoms of developments of much greater significance. To begin with, they were symbolic of a fundamental shift of the constitutional center of power in the colonies from the executive to the elected branch of the legislature. With the exception of the Georgia and Nova Scotia bodies, both of which had less than a decade of political experience behind them, the houses had by 1763 succeeded in attaining a new status, raising themselves from dependent lawmaking bodies to the center of political authority in their respective colonies.

But the lower houses had done more than simply acquire a new status in colonial politics. They had in a sense altered the structure of the constitution of the British empire itself by asserting colonial authority against imperial authority and extending the constitutions of the colonies far beyond the limitations of the charters, instructions, or fixed notions of imperial authorities. The time was ripe for a re-examination and redefinition of the constitutional position of the lower houses. With the rapid economic and territorial expansion of the colonies in the years before 1763 had come a corresponding rise in the responsibilities and prestige of the lower houses and a growing awareness among colonial representatives of their own importance, which had served to strengthen their long-standing, if still imperfectly defined, impression that colonial lower houses were the American counterparts of the British House of Commons. Under the proper stimuli, they would carry this impression to its logical conclusion: that the lower houses enjoyed an equal status under the Crown with Parliament. Here, then, well beyond the embryonic stage, was the theory of colonial equality with the mother country, one of the basic constitutional principles of the American Revolution, waiting to be nourished by the series of crises that beset imperial–colonial relations between 1763 and 1776.

The psychological implications of this new political order were profound. By the 1750's the phenomenal success of the lower houses had generated a soaring self-confidence, a willingness to take on all comers. Called upon to operate on a larger stage during

the Seven Years' War, they emerged from that conflict with an
increased awareness of their own importance and a growing consciousness of the implication of their activities. Symptomatic of
these developments was the spate of bitter controversies that characterized colonial politics during and immediately after the war.
The Gadsden election controversy in South Carolina, the dispute
over judicial tenure in New York, and the contests over the
pistole fee and the two-penny act in Virginia gave abundant evidence of both the lower houses' stubborn determination to preserve their authority and the failure of Crown officials in London
and the colonies to gauge accurately their temper or to accept the
fact that they had made important changes in the constitutions
of the colonies.

With the shift of power to the lower houses also came the development in each colony of an extraordinarily able group of politicians. The lower houses provided excellent training for the leaders of the rapidly maturing colonial societies, and the recurring
controversies prepared them for the problems they would be called
upon to meet in the dramatic conflicts after 1763. In the decades
before Independence there appeared in the colonial statehouses
John and Samuel Adams and James Otis in Massachusetts Bay;
William Livingston in New York; Benjamin Franklin and John
Dickinson in Pennsylvania; Daniel Dulany the younger in Maryland; Richard Bland, Richard Henry Lee, Thomas Jefferson, and
Patrick Henry in Virginia; and Christopher Gadsden and John
Rutledge in South Carolina. Along with dozens of others, these
men guided their colonies through the debate with Britain, assumed direction of the new state governments after 1776, and
played conspicuous roles on the national stage as members of the
Continental Congress, the Confederation, and, after 1787, the
new federal government. By the 1760's, then, almost every colony
had an imposing group of native politicians thoroughly schooled
in the political arts and primed to meet any challenge to the
power and prestige of the lower houses.

Britain's "new colonial policy" after 1763 provided just such a challenge. It precipitated a constitutional crisis in the empire, creating new tensions and setting in motion forces different from those that had shaped earlier developments. The new policy was based upon concepts both unfamiliar and unwelcome to the colonists such as centralization, uniformity, and orderly development. Yet it was a logical culmination of earlier trends and, for the most part, an effort to realize old aspirations. From Edward Randolph in the last decades of the seventeenth century to the Earl of Halifax in the 1750's colonial officials had envisioned a highly centralized empire with a uniform political system in each of the colonies and with the imperial government closely supervising the subordinate governments. But, because they had never made any sustained or systematic attempt to achieve these goals, there had developed during the first half of the eighteenth century a working arrangement permitting the lower houses considerable latitude in shaping colonial constitutions without requiring crown and proprietary officials to give up any of their ideals. That there had been a growing divergence between imperial theory and colonial practice mattered little so long as each refrained from challenging the other. But the new policy threatened to upset this arrangement by implementing the old ideals long after the conditions that produced them had ceased to exist. Aimed at bringing the colonies more closely under imperial control, this policy inevitably sought to curtail the influence of the lower houses, directly challenging many of the powers they had acquired over the previous century. To American legislators accustomed to the lenient policies of Walpole and the Pelhams and impressed with the rising power of their own lower houses, the new program seemed a radical departure from precedent, a frontal assault upon the several constitutions they had been forging over the previous century. To protect gains they had already made and to make good their pretensions to greater political significance, the lower houses thereafter no longer had merely to deal with weak governors or casual imperial administrators; they now faced an aggressive group of officials bent upon using every means at their disposal, including the legislative authority of Parliament, to gain their ends.

Beginning in 1763 one imperial action after another seemed to threaten the position of the lower houses. Between 1764 and 1766 Parliament's attempt to tax the colonists for revenue directly challenged the colonial legislatures' exclusive power to tax, the cornerstone of their authority in America. A variety of other measures, some aimed at particular colonial legislatures and others at general legislative powers and practices, posed serious threats to powers that the lower houses had either long enjoyed or were trying to attain. To meet these challenges, the lower houses had to spell out the implications of the changes they had been making, consciously or not, in the structures of their respective governments. That is, for the first time they had to make clear in their own minds and then to verbalize what they conceived their respective constitutions in fact were or should be. In the process, the spokesmen of the lower houses laid bare the wide gulf between imperial theory and colonial practice. During the Stamp Act crisis in 1764–1766 the lower houses claimed the same authority over taxation in the colonies as Parliament had over that matter in England, and a few of them even asserted an equal right in matters of internal policy. Although justified by the realities of the colonial situation, such a definition of the lower houses' constitutional position within the empire was at marked variance with imperial ideals and only served to increase the determination of the home government to take a stricter tone. This determination was manifested after the repeal of the Stamp Act by Parliament's claim in the Declaratory Act of 1766 to "full power and authority" over the colonies "in all cases whatsoever."

The pattern over the next decade was on the part of the home government one of increasing resolution to deal firmly with the colonies and on the part of American lawmakers a heightened consciousness of the implications of the constitutional issue and a continuously rising level of expectation. In addition to their insistence upon the right of Parliament to raise revenue in the colonies, imperial officials also applied, in a way that was increasingly irksome to American legislators, traditional instruments of royal control like restrictive instructions, legislative review, the governors' power to dissolve the lower houses and the suspending clause requiring prior approval of the Crown before laws of an "extraordinary nature" could go into effect. Finally Parliament threatened the very existence of the lower houses by a measure suspending the New York Assembly for refusing to comply with the Quartering Act in 1767 and by another altering the substance of the Massachusetts constitution in the Massachusetts Government Act in 1774. In the process of articulating and defending their constitutional position, the lower houses acquired aspirations well beyond any they had had in the years before 1763. American representatives became convinced in the decade after 1766 not only that they knew best what to do for their constituents and the colonies and that anything interfering with their freedom to adopt whatever course seemed necessary was an intolerable and unconstitutional restraint but also that the only security for their political fortunes was in the abandonment of their attempts to restrict and define parliamentary authority in America and instead to deny Parliament's jurisdiction over them entirely by asserting their equality with Parliament under the Crown. Suggested by Richard Bland as early as 1766, such a position was openly advocated by James Wilson and Thomas Jefferson in 1774 and was officially adopted by the First Continental Congress when it claimed for Americans in its declarations and resolves "a free and exclusive power of legislation in their several provincial legislatures, where their right of representation can alone be preserved, in all cases of taxation and internal polity."

Parliament could not accept this claim without giving up the principles it had asserted in the Declaratory Act and, in effect, abandoning the traditional British theory of empire and accepting the colonial constitutional position instead. The First Continental Congress professed that a return to the *status quo* of 1763 would satisfy the colonies, but Parliament in 1774–1776 was unwilling even to go that far, much less to promise them exemption from parliamentary taxation. Besides, American legislators now aspired to much more. James Chalmers, Maryland planter and later loyalist who was out of sympathy with the proceedings of American patriots between 1774 and 1776, correctly charged that American leaders had "been constantly enlarging their views, and stretching them beyond their first bounds, till at length they have wholly changed their ground." Edward Rutledge, young delegate from South Carolina to the First Continental Congress, was one who recognized that the colonies would not "be satisfied with a restoration of such rights only, as have been violated since the year '63, when we have as many others, as clear and indisputable, that will even then be infringed." The simple fact was that American political leaders, no matter what their professions, would not have been content to return to the old inarticulated and ambiguous pattern of accommodation between imperial theory and colonial practice that had existed through most of the period between 1689 and 1763. They now sought to become masters of their own political fortunes. Rigid guarantees of colonial rights and precise definitions of the constitutional relationship between the mother country and the colonies and between Parliament and the lower houses on American terms—that is, imperial recognition of the autonomy of the lower houses in local affairs and of the equality of the colonies with the mother country—would have been required to satisfy them.

No analysis of the charges in the Declaration of Independence can fail to suggest that the preservation and consolidation of the rights and powers of the lower houses were central in the struggle with Britain from 1763 to 1776, just as they had been the most important issue in the political relationship between Britain and the colonies over the previous century and a half. Between 1689 and 1763 the lower houses' contests with royal governors and imperial officials had brought them political maturity, a considerable measure of control over local affairs, capable leaders, and a rationale to support their pretensions to political power within the colonies and in the empire. The British challenge after 1763 threatened to render their accomplishments meaningless and drove them to demand equal rights with Parliament and autonomy in local affairs and eventually to declare their independence. At issue was the whole political structure forged by the lower houses over the previous century. In this context the American Revolution becomes in form, if not in essence, a war for political survival, a conflict involving not only individual rights as traditionally emphasized by historians of the event but assembly rights as well.

Foundations of the American Republic

The American Science of Politics

by Gordon S. Wood

Almost two hundred years ago, at a time when kings and nobles ruled everywhere else, Americans founded the first great republic of modern history. The idea of a nation conceived on the basis of popular sovereignty was perilously novel for its time, and has yet to prove its practicability in most parts of today's world. Here, in a chapter from his larger study, The Creation of the American Republic, *Gordon S. Wood describes the new science of politics and government as it evolved in the Revolutionary and post-Revolutionary eras.*

The Revolution had not transformed America's economic system—that had to wait for the Industrial Revolution of the nineteenth century—nor did it turn the social structure upside down. The most creative consequences of the Revolution were political—the reconstruction of authority in the states and the creation of an effective national government. British withdrawal forced Americans to think critically about appropriate forms of government. First, each of the new states adopted republican constitutions, acts which in themselves proved profoundly revolutionary. They established new rules for politics which officeholders and other citizens would thereafter have to observe. As colonists,

Americans had discovered that the British constitution offered no protection from tyranny, since Parliament enjoyed unlimited authority. Before 1776, a constitution was simply a description of the laws and forms of government that existed in a nation at any given time, and those laws and forms could be altered with ease. But Americans saw in a constitution a higher law, deriving its legitimacy from the people who sanctioned it, and placing limitations on the rulers. Moreover, they were convinced that a constitution should not be easily changed.

Just as Americans groped toward new conceptions of constitutionality, so too they worked out through trial and error new forms of government they hoped would provide a fair chance to reconcile liberty with public order. At first, legislatures dominated the new state governments, but Americans quickly discovered the dangers of legislative despotism and erected safeguards against it through a complex series of checks and balances. Similarly, Americans initially identified the preservation of liberty with political power lodged close to the people, in state and local governments. But a decade's experience under weak central government and the Articles of Confederation convinced many of the need to shift some authority away from the states to a strengthened national government.

The ultimate aim, Wood argues, was to guarantee a maximum of meaningful liberty to the individual. A critical study of the American political experience since 1789 will allow students to decide whether the Founding Fathers were justified in their belief that by fragmenting power, by placing limits on government, and by freeing individuals to pursue private interests, citizens would be able to attain the goal of ordered liberty.

1. Democratic Republics

Undoubtedly John Taylor was right about the source of the new principles of politics discovered during the Revolutionary era.

From *The Creation of the American Republic, 1776–1787* (Chapel Hill: University of North Carolina Press, for The Institute of Early American History and Culture, 1969), pp. 593–615. Reprinted by permission; footnotes omitted.

The creation of a new political theory was not as much a matter of deliberation as it was a matter of necessity. The blending of diverse views and clashing interests into the new federal system, Madison told Jefferson in October 1787, was nothing "less than a miracle." Although no one person had done so much to create the Constitution, Madison generously but rightly stressed to the end of his life that it was not "the offspring of a single brain" but "the work of many heads and many hands." The formation of the new government, as Franklin observed to a European correspondent in 1788, was not like a game of chess, methodically and consciously played. It was more like a game of dice, with so many players, "their ideas so different, their prejudices so strong and so various, and their particular interests, independent of the general, seeming so opposite, that not a move can be made that is not contested." Yet somehow out of all these various moves the Constitution had emerged, and with it had emerged not only "a wonder and admiration" among the members of the Convention themselves, but also a growing awareness among all Americans that the Constitution had actually created a political system "so novel, so complex, and intricate" that writing about it would never cease. The Constitution had become the climax of a great revolution. "Till this period," declared Aaron Hall of New Hampshire in a 1788 oration, "the revolution in America has never appeared to me to be completed; but this is laying on the cap-stone of the great American Empire." It was not the revolution that had been intended but it was a real revolution nonetheless, marked by a momentous upheaval in the understanding of politics where the "collected wisdom of ages" was "interwoven in this form of government." "The independence of America considered merely as a separation from England, would have been a matter but of little importance," remarked Thomas Paine, "had it not been accompanied by a revolution in the principles and practise of governments." "There are some great eras," said James Wilson, "when important and very perceptible alterations take place in the situation of men and things." And America, added David Ramsay, was in the midst of one of those great eras.

Americans now told themselves with greater assurance than ever that they had created something remarkable in the history of politics. "The different constitutions which have been adopted by these states," observed John Stevens in 1787, "are experiments in government entirely new; they are founded upon principles peculiar to themselves." Admittedly they had not fully understood politics at the outset of the Revolution; but within a decade they believed that most of the defects of their early state constitutions had been discovered and were on the way to being remedied. And the new federal Constitution expressed all they had learned. "The government of the United States," wrote Nathaniel Chipman of Vermont in 1793, "exhibits a new scene in the political history of the world, . . . exhibits, in theory, the most beautiful system, which has yet been devised by the wisdom of man." With their governments the Americans had placed the science of politics on a footing with the other great scientific discoveries of the previous century. Their governments, said William Vans Murray, represented "the most finished political forms" in history and had "deservedly attracted the attention of all speculative minds." It was therefore important for "the cause of liberty all over the world, that they should be understood." And by the end of the 1780's and the early nineties Americans increasingly felt compelled to explain to themselves and to the world the uniqueness of what they had discovered.

Their governments were so new and so distinctive that they groped for political terms adequate to describe them. By the late 1780's Americans generally were calling their governments democracies, but peculiar kinds of democracies. America, said Murray, had established governments which were "in their principles, structure, and whole mass, purely and unalterably Democratic." The American republics, remarked John Stevens, approached "nearer to perfect democracies" than any other governments in the world. Yet democracy, as eighteenth-century political scientists generally understood the term, was not, they realized, a wholly accurate description of their new governments. They were "Democratic Republics," as Chipman called them, by which was "meant, a Representative Democracy." In *The Federalist*, Number 10, Madison called the American governments republics, as distinct from a "pure democracy" in which a small number of citizens assembled and administered the government in person. For Madison a republic had become a species of government to be classed alongside aristocracy or democracy, a distinctive form of government "in which the scheme of representation takes place." Representation—that was the key conception in unlocking an understanding of the American political system. America was, as Hamilton said, "a *representative democracy*." Only the American scheme, wrote Thomas Paine, was based "wholly on the system of representation," and thus it was "the only real republic in character and practise, that now exists." The American polity was "representation ingrafted upon democracy," creating "a system of government capable of embracing and confederating all the various interests and every extent of territory and population."

2. *The Pervasiveness of Representation*

It was representation then—"the delegation of the government . . . ," said Madison, "to a small number of citizens elected by the rest"—that explained the uniqueness of the American polities. "The *principle* on which all the American governments are founded," wrote Samuel Williams of Vermont, "is *representation*." No other nation, said Charles Pinckney of South Carolina, so enjoyed the right of self-government, "where the true principles of representation are understood and practised, and where all authority flows from and returns at stated periods to, the people." Representation, said Edmund Randolph, was "a thing not understood in its full extent till very lately." Neither the Israelites nor the ancients had properly comprehended the uses of representation—"a very excellent modern improvement in the management of republics," said Samuel Langdon of New Hampshire. "It is surprising, indeed," said Wilson, "how very imperfectly, at this day, the doctrine of representation is understood in Europe. Even Great Britain, which boasts a superior knowledge of the subject, and is generally supposed to have carried it into practice, falls far short of its true and genuine principles." Representation, remarked Wilson, barely touched the English constitution, since it was not immediately or remotely the source of executive or judicial power. Even in the legislature representation was not "a pervading principle," but actually was only a check, confined to the Commons. The Lords acted either under hereditary right or under an authority granted by the prerogative of the Crown and hence were "not the representatives of the people." The world, it seemed, had "left to America the glory and happiness of forming a government where representation shall at once supply the basis and the cement of the superstructure." "In America," said Williams, "every thing tended to introduce, and to complete the system of representation." America, wrote Madison, had created the first example of "a government wholly popular, and founded at the same time, wholly on that principle [of representation]." Americans had made their entire system from top to bottom representative, "diffusing," in Wilson's words, "this vital principle throughout all the different divisions and departments of the government." Since Americans, influenced by the implications of the developing conception of actual representation, now clearly believed that "the right of representing is conferred by the act of electing," every part of the elective governments had become representative of the people. In truth, said Madison, representation was "the pivot" on which the whole American system moved.

Although the members of the houses of representatives were perhaps the more "immediate representatives," no longer were they the full and exclusive representatives of the people. "The Senators," said Nathaniel Chipman, "are to be representatives of the people, no less, in fact, than the members of the other house."

Foreigners, noted William Vans Murray, had mistaken the division of the legislatures in America as some sort of an embodiment of an aristocracy. Even in Maryland and in the federal Constitution where the senates were indirectly elected, the upper house was derived mediately from the people. "It represents the people. It represents no particular order of men or of ranks." To those who sought to comprehend fully the integrity of the new system the senate could only be a weight in the powers of legislative deliberation, not a weight of property, of privileges, or of interests. Election by the people, not the number of chambers in the legislature, declared John Stevens, had made "our governments the most democratic that ever existed anywhere." "With us," concluded Wilson, "the power of magistrates, call them by whatever name you please, are the grants of the people."

Therefore all governmental officials, including even the executive and judicial parts of the government, were agents of the people, not fundamentally different from the people's nominal representatives in the lower houses of the legislatures. The Americans of 1776, observed Wilson, had not clearly understood the nature of their executives and judiciaries. Although the authority of their governors and judges became in 1776 as much "the child of the people" as that of the legislatures, the people could not forget their traditional colonial aversion to the executive and judiciary, and their fondness for their legislatures, which under the British monarchy had been the guardians of their rights and the anchor of their political hopes. "Even at this time," Wilson noted with annoyance, "people can scarcely devest themselves of those opposite prepossessions." The legislatures often were still called "the *people's representatives*," implying, "though probably, not avowed upon reflection," that the executive and judicial powers were not so strongly or closely connected with the people. "But it is high time," said Wilson, "that we should chastise our prejudices." The different parts of the government were functionally but not substantively different. "The executive and judicial powers are now drawn from the same source, are now animated by the same principles, and are now directed to the same ends, with the legislative authority: they who execute, and they who administer the laws, are so much the servants, and therefore as much the friends of the people, as those who make them." The entire government had become the limited agency of the sovereign people.

The pervasive Whig mistrust of power had in the years since Independence been increasingly directed not only against the traditional rulers, but also against the supposed representatives of the people, who now seemed to many to be often as distant and unrepresentative of the people's interests as Parliament once had been. "The representatives of the people, in a popular assembly," said Hamilton, "seem sometimes to fancy that they are the people themselves." The constitutional reformers seized on the people's growing suspicion of their own representatives and reversed the perspective: the houses of representatives, now no more trusted than other parts of the government, seemed to be also no more representative of the people than the other parts of the government. They had lost their exclusive role of embodying the people in the government. In fact the people did not actually participate in the government any more, as they did, for example, in the English House of Commons. The Americans had taken the people out of the government altogether. The "true distinction" of the American governments, wrote Madison in *The Federalist*, "lies *in the total exclusion of the people, in their collective capacity, from any share*" in the government. Or from a different point of view the Americans could now argue that the people participated in all branches of the government and not merely in their houses of representatives. "The whole powers of the proposed government," said Hamilton in *The Federalist*, "is to be in the hands of the representatives of the people." All parts of the government were equally responsible but limited spokesmen for the people, who remained as the absolute and perpetual sovereign, distributing bits and pieces of power to their various agents.

Confrontation with the Blackstonian concept of legal sovereignty had forced American theorists to relocate it in the people-at-large, a transference that was comprehensible only because of the peculiar experience of American politics. "Sovereignty," said James Sullivan, "must in its nature, be absolute and uncontrolable by any civil authority. . . . A subordinate sovereignty is non-sense: A subordinate, uncontrolable power is a contradiction in terms." In America this kind of sovereignty could only exist in the people themselves, who "may invest the exercise of it in whom they please; but where the power delegated by them is subordinate, or controlable by any other delegated civil power, it is not a sovereign power." Thus it was obvious that in America "there is no supreme power but what the people themselves hold." "The supreme power," said Wilson, "is in them; and in them, even when a constitution is formed, and government is in operation, the supreme power still remains." The powers of the people were thus never alienated or surrendered to a legislature. Representation, in other words, never eclipsed the people-at-large, as apparently it did in the English House of Commons. In America the people were never really represented in the English sense of the term. "A portion of their authority they, indeed, delegate; but they delegate that portion in whatever manner, in whatever measure, for whatever time, to whatever persons, and on whatever conditions they choose to fix." Such a delegation, said Sullivan, was necessarily fragmentary and provisional; "it may extend to some things and not to others or be vested for some purposes, and not for others." Only a proper understanding of this vital principle of the sovereignty of the people could make federalism intelligible. The representation of the people, as American politics in the Revolutionary era had made glaringly evident, could never be virtual, never inclusive; it was acutely actual, and always tentative and partial. "All power whatever," said John Stevens, "is vested in, and immediately derived from, the people only; the rulers are their deputies merely, and at certain short periods are removable by them: nay," he added, "the very government itself

is a creature formed by themselves, and may, whenever they think
it necessary, be at any time new modelled."

3. The Equation of Rulers and Ruled

This conception of the sovereignty of the people used to create
the new federal government had at last clarified the peculiar
American idea of a constitution. A constitution, as James Iredell
said, was "a declaration of particular powers by the people to their
representatives, for particular purposes. It may be considered as a
great power of attorney, under which no power can be exercised
but what is expressly given." A constitution for Americans, said
Thomas Paine, was "not a thing in name only; but in fact. . . .
It is the body of elements, to which you can refer, and quote
article by article; and which contains . . . every thing that relates
to the complete organization of a civil government, and the principles on which it shall act, and by which it shall be bound."
A constitution was thus a "thing *antecedent* to a government,
and a government is only the creature of a constitution." It was
truly, said Wilson, the act of the people, and "in their hands it is
clay in the hands of the potter: they have the right to mould, to
preserve, to improve, to refine, and to furnish it as they please."
Only by conceiving of a constitution as a written delimitation of
the grant of power made by the people to the government was
"the important distinction so well understood in America, between a Constitution established by the people and unalterable
by the government, and a law established by the government and
alterable by the government" rendered truly comprehensible.

In America a constitution had become, as Madison pointed out,
a charter of power granted by liberty rather than, as in Europe,
a charter of liberty granted by power. Magna Carta and the English Bill of Rights were not constitutions at all. They "did not,"
said Paine, "create and give powers to Government in the manner
a constitution does." They were really only "restrictions on as-

sumed power," bargains "which the parts of the government made with each other to divide powers, profits and privileges." "The far famed social compact between the people and their rulers," declared David Ramsay, "did not apply to the United States." "To suppose that any government can be a party in a compact with the whole people," said Paine, "is to suppose it to have existence before it can have a right to exist." In America, said Ramsay, "the sovereignty was in the people," who "deputed certain individuals as their agents to serve them in public stations agreeably to constitutions, which they prescribed for their conduct." Government, concluded Paine, "has of itself no rights; they are altogether duties."

Yet if the ancient notion of a contract was to be preserved in American thinking, then it must be a Lockean contract, one formed by the individuals of the society with each other, instead of a mutual arrangement between rulers and ruled. In most countries, declared Charles Backus in 1788, the people "have obtained a partial security of their liberties, by extorted concessions from their nobles or kings. But in America, the *People* have had an opportunity of forming a compact *betwixt themselves*; from which alone, their rulers derive all their authority to govern." This image of a social contract formed by isolated and hostile individuals was now the only contractual metaphor that comprehended American social reality. Since an American constitution could no longer be regarded as a contract between rulers and people, representing distinct and unified interests, considerations like protection and allegiance lost their relevance. "Writers on government have been anxious on the part of the people," observed Nathaniel Chipman in 1793, "to discover a consideration given for the right of protection. . . . While government was supposed to depend on a compact, not between the individuals of a people, but between the people and the rulers, this was a point of great consequence." But not any longer in America, where government was based on a compact only among the people. Obedience to the government in America followed from no such traditional consideration. The flow of authority itself was reversed, and *"consent,"* which had not been the basis of magisterial authority in the past, now became "the sole obligatory principle of human government and human laws." Because of the pervasiveness of representational consent through all parts of the government, "the judgments of our courts, and the commissions constitutionally given by our governor," said John Jay, "are as valid and as binding on all our persons whom they concern, as the laws passed by our legislature." The once important distinction between magisterial authority and representative legislative authority was now obliterated. "All constitutional acts of power, whether in the executive or in the judicial department, have as much legal validity and obligation as if they proceeded from the legislature." No more revolutionary change in the history of politics could have been made: the rulers had become the ruled and the ruled the rulers.

4. *The Parceling of Power*

The American governments, wrote Samuel Williams in his *Natural and Civil History of Vermont* of 1794, "do not admit of sovereignty, nobility, or any kind of hereditary powers; but only of powers granted by the people, ascertained by written constitutions, and exercised by representation for a given time." Hence such governments "do not admit of monarchy or aristocracy; nor do they admit of what was called democracy by the ancients." The old classification of politics by the number and character of the rulers no longer made sense of American practice where "all is transacted by representation" expressed in different ways. The government in the several states thus "varies in its form; committing more or less power to a governor, senate, or house of representatives, as the circumstances of any particular state may require. As each of these branches derive their whole power from the people, are accountable to them for the use and exercise they make of it, and may be displaced by the election of others," the liberty and security of the people, as Americans had thought in

1776, no longer came from their participation in one part of the government, as the democracy balanced against the monarchy and aristocracy, "but from the responsibility, and dependence of each part of the government, upon the people."

In slightly more than two decades of polemics the Americans had destroyed the age-old conception of mixed government and had found new explanations for their polities created in 1776, explanations that rested on their expansion of the principle of representation. America had not discovered the idea of representation, said Madison, but it could "claim the merit of making the discovery the basis of unmixed and extensive republics." And their republics were now peculiarly unmixed, despite the presence of senates and governors. They could in fact intelligibly be considered to be democracies, since, as James Wilson said, "in a democracy" the supreme power "is inherent in the people, and is either exercised by themselves or their representatives." Perhaps no one earlier or better described the "new and rich discoveries in jurisprudence" Americans had made than did Wilson. The British constitution, he said, had attempted to combine and to balance the three different forms of government, but it had obviously failed. And it was left to the Americans to realize that it was "not necessary to intermix the different species of government" in order to attain perfection in politics. "We have discovered, that one of them—the best and purest—that, in which the supreme power remains with the people at large, is capable of being formed, arranged, proportioned, and organized in such a manner, as to exclude the inconveniences, and to secure the advantages of all three." The federal Constitution, said Wilson, was therefore "purely democratical," even though in its outward form it resembled the conventional mixed government: "all authority of every kind *is derived by* REPRESENTATION *from the* PEOPLE *and the* DEMOCRATIC *principle is carried into every part of the government.*" The new government was in fact, incongruous as it sounded, a mixed or balanced democracy.

Americans had retained the forms of the Aristotelian schemes of government but had eliminated the substance, thus divesting the various parts of the government of their social constituents. Political power was thus disembodied and became essentially homogeneous. The division of this political power now became (in Jefferson's words) "the first principle of a good government," the "distribution of its powers into executive, judiciary, and legislative, and a sub-division of the latter into two or three branches." Separation of powers, whether describing executive, legislative, and judicial separation or the bicameral division of the legislature (the once distinct concepts now thoroughly blended), was simply a partitioning of political power, the creation of a plurality of discrete governmental elements, all detached from yet responsible to and controlled by the people, checking and balancing each other, preventing any one power from asserting itself too far. The libertarian doctrine of separation of powers was expanded and exalted by the Americans to the foremost position in their constitutionalism, premised on the belief, in John Dickinson's words, that "government must never be lodged in a single body." Enlightenment and experience had pointed out "the propriety of government being committed to such a number of great departments"— three or four, suggested Dickinson—"as can be introduced without confusion, distinct in office, and yet connected in operation." Such a "repartition" of power was designed to provide for the safety and ease of the people, since "there will be more obstructions interposed" against errors and frauds in the government. "The departments so constituted," concluded Dickinson, "may therefore be said to be balanced." But it was not a balance of "any intrinsic or constitutional properties," of any social elements, but rather only a balance of governmental functionaries without social connections, all monitored by the people who remained outside, a balanced government that worked, "although," said Wilson, "the materials, of which it is constructed, be not an assemblage of different and dissimilar kinds."

Abuse of governmental power, especially from the legislature, was now best prevented, as Madison put it in *The Federalist*,

Number 51, one of the most significant expressions of the new political thinking, "by so contriving the interior structure of the government as that its several constituent parts may, by their mutual relations, be the means of keeping each other in their proper places." Perhaps the most rigorous separation of powers could be attained, suggested Madison in a revelation of the assumptions behind the new conception of government, by having all the departments of government drawn directly from the same fountain of authority, the people, "through channels having no communication whatever with one another." However, since such a plan was probably impractical, some deviations from "the principle" were necessary. Yet every effort, emphasized Madison, should be made to keep the separate departments independent, or else they could not effectively check and balance each other. The legislature must be divided and the executive fortified with a veto in order to distribute power and guard against encroachments. Moreover, continued Madison with mounting enthusiasm, the new federal government—with its new kind of "mixed character" —possessed an immense advantage over the conventional single republics which were limited in the amount of separating and dividing of powers they could sustain. "In the compound republic of America," said Madison, "the power surrendered by the people is first divided between two distinct governments, and then the portion allotted to each subdivided among distinct and separate departments." Furthermore, the partitioning of power in America would be intensified by "the extent of country and number of people comprehended under the same government," so that "the society itself will be broken into so many parts, interests and classes of citizens, that the rights of individuals, or of the minority, will be in little danger from interested combinations of the majority."

It was an imposing conception—a kinetic theory of politics— such a crumbling of political and social interests, such an atomization of authority, such a parceling of power, not only in the governmental institutions but in the extended sphere of the society itself, creating such a multiplicity and a scattering of designs and passions, so many checks, that no combination of parts could hold, no group of evil interests could long cohere. Yet out of the clashing and checking of this diversity Madison believed the public good, the true perfection of the whole, would somehow arise. The impulses and passions would so counteract each other, so neutralize their potencies, as America's contending religious sects had done, that reason adhering in the natural aristocracy would be able to assert itself and dominate.

5. *The End of Classical Politics*

The Americans had reversed in a revolutionary way the traditional conception of politics: the stability of government no longer relied, as it had for centuries, upon its embodiment of the basic social forces of the state. Indeed, it now depended upon the prevention of the various social interests from incorporating themselves too firmly in the government. Institutional or governmental politics was thus abstracted in a curious way from its former associations with the society. But at the same time a more modern and more realistic sense of political behavior in the society itself, among the people, could now be appreciated. This revolution marked an end of the classical conception of politics and the beginning of what might be called a romantic view of politics. The eighteenth century had sought to understand politics, as it had all of life, by capturing in an integrated, ordered, changeless ideal the totality and complexity of the world—an ideal that the concept of the mixed constitution and the proportioned social hierarchy on which it rested perfectly expressed. In such an ideal there could be only potential energy, no kinetic energy, only a static equilibrium among synthetic orders, and no motion among the particular, miscellaneous parts that made up the society. By destroying this ideal Americans placed a new emphasis on the piecemeal and the concrete in politics at the expense of order and completeness. The Constitution represented both the climax and the finale of the American Enlightenment, both the fulfillment and the end of the belief that the endless variety and perplexity of society could be reduced to a simple and harmonious system. By attempting to formulate a theory of politics that would represent reality as it was, the Americans of 1787 shattered the classical Whig world of 1776.

Americans had begun the Revolution assuming that the people were a homogeneous entity in society set against the rulers. But such an assumption belied American experience, and it took only a few years of independence to convince the best American minds that distinctions in the society were "various and unavoidable," so much so that they could not be embodied in the government. Once the people were thought to be composed of various interests in opposition to one another, all sense of a graduated organic chain in the social hierarchy became irrelevant, symbolized by the increasing emphasis on the image of a social contract. The people were not an order organically tied together by their unity of interest but rather an agglomeration of hostile individuals coming together for their mutual benefit to construct a society. The Americans transformed the people in the same way that Englishmen a century earlier had transformed the rulers: they broke the connectedness of interest among them and put them at war with one another, just as seventeenth-century Englishmen had separated the interests of rulers and people and put them in opposition to each other.

As Joel Barlow noted in 1792, the word *"people"* in America had taken on a different meaning from what it had in Europe. In America it meant the whole community and comprehended every human creature in the society; in Europe, however, it meant "something else more difficult to define." "Society," said Enos Hitchcock in 1788, "is composed of individuals—they are parts of the whole." And such individuals in America were the entire society: there could be nothing else—no orders, no lords, no monarch, no magistrates in the traditional sense. "Without the distinctions of titles, families, or nobility," wrote Samuel Williams, "they acknowledged and reverenced only those distinctions which nature had made, in a diversity of talents, abilities, and virtues. There were no family interests, connexions, or estates, large enough to oppress them. There was no excessive wealth in the hands of a few, sufficient to corrupt them." The Americans were thus both equal and unequal at the same time.

They all feel that nature has made them equal in respect to their rights; or rather that nature has given to them a common and an equal right to liberty, to property, and to safety; to justice, government, laws, religion, and freedom. They all see that nature has made them very unequal in respect to their original powers, capacities, and talents. They become united in claiming and in preserving the equality, which nature has assigned to them; and in availing themselves of the benefits, which are designed, and may be derived from the inequality, which nature has also established.

Politics in such a society could no longer be simply described as a contest between rulers and people, between institutionalized orders of the society. The political struggles would in fact be among the people themselves, among all the various groups and individuals seeking to create inequality out of their equality by gaining control of a government divested of its former identity with the society. It was this disembodiment of government from society that ultimately made possible the conception of modern politics and the eventual justification of competing parties among the people. Those who criticized such divisive jealousy and opposition among the people, said William Hornby of South Carolina in 1784, did not understand "the great change in politics, which the revolution must have necessarily produced. . . . In *these* days we are equal citizens of a DEMOCRATIC REPUBLIC, in which *jealousy* and *opposition* must naturally exist, while there exists a difference in the minds, interests, and sentiments of mankind." While few were as yet willing to justify factionalism so blatantly, many now realized with Madison that "the regulation of these various and interfering interests forms the principal task of modern legislation, and involves the spirit of party and faction

in the necessary and ordinary operations of the government."
Legislation in such a society could not be the transcending of the
different interests but the reconciling of them. Despite Madison's
lingering hope, the public good could not be an entity distinct
from its parts; it was rather "the general combined interest of all
the state put together, as it were, upon an average."

Under the pressure of this transformation of political thought
old words and concepts shifted in emphasis and took on new
meanings. Tyranny was now seen as the abuse of power by any
branch of the government, even, and for some especially, by the
traditional representatives of the people. "The accumulation of
all powers," said Madison, "legislative, executive, and judiciary,
in the same hands, whether of one, a few, or many, and whether
hereditary, self-appointed, or elective, may justly be pronounced
the very definition of tyranny." The separation of this governmental power, rather than simply the participation of the people
in a part of the government, became the best defense of liberty.
Therefore liberty, as the old Whigs had predominantly used the
term—public or political liberty, the right of the people to share
in the government—lost its significance for a system in which the
people participated throughout.

The liberty that was now emphasized was personal or private,
the protection of individual rights against all governmental encroachments, particularly by the legislature, the body which the
Whigs had traditionally cherished as the people's exclusive re-
pository of their public liberty and the surest weapon to defend
their private liberties. Such liberties, like that of freedom of the
press, said both Madison and Paine, were now in less danger from
"any direct attacks of Power" than they were from "the silent
awe of a predominant party" or "from a fear of popular resentment." The assumptions behind such charges were radically new
and different from those of the Whigs of 1776: men now began
to consider "the interests of society and the rights of individuals
as distinct," and to regard public and private liberty as antagonistic rather than complementary. In such circumstances the aim of

government, in James Iredell's words, became necessarily two-fold: to provide "for the security of every individual, as well as a fluctuating majority of the people." Government was no longer designed merely to promote the collective happiness of the people, but also, as the Tories had urged in the early seventies, "to protect citizens in their personal liberty and their property" even against the public will. Indeed, Madison could now say emphatically, "Justice is the end of government. It is the end of civil society." Unless individuals and minorities were protected against the power of majorities no government could be truly free.

Because of this growing sense of discrepancy between the rights of the society and the rights of individuals and because the new federal government was designed to prevent the emergence of any "common passion" or sense of oneness among large numbers of persons "on any other principles than those of justice and the general good," comprehensible only by a natural elite, the older emphasis on public virtue existing throughout the society lost some of its thrust; and men could now argue that "*virtue*, patriotism, or love of country, never was nor never will be till men's natures are changed, a fixed, permanent principle and support of government." The problem was, as Charles Thompson lamented in 1786, that most Americans had no other "Object" than their own "individual happiness." While Thompson still hoped that the people would eventually become "sufficiently impressed with a sense of what they owe to their national character," others began recasting their thinking. As early as 1782 Jefferson told Monroe that it was ridiculous to suppose that a man should surrender himself to the state. "This would be slavery, and not that liberty which the bill of rights has made inviolable, and for the preservation of which our government has been changed." Freedom, said Jefferson, would be destroyed by "the establishment of the opinion that the state has a *perpetual* right to the services of all it's members." The aim of instilling a spartan creed in America thus began to seem more and more nonsensical. By 1785 Noah Webster was directly challenging Montesquieu's opinion that

public virtue was a necessary foundation for democratic republics. Such virtue or patriotism, said Webster, could never predominate. Local attachments would always exist, self-interest was
all there ever was. But under a democracy, argued Webster, a self-
interested man must court the people, thus tending to make self-
love coincide with the people's interest.

William Vans Murray devoted an entire chapter of his *Political
Sketches*, published in 1787, to a denial of the conventional view
that republicanism was dependent upon virtue. The compulsion
for such arguments was obvious. America, as Murray admitted,
was "in a state of refinement and opulence," and was increasingly being permeated by "luxurious habits"—characteristics which
time-honored writers on politics had declared incompatible with
republican virtue and simplicity, and thus foreboding signs of
an inevitable declension of the state. Yet the political scientists
who spouted these maxims of republicanism had never known
America. "The truth is," said Murray, "Montesquieu had never
study'd a free Democracy." All the notions of these "refining
speculists" had come from impressions of the ancient republics
which possessed only "undefined constitutions, . . . constructed
in days of ignorance." The republics of antiquity had failed because they had "attempted to force the human character into
distorted shapes." The American republics, on the other hand,
said Murray, were built upon the realities of human nature. They
were free and responsive to the people, framed so as to give "fair
play" to the actions of human nature, however unvirtuous. They
had been created rationally and purposefully—for the first time
in history—without attempting to pervert, suppress, or ignore
the evil propensities of all men. Public virtue—the "enthusiasm,"
as Murray called it, of a rude and simple society, the public
proscription of private pursuits for luxury—had at last "found a
happy substitution in the energy of true freedom, and in a just
sense of civil liberty." The American governments possessed "the
freedom of Democracy, without its anarchy."

Although they were "so extremely popular," wrote John Stevens, "yet the checks which have been invented (particularly in some of them) have rendered these governments capable of a degree of stability and consistency beyond what could have been expected, and which will be viewed with surprise by foreigners." Undoubtedly virtue in the people had been an essential substitute for the lack of good laws and the indispensable remedy for the traditional defects of most democratic governments. But in America where the inconveniences of the democratic form of government had been eliminated without destroying the substantial benefits of democracy—where there was introduced, said James Wilson, "into the very form of government, such particular checks and controls, as to make it advantageous even for bad men to act for the public good"—the need for a society of simple, equal, virtuous people no longer seemed so critical. America alone, wrote Murray, had united liberty with luxury and had proved "the consistency of the social nature with the political happiness of man."

Such depreciations of public virtue were still sporadic and premature, yet they represented the beginnings of a fundamental shift in thought. In place of individual self-sacrifice for the good of the state as the bond holding the republican fabric together, the Americans began putting an increasing emphasis on what they called "public opinion" as the basis of all governments. Montesquieu in his *Spirit of the Laws*, wrote Madison in 1792, had only opened up the science of politics. Governments could not be divided simply into despotisms, monarchies, and republics sustained by their "operative principles" of fear, honor, and virtue. Governments, suggested Madison, were better divided into those which derived their energy from military force, those which operated by corrupt influence, and those which relied on the will and interest of the society. While nearly all governments, including the British monarchy, rested to some extent on public opinion, only in America had public consent as the basis of government attained its greatest perfection. No government, Americans told themselves over and over, had ever before so completely set its roots in the sentiments and aims of its citizens. All the power of America's governments, said Samuel Williams, was "derived from the public opinion." America would remain free not because of any quality in its citizens of spartan self-sacrifice to some nebulous public good, but in the last analysis because of the concern each individual would have in his own self-interest and personal freedom. The really great danger to liberty in the extended republic of America, warned Madison in 1791, was that each individual may become insignificant in his own eyes—hitherto the very foundation of republican government.

Such a total grounding of government in self-interest and consent had made old-fashioned popular revolutions obsolete. Establishments whose foundations rest on the society itself, said Wilson, cannot be overturned by any alteration of the government which the society can make. The decay and eventual death of the republican body politic now seemed less inevitable. The prevailing opinion of political writers, noted Nathaniel Chipman, had been "that man is fatally incapable of forming any system which shall endure without degeneration," an opinion that appeared "to be countenanced by the experience of ages." Yet America had lighted the way to a reversal of this opinion, placing, as David Ramsay put it, "the science of politics on a footing with the other sciences, by opening it to improvements from experience, and the discoveries of future ages." Governments had never been able to adjust continually to the operations of human nature. It was "impossible," said Chipman, "to form any human institution, which should accommodate itself to every situation in progress." All previous peoples had been compelled to suffer with the same forms of government—probably unplanned and unsuitable in the first place—despite extensive changes in the nature of their societies. "The confining of a people, who have arrived at a highly improved state of society, to the forms and principles of a government, which originated in a simple, if not barbarous state of men and manners," was, said Chipman, like Chinese foot-binding, a "perversion of nature," causing an incongruity between the form

of government and the character of the society that usually ended
in a violent eruption, in a forceful effort to bring the government
into accord with the new social temperament of the people.

However, the American republics possessed what Thomas Pow-
nall called "a *healing principle*" built into their constitutions.
Each contained "within itself," said Samuel Williams, "the means
of its own *improvement*." The American governments never pre-
tended, said Chipman, to perfection or to the exclusion of future
improvements. "The idea of incorporating, in the constitution
itself, a plan of reformation," enabling the people periodically and
peacefully to return to first principles, as Machiavelli had urged,
the Americans realized, was a totally new contribution to politics.
The early state constitutions, David Ramsay admitted, possessed
many defects. "But in one thing they were all perfect. They left
the people in the power of altering and amending them, whenever they pleased." And the Americans had demonstrated to the
world how a people could fundamentally and yet peaceably alter
their forms of government. "This revolution principle—that, the
sovereign power residing in the people, they may change their
constitution and government whenever they please—is," said
James Wilson, "not a principle of discord, rancour, or war: it
is a principle of melioration, contentment, and peace." Americans
had in fact institutionalized and legitimized revolution. Thereafter, they believed, new knowledge about the nature of government could be converted into concrete form without resorting to
violence. Let no one, concluded Chipman, now rashly predict
"that this beautiful system is, with the crazy empires of antiquity,
destined to a speedy dissolution; or that it must in time, thro' the
degeneracy of the people, and a corruption of its principles, of
necessity give place to a system of remediless tyranny and oppression." By actually implementing the old and trite conception
of the sovereignty of the people, by infusing political and even
legal life into the people, Americans had created, said Wilson,
"the great panacea of human politics." The illimitable progress
of mankind promised by the Enlightenment could at last be made

coincident with the history of a single nation. For the Americans at least, and for others if they followed, the endless cycles of history could finally be broken.

The Americans of the Revolutionary generation believed that they had made a momentous contribution to the history of politics. They had for the first time demonstrated to the world how a people could diagnose the ills of its society and work out. a peaceable process of cure. They had, and what is more significant they knew they had, broken through the conceptions of political theory that had imprisoned men's minds for centuries and brilliantly reconstructed the framework for a new republican polity, a reconstruction that radically changed the future discussion of politics. The Federalists had discovered, they thought, a constitutional antidote "wholly popular" and "strictly republican" for the ancient diseases of a republican polity—an antidote that did not destroy the republican vices, but rather accepted, indeed endorsed and relied upon them. The Federalist image of a public good undefinable by factious majorities in small states but somehow capable of formulation by the best men of a large society may have been a chimera. So too perhaps was the Federalist hope for the filtration of the natural social leaders through a federal sieve into political leadership. These were partisan and aristocratic purposes that belied the Federalists' democratic language. Yet the Federalists' intellectual achievement really transcended their particular political and social intentions and became more important and more influential than they themselves anticipated. Because their ideas were so popularly based and embodied what Americans had been groping towards from the beginning of their history, the Federalists' creation could be, and eventually was, easily adopted and expanded by others with quite different interests and aims at stake, indeed, contributing in time to the destruction of the very social world they had sought to maintain. The invention of a government that was, in James Sullivan's words, "perhaps without example in the world" could not long remain a strictly Federalist achievement. "As this kind of government," wrote

Samuel Williams, "is not the same as that, which has been called monarchy, aristocracy, or democracy; as it had a conspicuous origin in America, and has not been suffered to prevail in any other part of the globe, it would be no more than just and proper, to distinguish it by its proper name, and call it, *The American System of Government*."

So piecemeal was the Americans' formulation of this system, so diverse and scattered in authorship, and so much a simple response to the pressures of democratic politics was their creation, that the originality and the theoretical consistency and completeness of their constitutional thinking have been obscured. It was a political theory that was diffusive and open-ended; it was not delineated in a single book; it was peculiarly the product of a democratic society, without a precise beginning or an ending. It was not political theory in the grand manner, but it was political theory worthy of a prominent place in the history of Western thought.

The Emergence of Political Parties

The First American Party System

by Paul Goodman

Today, as in the past, American politics is on trial. Because political parties—private, voluntary institutions not mentioned in the Constitution—conduct much of the vital business of government in America, deciding who gets what, when, and how, politics in America has largely been the history of political parties. Yet that was not always so. Modern political parties emerged in the United States only as late as the 1790's, and not until much later in Western Europe. America gave birth to political parties after it rediscovered popular government.

As revolutionaries, Americans repudiated the sovereignty of king and Parliament and proclaimed instead the sovereignty of the people. The first American parties, however, did not spring up suddenly in the wake of the Revolution or because of increasing democratization of politics produced in that era. As in the colonial past, so in revolutionary America, many citizens were inclined to defer to the leadership of elites which traditionally claimed the right and enjoyed the power to govern. Groups of ambitious politicians, both in and out of office, jockeyed for control and occasionally appealed to voters for public support. In time of great voter apathy, the factious politics of a few had ample room in which to flourish. The Revolution, however, increased the potential for change. Since independent Americans, no longer owing allegiance to a distant Crown, had become theoretical masters of their own republican fate, they began to show more interest in government as a vehicle through which they could advance their well-being.

The Revolution politicized the citizenry, lowered obstacles to political participation, and heightened expectations. The adoption of the Constitution in 1789 created, in addition, a national political arena—the presidency and Congress—in which rival interests in a large, complex republic competed for advantage. Cliques accustomed to running things in their own states often found their will thwarted on the national scene. Only by forming coalitions with others whose votes might dominate Congress or elect a President could any single group hope to exert influence at the national capital. Political parties appeared to fulfill this and other needs. By nominating candidates and gathering behind them a broad base of support committed to programs and policies that appealed to the party's constituency, the first parties provided Americans with instruments for capturing power and making government serve their interests.

Paul Goodman analyzes the complex process through which the first modern political parties arose in the United States. Created by men who professed to abhor "parties"—any organized groups seeking power—the first political parties rescued popular government from the realm of theory and helped to mold it into a practical, political system.

The fears that haunted Americans in the decades preceding the Revolution continued to trouble the Revolutionary generation as it reconstructed political authority on "pure" republican foundations. No longer feeling themselves subjects of a corrupt kingdom,

From William N. Chambers and Walter Dean Burnham, *The American Party Systems: Stages of Political Development* (New York: Oxford University Press, 1967), pp. 56–77, 85–89. Copyright © 1967 by Oxford University Press Inc. Reprinted by permission; footnotes omitted.

Americans were free at last to devise political arrangements that would reconcile the competing claims of liberty and authority, protecting them from the aggressive and tyrannical propensities of power, and yet restraining those forces which threatened to disrupt communal order.

The solution was expected to come from a diligent study of politics, "the divine science." For two decades Americans wrote and rewrote constitutions, confident that appropriate constitutional mechanisms would tame faction, enable diverse and conflicting interests to secure justice, and lay the foundations of a great republic which was strong yet free. These high hopes, elaborately expounded during the formation of the federal Constitution, generated expectations that the young nation would avoid the rivalry and corruption, the tumult and violence that had infected and doomed earlier experiments in free government. The new frame of government was supposed to deliver Americans from the squabbling petty interests whose representatives schemed for the immediate, selfish advantage of their parochial constituencies.

The first decade's experience under the new regime was profoundly disillusioning. In the eyes of many the republic seemed to split into warring factions as dangerous as citizens had feared; as they saw it, forces lurked everywhere bent on subverting the carefully wrought structure of 1787 and overturning the social order. Networks of aristocrats, monarchists, and Jacobins, financial manipulators, "wild Irishmen," clerical bigots and blaspheming Illuminati, paid foreign agents and sowers of sedition and treason, they thought, roamed the republic plotting its destruction. In the decade preceding the Revolution, and recurrently throughout their history, Americans believed that sinister elements threatened their existence.

These perceptions of experience and the actual realities of public affairs were disturbingly incongruent. Those who built the first political party system in the 1790's mistook parties for factions, assuming that those with whom they differed were disloyal to the nation and its ideals. Though vastly different in structure and function from earlier forms of political organization, the first parties were confused with factions because the modern political party was outside the range of this generation's experience as well as its historical consciousness. Federalists and Republicans alike regarded themselves not as parties but as embodiments of the nation's will. When out of office, their duty was to recapture power from those temporarily and illegitimately exercising it; when in office, their task was to keep it from those ready to usurp and misuse it. Unconscious builders of political parties, Federalists and Republicans were prisoners of inherited political assumptions which distorted their understanding of the innovations stemming from the creation of a strong central government in a federal system. Viewing the political parties of the 1790's as alliances of factious elements, many Americans believed that factions had achieved cohesiveness, organization, and unity which made them more dangerous than ever, capable of overwhelming the consitutional mechanisms designed to restrain them.

Yet Americans were slowly learning from experience to accept the legitimacy of organized political activity in support of or in opposition to those who exercised the powers of government. In time political parties came to be recognized as institutions essential to the survival of free government, providing an orderly means of articulating the majority's wishes and settling differences among contending groups. The acceptance of parties, and their incorporation into the structure of American politics, constituted a recognition that the forces which generated them were inherent in an open society.

Unlike later nation-builders, the Americans had no contemporary models for guidance; nor were the lessons of history useful except as they helped them avoid the errors of others. Though unaware that they were experiencing political modernization, the necessities of circumstance forced them to change their ways of managing public business.

If crises in participation promote the growth of political parties, the contours of such crises in America differed noticeably from similar phenomena in other times and places. No fundamental social or economic transformation preceded the emergence of the early party system, nor was "the extension of the suffrage," as LaPalombara and Weiner, and others, have suggested, "the real impetus for the creation of some form of party organization at the local level." The Revolution did not radically alter the productive system or the social structure, and suffrage had not been monopolized by a few even before independence. The absence of a native hereditary aristocracy, the superficiality of royal control, the great instability in the fortunes of leading men, and the constant need to recruit additional leadership to govern a new and rapidly expanding society, made it difficult to exclude the most talented and persistent elements which sought to participate in public affairs. The colonists did not experience full-scale democracy, but those who exercised power had never been as secure as their counterparts in the Old World were.

The movement for independence which expressed the Americans' determination to preserve self-government had failed to generate parties such as those which appeared in the 1790's. The Revolutionary leaders did not, as later ones did, need to create a party to mobilize support outside the government, because they already dominated much of the existing political structure. They were not conspirators forced to operate outside the framework of established authority, but parliamentary leaders, accustomed to exercise power and able to work through established institutions. . . . The Revolutionary forces thus always enjoyed the legitimacy of being part of constituted authority. Accustomed to authority, the revolutionary leaders did not depend primarily on mass movements to organize resistance.

When political parties did emerge in the 1790's, they did not effect radical change in the *formal* terms of participation in government. Rather they mobilized previously inactive elements, bringing into the political arena citizens and groups that had had the right but not the desire or incentive to participate. Far more important in broadening the base of popular government than liberalization of the suffrage was erosion of the habits of deference which had enabled those claiming social superiority to command the respect and support of their inferiors. The decline of deference had its roots in the social disorganization accompanying the transplantation of traditional English institutions and attitudes to America. Because the American social order lacked either a nobility or other familiar ruling elements, its leadership strata was self-made and recruited from the middle and lower strata; and because abundant resource opportunities enabled the shrewd and enterprising to rise, the composition of the leading strata lacked permanence, as newcomers edged their way to prominence. The Revolution intensified the degree of social disorganization, as established elements were swept away by war, and further undermined the capacity of leaders to lead, making it harder than ever for citizens to know to whom they should defer when so many, often new faces, competed for their favor. Political parties hastened the decline of deference by legitimizing and institutionalizing competition for the electorate's favor and by enhancing the likelihood that challengers might succeed in ousting established elements. Thus instead of being the product of an enlarged franchise, the first American party system generally sharply increased the level of voter participation.

In addition to resolving crises of participation, political parties, as LaPalombara and Weiner suggest, emerge during crises of legitimacy. By proclaiming themselves instruments of the majority, parties authenticate a regime's claim to represent the popular will. The new Revolutionary regimes in America, following the Declaration of Independence, enjoyed legitimacy from the outset without the aid of modern parties to express majority will. The Revolutionary cause never became a party cause because it was seen as a defense of established units of local government against the usurpations of king and parliament. The colonists believed they were upholding the British constitution against those who sought to subvert it, and with relatively little difficulty the new regimes quickly assumed the right to exercise all the functions of government. These regimes suffered few doubts about their legitimacy, for the logic of the Revolutionary argument left no other conceivable claimant to sovereign power. Those Americans who opposed the Revolutionary movement either went into exile or quietly submitted, so the new republic was spared the challenges of potentially disloyal elements receptive to opportunities for restoring the old regime. . . .

The most troublesome problem of authority arose over the establishment of the national government. Those who favored strengthening the Confederation at the expense of the states, and who later wanted to scrap the Articles entirely, attacked the adequacy rather than the legitimacy of existing arrangements. And those who unsuccessfully but vigorously fought adoption of the new federal Constitution quietly and rapidly submitted to the new regime, without entirely abandoning their doubts. In the 1790's also, Americans often divided over the course the new government was steering, but few wished to undo the settlement of 1787. From time to time the disaffected lost hope that their interests could be advanced within the established political framework. Some of these elements joined the Whisky Rebellion in 1793 or Fries's Rebellion in 1799, or toyed with separating from the Union, as did some Republicans in the Old Southwest in the 1790's and some Federalists in New England after 1800. On the whole, however, while political activists professed to believe that their opponents plotted their downfall and endangered the social order, they argued that the evil stemmed from a perversion of legitimate authority which could be cured not by rejecting authority as such but by changing the men who held the reins of power. No *Putsch* could hope to succeed as long as most citizens had faith in peaceful change, and hence no group, however alienated, could reasonably expect to get its way through violence. Even hopelessly discouraged minorities, such as the later Federalists, became resigned to their fate.

The establishment of a national center of decision-making generated greater tensions than the framers had foreseen. Many feared

for the stability of the social order or doubted that the new framework of government would enable Americans to master the forces
that threatened survival. By 1815, however, these fears and doubts
had subsided. The nation experienced a series of internal and
external challenges but emerged with its constitutional fabric intact
and its citizens more nearly united than ever. By providing orderly
means of determining the majority's will and enabling conflicting
forces to settle their differences peacefully, the first political parties
authenticated government's claim to represent the people. Yet in
the early years of party development their functions were obscured
because no one had anticipated how difficult it would be to
articulate the national will in a republic that was larger in territory,
and more diverse in its social components, than any in the past.
The new government immediately faced a series of decisions on
problems whose specific outlines and complex dimensions could
not be foreseen in 1787, and whose solutions were likely to lead
to disagreements. Though nearly all agreed that public policy
must be based on the majority's wishes, no one could authoritative-
ly know or interpret the majority's wishes because the people
themselves often had no opinion, and when they did, it was hopelessly divided or fragmented. The task of the early political parties
was to attempt to clarify, to articulate and channel, the majority's
preferences. Though the clash of parties helped to give legitimacy
to the policies adopted by government, citizens often found it
difficult to accept this mode of decision-making because the deferential style of politics lingering from the past assumed that a
disinterested, virtuous, and wise few were to be entrusted with
power. But party politics assumed that no group had either a
prescriptive right to govern or an inherent monopoly of wisdom or
competence.

Like the crisis in participation and legitimacy, the American
version of the crisis of national integration also diverged from the
experience of many other new nations. In certain critical respects,
a large measure of integration had been achieved before the 1790's.

From the beginning the republic enjoyed territorial integration, with territorial limits defined by the boundaries of the colonies which the new nation automatically incorporated. Predominantly English in nationality and Protestant in religion, the colonists had also long shared a common culture inherited from Britain. Even more important were experiences which shaped a new sense of identity, transforming Britons into Americans. "What is an American?," Crèvecœur asked, and announced that "a new race of men" had appeared whose ideas and institutions distinguished them from those they had left behind in Europe. Long before Americanness was embodied in a sovereign state, the colonists had sensed that they shared a common nationality born of their unique experiences—the product not simply of a common language, culture, religion, or long identification with place, but of being uprooted and replanted in the wilderness. The Americans assumed that they were unique and superior because they assumed that their society was enlightened beyond any other. . . .

Yet integration was incomplete; like the crises of participation and legitimacy, the crisis of integration was subdued and prolonged. At first Americans misjudged the extent to which independence required the centralization of authority. They believed that by locating sovereignty in the states, power would be less dangerous to liberty; diversity, they thought, was not inconsistent with national prosperity and survival. The experiment in decentralization foundered when citizens discovered that their well-being required a redistribution of power. The new federal Constitution attempted to achieve a greater degree of national integration, sufficient to promote "the general welfare" without eliminating local authority but limiting its scope. The Constitution created a new locus of power which promoted greater integration by requiring the articulation of a national will to decide those policy questions which had become the responsibility of all the people, the voters in the Union. But it provided no mechanism for focusing national attention on the pressing issues of the day or for collecting popular sentiment. The first political parties, off-springs of a national center of decision-making, performed that task.

As long as the states had been sovereign during the Confederation, conflicts of interest were played out within the arenas of state politics. The members of Congress in the Confederation were ambassadors from their states, and in most matters local perspectives were decisive. The new Constitution shifted the locus of decision-making, and for the first time citizens elected a Congress and President to grapple with problems on a scale and in a context that were new. Whether the nation survived and prospered now depended on what happened at the national capital. Federal power was not distant and abstract but could reach into a citizen's pocketbook, hale him before the courts, and determine whether he lived at peace or war with other nations. Centralization also vastly multiplied the numbers and complexity of the groups competing for advantage. By throwing representatives of diverse elements together under one jurisdiction, the Constitution heightened the sense of group differences and local senses of identity. Frustrated Virginians became exploited planters and Southerners; disappointed Massachusetts men became aggrieved merchants and Easterners. The multiplication of heterogeneous elements, each prone to identify its own interests with what it regarded as the national welfare, certain that anything threatening its special interests jeopardized the common good, increased the intensity of political life. Groups used to getting their way at home were unused to being thwarted in the new arena. But there they repeatedly encountered frustration and discouragement, which aroused suspicions that "the general welfare" was being sacrificed to faction.

The only way to resist was to find new methods of arousing the electorate to the presumed dangers and to forge a national coalition to install in the legislative and executive branches men devoted to "the common good." To do this, electoral alliances among elements in the various states were indispensable, especially in the organization of Congress and the choice of a President. Paradoxically, though centralization promoted national integration, it also led to the polarization of the nation into parties by generating conflicts which required new institutions for their management and resolution. The parties divided people as they united them. Each party brought together diverse elements previously little known to one another, elements whose common fears and interests dictated their union and required the formulation of an ideology which defined their purpose and could claim to represent the national ideals. To form an effective party coalition, the diverse social materials were forced to accommodate to one another and to formulate a program and ideology vague and broad enough to carry a wide appeal. Once in power, parties learned that the compromises that had brought them into office could help keep them there by accommodating the opposition when feasible. Thus parties organized conflict and in doing so intensified it, but they also instituted an orderly means of settling differences without resorting to violence. Parties offered hope to the threatened or discouraged that the next election would bring a change in fortune and the restoration of virtue to the seats of power. And when that happened, the Union once more would be whole: "We are all republicans, we are all federalists," as Jefferson put it.

The first American party system made leadership and policy formulation sensitive to the conflicting demands of diverse elements scattered across an extensive republic and thereby helped to reconcile these heterogeneous elements to the Union. It did not, however, resolve the crisis in integration for the long run; by the middle of the nineteenth century, altered circumstances intensified the long smoldering crisis of national integration beyond the capacity of the party system of that time to resolve.

The course of party development in the 1790's was slow, uneven, and incomplete. Parties appeared earlier in some communities than elsewhere, and though they eventually spread into most states, they barely took root in some. In some states a strong two-party system developed and persisted; in others it did not survive much beyond the election of 1800, and one party dominated there-after. In some of the two-party states the contending forces were evenly balanced, but elsewhere they were unevenly matched. Some second parties became, after a struggle, the major party; others never achieved power. The peculiar circumstances of each state shaped the timing, direction, and precise course of party development.

Party evolution in the states was determined by conditions that preceded the appearance of stimuli to party growth and influenced the extent to which competitive politics flourished. The most important were the political infra-structure—the constitutional mechanisms and procedures, formal and informal, which defined the rules of the game—and the social structure, which influenced the range and intensity of group conflict. Both determined the strength with which habits of deference endured.

Some social structures nourished competitive politics while others discouraged it. States with a high degree of social differentiation and social change experienced tensions that weakened habits of deference and generated rivalry which promoted party development. Demographic patterns and shifts were one persistent important source of conflict. The influx of new population into an area was an index of the opportunities that attracted settlers to a region. The older and more densely settled areas, often the smaller states, exerted less pull on prospective emigrants because there was little good land left, and the few that might venture into such communities found it much harder to penetrate the established order. Unsettled areas not only offered land to new-comers but, since there was no pre-existing social structure, permitted settlers to fashion one themselves. All positions of influence were up for grabs where no established groups controlled them. Yet the unsettled areas were not the only ones experiencing high rates of population growth. Rapidly developing urban areas with expanding commercial economies, such as Baltimore, offered considerable opportunity to newcomers. Whatever reasons pulled men, the rapid influx of population into western Pennsylvania, up-country South Carolina and Georgia, Maine, and central and western New York introduced disruptive elements that required assimilation into the social structure; in turn, this usually meant a redistribution of power. Differential rates of growth within a state gave a sectional or regional pattern to politics as new groups concentrated in certain areas and challenged the authority of those situated in older, more stable communities.

Population growth often brought increased demographic heterogeneity. Some states already had highly differentiated populations before the Revolution. Pennsylvania had large numbers of Germans, fragmented into a variety of Protestant denominations, with the Lutherans the largest and most active; Scots-Irish who were also Presbyterians; and English and Welsh who were generally Quakers or Episcopalians. These ethnic and religious groups were concentrated in certain parts of the state which gave them a greater degree of self-consciousness, cohesiveness, and political force than they would have had were they distributed more evenly throughout the colonies or within the state. Similarly, in the 1790's a highly visible and often vocal influx of English and French *émigrés* from the tyranny and turmoil of Europe added troublesome new elements.

Memberships in ethnic and religious groups mediated an individual's relationships with authority. . . . Sometimes objective interests appear to explain partisan choice, as when religious dissenters supported the Republicans because they were opposed to religious bigotry and establishments. In other instances a group's party preference seemed to depend on its leaders' personal ambitions and antagonisms. These could, however, be reconciled with the group's interests, since support of its leaders was a way of asserting the group's dignity and expressing its desire for proper recognition in the community. Ethnic and religious influences on party preference were also complicated by the looseness of party identifications, which could easily be altered. Thus Pennsylvania Germans generally voted Federalist until the late 1790's, when the direct tax, reminding them of the hated hearth tax in

Europe which went to fill the coffers of Rome, turned them toward Jeffersonian Republicanism in 1800. A further complication was that individuals were subjected to multiple pressures, such as occupational and regional ones, which might reinforce or conflict with ethnic and religious ones.

Conflict rooted in competitive economic interests has traditionally become a primary focus of political history. The difficulty with the conventional economic interpretation is that economic or occupational groups in America did not form homogeneous classes and were usually deeply divided. Men differed on the best ways to advance their material well-being; but more importantly, their political preference was colored by the totality of their social situation, which included other roles besides occupational ones. Thus a Quaker merchant might have thought Federalist foreign policy was good for business, but his view might also have been shaped by his desire to harmonize his role as a merchant with his cultural ties with England, or with his fear of those who challenged his position through the Republican party. Though the conventional picture that the early parties stemmed from conflicts between agrarian, commercial, financial, and manufacturing interests is no longer persuasive, economic development was an important source of social differentiation. Some states and certain regions within a state experienced much less economic growth than other areas. Where rapid growth did occur, it generated rivalries that contributed to party development. Thus the emergence of Baltimore as a leading commercial center produced a powerful, ambitious group of Republican merchants, revolving around Robert and Samuel Smith and their connections, who successfully challenged the power of an old-line Federalist leadership entrenched in the rural counties. . . .

Sectional and provincial loyalties further complicated the political picture. Whether one left one's native region or stayed behind, place of birth was a source of pride. People thought of themselves as Virginians or Massachusetts men, Northerners or Southerners, as well as Americans. Presidential ticket makers knew this when they balanced George Washington with John Adams, Adams with Charles C. Pinckney of South Carolina, Thomas Jefferson with Aaron Burr, James Madison with Elbridge Gerry of Massachusetts. "How shall we conjure down this damnable rivalry between Virginia and Massachusetts?" John Adams asked Jefferson some years after they had done battle as representatives of their beloved rival commonwealths and regions.

Whatever its sources, diversity produced tensions in the social structure that undermined habits of deference, fostered competition, and promoted party growth. The variety of groups produced many different perceptions of self-interest and attitudes toward public policy, gave individuals an incentive to participate in public affairs to further their own group interests, and threw up leaders who expressed different perspectives. Wherever social diversity was greatest, it was most difficult for leadership to exercise power unchecked or to continue to receive uncritical deference from the citizenry. Where many competed for advantage in an open society, few could long resist pressures from the excluded. Hence states with highly differentiated social structures were likely to exhibit a more competitive politics than states with a low degree of differentiation. Since aristocracy also ran afoul of republican ideology, thwarted or endangered interests conventionally sought to discredit opponents by denouncing them as "aristocrats." Resistance to change was taken as proof that some Americans presumed illegitimately to possess a superior right to govern and sought to perpetuate temporary advantage, recently acquired, by transforming it into permanent privilege. The result, presumably, would be an hereditary aristocracy, without the birth, blood, or antiquity with which such groups traditionally justified their position. The father of Jeffersonian Republicanism proclaimed the party faith by demanding "equal rights for all, special privileges for none," a theme that reappeared in Republican rhetoric in endlessly different forms like a Wagnerian leitmotif. Here was a doctrine that, theoretically at least, tolled the death knell for the politics of deference.

Diversity of political interests and perspectives not only increased the desire of people to participate politically; it also created
obstacles to national integration. The great range of varying
interests competing for influence made the achievement of a
national consensus no easy task. The first American party system
played a critical role, not only in providing a means for various
groups to influence decision-making through alliances with others
which gave them effective political striking power, but also in
promoting trust and a willingness to compromise among disparate
forces separated by parochial perspectives and preferences. As the
first parties integrated diverse social materials into effective institutions, they provided an instrument by which the nation could
accommodate rivalries. For these reasons, not only was a heterogeneous social structure a precondition for the development of
political parties in general, but the special form party development
took in a particular community reflected in addition its own configuration of social forces. . . .

For almost a generation Americans engaged in a great deal of
constitution-making. The particular arrangement agreed upon was
the product of colonial experiences and existing power relationships, as well as historical investigation and philosophical reflection. Each state's constitution influenced the extent to which its
politics was competitive, for the rules of the game usually shaped
patterns of political expression. Thus, in states where informal
procedures had traditionally played an important role, inferiors
customarily deferred to their superiors; politics was likely to be
less competitive than it was in states where leadership recruitment
and decision-making were formalized as the result of open rivalry.
Formalization promoted political polarization on a statewide basis,
sharpened divisions between contending forces, and stimulated
coalitions among those with common interests. Where local offices
were largely appointive rather than elective, informal arrangements
were likely to prevail. Self-perpetuating town and country cliques
took turns in office with each member getting an opportunity to
enjoy the perquisites and profits of office, as long as he demon-

strated appropriate loyalty and patience. Ambitious newcomers were neutralized by admitting them to the favored circle, placing them at the bottom of the ladder but assuring them of eventual ascent. Since disaffected members of the group or excluded elements had no recourse to the electorate to gain access to office, it was nearly hopeless to fight the system, especially since the dominant loyal group easily controlled the county's only elected official, the representative in the legislature. Where local office was elective, on the other hand, political procedures were usually more formalized and open and the opportunities of electoral choice encouraged competition for office. The excluded and disaffected had a more reasonable chance to unseat an entrenched group, which found it much harder to monopolize patronage and office.

A deferential style of politics was strongest where informal procedures and appointive office went together with a constitution which dispersed decision-making in the towns and counties. The more the political structure was decentralized, the more difficult it was to organize on a colony-wide or statewide basis. A strong executive with patronage and the veto, independent of the legislature because he owed his election not to its favor but to a popular vote in a statewide constituency, and who could succeed himself repeatedly, was a centralizing force which promoted political competition. . . .

The political infra-structure of each state was the product of its own peculiar historical development. Whether a state relied on formal or informal procedures, recruited its leaders through election or appointment, centralized or decentralized power, or had a strong or a weak executive, was not entirely fortuitous but reflected the distribution of forces and power in the community and the way citizens thought it best to manage their public affairs. The shaping force in making constitutions was not logic but experience and expectations.

A competitive social and political structure was a necessary precondition for party growth, but not a precipitant. Before 1789 rivalries generally involved provincial interests within the states.

The federal Constitution, however, pushed citizens into a national political arena since the locus of decision-making was now divided between central and local governments. This change rendered inadequate the older methods by which public affairs were managed and stimulated the invention of new ones.

The parties which emerged in the 1790's were distinguished from the factions and *ad hoc* interest groups that had competed for advantage in the colonial and Revolutionary years by their elaboration of structures and functions. Parties systematically organized electoral processes by developing techniques for nominating candidates and persuading the citizens to vote for them on election day. The elaboration of ideologies and party structure, the recruitment of party leadership at different levels, the enlistment of a faithful cadre of party workers, and the development of party loyalty within the electorate gave the first American party system an institutional complexity and stability that earlier political forms lacked. As alliances of heterogeneous elements within a state and among groups in different states, parties also developed a territorial range and social density that made them national in scope and function.

The struggle over centralization during the 1780's, culminating in the federal Constitution, polarized the nation, as widely dispersed and diverse citizens collectively decided how best to manage the affairs of the republic. The newly established national government was also a potential source of continued polarization. The problems confronting the country and the policy choices adopted would affect citizens wherever they lived, and recognition of this fact worked against traditional parochial outlooks. The developing national perspectives of farmers, merchants, manufacturers, mechanics and artisans, holders of public securites, and others were now sharpened and deepened as they sought to shape public policy at the national capital after 1789. As the new government chose between competing courses, it won increased favor among some but disappointed others. Groups learned that they could effectively promote their interests only through national authority, but that rival groups could also thwart their desires through that same authority. Conflicts, compromises, bargains, and deals with distant and often unfamiliar elements were necessary before decisions could be reached. The first American party system became the principal means by which the complex array of interests and local perspectives sorted themselves out and joined together in electoral alliances to promote their welfare.

In the early 1790's Congress became a dramatic arena within which rival groups quarreled over policy questions. Should the state debts be assumed by the federal government, how should the federal debt be funded, how should the tax burden be distributed, should a national bank be established, how should the public domain be managed—these were some of the many vexing questions facing the new government. As a consequence of repeated clashes in the legislative chambers there was an increasing polarization within Congress around particular leaders and issues. As members of Congress articulated differences inherent in the electorate and fought to gain their way, newspapers and other communications media made citizens more aware than ever of the differences that divided them. As divisions emerged in Congress, legislative leaders became keenly interested in the outcome of congressional elections which would determine the strength of their troops at the next session. In this way, national leaders came to take a growing interest in the politics of the various states, while at the same time voters now were making choices that would influence, and were influenced by, national perspectives.

Presidential elections had a similar effect. The obvious preference for George Washington in the first two presidential elections delayed the nationalizing and polarizing impact of a contest for the presidency, and hence its contribution to political party development. The absence of consensus over the succession in 1796, however, encouraged leaders in the capital to form alliances and make arrangements with the various elements that influenced the choice of presidential electors in the states in order to mobilize support behind particular candidates. The previous divisions in the Congress, in the executive branch, and in the states simplified the task of presidential ticket-makers, since lines of opposition had been drawn more and more clearly in many communities before the intrusion of the presidential question.

Thus differences over policy produced national perspectives among interests and voters, splits in the Congress, and rivalry over the presidency, and in turn promoted party development. So too did personal rivalries and conflicts of interest within the states, many of which preceded party development but nonetheless fed the flames of party battle in the 1790's. In many states persisting antagonisms influenced the way people chose sides in the controversies which began to erupt in the capital. The Washington administration could not appoint all those who desired recognition, and those who were disappointed added to the numbers of the disgruntled. . . .

Yet none of these divisions aroused an often lethargic electorate in the way the ideological and diplomatic crisis generated by the French Revolution did. The outbreak of war in Europe in 1793 between Revolutionary France and the coalition of old regimes which were determined to crush republicanism agitated Americans profoundly. The Revolution in France forced them to choose between peace and war, between a French or a British alliance, between lining up with "the party of humanity" or backing "the forces of reaction." Determined to remain neutral in deed, if not in thought, Americans could not escape a choice. Their prosperity was closely bound to ties of trade with the belligerents, and their security and sense of destiny deeply involved in the fate of French republicanism.

At the center of party conflict in the mid-1790's, moreover, was a widespread belief that the future of the republic was threatened. Those who considered themselves Republicans had believed even earlier that the decisions made by the early, Federalist-dominated Congresses had departed from republican principles by benefiting the few at the expense of the many. But Federalists were equally

convinced that those measures, denounced as anti-republican by
their critics, actually promoted the stability and prosperity of the
nation and thereby helped to assure the success of the republican
experiment. When Federalists moved to prevent British interference with American trade with France from precipitating war,
they confirmed Republican suspicions that they were aristocrats
with British sympathies. When Republicans in turn sought to
block ratification of Jay's Treaty in 1795 and thereby risk war
with Britain, Federalists were confirmed in their suspicions that
the Republicans were Jacobins with French sympathies. The
crisis of the mid-1790's affected people wherever they lived and
whatever their local circumstances, and had a saliency that earlier
issues had lacked. By arousing widespread, deep, and fierce
partisan sentiments, it simplified and dramatized electoral choice.

The Republican party continued to attract many of those who
had already been alienated by the policies of the federal government. Now it also came to encompass others who had once
supported Federalist domestic policy but would not support Federalist foreign policy, and still others who had previously taken
little interest in public affairs but were aroused by what they saw
as new dangers. Although most Republicans prudently wished to
avoid involvement in foreign wars, they could not hide their
sympathies, and now perceived their own Revolution as the first
act in the drama of mankind's regeneration through the American
example. Should the votaries of superstition and oppression crush
republicanism in Europe, they thought, it could not long survive
in America. Moreover, French defeat would bring into question
the universality of America's own Revolutionary example and
strike a mortal blow at the party of humanity. The Jeffersonians,
along with many European *philosophes*, saw the American Revolution as the most important event in human affairs since the
coming of Christ. As Jesus had delivered mankind from the
tyranny of sin and death, so republicanism, inspired by the American model, promised to free mankind from civic inequality and
slavery.

Other Americans, of course, disagreed. Most had welcomed the French Revolution in its early years, but as it became violent and expansionist, and threatened to disrupt peaceful and profitable ties with the rest of the world, the consensus dissolved. Federalism expressed the fears and disillusionment of those who believed that France discredited republicanism by its inability to reconstruct a stable fabric of government at home and by its insatiable lust for conquest abroad. The future of republicanism rested not on the outcome of events abroad but on the establishment of a strong and stable republic at home, they thought, and the export of Jacobinism to the United States was now the most serious threat to the survival of the republic since the crisis of the 1780's. Thus the Federalist and Republican parties, both devoted to republicanism, each believed that the other threatened its survival at home. For the Republicans, those who favored a protective alliance with Britain and were willing to join the war against France betrayed the country's ideals and its mission. In turn, Federalists believed that men who were incapable of distinguishing between genuine republicanism and Gallic tyranny were at bottom American Jacobins who endangered the social order.

Whether citizens chose Federalism or Republicanism depended on their attitudes toward national authority and the way in which they thought it affected their vital interests. Federalist leadership was mainly drawn from elites who had achieved positions of prominence before or during the Revolution, but who were insecure because of challenges from below. These challenges they perceived as attacks on constituted authority, and thus they looked to the national government to protect them from disorder and the spread of "French principles." Republican leaders were more often ambitious newcomers, outsiders who had been excluded by dominant groups from positions of prestige and power. Denied equal access to government, they believed that they were the victims of an erstwhile aristocracy; and thus they regarded national authority as a potential instrument of local aristocracy and identified emotionally with French Revolutionary attacks on entrenched privilege. These alienated elements were galvanized, organized, made self-conscious through the leadership of elites in other states which did not feel threatened within and hence felt no fear of Jacobinism at home, but were disaffected from national authority because they believed they were denied their rightful place in the national councils. For them, the necessities of the national political arena required that they enlist support from among discontented elements in other states even though such allies might be their social inferiors. . . .

Even where conditions were most favorable to party growth, the first American party system failed to survive. In some states where the Republicans won majorities in 1800, Federalists perceived only the dimmest hopes of making a comeback, and many simply gave up the fight. Others invested new energies in party activity, though often with disappointing results. The crisis in foreign affairs after 1805, culminating in the unpopular Embargo of 1807 and the divisive decision to go to war in 1812, caused dissension among Republicans and led to a brief revival of Federalist strength, which, however, fell far short of enabling the party to recapture national power or even to regain it for long in many states. By 1815 Federalism and Republicanism no longer divided the nation into rival political formations. Party organizations decayed, ideological and programmatic differences were blurred, and many Federalists in search of office joined their erstwhile enemies. With each passing year, Jefferson's vision was increasingly coming to pass—"We are all republicans, we are all federalists" —although the emphasis fell on the former term.

Most explanations of the first party system's arrested development have focused on the Federalist decline. Some have argued that the party was deeply divided in the late 1790's between Hamiltonian war Federalists and Adams peace Federalists, and that this division cost the party dearly in the election of 1800 and unity was never restored. But why not? Why didn't the necessities of defeat, the experience of being a minority, force discordant elements to bury their differences sufficiently to form an effective opposition and regain power? Another analysis suggests that the Federalists were doomed by their conservative, aristocratic ideology, which was increasingly incongruous in a society of ongoing democratization. But why didn't the Federalists make a greater effort to adjust their ideology to political realities, as politicians usually do if they desire to regain power? And why were Republican elites so successful in building a party whose *raison d'être* was the destruction of aristocracy? Some have argued that Federalist principles made them loath to resort to the political methods and machinery which the Jeffersonians used so successfully to win office. But why should Federalist gentlemen have been less willing to innovate than Republican gentlemen? Moreover, recent studies suggest that younger Federalists did build elaborate party organizations in many states after 1800 without abandoning their basic ideology. Yet despite such efforts, the party failed to arrest decay.

Another course of explanation seems to be in order. It might begin with the fact that the first political parties were new and fragile institutions, lacking deep roots in political experience, and that party identification and loyalty was recent and weak. It is often difficult to fix clearly a politician's partisan identity in the 1790's and early 1800's, and shifts from one party to another occurred frequently. Party organization was also new and often rudimentary, falling short of stable institutional foundations; thus the early parties were not autonomous institutions, but hastily formed, loose alliances of individuals and groups. Should disaffection or apathy overtake these groups the party would wither away, because the party structure, as such, had only a weak claim to citizen support. Before the 1790's no one had been born a Federalist or Republican, and thus most ordinary citizens and voters did not inherit an ancestral party loyalty. The superficiality of party development helps explain why so many party leaders, especially Federalists, retired from battle, and why still others defected to the Republicans.

Party growth had thrived on the tensions of the 1790's, but

those tensions ebbed in the years that followed Jefferson's election. As the Republicans took power, most Federalists learned that, after all, their old fears of Jacobinism were unfounded. In office the Republicans left many important Federalist policies undisturbed, carefully cultivated support from moderate Federalists they hoped to convert, retained many Federalist jobholders and made removals covertly and piecemeal, so as not to alarm the opposition. Victory was also sobering for the Republicans. Their assumption of power reduced their fears of monarchy and restored their faith in peaceful means of effecting change. Controlling the presidency and Congress, Republicans were no longer hostile to national authority; and power gave them confidence, especially as their continued rule became assured. The more secure and dominant they became, the more they were prone to split into warring factions, especially in states where Federalists no longer effectively challenged them. On this count too, men of virtually all persuasions came to think less and less in party terms.

In this situation, the first party system withered away because most of its builders did not regard themselves as professional party politicians. Such leaders as Washington, Jefferson, and Hamilton had seen themselves as disinterested statesmen, not as political brokers among competing interests or as election managers, even when necessity forced them to behave as though they were. Confidence in their rectitude and the wisdom of their policies made Federalists insensitive and indifferent to the political dangers their rhetoric and programs entailed. In a social order where habits of deference still persisted, a statesman was accustomed to doing what he thought right regardless of personal risk, whereas a professional politician typically calculates risks and maneuvers accordingly within the mainstream of popular currents. The Federalists claimed to be statesmen, not professionals. To most early Republican as well as Federalist leaders too, politics was not a profession. It was rather a duty, a responsibility of gentlemen whose primary commitment was to planting, or trade, or law, or medicine, and the good life. Most hated to stand for or serve in public office. Party leaders often had to plead with popular vote-getters to run for office and with men of special talent to accept major appointments. Despite grave fears for the future of the republic, Thomas Jefferson fled public life in 1793 for Monticello, and not to build an opposition party, as mythology tells it. While President, John Adams spent so much time at home amid comfortable surroundings, neglecting affairs of state, that he temporarily lost control of his own administration. Men unaccustomed to the stinging shafts of political attack, thin-skinned, unused to the rough and tumble of political warfare, preferred to retreat to their firesides rather than remain as targets for mudslingers. If a man was disappointed or defeated, he gracefully retired; one's career did not revolve around winning and holding office. Once again, this was particularly the case among Federalist leaders. For the professional whose occupation is politics, there is nothing else to do but plan, work, wait, and hope for the next election. He knows that there is rhythm in political life and that eventually his fortunes will improve; tomorrow's possible victory makes it easier to accept today's defeat and inspires new energies to hasten the time of his return to office. But for defeated Federalists there could be no such expectation, if only because they had no experience with the cyclical alternation of parties in and out of power. Defeat, when it came, was total.

The Revolutionary generation did produce some prototypes of the political professional, men like Aaron Burr and DeWitt Clinton of New York, whose careers revolved around the pursuit of office. But such individuals inspired distrust and contempt even among those temporarily allied with them, those who needed and used their skills and strength. One could never quite trust men who were governed exclusively by selfish desires, devoid of principle, willing to resort to almost any means to gain their ends. During the deadlocked presidential election of 1800 that ended in the House of Representatives, Alexander Hamilton urged Federalists to support Jefferson over Burr because he thought that the Virginia gentleman, for all his faults, was far less dangerous than the unscrupulous Manhattan politician. In the eyes of the patrician leaders of the first party system, men like Burr lacked the essential moral qualities political leadership demanded. Only those recruited from among the "real" interests of the republic— merchants, farmers, and planters—could understand and would serve the people's needs. Lawyers, the occupation from whom professional politicians were to be recruited, were suspect since they were widely viewed as social parasites, producing no wealth but prospering off the miseries of those who did. To keep public life pure, officials should receive small salaries that would discourage service by any except virtuous men motivated by civic responsibility. A hireling political leadership was as unacceptable in a republic, they thought, as a hireling clergy in a reformed church, and equally dangerous.

One day the republic would need the services and skills of professional politicians. The Revolutionary generation had already discovered that the tasks of governance were far more difficult and complex than they had at first realized. As nation-builders the Americans were amateurs who sailed into rough and uncharted waters, only vaguely aware of the difficult storms ahead. At each step of the journey, none could quite see where it all would lead; but each decision confronted citizens with pressing new problems and choices. Winning independence did not so much create a nation as give men a chance to discover arrangements by which power could be harnessed in the service of liberty and the common good, so that a republic justified by the principles of the Declaration would be more than a short-lived utopian dream. The first efforts to reconstruct political authority in the Confederation by centering power in the states proved incomplete, but the new federal system invented by the Constitution-makers of 1787 was likewise no magic solution. Neither was the first American party system, although it did offer new hope and provide experience on which the organizers of later party systems could draw.

The New Politics and Political Innovation

Changing Concepts of Party in the United States: New York 1815–1828

by Michael Wallace

In the first quarter of the nineteenth century, the form and style of American politics underwent important changes. By the late 1820's popular participation had become a leading factor in American politics. Not only did more men exercise their right to vote, but the symbolic importance of the campaigns against property qualifications for the franchise and for officeholding contributed significantly to the replacement of the old elitist political order by a more egalitarian one.

The new order rested on modern forms of political organization and voter stimulation. Not only did strong national parties begin to appear, ending the Republican one-party reign, but such practices as the nominating convention became common and useful to the politicos organizing the emerging parties. The convention device could be used for the dual purpose of strengthening the party apparatus, while simultaneously providing the illusion of greater popular participation in the nominating process. The older caucus nominating system—either in state legislatures or in Congress—had been successfully denounced as aristocratic, and whatever its practical uses, had to be abandoned. The convention proved an ideal substitute, one that party managers quickly utilized to strengthen their machines.

But an even more fundamental change took place in the minds of Americans—the acceptance of the idea *of parties. Following adoption of the Federal Constitution which created a national political arena, Americans organized the first modern parties. Yet they refused to recognize the legitimacy of their own offspring, attacking the very idea of party on the ground that in a good society, community of interest should take precedence over personal interest, or the political interest of one group. Parties, scored as "factions," were supposedly lethal to republicanism, since they were vehicles by which selfish groups advanced their interests at public expense. By the 1820's, however, a new generation of American politicians began to see the problem more realistically and to square their professions with their actions. Political machines sprang up in several states, machines which not only operated on a different doctrine but whose spokesmen openly defended the necessity and morality of party organization. They rejected the charge that parties were no more than expanded cliques, arguing instead that parties were popular, democratically run bodies, and a distinctively American innovation.*

The new politicians clearly exaggerated the democratic aspect of parties, but egalitarian policies required the mobilization of popular support, an end that party organization served efficiently. Michael Wallace's analysis shows how the best-run of these political machines, New York's Albany Regency, fought a long and successful war for domination of that state's politics, and how acceptance of the idea of party became a cohesive factor that kept together the Regency leaders and their followers.

❧ During the first thirty years of its existence the United States developed, quite unintentionally, a party system. Organized popular parties regularly contested for power; Federalists and Republicans fought passionately and acrimoniously in Congress and cabinet, in town squares and county courthouses throughout the nation. The

From *The American Historical Review*, LXXIV (December 1968), 453, 456–60, 468–71, 476–77, 479–91. Reprinted by permission of the author; most footnotes omitted.

evidences of party spirit alarmed many Americans, for the existence of parties and their constant contention violated powerful and ancient traditions of proper political behavior. According to cannons inherited from British and colonial thought and practice, parties were evil: they were associations of factious men bent on self-aggrandizement. Political competition was evil: the ideal society was one where unity and consensus prevailed, where the national interest was peacefully determined by national leaders. Because partisan behavior violated normal ethical standards, many men, politicians among them, saw in the rise of parties a sign of moral decline. Not until a new generation of politicians emerged— men who had been raised in parties and had grown to maturity in a world that included party competition as a fixture of political life —were Americans able to re-evaluate the ancient traditions and establish new ones that justified their political activities.

Much of this re-evaluation and development of new ideals took place in New York State in the 1820's. There a group of professional politicians, leaders of the Republican party known as the Albany Regency, developed the modern concept of a political party and declared party associations to be eminently desirable. They adhered to a set of values that insisted on preserving, not destroying, political parties. They denounced and derided the consensus ideal and praised permanent political competition as being beneficial to society. . . .

In New York, after the War of 1812, a new conception of party emerged, modeled more closely on reality; in turn, the new definition of what a party ought to be legitimated existing structures. This re-evaluation developed out of what at first seemed just one more intraparty feud among New York Republicans, but that rapidly took a new and significant turn. The focus of the struggle was De Witt Clinton, in 1817 the leader of the party. Clinton held to the old view of party: he was a patrician politician who considered the party his personal property. This attitude is not surprising, given the nature of his career. Clinton assumed his position of leadership effortlessly, inheriting control of the faction

that had been led by his uncle, George Clinton, New York's Revolutionary War governor. Despite the fact that the organization
he headed in 1817 was quite different from what it had been
when he entered politics in the 1790's, his style of leadership remained characteristic of the earlier period. Snobbish, spiteful, and
supercilious, he was forbiddingly aristocratic. He craved flattery,
he rejected advice from subordinates that conflicted with his own
political judgments, and he directed the party largely as he saw
fit. Above all, he dispensed the rewards of the party—political
patronage and party nominations—as he pleased, often to personal friends, often to Federalists at the expense of deserving
Republicans.

This type of leadership became increasingly unacceptable to a
group of younger politicians in the party. As the party had become
richer, more powerful, more obviously a vital route to a successful
career in public life, many men whose allegiance lay not to any
person or family but to the party itself had joined the organization.
Inevitably such men would resent the idiosyncratic and unpredic-
table quality of party life, particularly the capricious dispensation
of party rewards. Beginning about 1817, a group of these younger
politicians known as the Bucktails began a quiet campaign to oust
Clinton from the leadership. They were not interested merely in
substituting one set of leaders for another. Rather their position
may be likened to that of a group of young executives in a family
firm who think that the business is being misrun because familial,
not managerial, standards govern its operation.

By 1819 the Bucktails, who included such able men as Martin
Van Buren, Benjamin Franklin Butler, Silas Wright, William
Learned Marcy, and Azariah Cutting Flagg, felt ready to challenge Clinton openly. At first they attacked him personally, charging that he put his own interests above those of the organization.
"De Witt Clinton, has acted incompatibly with his situation as the
head of the republican party of this state, and in direct hostility
to its best interest and prosperity. . . ." "Personal aggrandize-
ment," they declared, "has been his personal maxim, even at the

sacrifice of the republican party." As one Bucktail wrote in the Albany *Argus*, the organ of the insurgents, "notwithstanding his capacity, his manners are too repulsive, his temper too capricious and imperious, his deportment too dictatorial and tyrannical to acquire the affections or retain the confidence of any party."

The Bucktails wanted to go beyond indicting Clinton's personal style and to get at the anachronistic system of personal politics that he represented. Yet it was difficult to criticize Clinton's kind of leadership within the traditional framework of ideas about parties, for he was acting in accord with centuries-old standards of behavior. They were thus forced to proclaim a new definition of party and new standards of proper behavior for party politicians that would discredit both Clinton and his style of politics. They accomplished this task by adopting the rhetoric of democracy and egalitarianism and applying it to intraparty organization. Parties, they declared, should be democratic associations, run by the majority of the membership. It was a simple assertion, but it immediately put them in a position of strength. The ideal was virtually unassailable; to undermine the Bucktail position, critics would have to denounce republicanism itself—in the 1820's a political impossibility. Republican ideals became the Bucktails' weapons, and they were weapons that Clinton could not counter.

The Bucktails asserted that a party organized about an individual or patrician family was unacceptable as it was not republican. Personal parties were not parties at all, but factions, aristocratic remnants from the deferential days of colonial politics. Clinton was denounced as "raising up not only an aristocracy, but what has more hideous features, a species of monarchy." He was "the chieftain and head of an aristocracy"; his followers, "governed by no principle or party discipline," were "servile dependents . . . solely devoted to his views"; they were a "dangerous faction, bearing the badge of his family name," and solely concerned with "ministering to personal ambition." His patronage policy was denounced, not simply as unfair, but as producing undemocratic concentrations of power: "Devotion to the person of a chief becomes a

passport to public distinction, and servility to men in power is
rewarded . . . by honors and emoluments." In sum, Clinton's
whole vision of politics, "characterized by personal attachments
on the one hand and by personal antipathies on the other," was
"highly prejudicial to the interests of the people, and if successful
[would] have a tendency to subvert our republican form of government."

The proper form of political organization in a democratic state,
the Bucktails argued, was not a personal faction but a political
party. A true party was not the property of a man or a family, but
transcended any of its members. Like a corporation it outlived its
officers and did not, as had been the rule, expire when its leaders
died or were removed from office. The proper party was "bound to
the fortunes of no aspiring chief." A political party, moreover, was
responsible to the mass of its members: it was a democratic organization. The "cardinal maxim with the great republican party
[should be] . . . always to seek for, and when ascertained, always
to follow the will of the majority." Politicians like Clinton, who
felt themselves to be above the majority, could no longer be tolerated. "Those who refuse to 'abide by the fairly expressed will of
the majority' . . . forfeit all claims to the character of republicans, and become recreant to the principles of that party." This
did not mean an end to leadership: "Republicans know full well
that . . . some must bear the brunt of the battle, and that to
some hands must be consigned the interest and honor of the
party; the system, the management, the labor and the anxiety."
But leaders were expected to consider themselves the instruments
or agents of an organization, not its owners. He "whose talents
and zeal have benefitted the republican party will be supported as
long as he consults the interests and ascendancy of that party, and
no longer." The proper criteria for advancement were faithful
dedication to the party and long service in its support, not pedigree or property.

By these standards, Van Buren was a model party leader. He
proclaimed his obligation to the organization: "There are few

men in the state," he told a gathering of the faithful, "more indebted to the favor of the Republican Party than myself and none
more willing to acknowledge it." He rose to power in the prescribed fashion: "We speak of him with pride," declared a mass
meeting of Albany Republicans in 1820, "because without the
influence of fortune, or the factitious aid of a family name, he
has, by his entire devotion to the republican cause, raised himself
to the first grade as a statesman and a patriot."

By 1820 the Bucktail revolt had succeeded. Largely because
they were able to convince many of the party that they were more
faithful to the organization and the will of its majority than was
Clinton, they managed to oust Clinton and his adherents; they
then appropriated the apparatus and symbols of the Republican
party entirely for themselves. Despite vigorous protests at being
read out of the party because they failed to measure up to the
new criteria, the Clintonians were relegated to the status of a
distinct personal party. Van Buren and his fellow Republicans
entrenched themselves in the legislature and all of the executive
branch but the governorship and came to be characterized, by
Clintonian and Federalist opponents, as the Albany Regency.

The Bucktails thus succeeded in distinguishing between party
and faction in both the theory and actuality of New York politics.
A party (such as their own) was a democratically structured, permanent organization; a faction (such as the Clintonians) was a
transient, aristocratic, personal clique. "On one side is arrayed the
old republican party, and on the other the followers of a man."
Personal factions were bad: they were aristocratic and concerned
only with enriching their leader. But parties were good: they allowed all members an equal voice; gave all members an equal
chance to rise to positions of leadership and to receive party nominations for important elective positions; and provided all members
an equal chance at receiving patronage, now no longer dispensed
at the whim of an arbitrary leader. The degree to which the newer
politicians rejected the antiparty tradition and the personal basis
of politics can be seen in their extraordinary degree of attachment

to their organization. They went far beyond merely justifying the
existence of their party in ideological and practical terms and developed a system of political discipline that enjoined every politician, at whatever cost to himself, to preserve and perpetuate the
party. It is to the development of their doctrines of party loyalty
and party discipline that we now turn. . . .

The unity and thus the continuity of the party were to be
achieved by party discipline, the willingness of members to set
aside personal considerations for the greater good.[1] But there is a
final point to be made about this code of political ethics, one that
takes us to the core of the regency mind. As we have noted, the
Bucktails distinguished a true party as one responsive to the majority of its members. Party discipline and such practices as the
caucus were the devices that enabled the majority to rule; they
ensured, moreover, that it would rule. They were thus the guarantees of intraparty democracy. They were also believed to be
bulwarks of democracy in a larger arena. Party unity allowed the
common people (most of whom, of course, were assumed to be
Republicans) to deal as equals with aristocratic opponents like
the Federalists; the power and influence of family and fortune
could be offset by banding together and presenting a united front

1. The reasons for this mass acceptance of party loyalty were many and complex. One point is that the caucus system, to regency followers, did not
connote a locked room full of political bosses hacking out nominations.
Rather it betokened an elaborate network of ward, city, village, county, and
district conventions (a term virtually synonymous with caucus on levels below
the legislature) that laced the state into a pyramidal party structure open to
the public through most of its tiers. At the top, the caucus of the state
legislature was free from direct public influence, though after 1817 it was
broadened to include some elected party delegates. Local nominations, however, were the prerogative of the local caucuses, composed of all local Republicans (and often opponents as well, for there were no clear criteria of
party membership). While these bodies were often manipulated by local
leaders, and while the party as a whole was, like most other mass organizations, subject to Michels's "iron law of oligarchy," the caucus system (broadly
conceived) did allow for much participation by the party rank and file.
Another reason for mass support of the doctrine of regularity involves the
psychological function of party loyalty and the role that inherited affiliation
to an organization plays in allowing individuals to cope with a complex
political world.

at the polls. Again, party discipline was an agent of democracy.[2]

In the 1820's a subtle but important shift occurred: party discipline, from being essential to democracy, became the essence of democracy. What had been the practices became the principles of the party. Noah put the matter precisely.

Regular nominations . . . are not so much the engines as they are the principles of a party, because any system which tends to unite the people, to give them their rights, to promote harmony and unanimity, to effect reconciliation and a submission to the will of the majority, and a relinquishment of private attachments, such a system we call a cardinal principle in the administration of a representative government [italics mine].

The practices that tended to preserve the party became the real "principles" of the party, for the ultimate "principle" was self-preservation. The fact that republicans "were cordially disposed to respect and sustain the regular nominations of the party" was deemed "a principle of essential importance," indeed "a criterion of political orthodoxy." The system of discipline "which enjoins upon its members, the obligation of submitting to nominations fairly and regularly made" was declared to be "a great PRINCIPLE," and "adherence to regular nominations" was pronounced "a sacred and inviolable principle. . . ."

Because their goal was the preservation of the party, the politicians lost interest in other, more ideological objectives. This is evident from their election appeals and campaign rhetoric. There

2. Thus, "the caucus . . . was highly instrumental in enabling [the party] to wrest the power of this state . . . from the hands of its aristocratic opponents." Only the caucus doctrine, by clearly affixing a well-known party label to a man, could coalesce the needed support behind candidates otherwise unknown (members of the middle or lower classes) and thus neutralize the aristocracy's greatest asset, the familiarity of their family names. Van Buren said that, conversely, whenever the Republican party was "wise enough to employ the caucus or convention system, and to use in good faith the influence it is capable of imparting to the popular cause," it was successful.

were virtually no substantive planks in regency platforms—no programs of internal improvements, no plans for expanded education or agricultural improvements, no demands for expansion of the franchise, virtually no demands at all. There were many declarations that Republicans were the party of democracy, and their opponents the standard-bearers of aristocracy, but these were either vague statements asserting differences in temperament and style or, when made specific, differences in the structure of their organizations. Their basic campaign appeal was aimed at those who already identified with them, and it was simple enough: now is the time for all good men to come to the aid of their party. Most of their political advertisements were in fact apolitical; they were calls to the colors, exhortations to keep the organizational faith. Classic in its simplicity was this broadside: "Republicans, will you abandon that party which has done so much for your country? Remember the dying words of the brave Lawrence and 'DON'T GIVE UP THE SHIP!!' " Republicans were reminded of their party's glorious history. "Let scenes gone by, and blessings enjoyed, arouse every republican to a sense of his duty. Remember that republicans saved the nation from anarchy; that republicans stood firm in the 'trying times' of '98; . . . O Ye patriots of '76! Ye preservers of Democracy in '98; ye defenders of our rights in '12, '13, '14; come forth. . . ." The most popular issues in regency campaigns were those that had been safely dead for twenty years. Republicans were enjoined to ignore objections to particular regency policies, as they were simply threats to the safety of the organization; complaints about the defeat of the electoral bill, while seemingly legitimate, masked an insidious design. "It is not a question about the electoral law . . . that is now pending. It is whether the republican party shall stand or fall."

Such ideological urges as Republicans had were satisfied by their association in a democratic political party. Unlike the party's founders, they felt no need to use the party to achieve certain goals, for the perpetuation of a democratic organization was goal enough. The second-generation politicians were operational democrats.[3]

The "defense" of party association outlined in the preceding pages was relatively simple. Except for harnessing the legitimizing force of majoritarianism, the Republicans had merely recognized and ratified actual changes in the structure and function of parties. The more serious traditional rejection of party had always been closely associated with the rejection of political competition; to justify party fully, it was necessary to justify competition. . . .

The primary goal of regency politicians was to preserve their party. This is of utmost importance for understanding their attitudes toward their opponents in New York politics. Their goal was not to destroy, overwhelm, or eliminate their opponents; they were not ideologues bent on the destruction of evildoers. They were able, therefore, to realize that the continued existence of an opposition was necessary, from the perspective of perpetuating their own party; opposition was highly useful, a constant spur to their own party's discipline. While the party might, it was argued, "suffer temporary defeats" in the interparty struggle, "it is certain to acquire additional strength . . . by the attacks of adverse parties." Indeed, the party was "most in jeopardy when an opposition is not sufficiently defined." As another writer noted, "there is such a thing as a party being too strong; a small and firm majority is more to be relied upon than an overwhelming and loose one." The politicians were aware that during "the contest between the great rival parties . . . each found in the strength of the other a powerful motive of union and vigor."

3. Not only were what were called "abstract" principles increasingly ignored because of the overriding concern with organizational support, but, in the rush of politics, they were increasingly betrayed. Edwin Croswell, editor of the Albany *Argus*, reflected on the problems the incontrovertibly democratic electoral bill raised for the party: "Admit the general correctness of it & yet is this the proper time for its introduction? Ought the question of expediency to be entirely disregarded; or ought it with Republicans, to be one of the first consideration?" Expediency triumphed increasingly. The notion that legislators should vote as their constituents wished also became a hindrance to men like Marcy, who wanted legislators to vote as their party directed.

This need for opposition led to a fertile paradox. The Federalists and their latter-day avatars, the Clintonians, were, of course, guilty of heinous political sins: they were aristocrats, personalists, factionalists, no-party heretics. Yet they were also the opposition. As a consequence, the Federalist party (a label Republicans attached to their major opponents of the moment), while condemned, was simultaneously praised; it was the strong, flourishing, and virtuous organization to which Republicans would accede should it obtain the support of the state's majority. From the need for a sustained opposition came verbal bouquets like the following:

From the first organization of the government . . . this country has been divided into two great parties. . . . Neither party has yielded to the other in the zeal with which it has sought to procure concert among its members, or to give ascendancy to its principles, and although we may lament the occasional inconsistencies and the dangerous excesses into which both have unavoidably been betrayed, . . . we cannot for a minute admit that the majority of either have been actuated by any other than the purest, the most patriotic, and the most disinterested motives.

The *Argus* declared that "we wish not to be understood as having the slightest objection to the maintenance of the old federal party, broadly and with the spirit of other times." The two competing parties, the paper observed, "have existed among us almost from the formation of our constitution, and we are content with their present organization."

The regency, then, had no desire to eliminate its opponents. Rather it hoped for a "tranquil though determined opposition." It is significant that during the 1820's the word "opposition" itself gained popularity in Republican circles. They noted things in "the conduct of the Opposition which afford both amusement and instruction"; rejoiced in frustrating "the hopes and expectations of the Opposition"; and discussed in their papers "the views and opinions of what may now be termed the Opposition to the Democratic Party. . . ."

These were the attitudes regency politicians developed toward their opponents amid daily political struggles. Their lack of ideological fervor and their emphasis on preserving their institution contributed to a lowering of the political temperature. In the cooler atmosphere of the 1820's the politicians perceived that an opposition was necessary, and they came to think in terms of the continued existence of two parties, each sincere, legitimate, and capable of administering the government. Within this framework of attitudes a re-evaluation of the consensus ideal could easily emerge. But ideas seldom spring forth without some encouragement, no matter how conducive the times. A stimulus was needed, some reason to force the regency men to think about their political universe and to make them articulate their attitudes toward political parties. The stimulus came in the mid-twenties with a barrage of antiparty criticism from their New York opponents. Only confronted with a severe challenge to their habits and practices would they formulate a rebuttal. A brief look at the position of the New York antiparty spokesmen may help us understand what provoked the regency response.

The New York opponents of the Albany Regency, drawing on the antiparty spirit of the national leaders, reasserted the old consensus ideal. Clinton, for example, declared that the clash of parties has "rent us asunder, degraded our character, and impared our ability for doing good." He too felt there was no need for a division:

I hardly understand the nomenclature of parties. They are all republicans, and yet a portion of the people assume the title of republican, as an exclusive right. . . . It is easy to see that the difference is nominal —that the whole controversy is about office, and that the country is constantly assailed by ambitious demagogues for the purpose of gratifying their cupidity.

Many New Yorkers shared Clinton's attitude. They correctly observed that no deep differences of principle divided the parties:

"We ask [the regency] to lay down what it considers to be the republican creed, and then to designate any considerable body of men in this country whom it would not embrace." But they went on to conclude that no matters of controversy remained that required opposing political organizations. "What does the great mass of the people . . . care for party? Why should the people be divided into a thousand different interests without knowing for what, and made hostile to each other, when their true and only interest is to be united?" Many assumed that the politicians, with their vested interest in discord, were perpetuating artificial divisions among a happy and passive people. Regency leaders like Erastus Root were charged with engaging in a "mean and contemptible effort to revive party names, and to excite prejudices by cant phrases."

The solution was obvious: eliminate parties. If one could "knock aside all artificial arrangements and the whole machinery of party," it would prevent the "citizens of the state having their sentiments perverted by intrigue and corruption." If parties could not be exorcised, they could at least be merged and amalgamated, particularly as there existed no difference between them. The critics proclaimed an end of parties. The Federalists, "having no longer any ground of principle to stand on, [have] necessarily ceased to exist as a party." Again "[both parties] have manifested a willingness to drop old animosities and obsolete names, and to unite with their former political opponents." And again, "the barriers of party are completely broken down and the lines of political demarcation cannot be again drawn."

When it became apparent that the Republicans had no intention of merging with their opponents, much less of dissolving, the antiparty men moved beyond rhetoric. They organized. They formed, of all things, a party, an antiparty party, a party to end parties. The People's party, formed in 1823 by Clintonians, Federalists, and dissident Republicans, appealed to the electorate "not in the spirit of *party* warfare, for this is emphatically the cause of the People. . . ." They offered their party as a means whereby members of all groups could unite, but it was highly unlikely that many regency Republicans would be lured into support of the fledgling party in light of the candidate it chose to support in 1824 —De Witt Clinton. Yet here a theoretical assault on party was linked to a potentially powerful organization and a popular candidate. If the antiparty message appealed to many in the electorate, the regency was in trouble. The emergence of the People's party threatened regency hegemony and forced its members to defend the party system that had evolved in New York. This they consciously set about to do. . . .[4]

The regency defense against the amalgamation attack took five forms. Their first, most parochial, and probably most effective position was that the philosophy of amalgamation, for all its seeming disinterestedness, was actually an opposition trick, the purpose of which was not to unite the country but to destroy the Republican party. Secondly, on a more theoretical level, regency Republicans denied that parties had dissolved, but rather that they continued in undiminished strength, a result traceable to powerful ideological and historical forces perpetuating them, which the Good Feeling men had ignored. Thirdly, they rejected the entire vision of a society based on consensus; the proper political universe was characterized by constant contention; the truly moral man was not one who put himself above party, but was a committed partisan. Fourthly, echoing the English justification of opposition, they declared that parties had to exist in a free state, that the elimination of parties occurred only under despotism. Fifthly, and most broadly, they declared that, for several reasons, competition be-

4. There was another, equally conscious conflict on the national level, waged primarily against Monroe. Van Buren reminisced about the "degree of odium" brought upon him by his staunch resistance to amalgamation doctrines "within the precincts of the White House and in most of the circles, political and social, of Washington." "The noisy revels," he recalled, "of bacchanalians in the Inner Sanctuary could not be more unwelcome sounds to devout worshippers than was this peal of the party tocsin in the ears of those who glorified the 'Era of Good Feeling.' "

tween parties benefited the state. We must examine each of these arguments in detail.

Republicans declared that advocacy of Good Feeling was a Federalist plot. By persuading Republicans that parties no longer existed, or by convincing them that they no longer should exist, the Federalists would loosen the bands of party discipline so vital to the party, and it would dissolve; then the Federalists would step in and recapture the government. . . .

At the heart of the appeal of Good Feeling was the assertion that no differences in principle divided the country; therefore, no legitimate basis for party competition existed. This proved a difficult argument to answer, for it contained much truth, but regency men responded in two ways. One was an exercise in exaggeration, the other an observation of great shrewdness. Their first answer was to assert that a great division did exist in the country, based upon differing constructions of the Constitution and disagreements over the value of republicanism. Van Buren's formulation of this Republican equivalent of a Whig history is among the more concise:

The origin of the two great political parties which have divided the country, from the adoption of the Constitution to the present day . . . has . . . been attributed to causes which had either become obsolete, or been compromised by mutual concession. . . . [In reality] they arose from other and very different causes. They are, in truth . . . mainly to be ascribed to the struggle between the two opposing principles that have been in active operation in this country from the closing scenes of the revolutionary war to the present day—the one seeking to absorb, as far as practicable, all power from its legitimate sources, and to condense it in a single head. The other, an antagonist principle, laboring as assiduously to resist the encroachments and limit the extent of executive authority. . . . The former is essentially the monarchical, the latter the democratical spirit, of society.

There was, of course, some truth at the core of the argument: there had been important distinctions in ideology and style between the two parties in the [preceding] generation. But this portrait of

politics had much less relevance to the state of parties in New
York in the 1820's; the attribution of a monarchical spirit to the
Federalists was clearly overdrawn. . . . But regency men simply
pointed to past party performance and declared that no real
change had occurred. "The whole Federal party cannot so suddenly
have altered their opinions nor abandoned their distinctive principles. As well might the Ethiopian change his skin or the leopard
his spots." And they insisted that differences in principle remained
so striking that it was impossible "to destroy the old landmarks
of party," impossible to "draw men into a political union who were
never united before, and who, from the utter dissimilarity of their
views and notions, never could act cordially together."

The regency's second, more muted response to the amalgamationists was also more radical. Parties, they declared, were not
simply ideologically coherent organizations, at odds over fundamental issues. They were social institutions in their own right,
largely independent of their earlier ideological stances. The men
who advocated Good Feeling had confused competition between
parties with the bickering of factions. . . . New issues did not require new parties; rather the two traditional organizations remained to act as vehicles for opposing positions. The parties maintained themselves not so much by love of "principle" as by the
attachment of the members to the organization itself. . . .

Association with a political party, therefore, was not simply the
result of a conscious decision; parties were not to be dissolved after
certain issues were resolved. Rather, party affiliation and thus party
divisions were handed down, like heirlooms, from generation to
generation. Once again, amalgamation was precluded.

The Republicans' third rejection of amalgamation was perhaps
their most radical, for it condemned the consensus ideal itself, de-
claring that it led to politically immoral behavior. The regency
conception of what comprised political honesty and morality was
not an avoidance of party, but a consistent adherence to party.
Amalgamationists insisted that party men of opposite faiths should
come together; with Republicans it was an article of political
morality for them to remain apart. The Republicans did not re-

spect the man who, following the consensus tradition, put himself above party. They were partisans and respected only other partisans. . . .

Men who abandoned one party for another were thoroughly denounced. They were condemned, with almost ecclesiastical fervor, as "apostates." [5] But even worse than apostasy was vacillation. The politician who drifted from party to party was condemned as "inconsistent"; Butler lucidly outlined the immorality of this attitude. Writing to Van Buren, Butler declared that *"political consistency* [is] as indispensable as any other *moral qualification.* For say what you will it is a *moral* qualification." This was so because the "man who is dishonest and unstable in his politics" is "equally dishonest and unstable in the relations of his private life. . . ." This partisan spirit proved the deadliest foe of the consensus mentality. It governed relations between party organizations, not just party members, and thus barred amalgamation. Partisans did not switch, and parties did not mix: organizations as well as individuals were consistent.

The terminology of morality, not tactics, was used when discussing interparty relations. Alliances, temporary joining of party forces, were frowned upon. . . .

The fourth argument advanced by the Republicans concerned the inevitability of parties in a free state; their absence or amalgamation was evidence of repression. Republicans assumed that in any society there would be more than one conception of the national interest. In order to express these differences, men form parties: those whose "general interests are the same" will always combine to promulgate their ideas, for "all experience has shown, that efforts to be powerful, must be concentrated." It followed that society normally contained parties contending with one another. . . .

Yet they might not exist, if repressed: parties developed only in

5. It must be admitted that the regency could more readily stomach apostates if they were arriving rather than departing. In 1820, for example, a portion of the old Federalist party known as "the high-minded" moved into the Republican ranks.

societies that tolerated organized dissent. The very existence of
parties was, therefore, an indication that freedom of expression
existed. Parties "will prevail where there is the least degree of liberty of action on the part of the public agents, or their constituents; . . . they are . . . inseparable from a free government." The
association of parties and freedom was a basic theme of the regency
defense. "Parties," they declared, "will ever exist, in a free state."
The maintenance of parties, they asserted, was "necessary to the
just exercise of the powers of free governments." Because this was
such an obvious equation, they hinted darkly that their Good Feeling opponents, in calling for an end to parties, were contemplating
an end of freedom. It was much commented on that military men
like Jackson were fervent advocates of eliminating parties, and they
contrasted such behavior with their own: "Fortunately for our
country, and its institutions, there is another class of politicians,
whom we delight to honor, who believe, that when party distinctions are no longer known and recognized, our freedom will be
in jeopardy, as the 'calm of despotism' will then be visible." Party
competition was the hallmark of a free society.[6]

The fifth ground for rejecting the consensus ideal derived from
the belief that permanent competition between political parties
was a positive benefit to the state. This was their broadest argument, most likely to appeal to nonpoliticians. "We are party men,
attached to party systems," they declared, but added, "we think
them necessary to the general safety. . . ." And again, "for the
safety of the republic & the good of the people" it was imperative
to "keep up and adhere to old party distinctions." How did they
justify this position? For one thing, party competition provided a
check upon the government; it was an extraconstitutional aid to

6. When Van Buren decided to support Jackson for the presidency in 1828,
he had a difficult time convincing his party to do the same. Most regency
politicians considered Jackson a no-party heretic. Even someone as high in
party circles as Marcy proved recalcitrant: "I am somewhat thick skulled
about making distinctions," he wrote Van Buren acidly. "I do not very
clearly see how I can prefer with a strong preference an anti-caucus—amalgamation—no party candidate to another who has held the same heretical
doctrines."

the people. "The spirit of party," they declared, was "the vigilant watchman over the conduct of those in power." The parties were "among the firmest bulwarks of civil liberty," and politicians insisted that they were "necessary to keep alive the vigilance of the people, and to compel their servants to act up to principle." But exactly how did they do this? One of their major functions was to inform the people.   •

[Parties] on either side of the question, become the counsel who argue the cause before the people. . . . The solicitude and interest of political rivalship, will sufficiently expose the crimes, and even the failings, of competitors for the people's confidence. Competitors of this description *force* into notice facts, . . . which the people at large could never have derived from the ordinary commerce of thought.

The people are thus presented with expert watchdogs: "leading men, on both sides of the question check one another," and the people, presented with informed alternatives, "know when to support and when to oppose." Governor Enos Throop asserted that the party system allowed the people to participate intelligently in government.

Those party divisions which are based upon conflicting opinions in regard to the constitution of the government, or the measures of the administration of it, interest every citizen, and tend, inevitably, in the spirit of emulation and proselytism, to reduce the many shades of opinion into two opposing parties. . . . [The] organized parties watch and scan each other's doings, the public mind is instructed by ample discussions of public measures, and acts of violence are restrained by the convictions of the people, that the prevailing measures are the results of enlightened reason.

Party competition had another value: it agitated the public and kept the mass of people interested in the operation of the government. It produced discord, and discord, despite the attitudes of the men who advocated Good Feeling, was of utmost value to republics. For, in the eyes of the Bucktails, the real danger to republics was not division, as in consensus cosmology, but apathy. And the surest cure for apathy was party competition. This idea is most closely associated with Van Buren. From the beginning of his political life he had appreciated the value of conflict. In 1814, for example, amidst the bitter animosities of the war, he said that

on the various operations of government with which the public welfare are connected, and honest difference of opinion may exist—[and] when those differences are discussed and the principles of contending parties are supported with candor, fairness, and moderation, the very discord which is thus produced, may in a government like ours, be conducive to the public good.

Then, paradoxically, party competition bound the country together. Here was one of the shrewdest observations that the politicians made. While only in its formative stages in the 1820's, the idea would quickly enter the main current of antebellum thought. Van Buren and his colleagues realized that contrary to antiparty mythology, the really divisive threat to the nation was not party, but section. Party associations that cut across sectional lines were, in fact, an antidote to interregional stress. The Good Feeling men, by calling for the elimination of parties, were exacerbating sectionalism. Republicans accused them of wanting "to ABROGATE THE OLD PARTY DISTINCTIONS" in order to "organize new ones founded in the territorial prejudices of the people." The consequence of abolishing the old political distinctions would be "to array republicans against each other under such new and artificial distinctions . . . as geographical locations, such as North and South, East and West." Van Buren rested much of his case for the maintenance of the old parties on this ground: "We must always have party distinctions, and the old ones are the best. . . . If the old ones are suppressed, geographical differences founded on local instincts or what is worse, prejudices between free & slave holding states will inevitably take their place."

Finally, contests between political parties benefited society by eliminating the fierce contentions of personal parties. . . . It was now obvious, as Throop noted, that it was "one of the peculiar benefits of a well-regulated party spirit in a commonwealth, that it employs the passions actively in a milder mood, and thus shuts the door against faction. . . ."

By the end of the 1820's, the amalgamation attack had been met, the consensus tradition rejected. "Let us be greeted no more," demanded the Albany *Argus*, "by the cant and whining about the extinction of party feelings and the impropriety of endeavoring to keep them alive." "Parties of some sort must exist. 'Tis in the nature and genius of our government."

Nationalizing the Presidential Vote

New Perspectives on Jacksonian Politics

by Richard P. McCormick

The extension of the suffrage and the growing acceptance of party organization eventually reshaped presidential politics. The founding fathers had by design kept election of the President far from the people, and the presidential electors were supposed to exercise judgments free from popular pressures. But the course of American political practices ruled otherwise. Although the electoral college continued in existence, the electors lost their independence and became subject to party discipline. The congressional nominating caucus, by which the first parties nominated presidential candidates, also gave way to the national convention as the nominating device. Politicians once again fought openly over the presidency and the resulting competition sharpened voter interest in the outcome.

The renewed interest in national affairs rested on a firm and well-established foundation: state politics. In the following article, Richard P. McCormick probes beneath the surface of the fact that in 1828, Andrew Jackson won the presidency with a vote considerably larger than the entire presidential vote for all candidates four years before, and he shows that although Jackson's election held great significance, it did not signify a "popular revolution" in voting as described by several generations of historians. Mc-

*Cormick tabulated the percentage of eligible voters who partici-
pated in presidential elections (1824–44), a much more meaningful
figure than the raw vote alone.*

*This article upset many previously held notions about the Jack-
sonian "explosion at the polls"; nevertheless, the student should
not lose sight of an equally important and positive fact. As clearly
demonstrated in McCormick's data, the Jackson campaign of 1828,
while no revolution, did begin to nationalize American voting by
bringing the percentage of eligible voters participating in a presidential election up to the levels of previous participation in state
elections. In 1828 the presidential election began to lose its "clubby"
aspect, and it started to assume its modern shape, as a two-way
and highly organized contest for political preferment.*

🕸 The historical phenomenon that we have come to call Jacksonian Democracy has long engaged the attention of American political historians, and never more insistently than in the past decade.
From the time of Parton and Bancroft to the present day, scholars
have recognized that a profoundly significant change took place in
the climate of politics simultaneously with the appearance of
Andrew Jackson on the presidential scene. They have sensed that a
full understanding of the nature of that change might enable them
to dissolve some of the mysteries that envelop the operation of the
American democratic process. With such a challenging goal before
them, they have pursued their investigations with uncommon intensity and with a keen awareness of the contemporary relevance
of their findings.

A cursory view of the vast body of historical writing on this subject suggests that scholars in the field have been largely preoccupied with attempts to define the content of Jacksonian Democracy and identify the influences that shaped it. What did Jacksonian Democracy represent, and what groups, classes, or sections
gave it its distinctive character? The answers that have been given
to these central questions have been—to put it succinctly—bewil-

From *The American Historical Review*, LXV (January 1960), 288–301.
Reprinted by permission of the author; most footnotes omitted.

dering in their variety. The discriminating student, seeking the essential core of Jacksonianism, may make a choice among urban workingmen, southern planters, venturous conservatives, farm-bred *nouveaux riches*, western frontiersmen, frustrated entrepreneurs, or yeoman farmers. Various as are these interpretations of the motivating elements that constituted the true Jacksonians, the characterizations of the programmatic features of Jacksonian Democracy are correspondingly diverse. Probably the reasonable observer will content himself with the conclusion that many influences were at work and that latitudinarianism prevailed among the Jacksonian faithful.

In contrast with the controversy that persists over these aspects of Jacksonian Democracy, there has been little dissent from the judgment that "the 1830's saw the triumph in American politics of that democracy which has remained pre-eminently the distinguishing feature of our society." The consensus would seem to be that with the emergence of Jackson, the political pulse of the nation quickened. The electorate, long dormant or excluded from the polls by suffrage barriers, now became fired with unprecedented political excitement. The result was a bursting forth of democratic energies, evidenced by a marked upward surge in voting. Beard in his colorful fashion gave expression to the common viewpoint when he asserted that "the roaring flood of the new democracy was . . . [by 1824] foaming perilously near the crest. . . ." Schlesinger, with his allusion to the "immense popular vote" received by Jackson in 1824, creates a similar image. The Old Hero's victory in 1828 has been hailed as the consequence of a "mighty democratic uprising."

That a "new democracy, ignorant, impulsive, irrational" entered the arena of politics in the Jackson era has become one of the few unchallenged "facts" in an otherwise controversial field. Differences of opinion occur only when attempts are made to account for the remarkable increase in the size of the active electorate. The commonest explanations have emphasized the assertion by the common man of his newly won political privileges, the democratic influences that arose out of the western frontier, or the magnetic attractiveness of Jackson as a candidate capable of appealing with singular effectiveness to the backwoods hunter, the plain farmer, the urban workingman, and the southern planter.

Probably because the image of a "mighty democratic uprising" has been so universally agreed upon, there has been virtually no effort made to describe precisely the dimensions of the "uprising." Inquiry into this aspect of Jacksonian Democracy has been discouraged by a common misconception regarding voter behavior before 1824. As the authors of one of our most recent and best textbooks put it: "In the years from the beginning of the government to 1824, a period for which we have no reliable election statistics, only small numbers of citizens seemed to have bothered to go to the polls." Actually, abundant data on pre-1824 elections is available, and it indicates a far higher rate of voting than has been realized. Only by taking this data into consideration can voting behavior after 1824 be placed in proper perspective.

The question of whether there was indeed a "mighty democratic uprising" during the Jackson era is certainly crucial in any analysis of the political character of Jacksonian Democracy. More broadly, however, we need to know the degree to which potential voters participated in elections before, during, and after the period of Jackson's presidency as well as the conditions that apparently influenced the rate of voting. Only when such factors have been analyzed can we arrive at firm conclusions with respect to the dimensions of the political changes that we associate with Jacksonian Democracy. Obviously in studying voter participation we are dealing with but one aspect of a large problem, and the limitations imposed by such a restrictive focus should be apparent.

In measuring the magnitude of the vote in the Jackson elections it is hardly significant to use the total popular vote cast throughout the nation. A comparison of the total vote cast in 1812, for example, when in eight of the seventeen states electors were chosen by the legislature, with the vote in 1832, when every state except South Carolina chose its electors by popular vote, has limited meaning. Neither is it revealing to compare the total vote in 1824 with that in 1832 without taking into consideration the population increase during the interval. The shift from the legislative choice of electors to their election by popular vote, together with the steady population growth, obviously swelled the presidential vote. But the problem to be investigated is whether the Jackson elections brought voters to the polls in such enlarged or unprecedented proportions as to indicate that a "new democracy" had burst upon the political scene.

The most practicable method for measuring the degree to which voters participated in elections over a period of time is to relate the number of votes cast to the number of potential voters. Although there is no way of calculating precisely how many eligible voters there were in any state at a given time, the evidence at hand demonstrates that with the exception of Rhode Island, Virginia, and Louisiana the potential electorate after 1824 was roughly equivalent to the adult white male population.[1] A meaningful way of expressing the rate of voter participation, then, is to state it in terms of the percentage of the adult white males actually voting. This index can be employed to measure the variations that occurred in voter participation over a period of time and in both national and state elections. Consequently a basis is provided for comparing the rate of voting in the Jackson elections with other presidential elections before and after his regime as well as with state elections.[2]

Using this approach it is possible, first of all, to ascertain whether or not voter participation rose markedly in the three presidential elections in which Jackson was a candidate. Did voter participation

1. The only states in which property qualifications were a factor in restricting voting in presidential elections after 1824 were Virginia and Rhode Island. New York did not completely abolish property qualifications until 1826, but the reform of 1821 had resulted in virtually free suffrage. In Louisiana, where voters were required to be taxpayers, the nature of the system of taxation operated to confine the suffrage to perhaps half of the adult white males. See Joseph G. Tregle, "Louisiana in the Age of Jackson: A Study in Ego Politics," doctoral dissertation, University of Pennsylvania, 1954, 105–108. To be perfectly accurate, estimates of the size of the potential electorate would have to take into account such factors as citizenship and residence requirements and, in certain states, the eligibility of Negro voters.

2. After 1840 when the proportion of aliens in the population increased markedly and citizenship became an important requirement for voting, the

in these elections so far exceed the peak participation in the pre-1824 elections as to suggest that a mighty democratic uprising was taking place? The accompanying data (Table 1) provides an answer to this basic question.[3]

In the 1824 election not a single one of the eighteen states in which the electors were chosen by popular vote attained the percentage of voter participation that had been reached before 1824. Prior to that critical election, fifteen of those eighteen states had recorded votes in excess of 50 per cent of their adult white male population, but in 1824 only two states—Maryland and Alabama exceeded this modest mark. The average rate of voter participation in the election was 26.5 per cent. This hardly fits the image of the "roaring flood of the new democracy . . . foaming perilously near the crest. . . ."

adult-white-male index becomes less reliable. In order to calculate accurately the number of qualified voters in 1850, the alien adult white males would have to be deducted in those states where citizenship was a qualification for voting. Unfortunately, federal census data on aliens is not obtainable prior to 1890, except for the censuses of 1820 and 1830. In the latter year there were only 107,832 aliens out of a total population of nearly thirteen millions, a fraction so small as to be insignificant. But by 1850, according to one calculation, adult male aliens may have amounted to one-twelfth of the total voting population. J. D. B. De Bow, *Statistical View of the United States* (Washington, D.C., 1854), 50. In certain eastern states the proportion of aliens was higher than the national average. In New York, for example, 18.5 per cent of the total population in 1855 were aliens; the proportion in 1835 had been only 3.79 per cent. Franklin B. Hough, *Census of the State of New York for 1855* (Albany, 1857), xiv, xliii.
3. The figures on voter participation have been computed from a compilation I have made of returns of state-wide elections covering twenty-five states over the period from 1800 to 1860. For the post-1836 years the returns may be consulted in the *Whig Almanacs* and *Tribune Almanacs* issued by Horace Greeley and, for presidential elections, in W. Dean Burnham's *Presidential Ballots, 1836–1892* (Baltimore, Md., 1955). For the period prior to 1836 the best general sources are the official manuals of certain states, the legislative journals, and the contemporary newspapers. For several states, among them Massachusetts, Connecticut, New Jersey, Maryland, Virginia, North Carolina, and Georgia, it is necessary to use the manuscript sources. The estimate of the adult white male population was computed for each decennial year from the federal census, and the figure for the particular election year was obtained by interpolation. I have computed for each gubernatorial and presidential election in the twenty-five states admitted to the Union by 1836 (exclusive of South Carolina) the percentage of adult white males voting.

Table 1

Percentages of Adult White Males Voting in Elections

	Highest Known % AWM Voting before 1824		Presidential Elections					
State	Year	% AWM	1824	1828	1832	1836	1840	1844
Maine	1812 g	62.0	18.9	42.7	66.2 *	37.4	82.2	67.5
New Hampshire	1814 g	80.8	16.8	76.5	74.2	38.2	86.4 *	65.6
Vermont	1812 g	79.9	—	55.8	50.0	52.5	74.0	65.7
Massachusetts	1812 g	67.4	29.1	25.7	39.3	45.1	66.4	59.3
Rhode Island	1812 g	49.4	12.4	18.0	22.4	24.1	33.2	39.8
Connecticut	1819 l	54.4	14.9	27.1	45.9	52.3	75.7 *	76.1
New York	1810 g	41.5	—	70.4 *	72.1	60.2	77.7	73.6
New Jersey	1808 p	71.8	31.1	70.9	69.0	69.3	80.4 *	81.6
Pennsylvania	1808 g	71.5	19.6	56.6	52.7	53.1	77.4 *	75.5
Delaware	1804 g	81.9	—	—	67.0	69.4	82.8 *	85.0
Maryland	1820 l	69.0	53.7	76.2 *	55.6	67.5	84.6	80.3
Virginia	1800 p	25.9	11.5	27.6 *	30.8	35.1	54.6	54.5
North Carolina	1823 c	70.0 †	42.2	56.8	31.7	52.9	83.1 *	79.1
Georgia	1812 c	62.3	—	35.9	33.0	64.9 *	88.9	94.0
Kentucky	1820 g	74.4	25.3	70.7	73.9	61.1	74.3	80.3 *
Tennessee	1817 g	80.0	26.8	49.8	28.8	55.2	89.6 *	89.6
Louisiana	1812 g	34.2	—	36.3 *	24.4	19.2	39.4	44.7
Alabama	1819 g	96.7	52.1	53.6	33.3	65.0	89.8	82.7
Mississippi	1823 g	79.8	41.6	56.6	32.8	62.8	88.2 *	89.7
Ohio	1822 g	46.5	34.8	75.8 *	73.8	75.5	84.5	83.6
Indiana	1822 g	52.4	37.5	68.3 *	61.8	70.1	86.0	84.9
Illinois	1822 g	55.8	24.2	51.9	45.6	43.7	85.9 *	76.3
Missouri	1820 g	71.9	20.1	54.3	40.8	35.6	74.0 *	74.7
Arkansas	—					35.0	86.4	68.8
Michigan	—					35.7	84.9	79.3
National Average			26.5	56.3	54.9	55.2	78.0	74.9

Exceeded pre-1824 high
g Gubernatorial election
p Presidential election
† Estimate based on incomplete returns
c Congressional election
l Election of legislature

There would seem to be persuasive evidence that in 1828 the common man flocked to the polls in unprecedented numbers, for the proportion of adult white males voting soared to 56.3 per cent, more than double the 1824 figure. But this outpouring shrinks in magnitude when we observe that in only six of the twenty-two states involved were new highs in voter participation established. In three of these—Maryland, Virginia, and Louisiana—the recorded gain was inconsiderable, and in a fourth—New York—the bulk of the increase might be attributed to changes that had been made in suffrage qualifications as recently as 1821 and 1826. Six states went over the 70 per cent mark, whereas ten had bettered that performance before 1824. Instead of a "mighty democratic uprising" there was in 1828 a voter turnout that approached—but in only a few instances matched or exceeded—the maximum levels that had been attained before the Jackson era.

The advance that was registered in 1828 did not carry forward to 1832. Despite the fact that Jackson was probably at the peak of his personal popularity, that he was engaged in a campaign that was presumably to decide issues of great magnitude, and that in the opinion of some authorities a "well-developed two party system on a national scale" had been established, there was a slight decline in voter participation. The average for the twenty-three states participating in the presidential contest was 54.9 per cent. In fifteen states a smaller percentage of the adult white males went to the polls in 1832 than in 1828. Only five states bettered their pre-1824 highs. Again the conclusion would be that it was essentially the pre-1824 electorate—diminished in most states and augmented in a few—that voted in 1832. Thus, after three Jackson elections, sixteen states had not achieved the proportions of voter participation that they had reached before 1824. The "new democracy" had not yet made its appearance.[4]

4. It may be suggested that it is invalid to compare voter participation in each state in the presidential contests of 1824, 1828, and 1832 with the highs, rather than the average participation in each state prior to 1824. The object of the comparison is to ascertain whether the Jackson elections brought voters

A comparison of the Jackson elections with earlier presidential contests is of some interest. Such comparisons have little validity before 1808 because few states chose electors by popular vote, and for certain of those states the complete returns are not available. In 1816 and 1820 there was so little opposition to Monroe that the voter interest was negligible. The most relevant elections, therefore, are those of 1808 and 1812. The accompanying table (Table 2) gives the percentages of adult white males voting in 1808

Table 2

Percentages of Adult White Males Voting in Presidential Elections

State	1808	1812	1824	1828
Maine	Legis.	50.0	18.9	42.7
New Hampshire	62.1	75.4	16.8	76.5
Massachusetts	Legis.	51.4	29.1	25.7
Rhode Island	37.4	37.7	12.4	18.0
New Jersey	71.8	Legis.	31.1	70.9
Pennsylvania	34.7	45.5	19.6	56.6
Maryland	48.4	56.5	53.7	76.2
Virginia	17.7	17.8	11.5	27.6
Ohio	12.8	20.0	34.8	75.8

Note: No complete returns of the popular vote cast for electors in Kentucky or Tennessee in 1808 and 1812 and in North Carolina in 1808 could be located.

and 1812 in those states for which full returns could be found, together with the comparable percentages for the elections of 1824 and 1828. In 1824 only one state—Ohio—surpassed the highs established in either 1808 or 1812. Four more joined this list in 1828

to the polls in unprecedented numbers, as has so often been asserted. Moreover, it is hardly feasible to compare average participation in elections before and after 1824 in many states because of the changes that were made in the methods of electing governors and presidential electors or—in certain instances —because the state had only recently entered the Union. However, among those states in which average voter participation was obviously higher before 1824 than it was in the three Jackson elections were Alabama, Connecticut, Georgia, Massachusetts, Mississippi, New Hampshire (1809–1817), Pennsylvania, Rhode Island, Tennessee, and Vermont (1807–1815).

—Virginia, Maryland, Pennsylvania, and New Hampshire—although the margin in the last case was so small as to be inconsequential. The most significant conclusion to be drawn from this admittedly limited and unrepresentative data is that in those states where there was a vigorous two-party contest in 1808 and 1812 the vote was relatively high. Conversely, where there was little or no contest in 1824 or 1828, the vote was low.

When an examination is made of voting in other than presidential elections prior to 1824, the inaccuracy of the impression that "only small numbers of citizens" went to the polls becomes apparent. Because of the almost automatic succession of the members of the "Virginia dynasty" and the early deterioration of the national two-party system that had seemed to be developing around 1800, presidential elections did not arouse voter interest as much as did those for governor, state legislators, or even members of Congress. In such elections at the state level the "common man" was stimulated by local factors to cast his vote, and he frequently responded in higher proportions than he did to the later stimulus provided by Jackson.

The average voter participation for all the states in 1828 was 56.3 per cent. Before 1824 fifteen of the twenty-two states had surpassed that percentage. Among other things, this means that the 1828 election failed to bring to the polls the proportion of the electorate that had voted on occasion in previous elections. There was, in other words, a high potential vote that was frequently realized in state elections but which did not materialize in presidential elections. The unsupported assumption that the common man was either apathetic or debarred from voting by suffrage barriers before 1824 is untenable in the light of this evidence.

In state after state (see Table 1) gubernatorial elections attracted 70 per cent or more of the adult white males to the polls. Among the notable highs recorded were Delaware with 81.9 per cent in 1804, New Hampshire with 80.8 per cent in 1814, Tennessee with 80.0 per cent in 1817, Vermont with 79.9 per cent in 1812, Mississippi with 79.8 per cent in 1823, and Alabama with a highly improbable 96.7 per cent in its first gubernatorial contest in 1819. There is reason to believe that in some states, at least, the voter participation in the election of state legislators was even higher than in gubernatorial elections. Because of the virtual impossibility of securing county-by-county or district-by-district returns for such elections, this hypothesis is difficult to verify.

Down to this point the voter turnout in the Jackson elections has been compared with that in elections held prior to 1824. Now it becomes appropriate to inquire whether during the period 1824 through 1832 voters turned out in greater proportions for the three presidential contests than they did for the contemporary state elections. If, indeed, this "new democracy" bore some special relationship to Andrew Jackson or to his policies, it might be anticipated that interest in the elections in which he was the central figure would stimulate greater voter participation than gubernatorial contests, in which he was at most a remote factor.

Actually, the election returns show fairly conclusively that throughout the eight-year period the electorate continued to participate more extensively in state elections than in those involving the presidency. Between 1824 and 1832 there were fifty regular gubernatorial elections in the states that chose their electors by popular vote. In only sixteen of these fifty instances did the vote for President surpass the corresponding vote for governor. In Rhode Island, Delaware, Tennessee, Kentucky, Illinois, Mississippi, Missouri, and Georgia the vote for governor consistently exceeded that for President. Only in Connecticut was the reverse true. Viewed from this perspective, too, the remarkable feature of the vote in the Jackson elections is not its immensity, but rather its smallness.

Finally, the Jackson elections may be compared with subsequent presidential elections. Once Jackson had retired to the Hermitage, and figures of less dramatic proportions took up the contest for the presidency, did voter participation rise or fall? This question can be answered by observing the percentage of adult white males who voted in each state in the presidential elections of 1836 through

1844 (Table 1). Voter participation in the 1836 election remained near the level that had been established in 1828 and 1832, with 55.2 per cent of the adult white males voting. Only five states registered percentages in excess of their pre-1824 highs. But in 1840 the "new democracy" made its appearance with explosive suddenness.

In a surge to the polls that has rarely, if ever, been exceeded in any presidential election, four out of five (78.0 per cent) of the adult white males cast their votes for Harrison or Van Buren.[5] This new electorate was greater than that of the Jackson period by more than 40 per cent. In all but five states—Vermont, Massachusetts, Rhode Island, Kentucky, and Alabama—the peaks of voter participation, reached before 1824 were passed. Fourteen of the twenty-five states involved set record highs for voting that were not to be broken throughout the remainder of the antebellum period. Now, at last, the common man—or at least the man who previously had not been sufficiently aroused to vote in presidential elections—cast his weight into the political balance. This "Tippecanoe Democracy," if such a label is permissible, was of a different order of magnitude from the Jacksonian Democracy. The elections in which Jackson figured brought to the polls only those men who were accustomed to voting in state or national elections, except in a very few states. The Tippecanoe canvass witnessed an extraordinary expansion of the size of the presidential electorate far beyond previous dimensions. It was in 1840, then, that the "roaring flood of the new democracy" reached its crest. And it engulfed the Jacksonians.

The flood receded only slightly in 1844, when 74.9 per cent of the estimated potential electorate went to the polls. Indeed, nine

---

5. It can be calculated that the total of adult white males in the twenty-five states was 3,090,708. The total popular vote was 2,409,682. In the presidential election of 1896 the total vote approximated 80 per cent of the potential electorate. In 1940 and 1952 the comparable figures would be 63 per cent and 65 per cent respectively. These percentages have been calculated on the assumption that the potential electorate in 1896 included all adult male citizens and in 1940 and 1952 all adult citizens.

states attained their record highs for the period. In 1848 and 1852 there was a general downward trend in voter participation, followed by a modest upswing in 1856 and 1860. But the level of voter activity remained well above that of the Jackson elections. The conclusion to be drawn is that the "mighty democratic uprising" came after the period of Jackson's presidency.

Now that the quantitative dimensions of Jacksonian Democracy as a political phenomenon have been delineated and brought into some appropriate perspective, certain questions still remain to be answered. Granted that the Jacksonian electorate—as revealed by the comparisons that have been set forth—was not really very large, how account for the fact that voter participation doubled between the elections of 1824 and 1828? It is true that the total vote soared from around 359,000 to 1,155,400 and that the percentage of voter participation more than doubled. Traditionally, students of the Jackson period have been impressed by this steep increase in voting and by way of explanation have identified the causal factors as the reduction of suffrage qualifications, the democratic influence of the West, or the personal magnetism of Jackson. The validity of each of these hypotheses needs to be re-examined.

In no one of the states in which electors were chosen by popular vote was any significant change made in suffrage qualifications between 1824 and 1828. Subsequently, severe restrictions were maintained in Rhode Island until 1842, when some liberalization was effected, and in Virginia down to 1850. In Louisiana, where the payment of a tax was a requirement, the character of the state tax system apparently operated to restrict the suffrage at least as late as 1845. Thus with the three exceptions noted, the elimination of suffrage barriers was hardly a factor in producing an enlarged electorate during the Jackson and post-Jackson periods. Furthermore, all but a few states had extended the privilege of voting either to all male taxpayers or to all adult male citizens by 1810. After Connecticut eliminated its property qualification in 1818, Massachusetts in 1821, and New York in 1821 and 1826, only Rhode Island, Virginia, and Louisiana were left on the list of "restrictionist" states. Neither Jackson's victory nor the increased vote in 1828 can be attributed to the presence at the polls of a newly enfranchised mass of voters.

Similarly, it does not appear that the western states led the way in voter participation. Prior to 1824, for example, Ohio, Indiana, and Illinois had never brought to the polls as much as 60 per cent of their adult white males. Most of the eastern states had surpassed that level by considerable margins. In the election of 1828 six states registered votes in excess of 70 per cent of their adult white male populations. They were in order of rank: New Hampshire, Maryland, Ohio, New Jersey, Kentucky, and New York. The six leaders in 1832 were: New Hampshire, Kentucky, Ohio, New York, New Jersey, and Delaware. It will be obvious that the West, however that region may be defined, was not leading the "mighty democratic uprising." Western influences, then, do not explain the increased vote in 1828.

There remains to be considered the factor of Jackson's personal popularity. Did Jackson, the popular hero, attract voters to the polls in unprecedented proportions? The comparisons that have already been made between the Jackson elections and other elections—state and national—before, during, and after his presidency would suggest a negative answer to the question. Granted that a majority of the voters in 1828 favored Jackson, it is not evident that his partisans stormed the polls any more enthusiastically than did the Adams men. Of the six highest states in voter participation in 1828, three favored Adams and three were for Jackson, which could be interpreted to mean that the convinced Adams supporters turned out no less zealously for their man than did the ardent Jacksonians. When Van Buren replaced Jackson in 1836, the voting average increased slightly over 1832. And, as has been demonstrated, the real manifestation of the "new democracy" came not in 1828 but in 1840.

The most satisfactory explanation for the increase in voter participation between 1824 and 1828 is a simple and obvious one.

During the long reign of the Virginia dynasty, interest in presidential elections dwindled. In 1816 and 1820 there had been no contest. The somewhat fortuitous termination of the Virginia succession in 1824 and the failure of the congressional caucus to solve the problem of leadership succession threw the choice of a President upon the electorate. But popular interest was dampened by the confusion of choice presented by the multiplicity of candidates, by the disintegration of the old national parties, by the fact that in most states one or another of the candidates was so overwhelmingly popular as to forestall any semblance of a contest, and possibly by the realization that the election would ultimately be decided by the House of Representatives. By 1828 the situation had altered. There were but two candidates in the field, each of whom had substantial sectional backing. A clear-cut contest impended, and the voters became sufficiently aroused to go to the polls in moderate numbers.

One final question remains. Why was the vote in the Jackson elections relatively low when compared with previous and contemporary state elections and with presidential votes after 1840? The answer, in brief, is that in most states either Jackson or his opponent had such a one-sided advantage that the result was a foregone conclusion. Consequently there was little incentive for the voters to go to the polls.

This factor can be evaluated in fairly specific quantitative terms. If the percentage of the total vote secured by each candidate in each state in the election of 1828 is calculated, the difference between the percentages can be used as an index of the closeness, or one-sidedness, of the contest. In Illinois, for example, Jackson received 67 per cent of the total vote and Adams 33; the difference—thirty-four points—represents the margin between the candidates. The average difference between the candidates, taking all the states together, was thirty-six points. Expressed another way this would mean that in the average state the winning candidate received more than twice the vote of the loser. Actually, this was the case

Table 3

Differential between Percentages of Total Vote Obtained by Major Presidential Candidates, 1828–1844

State	1828	1832	1836	1840	1844
Maine	20	10	20	1	13
New Hampshire	7	13	50	11	19
Vermont	50	10	20	29	18
Massachusetts	66	30	9	16	12
Rhode Island	50	14	6	23	20
Connecticut	50	20	1	11	5
New York	2	4	9	4	1
New Jersey	4	1	1	4	1
Pennsylvania	33	16	4	1	2
Delaware	—	2	6	10	3
Maryland	2	1	7	8	5
Virginia	38	50	13	1	6
North Carolina	47	70	6	15	5
Georgia	94	100	4	12	4
Kentucky	1	9	6	29	8
Tennessee	90	90	16	11	1
Louisiana	6	38	3	19	3
Alabama	80	100	11	9	18
Mississippi	60	77	2	7	13
Ohio	3	3	4	9	2
Indiana	13	34	12	12	2
Illinois	34	37	10	2	12
Missouri	41	32	21	14	17
Arkansas	—	—	28	13	26
Michigan	—	—	9	4	6
Average Differential	36	36	11	11	9

in thirteen of the twenty-two states (see Table 3).[6] Such a wide margin virtually placed these states in the "no contest" category.

A remarkably close correlation existed between the size of the

6. The index figures in the table represent the difference between the percentages of the total popular vote secured by the two major candidates in each state. For the election of 1832, the figures represent only the difference between the votes obtained by Clay and Jackson.

voter turnout and the relative closeness of the contest. The six states previously listed as having the greatest voter participation in 1828 were among the seven states with the smallest margin of difference between the candidates. The exception was Louisiana, where restrictions on the suffrage curtailed the vote. Even in this instance, however, it is significant that voter participation in Louisiana reached a record high. In those states, then, where there was a close balance of political forces the vote was large, and conversely, where the contest was very one sided, the vote was low

Most of the states in 1828 were so strongly partial to one or another of the candidates that they can best be characterized as one-party states. Adams encountered little opposition in New England, except in New Hampshire, and Jackson met with hardly any resistance in the South. It was chiefly in the middle states and the older West that the real battle was waged. With the removal of Adams from the scene after 1828, New England became less of a one-party section, but the South remained extremely one sided. Consequently it is not surprising that voter participation in 1832 failed even to match that of 1828.

Here, certainly, is a factor of crucial importance in explaining the dimensions of the voter turnout in the Jackson elections. National parties were still in a rudimentary condition and were highly unbalanced from state to state. Indeed, a two-party system scarcely could be said to exist in more than half of the states until after 1832. Where opposing parties had been formed to contest the election, the vote was large, but where no parties, or only one, took the field, the vote was low. By 1840, fairly well-balanced parties had been organized in virtually every state. In only three states did the margin between Harrison and Van Buren exceed twenty points, and the average for all the states was only eleven points. The result was generally high voter participation.[7]

7. Careful analysis of the data in Table 3 will suggest that there were three fairly distinct stages in the emergence of a nationally balanced two-party system. Balanced parties appeared first in the middle states between 1824 and 1828. New England remained essentially a one-party section until after

When Jacksonian Democracy is viewed from the perspectives employed in this analysis, its political dimensions in so far as they relate to the behavior of the electorate can be described with some precision. None of the Jackson elections involved a "mighty democratic uprising" in the sense that voters were drawn to the polls in unprecedented proportions. When compared with the peak participation recorded for each state before 1824, or with contemporaneous gubernatorial elections, or most particularly with the vast outpouring of the electorate in 1840, voter participation in the Jackson elections was unimpressive. The key to the relatively low presidential vote would seem to be the extreme political imbalance that existed in most states as between the Jacksonians and their opponents. Associated with this imbalance was the immature development of national political parties. Indeed, it can be highly misleading to think in terms of national parties in connection with the Jackson elections. As balanced, organized parties subsequently made their appearance from state to state, and voters were stimulated by the prospect of a genuine contest, a marked rise in voter participation occurred. Such conditions did not prevail generally across the nation until 1840, and then at last the "mighty democratic uprising" took place.

Adams had passed from the scene; then competing parties appeared. In the South and the newer West, a one-party dominance continued until divisions arose over who should succeed Jackson. Sectional loyalties to favorite sons obviously exerted a determining influence on presidential politics, and consequently on party formation, in the Jackson years.

Rich Men and Politics

Money and Party in Jacksonian America

by Frank Otto Gatell

Jackson's presidency was one of the most controversial in American history. Every political battle became a crisis, a battle between Light and Darkness in the minds of the President and his opponents, fought at peaks of emotional intensity far exceeding the objective importance of even such significant issues as internal improvements, the tariff, or the location of the Federal government's financial accounts. In particular, banking and finance— the money question—set the tone for Democratic politics during the 1830's. By the end of that decade, many wealthy Americans had become frightened, and they blamed the Jacksonians for stimulating anti-business feeling that threatened the rights of property. They labeled that feeling, and whatever else displeased them politically, Loco-Focoism, a scareword connoting wild-eyed radicalism.

The aftermath of the Panic of 1837 intensified conservative fears in a way that paralleled the constant anxieties of Southerners over the possibility of slave revolts. Northern businessmen reacted apprehensively to social protest movements, and to the rising tide of urban violence. A monied man who might well have supported Jackson's vague program in 1828 was far less likely to do so in 1840, when the Democratic party attacked bankers and other businessmen. Neither Jackson nor his chosen successor, Martin Van Buren, were anti-capitalist, but the Bank War and the subsequent alignment of most businessmen in the anti-Jackson or Whig camp injected an obvious class element into the two-party system. During these years a major reshuffling occurred that altered the political structure for a time, and gave the parties after 1837 a greater class orientation than before.

The following study of the political behavior of the wealthiest men in New York between 1828 and 1844 shows the emergence of the class basis of party preference. Frank Otto Gatell found that a clear preference had developed for Whiggery over Jacksonian Democracy, and he contends that many rich men acquired their anti-Jacksonian bias during the 1830's as a fearful response to Democratic banking and financial policies.

In olden times, that is, a generation or more ago, American historians proceeded upon a basic assumption when discussing the Jacksonian period: the Democratic party was the party of the people, and the Whig party was the party of economic privilege. The Democrats included in their ranks the common man, the farmers, the artisans, and the mechanics, the poor but honest sinew of Jacksonian Democracy. Conversely, the Whigs were the rich merchants and the wealthy planters who made up a self-styled "better sort." They were thinly disguised Federalists, vainly striving to stem the populistic tide.

This economic class interpretation of political divisions came under severe attack during the two decades following the Second World War. First the entrepreneurial or "Columbia" school argued that Jacksonians shared the capitalistic ethos of their Whig antagonists, and that they were merely demanding equal time at the feeding trough. A short time later, the writers of the complementary consensus school went beyond the identity of outlook

From the *Political Science Quarterly*, LXXXII (June 1967), 235–52. Reprinted by permission; most footnotes omitted.

that supposedly existed between established Whig capitalists and
nascent Jacksonian capitalists, and argued that agreement on fundamental issues has been the hallmark of American politics at all
levels. They insisted that meaningful correlations between voting
behavior and economic status were hard to come by, if not non-
existent.

In the latter category, the work of Lee Benson stands as an influential example. His study of voting behavior in New York State
in 1844, *The Concept of Jacksonian Democracy*,[1] has in the few
years since its publication in 1961 gone through several printings,
including two paperback editions, and has become one of the most
widely discussed volumes on Jacksonianism, even gaining the rare
accolade of a session at a historical convention devoted entirely to
its appraisal. Benson's book has not swept all before it—the conservatism of the historical profession is guarantee against such
sweeping triumphs whatever the new viewpoint may be—but even
critics have conceded that it made a breakthrough in methodology,
a departure which afforded a fresh approach to the Age of Jackson,
and perhaps to American politics in general.

Benson's methodology breathed academic modernity from every
pore. He employed the rhetorical and structural paraphernalia of
the social sciences. And particularly in those passages which demol-
ished historiographical shibboleths, Benson ardently championed
a marriage of historical dilletantism with the virile social sciences
—an alliance meant to rescue history from old-maid antiquarian-
ism. Such a union will be solemnized before long, and the historical discipline will profit by it; so say most of the younger practitioners of the historian's craft. Thus Benson placed himself in
the vanguard, and his methodological *tour de force* gave almost
irresistible impetus to his thesis.

Benson was especially assiduous in attacking the older view that
in the Jacksonian era parties divided along class lines. In a section

1. Benson does not write of an America without social conflicts, but he gives
primacy to ethnic and religious factors as determinants for group behavior,
discarding the haves-versus-the-have-nots basis of liberal historiography.

on party leadership, he attempted to establish a sociological identity among New York State Democrats and Whigs at the top rank, and his analysis extended with similar results into "Middle-Grade Leaders." But in the process, to borrow a figure from the politics of New York in the eighteen-forties, Benson may have turned Barnburner to get rid of a few rats. A closer inspection of a small but important part of the smoldering ashes than has previously been attempted is called for. The comments which follow are not offered as an assessment of Benson's book as a whole. His theory of voting cycles and his call for a multivariate analytical approach to voting behavior are stimulating, and they will doubtless receive careful appraisal and criticism as his hypotheses are tested.

I

"Partial answers," Benson declared at the beginning of his section on party leadership, "frequently give rise to misleading or erroneous conclusions." No one can fault that observation, but in practice Benson himself emerged with answers that were partial, misleading, and erroneous. The questions he posed in that section went beyond the stated initial problem of the social composition of middle grade political leadership. In addition, and much more significantly, he asked: "Did men of wealth strongly tend to give their resources, talents, and prestige to the Whigs rather than to the Democrats? Did a large proportion of the business community —however defined—adhere to the Whig faith?" [2] In arguing for the negative, Benson cited an unnamed Whig orator to the effect that New York's rich men were divided politically and that many Democrats were in fact wealthy. The orator did not contend, however, that the wealthy men were divided *evenly* between the parties. But according to Benson, "by exploiting the clue" provided by the orator's imprecise claim, "historians may be able to clear away

2. Two questions (composition of middle-grade political leadership and voting behavior of wealthy citizens) run through the discussion. I am concerned with the second.

the rhetorical rubbish and reveal the social structure of party leadership during the Age of Egalitarianism." Rhetorical rubbish, or
the injection of something resembling class conflict into the Demo-
cratic-Whig struggle of the late eighteen-thirties, thus became the
impediment. "Who from 1834 to 1844 took the [Democratic] campaign claptrap literally?" Benson asked derisively. A fairer question might be: Who took the campaigning seriously? and the
answer would be: A great many people. For, as is the case of
twentieth-century advertising, which is also not to be taken literally, the effectiveness of rhetorical claptrap cannot be dismissed.

So much for rhetoric. What about verifiable data? Benson
quoted from an editorial in Greeley's *Tribune* which tried to distribute part of the odium attached to the possession of wealth to
the Democrats: "The Whigs are by no means all wealthy, nor
are the wealthy all Whigs," etc., etc. Some of Greeley's statements were themselves rhetorical claptrap. For example, Greeley
"charged" that Democrats chartered most of New York City's
banks. Since the Democratic Albany regency had controlled the
legislature almost continuously for a generation, the statement was
a truism. But Greeley also specified that many New York City
Democrats were worth $100,000 or more. Benson explained that
"the design of this study does not permit the research necessary to
test all the claims" Greeley made, but one assertion (the presence
of $100,000-or-over Democrats) could be tested precisely to learn
about "party division among economic groups in New York."

Eventually, all discussions of New York City wealth in the
eighteen-forties depend upon those exasperating, fascinating, incomplete, and indispensable compendia of the city's economic
elite, *Wealth and Biography of the Wealthy Citizens of New
York City* . . . , published annually during most of the eighteen-
forties and fifties by Moses Y. Beach, editor of the New York *Sun*.
Many historians have used them, Robert G. Albion wrote an article about them, and Benson took samples from the sixth edition
of 1845.

Beach's list of wealthy citizens for that year included about one thousand names. Benson chose not to analyze the list *in toto*, despite his stated intention to evaluate this specific Greeley claim. Therefore, "some sampling procedure must be devised." He first matched the names of men who were officers of "ratification meetings" held in New York City in 1844 by both major parties with the names on the Wealthy Citizens list, and found that twelve Whig officers (or 34 per cent) qualified, as did thirteen (or 26 per cent) of the Democratic officers. Although Benson dismissed the percentage differential of 8 per cent as "not large enough to be significant in any case," he nevertheless took the trouble to explain it away by the claim of "rank order position." In other words, the importance of Middle Grade Leaders decreased as one read down from the top of the list. Thus if one took the first ten names, both parties supplied six (or 60 per cent) Wealthy Citizens. If one took only the first thirty-five names, the Democrats supplied 34 per cent Wealthy Citizens to the Whigs' 35 per cent. This reduction procedure, although ingenious was questionable to say the least. Benson nowhere established that the men were listed in order of social or political prominence. The Democrats may have been listed that way (although that is doubtful); the Whigs certainly were not. They appeared arranged not in "rank order," but by city wards. The eighth name among the many Whig vice-presidents, for example, was not that of the eighth most important New York City Whig, but that of the Whig sent to the city-wide party convention to represent the Eighth Ward. And it should also be remembered that Benson's "ratification meeting sample" involved but twenty-five men out of the thousand Wealthy Citizens.

Benson's second sampling procedure was simpler but equally unsatisfactory. Taking the list at face value, he scanned Beach's biographical vignettes for political identifications and found information concerning the party affiliations of another twenty-five men, thirteen Democrats (52 per cent) and twelve Whigs (48 per cent). Again, a consensus historian's dream. But the stumbling block here was the inaccuracy of the identifications. Beach, or his

compilers, called two of the alleged Jacksonian Democrats, Jonathan Thompson and William W. Todd, "democrats." Both men
were in fact National Republicans who supported John Quincy
Adams in 1828 and Whig candidates thereafter. Thompson was
Adams's collector of the port, whom Jackson removed in 1829.
Corrected, the second sample then becomes fourteen Whigs (56
per cent) and eleven Democrats (44 per cent). But the "sample"
is not useful in any case. Beach's political identification of his
Wealthy Citizens was arbitrary. Some men of political prominence
were not identified by party (Benjamin F. Butler, for example),
and some were identified incorrectly.

So, on the basis of these forty-five individuals (five were repeaters) out of one thousand (or 4.5 per cent of the total), Benson asked us to believe that his "hypotheses appear potentially
verifiable." This is a very tall order for such scanty research to
accomplish, however tentative the claims. Obviously, the only con-
structive way to resolve the problem is to direct attention to the
remaining 95 per cent and examine the Wealthy Citizens list in
its entirety.

II

As already noted, the principal recommendation for the use of
Beach's list is its availability. It contained no explanation of the
selection procedure employed, but merely implied that *every* New
Yorker of 1845 worth $100,000 or more could be found on the list.
Nor was there any assurance of accuracy concerning the estimates
of wealth (usually rounded off to the "nearest" $50,000).

Striking omissions were plentiful. Take, for example, William E.
Dodge of the important metals firm, Phelps, Dodge & Company.
Dodge, aptly termed a "merchant prince" by his biographer, was
already a very wealthy citizen at the time of the Beach compilation. Even more perplexing is the fact that Dodge was omitted although the company's senior partner, Anson G. Phelps, was listed
at one million dollars, and junior partners Anson G. Phelps Jr.,

and Daniel James (worth $400,000 each), were both included. Similarly, Edwin D. Morgan, merchant and politician, did not receive a listing; nor did Marshall O. Roberts, a young capitalist worth $250,000 by 1847. Dodge, Morgan, and Roberts were all Whigs, but one can probably produce names of some prominent Democrats of means who did not gain inclusion. Obviously, Moses Beach was as capricious a practitioner of the art of "elite listing" as any of his predecessors or successors.

Theoretically, one might spurn Beach's offering and try to draw up a comprehensive and accurate list of New York City wealth in the eighteen-forties or any other decade of the period. But the task would involve a lifetime of research in the city directories and tax lists, among other sources. The scope of *this* inquiry does not permit such a luxuriance of preliminary investigation. I propose to limit myself to the one thousand individuals found in the Beach list of 1845.

The figure "one thousand" has cropped up several times. It is an approximation, since the precise number of "workable" names is actually 909. The elimination of some names was advisable for several reasons. Female wealthy citizens could not vote or participate politically, whatever their views. Men who died before 1828 (the first year of a meaningful pro- or anti-Jackson alignment) have been eliminated, as have those identified by a last name only. There were also a dozen names repeated on the list.

Among the remaining 909 names, problems of identification arose. In some cases, men shared the same name, sometimes with another man on the list and far more often with another citizen who was not listed. There are two wealthy citizens named David Banks, and two men named George Douglass. In these instances, separate identifications were possible, and each pair split politically. But significantly, perhaps, at least as far as this study is concerned, the two Whigs were wealthier than their namesakes. There was also the problem of identifying the politics of men with common given and family names. For example, many John Wards lived in New York City at the time, but businessmen (who made up the

vast majority of those on the list) often signed their firms' names
to political pronouncements, such as calls for ratification meetings,
or patronage petitions. Thus the presence of "Prime, Ward &
King" on a Whig call or petition provided the political stand of
John Ward, as well as that of Edward Prime, Samuel Ward, and
James G. King, his partners in that well known brokerage firm.
Of course, not all the names were that "common." Happily for
the investigator, there was only one Aquilla G. Stout in New York
City in 1845, and, of course, only one Preserved Fish.

Whatever the deficiencies and difficulties, the list still beckons.
An intensive search in both primary and secondary sources, Whig
and Democratic, produced the political identification of 642 men,
or 70.6 per cent. The extent of political involvement varied widely.
Thus, among the Whigs, the men ranged from Moses H. Grinnell, a Whig congressman, and Jonathan Goodhue, president of
many an anti-Jackson New York City rally, to merchants such
as George T. Trimble and Oliver T. Hewlett, who apparently were
not lured into participating in political meetings but who publicly
opposed Democratic policies, such as the removal of the deposits
and the refusal to charter a new national bank. The Democratic
minority showed a similar spread, from ex-cabinet member Benjamin F. Butler to Democratic merchants such as Reuel Smith, who
voiced general approval of the Van Buren administration in 1840.
In any case, of the 642 men identified politically, the overwhelming majority (541, or 84.3 per cent) were of the Whig persuasion.
New York City money in 1845 was decidedly Whig.

Not only was New York City wealth Whiggish to the general
extent of 84.3 per cent but big money showed an even more pronounced affinity for the party of "sound principles." If we divide
the Wealthy Citizens into groups according to the size of their
estates, at the highest levels the incidence of Democratic affiliation
shrinks well below the already miniscule over-all average of 15.7
per cent. All four men worth five million dollars or more were anti-
Jacksonians. And at the next three levels, the Democrats averaged
only 8.4 per cent of those identified. Thus among those worth

$400,000 or more (with one hundred identified out of a total of 129), ninety-two men (92 per cent) were Whigs. Democrats fared better in the categories $300,000 to $399,000 and $250,000 to $299,000, dropping off again sharply in the $200,000 to $249,000 class. But to revert to America's common yardstick for measuring great wealth, of the seventeen millionaires identified out of a total of twenty-two, sixteen (94.1 per cent) were Whigs.[3]

Table 1

Party Affiliation by Amount of Wealth

	Total No.	Politics Identified No. %	Whigs No. %	Democrats No. %
$5,000,000 or more	4	4 (100.0)	4 (100.0)	0 (0.0)
$1,000,000 to $4,999,000	18	13 (72.2)	12 (92.3)	1 (7.7)
$500,000 to $999,000	80	59 (73.8)	54 (91.5)	5 (8.5)
$400,000 to $499,000	27	25 (92.6)	23 (92.0)	2 (8.0)
$300,000 to $399,000	101	67 (66.3)	50 (74.6)	17 (25.4)
$250,000 to $299,000	63	47 (74.6)	37 (78.7)	10 (21.3)
$200,000 to $249,000	162	110 (67.9)	98 (89.1)	12 (10.9)
	455	325 (71.4)	278 (85.5)	47 (14.5)

III

Benson could not have chosen a less suitable point in time than 1844–45 to seek validation for his thesis. In fact, his study of Jacksonian Democracy is curiously unhistorical in its neglect of chronology. True, he provided a summary of New York political history from 1815 to 1844 which set the Fox-Schlesinger accounts topsy-turvy, and he specifically chided political historians for their unhistorical use of isolated election returns, but in essence his study concentrated upon voting behavior in 1844. With regard to a negative correlation between upper-class membership and party, 1828 would have served far better.

3. The only millionaire identified as a Democrat, Jacob Lorillard, died in 1838. Had he lived on into the forties he might well have become one of the many wealthy Democratic defectors to Whiggery.

In 1828, a New York City businessman or professional might as easily have supported Jackson as Adams. Or with equal probability, he might have ignored the organized aspects of politics and done no more than cast his vote. This was no longer the case in 1844. In the intervening sixteen years, businessmen had soured on Jacksonism–Loco-Focoism in a series of revolts which culminated in opposition to Van Buren's subtreasury proposal during the late eighteen-thirties and in the feverish enthusiasm of the election of 1840. The defection process began in New York City as early as 1827, when several Tammany sachems supported Adams instead of Jackson. Then during the Bank Veto campaign of 1832 several Democratic leaders bolted (among them Gulian Verplanck and Moses Grinnell), and a year later the crisis brought on by the removal of federal deposits from the Bank of the United States caused further defections. The Panic of 1837 and the subtreasury proposal, which ostensibly would have cut the ties between the national government and the bank credit system, produced the major party split known as the conservative revolt, and created more recruits for the Whig column. Most conservatives found their way back to the Democratic party in time, but not all.

Among the Wealthy Citizens of 1845, many such defectors from the Democracy can be found. Of the men identified as Whigs by the eighteen-forties, fifty-two (or almost 10 per cent) were former Democrats. The total of men identified as having been Democrats at one time or other was 153 (101 in good standing by 1845, and 52 defectors). Thus fully one-third of the wealthy who had originally been Democrats reacted violently to their party's policies in the eighteen-thirties and joined the enemy. One simply cannot dismiss the "Loco-Focoizing" of the Democratic party in the middle and late eighteen-thirties as rhetorical claptrap; *something* caused a third of the wealthy Democrats to bolt. And there was no corresponding reversal of the process. Not a single individual among the 101 Democrats of 1845 had previously been an anti-Jacksonian.

As important as were the defections, perhaps even more significant was the fact that the Democratic response to the Bank War and Panic of 1837 temporarily solidified the New York City business community into an anti-Democratic force. It may be difficult now to comprehend what terrors the subtreasury scheme would have imposed on the merchants, or to tremble at the Loco-Foco oratory, but the businessmen of that day did not have the balm of historical perspective to soothe them. Many believed that they were standing on the "ragged edge of anarchy," to employ a conservative pronouncement of the latter part of the nineteenth century. In the late eighteen-thirties, New York City businessmen displayed their colors, many of them for the first time. A contemporary observer described a leading merchant financier's reaction:

With very clear and decided notions on public subjects, Mr. Ward had yet kept himself—as was, indeed, until 1834, the case with very many of the leading and active commercial men in New York—free from party strife. . . . When, however, in 1834, that series of disastrous measures commenced, which, under the auspices of General Jackson and his successor, have caused such accumulated ruin and misery, Mr. Ward . . . entered the political arena.

Merchants supporting the Whig ticket convened a meeting in September 1840 in front of the Merchants Exchange. Over two thousand firms signed the call for the meeting, a list which took up the entire front page of the Whig newspapers. The Whig diarist Philip Hone was both exultant and accurate when he wrote:

The great meeting of Whig merchants took place to-day. . . . The appearance of the mass of people was perfectly sublime. It was a field of heads, occupying a space about six times as large as the area of Washington hall, from which I calculated the number at fifteen thousand; all respectable and orderly merchants and traders. . . .

The Democratic merchants also held a meeting. Its call, again in the form of company names tabulated in small print, consumed one-tenth the space in newspaper columns that the Whig call had used. As Democrat Joseph A. Scoville (the "Old Merchant") put it, colorfully but not exultantly: "Very few merchants of the first

class have been Democrats. . . . The Democratic merchants could
have easily been stowed in a large Eighth avenue railroad car."

Table 2 illuminates the intensification of political activity on
the part of New York City businessmen following the initiation of
the Bank War. In the period 1828–31 slightly less than 10 per cent
of the Wealthy Citizens could be identified politically and, of
them, nearly half were Democrats. But in the next four-year
period, 1832–35, a span which coincided with the Bank Veto and
the Removal of Deposits, the number of Wealthy Citizens taking
a political stand more than quadrupled, and the proportion of
Democrats fell to 23.2 per cent. The Democratic percentages continued to dip in the late eighteen-thirties and early forties. By the
mid-forties the incidence of political identification declined as the
fires of the Bank and currency questions died down, but by then
the bond between the business community and the Whig party
had been established. Of course, these figures are not a mirror of
the political loyalties of all the Wealthy Citizens from 1828 to
1851, but they do reflect the willingness of the elite economic
groups to make public their political preferences at certain times.
We can reasonably assume that nearly all of the Wealthy Citizens
voted in 1828, but the fact that only 10 per cent were part of the
visible political superstructure indicates a lack of mercantile hostility toward the Jacksonians before the coming of the Bank Wars.

Table 2

Party Affiliation by Time Period

	Total No.*	Politics Identified No. %	Whigs No. %	Demo- crats No. %
1828–31	909	90 (9.9)	48 (53.4)	42 (46.6)
1832–35	909	379 (41.9)	291 (76.8)	88 (23.2)
1836–39	905	298 (32.9)	244 (81.9)	54 (18.1)
1840–43	900	324 (36.0)	270 (83.4)	54 (16.6)
1844–47	892	190 (21.3)	156 (82.2)	34 (17.8)
1848–51	880	134 (15.2)	106 (79.2)	28 (20.8)

* Twenty-nine Wealthy Citizens died between 1828 and 1847.

IV

It is abundantly clear that by 1845 New York City wealth was allied to Whiggery, and that the process had taken place progressively during the preceding fifteen years. Were there other factors which might have produced this pattern of political allegiance? Religious and ethno-cultural variables as determinants of political behavior are being investigated more and more, and I shall follow the trend.

Not surprisingly, the denomination with by far the largest representation among the Wealthy Citizens was the Episcopalian. Presbyterians followed next, and then Quakers and Dutch Reformed. The striking thing about the political breakdown for these four dominant denominations is that the percentages of Whig affiliation ran close to the over-all Whig average of 84 per cent. Thus 84 per cent of the Episcopalians were Whig; 88 per cent of the Presbyterians; 84 per cent of the Dutch Reformed; and 92 per cent of the Quakers. Benson observed that Protestant denominationalism was of little use in pinpointing political alignment, and this seems to be true for the wealthy. What we can observe is such a well known phenomenon as denominational social climbing. Of twenty-three men who switched religions, twelve became Episcopalians and joined, if not the established church, then the church of the establishment.

The number of Wealthy Citizens in the remaining denominations was too small for generalizations. Unitarians were Democratic by 66 per cent, but only two men were involved. Congregationalists and Jews were 100 per cent Whig—all four Congregationalists and all seven Jews. There were only eight Catholics, including a mathematician from Columbia College who converted as an adult, and the Delmonico brothers, the Italian-Swiss restauranteurs, but only one man from Ireland (a Democrat).

On the ethnocultural front, I have followed the native-immigrant division (and sub-categorization) employed by Benson. He also provided rough estimates of political affiliation among the groups—native Dutch, for example, he estimated to have been 60 per cent Democratic. Although the estimates are expressed in percentages, Benson requested that the figures not be taken "literally." Their precision cannot be verified, but precise or not, there is a pronounced dissimilarity between Benson's ethnocultural estimates for the New York electorate as a whole, and the ethnocultural breakdown of wealthy New Yorkers.

Table 3

Religious Affiliation

	No.	Politics Known No.	%	Whigs No.	%	Demo- crats No.	%
Baptists	8	7	(87.5)	5 [1] *	(71.4)	2	(28.6)
Catholics	8	4	(50.0)	2	(50.0)	2	(50.0)
Congregationalists	6	4	(66.7)	4	(100.0)	0	(0.0)
Dutch Reformed	33	25	(75.8)	21 [2]	(84.0)	4	(16.0)
Episcopalians	204	157	(78.0)	132 [13]	(84.0)	25	(16.0)
Jews	8	7	(87.5)	7	(100.0)	0	(0.0)
Methodists	9	8	(89.0)	7	(87.5)	1	(12.5)
Moravians	2	2	(100.0)	2	(100.0)	0	(0.0)
Presbyterians	118	99	(83.9)	87 [4]	(87.8)	12	(12.2)
Quakers	45	36	(80.0)	33 [1]	(91.7)	3	(8.3)
Unitarians	3	3	(100.0)	1	(33.3)	2	(66.7)
Fundamentalists	1	0	(0.0)	0	(0.0)	0	(0.0)
No Religion	2	1	(50.0)	1	(100.0)	0	(0.0)
	447	353	(79.0)	302 [21]	(85.5)	51	(14.5)

* Numbers in brackets indicate Democrats who defected.

Among the natives, Benson estimated that the Old British and Dutch were both 60 per cent Democratic; but among the wealthy, the Old British were 80 per cent Whig, and the Dutch were 83 per cent Whig. These two categories were large, but the largest single native category was the "Yankees," or as Albion put it "the swarm of New Englanders who were seeking their fortunes in New York City, just as it was clinching its leadership over the rival

American ports." Benson estimated that New York Yankees as a whole voted Whig by 55 per cent; wealthy New Englanders in New York City voted Whig by 92 per cent. Two other native groups identified as Democratic by Benson, Germans (60 per cent) and Penn-Jerseyites (55 per cent), were also Whig by 75 per cent and 72 per cent respectively. There were a dozen native Southerners. Though they came from Jackson's banner region, they were 83 per cent Whig.

Table 4

Ethnocultural Background

	Total No.	Politics Identified No. %	Whigs No. %	Benson's Estimates for Whigs %	Demo-crats No. %
Natives					
British	146	106 (72.6)	85 [10] * (80.2)	40	21 (19.8)
Dutch	102	77 (75.5)	64 [7] (83.1)	40	13 (16.9)
German	11	8 (72.8)	6 (75.0)	40	2 (25.0)
Huguenot	7	3 (42.8)	2 (66.7)	75	1 (33.3)
Penn.–Jersey	26	21 (80.8)	15 [3] (71.5)	45	6 (28.5)
Southern	13	12 (92.3)	10 (83.3)	—	2 (16.7)
Yankee	147	122 (83.0)	112 [3] (91.8)	55	10 (8.2)
Sub-totals	452	349 (78.0)	294 [23] (84.2)		55 (15.8)
Immigrants					
Dutch	4	4 (100.0)	4 [1] (100.0)	—	0 (0.0)
English	32	14 (43.7)	14 (100.0)	75	0 (0.0)
French	12	7 (58.4)	6 [1] (85.7)	10	1 (14.3)
German	15	13 (86.6)	7 [1] (53.8)	20	6 (46.2)
Cath.-Irish	1	1 (100.0)	0 (0.0)	5	1 (100.0)
Prot.-Irish	17	14 (82.4)	10 [3] (71.4)	90	4 (28.6)
Scottish	31	29 (93.6)	27 [2] (93.1)	90	2 (6.9)
Swiss	5	0 (0.0)	0 (0.0)	—	0 (0.0)
West Indian	1	1 (100.0)	1 (100.0)	—	0 (0.0)
Polish	1	0 (0.0)	0 (0.0)	—	0 (0.0)
Sub-totals	119	83 (69.7)	69 [8] (83.2)		14 (16.8)
Totals	571	432 (75.7)	363 [31] (84.0)		69 (16.0)

* *Numbers in brackets indicate Democrats who defected.*

The immigrant categories reveal the same patterns. All but one group represented among the wealthy were Whig. There was only one Irish Catholic, no French Canadians, no Welsh, and no Negroes on the Wealthy Citizens list. Immigrant French, supposedly 90 per cent Democratic, were 86 per cent Whig (but that includes only seven men). The immigrant English, estimated at 75 per cent Whig, were 100 per cent Whig (fourteen of fourteen). The Scots, estimated at 90 per cent Whig, were 93 per cent Whig. The lowest Whig percentage among immigrant groups (excluding the one Irish Catholic), was the German (54 per cent), a group estimated at 80 per cent Democratic. Although the German percentage involves but a dozen men, it seems to demonstrate the tug of various factors operating on a man's political decision-making process. One can accept, almost axiomatically, the proposition that religious and ethnocultural background will influence his response to politics, but surely one need not have to argue excessively for considering the possession of great wealth as an important factor, perhaps the preponderant factor, in analyzing the American wealthy as political men.

V

What do these data prove about the political alignment of America's wealthy classes in cities other than New York? Nothing. To what extent New York, City or State, represents the country at large, or to what extent it can usefully be called a "test case," remains to be determined, especially among non-commercial, rural elites. Several additional studies using other "Wealthy Citizens" lists (they exist for Boston and Philadelphia, for example) would be feasible and profitable. Even the absence of such lists does not close the door to counting the heads of the elite. There are directories for all major cities in the Jackson period, and in some cases they go beyond a mere alphabetical listing of heads of households to include classified business and professional directories. From these one might "do" the politics of, say, the importing merchants of Providence, or the lawyers of Pittsburgh, or the physicians of Charleston.

But it is important to begin with men of a non-political grouping and then proceed to their political identification. To start with vice-presidents of ratification meetings or with members of Congress from Tennessee in the antebellum period is to beg the question, since a sociological identity, or near-identity, is almost predictable in those instances. In the case of ratification-meeting vice-presidents we can expect that both parties, whatever their rhetoric, produced lists of solid men—that is, men of material substance—even though one party might have had a much smaller reservoir of "vice-presidential types" to draw upon.[4] It was not likely that the New York City Democracy, whatever its Loco-Foco professions, would put a score of illiterate and inarticulate hod carriers on the Tammany Hall platform. In the second case cited, it was no surprise that the Tennessee congressmen were usually middle-aged lawyers of similar social background. The nature of the group chosen for investigation predetermined that result. But what of the Tennessee professional and commercial classes, the upper crust of the state (and other states as well), taken as solid blocs? Only after such groups have been isolated and examined can we begin to speak with certainty about upper class and party in Jacksonian America.

Much of the previous debate has floundered upon the semantic difficulty of whether Whigs were wealthy. Once again, the terms are in reverse order; the question should read: Were wealthy Americans Whigs? If by "Whigs" we mean all who voted for that party, or even the party functionaries at all levels, it is obvious that the possession of great wealth was not a prerequisite to association with Whiggery. The party had to appeal to a mass electorate in an age of ballot-box egalitarianism. By definition, a man

4. Yet even among the vice-presidents of ratification meetings who were Wealthy Citizens there was considerably more Whig money than Democratic. The thirteen Democrats were worth, collectively, 2.5 million dollars; the twelve Whigs were worth 13.4 million.

of wealth was one who owned more than the majority of his neighbors, and there were simply not enough of the "wealthy" available to achieve election-day victories without the creation of an exclusive, high-level electorate. One Democratic editor described the situation in 1840 in simple terms: "There was a meeting of Whig merchants in Wall Street, and a meeting of the people in the Park, both of which were very large, but the latter much the larger, for the very simple reason that there are more people,—more mechanics and laborers,—than there are merchants." If we begin with the parties, and especially with the entire electorate, it is indeed difficult to find "any evidence that the party situation reflected basic economic or social cleavages in the population," as has recently been remarked of New Jersey. But perhaps the judgment would be altered if one plotted the location of economic status groups in the New Jersey political spectrum, especially for the eighteen-forties.

In a viable two-party system, operating within the context of universal white manhood suffrage, the class nature of political alignment must be sought in areas other than a pristine partisan division of rich versus poor. The validity of projecting the New York City experience to points beyond has yet to be established, but I suspect that the monied men of New York City in the eighteen-forties were not out of step with their peers elsewhere in thinking that the Whig party of that decade better served their interests and better calmed their fears than did the Democracy.

The Politics of Compromise

Democratic Senate Leadership and the
Compromise of 1850

by Holman Hamilton

The building of a successful Jacksonian coalition made the Demo-
crats the majority party in America. They lost the White House
only twice in the thirty-two years between the election of Jackson
in 1828 and the election of Lincoln in 1860. When, after the
Mexican War (1846–48), sectionalism and slavery re-emerged as
dominant issues which threatened to bring the machinery of
national politics to a halt, leading politicians rushed to head off
this disaster. The Democrats proved especially receptive to com-
promise moves, since they had the most to lose if the political
system broke down.

To them—and to compromise-minded Whigs, too—the alter-
natives were limited to either accommodation or confrontation.
They chose accommodation in preference to the dissolution of the
Union and the bloodshed that was sure to follow. This attitude
produced the Compromise of 1850, a catch-all phrase for the half-
dozen measures designed to cool political passions, ease sectional
conflict, and, hopefully, bring Americans peace in their time.
Getting the bills through Congress required complex political bar-
gaining and legwork, and as Holman Hamilton here makes clear,
once the "big guns" of the United States Senate, John C. Cal-

*houn, Henry Clay, and Daniel Webster, had had their say—the
first against compromise, the latter two in favor—others took
charge of the serious legislative business. Stephen A. Douglas and
other Senate Democrats first took the compromise "omnibus"
apart, and then reassembled it after separate passage of each
measure.*

*Douglas seemingly accomplished the impossible: he put
Humpty-Dumpty together again. The nation had accepted the
Compromise and rejected extremism. Democrats would continue
to rule throughout the 1850's, and they would continue to call
themselves the party of compromise and popular sovereignty. Yet
Douglas's efforts did not end in his politcal advancement. Instead,
his party made presidents out of nonentities, Franklin Pierce
(1852) and James Buchanan (1856), and when Douglas made his
most serious bid for the presidency in 1860, the Democratic
coalition shattered.*

In approaching the Compromise of 1850, the modern historian
is likely to find himself on ground previously and even repeatedly
traversed. The last appearance of Clay, Calhoun, and Webster in
the Senate spotlight, the shadow of the second Fugitive Slave Law,
the growing prominence of William H. Seward and Salmon P.
Chase—these and similar landmarks make the usual roads to the
Compromise familiar terrain.

Yet one wonders whether the old historical highways can lead
to a successful reappraisal of an oft-accepted story, which the
eloquent triumvirate of "America's silver age" has all but monopolized. A number of facts project reasonable doubt. Despite the repeated emphasis which writers have placed on Daniel Webster's
"Seventh of March Speech," only one northern Whig senator,
James Cooper of Pennsylvania, supported Webster as long as
President Zachary Taylor lived. Owing to Henry Clay's prominence in the debates, readers are disposed to assume that Whigs

From *The Mississippi Valley Historical Review*, XLI (December 1954),
403–18. Reprinted by permission; footnotes omitted.

provided most of the votes for Clay's "Omnibus Bill." Actually, it was a Whig, James A. Pearce of Maryland, who spiked Clay's efforts on July 31, 1850; nearly all the Whigs then deserted Clay, and the bulk of the backing given first to Clay and later to Stephen A. Douglas stemmed from Democratic ranks. It is known, of course, that John C. Calhoun died when the "Great Debate" was barely under way. But the role of another southern senator, Henry S. Foote of Mississippi, from the mild winter days of early 1850 through the steamy Washington summer, has been obscured —perhaps by Calhoun's reputation and death.

Although such truths as these have been touched upon by a number of writers, there has been no documented synthesis of the detached parts of the picture puzzle. Some of the fragmentary parts have but recently been discovered. Others, large and small, remain missing today. Still, the major outlines of the picture can be re-created through a point-by-point analysis of aims, methods, votes, and contributions of Senate Whig and Democratic leaders. Such an analysis provides a key or clue to precisely what was going on behind the spectacular façade of rhetoric and drama.

Albert Bushnell Hart, Albert J. Beveridge, and Charles A. and Mary R. Beard are only a few of the numerous authors who have magnified Clay's and Webster's influence far beyond the limits of the facts. According to Hart, in early 1850 "the Compromise was already decided, since the agreement of Clay and Webster meant the effective coalition of Southern Whigs and Northern 'Cotton Whigs.'" Also, said Hart, Webster's Seventh of March Speech "was virtually an announcement that the Senate would vote for the Compromise." Actually, President Taylor's death in July and Millard Fillmore's accession—together with the switch from Clay's methods to Douglas's methods—provided the deciding factors, and none of these things could have been foreseen in March.

Beveridge went into considerable detail to do justice to the remarks of Jefferson Davis, Seward, Douglas, and Chase. For this he deserves commendation. But, in the pages of his second volume on Abraham Lincoln, his lucid discussion suddenly breaks down.

The importance of Taylor's death is slighted. Beveridge seems satisfied to say: "So opposition disintegrated and, one after another, the measures suggested by Clay were enacted." A poorly informed reader of Beveridge's book is at a loss to know how and why the Compromise finally survived.

Charles A. and Mary R. Beard, in *The Rise of American Civilization*, have no doubt influenced students by the tens of thousands. Yet the Beards declared: "Once more, as in 1820 and 1833, Clay was to prevail. But he won this time only through the aid of Webster." Still another facet of the same fallacy was later presented by Burton J. Hendrick, who wrote that Howell Cobb "deserted his Democratic party in 1850 and joined forces with the antislavery Whigs in upholding the Compromise measures of that year." In other words, we are asked to believe that the Democratic party opposed the Compromise; that the antislavery Whigs were outstanding in its support; that Clay pushed through the Compromise, but only with the aid of Webster; and that an effective coalition of northern and southern Whigs spelled success for the Compromise as early as March. With each and all of the allegations, the facts themselves take issue.

Lest it be objected that most of these scholars belonged to a past generation, it may be instructive to look into Allan Nevins's *Ordeal of the Union*. Published as recently as 1947, the *Ordeal* contains much that the specialist should value. Nevins does not fall into Edward Channing's error in terming the pro-Compromise position of Cobb a "marked overturn" in the Georgian's sentiments. Nor does he say with James Ford Rhodes that "Webster's influence was of the greatest weight in the passage of the compromise measures," or that "Clay's adroit parliamentary management was necessary to carry them through the various and tedious steps of legislation." But the *Ordeal* does describe Clay's influence as "unrivalled," and the Seventh of March Speech as 1850's "great turning point."

The record shows that the speech of March 7 was not nearly as great a "turning point" as President Taylor's death or the subsequent adoption of the Douglas strategy. The votes demonstrate that Clay's influence was not only rivaled but surpassed by that of the Douglas–Cass Democrats. An equally pertinent criticism lies in the area of Nevins' emphasis. He mentions aspects of the Compromise tangle to which the Beards, Beveridge, and the others appeared oblivious. The irony is that, time and again, he relegates significant material to mere footnote status and neglects to integrate it with his text and conclusions.

In one footnote, Nevins cites Orlando Brown's reference to Lewis Cass's broaching a compromise on January 11, nearly three weeks before Clay's first compromise proposal. In a second footnote, he quotes Robert C. Winthrop's luminous prediction that "any other course" than Taylor's "will kill Whiggery at our end of the Union." In a third footnote, he gives a little space to the contribution of Foote and Thomas Ritchie in forming the Committee of Thirteen. These happen to be a few of the vital links in the chain, but the chain as a whole remains to be forged.

Among the papers of William M. Meredith is a letter written on June 1, 1850, by Whig Senator John H. Clarke of Rhode Island. Clarke was anti-Compromise, as was Secretary of the Treasury Meredith. Reporting to the secretary, Clarke expressed his belief that "from the North & West we can safely depend upon" Senators John Davis, Samuel S. Phelps, William Upham, Albert C. Greene, Truman Smith, Roger S. Baldwin, William H. Seward, William L. Dayton, Jacob W. Miller, Thomas Corwin, and Clarke (Whigs); Hannibal Hamlin, James W. Bradbury, Alpheus Felch, Isaac P. Walker, and Henry Dodge (Democrats), plus John P. Hale and Salmon P. Chase (Free Soilers). When Clarke wrote "we," he referred to the anti-Compromise people who followed President Taylor and Senator Thomas H. Benton. Of the Delaware senators, John Wales was a pro-Taylor and anti-Compromise Whig; Presley Spruance wavered, but Clarke expected him to vote against Clay's Omnibus Bill.

Clarke's summation is echoed, in almost every detail, in a revealing document written by Senator Lewis Cass twelve days later, and addressed to his son-in-law, Henry Ledyard. Cass was pro-Compromise and anti-Taylor, which lends special credence to his assertion that his own Michigan colleague, Felch, was deserting him and lining up with Taylor and Benton.

A third manuscript, until recently in private hands, was sent by Illinois Senator Douglas to the two Democratic journalists responsible for his paper in Springfield. Dated August 3, 1850, the Douglas communication disclosed some of the reasons for the failure of Clay's attempt to pass the Compromise in what was known as the "omnibus" form, even after the death of Taylor. From the first, Douglas and Clay had seen eye to eye respecting the Compromise end-product in which each was interested. The "Little Giant," however, wanted component parts of compromise legislation voted on separately, one at a time. Clay, on the other hand, was determined to rush the program through Congress at one swoop. Realizing that he could not bring Clay around to the methods he himself preferred, the younger man gave way to the elderly Kentuckian in the late winter and spring (when Taylor was living), and even as late as the end of July (when Fillmore occupied the White House). Douglas did this although, as chairman of the Senate committee on territories, he had at least as good a claim to the authorship of the Compromise as anyone else.

The certainty that Clay's "Omnibus Bill" would have failed with Zachary Taylor in the Executive Mansion is indicated by its recorded failure when the favorably disposed Fillmore resided there, with the patronage power ranged on Clay's side. After Clay saw his measure vanquished, the exhausted old Whig beat a retreat to Newport's beaches, while Douglas captained Compromise forces and succeeded where he had failed. Douglas did exactly what he had thought he could do at the outset, masterfully promoting piecemeal, instead of combined, legislation. Douglas's letter of August 3 to Charles H. Lanphier and George Walker accurately prophesied that what did happen would happen.

The ultimate passage of the Compromise, under Douglas's guidance, raises the question as to the nature of the strength behind it. It also leads to inquiry concerning the origin of the parts of the compromise arrangement, which from 1850 to 1854 was thought to have settled the sectional controversy.

An analysis of the Senate votes on the integral portions of the Douglas-sponsored Compromise, between August 9 and September 16, shows only four senators supporting all five bills. These were Augustus C. Dodge, Democrat of Iowa; Sam Houston, Democrat of Texas; Daniel Sturgeon, Democrat of Pennsylvania; and John Wales, Whig of Delaware. Eight other senators voted "yea" on four occasions and abstained from casting ballots on a fifth. With the exceptions of Dodge, Houston, Sturgeon, and Wales, these men came closest to giving the Compromise their complete backing in August and September. The eight were Jesse D. Bright, Democrat of Indiana; Lewis Cass, Democrat of Michigan; Stephen A. Douglas, Democrat of Illinois; Alpheus Felch, Democrat of Michigan; Moses Norris, Democrat of New Hampshire; James Shields, Democrat of Illinois; Presley Spruance, Whig of Delaware; and James Whitcomb, Democrat of Indiana. Of the twelve senators who lent the Compromise the greatest strength under Douglas's sponsorship, ten were Democrats and two were Whigs.

For the individual bills, Democrats likewise provided the greatest share of needed support. On August 9, sixteen Democrats and fourteen Whigs approved the Texas boundary measure. On August 13, seventeen Democrats joined fourteen Whigs and two Free Soilers in voting statehood to California. Two days later, nineteen Democrats and only eight Whigs supplied the winning total for New Mexico's territorial legislation. The *Congressional Globe* does not contribute a yea-and-nay breakdown on the fugitive slave bill, but August 23 found eighteen Democrats and nine Whigs assenting to its engrossment for a third reading—virtually tantamount to passage. Finally, on September 16, the abolition of the slave trade in the District of Columbia was due to eighteen Democrats, thirteen Whigs, and two Free Soilers. In every one of the five tests, the Democratic part of the pro-Compromise majority was larger than the Whig part. For the fugitive slave and New Mexico measures, the ratio was at least two to one.

By the same token, when three sections of Clay's Omnibus Bill had been defeated on July 31, only five of the Kentuckian's fellow-Whigs sustained him on the New Mexico question while sixteen Democrats followed his "lead." On the Texas boundary, Clay and ten other Whigs went down with seventeen Democrats in an extremely close vote. And on the California statehood issue, Clay had only six Whigs in his camp together with sixteen Democrats and two Free Soilers. Senators siding with Clay on all three tests were Daniel S. Dickinson of New York, George W. Jones of Iowa, Bright, Cass, Augustus C. Dodge, Norris, Spruance, Sturgeon, and Whitcomb. Eight of the nine were Democrats. In defeat as in subsequent victory, under Clay's aegis as well as Douglas's, Democrats stood for the Compromise more consistently and faithfully than Whigs.

It will be observed that there were shifts of sentiment on the part of some members of the Senate between the dates of Clarke's and Cass's letters and the critical votes of July 31, August, and September. Most of these changes involved Whigs. Spruance, whose position had been uncertain in June, was pro-Compromise in July and August. Wales had been correctly considered an anti-Compromise man by Clarke; and even Clay characterized him as such. Yet in August, Wales took new ground. Clarke himself and his fellow Rhode Islander, Albert C. Greene, supported Douglas's Texas boundary bill; Clarke did not vote on three of the August trials, and Greene voted "nay" on two of them. But the approval given the Texas boundary on August 9 by Clarke, Greene, John Davis, Phelps, Smith, Spruance, and Wales (together with the absence of Dayton and Miller) made the difference between defeat and victory.

A case might be made that Whig deviations from anti-Compromise to pro-Compromise positions were of transcendent importance in the reckoning. Admittedly, last-minute additions to the

Compromise forces transformed disaster into triumph for the compromisers. These additions also demonstrated the effect of Taylor's death and Fillmore's succession on Whig late-comers whose votes were sorely needed by the Douglas high command. There also is no gainsaying the fact that, even as some Whigs favored the Compromise first under Clay and then under Douglas, not a few Democrats were ranged in opposition before and during Clay's seashore vacation. But both the hard core and the greater number of Compromise votes in the dramatic and decisive contests were Democratic in origin. This fact is fundamental in gaining a clear comprehension of the story as a whole.

It is equally imperative, in clarifying political attitudes and votes of senators, to determine the connection between legislative instructions and the Compromise of 1850. Over fifty years ago, William E. Dodd observed that in the second quarter of the nineteenth century the principle of state legislatures instructing United States senators was "accepted fully by one party and partially by the other." Although Dodd and other scholars have stressed the importance of the practice during the Jackson–Van Buren period, no comparable studies of the 1850 scene have been printed. From 1846 to 1850, fourteen northern legislatures sent resolutions to Washington, and southern capitols lagged but little. All this was done on the theory that since the state legislators elected the senators they had a right to tell them what to do. Whereas Whigs had been the chief victims of instructions from 1834 to 1840, now Democrats were impaled on their own precedents; this was especially true of Northwesterners. No one resigned from the Senate on account of instructions in 1850, but Cass threatened to do so unless Michigan withdrew its instructions—whereupon Lansing at once complied. Douglas was embarrassed by instructions, while John P. Hale made light of the instructions idea. Generally, instructions showed that politicians at home were less inclined to compromise than were a majority of the men they had elected to the Senate.

Ever since the annexation of Texas and the onset of the Mexi-

can War, extremist and moderate arguments and plans of settlement had been advanced and presented in Washington. The ill-
starred Clayton Compromise of 1848, which Clay stated he had
never read, proved no model two years later. Extension of the
Missouri compromise line to the Pacific, advocated by such Southerners as Jefferson Davis and Hopkins L. Turney, held no attraction for Clay or the Douglas Democrats. The new fugitive slave
bill was primarily sponsored by James M. Mason of Virginia, a
Calhoun–Davis Democrat; in its final form, it contained harsher
provisions (in northern eyes) than the ones Daniel Webster desired. California statehood had been promoted in the Thirtieth
Congress by the Democrat Douglas and the Whig William B.
Preston. Yet the boundaries of the California state envisioned by
Douglas and Preston were far from those defined in the Compromise of 1850, and the California picture had been altered economically and politically by the discovery of gold. The Texas
boundary solution of 1850 was premised on ideas backed by successive Texas governors. Abolition of the slave trade in the District
of Columbia, frequently broached in the past, commanded the
assent of many northern Whigs and Democrats.

If California statehood and ending the slave trade in the District were predominantly northern measures in 1850, and if the
fugitive slave and Texas boundary bills derived most of their support from Southerners, two other parts of the Compromise had a
different appeal. Designed to dispose of the New Mexico and
Utah problems, they gave territorial governments to those western
regions, with a proviso that states formed from them would be
admitted with or without slavery as their constitutions should
provide.

The New Mexico territorial bill was the issue which wrecked
Clay's omnibus plan, and perhaps it ought to be remembered that
about three-fourths of the Senate Whigs contributed to its fate.
When Douglas took control, he did not promote the New Mexico
bill until after the Texas boundary and California statehood measures had been passed. With a considerable show of skill he then
directed the adoption of the New Mexico measure.

In achieving his New Mexico aim, Douglas was aided directly by eighteen Democrats and eight Whigs, and indirectly by twenty-three absentees. Only three Democrats—Hamlin, Walker, and Henry Dodge—spoiled the Democratic record. When one realizes that these three were also the only Senate Democrats out of thirty-three to oppose the Utah bill of July 31, it is evident that Democrats had the key role with regard to both New Mexico and Utah.

This was no accident. For upwards of two years, the majority or national element of the Democratic party had initiated and repeated the "non-intervention" or "popular sovereignty" doctrine embodied in this territorial plan. As far back as December 14, 1847, Dickinson, the New York Democrat, had introduced resolutions specifying that territorial legislatures should decide all questions of domestic policy within the territories. Ten days later, Lewis Cass addressed his famous "Nicholson Letter" to Alfred O. P. Nicholson of Tennessee. Cass's position, comparable to Dickinson's, was summarized by the injunction: "Leave to the people who will be affected" by the slavery issue "to adjust it upon their own responsibility and in their own manner." The Nicholson letter became Cass's personal platform in his campaign for the 1848 Democratic presidential nomination. Dickinson, who publicly enunciated the idea before Cass did, served as the Michigan Democrat's lieutenant both in that contest (which Cass won handily) and in the post-convention canvass. The Democratic national platform was vague, but was capable of being interpreted along the lines of the Dickinson resolutions and the Nicholson letter. In fact, it was thus interpreted by Jefferson Davis and by the host of northern Democrats loyal to Cass in his presidential quest.

Historians have commented on the antipodal contrast between what Cass and Dickinson seemed to mean by non-intervention and what John C. Calhoun certainly did mean. Before Cass said a word on the subject, Calhoun had employed the same label to mark a radically different doctrine. Calhoun's non-intervention was designed to permit Southerners to take their slaves into the western territories, without interference by the federal government or by the territories themselves. During the Taylor–Cass–Van Buren struggle of 1848, most southern Democrats said that Cass's non-intervention was the same as Calhoun's. Davis suspected that this was not the case at all. Cass himself in 1850, becoming more candid than in 1847 or 1848, verified the Davis suspicion. According to Cass's remarks in the "Great Debate," territorial legislatures could sanction or prohibit slavery as they preferred.

Regardless of whether Cass's 1850 contention was justified or consistent, not a few of the southern Democratic senators went along with the New Mexico and Utah arrangement in the Compromise of 1850, just as most northern Democratic senators did. At various stages, Foote, Houston, William R. King of Alabama, and others joined Northerners along the non-intervention route. A single phrase in the bills, "consistent with the Constitution," made it possible for Southerners to put their own gloss on the Compromise keystone. Anomalous or hazy as the territorial provisions were, they were Democratic provisions. Created by Democrats and supported by Democrats from both the sections, they were championed late and secondarily by Henry Clay and Daniel Webster.

Whether Webster would assent to what tradition has termed "Clay's plan" remained in doubt until March 7, 1850. How late Clay was can best be illustrated by an exchange of views between Foote and Clay on February 14. Foote had first presented a plan closely resembling what came to be the Compromise. He had called for a select committee of fifteen, to pass upon the sectional problems and united most or all of them in a single bill. Foote said he made this move on the assumption that Clay favored just such strategy in his remarks of February 5 and 6, supporting his own resolutions of January 29. Clay, however, denied that this was his aim. In fact, the Kentucky Whig disparaged the Democrat's "omnibus speech, in which he introduced all sorts of things and every sort of passenger, and myself among the number."

"My desire," Clay explained, "was that the Senate should express its sense upon each of the resolutions in succession, beginning with the first and ending with the eighth. If they should be affirmatively adopted, my purpose was to propose the reference of them to appropriate [standing] committees. There are some of the subjects which may be perhaps advantageously combined. . . . But never did I contemplate embracing in the entire scheme of accommodation and harmony . . . all these distracting questions, and bringing them all into one measure." Foote, on the contrary, "certainly thought that all or most of these matters could be embraced in one bill, at least so far as positive legislative action was concerned. I think so yet; and, acting upon this opinion, I have actually embraced them in the bill introduced by me." The Mississippian went on to charge Clay with "playing the game of political power with our neighbors of the North in a manner decidedly unskillful. He is throwing into the hands of his adversaries all the *trump cards* in the pack."

Whoever may have held the trump cards in 1850, evidently by 1852 it was the Democratic party that benefited from the Compromise. Although its platform was scarcely less ambiguous than in 1848, Franklin Pierce rode confidently to the White House on the magic carpet of the most important letter of his life, in which he pronounced himself a Compromise Democrat. In 1854, another twist of the popular sovereignty doctrine resulted in the Kansas–Nebraska Act. In 1856, James Buchanan's banner proclaimed a variety of non-intervention, and the 1850's saw Douglas making popular sovereignty his political steed. Thus what was done on Capitol Hill in August and September, 1850, was in line with Democrats' policies—enunciated in 1847, 1848, and 1852, and often echoed by leading Democrats in the post-Compromise decade.

Both the Democratic and the Whig spokesmen and leaders most intimately identified with the Compromise of 1850 then and thereafter gave proof of this interpretation. Just as the Democrats produced most votes, such Democratic stalwarts as Douglas, Cass, Foote, Houston, Dickinson, and King were on Clay's side in successive tests. Were they siding with him? Or was he siding with them? Here another question of emphasis confronts the historian.

Douglas asserted in the Senate, without Whig denials, that nearly all the omnibus measures advanced by Clay's Committee of Thirteen had previously been considered and approved by the territorial committee, which had a Democratic majority and of which Douglas was chairman. What Clay did was to connect old bills, change some of them slightly, and cause the enactment of one to depend on the enactment of all. This was a procedure Clay lifted from Foote, and one Douglas's committee had decided against. Clay was less the originator and more the improviser. Incorporated in his recommendations, indeed the epitome of them, was the non-intervention theory of Dickinson and Cass.

Several persons claimed the role of originator of the compromise settlement. One, on the Senate floor, was Foote, who said "without egotism" (his own words) that "the report of the Committee on Territories was based upon bills introduced by myself." Jefferson Davis' response to this sally was a relaxed "Oh, yes, I am willing to give you all the credit for that." Referring to the Compromise itself, however, Davis added: "If any man has a right to be proud of the success of these measures, it is the Senator from Illinois." Years afterward, Foote traced popular sovereignty's inception back past his own contribution and Cass's Nicholson letter to Dickinson's resolutions. Without subtracting an inch from the Little Giant's stature, credit must also be given to Cass, Foote, and Dickinson—Democrats all—as well as to Douglas.

The Whigs' point of view, and especially that of Webster and Clay, should be borne in mind. Daniel Webster was in a tiny minority where opinion of Senate Whigs from the North was concerned as long as President Taylor lived. Webster hoped to obtain the presidential nomination in 1852. But the Whig delegates rebuffed Webster and Fillmore, bestowing the worthless palm on Winfield Scott. Webster died on October 24, 1852. His biographer, Claude M. Fuess, has written: "If Webster had lived and had been able to go to the polls, he would undoubtedly have cast his ballot for Franklin Pierce."

Clay, who died on June 29, 1852, had favored Fillmore, in

opposition to Scott and Webster, for the Whig nomination. Because of his death at that particular time, no one can say with precision what he would have done on November 2. Possibly he might have taken the road which Webster had begun to follow. Clay's statement in Frankfort, Kentucky, in the autumn of 1850, strongly suggests that he could not have voted for the Whig ticket two years later—with Scott running under the aegis of William H. Seward and Thurlow Weed. Earlier in 1850, Clay insisted that he was not the least interested in parties, party maneuvers, or party statutes; and in 1851, he was brought forward as a Democratic or Union presidential possibility, with Cass for vice-president. Throughout the 1850 controversy, Clay's speeches emphasized the placing of national interests ahead of party interests. This has been interpreted as a sure proof of statesmanship. Yet could it not as logically mean abandonment of allegiance to the majority element within the Whig party, and adherence to the non-intervention program of the Democrats?

Dickinson's resolutions of 1847, Cass's Nicholson letter of 1847, the territorial aspect of Cass's candidacy in 1848, and Foote's proposals of late 1849 were Democratic contributions. The majority of Douglas's committee on territories was Democratic, as were most of the Compromise leaders on the floor. If Douglas the Democrat guided the Compromise through to success, if Democrats supplied most of the votes, and if Democrats were far more consistent than Whigs in underwriting component parts, small wonder that in 1852 the Democrats ran a pro-Compromise nominee—and that the Whigs went down to party defeat and party death.

Two other matters merit mention. One is the likelihood that the Whig party was hopelessly split on the sectional question, in 1850 and even before. Unable to elect one of their seasoned statesmen to the presidency, the Whigs had to rally their faltering forces and appeal to independents behind the glamor of military heroism; this mirrored intrinsic weaknesses. During Taylor's lifetime, the bulk of the Whig senators stoutly opposed the Compromise.

After his death, Clay's "omnibus" was halted despite the push Democrats gave it. Even under Fillmore, and with Douglas in command in the Senate, the piecemeal measures could not have passed if many Whigs had not absented themselves when the yea-and-nay roll was called. Thus opposition, followed by negation, should be highlighted in accounts of the Compromise and integrated with the decline of Whiggery.

The second vital corollary is related to the first. Why the underscored prominence of Clay and Webster in virtually every version of the debates? Why the exaggerated emphasis on what they are presumed to have contributed? True, Clay returned to the Senate from retirement and for months did take charge of the Compromise efforts in the public gaze. Webster delivered one of the most brilliant speeches in American annals under circumstances loaded with drama. Such facets certainly deserve to be taken into account. Yet on the basis of many another fact developed here, from the standpoint of strength, of votes, of practical influence, the Clay–Webster contribution was merely secondary and supplemental alongside the major and primary Democratic backing of the Compromise.

Democratic senators and representatives, Democratic newspapers, Democratic party chieftains did much to play up Clay's and Webster's co-operation with them. It was not unlike what we have seen in our own era, in connection with Democratic foreign policy —to which such Republicans as the late Arthur H. Vandenberg, the present Henry Cabot Lodge, and other senators gave allegiance. Who loomed largest during the 1940's in the internationalist phase of Senate foreign policy? Was it Alben W. Barkley of Kentucky, James E. Murray of Montana, Brien McMahon of Connecticut, Elbert D. Thomas of Utah, or one of the numerous other Democrats who were steadfast in this regard? Or was it Vandenberg of Michigan? The popular interpretation appears to favor Vandenberg. There is something so sensational about a man who bucks the majority element within his minority party, to join the majority party on a fundamental issue, that this seems to ensure a certain kind of immortality.

According plenty of credit to Clay and Webster, as also we give it to Vandenberg and Lodge, should not historians take a closer look at what the protagonists represented? Are men who deliver two or eight votes more significant than those who speak for twenty? By what strange alchemy was Douglas long relegated to a really negligible part in the Compromise achievement? Did the relationship of Daniel Pomeroy Rhodes to the Douglas estate have anything to do with James Ford Rhodes's assigning Douglas to the limbo in 1850? Is the prominence of Republicans among historical writers from 1865 to 1920 to be equated with Clay–Webster Whig emphasis? These questions are packed with possibilities, warranting thorough investigation.

Nearly forty years ago, in the *Mississippi Valley Historical Review*, St. George L. Sioussat emphasized the need of re-exploring the Compromise of 1850. Not all that Sioussat found wanting has yet been supplied. The evidence is never all in. But benefiting from the discovery of old manuscripts penned by Senators Cass, Clarke, and Douglas, and from a rereading and perhaps a more extensive reading of the *Congressional Globe* and kindred sources, it is possible to come closer now to the realities of 1850, and to view the true structure behind the façade.

The Labor of Free Men

Free Labor, Slavery, and the
Republican Ideology

by Eric Foner

A *specter had been haunting the American Republic ever since its
inception, the specter of sectional politics. The successes of the
first two American party systems—limited and short-lived though
they were—depended in large measure on the suppression of the
sectional irritant and its most obvious manifestation: the debate
over slavery. When this proved impossible, and the North grew in
population and developed its resources at rates far exceeding the
Southern experience, it was but a matter of time before an assertive Northern party would appear to compete for national political power. The rise of the Republican party fulfilled that prophecy.
The new grouping, unlike its national predecessors, was a sectional
party, its strength confined exclusively to the North. And the
Democratic party, though it survived in the North, became a
political captive of Southern demands.*

*Southern nationalists and Northern antislavery men agreed that
fundamental sectional differences existed. Republicans tended to
look upon the South in some ways as a foreign country, whose
institutions and attitudes clashed with those they regarded as
truly American. The South, Republicans charged, was an undemocratic, hierarchical society dominated by a coterie of near-*

*sighted planters; a society based on slavery which must remain
hopelessly inefficient and economically backward, a drag on the
nation as a whole. In contrast, the free North accepted Europe's
restless millions, attracted by unmatched opportunity for self-
improvement. Northerners honored free labor and rewarded it,
whereas Southerners associated physical toil with slavery and
degradation.*

*Northern fear that Southern expansion would force white labor
to compete with slave labor, and that the spread of slavery in the
West would deprive white Americans of their birthright, gave
Republicans a powerful issue that appealed to millions who would
never have joined a purely antislavery movement. Nonetheless,
dynamic leadership for the party also came from such radical Republicans as Senator Charles Sumner of Massachusetts and Senator
Salmon P. Chase of Ohio, men who thought slavery would
crumble within the South itself if it were not allowed to expand,
and other men who sought full equality for the black men. Nevertheless, many more Republican moderates, like Abraham Lincoln,
saw the evil in slavery yet would accept its continuation in the
South; moreover, these moderates did not espouse racial equality.
Such basic differences laid the foundation for the Republican
party's flip-flop course during postwar Reconstruction on the race
question.*

*Republican ideology thus mixed white racism with white ideal-
ism, and then joined the two with a commitment to block further
expansion of slavery. That commitment remained non-negotiable,
however, and gave the party its backbone in the 1850's, as the
analysis by Eric Foner clearly demonstrates.*

On May 26, 1860, one of the Republican party's leading
orators, Carl Schurz of Wisconsin, addressed a Milwaukee audience which had gathered to endorse the nomination of Abraham Lincoln. "The Republicans," Schurz declared, "stand before

From Eric Foner, *Free Soil, Free Labor, Free Men: The Ideology of the
Republican Party before the Civil War*, pp. 11–18, 301–17. Copyright ©
1970 by Oxford University Press, Inc. Reprinted by permission; footnotes
omitted.

the country, not only as the antislavery party, but emphatically as the party of free labor." Two weeks later, Richard Yates, the gubernatorial candidate in Illinois, spoke at a similar rally in Springfield. "The great idea and basis of the Republican party, as I understand it," he proclaimed, "is free labor. . . . To make labor honorable is the object and aim of the Republican party." Such statements, which were reiterated countless times by Republican orators in the 1850's, were more than mere election-year appeals for the votes of laboring men. For the concept of "free labor" lay at the heart of the Republican ideology, and expressed a coherent social outlook, a model of the good society. Political antislavery was not merely a negative doctrine, an attack on southern slavery and the society built upon it, it was an affirmation of the superiority of the social system of the North—a dynamic, expanding capitalist society, whose achievements and destiny were almost wholly the result of the dignity and opportunities which it offered the average laboring man.

The dignity of labor was a constant theme of ante-bellum northern culture and politics. Tocqueville noted that in America, "not only work itself, but work specifically to gain money," was considered honorable, and twenty years later, the New York editor Horace Greeley took note of "the usual Fourth-of-July declamation in behalf of the dignity of labor, the nobleness of labor." It was a common idea in both economic treatises and political pronouncements that labor was the source of all value. Lincoln declared in 1859 that "Labor is prior to, and independent of capital . . . in fact, capital is the fruit of labor," and the New York *Tribune* observed that "nothing is more common" than this "style of assertion." Republican orators insisted that labor could take the credit for the North's rapid economic development. Said William Evarts in 1856, "Labor, gentlemen, we of the free States acknowledge to be the source of all our wealth, of all our progress, of all our dignity and value." In a party which saw divisions on political and economic matters between radicals and conservatives, between former Whigs and former Democrats, the glorification of labor provided a much-needed theme of unity. Representatives of all these segments included paeans to free labor in their speeches; even the crusty old conservative Tom Corwin delivered "a eulogy on labor and laboring men" in an 1858 speech.

Belief in the dignity of labor was not, of course, confined to the Republican party or to the antebellum years; it has been part of American culture from the very beginning. In large part, it can be traced to the fact that most Americans came from a Protestant background, in which the nobility of labor was an article of faith. One does not need to accept in its entirety Max Weber's association of the "Protestant ethic" with the rise of capitalism in Europe to believe that there is much validity in Weber's insight that the concept of "calling" provided the psychological underpinning for capitalist values. Weber pointed out that in Calvinist theology each man had an occupation or calling to which he was divinely appointed. To achieve success in this calling would serve the glory of God, and also provide visible evidence that an individual was among the few predestined to enter heaven. The pursuit of wealth thus became a way of serving God on earth, and labor, which had been imposed on fallen man as a curse, was transmuted into a religious value, a Christian duty. And the moral qualities which would ensure success in one's calling—honesty, frugality, diligence, punctuality, and sobriety—became religious obligations. Weber described the Protestant outlook on life as "worldly asceticism," since idleness, waste of time, and conspicuous display or expenditure for personal enjoyment were incompatible with its basic values.

There was more to the Republican idea of free labor, however, than the essentials of the Protestant ethic, to which, presumably, the South had also been exposed, for the relation of that ethic to the idea of social mobility was highly ambiguous. On the one hand, the drive to work zealously in one's calling, the capital accumulation which resulted from frugality, and the stress on economic success as a sign of divine approval, all implied that men would work for an achievement of wealth and advancement in their chosen professions. But if one's calling were divinely ordained, the implication might be that a man should be content with the same occupation for his entire life, although he should strive to grow rich in it. In a static economy, therefore, the concept of "a calling" may be associated with the idea of an hierarchical social order, with more or less fixed classes. But Republicans rejected this image of society. Their outlook was grounded in the Protestant ethic, but in its emphasis on social mobility and economic growth, it reflected an adaptation of that ethic to the dynamic, expansive, capitalist society of the antebellum North.

Contemporaries and historians agree that the average American of the antebellum years was driven by an inordinate desire to improve his condition in life, and by boundless confidence that he could do so. Economic success was the standard by which men judged their social importance, and many observers were struck by the concentration on work, with the aim of material advancement, which characterized Americans. Tocqueville made the following observation during Jackson's presidency: "The first thing that strikes one in the United States is the innumerable crowd of those striving to escape from their original social condition." On the eve of the Civil War, the Cincinnati *Gazette* reported that things had not changed. "Of all the multitude of young men engaged in various employments of this city," it declared, "there is probably not one who does not desire, and even confidently expect, to become rich, and that at an early day." The universal desire for social advancement gave American life an aspect of almost frenetic motion and activity, as men moved from place to place, and occupation to occupation in search of wealth. Even ministers, reported the Cincinnati *Gazette*, "resign the most interesting fields of labor to get higher salaries." The competitive character of northern society was aptly summed up by Lincoln, when he spoke of the "race of life" in the 1850's.

The foremost example of the quest for a better life was the steady stream of settlers who abandoned eastern homes to seek their fortunes in the West. The westward movement reached new heights in the mid-1850's, and it was not primarily the poor who migrated westward, but middle class "business-like farmers," who sold their farms to migrate, or who left the eastern farms of their fathers. "These emigrants," said a leading Republican newspaper of Ohio, "are not needy adventurers, fleeing from the pinchings of penury. They are substantial farmers." Those without means who came to the West were interested in obtaining their own farms as quickly as possible, because to the American of the nineteenth century land was not the bucolic ideal of the pre-capitalist world, but another means for economic advancement. Tocqueville noted that the small farmer of the West was really a landed businessman, an entrepreneur who was prepared to sell his farm and move on, if he could get a good price. What Horace Greeley called "the nomadic tendency" of Americans contributed to the rapid expansion of the western frontier. "The men who are building up the villages of last year's origin on the incipient Railroads of Iowa," said the New York editor, "were last year doing the like in Illinois, and three years since in Ohio." The acquisitive instincts of western settlers were described by Kinsley Bingham, the first Republican governor of Michigan: "Like most new States, ours has been settled by an active, energetic and enterprising class of men, who are desirous of accumulating property rapidly."

The Republican idea of free labor was a product of this expanding, enterprising, competitive society. It is important to recognize that in antebellum America, the word "labor" had a meaning far broader than its modern one. Andrew Jackson, for example, defined as "the producing classes" all those whose work was directly involved in the production of goods—farmers, planters, laborers, mechanics, and small businessmen. Only those who profited from the work of others, or whose occupations were largely financial or promotional, such as speculators, bankers, and lawyers, were excluded from this definition. Daniel Webster took a similarly all-embracing view. In his famous speech of March 7,

1850, Webster asked, "Why, who are the laboring people of the North? They are the whole North. They are the people who till their own farms with their own hands; freeholders, educated men, independent men." And the Republican definition, as it emerged in the 1850's, proved equally broad. Some Republicans did exclude commercial enterprise from their idea of labor—the Springfield *Republican*, for example, suggested that three-quarters of the traders in the country should go into some field of "productive labor." In general, however, Republicans would agree with Horace Greeley that labor included "useful doing in any capacity or vocation." They thus drew no distinction between a "laboring class" and what we could call the middle class. With Webster, they considered the farmer, the small businessman, and the independent craftsmen, all as "laborers."

If the Republicans saw "labor" as substantially different from the modern-day notion of the "working class," it was partly because the line between capitalist and worker was to a large extent blurred in the antebellum northern economy, which centered on the independent farm and small shop. Moreover, for the Republicans, social mobility was an essential part of northern society. The antebellum Republicans praised the virtues of the enterprising life, and viewed social mobility as the glory of northern society. "Our paupers to-day, thanks to free labor, are our yeomen and merchants of tomorrow," said the New York *Times*. Lincoln asserted in 1859 that "advancement, improvement in condition—is the order of things in a society of equals," and he denounced southern insinuations that northern wage earners were "fatally fixed in that condition for life." The opportunity for social advancement, in the Republican view, was what set Americans apart from their European forebears. As one Iowa Republican put it:

What is it that makes the great mass of American citizens so much more enterprising and intelligent than the laboring classes in Europe? It is the stimulant held out to them by the character of our institutions.

The door is thrown open to all, and even the poorest and humblest in the land, may, by industry and application, attain a position which will entitle him to the respect and confidence of his fellow-men.

Many Republican leaders bore witness in their own careers to how far men could rise from humble beginnings. Lincoln's own experience, of course, was the classic example, and during the 1860 campaign Republican orators repeatedly referred to him as "the child of labor," who had proved how "honest industry and toil" were rewarded in the North. Other Republican leaders like the former indentured servant Henry Wilson, the "bobbin boy" Nathaniel P. Banks, and the ex-laborer Hannibal Hamlin also made much of their modest beginnings in campaign speeches.

In the free labor outlook, the objective of social mobility was not great wealth, but the middle-class goal of economic independence. For Republicans, "free labor" meant labor with economic choices, with the opportunity to quit the wage earning class. A man who remained all his life dependent on wages for his livelihood appeared almost as unfree as the southern slave. There was nothing wrong, of course, with working for wages for a time, if the aim were to acquire enough money to start one's own farm or business. Zachariah Chandler described in the Senate the cycle of labor which he felt characterized northern society: "A young man goes out to service—to labor, if you please to call it so—for compensation until he acquires money enough to buy a farm . . . and soon he becomes himself the employer of labor." Similarly, a correspondent of the New York *Tribune* wrote in 1854, "Do you say to me, hire some of the thousands and thousands of emigrants coming to the West. Sir, I cannot do it. They come West to labor for themselves, not for me; and instead of laboring for others, they want others to labor for them." The aspirations of the free labor ideology were thus thoroughly middle-class, for the successful laborer was one who achieved self-employment, and owned his own capital—a business, farm, or shop.

The key figure in the Republicans' social outlook was thus the small independent entrepreneur. "Under every form of govern-

ment having the benefits of civilization," said Congressman Timothy Jenkins of New York, "there is a middle class, neither rich
nor poor, in which is concentrated the chief enterprise of the
country." Charles Francis Adams agreed that the "middling class
. . . equally far removed from the temptations of great wealth
and of extreme destitution," provided the surest defense of democratic principles. In a nation as heavily agricultural as the antebellum United States, it is not surprising that the yeoman received the greatest praise. "The middling classes who own the soil,
and work it with their own hands," declared Thaddeus Stevens,
"are the main support of every free government." But the exponents of the development of manufactures also looked to the small
capitalist, not the very wealthy, as the agents of economic progress. "The manufacturing industry of this country," said Representative Samuel Blair of Pennsylvania, "must look to men of
moderate means for its development—the men of enterprise being, as a class, in such circumstances." In their glorification of
the middle class and of economic independence, the Republicans
were accurately reflecting the aspirations of northern society. As
Carl Schurz later recalled of his first impressions of the United
States, "I saw what I might call the middle-class culture in process of formation. . . ."

"Of the American Civil War," James Ford Rhodes wrote over
a half a century ago, "it may safely be asserted that there was a
single cause, slavery." In this opinion, Rhodes was merely echoing
a view which seemed self-evident to Abraham Lincoln and many
other participants in the sectional conflict. Their interpretation
implicitly assumes that the antebellum Republican party was primarily a vehicle for antislavery sentiment. Yet partly because historians are skeptical of explanations made by participants of their
own behavior, Rhodes's view quickly fell under attack. Even be-
before Rhodes wrote, John R. Commons had characterized the
Republicans as primarily a homestead party, and Charles and
Mary Beard later added the tariff as one of its fundamental con-

cerns. More recently, historians have stressed aversion to the presence of blacks—free or slave—in the western territories as the Republicans' motive for opposing the extension of slavery. Because the Republicans disavowed the intention of attacking slavery in states where it already existed by direct federal action, their antislavery declarations have been dismissed by some historians as hypocritical. And recently, a political analyst, not a professional historian, revealed how commonplace a cynical attitude toward the early Republican party has become when he wrote: "The Republican Party succeeded by soft-pedalling the issue of slavery altogether and concentrating on economic issues which would attract Northern businessmen and Western farmers."

Controversy over the proper place of antislavery in the Republican ideology is hardly new. During the 1850's, considerable debate occurred within abolitionist circles on the proper attitude toward Republicanism. In part, this was simply an extension of the traditional schism between political and non-political abolitionists, and it is not surprising that William Lloyd Garrison and his followers should have wasted little enthusiasm on the Republicans. Yet many abolitionists who had no objection on principle to political involvements considered the antislavery commitment of the Republican party insufficient to merit their support. Gerrit Smith and William Goodell, for example, who had been instrumental in organizing the Liberty party in New York State, declared that they could not support a party which recognized the constitutionality of slavery anywhere in the Union. The Republican party, Smith charged, "refuses to oppose slavery where it is, and opposes it only where it is not," and he continuously urged radicals like Chase and Giddings to take an abolitionist stance. Theodore Parker made the same criticism. When Chase declared in the Senate that the federal government would not interfere with slavery in the states, Parker wrote that while he did not object to attacking slavery one step at a time, he "would not promise *not to take other steps.*"

Yet it is important to remember that despite their criticisms of the Republican party, leading abolitionists maintained close personal relations with Republican leaders, particularly the radicals. The flow of letters between Chase and Smith, cordial even while each criticized the attitude of the other, is one example of this. Similarly, Parker kept up a correspondence with Henry Wilson, Charles Sumner, and William Seward as well as Chase. And he and Wendell Phillips, both experts at the art of political agitation, recognized the complex interrelationship between abolitionist attempts to create a public sentiment hostile to slavery, and the political antislavery espoused by Republicans. "Our agitation, you know, helps keep yours alive in the rank and file," was the way Wendell Phillips expressed it to Sumner. And Seward agreed that the abolitionists played a vital role in awakening the public conscience—"open[ing] the way where the masses can follow." For their part, abolitionists like Theodore Parker were happy to borrow statistics and arguments from the antislavery speeches of politicians.

The evidence strongly suggests that outside of Garrison's immediate circle, most abolitionists voted with the Republican party despite their wish that the party adopt a more aggressive antislavery position. Indeed, abolitionist societies experienced financial difficulties in the late 1850's, as former contributors began giving their money to the Republicans. Even Gerrit Smith, who insisted he could "never vote for any person who recognizes a law for slavery," contributed five hundred dollars to the Frémont campaign. The attitude of many abolitionists was summed up by Elizur Wright, a proponent of Smith and Goodell's brand of political antislavery who nonetheless voted for Lincoln in 1860. While Wright criticized the Republicans for their shortcomings on slavery, he acknowledged that "the greatest recommendation of the Republican Party is, that its enemies do not quite believe its disclaimers, while they do believe that [it is] sincerely opposed to slavery as far as it goes." Prophetically, he added: "Woe to the slave power under a Republican President if it strikes the first blow."

The fact that so many abolitionists, not to mention radical Republicans, supported the Republican party, is an indication that antislavery formed no small part of the Republican ideology. Recent historians have concluded, moreover, that writers like Beard greatly overestimated the importance of economic issues in the elections of 1856, 1858, and 1860. We have already seen how tentative was the Republican commitment to the tariff. As for the homestead issue, Don E. Fehrenbacher has pointed out that the Republicans carried most of the Northwest in 1856 when free land was not a political issue, and that in 1860, Douglas Democrats supported the measure as ardently as Republicans. More important, it would have been suicidal for the Republicans to have put their emphasis on economic policies, particularly the neo-Whiggism described by Beard. If one thing is evident after analyzing the various elements which made up the party, it is that antislavery was one of the few policies which united all Republican factions. For political reasons, if for no other, the Republicans were virtually obliged to make antislavery the main focus of their political appeal. Such questions as the tariff, nativism, and race were too divisive to be stressed, while the homestead issue could be advanced precisely because it was so non-controversial in the North.

Conservative Republicans and radicals, ex-Democrats and former Whigs, all agreed that slavery was the major issue of the 1850's. It was not surprising that Giddings should insist that "there is but one real issue between the Republican party and those factions that stand opposed to it. That is the question of slavery," or that Salmon P. Chase should declare that the election of 1860 had not turned on "subordinate questions of local and temporary character," but had vindicated the principle of "the restriction of slavery within State limits." But Orville H. Browning, as conservative as Giddings and Chase were radical, appraised the politics of 1860 in much the same way. "It is manifest to all," he declared, "that there is an unusual degree of political interest pervading the country—that the people, everywhere, are excited, . . . and yet, from one extremity of the Republic to the other, scarcely any other subject is mentioned, or any other question discussed . . . save the question of negro slavery. . . ." Ex-Democrats in the Republican party fully agreed. Both Francis Spinner and Preston King rejected suggestions that Democratic economic policies be engrafted onto the Republican platform, on the ground that these must await settlement until the slavery issue had been decided. As Spinner tersely put it, "Statesmen cannot make issues for the people. As live men we must take the issues as they present themselves." The potency of the slavery issue, and the way in which it subordinated or absorbed all other political questions, was noted by the anti-Lecompton Democrat from New York, Horace Clark, on the eve of the 1860 campaign:

It is not to be controverted that the slavery agitation is not at rest. It has absorbed and destroyed our national politics. It has overrun State politics. It has even invaded our municipalities; and now, in some form or other, everywhere controls the elections of the people.

In a recent study of Civil War historiography, Roy F. Nichols observed that we still do not know whether either section had reached its own consensus on major issues by 1861. Some historians have interpreted the strong showing of Stephen A. Douglas in the free states as proof that a substantial portion of the electorate rejected the Republican brand of antislavery. Though there is some truth in this view, it is important to remember that by 1860 the Douglas Democrats shared a good many of the Republicans' attitudes toward the South. One of the most striking aspects of the Democratic debate over the Lecompton constitution was the way in which the Douglasites echoed so many of the anti-southern views which anti-Nebraska Democrats had expressed only a few years earlier. There is a supreme irony in the fact that the same methods which Douglas had used against dissident Democrats in 1854 were now turned against him and his supporters. Buchanan applied the patronage whip ruthlessly, and anti-Lecompton Democrats complained that a new, proslavery test had suddenly been imposed upon the party. And like the anti-Nebraska Democrats, who were now members of the Republican party, the Douglasites insisted that they commanded the support of most northern Democrats. Historians have tended to agree with them. Roy Nichols suggests that the enthusiasm Douglas's anti-southern stand aroused among rank and file Democrats was one reason why he refused to accept the compromise English bill to settle the Lecompton controversy, and recent students of Pennsylvania and Indiana politics agree that the vast majority of the Democracy in those states favored Douglas against the administration.

The bitterness of Douglas Democrats against the South did not abate between 1858 and 1860. They believed that the South had embarked upon a crusade to force slavery into all the territories, and protested that endorsement of such a goal would destroy the northern Democracy. "We have confided in their honor, their love of justice, their detestation of what is wrong," Henry Payne, a prominent Ohio Democrat, said of his southern colleagues in 1858, *"but we can do it no more."* And many Republicans believed that, even if Douglas made his peace with the Democratic organization, many of his followers had acquired "a feeling against Slavery and its arrogant demands which *if cherished* will prevent their going back. . . ." A few Democrats did defect to the Republican party in 1858, 1859, and 1860, including a former chairman of the Iowa Democracy, several anti-Lecompton Congressmen, and F. P. Stanton, the former Democratic governor of Kansas. That there were not more defections largely reflected the continuation into 1860 of Douglas's contest with the administration, which increasingly took on what one historian calls "a semi-free-soil" tone. And when the 1860 Democratic national convention broke up over the South's insistence on a platform guaranteeing slavery in the territories, the bitterness of the Douglasites knew no bounds. The reporter Murat Halstead observed that he had "never heard Abolitionists talk more rancorously of the people of the South than the Douglas men here." For their part, southerners insisted they would not accept popular sovereignty since this would be as effective as the Wilmot Proviso in barring slavery from the territories.

There were, of course, many important differences between the Douglasites and Republicans. Douglas still insisted in 1860 that the slavery question was not important enough to risk the disruption of the Union, he was much more inclined to use racism as a political weapon, and, as one Republican newspaper put it, in words echoed by several recent scholars, Douglas "does not recognize the moral element in politics. . . ." Yet in their devotion to the Union and their bitter opposition to southern domination of the government, Republicans and Douglasites stood close together in 1860. There was much truth in the observation of one Republican that "the rupture between the northern and southern wing of the democracy, is permanent with the masses . . . ," and the experiences of the Douglas Democrats in the years preceding the Civil War go a long way toward explaining the unanimity of the North's response to the attack on Fort Sumter.

The attitude of the Douglasites toward the South on the eve of the Civil War partially reflected their assessment of northern opinion regarding slavery. Politicians of all parties agreed that northerners opposed slavery as an abstract principle, although they disagreed on the intensity of this sentiment. John C. Calhoun had estimated in 1847 that while only 5 per cent of northerners supported the abolitionists, more than 66 per cent viewed slavery as an evil, and were willing to oppose its extension constitutionally. Similarly, a conservative Republican declared in 1858, "There is no man [in the North] who is an advocate of slavery. There is no man from that section of the country who will go before his constituents and advocate the extension of slavery." Northern Democrats had the same perception of northern sentiments. Even the Hunkers of New York, who consistently opposed the Wilmot Proviso, refused to say "that they are not opposed to slavery." For as William L. Marcy declared in 1849, "In truth we all are."

Antislavery as an abstract feeling had long existed in the North. It had not, however, prevented abolitionists from being mobbed, nor antislavery parties from going down to defeat. Democrats and Whigs had long been able to appeal to devotion to the Union, racism, and economic issues, to neutralize antislavery as a political force. "The antislavery sentiment," Hamilton Fish explained in 1854, "is inborn, and almost universal at the North . . . but it is only as a *sentiment* that it generally pervades; it has not and cannot be inspired with the activity that even a very slight interest excites." But Fish failed to foresee the fundamental achievement of the Republican party before the Civil War: the creation and articulation of an ideology which blended personal and sectional interest with morality so perfectly that it became the most potent political force in the nation. The free labor assault upon slavery and southern society, coupled with the idea that an aggressive Slave Power was threatening the most fundamental values and interests of the free states, hammered the slavery issue home to the northern public more emphatically than an appeal to morality alone could ever have done.

To agree with Rhodes that slavery was ultimately the cause of the Civil War, therefore, is not to accept the corollary that the basis of the Republican opposition to slavery was simple moral fervor. In a speech to the Senate in 1848, John M. Niles listed a dozen different reasons for his support of the Wilmot Proviso—but only once did he mention his belief that slavery was morally repugnant. And thirteen years later, George William Curtis observed that "there is very little moral mixture in the 'Anti-Slavery' feeling of this country. A great deal is abstract philanthropy; part is hatred of slaveholders; a great part is jealousy for white labor, very little is consciousness of wrong done and the wish to right it." The Republican ideology included all these elements, and much more. Rhodes argued that northerners wished to preserve the Union as a first step toward abolition. A more accurate formulation would reverse the equation and say that many Republicans were antislavery from the conviction that slavery threatened

the Union. Aside from some radicals, who occasionally flirted
with disunion, most Republicans were united by the twin principles of free soil and Unionism. Cassius M. Clay even suggested
that the Free-Soilers in 1851 adopt the name "Liberty and Union"
party, in order to impress their essential goals upon the electorate.
The New York *Times* emphasized this aspect of Republican
thought in 1857: "The barbaric institution of slavery will become
more and more odious to the northern people because it will
become more and more plain . . . that the States which cling
to Slavery thrust back the American idea, and reject the influences
of the Union."

Still, Unionism, despite its importance to the mass of northerners, and obviously crucial to any explanation of the Republicans'
decision to resist secession, was only one aspect of the Republican
ideology. It would have been just as logical to compromise on the
slavery question if the preservation of the Union were the paramount goal of Republican politics. Nor should Republicanism be
seen merely as the expression of the northern drive toward political power. We have seen, to be sure, that resentment of southern
power played its part, that many Democratic-Republicans had
watched with growing jealousy the South's domination of the
Democratic party and the national government, and that many
former Whigs were convinced that the South was blocking economic programs essential for national economic development. But
there is more to the coming of the Civil War than the rivalry of
sections for political power. (New England, after all, could accept its own decline in political power without secession.)

In short, none of these elements can stand separately; they dissolve into one another, and the total product emerges as ideology.
Resentment of southern political power, devotion to the Union,
antislavery based upon the free labor argument, moral revulsion to
the peculiar institution, racial prejudice, a commitment to the
northern social order and its development and expansion—all
these elements were intertwined in the Republican world-view.
What they added up to was the conviction that North and South

represented two social systems whose values, interests, and future prospects were in sharp, perhaps mortal, conflict with one another. The sense of difference, of estrangement, and of growing hostility with which Republicans viewed the South, cannot be over-emphasized. Theodore Sedgwick of New York perhaps expressed it best when he declared during the secession crisis: "The policy and aims of slavery, its institutions and civilization, and the character of its people, are all at variance with the policy, aims, institutions, education, and character of the North. There is an irreconcilable difference in our interests, institutions, and pursuits; in our sentiments and feelings." Greeley's *Tribune* said the same thing more succinctly: "We are not one people. We are two peoples. We are a people for Freedom and a people for Slavery. Between the two, conflict is inevitable." An attack not simply on the institution of slavery, but upon southern society itself, was thus at the heart of the Republican mentality. Of all historians, I think Avery Craven caught this feature best: "By 1860, slavery had become the symbol and carrier of *all* sectional differences and conflicts." Here and elsewhere, Craven describes the symbolic nature of the slavery controversy, reflected as it was in the widespread acceptance among Republicans of the Slave Power idea—a metaphor for all the fears and resentments they harbored toward the South. But Craven did leave out something crucial. Slavery was not only the symbol, but also the real basis of sectional conflict, for it was the foundation of the South's economy, social structure, aspirations, and ideology.

"Why do we Meddle with Slavery?" the New York *Times* asked in an 1857 editorial. The answer gives us a penetrating insight into the Republican mind on the eve of Civil War:

The great States of the North are not peopled exclusively by quid-nuncs and agitators. . . . Nevertheless, we do give ourselves great and increasing concern about the existence of Slavery in States over whose internal economy we have no right and no wish to exercise any control whatever. Nevertheless, we do feel, and the feeling is growing deeper in the northern heart with every passing year, that our character, our prosperity, and our destiny are most seriously involved in the question of the perpetuation or extinction of slavery in those States.

What is striking about this statement is a concern directed not only against the extension of slavery, but against its very existence. Lincoln put the same concern even more succinctly to a Chicago audience in 1859, "Never forget," he said, "that we have before us this whole matter of the right or wrong of slavery in this Union, though the immediate question is as to its spreading out into new Territories and States."

Lincoln and the editors of the *Times* thus made explicit that there was more to the contest over the extension of slavery than whether the institution should spread to the West. As Don E. Fehrenbacher puts it, the territorial question was the "skirmish line of a more extensive struggle." Only by a comprehension of this total conflict between North and South, between Republican and southern ideologies, can the meaning of the territorial issue be fully grasped. Its importance went even beyond the belief shared widely in both sections that slavery required expansion to survive, and that confinement to the states where it already existed would kill it. For in each ideology was the conviction that its own social system must expand, not only to ensure its own survival but to prevent the expansion of all the evils the other represented. We have already seen how Republicans believed that free society, with its promise of social mobility for the laborer, required territorial expansion, and how this was combined with a messianic desire to spread the benefits of free society to other areas and peoples. Southerners had their own grandiose design. "They had a magnificent dream of empire," a Republican recalled after the war, and such recent writers as C. Stanley Urban and Eugene Genovese have emphasized how essential expansionism was in the southern ideology. The struggle for the West represented a contest between two expansive societies, only one of whose aspirations could prevail. The conflict was epitomized by two statements which appeared in the Philadelphia *North Amer-*

ican in 1856. Slavery, the *North American* argued, could not be allowed to expand, because it would bring upon the West "a blight whose fatal influence will be felt for centuries." Two weeks later the same paper quoted a southern journal, which, in urging slavery expansionism, used precisely this logic in reverse. Such expansion, the southern paper argued, would "forbid the extension of the evils of free society to new people and coming generations."

Here then was a basic reason why the South could not accept the verdict of 1860. In 1848, Martin Van Buren had said that the South opposed the principle of free soil because "the prohibition carries with it a reproach to the slaveholding states, and . . . submission to it would degrade them." Eight years later, the Richmond *Enquirer* explained that for the South to abandon the idea of extending slavery while accepting Republican assurances of non-interference in the states would be "pregnant with the admission that slavery is wrong, and but for the constitution should be abolished." To agree to the containment of slavery, the South would have had to abandon its whole ideology, which had come to view the institution as a positive good, the basis of an enlightened form of social organization.

Although it has not been the purpose of this study to examine in any detailed way the southern mind in 1860, what has been said about the Republican ideology does help to explain the rationale for secession. The political wars of the 1850's, centering on the issue of slavery extension, had done much to erode whatever good feeling existed between the sections. The abolitionist Elihu Burrit suggested in 1857 that a foreigner observing American politics would probably conclude "that the North and South were wholly occupied in gloating upon each others' faults and failings." During the 1856 campaign, Burrit went on, sectional antagonisms had been brought "to a pitch of rancor, never reached before" in American politics. This was precisely the reason that Union-loving conservatives like Hamilton Fish dreaded the mounting agitation. "I cannot close my eyes to the fact which all history shows," Fish wrote Thurlow Weed in 1855, "that every physical revolution (of governments) is preceded by a moral revolution. [Slavery agitation] leads to estrangement first, and next to hostility and hatred which end inevitably in separation." By the time of the secession crisis another former Whig could observe that "the people of the North and of the South have come to hate each other worse than the hatred between any two nations in the world. In a word the moral basis on which the government is founded is all destroyed."

It is thus no mystery that southerners could not seriously entertain Republican assurances that they would not attack slavery in the states. For one thing, in opposing its extension, Republicans had been logically forced to attack the institution itself. This, indeed, was one of the reasons why radicals accepted the emphasis on non-extension. "We are disposed to select this single point," Sumner explained to Chase, "because it has a peculiar practical issue at the present moment, while its discussion would, of course, raise the whole question of slavery." Frederick Douglass agreed that agitation for the Wilmot Proviso served "to keep the subject before the people—to deepen their hatred of the system—and to break up the harmony between the Northern white people and the Southern slaveholders. . . ." As we have seen, many Republicans, both radicals and moderates, explicitly stated that non-extension was simply the first step, that there would come a day when slavery would cease to exist.

As southerners viewed the Republican party's rise to power in one northern state after another, and witnessed the increasingly anti-southern tone of the northern Democrats, they could hardly be blamed for feeling apprehensive about the future. Late in 1859, after a long talk with the moderate Unionist Senator from Virginia, R. M. T. Hunter, Senator James Dixon of Connecticut reported that the Virginian was deeply worried. "What seems to alarm Hunter is the *growth* of the Anti-slavery feeling at the North." Southerners did not believe that this antislavery sentiment would be satisfied with the prohibition of slavery in the territories, although even that would be bad enough. They also feared that a Republican administration would adopt the radicals' program of indirect action against slavery. This is why continued Democratic control of Congress was not very reassuring, for executive action could implement much of the radicals' program. Slavery was notoriously weak in the states of Missouri, Maryland, and Delaware. With federal patronage, a successful emancipation movement there might well be organized. And what was more dangerous, Lincoln might successfully arouse the poor whites in other states against the slaveholders. "Cohorts of Federal office-holders, Abolitionists, may be sent into [our] midst," a southern Senator warned in January 1861; ". . . Postmasters . . . controlling the mails, and loading them down with incendiary documents," would be appointed in every town. One southern newspaper declared that "the great lever by which the abolitionists hope to extirpate slavery in the states, is the aid of the non-slaveholding citizens of the South." The reply of Republicans to these warnings was hardly reassuring. Commenting on one southern editorial, the Cincinnati *Commercial* declared that the spread of antislavery sentiment among southern poor whites was "an eventuality against which no precautions can avail." And by December 1860, Republican Congressmen were already receiving applications for office from within the slave states.

For many reasons, therefore, southerners believed that slavery would not be permanently safe under a Republican administration. Had not William H. Seward announced in 1858, "I know, and you know, that a revolution has begun. I know, and all the world knows, that revolutions never go backward." Did not Republican Congressmen openly express their conviction that "slavery must die"? The Republican policy of preventing the spread of slavery, one southerner wrote to William T. Sherman, "was but the entering wedge to overthrow it in the States."

The delegates to South Carolina's secession convention, in their address to the people of the state, explained why they had dissolved the state's connection with the Union:

If it is right to preclude or abolish slavery in a Territory, why should it be allowed to remain in the States? . . . In spite of all disclaimers and professions, there can be but one end by the submission of the South to the rule of a sectional anti-slavery government at Washington; and that end, directly or indirectly, must be—the emancipation of the slaves of the South.

Emancipation might come in a decade, it might take fifty years. But North and South alike knew that the election of 1860 had marked a turning point in the history of slavery in the United States. To remain in the Union, the South would have had to accept the verdict of "ultimate extinction" which Lincoln and the Republicans had passed on the peculiar institution.

The decision for civil war in 1860–61 can be resolved into two questions—why did the South secede, and why did the North refuse to let the South secede? As I have indicated, I believe secession should be viewed as a total and logical response by the South to the situation which confronted it in the election of Lincoln—logical in the sense that it was the only action consistent with its ideology. In the same way, the Republicans' decision to maintain the Union was inherent in their ideology. For the integrity of the Union, important as an end in itself, was also a prerequisite to the national greatness Republicans felt the United States was destined to achieve. With his faith in progress, material growth, and the spread of both democratic institutions and American influence throughout the world, William Seward brought the Republican ideology to a kind of culmination. Although few Republicans held as coherent and far-reaching a world view as he, most accepted Lincoln's more modest view that the American nation had a special place in the world, and a responsibility to prove that democratic institutions were self-sustaining. Much of the messianic zeal which characterized political antislavery derived from this faith in the superiority of the political, social, and economic institutions of the North, and a desire to spread these to their ultimate limits.

When a leading historian says, therefore, that the Republican party in 1860 was bound together "by a common enmity rather than a common loyalty," he is, I believe, only half right. For the Republicans' enmity toward the South was intimately bound up with their loyalty to the society of small-scale capitalism which they perceived in the North. It was its identification with the aspirations of the farmers, small entrepreneurs, and craftsmen of northern society which gave the Republican ideology much of its dynamic, progressive, and optimistic quality. Yet paradoxically, at the time of its greatest success, the seeds of the later failure of that ideology were already present. Fundamental changes were at work in the social and economic structure of the North, transforming and undermining many of its free-labor assumptions. And the flawed attitude of the Republicans toward race, and the limitations of the free labor outlook in regard to the Negro, foreshadowed the mistakes and failures of the post-emancipation years.

The Uses of Politics

Party Politics and the Union and
Confederate War Efforts

by Eric L. McKitrick

"It is a safe bet," observed one historian during the war's centennial celebration, "that the Civil War has spilt more ink than blood." In both cases, the spillage has been tremendous. The conflict produced a million casualties, and its military, diplomatic, and social history have indeed been dealt with in thousands of books written since Appomattox. No other period in American history except the time of the Revolution can claim to have received more exhaustive treatment. Until recently, however, most political studies of the Civil War have focused either on the careers of Union and Confederate generals or political leaders, notably Lincoln and Lee, or on controversial factions such as the Radical Republicans or the Southern fire-eaters. Few scholars paid much attention to the actual functioning of political parties in the North during the war or to how the formation of the Confederacy all but destroyed the South's political life. Even fewer scholars were attracted to the problem of how political behavior in each region influenced the course of the war itself.

Instead, historians concentrated on comparing the relative merits of Lincoln and Jefferson Davis as "statesmen," or on the relationship between Lincoln and Republican groups such as the war governors or the Radicals, and they believed, until recently, that partisan conflicts within the Republican party seriously hampered the Northern war effort. Similarly, scholars had been in the habit of crediting the high degree of Confederate "unity," and endurance through four bloody years partly to the absence of bitterly devisive two-party political contests.

In an essay published in 1960 on "Jefferson Davis and the Political Factors in Confederate Defeat," David M. Potter questioned both these assumptions, suggesting instead that the Southern war effort lost much of its effectiveness because of the absence of adequate channels for organized, partisan, political life. In his view, the North's conduct of the war benefited from the Lincoln administration's effort to continue most normal political processes. Eric L. McKitrick here amplifies that hypothesis, providing the most important summary and reassessment of Civil War politics published in recent years.

The Civil War has always lent itself naturally and logically to the comparative method. Comparing the resources of the Union and the Confederacy in everything conceivable—manpower, brainpower, firepower—has been highly productive in helping us to understand the process whereby the North ultimately overwhelmed the South. But it is in the realm of government, where the process of historical comparison normally begins, that the results are on the whole least conclusive and least satisfying. The two sets of institutions exhibit a series of uncanny similarities. We may think we can detect in the Southern body politic a certain pallor, a lack of muscle tone that is in some contrast to the apparent resiliency of the North. But this is only a suspicion. We have not been very certain about how to get at such a subjective matter as the health of a metaphorical organism.

From William N. Chambers and Walter D. Burnham, *The American Party Systems: Stages of Political Development* (New York: Oxford University Press, 1967), pp. 117–20, 122–23, 128–29, 131–39, 141–51. Copyright © 1967 by Oxford University Press, Inc. Reprinted by permission; footnotes omitted.

The Union and Confederate governments, as set down on paper, were almost identical. The Confederacy deliberately adopted the federal Constitution with very few changes, some of which might have been improvements had they been carried fully into effect. Cabinet members might sit in Congress, though few did; the executive had an itemized veto on appropriation bills, though it was a power he did not use; and bills for departmental appropriations had to be initiated with an estimate from the department concerned. The general welfare clause was dropped, but the "necessary and proper" clause—so useful for expanding national power—was kept. The states were "sovereign" but had no power to make treaties, which meant that they were in fact not sovereign. Nothing was said about the right of secession, and it was not as though no one had thought of it. The relations of the states to the central government would, in the course of things, reveal some crucial differences, but it is hard to find much evidence for this in the organic law of the two governments. A trend toward centralized power was perfectly possible within either of the two constitutions, and it could proceed just as far under the one as under the other. The co-ordinate branches of government were constitutionally the same, though in the election and term of office of the executive there were certain differences. As for the judiciary, the Confederacy too was to have had a Supreme Court, though it never actually got around to establishing one. In the Confederacy judicial review (with generous citations from *The Federalist*, as well as from the opinions of Marshall and Story) occurred in the states. How much difference this made may be debated, though historians have not in general made an issue of it. In any case, of the three branches of government on either side, the judiciary seems to have made the least impact on the waging of war. With regard to the two Congresses, the practices and procedures were strikingly similar. It might be said that even their membership overlapped, since a number of men had served in both. . . .

All such comparisons as those just surveyed, enlightening as they are, must be made within certain limits. Attention is always in some way directed to the formal structure of government and to the individuals occupying the formal positions established by that structure. But comparing these formal arrangements, even in the broadest and most extended way, still does not bring us a very clear idea of why the North won and where it drew the necessary energy for sustaining a long drawn out war effort. At this point one normally retreats to the "concrete realities" of military power and material resources, the logic of which has a reassuring finality. Military and economic organization—"in the last analysis," as we say—is what tells.

Still there may be, as I think, much more to be said for the way in which political organization, in and of itself, affected the respective war efforts. And if so, it is most likely to be found by moving to another level altogether: by turning from the formal to the informal functions of politics, from its official to its unofficial apparatus, from the explicit formulations to the implicit understandings. For at least a generation prior to the Civil War, the most salient unofficial structure in American public life was its system of political parties. No formal provision was ever made for such a system. Yet in this system of parties may be found historically the chief agency for mobilizing and sustaining energy in American government. It thus seems reasonable to consider how, as a matter of actual practice, the energies of government may have been affected by the workings of this unofficial system in waging the American Civil War.

In an essay published in 1960, David Potter suggested "the possibility that the Confederacy may have suffered real and direct damage from the fact that its political organization lacked a two-party system." This, with its implications, constitutes in my opinion the most original single idea to emerge from the mass of writing that has been done on the Civil War in many years. It implicitly challenges two of our most formidable and consistently held assumptions regarding political life of the time, assumptions which until recently have gone unquestioned. One is that Lin-

coln's leadership of the Union war effort was severely and danger-
ously hampered by political partisanship—that is, by obstructions
put in his path by Democrats on the one hand and, on the other,
by extremists within his own Republican party. The other assumption is that Davis and the Confederate government, by deliberately setting aside partisanship, avoided this difficulty. There
were no parties in the Confederacy, and thus the South, in this
respect at least, had the advantage. . . .

The rapid growth of the Republican party in the brief span of
five or six years prior to 1860 had generated certain by-products.
It had certainly dissipated the malaise of the early 1850's in which
the expanding antislavery and free-soil sentiment of the North
had been, for a time, without any clear vehicle for political organization. There were, moreover, established public men who
had come to be identified with this sentiment, and whose careers
could no longer be promoted without stultification amid the dissolution of the Whig party and the conservatism of the regular
Democrats. Such men, of whom William H. Seward and Salmon P.
Chase were conspicuous examples, now found in the Republican
party a welcome field for their talents and leadership. In addition,
the very effort required in organizing the new party in state after
state brought to the fore hundreds of new men within the same
short space of time. The very marching clubs which sprang up
everywhere—the so-called "Wide Awakes"—amounted to much
more than a freakish social phenomenon. They represented the
"progressive" element of the community. That the Republicans
by 1860 had elected governors in every Northern state, to say
nothing of capturing the national government, is evidence of a
vitality going far beyond the ordinary. The period was one of
mounting public crisis; what has been less noticed is that precisely at this time public life began to present an expanding field
for younger men of talent, ambition, and energy.

By the time the Confederacy was being established, politics was
not attracting the South's best men to anywhere near this degree.
An obvious immediate reason, of course, was that the war crisis

naturally brought many of the Southern elite into the army, and many writers have commented on this. But antecedent factors were more pervasive. The chief mechanism for managing political talent and bringing it forward—party organizations—had in effect disintegrated in the South by the time the war began. . . . Thus the collapse in the South of the existing parties—the Whigs in the early 1850's and the Democrats in 1860—had created a setting in which the only real political issue came down to that of whether a man did or did not support secession. . . .

A further contrast between the Federal and Confederate governments, looking now at their formation from still another viewpoint, might consist in the standards whereby the cabinets as a whole were organized. For Davis, the chief concern was that each state had to be represented. For Lincoln also, geography counted as a strong consideration; but for him, both merit and geography as factors in choice had to operate within the limits of another criterion, which gave the problem a certain focus and required a certain precision. His cabinet had to be primarily a party alliance, which was its true functioning character, and its character as a coalition of state interests was thus quite secondary. He wanted every shade of commitment within the party, from border-state conservative to antislavery radical—and the influence they commanded—represented in his cabinet and, as it were, under his eye. A further nicety was that, owing to the comparative newness of the party, considerations of present and future support required that a man's antecedents also be weighed: there should be some balance between former Whigs and former Democrats. On the other hand, Davis had no choice but to follow the principle of state representation, and had he not done so he would undoubtedly have suffered even more general dissension and public attacks on his cabinet than he did. But judging both from this and from the cabinet's own instability, the political symbolism of a coalition of states, just in itself, as a focus for loyalty was somehow abstract, lacking in sharpness, and not very compelling. . . .

There were relatively few changes in Lincoln's cabinet, and

they were all made under circumstances firmly controlled by
Lincoln himself. The historian of Jefferson Davis's cabinet is unable to account satisfactorily for its lack of stability, except to
chronicle a long series of resignations, most of them under fire.
(There were six secretaries of war, five attorneys-general, and four
secretaries of state.) The legislative branch of government has no
constitutional right to interfere in the business of the President's
cabinet, and in this light Lincoln would have been quite justified
in refusing to deal with the senatorial delegation that challenged
him on Seward. But constitutional formality was only one of the
guidelines. These men confronted him in at least two capacities,
as senators and as leaders of the party, and in their latter capacity,
is Lincoln well knew, they could not safely be turned away. The
resulting adjustment, though exhausting and worrisome, brought
rich dividends in the repair of morale. Davis was not required to
adjust to any such principle. He too was harassed by informal
groups of legislators on similar missions. In February 1865, with
the Confederacy rapidly deteriorating, the legislative delegation
of Virginia urged him to make certain changes in his cabinet.
He thought it proper to declare, as he had on other occasions:
"The relations between the President and the Heads of the Executive Departments are . . . of the closest and most intimate
character . . . and it is not a Constitutional function of the Legislative Department to interfere with these relations. . . ." Lincoln's cabinet represented an ever-uneasy alliance, which is why
it required so much of his attention. But in the very process of
managing it he was, in effect, at the same time managing the
party and fashioning it into a powerful instrument for waging
war. In reference to that cabinet, it is not too much to say that
the choice of its members, its stability, its management, and the
major changes made in it, are all to be understood largely with
reference to a single principle, the exigencies of party politics.

The whole corps of federal officeholders may be understood in
much the same light. We have no full study of Jefferson Davis's
patronage policies, which is probably symptomatic; there may

never be much of a basis for generalizing about them. But there
certainly was one striking, self-evident difference between Lincoln's
and his, which was clarity of standards. Davis wanted merit, zeal,
and loyalty. (As one writer puts it, he "favored civil service reform.") Lincoln also, naturally, wanted merit, zeal, and loyalty.
But he also had some very straightforward criteria for determining
in a hurry what those qualities actually meant and how they were
to be found. The appointee had to be a Republican—which was
at least helpful in narrowing a swarming field by roughly half—
and the most dependable general standard for assessing loyalty
and zeal was services to the party. It was within this category that
he made his choices on "merit." The rules of procedure were also
quite precise. For example:

The appointments of postmasters, with salaries less than $1000 per
annum, will be made upon the recommendations of the [Republican]
members of Congress in the different districts. Applications addressed
to them will receive attention earlier than if sent to the Department,
and save much delay and trouble.

Lincoln was, moreover, very meticulous about "senatorial cour-
tesy."

Though Davis, as might naturally be supposed, accepted the
recommendations of others, he does not seem to have felt bound
by any given rule in acting upon them. For example, by insisting
on having his own way over the postmastership of Montgomery,
Davis deeply alienated both the senators from Alabama. . . .

Patronage is a care and a worry; it is also a cherished prerogative, with gratifications for those who give as well as those who
receive. They are all part of the same sensitive network. The re-
sponsiveness and *esprit* of such a network thus require that both
the giving and the receiving be widely shared, and on some understood basis. We have no way of measuring the energy with which
the men who made up these two patronage systems supported
their respective administrations and worked to carry out their
purposes. But we do know that one administration had an intri-

cate set of standards for appraising energy and rewarding it—in
addition always, of course, to standards of patriotism—which was
not available to the other.

The field of comparison in which contrasts between the two
governments are perhaps most grossly striking is that of state–
federal relations. In both cases there was a set of natural fault-
lines, inherent in a federal structure, between the state and national governments. In the Confederacy, these cracks opened ever
more widely as the war went on. Toward the end, indeed, some
states were in a condition of virtual rebellion against the Confederate government. In the North, the very opposite occurred.
The states and the federal government came to be bound more
and more closely in the course of the four years, such that by the
end of that time the profoundest change had been effected in
the character of their relations. In the course of things, moreover,
the people themselves would come to be more closely bound to
their national government. But the mechanisms are by no means
self-evident. It cannot be taken for granted that in the nature of
things such a process was bound to occur.

For the Confederacy, the great problem in raising and organizing armies was far less a matter of insufficient manpower than it
was of divided authority. The various efforts of the Confederate
government to get full access to and control over military manpower in the states were successfully obstructed throughout the
war by the state governors. The patriotic ardor of the governors
for mobilizing troops need not in itself be doubted. The perpetual
question was rather how it ought to be managed and how troops
were to be used; state resistance to Confederate policy always
came down to one of two principles: local defense, or the dangers
of a centralized military despotism. . . .

The organization of the army in the spring and summer of 1861
was held up by shortages not of men but of arms, substantial
amounts of which were in possession of the state governments.
They were held back partly for what were seen as local needs, and
partly in pique at the War Department's receiving of volunteers

raised without the intermediary of the governor. Efforts of the states to control the appointment of field officers led them either to hold back regiments until they were fully formed—instead of sending them forward by companies—or else by tendering "skeleton regiments" with a full complement of state-commissioned officers and only a few privates. Their insistence on controlling the clothing and supply of their own state troops in Confederate service led to consequences that were almost disastrous. Resources being not only unequal but at the very best limited, the maximum co-ordination of both purchasing and distribution was imperative. Yet as it was, Confederate purchasing agents had to engage everywhere in the most ruinous competition with agents from the states for sources of supply at home and abroad, while at the same time the output of state-controlled factories was kept consistently out of general reach. Governor Zebulon B. Vance of North Carolina actually boasted that, at the time of Robert E. Lee's surrender (of a tattered and starving army), he himself had huge stores of uniforms, blankets, cloth, leather, overcoats, and bacon in his state warehouses.

Conscription was adopted in the Confederacy in April 1862, a full year before the same step was taken in the North. One of the objects was to reorganize the twelve-months' volunteers whose terms were then running out; the other was to get control of the aggregations of militia which had been built up during the previous year and held in the states for local defense. This latter purpose was never properly achieved. State guards were once again built up, the condition of whose discipline and training made them worthless for almost any purpose so long as they were withheld from general service; and conscription itself, especially after the Act of February 1864, was resisted by the governors in a variety of ways. The chief device was that of exemptions, wherein wide categories of persons were sweepingly redefined as "state officers.". . .

In the North, the story of the recruitment and control of the army was, at least by comparison, relatively straightforward. The raising of troops was at the outset fully in the hands of the state governors, and so in a nominal sense it remained throughout. And yet by a series of steps the actual initiative tended to pass increasingly to the national government. By calling for three-year volunteer enlistments during the first month of hostilities and enlarging the regular army without the authority of law before the assembling of Congress, Lincoln took clear control of the national forces. Through most of the first year the recruiting activities of the governors proceeded with the utmost energy. The first major shift in initiative occurred after the failure of the Peninsular Campaign, when patriotic fervor began wearing thin and volunteers became increasingly harder to find. At this point Secretary Seward persuaded all the governors to unite in memorializing the President to call for 150,000 more volunteers, whereupon Lincoln promptly called for twice that many, together with 300,000 nine-months' militia. Both calls were more than met. Under the threat of a militia draft, the governors threw themselves with renewed zeal into a very aggressive campaign of recruiting. After the Emancipation Proclamation, the administration agreed to the enrolling of Negro troops. Aside from the raising of a few independent regiments, this recruiting was done directly by field commanders, entirely outside the control of any state government, and approximately 186,000 men were thus added to the national army. A further step was the adoption of conscription with the National Enrollment Act of March 1863, which gave the President full power to raise and support armies without state assistance. The unpopular Act was not fully exploited, and conscription as such accounted for no more than about 6 per cent of the total Union forces. It was successfully used, however, from 1863 to the end of the war, as a device for filling deficiencies in state volunteer quotas and for encouraging the governors to see that such deficiencies did not occur. In the mobilization of military manpower the state governors on the whole performed their function with exceptional vigor, even while becoming—as one writer somewhat extravagantly puts it—"mere agents" of the national government.

The energy of the Union government may be seen with even greater clarity in its actions against disaffection and disloyalty. Without any special legislation, Lincoln immediately assumed executive authority to suspend the writ of habeas corpus and make summary arrests in areas particularly endangered by disloyal activities; and in handling such cases the government made very little use of the courts. . . . Congress made some effort to define the President's powers in the Habeas Corpus Act of March 3, 1863, but whether the Act intended to grant these powers for the first time or to recognize powers he had exercised all along was not clear, and in any event executive policy and practice proceeded unaltered. . . .

No such freedom or directness of action was ever permitted to Jefferson Davis. He could make no summary moves against practices whose effect was to obstruct the war effort until the badly unsettled conditions of early 1862 finally persuaded the Confederate Congress that something needed to be done. The Act passed on February 27 thereupon permitted the executive to suspend habeas corpus and apply martial law to places threatened by invasion. But though Davis used his power in a very restricted way, the resulting hostility to martial law as imposed on Richmond and certain other places was such that Congress in April felt constrained to put further limits on the executive and to amend the law by giving it a fixed date of expiration. . . . That opposition had, indeed, been so bitter that Confederate law was in many places rendered practically unenforceable. Governor Brown insisted that the people of Georgia had "more to apprehend from military despotism than from subjugation by the enemy," and when Alexander Stephens harangued the Georgia legislature in March 1864 on the government's "despotic" suspension of habeas corpus, Brown had the speech printed and mailed to the company officers of every Georgia regiment and to every county clerk and county sheriff in Confederate territory. The legislature of North Carolina passed an Act making it compulsory for state judges to issue the writ, in effect nullifying Confederate

law. A meeting of governors in October 1864 adopted a resolution "virtually condemning" the suspension of habeas corpus.

One result was a serious weakening of the South's military system. State judges in Virginia, Texas, North Carolina, and elsewhere issued writs of habeas corpus indiscriminately to persons
accused of desertion or evading military service, and Governor
Vance used his militia to enforce them. Robert E. Lee complained to the Secretary of War that the drain on the army thus
caused by the use of habeas corpus was "more than it can bear."
Moreover, the deterioration of civil government in many areas
made a wide field for lawless bands, disloyal secret societies, and
trading with the enemy. Persons arrested for such activities were
again and again freed by habeas corpus on grounds of insufficient
evidence. All this despite Davis's plea that "the suspension of the
writ is not simply advisable and expedient, but almost indispensable to the successful conduct of the war."

The chief mechanism that prevented such centrifugal tendencies from developing in the Northern states, as William B. Hesseltine pointed out some years ago, was the Republican party. It
was the energy of the Republican party that established the political structure with which the North began the war, and through
which the war was prosecuted to the end. More specifically, the
governors of every Northern state in 1861 had been put there
through the efforts of that party, and these men represented both
the state organizations and the national coalition responsible for
bringing a Republican administration to Washington. They were
politically committed from the very first to positive measures for
suppressing disunion. With remarkable unanimity they invited
Lincoln at the outset to take steps—indeed, they insisted he take
them—which could only draw more and more power into his
hands, leaving them with less and less initiative. As with the raising of armies, there was something cumulative about this process;
it came to take on a life of its own.

In turn, the various state administrations—especially after the
resurgence of the Democratic party with the reverses of 1862—

came more and more, despite their traditions of particularism, to realize their growing dependence on the federal government for political support. . . .

In the broadest sense the dependence of the state and national administrations was mutual, and was mutually acknowledged; but in any case the binding agency and energizing force was the Republican party. And this in turn was maintained—indeed, made possible—through the continued existence of the Democrats.

There is certainly no need here to discuss the beneficial functions of a "loyal opposition." But something might be said about the functions of an opposition which is under constant suspicion of being only partly loyal. The Northern Democratic party during the Civil War stood in precisely this relation to the Union war effort, and its function in this case was of a double nature. On the one hand, its legitimacy as a quasi-formal institution would remain in the last analysis unchallenged, so long as it kept its antiwar wing within some sort of bounds. But by the same token there was the rough and ready principle that "every Democrat may not be a traitor, but every traitor is a Democrat."

Thus, the very existence of the Democratic party provided the authorities (who badly needed some standard) with a ready-made device for making the first rough approximation in the identification of actual disloyalty. It also provided a kind of built-in guarantee against irrevocable personal damage should the guess turn out to be wrong. When in doubt they could always round up local Democrats, as many a time they did, and in case of error there was always a formula for saving face all around: it was "just politics." There was, in short, a kind of middle way, an intermediate standard that had its lighter side and alleviated such extremes in security policy as, on the one hand, the paralysis and frustration of doing nothing, and, on the other, the perversions of power that accompany political blood-baths. . . .

Two state governments, those of New York and New Jersey, actually did fall into Democratic hands for a time during the war.

But despite much talk of states' rights and arbitrary central authority, neither of these administrations did anything that materially hindered the war effort. Both, in fact, did much to promote it, and it was not as though either state was lacking in Democrats ready for almost any measure which might tie up the federal government. But a strong stimulus to the Democratic governors, as well as to the state Democratic organizations, for keeping such elements in check was the existence in each state of a formidable Republican organization which was watching their every move.

Meanwhile Jefferson Davis also had opposition, in his Congress as well as in the states, and it grew ever larger. But it was not "an" opposition in any truly organized sense. It was far more toxic, an undifferentiated bickering resistance, an unspecified something that seeped in from everywhere to soften the very will of the Confederacy. Davis could not move against this; he had no real way of getting at it. He had no way, for example, without either an organized opposition party or an organized administration party, of dealing with a man like Joseph E. Brown. Had there been such organizations, and had Brown himself been at the head of either the one or the other of them in the state of Georgia, the administration forces would have had some sort of check on him. . . . Unlike the Northern governors, Brown had no informal national structure with a clear set of organizational interests, and on which his own power depended, to persuade him otherwise. . . .

A further note on "opposition" might involve the relations of Lincoln with the "Radical" faction of his own party. This question has produced some strong debate among historians, though the principal issues appear by now to have been largely settled. . . .

The . . . point . . . is that these Radicals, whatever may have been their many differences, represented the most articulate, most energetic, most militant wing of the Republican party. The one thing that did unite such men as Trumbull, Wade, Greeley,

Chandler, Fessenden, Julian, and the rest was their implacable insistence that the war be prosecuted with ever more vigor, and that the President use the national power to the utmost in doing it. There is every evidence that in this over-all objective they and the President were at one, inasmuch as the war was, in the end, so prosecuted. Whether Lincoln welcomed his tormentors is doubtful. But whether he or anyone else would have moved as decisively without them is equally doubtful, and what the Union war effort as a whole would have been without the energy they represented is more doubtful still. The tensions and conflicts of the Lincoln administration—such as those having to do with emancipation, the use of Negro troops, and the complexion of the government that was to stand for re-election in 1864—were, as we know, considerable. But without a party apparatus to harness and direct them, they would surely have been unmanageable.

In any event, we might imagine Jefferson Davis as being quite willing to exchange this sort of "opposition" for the one he had. In the Confederate Congress there seem to have been some who pressed for greater vigor than Davis's in fighting the war; a much larger number inclined to measures that would have resulted in less. But perhaps more fundamental was that these men were all mixed in together. There was no recognized way of segregating or defining them, no basis of expectations, no clear principle for predicting what they might do. "There were no political organizations seeking undivided loyalty," as the historian of that Congress puts it, "nor was there consistent pressure from the electorate. Conditions changed, opinions changed, consequently administration sympathies changed." This lack of sharpness seems to have been accompanied by a . . . lack of initiative which is quite noticeable when contrasted with the wartime federal Congress, and it is apparent that lack of party responsibility had much to do with it. . . . Certainly Davis had no counterpart of Lincoln's "Radicals" to spur him on. Could the rabid secessionists of the 1850's, the so-called Southern "fire-eaters," the Robert Barnwell Rhetts, the William Lowndes Yanceys, the Edmund Ruffins, have made such a counterpart? There is little evidence that they could, or would. Such men are quite absent from the roll of the Confederacy's leading statesmen. The most dynamic "fire-eaters" who came into their own in the war years were two obstructionist state governors, already mentioned, Zebulon Vance and Joseph E. Brown.

It has been asserted throughout this essay that the Republican party, in the presence of an organized party of opposition, performed a variety of functions in mobilizing and managing the energies needed for sustaining the Union war effort. These were carried on both inside and outside the formal structure of government, and by men active in party affairs whether they held office or not. The absence of such a system in the Confederacy seems to have had more than a casual bearing on the process whereby Southern energies, over and beyond the course of military events, became diffused and dissipated. National commitments in the North were given form and direction by an additional set of commitments, those of party. This hardly means that the Republican party is to be given sole credit for the success of the war effort, which was in fact supported by overwhelming numbers of Democrats. But it does mean, among other things, that there were political sanctions against the Democrats' *not* supporting it, sanctions which did not exist in the Confederacy. When Democratic leaders were inclined to behave irresponsibly they could not, like Brown and Vance, play the role of state patriots. A hint of Democratic disloyalty anywhere tightened the Republican organization everywhere.

The emphasis hitherto has been upon leadership, upon how the process of politics affected the workings of government, but a final word should be said about how that process affected the body of citizenry. What may have been the function of a party system as a vehicle of communication? What did it do toward making popular elections a mode whereby the people were in effect called upon to define and reaffirm their own commitment to the national cause? In 1862, 1863, and 1864, through a series of elections which made the heaviest psychological demands on the entire country, the North had annually to come to terms with the war effort. The Republicans, with varying degrees of success, everywhere made attempts to broaden their coalition by bringing as many Union Democrats into it as possible, and naturally tried to attract as many Democratic voters to it as they could. The national party even changed its name in 1864, calling itself the "Union" party to dramatize the breadth of its appeal. And yet the result was in no true sense an all-party front or bipartisan coalition; rather it was a highly successful device for detaching Democrats from their regular party loyalties. The distinction is of some importance. The initiative for this effort remained throughout in Republican hands, and the Democrats everywhere maintained their regular organizations. The structure of parties was therefore such that every election became, in a very direct way, a test of loyalty to the national government.

The tests were by no means consistently favorable. In the fall of 1862, the time of the mid-term elections, the Republicans were significantly divided on the President's policy of emancipation, and a heavy majority of Democrats opposed it. This was reflected in the state and congressional election results, which were deeply depressing to the administration. The Democrats elected governors in two states and majorities in the legislatures of several, and substantially increased their numbers in Congress. This had several important consequences. One was that, inasmuch as the Republicans still maintained their control of Congress, the weakened state organizations were brought a step farther in that progress, already described, of growing dependency on the national party and the national administration for leadership and support. Another was that the Republicans were inspired to great exertions in justifying emancipation as an integral feature of the party program and in minimizing the Democrats' claim that the purposes of the war had been altered to make it an abolition crusade. Still a further consequence was that the Democrats were sufficiently emboldened by their successes that in a number of places they overstepped themselves. The "peace" theme in the Democrats' case against the administration emerged with a clarity that had hitherto been muted, making them much more vulnerable than before to the Republicans' "treason" theme, and drawing clear lines for the state elections of 1863. . . .

Once again in 1864, the Democrats, amid the military discouragements of the summer, assisted in clarifying the choices by writing a peace plank into their national platform and nominating a general, George B. McClellan, who had been dismissed for the failure of the operations of 1862 in the Eastern theater. The re-election of Lincoln was accompanied by the restoration of Republican majorities to every legislature and every congressional delegation, and of Republican governors to every state.

The people of the Confederacy, of course, continued to hold elections. Yet we know surprisingly little—indeed, almost nothing —about these elections. No study has ever been made of them, which is some measure of how comparatively little importance was attached to them at the time. The people were asked in November 1861 to choose Davis and Stephens as heads of the "permanent" government. The election "was marked, however, by general apathy." The first elections to Congress, according to Professor Yearns, "went off quietly." There was virtually no campaigning, and "balloting everywhere was light, as is usual when issues are absent." The elections of 1863, from what little glimpse we have of them, seem aggressive only by contrast. The increased activity at that time was principally a product of increased dissatisfaction with Davis's government. Yet even here the opposition was unorganized and unfocused, and candidates "failed to offer any clear substitute for policies they denigrated." "Mixed with rodomontade was the familiar state rights ingredient which gave much criticism a respectable flavor. All of the strong war measures were condemned as evidence of centralized despotism which was abusing the states."

The sluggishness of communication in the Confederacy has

often been commented on, and yet here the contrast with the North is one which the disparity in technology does not quite fully account for. There was no counterpart in the South of the resonance which party elections provided for the Northern cause. The historian of Confederate propaganda asserts that official efforts in this direction were very deficient, which is not surprising when it is recalled how preponderantly such efforts in the North were handled through party agencies. We have a description of how such activities were carried on in Washington with the heartiest co-operation of the national government during the fall of 1864:

> The National Republican Committee have taken full possession of all the Capitol buildings, and the committee rooms of the Senate and House of Representatives are filled with clerks, busy in mailing Lincoln documents all over the loyal States. . . .
> The Post Office Department, of course, is attending to the lion's share of this work. Eighty bags of mail matter, all containing Lincoln documents, are daily sent to Sherman's army.

Not long after this time, a measure was timidly offered in the Confederate Congress whereby the government frank might be used for mailing newspapers to soldiers in the field. The Confederate Postmaster-General was distressed. His department was required by law to be self-supporting, and he was very proud of its being the only one to show a surplus, which he had achieved by doing away with all but the bare minimum services. He spoke to the President about this new bill, and the latter solemnly vetoed it as being unconstitutional.

Whether Northern wartime elections served to give refinement and precision to the issues is perhaps less important than that they served to simplify and consolidate them. When the people of Indiana were urged in 1863 to vote for Republicans in their local elections, they were really being asked to do more than elect a few county officers. And by the same token the candidate for such an office accepted, along with his nomination, a whole train of extraordinary responsibilities: Governor Morton, President Lincoln, emancipation, arbitrary arrests, and war to the end. There was no separating them; under the circumstances of war, the voter who took the Republican candidate took them all. And the candidate, if successful in his debates with his Democratic opponent, would have enacted something akin to the principle of the self-fulfilling prophecy. He defined his position, he defended the administration, he persuaded his audience, and in the process he repersuaded and recommitted himself.

It may be quite proper to say that it was, after all, the Union's military success that made political success possible. The fall of Atlanta in September 1864, for example, certainly rescued Lincoln's chances for re-election. But conceivably it was not that simple, and short-term correlations may be deceiving. How was the Northern will sustained for the three and a half years that were needed before it could reap successes of any kind in late 1864? A continual affirmation and reaffirmation of purpose was built into the very currents of political life in the Northern states. It is altogether probable that the North's political energies and its military will were, all along, parts of the same process.

Every election, moreover, was a step in nationalizing the war. The extension of local and state loyalties into national loyalties during this period was something of a revolution, and it did not occur easily. This profound change cannot be taken for granted, nor is it best undertsood simply by examining the formal federal structure through which it began. It is revealed rather through the far less formal political process whereby the national government in the Civil War was able to communicate its purposes, to persuade, and to exercise its will directly upon individuals in state, city, town, and local countryside.

Reconstruction: A National View

Negro Suffrage and Republican Politics

by La Wanda and John H. Cox

The nation emerged from four years of Civil War only to plunge at once into a decade of political conflict for control of the former slave states. Radical Republicans and Johnson Democrats, freedmen and ex-rebels all shared at least one fundamental perception throughout the "Reconstruction Era," namely a common recognition of its uniqueness. The partisan quarrels of the years 1865–1877 were grounded on a dilemma which all politicians faced: the singular absence of precedents to guide political decision-making.

At war's end, there existed an unwieldly governing coalition in the North, the "Union party" composed of Republicans and some "War Democrats" such as President Andrew Johnson. As Johnson and the congressional Radicals struggled for power, both confronted a revolutionary situation for which neither the Constitution nor the ordinary processes of American government had made provision. What political rights, if any, remain for leaders and followers of a defeated secessionist movement? What place in the Republic's political life should a freed Negro population assume—be given, rather? Which branch of the national government, executive or legislative, should dominate postwar policy formation? The confrontation between Andrew Johnson and the Radicals arose out of these unanswered constitutional and moral questions. Not even the takeover of national government by Republican congressional leaders in 1867 provided firm answers either to the legal or political questions involved. In the process, however, Congress assumed responsibility for imposing its own version of Reconstruction upon the South.

Who were the Radicals and what were their major goals? Historians have argued over these problems almost from the moment Reconstruction ended, often disagreeing vehemently on Republican motives in supporting Negro suffrage through passage of the Reconstruction Acts and the Fourteenth and Fifteenth Amendments. Some have labeled the Radicals either self-serving political opportunists or pro-black zealots, bent upon cynically manipulating a Southern Negro electorate in order to ensure their own continued domination of national politics and to punish former Confederates. Others have seen congressional Radicals as tools of Northern industrialists determined to block the Democrats' return to power and preserve the economic benefits of Republican rule. Still others have pointed to the contradictions between the general opposition of most white Northerners to Negro suffrage in their own states and Radical support for such legislation in the South. Were Republican politicians "sincerely" in favor of federal support for the freedman—including his enfranchisement—and, if so, how did their policies triumph temporarily in spite of their constituents' strong anti-Negro bias? In the following article La Wanda and John Cox explore these questions by reviewing the historiography of Negro suffrage and interpreting the complexities of Republican motivation.

❧ Republican party leadership of the 1860's was responsible for establishing the legal right of Negro citizens to equal suffrage, first in the defeated South by act of Congress and then through-

From *The Journal of Southern History*, XXXIII (August 1967), 303–30. Copyright 1967 by the Southern Historical Association. Reprinted by permission of the Managing Editor; most footnotes omitted.

out the nation by constitutional amendment.[1] Whether historians have condemned or applauded the grant of suffrage to Negroes in the post–Civil War years, they have more often than not viewed the motives behind this party action with considerable cynicism. The purpose of this article is to review their treatment and to raise for re-examination the question of what moved Republicans in Congress to such far-reaching action.

The earliest study of the origins of the Fifteenth Amendment was prepared by a scholarly lawyer from western Virginia, Allen Caperton Braxton, for presentation to the state bar association in 1903. The work is still cited, and a new edition was printed in the 1930's. Braxton held that Negro suffrage was the result of "gratitude, apprehension and politics—these three; but the greatest of these was politics." To Radical leaders of the Republican party, enfranchisement early appeared "a promising means of party aggrandisement"; it soon became "essential to the perpetuation of their power." In the struggle with President Andrew Johnson over Reconstruction, they had alienated "the entire white race of the South" for at least a generation to come. Once the Southern states were restored to the Union and the white vote of the South added to the Democratic vote of the North, the Republican party would face hopeless defeat; the only means of escape lay through the Southern Negro. In the legislation of March 1867 Radicals effected "a *coup d'etat* of the first magnitude," but it was not a stable foundation on which to build future political power. The law might be rescinded by Congress, overturned by judicial decision, or defied by the Southern states after their readmission. Only a constitutional amendment could provide security. It would also mean votes from an increasing Negro pop-

1. The First Reconstruction Act, passed over President Andrew Johnson's veto March 2, 1867, and the Fifteenth Amendment, passed by Congress February 26, 1869, and declared ratified March 30, 1870. In 1860 the only states with equal suffrage for Negroes were Maine, New Hampshire, Vermont, Massachusetts, and Rhode Island. New York permitted Negroes with a $250 freehold estate to vote. By 1869 the following Northern states had been added to the above list: Nebraska, Wisconsin, Minnesota, and Iowa.

ulation in the North as a potential balance of power in close elections. A few footnotes and quotations, notably one from Charles Sumner, appear as illustrative, and there is a flat assertion that debates in Congress on the Fifteenth Amendment "leave no room to doubt" its political inspiration. It is clear, however, that the author felt no need either to scrutinize or to document his interpretation; a primary relationship between Negro suffrage and party expediency appeared to him self-evident.

Braxton did examine in detail a thesis and the historic contradiction that it implied. "One may well question," he wrote in conclusion, "whether the popular will was executed or thwarted when negro suffrage was written into the fundamental law of this nation." No reader would doubt that the author's answer was "thwarted." Despite some overstatement and minor distortions of fact, this thesis is sound history. The national guarantee of an equal vote to the Negro did not reflect a popular consensus, even in the North. Braxton's attempt to explain how an unwanted policy became the fundamental law of the land, though less convincing, raised an important historical problem.

Despite his emphasis upon political expediency as the impelling causal element behind equal suffrage, the Virginia attorney might have considered Republican leaders who had imposed this result upon the nation, at least a few of their number, men sincerely concerned with the Negro's right to vote. References to "fanaticism," "bigotry," and "negrophiles" suggest that he did, though obviously without sympathy. This implication, however, is explicitly disavowed and with specific reference to Senator Sumner. Braxton found "shocking" evidence of insincerity in the fact that men who argued for the inalienable right of the Negro to vote agreed to exclude Indians and Chinese from the franchise. He considered leaders of the party to be distinguished from the rank and file of Northerners neither by principle nor by lack of prejudice. Unlike their constituents, congressmen were removed from personal competition with the Negro, and their national perspective made them aware of the dependence of Republican party power upon Negro enfranchisement. Braxton's indictment of Republican motivation showed charity on just one count. He granted that some leaders were moved neither by "malice toward the South" nor by "heartless political ambition." They had come to equate the life of the Republican party with the life of the nation and honestly feared a Democratic victory as a national disaster.

The second study of the fifteenth Amendment, by John M. Mathews, appeared in 1909 and was to remain the standard historical account for more than half a century. Originally prepared as a paper for a seminar in political science at Johns Hopkins University, it is a most unhistorical history in the sense that its author was more concerned to analyze concepts than men or events. He narrowly delimited the chronology and substance of his "legislative history" and showed special interest in the judicial interpretation of the amendment. Neither the historic problem posed by Braxton's study nor the question of men's motives as individuals or as party leaders presented a challenge to Mathews; he did not even consider it important to identify with particular congressmen or with political parties the four elements in his analysis—the humanitarians, the nationalists, the politicians, and the local autonomists. Indeed, he explicitly stated that "These forces were primarily principles, rather than men or groups of men. They were not always separable except in thought, for the same senator or representative was often influenced by more than one of them at the same time."

Yet the Mathews monograph does carry certain implications in respect to motivation. The statement that "There was little real difference of opinion among the leaders in Congress as to the desirability of enlarging the sphere of political liberty for the negro race" might be read as an assumption of genuine concern for the Negro on the part of the lawmakers. On the other hand, a quite different interpretation could be given to statements that "The politician was the initiator and real engineer of the movement," that he labored for a concrete objective "fraught with definite,

practical results," and that he was not altogether satisfied with
the final form of the amendment "because it did not directly and
specifically guarantee the African's right to vote" and hence might
be evaded. In this study so long considered authoritative, there
is nothing to confirm Braxton's identification of equal suffrage
with partisan advantage, but neither is there anything that would
cause its readers to question that assumption.

The writings of William A. Dunning and of James Ford
Rhodes, the two most influential scholars with accounts of Reconstruction published during the first decade of the twentieth
century, did sound a warning. To Southerners it had been "incon-
ceivable," Dunning pointed out, that "rational men of the North
should seriously approve of negro suffrage *per se*"; hence they assumed that the only explanation was "a craving for political
power." Dunning was implying a fallacy in their understanding.
Yet he himself attributed Republican sponsorship of Negro suffrage in the First Reconstruction Act of 1867 to the "pressure of
party necessity and of Sumner's tireless urging." In writing of the
Fifteenth Amendment, Dunning assumed that he had established the motivation behind it. He cited an earlier paragraph as
support for the statement: "We have already seen the partisan
motive which gave the impulse to the passage of the Fifteenth
Amendment." Any reader who took the trouble to turn back the
pages would find a passage which, far from proving the contention, did not necessarily imply it. Dunning had written that after
the presidential election of 1868 in which Democrats gained majorities in Georgia and Louisiana through the use of violence,
moderate Republicans had no uncertainty as to "the policy
of maintaining what had been achieved in enfranchising the
blacks."

Rhodes was more explicit in his warning and more direct in
crediting to humanitarian feelings within Republican party ranks
an influence in "forcing negro suffrage upon the South." He cautioned readers not to lose sight of the high motives involved "for
it would be easy to collect a mass of facts showing that the sole

aim of congressional reconstruction was to strengthen the Republican party." Neither the statement quoted nor his account as a whole would stir to skepticism anyone who had assumed with Braxton the predominance of political expediency. He did not analyze or criticize the Braxton assumption but rather supplemented it. In Rhodes's view, there were men with "intelligence and high character" who were "earnest for the immediate enfranchisement of the freedmen," but they were "numerically small." His writing at times carried an unintended innuendo. For example, he stated that the majority of Republicans in Congress when they reassembled after the Christmas holidays of 1866 did not favor the imposition of Negro suffrage upon the South, a policy which they sustained by a two-thirds vote a few weeks later. The explanation lay in "The rejection of the Fourteenth Amendment by the South, the clever use of the 'outrages' argument, the animosity to the President . . . which was increased to virulence by his wholesale removals of Republicans from office," factors that "enabled the partisan tyranny of Stevens and the pertinacity of Sumner to achieve this result."

The ambivalence in Rhodes's treatment arose primarily from his strong conviction that the grant of suffrage to the Negro during Reconstruction was a major mistake in policy. This judgment was evident in a paper which he delivered before the Massachusetts Historical Society while writing his account of Reconstruction and also in the volumes of his *History of the United States* which appeared two years later. Suffrage had been an abysmal failure which "pandered to the ignorant negroes, the knavish white natives and the vulturous adventurers who flocked from the North" and "neutralized the work of honest Republicans. . . ." Experience in the North, in his opinion, also discredited the grant of equal suffrage to the Negro—he had shown little political leadership, rarely identified himself "with any movement on a high plane," such as civil service, tariff reform, honest money, or pure municipal government, and "arrogantly asserts his right to recognition" because he is "greedy for office and emolument." All this had not been the Negro's fault; he had been "started at the top" despite "all the warnings of science and political experience." Rhodes believed that the findings of science were clear and that they had been available to Sumner and his fellow advocates of Negro enfranchisement through the distinguished Harvard scientist Louis Agassiz, who was Sumner's friend. He did not place all blame on Sumner, however, but indicated that the fault lay in our national character. "I think that England or Prussia would have solved the negro problem better"; they would have "studied the negro scientifically"; in the "age of Darwin and Huxley" Americans had made no attempt to do so.

In discussing the problem with fellow historians, Rhodes revealed more sharply than in his writings his personal assessment of motivation: "From a variety of motives, some praiseworthy and others the reverse, we forced negro suffrage upon the South. . . . Party advantage, the desire of worthless men at the North for offices at the South, co-operated with a misguided humanitarianism." The warning which he sounded, and the less explicit one from Dunning as well, reflected a conscientious desire on the part of these distinguished historians to be fair, restrained, and judicious. The assumption that most Republican members of Congress who voted for equal Negro suffrage did so primarily if not solely, for reasons of political expediency, was an assumption they accepted; it apparently did not occur to either man that there was need for any careful scrutiny to establish the validity of this accusation.

For three decades, until the post–World War II years, few historians handled the question of Republican motivation with as much fairness as had Rhodes and Dunning. Ellis P. Oberholtzer, in his multivolume *History of the United States Since the Civil War*, wrote that "Just as the war had not been waged to free the negro from bondage" so the postwar strife "except to a few minds, had little enough to do with the improvement of the lot of the black man." He continued: "The project to make voters out of black men was not so much for their social elevation as for the further punishment of the Southern white people—for the capture of offices for Radical scamps and the intrenchment of the Radical party in power for a long time to come in the South and in the country at large." The small but influential volume in the Yale *Chronicles of America* series written by Dunning's foremost student, Walter L. Fleming, made the indictment specific. The election of 1868, Fleming wrote showed that Democrats could command more white votes than could Republicans "whose total included nearly 700,000 blacks." This prompted the Radicals to frame the Fifteenth Amendment which, as it appeared to them, would not only "make safe the negro majorities in the South" but also add strength from Negroes previously denied the ballot in the North, thus assuring "900,000 negro voters for the Republican party."

During the late 1920's and the 1930's, a period in Reconstruction historiography which saw the "canonization" of Andrew Johnson, little charity was shown to those who had been Johnson's opponents. Claude G. Bowers developed the "conspiracy" approach to Negro suffrage, seeing it as the culmination of a plot hatched by Sumner and a few Radicals and dating back at least to the early days of 1865. He quoted approvingly the Georgian, Benjamin H. Hill, who charged that Negro suffrage was a matter of knaves using fools " 'to keep the Radical Party in power in the approaching presidential election, . . . to retain by force and fraud the power they are losing in the detection of their treason in the North.' " George Fort Milton recognized that "The Radicals had mixed motives in this insistence on negro suffrage," but his lack of sympathy for the "old Abolitionists" led him to gibe at Sumner. From a letter of the Senator, he quoted, " 'We need the votes of all,' " then observed, "Could it be that practical political necessities moved him as well as lofty idealistic views?" Milton did little more than mention the Fifteenth Amendment but could not resist using the opportunity to belittle its Republican sponsors: ". . . one or two Senators shamefacedly admitted that perhaps an intelligent white woman had as much right as an ignorant negro plow-hand to determine the destinies of the nation. But there seemed little political advantage in women suffrage. . . ." James G. Randall, whose substantial volume on the Civil War and Reconstruction served as a standard college textbook from the 1930's to the 1960's, handled the subject of Negro suffrage with restraint; yet in substance he accepted a mild version of Bowers' conspiracy thesis. Randall's variant was that "the importance of the Negro vote to the Republican party North and South caused leading Radicals to keep their eye upon the issue" although Northern sentiment would not support nationwide Negro suffrage. Gradually, as the power of the Radicals increased, they moved toward their goal. "Step by step they were able to enact laws promoting Negro suffrage without an amendment, and finally to carry the suffrage amendment itself in the first year of Grant's administration." This account was allowed to stand without modification when the volume was revised in 1961 by David Donald.

The chronological limits of Howard K. Beale's study of the election of 1866, perhaps the most influential scholarly product of the pro-Johnson historiography, precluded an examination of the Reconstruction Acts of 1867 and the Fifteenth Amendment. However, there is a chapter devoted to Negro suffrage as a general issue. Beale divided its Radical proponents into four groups —old abolitionists, who believed in the principle of equal suffrage; friends of the Negro, who saw the ballot as his only means of defense; men hostile to racial equality, who would use Negro suffrage to humiliate the defeated South; and, lastly, "a more numerous group" to whom "expediency was the motive." Curiously, his classification had the same weakness as Mathews' disembodied analysis; it offered the reader no evidence that any one of the four "groups" was identifiable in terms of specific individuals. In fact, despite a deep personal commitment to Negro equality and intensive manuscript research, Beale added little new except to link the suffrage issue with his general thesis that Radical leaders were motivated by economic as well as political ends.

"If the South could be excluded, or admitted only with negro suffrage," he wrote, "the new industrial order which the Northeast was developing, would be safe."

Yet Beale did not dismiss the suffrage issue as summarily as had the Republicans in the 1866 campaign. His treatment suggests his interest in the subject, and particularly in the claim made during 1865 and after that the Negro would never be safe unless protected by the ballot. Beale considered it "a powerful [argument]" even though he looked with sympathy upon those who mistrusted a grant of unqualified suffrage to naïve and uneducated freedmen. After struggling with the argument for several pages, he concluded that no one could say with certainty whether without the ballot the status of the newly freed slave among white Southerners would have been shaped by "the fair-minded" or "the vicious." Then he added: "Few cared to know. Extreme Radicals wanted negro suffrage; outrages against the negroes, and an exaggeration of cruel codes would reconcile Northerners to it." In other words, the "powerful argument" was essentially a propaganda device; its prevalence in the 1860's would not lighten the charges against the Republican Radical leadership.

Another election study, Charles H. Coleman's analysis of the Grant–Seymour campaign of 1868, was published in the 1930's and at once took its place as the standard, perhaps definitive, account. Coleman's discussion of the Negro suffrage issue in the elections of 1867 and 1868 is exceptionally fair and informative. Without raising the question of motivation or passing judgment, it yet provides considerable material pertinent to the problem. Also, Coleman, like Walter Fleming, was interested in the importance of the Negro vote. He estimated that it had provided Grant with 450,000 of his total, without which the Republicans would not have gained a popular majority. While Coleman believed that a majority of the white voters of the country favored the Democratic party in 1868 and implied that this remained true until 1896, unlike Fleming, he did not point to any connection between the 1868 election results and the movement immediately

thereafter for an equal-suffrage amendment. The omission may
have been due to his clear recognition that Grant's victory in the
electoral college would have been secure without any Negro votes.
The Democrats with better leadership, according to Coleman,
might have contended with the Republicans on almost equal
terms in 1868, but they did not lose the election "through the
operation of the reconstruction acts." Despite a generally careful
and balanced presentation, in his opening paragraphs Coleman
made reference incidentally and uncritically to "Republican
ascendancy" as the motive behind the Fifteenth Amendment.
He had not given thought to the relationship between his findings and the time-honored charges of Braxton and Fleming.

By the 1950's a new direction was evident in historical writings
dealing with the Negro in nineteenth-century America, one that
rejected the assumption of racial inferiority and cherished the
quest for racial equality. This trend, which reached major proportions in the 1960's, drew stimulus and support both from the
contemporary social and intellectual climate and from interior
developments within historical research. During the thirties revisionist articles dealing with so-called "Black" Reconstruction in
the South had anticipated postwar attitudes toward race relationships and had upset the negative stereotypes of "scalawags,"
"carpetbaggers," and "Radical" regimes. In the forties the National Archives provided material for new departures in Reconstruction scholarship by making available the manuscript records
of the Freedmen's Bureau with a useful checklist. The extremes
to which vindication of Andrew Johnson had been carried in the
thirties, together with a program to assemble and publish his papers, led to re-examination of his record and that of his opponents. Military confrontation with Hitler stimulated a challenge
to the "needless war" interpretation of the American civil conflict,
redirecting attention to slavery as a moral issue. Antislavery agitators became the focus of renewed interest and sympathy, the
latter reinforced by a growing sophistication in the historian's
borrowings from psychology and sociology. Leadership of Negroes

in the contemporary struggle for equality found a counterpart in an increased recognition of the role of Negro leadership during the nineteenth century. Through new biographies and analytical articles, a beginning was made in reassessing the record and motives of leading Radicals. Finally, the coincidence of the Civil War centennial with the great public civil rights issues of the 1960's quickened the pace of historical writings concerned with the status of the Negro.

Out of these recent studies has come a new perspective on the post–Civil War grant of suffrage to the Negro, once widely regarded with dismay. The Fifteenth Amendment is now seen as a "momentous enactment." It included Negroes within "the American dream of equality and opportunity," gave the United States distinction as being the first nation committed to the proposition that in a "bi-racial society . . . human beings must have equal rights," and established an essential legal substructure upon which to build the reality of political equality.

There has also emerged an explanation of political Radicalism during Reconstruction, even of Republicanism generally, in terms of ideas and idealism. The case has been subtly argued and dramatically summarized by Kenneth M. Stampp: ". . . radical reconstruction ought to be viewed in part as the last great crusade of the nineteenth-century romantic reformers." If anything, Radicals were less opportunistic and more candid than the average politician. "To the practical motives that the radicals occasionally revealed must be added the moral idealism that they inherited from the abolitionists." The case for Radicalism has also been persuasively presented by the English historian William Ranulf Brock, who has written that the cement binding together the Radicals as a political group was "not interest but a number of propositions about equality, rights, and national power." In fact, Brock does not limit this generous interpretation of motives to the Radicals, but includes moderate Republicans as well. He was gone even further and identified "the great moving power behind Reconstruction" with "the conviction of the average Republican that the objectives of his party were rational and humane." The study by the present authors led to the conclusion that the moderates in Congress broke with the President in 1866 primarily because of their genuine concern for equal civil rights short of suffrage.

With the ferment and new direction of Reconstruction historiography, the old Braxton–Rhodes–Fleming assumption of party expediency as the controlling motive behind support for Negro suffrage by Republican congressmen might reasonably be expected to meet one of three fates: it might be quietly replaced by the opposite assumption that congressional votes reflected in large measure the strain of idealism in Republicanism; it could be dismissed on the ground that there had been a fusion of principle and expediency so intimate and indivisible as to preclude further inquiry; or it could be subjected to an incisive, detailed, and comprehensive examination. At the present writing neither the first nor third alternative appears at all likely. As for the second, the problem of motivation deserves a better resolution, for it is important both to our understanding of the past and to our expectations of the future.

The "practical" view of Republican motivation is too casually accepted in historical writings and too consonant with prevailing attitudes toward politicians and parties to be in danger of just disappearing. Leslie H. Fishel, Jr., Emma Lou Thornbrough, and Leon F. Litwack in their sympathetic pioneering studies of Negroes in the North all assume that Republican politicians had little interest in the Negro except to obtain his vote. In staking out the well-merited abolitionist claim of credit for having championed the cause of Negro equality during the Civil War and Reconstruction, James M. McPherson perpetuates the traditional attitude toward Republicans: the abolitionists provided moral justification, but party policies "were undertaken primarily for military or political reasons." Indeed, McPherson condemns the whole North for a failure of conscience and belittles the public support given to equal rights as "primarily a conversion of expediency

rather than one of conviction." David Donald has attempted to
bypass the "difficulty of fathoming . . . motives" by disregarding
individuals in favor of "objective behavior patterns" and "quanti-
tatively measurable forces." His procedures and logic, however,
start with the assumption that politicians wish either re-election
or higher office and that this fact is controlling in presidential
policy and congressional voting. It is startling to read that Lincoln's policies could have been arrived at by "A rather simple
computer installed in the White House, fed the elementary statistical information about election returns and programed to solve
the recurrent problem of winning re-election. . . ."

Even Stampp, who restates the old hostile arguments regarding
the political motivation of Radicals in order to challenge them,
replies directly only with the observation that conservatives as
well were thinking how best to keep the Republican party in
power—to them Negro suffrage simply appeared an obstacle
rather than an instrument of party unity and control. Stampp also
strikes a disparaging note evident elsewhere in recent scholarship.
This is the charge of "timidity" and "evasion" leveled against Republican politicians on the question of Negro suffrage. There is
irony in the shifting basis of attack upon the reputation of Republican politicians. Once berated from the right for plots and
maneuvers to thwart the popular will and establish Negro suffrage, these whipping boys of history are now in danger of assault from the left for having lacked the boldness, energy, and
conviction needed for an earlier and more secure victory.

There finally appeared in 1965 to supersede the Mathews
monograph an intensive, scholarly work by a young historian,
William Gillette, on the passage and ratification of the Fifteenth
Amendment. Reflecting the modern temper in its rejection of caste
and commitment to equality, the new study nevertheless represents a vigorous survival of the Braxton-Fleming tradition. Gillette's thesis transfers to the North the emphasis formerly placed
on the South, but political expediency remains the heart of the
matter: "The primary object of the Amendment was *to get the*

Negro vote in the North. . . ." As revealed by the election results of 1868, "prospects for both northern and southern Republicans were not bright" and, according to Gillette, "Republicans
had to do something." They were pessimistic about reliance upon
the Negro vote in the South but alert to its potential in the
North. This prospect motivated the framing of the amendment
and accounted for ratification in the face of widespread opposition since it "made political sense to shrewd politicians. . . ." In
effect, Gillette accepts as his thesis the judgment pronounced in
1870 by the Democratic party-line newspaper, the New York
World, that Republican leaders " 'calculated that the Negro vote
in the doubtful Northern states would be sufficient to maintain
the Republican ascendancy in those states and, through them, in
the politics of the country. It was with this in view that they
judged the Fifteenth Amendment essential to the success of their
party.' "

In challenge to the dominant pattern of interpretation from
Braxton through Gillette, we should like to suggest that Republican party leadership played a crucial role in committing this
nation to equal suffrage for the Negro not because of political expediency but *despite* political risk. An incontestable fact of Reconstruction history suggests this view. Race prejudice was so
strong in the North that the issue of equal Negro suffrage constituted a clear and present danger to Republicans. White back-
lash may be a recently coined phrase, but it was a virulent political phenomenon in the 1860's. The exploitation of prejudice by
the Democratic opposition was blatant and unashamed.

The power base of the Republican party lay in the North. However much party leaders desired to break through sectional boundaries to create a national image or to gain some measure of security from Southern votes, victory or defeat in the presidential
elections of the nineteenth century lay in the Northern states.
With the exception of the contested election of 1876, electoral
votes from the South were irrelevant—either nonexistent or unnecessary—to Republican victory. It was the loss of Connecticut,

Indiana, and New York in 1876 and 1884, and of those states plus Illinois in 1892, which was critical; had they remained in the Republican column, Democrats would have waited until the twentieth century to claim residence for one of their own in the White House.[2]

What has been charged to timidity might better be credited to prudence. The caution with which Republicans handled the Negro suffrage issue in 1865, 1866, and again in 1868 made political sense. Had the elections of 1866 and 1868 been fought on a platform supporting equal suffrage, who could say with certainty, then or now, that Republicans would have maintained their power?[3] In the state elections of 1867, when Negro suffrage was a major issue, the party took a beating in Connecticut, New York, Pennsylvania, and New Jersey, suffered losses in local elections in Indiana and Illinois, and came within 0.4 per cent of losing the Ohio governorship despite the personal political strength of their candidate Rutherford B. Hayes. In Ohio the issue was clearly drawn, for, in addition to the nationwide commitment to Negro suffrage in the South made by the First Re-

2. For the election of 1868, see Coleman, *Election of 1868*, p. 363. Calculations for the other years are based upon the electoral vote as given in W. Dean Burnham, *Presidential Ballots, 1836–1892* (Baltimore, 1955), 888–89. In 1872 Republicans had 286 electoral votes and would have held a substantial majority without the six Southern states and the two border states which were included in the total. Republicans could have won in 1876 without the 19 contested votes of Florida, Louisiana, and South Carolina had they retained either New York (35 votes) or both Connecticut (6) and Indiana (15). In the elections of 1880, 1884, 1888, and 1892, the Republican candidate gained no electoral votes from any former slave state. In 1884, as in 1876, either the New York vote or a combination of those of Indiana and Connecticut would have won the election for the Republicans. In 1892 the electoral count was 277 Democratic, 145 Republican, and 22 Populist. Republicans needed an additional 78 votes for a majority, which could have come from New York (36), Illinois (24), Indiana (15), and Connecticut (6). The party kept Pennsylvania and Ohio (except for one vote); it had not held New Jersey (10 votes) since 1872.
3. More than a simple majority would have been necessary to retain control of Reconstruction in the face of President Johnson's vetoes and to pass the Fifteenth Amendment. Johnson supporters welcomed Negro suffrage as an issue on which they expected to redress their 1866 defeat.

construction Act of March 1867, the Republican party bore
responsibility for a state-wide referendum on behalf of equal
suffrage at home. The proposed suffrage amendment to the state
constitution went down to defeat with less than 46 per cent of
the votes cast. Democrats gained control of both houses of the
state legislature, turning a comfortable Republican margin of
forty-six into a Democratic majority of eight. Even judged by
the gubernatorial vote, Republicans suffered a serious loss of support, for the popular Hayes gained 50.3 per cent of the vote as
compared to 54.5 per cent won by the Republican candidate
for secretary of state in 1866.

There was nothing exceptional about Ohioans' hostility to
Negro suffrage. In Republican Minnesota and Kansas equal-
suffrage amendments also went down to defeat in the fall elections of 1867, with a respectable 48.8 per cent of the vote in the
former but with less than 35 per cent in the latter despite the
fact that Kansas Repubilcans in the 1860's constituted 70 per
cent of the electorate. From 1865 through 1869 eleven referendum votes were held in eight Northern states on constitutional
changes to provide Negroes with the ballot; only two were successful—those held during the fall of 1868 in Iowa and Minnesota. The Minnesota victory, gained after two previous defeats,
has been attributed to trickery in labeling the amendment. The
issue was never placed before the white voters of Illinois, Indiana,
Pennsylvania, or New Jersey; and this fact probably indicated a
higher intensity of race prejudice than in Connecticut, New York,
and Ohio, where equal suffrage was defeated.[4] These seven were
marginal states of critical importance to the Republicans in national elections. The tenacity of opposition to Negro enfranchisement is well illustrated in New York, where one might have expected to find it minimal since Negroes had always voted in the
state although subjected to a discriminatory property qualification
since 1821. After a Republican legislature ratified the Fifteenth

4. The other two states where equal suffrage was defeated were Wisconsin
and Michigan.

Amendment in April 1869, New Yorkers defeated a similar change in the state constitution, swept the Republicans out of control at Albany and returned a Democratic majority of twenty, which promptly voted to rescind New York's ratification.

In short, Republican sponsorship of Negro suffrage meant flirtation with political disaster in the North, particularly in any one or all of the seven pivotal states where both the prejudice of race and the Democratic opposition were strong. Included among them were the four most populous states in the nation, with corresponding weight in the electoral college: New York, Pennsylvania, Ohio, and Illinois. Negroes were denied equal suffrage in every one of these critically important seven, and only in New York did they enjoy a partial enfranchisement. If Negroes were to be equally enfranchised, as the Fifteenth Amendment directed, it is true that Republicans could count upon support from an overwhelming majority of the new voters. It does not necessarily follow, however, that this prospect was enticing to "shrewd politicians." What simple political computation could add the number of potential Negro voters to be derived from a minority population that reached a high of 3.4 per cent in New Jersey and 2.4 per cent in Ohio, then diminished in the other five states from 1.9 to 1.1 per cent, a population already partially enfranchised in New York and to be partially disenfranchised in Connecticut by the state's nondiscriminatory illiteracy tests; determine and subtract the probable number of white voters who would be alienated among the dominant 96.6 to 98.9 per cent of the population; and predict a balance that would ensure Republican victory?

The impact of the Negro suffrage issue upon the white voter might be softened by moving just after a national election rather than just before one; and this was the strategy pursued in pushing through the Fifteenth Amendment. Yet risk remained, a risk which it is difficult to believe politicians would have willingly assumed had their course been set solely, or primarily, by political arithmetic. Let us, then, consider the nature of the evidence cited

to show that Republican policy sprang from narrow party interests.

Since the days of Braxton, historians have used the public statements of public men, straight from the pages of the *Congressional
Globe*, not only to document the charge of party expediency but
also to prove it by the admission of intent. The frequency with
which either Senator Charles Sumner or Thaddeus Stevens has
been quoted on the arithmetic of Negro enfranchisement might
well have suggested caution in using such oral evidence for establishing motivation. As craftsmen, historians have been alerted
against a proclivity to seize upon the discovery of an economic
motive as if, to quote Kenneth Stampp, they then were "dealing
with reality—with something that reflects the true nature of man."
Stampp cites Sumner as an example of the fallacy: ". . . when he
argued that Negro suffrage was necessary to prevent a repudiation
of the public debt, he may *then* have had a concealed motive—
that is, he may have believed that this was the way to convert
bondholders to his moral principles." An equal sophistication is
overdue in the handling of political motivation. With reference
to the Reconstruction legislation of 1867, Sumner did state—
frankly, as the cynically inclined would add—that the Negro
vote had been a necessity for the organization of "loyal governments" in the South. He continued with equal forthrightness:
"It was on this ground, rather than principle, that I relied most.
. . ." A man remarkably uncompromising in his own adherence
to principle, Sumner obviously did not believe it wise to rely
upon moral argument alone to move others. Thaddeus Stevens's
belief in the justice of equal suffrage and his desire ·to see it
realized were as consistent and genuine as Sumner's own, but
Stevens was a much shrewder practitioner of the art of politics. It
is worth noting, then, that Negro suffrage was not the solution
to which he clung most tenaciously in order to guarantee "loyal
governments" in the South; he looked more confidently to the
army and to white disfranchisement. In the last critical stage of
battle over Reconstruction policy, it was the moderate Repub-

licans who championed an immediate mandate for Negro suffrage in the South, while Stevens led the fight to delay its advent in favor of an interlude of military rule.

All this suggests the need for a detailed analysis of who said what, when, in arguing that Negro suffrage, South or North, would bring Republican votes and Republican victories. Did the argument have its origin with the committed antislavery men or with the uncommitted politician? Was it used to whet an appetite for political gain or to counter fear of losses? Such a study might start by throwing out as evidence of motivation all appeals to political expediency made after the Fifteenth Amendment was sent to the states for ratification. By that time Republicans were tied to the policy and could not escape the opprobrium it carried; a leadership that used every possible stratagem and pressure to secure ratification in the face of widespread opposition could be expected to overlook no argument that might move hesitant state legislators, particularly one that appealed to party loyalty and interest.

It has been implied that election results in the 1870's and 1880's were evidence of political motivation behind the Fifteenth Amendment. The logic is faulty. Consequences are not linked causally to intentions. Favorable election returns would not constitute proof that decision-making had been dependent upon calculation, nor would election losses preclude the existence of unrealistic expectations. Yet it would be of interest to know the effect of the enfranchisement of Negroes upon Republican fortunes, particularly in the marginal Northern states. Election returns might serve to test the reasonableness of optimistic projections of gain by adding black voters, as against the undoubted risk of losing white voters. If the end result of Negro enfranchisement in the North was one of considerable advantage to Republicans, we may have overestimated the element of political risk. If enfranchisement brought the Republicans little benefit, the case for a careful re-examination of Republican motivation is strengthened. Inquiry can reasonably be restricted to the results

of presidential and congressional contests, since these were of
direct concern to the Republicans in Congress responsible for the
Fifteenth Amendment.[5]

Negro votes in the critical Northern states were not sufficient
to ensure victory in three of the six presidential elections following ratification of the Fifteenth Amendment in 1870. For purposes of comparing the "before" and "after" vote, the election of
1872 is unfortunately of no utility. Horace Greeley proved so
weak a Liberal Republican-Democratic candidate that in every
one of the critical seven states Grant would have won without
a single Negro ballot.[6] In the 1876 contest, which affords the best
comparison with 1868, the Republican percentage of the vote
dropped in every one of the marginal states, four of which were
lost to the Democrats. Comparison of the number of Republican
losses in the seven states for the three elections before 1872 with
those for the three elections after 1872, shows four losses in the
earlier period as against nine losses after Negro enfranchisement.[7]
Of course, it could be argued that Republicans would have done
even worse without the Negro vote and the politicians in 1869
could not have anticipated the depression of 1873. Politicians
would have known, however, that Negroes in the North, outside
the border states, were too few to constitute a guarantee of victory

5. Local elections did, of course, have consequences for senators, who were
elected by state legislatures; and a shift of political fortune in a critical state
was always of national interest. However, the Fifteenth Amendment was not
generated from local politics. The argument of political expediency implies
political profit in national elections.
6. The percentage of Negroes in the population as compared with the percentage margin of victory in 1872 follows: Connecticut, 1.8 per cent with 2.4;
New York, 1.2 per cent with 3.1; Pennsylvania, 1.9 per cent with 12.1; New
Jersey, 3.4 per cent with 4.4; Ohio, 2.4 per cent with 3.2; Indiana, 1.5 per
cent with 3.2; Illinois, 1.1 per cent with 6.2. The Negro percentage is from
Gillette's convenient chart, Right to Vote, 82; the percentage of the Republican vote was calculated from the election figures in Burnham, Presidential
Ballots, as was that of 1868 and 1876.
7. Before 1872: New Jersey in 1860 (in part), 1864, and 1868, and New
York in 1868. After 1872: Connecticut, New York, and Indiana in 1876 and
1884; New Jersey in 1876, 1880, and 1884.

in the face of any major adversity. In 1880 and 1888, years of success, Republicans might have lost Indiana without the Negro, but they would not have lost the Presidency. The only presidential contest in the nineteenth century in which Negro voters played a critical role was that of 1876, and the voters lived not in the North but in the South. Analysis of ballots in the 1870's and 1880's does not confirm the reasonableness of expectations for a succession of Republicans in the White House as the result of Negro enfranchisement.

As to Congress, Republicans could hope to gain very little more than they already held in 1869. Of thirty-six Democrats seated in the House of Representatives from the seven marginal states, only four came from districts with a potential Negro electorate large enough to turn the Republican margin of defeat in 1868 into a victory.[8] Of the four, Republicans gained just one in 1870, in Cincinnati, Ohio. Their failure to profit from the Negro vote in the Thirteenth District of Illinois, located at the southern tip of the state, is of particular interest. The district had gone Republican in 1866 and had a large concentration of Negro population. In 1868 the Republican share of the vote had been a close 49.1 per cent; in 1870 it actually decreased with the Democratic margin of victory rising from 503 to 1,081. In the two counties with the highest proportion of Negroes to whites, over 20 per cent, a jump in the Republican percentage plus an increase in the actual number of Republican votes cast—unusual in a nonpresidential year—indicate that Negroes exercised their new franchise. How-

8. The four were the Second District in New Jersey, the First in Ohio, the Sixth in Indiana, and the Thirteenth in Illinois. This conclusion is based upon an inspection of election returns as reported in the *Tribune Almanac*, comparing the margin of victory for Democratic winners in 1868 with an approximation of the number of potential Negro voters estimated as one-fifth of the Negro population in the counties comprising each district. Population figures were taken from the *Ninth Census of the United States*, 1870 (Washington, 1872). Districts where Republican candidates were seated as the result of a contest were not counted as Democratic even though a Democratic majority was shown in the *Tribune Almanac* election returns.

ever, this apparently acted as a stimulus for whites to go to the polls and vote Democratic. In three of the five counties in the district where Negroes constituted over 5 per cent of the population, more Democratic votes were recorded in 1870 than in 1868.[9]

The Republicans did better in holding seats won by slim margins in 1868 than in winning new ones. Eighteen congressional districts in the critical seven states had gone to Republicans by a margin of fewer than five hundred votes. Of these, Republicans retained fourteen and lost four to the Democrats in 1870.[10] Three of the four districts lost had a potential Negro electorate large enough to have doubled the Republican margins of 1868. The record of voting in congressional elections from 1860 through 1868 in the fourteen districts retained suggests that half might have remained Republican without any benefit of the Fifteenth Amendment.[11] It is doubtful whether three of the other seven, all districts in Ohio, would have been placed in jeopardy had Negro suffrage not been raised as an issue in 1867 both at home and in Washington, for the margin of victory dropped sharply from 1866

9. That Negroes were responsible for the increase in the Republican vote cannot, of course, be proved but appears highly probable; similarly, the explanation for the larger Democratic vote is inference. The Republican vote in Alexander County with a Negro population of 21.73 per cent rose from 656 to 804 (37.8 to 45.6 per cent); in Pulaski with a Negro population of 27.4 per cent from 543 to 844 (46 to 55.59 per cent). The three counties showing an increase in the number of Democratic votes were Jackson (Republican votes increased there also), Massac, and Pulaski.

10. Districts lost were the Sixteenth Pennsylvania, the Third and Fourth Ohio, and the Seventh Indiana. Districts retained were the Second Connecticut, the Eleventh and Twelfth New York, the Third, Fifth, Tenth, and Thirteenth Pennsylvania, and Fourth New Jersey, the Second, Sixth, Seventh, Fourteenth, and Sixteenth Ohio, and the Fourth Indiana.

11. This tentative conclusion is based upon Republican victories in at least four of the five congressional elections before 1870. The winner in 1860 had to be estimated on the basis of the county vote because district boundaries were changed in 1862. In only one of the seven had the margin of Republican victory in 1866 been less than five hundred. This district, the Fifth in Philadelphia, may have needed Negro votes for victory in 1870 despite its Republican record. Together with it, the Thirteenth in Pennsylvania and the Fourth in Indiana had slim majorities in 1870. In the latter two, however, the margin decreased as compared with 1868, making it unlikely that Negro enfranchisement helped more than it hurt the Republican candidates.

to 1868.[12] One of the remaining four, the Second District in Connecticut, consisted of two counties, Middlesex with a Negro population of 372 and New Haven with 2,734, the largest concentration of Negroes in the state. New Haven had gone Democratic in
1869 (Connecticut elected its congressmen in the spring) by 62
votes, though the Republican won the district; two years later,
with Negroes enfranchised, the Democratic margin in New Haven actually increased to 270! Middlesex saved the day for the incumbent, who barely survived by 23 votes. This suggests that the
district remained Republican not because of Negro enfranchisement, but despite it. Two seats, one in Pennsylvania and the
other in New Jersey, were retained by an increase in the margin of
victory larger than the number of potential Negro voters.[13] The
last of the fourteen districts, the Eleventh of New York, consisting of Orange and Sullivan counties, may have been saved by
Negro voters, although the election results there are particularly
difficult to interpret.[14]

If we consider the total picture of the 1870 congressional races,
we find that the Republican share of the vote decreased in five of
the seven critical states, remained practically constant in Ohio,
and increased in New Jersey. The party did best in the two states
with the highest percentages of Negroes in their population,

12. In every one of the seven close Ohio districts, the majority vote had been
against the state's Negro suffrage amendment in 1867. Their congressmen,
however, supported Negro suffrage, all having voted for the First Reconstruction Act of March 1867, and also for Negro suffrage in the District of
Columbia on January 18, 1866, and again on December 14, 1866. These
men, each of whom served both in the Thirty-ninth and Fortieth Congresses
(1865–1869) were Rutherford B. Hayes, Robert C. Schenck, William Lawrence, Reader W. Clarke, Samuel Shellabarger, Martin Welker, and John A.
Bingham.
13. The Tenth District in Pennsylvania, made up of Lebanon and Schuylkill
counties, had a Negro population of 458, or about 90 potential voters. The
Republican margin increased by 404 votes. The Fourth District in New Jersey
had a larger Negro population, but the incumbent's margin jumped from 79
to 2,753.
14. The Republican incumbent lost in 1868 by 322 votes but contested the
outcome and was seated. In 1870 another Republican won by 500 votes.
There were 2,623 Negroes, somewhat more than 500 possible voters, of whom
some would have qualified under the old freehold requirement.

Ohio and New Jersey, netting one additional seat in each. However, in the seven states as a whole Republicans suffered a net
loss of nine representatives. Democrats gained most in New York
and Pennsylvania, almost doubling their congressional delegation in the latter from six to eleven out of a total of twenty-four.
Republicans retained control in Congress but with a sharply reduced majority. In short, results of the Northern congressional
elections of 1870 suggest that Negro voters may have offset to
some extent the alienation of white voters by the suffrage issue,
that they did little, however, to turn Republican defeats into
Republican victories, and that the impact of the Fifteenth
Amendment was in general disadvantageous to the Republican
party.

Election returns blanket a multitude of issues, interests, and
personalities. In an effort to relate them more precisely to the
impact of Negro enfranchisement, we have identified all counties
in the seven marginal states in which Negroes constituted a
higher-than-average percentage of the population. Using 5 per
cent, we found thirty-four such counties.[15] An analysis of the
number of Republican voters in 1868 as compared with 1870 and
of the changing percentage of the total vote won by Republicans
in 1866, 1868, 1870, and 1876 would indicate that Negroes did go

---

15. One in New York (Queens); three in Pennsylvania (Chester, Delaware,
Franklin); eight in New Jersey (Cape May, Cumberland, Salem, Camden,
Mercer, Monmouth, Somerset, Bergen); ten in Ohio (Meigs, Gallia, Pike,
Ross, Brown, Clinton, Fayette, Clark, Greene, Paulding); five in Indiana
(Clark, Floyd, Spencer, Vanderburgh, Marion); and seven in Illinois (Alex-
ander, Jackson, Gallatin, Massac, Pulaski, Randolph, Madison). The three
urban centers with the largest aggregate number of Negroes in 1870 did not
meet the 5 per cent criterion and are not included. Leslie Fishel has compiled
a revealing table showing Negro and foreign-born urban population: Table II,
Appendix III-B, "The North and the Negro, 1865–1900: A Study in Race
Discrimination" (unpublished Ph.D. dissertation, Harvard, 1954). For the
three cities with over 5,000 Negroes, the comparative figures in 1870 were:

	Colored	Foreign-born	Total
Philadelphia	22,147	183,624	674,022
New York	13,072	419,094	942,292
Cincinnati	5,900	79,612	216,239

to the polls and vote Republican in numbers which more than
offset adverse white reaction, but this appears to have been the
case in less than half the counties.[16] The net effect upon Republican fortunes was negligible, if not negative. Thus, in the first
congressional election after Negroes were given the ballot, three
of the thirty-four counties shifted from Democratic to Republican
majorities, but another three went from the Republicans to the
Democrats. The record was no happier for Republicans in the
1876 presidential election. Again, only six counties changed political alignment as compared with the 1868 balloting. Two were
added to the Republican column, and four were lost!

From whatever angle of vision they are examined, election returns in the seven pivotal states give no support to the assumption
that the enfranchisement of Northern Negroes would help Republicans in their struggle to maintain control of Congress and
the Presidency. This conclusion holds for all of the North. Any
hope that may have been entertained of gaining substantial
strength in the loyal border states was lacking in realism. It
failed to take into account the most obvious of facts—the intensity of hostility to any form of racial equality in communities
recently and reluctantly freed from the institution of Negro slavery. Only Missouri and West Virginia had shown Republican
strength in 1868; of the ten congressional seats which Republicans then won, half were lost in the elections of 1870. Kentucky
had the largest Negro population in the North, but in seven of
its nine congressional districts the Democratic margin of victory

16. Twelve counties showed an increase in both the number and percentage of
Republican votes in 1870 as compared with 1868; in nine of these, Republicans also made a better showing than in 1866. In 1876 twelve counties had a
higher percentage of Republican votes than in 1868. Of these, eight were
identical with counties showing marked gains in 1870. The eight, with an
indication of their pre-1870 party record, are: in New Jersey, Camden (R),
Mercer (D/R), and Somerset (D); in Ohio, Pike (D) and Ross (D/R); in
Indiana, Clark (D); in Illinois, Alexander (D) and Pulaski (D/R). The two
clear instances of contested counties turning Republican in 1870 and remaining Republican were Mercer in New Jersey and Pulaski in Illinois, the former
with a Negro population of 5.1 per cent and the latter with 27.3 per cent.

was so overwhelming that the state could not possibly be won by the Republican opposition, and, in fact, all nine seats remained Democratic in 1870. Although no Republican had won a seat from Maryland in 1868, there the odds were better. The outcome, however, was only a little more favorable. In 1870 Republicans failed to make any gain; in 1872 they were victors in two of the six congressional districts; these they promptly lost in 1874. The pattern of politics in Delaware was similar, consistently Democratic except in the landslide of 1872.

The lack of political profit from the Negro vote in pivotal states of the North reinforces the contention that Republican sponsorship of Negro suffrage in the face of grave political risk warrants a re-examination of motive. There is additional evidence which points to this need. Circumstances leading to the imposition of unrestricted Negro suffrage upon the defeated South are not consistent with an explanation based upon party expediency. Two detailed accounts of the legislative history of the Reconstruction Act of March 2, 1867, have recently been written, one by Brock and the other by David Donald; in neither is there any suggestion that the men responsible for the Negro suffrage provision, moderates led by John A. Bingham, James G. Blaine, and John Sherman, placed it there as an instrument of party advantage. They were seeking a way to obtain ratification of the Fourteenth Amendment, which the Southern states had rejected, and to restore all states to the Union without an indefinite interval of military rule or the imposition of more severe requirements.

The nature of the Fifteenth Amendment also suggests the inadequacy of the view that its purpose was to make permanent Republican control of the South. The amendment did not constitute a guarantee for the continuance of Radical Republican regimes, and this fact was recognized at the time. What it did was to commit the nation, not to universal, but to *impartial* suffrage. Out of the tangle of legislative debate and compromise there had emerged a basic law affirming the principle of nondiscrimination. A number of Republican politicians, South and

North, who measured it in terms of political arithmetic, were not happy with the formulation of the amendment. They recognized that under its provisions the Southern Negro vote could be reduced to political impotence by literacy tests and other qualifications, ostensibly equal.

If evidence of Republican concern for the principle of equal suffrage irrespective of race is largely wanting in histories dealing with Negro enfranchisment, it may be absent because historians have seldom considered the possibility that such evidence exists. With the more friendly atmosphere in which recent scholarship has approached the Radicals of Reconstruction, it has become apparent that men formerly dismissed as mere opportunistic politicians—"Pig Iron" Kelley, Ben Wade, Henry Wilson— actually displayed in their public careers a genuine concern for the equal status of the Negro. It is time to take a fresh look at the Republican party record as a whole. For example, let us reconsider the charge that Republicans were hypocrites in forcing equal suffrage upon the South at a time when Northern states outside New England did not grant a like privilege and were refusing to mend their ways. Aside from disregarding the sequence of events which led to the suffrage requirement in the legislation of 1867, this accusation confuses Republicans with Northerners generally. In the postwar referendums on Negro suffrage, race prejudice predominated over the principle of equality but not with the consent of a majority of Republican voters. Thus the 45.9 per cent of the Ohio vote for Negro suffrage in 1867 was equivalent to 84.6 per cent of the Republican electorate of 1866 and to 89 per cent of the Republicans who voted in 1867 for Rutherford B. Hayes as governor.[17] In truth, Republicans had

17. Republican support in Kansas was the weakest, with the 1867 referendum gaining only 54.3 per cent of the vote for the party's candidate for governor the previous year. In the 1867 defeat for Negro suffrage in Minnesota, the proposal had the support equal to 78.7 per cent of those voting for the Republican governor. The 1865 vote on the constitutional proposal in Connecticut amounted to 64 per cent of the vote for the Republican candidate for governor; that in Wisconsin, to 79 per cent of the Republican gubernatorial

fought many lost battles in state legislatures and in state referendums on behalf of Negro suffrage. What is surprising is not
that they had sometimes evaded the issue but that on so many
occasions they had been its champion. Even the most cynical of
observers would find it difficult to account for all such Republican effort in terms of political advantage. What need was there in
Minnesota or Wisconsin or Iowa for a mere handful of potential
Republican voters? In these states, as in others, the movement to
secure the ballot for Negroes antedated the Civil War and cannot be discounted as a mere maneuver preliminary to imposing
Negro suffrage upon a defeated South.

Historians have not asked whether Republicans who voted for
the Fifteenth Amendment were acting in a manner consistent
with their past public records. We do not know how many of
these congressmen had earlier demonstrated, or failed to demonstrate, a concern for the well-being of free Negroes or a willingness publicly to support the unpopular cause of Negro suffrage.
The vote in the House of Representatives in January 1866 on the
question of Negro suffrage in the District of Columbia offers an
example of neglected evidence. The issue was raised before a
break had developed between President Johnson and Congress; it
came, in fact, at a time when an overwhelming majority of Republicans accepted the President's decision not to force Negro
suffrage upon the South, even a suffrage limited to freedmen who
might qualify by military service, education, or property holding. In other words, this vote reflected not the self-interest but
the conscience of Republicans. They divided 116 for the measure, 15 against, and 10 recorded as not voting. In the next Congress, which passed upon the Fifteenth Amendment, support for
that measure came from seventy-two representatives elected from
Northern states which had not extended equal suffrage to Negroes. Were these men acting under the compulsion of politics

vote. New York rejected equal suffrage in 1869 with supporters equaling 60
per cent of the 1868 Republican vote for governor and 80 per cent of the
party's 1869 vote for secretary of state.

or of conscience? More than half, forty-four in all, had served in the House during the previous Congress. Every one of the forty-four had voted in favor of Negro suffrage for the District of Columbia. Why can they not be credited with an honest conviction, to use the words of a New York *Times* editorial, "that a particular color ought not of itself to exclude from the elective franchise . . . ?"

The motives of congressmen doubtless were mixed, but in a period of national crisis when the issue of equality was basic to political contention, it is just possible that party advantage was subordinated to principle. Should further study rehabilitate the reputation of the Republican party in respect to Negro suffrage, it would not follow that the 1860's were a golden age dedicated to the principle that all men are created equal. During the years of Civil War and Reconstruction, race prejudice was institutionalized in the Democratic party. Perhaps this very fact, plus the jibes of inconsistency and hypocrisy with which Democrats derided their opponents, helped to create the party unity that committed Republicans, and through them the nation, to equal suffrage irrespective of race.

Reconstruction: A Local View

The South Carolina Politicos

by Joel Williamson

World events have seriously undermined American mythology in recent decades, and one of the prominent casualties has been the national image of Reconstruction in the South. Having themselves undertaken to occupy and "reconstruct" Germany and Japan following World War II, Americans could no longer view the Southern experience as unique. Nor did growing knowledge of the usual manner in which victors dealt with vanquished in modern civil wars—whether in Russia, Spain, China, Cuba, or elsewhere—support the contention made by previous generations of American historians that Northern treatment of the South had been harsh beyond measure. The images conjured up by such films as "The Birth of a Nation" or "Gone With the Wind," which portrayed an entire region under the oppressive thumb of rapacious Radical carpetbaggers and bestial freedmen, seem from today's perspective more a product of desire than memory. There never was any Black Reconstruction, and the notion that "black excesses" turned Radical rule into a nightmare for the South endures largely as a monument to America's national neurosis—racism.

In light of the Black Revolution of the 1960's which helped produce changing American racial attitudes, changes already well underway in the academic community have undertaken a more thorough and less mythical assessment of the Negro's role during Reconstruction. No longer treating blacks solely as objects of fear and abuse, more sympathetic scholars have begun probing the manner in which Negroes experienced their new freedom. They have found that although blacks clearly did not dominate Reconstruction, they were much more than merely subservient and unwitting tools of ruling, white politicians. Despite the humble post-emancipation status of most Southern Negroes as landless farmers, the Fifteenth Amendment had promised Constitutional protection for their right to vote. In every Southern state under Radical rule, politicians eagerly competed for their ballots. Local Southerners or Northern emigrants, many of them black, often wrestled for power among themselves in the name of principle, economic privilege, or simple plunder—and all needed votes.

One of the period's most undeniably tragic aspects concerned the aborted development of a Negro leadership class, particularly in state and local politics. By the time the South had reverted completely to conservative white domination in 1877, the Negro's political leaders had either fled the South or been silenced. In the following selection, Joel Williamson describes the development of such a group and the problem it faced during the Reconstruction period in South Carolina.

The alliance of Negroes with the Republican party was a logical outgrowth of the pursuit by individuals of their own interests. Yet, some allowance must be made for the leadership that focused and organized the political energy of the Negro masses. The men who supplied this leadership and the manner in which they pursued their objectives are the subjects of this chapter.

The traditional story that Radical Republicans in the North dispatched paid organizers to South Carolina to encourage Ne-

From Joel Williamson, *After Slavery: The Negro in South Carolina During Reconstruction, 1861–1877* (Chapel Hill: University of North Carolina Press, 1965), pp. 363–83, 387–92, 394, 416–17. Reprinted by permission; footnotes omitted.

groes to claim their political rights and join the Republican party only after they plotted to pass the first Reconstruction Act is a patent exaggeration. Actually, Republican organization in South Carolina began during the war. As if by deliberate selection, the great majority of Northern civilians and the higher officers of the military who came to the Sea Islands before the surrender were of the Republican persuasion. In 1864, Republicans on the islands were well enough organized to send a delegation to the national convention of the party and in the following year to elect the Radical editor of the Beaufort *Free South*, James G. Thompson, to the otherwise all-Democratic state constitutional convention which met at Johnson's call. Many of these Sea Island Republicans were abolitionists who, after emancipation, passed on to Radicalism. Before 1867, however, most of them were much more avid in pursuing their professions than in organizing potential Negro voters as Republicans.

The tradition also asserts that governmental employees, military officials, and, particularly, the agents of the [Freedmen's] Bureau were hand-picked Republican emissaries. Assuming that subsequent political prominence would mark most such people, this, too, is clearly untrue. Indeed, with the exception of the educational department of the Bureau, less than a dozen Republican leaders emerged from the hundreds thus employed. Albert Gallatin Mackey, Daniel T. Corbin, and Charles P. Leslie were the only federal officials who took leading parts in organizing Republicanism in South Carolina. Mackey, a native Charlestonian and a persistent Unionist, received the choicest post in the state— that of collector of the port of Charleston. Mackey became the very able presiding officer of the convention that drafted the Constitution of 1868. Corbin, a Vermonter who had been a captain of Negro troops during the war, became the federal district attorney after the war. Corbin acted as a legal adviser to the Constitutional Convention of 1868, was a perennial senator from Charleston, and remained an active Republican leader in the state long after Redemption. Leslie came to the state as a collector of internal·revenue. By the spring of 1867, however, when he emerged an active Republican, he had already left the service of the treasury department and was eminently unsuccessful as a planter in Barnwell District.

The military was even less political. From early 1866 into the summer of 1867, the commanding general was Daniel Sickles, a close personal friend of Orr. Sickles's relief, E. R. S. Canby, evinced a mild Republicanism which even the native whites found inoffensive. Only two officers in the entire command became active Republicans. One of these, a Colonel Moore who commanded the Sixth Infantry, was relieved after appearing at several political meetings in the Columbia area. The other, A. J. Willard, pursued a peculiar political career. A New York lawyer who came South as the lieutenant-colonel of a Negro regiment, he remained to become a legal adviser to the commanding general. In 1867, he was given the duty of registering voters in the two Carolinas. There is no indication that he was an active Republican until after he was seated on the supreme court bench by the first Republican legislature.

Outside of its educational division, the Bureau was hardly more political. Saxton had never been able to make an abolitionist stronghold out of his various commands. His successor in the Bureau, Scott, became the first Republican governor and laid the Bureau open to the obvious charge. Yet, the Bureau under Scott was as often accused of anti-Republicanism as otherwise. Indeed, his staff seemed to tend away from Republicanism and certainly from Radicalism. "They are often more pro-slavery than the rebels themselves," scandalized Laura Towne, "and only care to make the blacks work. . . ." Leaving aside its educators and Scott, only three Bureau agents were active Republican organizers. R. C. De Large and Martin Delany held minor offices in the Bureau, and J. J. Wright was Scott's legal adviser.

It is true that before the passage of the first Reconstruction Act South Carolina Negroes were not organized by and as Republicans in any significant degree. They were, however, or-

ganized *for* Republicanism. They were associated in such a way
that when they were enfranchised, the establishment of the party
amounted to little more than formalizing a pattern which already
existed. The elements most responsible for this pre-conditioning
of the Negro voter-to-be were the Bureau schools, the Northern
churches, and the native Negro leadership. Moreover, these three
sources supplied a ready-made core of chiefs to South Carolina
Republicanism.

Many early Republican leaders found their first postwar employment in the educational division of the Bureau. Reuben Tomlinson, a Pennsylvania Quaker who had been among the first
experimenters to come to the Sea Islands during the war, was
for nearly three years the Bureau's superintendent of education
in South Carolina. In the summer of 1868, he took a seat in the
first Republican legislature. Two of Tomlinson's assistant super-
intendents, Whittemore and Randolph, were front rank leaders
in the organization of the state's Republicans. Whittemore was
particularly influential in the northeastern quarter of the state,
represented Darlington in the Constitutional Convention of 1868,
and became the first Republican congressman elected in that
area. Randolph was active in the vicinity of Orangeburg and was
that county's first Republican state senator. A number of North-
ern-born Negro soldiers also became Bureau teachers and passed
into the Republican leadership. London S. Langley and Stephen
A. Swails were two who belonged to this class.

In addition, the Bureau recruited as teachers a host of Charleston Negroes (many of whom had been free before the war) and
sent them into the hinterland. There they did yeoman work, not
only as educators, but in imparting a sense of political awareness
to the parents of their scholars. Many of them returned to
Charleston as delegates to the Constitutional Convention of 1868.
Examples of such cases are numerous and worth close attention
because they indicate one means by which Republicanism spread
among the Negro population before they actually obtained the
vote. These examples also reveal much of the character of what

might be called the second echelon of Republican leadership in the state. Henry L. Shrewsbury, twenty-one years old in 1868, a mulatto offspring of the free Negro population of Charleston and well educated, was sent to Cheraw as a Bureau teacher soon after the war. In 1868, he returned to Charleston as Chesterfield's Negro delegate to the Constitutional Convention. Henry E. Hayne, who had also been free before the war and became a sergeant in the First South, was sent to Marion as a Bureau teacher and returned to Charleston in 1868 as the leader of the three-man Negro delegation from that district. William J. McKinlay and T. K. Sasportas went to Orangeburg from Charleston as Bureau teachers. Both were scions of free Negro families which were prominent in the trades. Sasportas was the son of a butcher who had himself owned slaves before the war. Sasportas was educated in Philadelphia, remained there during the war, and was said to be intelligent and very well informed. The work of Randolph, Sasportas, and McKinlay goes far toward explaining the large Negro vote cast for the convention in Orangeburg District in the fall of 1867 and the subsequent development of Orangeburg as the stronghold of Republicanism, Northern Methodism, and Negro education. All three of these educators returned to Charleston in 1868 as delegates to the convention. What these men did in Orangeburg was duplicated by James N. and Charles D. Hayne in Barnwell District. Offspring of the free Negro society of Charleston, the brothers probably came to Barnwell as Bureau teachers and, along with Northern Methodist minister Abram Middleton, formed the core of Republican leadership in that district. James Hayne was apparently the leader of the trio which combined with ex-slave Julius Mayer to represent Barnwell in the Convention of 1868. Interestingly, in the convention, Sasportas voted with Randolph on every recorded vote, and the Negro delegates from Barnwell paralleled Randolph's vote six out of seven times. . . .

Technically all these teachers were employed by private parties, the function of the Bureau being simply to supply the physical materials necessary. Actually, however, as superintendent of education, Tomlinson had a large degree of control over recruiting, assigning, and overseeing the performance of teachers in schools supported by the Bureau.

Also prominent in early Republican organization in South Carolina and in the Constitutional Convention of 1868 were two Negroes who came to the state as the direct agents of the American Missionary Association for the purpose of establishing schools and, hence, were closely associated with the Bureau. These were F. L. Cardozo, who was the principal of the largest Negro school in the state, and J. J. Wright who passed into full Bureau service soon after entering the state.

Of the seventy-four Negroes who attended the Constitutional Convention of 1868, certainly eleven and probably thirteen . . . came by way of their involvement in Negro schools. Even though Tomlinson did not himself attend the convention, he followed the same path into the Republican legislature. It could hardly be denied that this phase of the Bureau's program in South Carolina was politically vital.

Probably as significant in conditioning the Negro population for Republicanism were the labors of religious missionaries from the North. The real meaning of their work was that they taught and practiced a religion which did not discriminate against the freedman because of his race. . . . Many leading ministers did manage to avoid direct political participation. Many others, however, devoted themselves wholeheartedly to promoting the interests of the Republican party.

Northern Methodists were especially prominent politically. French, Whittemore, and Randolph might well be considered politicians rather than ministers, but when formal Republican organization began in the spring of 1867 they moved easily and familiarly among the Northern Methodist congregations of the state. It is no coincidence that the very areas in which Northern Methodism was strongest—Camden, Greenville, Kingstree, Orangeburg, Summerville, Florence, Maysville, Sumter, Darlington,

Aiken, Barnwell, and Charleston—were also areas in which Republican organization proceeded comparatively rapidly and successfully. . . .

At least five of the 124 members of the Constitutional Convention of 1868 were Northern Methodist ministers. At least one delegate—Barney Burton, a forty-year-old ex-slave who had moved to Chester after the war—and perhaps several others were among the 102 local preachers in the conference.

Aside from Bishop Payne nearly every leading minister in the African Methodist Church was also a practicing politician. R. H. Cain was the most successful in both careers, but there were others who were hardly less active than he. William E. Johnston of Sumter was a delegate to the Constitutional Convention of 1868 and later the senator from that county. Richard M. Valentine was an early organizer for the African Church in Abbeville and, although not a delegate to the convention, he sat as a representative in the first Republican legislature. It is virtually a fact that the African Methodists moved their 30,000 members into the Republican party as a solid phalanx.

Individual ministries in other churches were also active politicians. Altogether at least thirteen of the seventy-four Negro delegates who sat in the convention of 1868 were professional or lay ministers.

By 1867 in South Carolina, a numerous resident leadership had already evolved among Negro laymen to make the work of Republican organization easy. The coastal Negro population who had won their freedom before the end of the war supplied a disproportionately large number of top-level leaders for their race. Many of these came directly out of the Union Army to assume prominent places in their communities. At least nine members of the Constitutional Convention of 1868 had been soldiers in the Negro regiments. Three of these had been in South Carolina regiments and became active Republican organizers in the interior districts—H. E. Hayne in Marion, Prince R. Rivers in Edgefield, and Richard Humbird in Darlington. Six were Northerners who had joined the Massachusetts regiments and remained in the coastal area after the war. . . .

Negroes in the interior were not without their natural leaders and some of these appeared in the Constitutional Convention of 1868. W. Beverly Nash, a middle-aged, ex-hotel waiter who had once belonged to William C. Preston, gained national attention in 1866 by his criticism of the Bureau's activities in the middle districts. By 1868, Nash was unquestionably the chief spokesman for the Negro electorate of Richland, a position which he maintained over all rivals throughout Reconstruction. Even in the most remote districts, Negro communities pressed forward a home-grown leadership. . . .

Utilizing the ready-made organization and leadership provided by Bureau schools, churches, and the native Negro community, Republicans in South Carolina rapidly marshaled their powers. Almost simultaneously, in mid-March, organizing meetings were held in Columbia and Charleston. Early in May, Republicans from as far away as Greenville met in Charleston for the purpose of establishing the party on a statewide basis. The Charleston meeting was decidedly not representative, but it did call for a Columbia convention in July and formed a committee to accelerate formal organization in areas not represented. . . . When the referendum on the calling of a constitutional convention was held in November, Republicans were able to present a slate of candidates in each district and to muster some 69,000 votes to secure their election.

Obviously, Republican organization in South Carolina was largely homespun rather than imported as tradition maintains. However, Northern emissaries were not entirely lacking. In March, 1867, heretofore strange Negro ministers from Washington appeared in Charleston and Columbia. In May, Senator Wilson (escorted by Parson French), was circulating through the state, and "Pig Iron" Kelley was expected to follow soon. A white woman residing in Abbeville in August saw some of the lesser lights in the field. "With Rev. Nick Williams's & Armstrong's lecturing our semi-chimpangee brethren at our very doors," she wailed, "God only knows what will come, & I have decided to hide my head." A few of the lesser Northern politicos remained to participate in the constitutional convention. William N. Viney, for instance, was an Ohio-born Negro who came to the state as a paid political organizer and went to the convention as a delegate from Colleton District. . . .

In 1867 and 1868, Union or Loyal Leagues were an important part of Republican activity in the state. Possibly, Leagues had existed in South Carolina in 1865 and 1866, but it was only after the passage of the first Reconstruction Act that the organizational device was widely used. Leagues were used to indoctrinate Negroes with Republicanism, but they were also schools to instruct Negroes in their civic responsibilities. It was perhaps no accident that the first president of the League in South Carolina was Gilbert Pillsbury, a long-time abolitionist who had first headed the military's school system in the Charleston area. Negroes must have found the Leagues entertaining. Visiting his low-country plantation near Adams Run in December, 1867, The Reverend Cornish found that "Sam—the then negro boy that waited on me when I lived at the Hermitage on Edisto Island— . . . is now president of the Loyal Leage [sic] & a very influential character among the Negroes—is Sam Small——" Leagues were not always harmless, however. Sometimes they assumed a militant front. Early in January, 1868, the mistress of Social Hall, also near Adams Run, noted that the Negroes in the vicinity were well organized. "The men have weekly meetings for the purposes of drill—fife, fine dinners, uniforms, drum, flags & c. Prince Wright acting Brig. Gen., Ned Ladson (R. knows him) Colonel!" As described above, in the mountain district of Oconee, the threat passed into open violence when members of a League killed a white boy in the course of a riot and proceeded to seize control of the community. Occasionally the whites retaliated. A year after the Oconee riot, Elias Kennedy, a Negro minister living in adjacent Anderson County and well known as a League organizer, was killed while on a League mission in a neighboring Georgia town. Leagues were numerous in South Carolina, but outside of the cities they were not durable. After the heated campaigns of 1867 and 1868, the great mass of Negro voters apparently faded out of the organization. The subsequent character of the League in South Carolina was accurately reflected in the politics of their president, F. L. Cardozo, one of the most conservative Negro politicians in the state.

Far more permanent and effective than the League was the regular party organization, which had developed in the traditional pattern. The grass roots were represented by individual Republicans who met either in township or, frequently, in county conventions to nominate candidates for local offices and to choose delegates to conventions representing larger districts—counties, congressional districts, or the state and nation. Each convention chose its permanent executive committee which, with its chairman, was responsible for carrying on the party's business until relieved by the next convention. At the peak of the pyramid was the state executive committee. After 1870, control of this committee by Negroes gave them important power in the heart and core of Republican politics in South Carolina.

The character of professional Republican politicians in South Carolina during Reconstruction has often been debated. The Redeemers, who wrote most of the history of the period, damned them all. The scalawags were poor whites without character, education, or position. The carpetbaggers—except those with money —were bootless ex-officers of the Union Army and unprincipled adventurers in search of political plunder. And Negro politicians were either Northern-sprung zealots in various stages of mental derangement or ignorant and deluded freedmen who moved directly from the cotton fields into office without so much as a change of clothes. Even a cursory survey of these groups reveals the inaccuracy of such a description.

Actually, scalawags represented—in economic status, education, and, to a large extent, social standing—every phase of Carolina society. The single quality found in the backgrounds of most native white Republican leaders was a spirit of Unionism distinctly deeper than that of their neighbors. Even here, however, scalawags as a group were still in some degree representative of the community, mustering a few first-line fire-eaters in their ranks. Franklin J. Moses, Jr., for instance, had been the secretary of the secession governor and had personally hauled the United States flag down from over Fort Sumter in 1861. Some scalawags were poor. Solomon George Washington Dill of Charleston and Kershaw, by his own report, had always been a poor man and identified himself with the interest of the poor. Others were rich. Thomas Jefferson Robertson, a United States senator throughout the period, was reputedly one of the wealthiest men in the state after the war. Precisely as South Carolina exhibited a high degree of illiteracy in its white population, so too were there ill-educated scalawags. Dill of Kershaw, Allan of Greenville, Owen and Crews of Laurens, and many others apparently possessed only common school educations. On the other hand, many scalawag leaders were at least as erudite as their conservative opponents. Dr. Albert Gallatin Mackey graduated first in his class in Charleston's Medical School, and a Northern correspondent, visiting him in the book-lined study in his Charleston home, found him highly learned. . . . Doubtless some native whites became Republicans out of expediency, but it is also certain that many adopted the party out of principle. John R. Cochran and John Scott Murray of Anderson and Simeon Corley of Lexington, for instance, were Republican leaders whose principles were above reproach even by the opposition. Although none of the self-styled aristocracy became open Republicans, a fair proportion of the scalawag leadership had been accepted in the elite social circle of their own communities before becoming Republicans, and in most cases, apparently they did not immediately lose social prestige by crossing the political divide. . . .

Carpetbaggers exhibited the same degree of variety. . . . The average carpetbagger was rather better educated than his Southern counterpart of the same age and economic background. . . .

Indeed, one seeks in vain among the leading carpetbaggers for one who was ill-educated, and many of those least educated in the formal sense were, like Timothy Hurley, intelligent men of wide experience. Few political carpetbaggers were received socially by the aristocracy, but they obviously remained fully acceptable in their home communities in the North. . . .

The Redeemers' estimate of Northern Negroes in the South was nearly correct—they were zealots. Some, like R. H. Gleaves, came to further their material fortunes by business pursuits. Others, like Whipper and the lawyer class in general, probably saw a chance for personal profit in representing the claims of the newly emancipated. But, most of them came (or, having left the army, remained) primarily as religious, educational, and cultural missionaries, hoping to accomplish an elevation of their racial brothers which was not possible in the restricted and less populous Negro communities in the North. Just as the Massachusetts Negro regiments drew off the cream of young manhood from the Northern Negro population during the war, Reconstruction attracted the cream in peace.

The one thing that most native Negro leaders were not was fresh from the cotton fields. Of the seventy-four Negroes who sat in the Constitutional Convention of 1868, fourteen were Northerners. Of the fifty-nine Negroes who had been born or settled in South Carolina before the war, at least eighteen and probably twenty-one had been free. A dozen of these were Charlestonians. Nearly all had been tradesmen. Roughly two-thirds of this group continued to pursue their trades after the war and at least until the time of the convention. The remainder took service as Bureau teachers. T. K. Sasportas, Henry Shrewsbury, and others had risen to the educational level of the high school graduate in the North. Most possessed the equivalent of a common school education, while several were, apparently, barely literate. F. L. Cardozo, of course, having attended the University of Glasgow and the London School of Theology, was as well educated as any man in the state.

Thirty-eight of the delegates were clearly former slaves. The occupations of twelve of these are not known, but not one was
described as an agricultural worker. Twenty-six were trades-, professional, or business men. Eight of the twenty-six were ministers
(some being tradesmen as well), four were carpenters, two black-
smiths, two shoemakers, two had been coachmen and the remaining eight included a businessman, a businessman and steamer
captain (Smalls), a tanner, a barber, a teacher, a waiter, a servant, and a carriage maker. Most of those who were tradesmen
had pursued the same occupation as slaves. For instance, John
Chesnut, the barber, was the son of a Camden barber whose father
had been freed by the first General James Chesnut. John was born
of a slave mother and, hence, was a slave but had been allowed to
learn his trade in his father's shop. The degree of education possessed by these freedmen was not high. However, nearly all appeared to be literate in some degree, and a few were amazingly
well read. Nash, for example, could quote Shakespeare with apparent ease and obviously read the leading Northern papers.
During the war, Robert Smalls had been taught intensively by
two professional educators while he was stationed for a year and
a half in the Philadelphia Naval Yard. It is true that conservatives had considerable grounds for complaint against the ignorance of their late-slaves become legislators, but their charges of
stupidity changed with the political climate. Early in 1866, the
Camden press lauded John Chesnut and Harmon Jones as "two
intelligent freedmen" for their speeches to the Negroes denying
that the government was to give them lands and urging them to
return to work. After 1867, when John Chesnut went into Republican politics, became a delegate to the convention which drafted
a new constitution, and served thereafter in the Republican legislature, words strong enough to describe Chesnut's lack of talent
were not available.

In view of the high degree of natural ability extant among
leading Republicans of both races, it is hardly surprising that the

higher offices were filled with men who were quite capable of executing their responsibilities.

In the executive area, the abilities of such white office holders as Dr. Ensor as the director of the insane asylum and H. L. Pardee as superintendent of the penitentiary and such Negro office holders as F. L. Cardozo and H. E. Hayne withstood the closest criticism. Although he was frequently overridden by a less careful legislature, Cardozo as treasurer of the state from 1872 until the summer of 1876 (after which his office was virtually nullified by a boycott of white taxpayers) revealed the highest capacities. . . .

Even political opponents generally recognized the capacity of leading Republican legislators. South Carolina's Negro congressmen—Elliott, Rainey, Ransier, De Large, Cain, and Smalls—were usually conceded to be able enough for their posts. Though Democrats in the House scoffed, Elliott's speech to Congress on the Ku Klux was widely celebrated. Capable Negro solons also appeared in the Constitutional Convention of 1868 and in the Republican legislatures which followed. Ransier, Gleaves, and Swails as presiding officers in the Senate and Samuel J. Lee and, again, Elliott as speakers of the house were remarkably effective managers in view of their sudden elevation to their posts. There were others, like Whipper, who were virtually professional legislators and became excellent parliamentarians.

It was inevitable that combinations of intelligence, education, experience, and natural ability were in short supply among Republicans in South Carolina. After all, there were comparatively few Negroes in South Carolina who could claim to possess a high level of education or significant experience in government. In the legislature, and in local offices in many areas, there was obviously a lack of competence among Republican leaders. This absence was usually identified with the presence of the Negro officeholder.

Yet, what one saw in the legislature was obviously determined by what one was conditioned to see. . . . The more astute visitors, however skeptical they may have been of the results, invariably saw something vital in the proceedings of Republican and Negro legislatures in the state. "It is not all sham, nor all burlesque," wrote James Pike after his celebrated visit in the winter of 1873. "They have a genuine interest and a genuine earnestness in the business of the assembly which we are bound to recognize and respect unless we would be accounted shallow critics."

Conservative native whites were distressed by what they saw even before they entered the legislative chambers. . . .

The proceedings of the House particularly offended whites. In August, 1868, an upcountry editor was shocked to find seven "dusky belles" seated on the platform with Speaker Moses. A year later, another observer noted that members frequently defied the chair, conversed with debaters on the floor, and, on one occasion, T. K. Sasportas answered an argument from Representative De Large with his fist. A Northern visitor in 1874 was amazed by the lack of respect accorded to some members by others. As an instance, he noted that Representative Holmes of Colleton called on the speaker for the yeas and nays on a measure, but the speaker refused to recognize him until the vote had been announced. Holmes then rose to a question of privilege and was overruled. He persisted and other members began to cough. Holmes tried to talk over the noise. The coughing grew louder. Finally, E. W. M. Mackey suggested that someone call a doctor and the house roared in amusement, while the exasperated Holmes collapsed in his chair.

Capacity and incompetence frequently traveled side by side in the legislature, but incapacity was often glaringly in evidence among officeholders of the lower echelons. "Our letters are often lost now," wrote a resident of Camden to her son, "Adamson is travelling Agent to distribute the letters and Boswell and Frank Carter, Ned's son, are Postmaster[s] here." The cause, of course, was apparent: "In Columbia and elsewhere, they have negroes in the Post office, and I have no doubt our letters go astray." County and city officers elicited similar complaints. Much distressed, the grand jury of Williamsburg County, in the spring of 1871, charged that the county commissioners permitted the county's prisoners to roam the streets of Kingstree after the jail burned in 1867, kept no records worthy of the name, and had allowed the roads and bridges of the county (some of which had not been worked upon in two years) to become almost impassable. Further, they feared that the county poor farm was "calculated to do more harm to the County than good."

The great problem of the Republican regime in South Carolina, however, was not so much a lack of capacity among its leaders as it was an absence of a sense of responsibility to the whole society, white as well as black. In the idealistic days of the Constitutional Convention of 1868, Republicans often reflected verbally upon the fact that their work was for the benefit of all. Yet, within two months after the close of the convention, election results showed that, willingly or not, the Republican party in South Carolina was the party of the Negro and for the Negro. Within a short time, it also became a party by the Negro. This was a line which the whites themselves had helped to draw. There emerged among Republican leaders a new concept that their first loyalty was due, not to their total constituency, but to that particular Republican and Negro element which had put them into office. This attitude was evident in the inclination of Republicans to drive Democrats and native whites of the conservative persuasion completely out of the government. It was also evident in a certain superciliousness which developed among members of the party in power toward the opposition. In this atmosphere, the protests of the white minority became proper subjects for Republican disdain and, indeed, ridicule. "Please read where I have marked, and judge the class of men which composed the late Taxpayer's convention of South Carolina," Negro Congressman Rainey jeered quietly in a confidential communiqué to President Grant's secretary early in 1874. Three years earlier, while the first taxpayers' convention was in session, A. O.

Jones, the mulatto clerk of the house, suggested to his partner in a corruption-laden ring of public printers that their Republican Printing Company enter a bid for the printing of "Ye Taxpayers." "R. P. C.," he jested, "That's as effective on the State Treasury as the other terrible triad is on Radical office holders—eh?" If the opposition had no political rights, they also had no economic rights. Attacks on the property by heavy taxation and then by the theft of those tax moneys was perhaps within the limits of this new morality.

Among Republican politicos in Reconstruction South Carolina, there is no correlation between intelligence, education, wealth, experience, and competence on the one hand and, on the other, integrity. The thieves included men who claimed all or most of these qualities, as well as men who could claim none. The relationship which did exist was the logical one: among those who did steal, the most successful thieves invariably combined high intelligence and large administrative talents with generous endowments of education, wealth, and experience. Petty frauds were numerous and widespread, but the truly magnificent peculations were conceived and executed by a relatively few men, usually residing in Columbia or Charleston. However, these larger schemes frequently required the purchase of the co-operation of scores of state officers and legislators, and thus corruption was spread.

The first and always the most gigantic steals consisted simply of issuing state bonds in excess of the amounts authorized by the legislature. In the summer of 1868, the legislature sanctioned the issue of one million dollars worth of bonds to pay the interest on the state debt and to re-establish its credit. The financial board, consisting of Governor Scott and the other leading officers in the state government, was authorized to market the bonds through a financial agent, H. H. Kimpton, in New York. The authorized issue was promptly made. Probably under Kimpton's management, another million was clandestinely added. Since Scott had to sign each bond and Treasurer N. G. Parker had to

issue them and honor payments of interest, it is certain that they
were implicated in the plot, but the involvement of other members of the board is not clear. When the legislature directed the
issue of another million dollars in bonds in 1869, the fraud was
repeated. After passing and repealing an act to re-finance the debt
through London sources, the legislature repudiated about half of
the state's twelve-million-dollar debt and converted the remainder
into a single loan guaranteed by about six million dollars' worth
of "Conversion Bonds." But again the actual issue almost doubled
the amount authorized. By flagrantly misrepresenting the state's
finances and by buying and selling his own issues, Kimpton kept
the bond bubble afloat. To its authors, a part of the appeal of the
bond scheme was that it needed the co-operation of the inner
few only and did not require the wide-scale bribery of state officials. Indeed, the fewer to profit the better. Moreover, the ring
only served its own interest when it encouraged efforts at financial
reform and re-establishing the state's credit, because these displays
tended to drive up the market price and to prepare the way for
further illicit issues. . . .

There were a number of other major "jobs" pushed through
the legislature. During the first Scott administration, a group of
native white conservative Charleston businessmen combined with
several carpetbag politicians to gain, over Scott's veto, a fabulously
lucrative monopoly of the mining of phosphates (for fertilizer)
from the river beds of the state. Agent for the job was Timothy
Hurly, a Boston-born Republican who reportedly came to Columbia carrying a carpetbag containing $40,000 which he used, partly
through scalawag Speaker Moses, to win the desired legislation.

The most effective jobber, however, was always Patterson. It
appears that the Pennsylvania financier enjoyed legislative bribery
as a game. In the fall of 1871, he and his henchman, H. C. Worthington, one-time Nevada congressman, Union general, and minister to Brazil, volunteered to defend Governor Scott from a
threatened impeachment. They used $50,000 of the state's money
provided by Scott. On the morning before the vote initiating pro-

ceedings was taken, Patterson arranged the usual caucus through Rivers, who "was always looked to as a leader of certain members, about fifteen or twenty." As host, Rivers served drinks, "viands," and cigars. Patterson and Worthington attended and spoke against the impeachment. Afterward, only Patterson and Rivers were in the room. "So when Patterson saw me in the room," Rivers later testified, "he just said: 'You go and vote against the impeachment and I'll give you $200;' and I said: 'All right.'" By the same methods, and at the cost of $40,000, Patterson bought himself a seat in the United States Senate and promptly had Worthington appointed collector of the port of Charleston where both doubtless soon earned several times that amount by soliciting bribes from merchants. In the fall of 1873, Senator Patterson again lent his special legislative talents to a friend, Hardy Solomon, and succeeded in getting legislation passed to pay the obligations of the state to that merchant and banker.

There were other patterns of corruption in the legislature. Presiding officers in both houses and their clerks conspired to issue fraudulent pay certificates and to honor claims for legislative expenses which were without justification. Between 1870 and 1874, a steady source of bribe money was the Republican Printing Company, an organization administered and ostensibly owned by the clerks of the two houses, A. C. Jones, a Negro, and Josephus Woodruff, a Charleston and Columbia journalist become scalawag. Through bribery, the clerks patched together enough support to secure the contract for state printing, but actually they were constantly pressed for funds by some legislators as if the company were co-operatively owned by the members and Woodruff and Jones merely the managers. Virtually every election by the legislature elicited a rash of bribery; but there were also other forms of graft. The sumptuous furnishings of Columbia committee rooms somehow seemed to find their way into the homes of members and of attachés in all parts of the state. A committee clerk from Aiken later testified that Speaker Samuel J. Lee, a Negro also from Aiken, during one session furnished rooms for himself and his wife over a Columbia restaurant as a "Committee Room." Later the clerk saw the same "marble-top table, settees, cushioned chairs, sideboards, &c" in the parlor of Lee's Aiken home. John Williams, the sergeant-at-arms for the house, furnished rooms for himself and Prince Rivers in the same way. Williams, too, carried furniture to his Hamburg residence and transferred other pieces so that "a house of ill fame kept by a colored woman named Anna Wells was also furnished."

Corruption at the local level was less spectacular, but it was prevalent enough. In many places, e.g., Beaufort, Negro officers maintained high standards of integrity, but all too often Negroes and whites were knaves together. The grand jury of Williamsburg, looking over the books—such as they were—of the clerk of the county commissioners in the spring of 1874, found that "upon many occasions when money was received, it was forthwith divided out between the members of the board and the clerk." Further, the commissioners had drawn pay for more than the maximum number of days allowed per year; the Negro school commissioner could not account for his funds; and the county treasurer paid only such claims as he chose to honor. By June, 1874, no less than twenty-four county commissioners, three county treasurers, two sheriffs, and one school commissioner had been presented by grand juries, indicted, or convicted. During Moses's gubernatorial term, punishment was neither swift nor certain for the guilty. . . . After 1874, when reform was in the air and public peculation had become precarious, thievery seemed almost entirely halted. . . .

Cities, too, frequently fell victim to the spoilers. Columbia, which underwent an expansion of its boundaries to give the Republicans absolute control and Negro officers from mayor to policeman, suffered an increase in its debt from some $426,000 in 1872 to $620,000 in 1874, and to $677,000 in 1875. Meanwhile, Charleston's debt swelled prodigiously beyond the two-million-dollar mark.

The average Negro officeholder realized very little profit by resorting to rascality. Those who became wealthy by thievery were
few, and all the most successful were white—Scott, Parker, Kimpton, Patterson, and, perhaps, Neagle and Woodruff. These were
the men who conceived, organized, and directed steals on a statewide basis. Key figures who abetted them in their predatory operations, either as officers of the government or as lobbyists, also received substantial sums—Moses, Hurley, Leslie, Worthington,
Whittemore, Elliott, Samuel J. Lee, and Swails—amounting over
the entire period from scores of thousands to several hundred
thousand dollars each. The average Negro legislator and officeholder, however, found that the wages of sin were pitifully small.
There were only four occasions when large sums of money were
passed out as bribes; other divisions were made of the printing
money, and occasionally some office seeker was willing to buy
votes. Senators were usually paid from $500 to $5,000 for their
support on such occasions. Members of the House received much
less. . . .

The real profits of the corruptionists, large and small, were
often much less than quoted. For instance, the bond ring sold its
issues to doubtful investors at much less than par value (usually
at about sixty cents on the dollar). As more bonds flooded the
market and criticism of the government rose, good issues and bad
dropped to fractions of their face value. One issue eventually fell
to 1 per cent of its nominal value. Blue Ridge Railroad scrip,
used to pay the largest bribe bill contracted during the Reconstruction Period, circulated at less than its face value. Legislative
pay certificates, whether or not legitimately obtained, were usually
sold at a considerable discount by impecunious members of businessmen like Hardy Solomon. Such circumstances existed because
the treasury was itself perennially empty and those having claims
against it had to await the pleasure or indulgence of the treasurer.
While Parker held that position, large sums of tax money were
sent North to Kimpton to keep the bond bubble inflated by in-

terest payments on both good and bad issues. Local obligations were very liable to be neglected. After 1872, each claimant had to face the suspicious Cardozo, who soon became the bane of every corruptionist's existence by his miserly management of the treasury. The officers of the Republican Printing Company, to which a generous legislature appropriated $385,000 for the state fiscal year 1873–1874, had the greatest difficulty during the summer of 1874 in squeezing $250 to $300 out of the treasurer every Saturday to meet their minimum operating expenses. Lecturers in history are fond of titillating their classes with the story of how the Negro legislature voted Speaker Moses a gratuity of $1,000 for his services as presiding officer after his having lost that amount to Whipper in a horse race. Yet, Moses probably thought the gesture something less than generous since pay certificates, if the holder were fortunate enough to find any buyer, seldom sold at more than three-fourths of face value. Moreover, Moses probably considered it an ordinary reward for the extra duty demanded by his office, a burden which many legislatures, North and South, customarily eased by voting special compensation.

There *was* plush living in Columbia during Reconstruction. The senators maintained a bar in one of their cloak rooms in the Capitol and fine food, smooth whiskey, and the best Havana cigars were copiously available. The legislative halls, the offices in the Capitol, and the committee rooms located in privately owned buildings (many were in Parker's Hall, often spelled "Haul" by contemporaries) were lavishly furnished. Yet the bar, which was allegedly supported by the senators from their private resources, was closed to other officers except by invitation, and the enjoyment of the accommodations afforded by other rooms were usually limited to those who used them officially.

The average Negro representative came to Columbia on his own money. He roomed and took his meals—usually on credit—in an ordinary boarding house with a dozen or so other legislators, clerks, and legislative attachés. Many could not afford appropriate clothing. Hardy Solomon found one member on the street so ill clad that he took him to his store and fitted him into a suit without requiring a vote in return. Occasionally some affluent Republican might offer the favorite "oyster supper" at a local dining room, or a caucus be held in which refreshments were served; but these were rare events. Such high living as was done by the legislators was done in the barrooms and, typically, on credit. . . .

Far from a jubilee, attending a session of the legislature was for many Negro members a prolonged torture. Occasionally, political excitement ran high, as during the Ku Klux troubles and recurrently during elections. But the typical legislator followed a dull, drab, daily routine. During the mornings, he attended committee meetings or caucuses, stood on the streets or about the Capitol grounds, or remained in his boarding house. Beginning at noon, he attended a three- or four-hour legislative session, most of which were uneventful and, indeed, unimportant. In the late afternoons, he repeated the morning's performances, had his communal dinner at his boarding house, and retired. Throughout the session, he was plagued by a lack of money and by a worrying uncertainty whether he would be able to collect his pay at all, regardless of how much he voted himself, and whether he would realize from his nominal salary enough cash to meet his debts in Columbia and his obligations at home, familial and otherwise. Retrospectively, the life of the Reconstruction Negro legislator was rather monkish when compared to the annual excursions to the capital of his antebellum counterpart. . . .

If, as Chamberlain alleged in the summer of 1874, the mass of Negro voters thought that public peculation was no less wrong than private thievery, the question arises of how the thieves remained in office year after year. The circumstances suggest a series of obvious answers. First, the period of blatant corruption was actually quite short, beginning when the railroad and printing schemes got out of hand in 1870 and ending as reform pressures became increasingly strong in the spring and summer of 1874. Further, the full extent of corruption became known only after

Redemption, if then. Very few Republican officials admitted to
any robbery before 1877, and even the conservative native whites,
in the Taxpayers' Convention of 1871, certified the soundness of
Republican fiscal administration.

Rumors there were of fraud, and probably many Negro voters
realized something of the state of affairs, but Republican politicos
sagaciously chose to accentuate the positive aspects of their activities and to call the roll of the offenses of the whites. With a fair
degree of honesty, Republican campaigners could point with pride
to a legislative program dedicated fully to the Negro's economic,
educational, and political interests, and the paper pattern had at
least some fraction of reality in every county. . . .

During their first dozen years of freedom in South Carolina,
Negroes realized a progressive expansion of the meaning of their
new liberty. From slaves and quasi-slaves they burgeoned into
soldiers, farmers, lawyers, businessmen, and investors; elders and
bishops; college students and teachers; jurors, voters, and politicians; family men, Masons, and, even, criminals. In a large
measure, this growth was made possible by an outside political
power which, early in the period, expanded the basis of that
power to include the Negroes themselves. Yet, an irony of the
post-Reconstruction history of the Negro is that the very political
freedom under which other liberties were early nurtured could not
sustain itself in a period in which those liberties continued to
grow. Negro losses in the political realm were largely the result of
the effectiveness of the Redeemer campaign in vilifying Republicanism in South Carolina. The extravagant charges levied in the
report of the Fraud Committee (attested to by scores of witnesses
who were confessed participants) seemed ample by its very volume and redundancy to cover the whole body of Republicanism
with layers of slime. The numerous indictments against absent
Republicans and the apparent ease with which convictions were
obtained where the state chose to prosecute was proof enough of
the guilt of all. It is hardly surprising that many native white

contemporaries convinced themselves and the following generation that Republicanism meant "corruption," and that Negro
Republicanism meant "corruption compounded." In time, Northerners accepted the Southern argument as it applied to the South
and found in it a certain measure of relief from a sense of guilt
for their apostasy. The results were unique; the men who had lost
the war in South Carolina had won the peace. Not many vanquished can claim such a victory.

The Business of Politics

National Party Structure in the
Gilded Age

by Robert D. Marcus

After the collapse of Radical rule in the South, national political debate clustered around a group of issues that defined most partisan conflict for the next two decades. No great constitutional crisis such as Andrew Johnson's impeachment trial nor any profound moral question such as Negro suffrage troubled Democratic and Republican politicos as they haggled over the tariff, silver policy, civil service reform, and regulation of trusts. While mass immigration, urban growth, and especially rapid industrialization transformed the contours of American society, most politicians responded to the process of change largely by aligning themselves with the industrial elites who dominated late-nineteenth-century economic life. Both parties contained business-oriented factions, primarily (but not exclusively) among Eastern politicians. No clear-cut ideological divisions separated the major parties after Reconstruction, in fact, until the silver issue split them both into sectional wings in 1896, a circumstance made possible by the growth of the Populist third-party threat and three years of depression.

Some historians have argued that the remarkable cohesion displayed by both parties during the "Gilded Age" (Mark Twain's

*catchy but meaningless label for the period) simply pointed up
the hollowness of most national political contests. In this view,
both major parties had been transformed largely into mouth-
pieces of the business community, and their quadrennial struggles
for the presidency turned into sham battles. Recently, however,
some scholars have reassessed the notion of Gilded Age politicians
as business-dominated and concluded instead that both major
parties showed considerable skill in absorbing business support
while retaining a large measure of independence in political
decision-making.*

*The selection by Robert D. Marcus that follows explores the
complicated, revealing, and often surprising interrelationships between national politics and the business community.*

American political parties are what Maurice Duverger calls
"cadre parties." They have no official roster of supporters. There
are no dues to pay or cards to carry and no rigid membership requirements. Before the twentieth century, the parties had no
definable legal status, nor was there any official listing of who had
a right to participate in their nominating procedures. They were
simply, as Lord Bryce observed, "extra-legal groupings of men."
The concept of party membership had "no meaning at all" in
the American system, Duverger correctly notes. Rather one could
only enumerate in the order of their importance the political roles
men played: "the militants who are part of the 'machine,' the
supporters who reinforce it during election campaigns, the people
who take part in 'primaries,' and the citizens who vote for the
party's candidates at election." The politician, not the party
member, had the central role.

In the Gilded Age, the men we would call professional politicians did not form a distinct interest group, as reformers then and
historians since have often supposed. The professional politician

did not necessarily earn his living directly from politics (although there were many who did). He was simply the man from whatever walk of life who made a continuous identification between his own political interests and that of an ongoing organization, which in American politics has always meant a state or local organization, a "machine."

These political leaders included a large number of businessmen. The great political boss of Michigan, Zachariah Chandler, was a wealthy lumber merchant; Pennsylvania's Simon Cameron a banker and railroad director; and New Yorker Tom Platt a banker, president of a lumber company, and director of an express company. Theodore Roosevelt conceded that Boss Platt's political lieutenants throughout New York State included "the leading and substantial citizens"—bankers, railroad and traction executives, and manufacturers. Most railroad company presidents engaged actively in politics in this era; and in fields facing public regulation, such as banking and insurance, some executives like John A. McCall, insurance company president and prominent Democrat, or Chauncey Depew, railroad counsel and important Republican, held positions that depended on their political activities.

The parties also included the actors kept alive in the textbooks: the letter carriers and veterans, the customs-house tide waiters and the ward heelers, the "shoulder-hitters" and thugs, as well as the ambitious lawyers, the butchers, the barbers, and the saloon keepers. Politics was a national pastime to a far greater degree than it would be in the twentieth century, and the personnel of the parties—although one could find spectacular local exceptions —constituted a fair cross-section of the population. The same social class would not provide both letter carriers and Senators, but the parties, in sharp contrast to twentieth-century experience, reached all the way across the social spectrum.

When the politician, however wide or narrow his gaze, viewed his electorate, what he counted on most was an overwhelming party regularity. From the seventies until 1889, national elections were close, voters tended to vote straight tickets—supporting the party generally, not just particular candidates—and voting turnout was very high. Walter Dean Burnham in a careful statistical study found that between 1876 and 1896, 78.5 per cent of the eligible voters turned out for presidential elections and 62.8 per cent for off-year elections, figures remarkably high by twentieth-century standards. He also found that about two-thirds of the voters habitually voted straight tickets, with about an additional 10 per cent voting with a relatively high frequency for one party's candidates. Moreover, this electorate constituted a genuine national cross-section: poor people, rural Americans, and (with numerous and shocking local exceptions) Negroes voted along with their more affluent and socially favored compeers in a way that is no longer typical of the American electorate.

The parties of the Gilded Age continued the political system that had matured before the Civil War. Political fervor remained high for a forty-year period after the log cabin campaign of 1840: campaigns were major events offering entertainment, information, and emotional satisfaction. Then in the 1880's politicians noted a slackening of enthusiasm as "the brass band, the red light, and the mass meeting seemed suddenly to have lost their power." This mood deepened until 1892, when politicians complained that it was "difficult to tell from the manners of the people that this [was] a presidential campaign." The decline in political enthusiasm and participation gave way momentarily to a new and intense interest in the battle of the standards, but in the twentieth century American voters have failed to show the level of interest in political contests which they manifested in the past.

The closeness of elections, high turnout, and party regularity of the period seemed to be mutually reinforcing phenomena. The voters who identified with a party were—then as now—those who cared enough about the election to vote, while the expectation that an election will be close spurred both the voter to make his franchise count and the political organization to get to the polls everyone likely to vote its way. Close elections also supported party regularity by raising the cost of expressing one's dissatisfaction with the party above what most voters were willing to pay. When Tom Platt during the depression year of 1894 hoped to get New York Democrats to vote for a Republican congressional candidate, he instructed his canvassers to remind voters that they were not threatening the Democratic majority in Congress, but only serving "a warning to the Democrats that they must go slow in the passage for laws that interfere with industry." In short, Platt did not think that voters ordinarily were willing to sacrifice a possible party victory to express their dissident opinions.

These three factors—close party balances, high turnout, and party regularity—gave a particular form to presidential contests of the Gilded Age. In the twentieth century, these elections have been marked by periodic "surges" of voter participation—the result of a charismatic and prominent candidate who could bring out the potential voters not in the habit of exercising their franchise, not bound by party ties, and needed to break the stranglehold of a majority party. The election of Dwight Eisenhower in 1952 and 1956 is, of course, the best example. Gilded Age presidential contests did not and indeed could not show such a trend. Since most eligible people voted, the possibility of a radical surge of otherwise non-participatory citizens was not the usual expectation and statistics clearly indicate that it did not occur. Also, the "independent" voters who might be swayed by an especially attractive candidate were not a huge statistical quantity as at present, but a small number of usually well-to-do and college-educated men whose role as publicists far out-shadowed their size as a voting group. Moreover, neither party felt the need for a presidential candidate with the independent and individual strength of the charismatic leader when they could very well hope to win with some regular party member so long as he was "available."

After 1880, when Republican politicians began to worry about the waning of the old-time enthusiasm of the Civil War era, the party turned for the first time to a "prominent" rather than an "available" leader. James G. Blaine, with a long, colorful, and controversial national record, was a man whom we would call charismatic and whom contemporaries described as "magnetic." He had a personal following, especially among Irish nationalists, in addition to normal Republican support, and he seemed capable of re-arousing the traditional dedication among party workers.

Modern students of voting behavior have discovered that Blaine's 1884 campaign was reasonably successful in retrieving significant losses suffered two years previously in the off-year elections. But his contemporaries saw only the more obvious results: that the new strategy of appealing to voters not normally Republican led to dangerous incidents upsetting the loyalties of both new and old Republicans, and most of all that Blaine had been the first unsuccessful Republican candidate since Frémont in 1856. And as Blaine's magnetism had seemed to fail in 1884, so did Grover Cleveland's issue-oriented tariff campaign four years later. These incidents of the eighties slowed the tendency to put prominence over party, postponing for several years longer the era of the charismatic, issue-oriented national leader that Theodore Roosevelt was to inaugurate.

There is a more sophisticated explanation of Blaine's and Cleveland's failure to inaugurate the era of presidential leadership and charisma. For the nineteenth-century analogue to the "surge" election was what we might call the "decline" election. One could expect the normal party vote for virtually any reasonable candidate. But someone of national prominence was liable to have made a few enemies in his political career. He was unlikely to gain opposition votes in an age of straight-ticket voting, there were few independent surge votes to pick up, and he might keep a few of the otherwise faithful who disliked his past record away from the polls. This in fact was the only kind of swing election the era saw: 1872, when Democrats stayed home rather than vote for Greeley; and probably 1892, when a few hundred thousand Republicans must have neglected to support Benjamin Harrison, who as President had committed enough sins of omission or commission to alienate many party members. Blaine in 1884 probably suffered this "decline" effect among Republicans, but apparently compensated for it by picking up normally Democratic support from Irish-Americans. Throughout the period, Presidents found it hard to win a second term for just this reason: they had become too prominent. The unpopular Lincoln had had to create a new "Union" party and needed the good fortune of major military victories to win re-election; Grant had been equally unpopular and had had to withstand a party split, triumphing only because the opposition party split even more completely. For the remainder of the era no other leader could do it until the fundamental facts of voting behavior had changed.

The leaders of the Gilded Age have long been excoriated for their colorlessness and their failure to confront significant issues. But this accusation—which is wholly just—must be understood in terms of the voting public the politicians represented. Recent students of voting behavior have demonstrated that the questions that voters of the Gilded Age found salient revolved almost exclusively about local cultural conflicts: native versus immigrant, Protestant versus Catholic, evangelical temperance-oriented church groups versus liturgical tradition-oriented Lutherans. National politicians avoided these explosive cultural issues, capitalized on immediate circumstances such as economic downturns, and depended on close party organization. Blaine's perennial problem as a presidential candidate was his facility for reflecting the deep-seated cultural issues, especially the overriding one of anti-Catholic prejudice among the Protestant electorate. His early advocacy of national campaigns based on the tariff was not—as many have interpreted it—an effort to rearrange the politics of the age, but an attempt to move personally to a more neutral national position.

The national political results of the era show clearly that anything which detracted from the overt appeal of partisanship, such as issues or personalities, brought a decline in support. Even the third parties, the era's characteristic expression of political dissatisfaction, bear this out. They not only withheld votes from the major parties, their presence actually was a sign of shrinking political participation. They flourished in off-year elections when fewer voters turned out; in the two presidential years of the Gilded Age in which third-party movements were serious forces, 1872 and 1892, voting turnout dipped significantly. The third-party issues of reform and economic regulation by which twentieth-century historians have judged the era apparently frightened and confused the electorate of the Gilded Age, who probably were either baffled into political impotence or sent scurrying back into the comfortable and familiar world of the old parties.

The major parties rapidly moved into a modern personality and issue-oriented style in the twentieth century. But the world in which McKinley could easily win re-election and in which Teddy Roosevelt became so outstanding a national leader that he dared create a party in his own image, was one in which the electorate had wholly changed: the Republicans were the clear majority party, voter turnout had mysteriously shrunk, and "insurgency" became a major political style. It was, in Burnham's image, a newly shaped political universe, stressing well-defined issues, much independent voting, active national leadership, and the confinement of the national political family to those with a stake in society. This last came about in part by systematic exclusion, as in the case of the Negro, and in part by the elaboration of electoral machinery that made the political system more accessible to, and more controlled by, educated issue-oriented elites, and also better buffered against the vagaries of a lower class that—under the new dispensation—became increasingly depoliticized.

II

The late nineteenth century was preoccupied, in Robert Wiebe's phrase, with a "search for order." Men grasped for elements of predictability and continuity amid furious social and physical change. Politics was one area where men sought a link with the past. This theme was especially prominent in the seventies and eighties when the events of the Civil War and Reconstruction continued to provide the main topics of national debate. These issues, in stabilizing political loyalties by keeping eyes focused on a past full of familiar friends and enemies, fulfilled some of the need for order, even if this psychological advantage came at the cost of any meaningful attempt to control the world of early industrialism.

The men actively engaged in party politics welcomed and encouraged the electorate's disposition to re-live and relieve the traumas of the sixties: it helped them maintain their own order in the world of politics by keeping the behavior of voters generally predictable. Politicians could usually tell how various groups would vote. They talked, as politicians usually do, about the "Germans" or the "wheat farmers" or the "wool-growing counties." They knew roughly where there were Democrats and where Republicans. They could predict with considerable accuracy sure victories, certain defeats, and which contests would be close and require attention. This was not because they possessed insight superior to that of the politicians of other eras, but because of three related factors: the predictable party voting of the electorate, the party structure which provided them with a range and level of information that the modern politician with all his computers and survey data clearly does not have, and the forms of political indoctrination to which their electorate was exposed.

Although the men of the nineteenth century knew about sampling the close counties where minor changes would mirror what a larger voting public was doing, it was not the main prop of their information structure. Instead they relied on virtually total polling. When they wanted information about the "condition" of an electorate, in some cases over as large an area as an entire state, they got it through an attempt at a full poll of the state. The state committee chairman would request the information from his county chairmen, who would enlist all available workers to visit every voter. These workers included the postmasters in the little villages, the editors of the party paper—and rare was the small town outside the South without its Republican and its Democratic newspapers—every federal official wherever he held a post, as well as men engaged in work for the state, county, or town governments, and any of a number of businesses (street cars, railroads, banks, utilities) having extensive dealings with these governments. In short, with politics a hobby to hundreds of thousands and a livelihood or part of one to hundreds of thousands more, there was usually enough labor to conduct a full survey.

The results were impressive. The "inside polls"—those for party use, not for scare tactics—often were amazingly accurate. Politicians complained that 1892 was a particularly hard year to tell in advance how the "silent vote" tended. Yet the Indiana Democratic poll showed a statewide margin of 6000 votes against an actual victory by 6482 votes. Similarly, the chairman of the Republican state committee of Maine figured a 12,000 vote victory against a final margin of 12,531 votes. Not all polls were so accurate, but they suggest the capability of the politicians to get accurate information when they required it.

Politicians calculated their chances by handfuls of votes. They pinpointed the areas where a few votes would make the difference, and sought means to gain them. Their principal method was to stir up "enthusiasm" to bring their potential voters to the polls, or, less frequently, to demoralize the opposition into staying home. They knew what students of voting behavior have since confirmed, that campaigns rarely change voters' minds, that "a candidate's major resources should go into getting out his supporters and latent supporters and only peripherally attempting to convert the opposition." Only in very special circumstances when voter allegiances seemed to be shifting did they actually expect to convert waverers.

Their other mainstay in making up votes which their polls told them were lacking was a set of hoary but not hallowed methods, which included buying up purchasable voters, intimidating fearful ones into staying away from the polls, voting "repeaters," stuffing ballot boxes, falsifying returns, and creating imaginary voters on the rolls and producing them from out of town on election day. Some of these techniques, such as intimidation and repeating, were apparently most common in the cities; others, such as out-right vote-buying, seem to have been practiced most often in the small towns and rural areas.

There is far too much evidence to dismiss these techniques as folklore, and sensible and successful politicians were too frank about their use to discount them as factors in over-all results. Surely many an election on every level was determined by who was in the best position for perpetrating frauds. One source of political stability must have been the built-in advantage a majority party had in any given area in being able to control the election machinery, or often simply the balance of physical force at a polling place. Its importance in the South was too overwhelming to question. But in many northern localities it was crucial as well, and "election-day expenses and operations" were a large item in the party managers' organization and expenditures.

Corruption was a real factor in political calculations. Nevertheless two major qualifications must be entered to place this force into a proper perspective. As charges and counter-charges during each campaign bear witness, both parties practiced it, so that in national politics over the long run much of the impact must have canceled out. And most important of all, the widespread fraud in this era must be understood as far more a product than a cause of the close elections. No one would pay as much as $15 per vote (as Indiana politicians did in 1888) in a runaway con-test. Only because the parties were so closely balanced did chica-nery have this importance in the calculations of the professionals. Historians today tend to underestimate this factor in response to the fantastic overestimation of it by the Progressives, but an image of clean politics in the Gilded Age would be much like Sophocles's *Philoctetes* without the wound.

The electorate itself helped mightily in the politicians' efforts to keep track of it. Crucial to party regularity in the era's voting pat-terns was the delimited body of political information available to most of the electorate. Charles Sellers has argued that the flow of political information in the antebellum period was probably greater than at present, even if far less varied. This appears true of the post–Civil War period as well. Rather than a mass of relatively independent media in competition for the attention of voters, most political information came in the direct party form: newspapers were party newspapers, and political conversations, which were clearly innumerable, were among committed party members. In short, the party in each area had a far larger degree of control of the political information flow than at present, and this in turn reinforced party loyalty.

Survey data has confirmed that voters with a clear party commitment are more easily swayed by propaganda during a campaign than those who are more party-oriented. In the nineteenth century few people would be greatly influenced by outside, independent sources of political information. This naturally discouraged the production of such material. The era sported independent political journalism of a high order in periodicals such as *Harper's Weekly* and *The Nation*, but their clientele was extremely restricted and their indirect political influence through that small but select readership seems also to have been slight. The world of the magazines was the world of sensibility which, as cultural historians have repeatedly observed, was ruled by women in the late nineteenth century. Roscoe Conkling scored a direct hit when he stigmatized George William Curtis, the editor of *Harper's Weekly* and a leading civil service reformer, as a "man-milliner." Men, the politicians shouted, had party labels. The caustic Kansas Republican Senator, John J. Ingalls, berated the "new school of political philosophers who announce that nonpartisanship is the panacea for all the evils that afflict the Republican party" as "the neuter gender not popular either in nature or society." They were "a third sex."

Politics, the Gilded Age believed, was masculine, and culture feminine. Men got their information from the stump speech, the party paper, and the smoke-filled tavern and meeting room, while women read magazines and novels and attended lectures and sermons. Judging from their rhetoric, practical politicians worked hard to maintain the artificial separation between these two realms.

They attacked political independence with its attendant interest in civil service, women's rights, prohibition, and general efforts to raise the tone of politics, with a vehemence that suggests they knew their real enemy. Politics was that generation's moral equivalent of war, and politicians did not welcome a middle ground between friend and foe. The party faithful were inured against enemy propaganda, but politicians knew from experience that an independent appeal could be seductive. In 1884, for example, an Iowa Republican reported to a party leader on the "Edmunds feeling . . . at Stanwood," caused, he explained, by *The Nation*, "which has a small circulation there." Politicians rejoiced that the audience for independent political attitudes remained small and its influence limited either by standards of literacy or by the official cultural dichotomy reinforced by the ridicule of politicians. Thus did these small men make their contribution to the great bifurcation between the masculine life of business and politics and the feminine genteel culture of the age.

Everything about this picture: the party regularity, the well-coordinated information structure of both parties, and the general party control of political information started to fade in the late eighties as voting habits began to shift in one of those mysterious cycles which have come once a generation throughout the history of the republic. Politicians worried all during the eighties over slackening enthusiasm and the weakening of old means of campaigning. They experimented unsuccessfully with new forms of political organization designed to appeal to more genteel citizens. They tried one makeshift after another to catch the changing moods of restless workingmen and immigrants. As the decade advanced the old moorings began to slip everywhere. The rise of the Knights of Labor, the Haymarket affair, and Henry George's strong showing in the New York mayoralty race of 1886 sent tremors throughout middle-class America. Agricultural depression shook the countryside. People expressed their fear of the "trusts," unhappiness over the railroads rose to a crescendo, and a new concern over the dangers of unlimited immigration settled upon the land. Even the

Negroes, the most loyal of Republican groups, manifested discontent by forming a short-lived "Afro-American National League" hoping to organize the entire black community independent of the Republican party.

The off-year election of 1889 showed that this discontent had reached the parties, as long-held voting patterns gave way, especially in the Midwest, revealing a significant trend away from the Republican party. In the cycle of fluctuation into which the parties plunged thereafter, the politician found himself no longer certain of his electorate. The degree of predictability had abruptly shrunk. Previously only a limited part of the electorate had eluded the politicians' estimates. Workingmen in times of economic hardship and restive Irish voters in periods of intense agitation of the "Irish question" in the British Isles were the outstanding examples. Other groups, such as the harder-pressed farmers, had gone through various third-party romances, but in most cases this had been a measurable quantity in political calculations and Republican party managers could closely gauge the size of such movements and the probabilities of arranging fusions with them or avoiding fusions with the Democrats. But after 1889 politicians were never sure of their votes. The congressional election of 1890 showed a massive defection from the Republicans, a revitalization of the Democratic party, and the growth of the Populists. On the other hand, four years later, the Republicans scored the greatest congressional victory in their party's history. The changeability of the electorate became as much a byword among politicians as its predictability had been years before. The most astute politicians shared the general feeling of crisis that so clearly marked the nineties.

The parties' control of the flow of political information was seriously diminished as well. Suddenly a spate of utopian and muckraking books appeared and commanded wide audiences. William Allen White recalled years later the "tremendous thrill" of "the books from the late Eighties and early Nineties" that broke down the conservatism of his upbringing. The most influential of these, and the one most indicative of their place in the political

changes of the nineties, was Edward Bellamy's *Looking Backward,
2000–1887*, published in 1888. The first and most successful of
some fifty utopias committed to paper in the few years after its
publication, this pleasant—if somewhat static—utopian romance
not only sold half a million copies, it also gave rise to a network
of Nationalist clubs which Bellamy and many of his supporters
hoped would become "a party aiming at a national control of industry with its resulting social changes."

That never happened, but many erstwhile Nationalists found
their way into the People's party and then into various socialist or
progressive movements in the ensuing years. An incipient American socialist movement which, Howard H. Quint has argued,
"owed more for its inspiration to Edward Bellamy's *Looking Backward* than it did to Karl Marx's *Das Kapital*" began to show the
first signs of what many expected would be a massive political future. Leading Americans voiced hysterical fears of social revolution, and some of the most sober politicians quietly calculated the
probabilities.

The gap between culture and politics, which, artificial as it was,
men like Henry Adams despaired of bridging, slowly gave way of
itself in the nineties. The older magazines suddenly confronted
competition from newer, cheaper, and more topical journals such
as *Munsey's, McClure's,* and *Cosmopolitan.* These magazines aimed
at capturing the middle-class family audiences of the age by appealing to the father of the household, not the mother. Under
pressure of this competition, the older magazines became increasingly political as well. Ministers started to become far more vocal
in their comments on the political order while reformers in numerous localities challenged the parties and their methods in ways
similar to the more successful challenges of the progressive era.

Beneath all of this was the obvious and palpable fact that the
voters' long-ingrained habits were changing, that some kind of
vast generational shift was occurring whose end no man could see
and no man—not even Mark Hanna—could hope to guide. Politicians could only guess at the direction in which the electorate was

moving and wonder if the party system they knew was capable of containing the new populations, the new pressures, and the new demands that all parts of an increasingly interconnected society made on the political system.

National leaders had their first glimmering of this changing electorate in 1888. The old world of hard, recognizable factions had become blurred and indefinite, and the landmarks of sure Republican or Democratic states with but a few marked "doubtful" had eroded to a grey mass of marginally doubtful states stretching across the country. Yet the older mold was strained rather than broken, and party leaders, puzzled but still basically confident, pushed on in the old way, discounting the alarms of local politicians, and concentrating their resources where they had in years past. In the end, 1888 proved an Indian Summer for the Gilded Age, the last moment before the optimism of the eighties gave way to the insecurities of the next decade.

Four years later there could be no doubt of the changed world that the politicians faced. The Republican party seemed in a continuing crisis with its traditional support threatened all over the country, its national structure chaotic, and its personnel demoralized. The rise of the Populists, the growth of the Democratic party, and the unpopularity of the administration suggested an unhappy future for the Grand Old Party. Its national leadership, confused by change and riddled with discontent, seemed at a loss to adjust to the equally confused discontent of the electorate.

Yet within two years, the whole political scene had been transformed. Instead of the Republican demise which many had feared, the Democrats collapsed under the pressure of a grinding depression, exacerbated ethnic tensions, and a national administration even more unpopular than its predecessor. In 1896, both parties had to make a major attempt to accommodate the new and mysterious electorate of this period of fluctuation, although neither effort disrupted the traditional forms of national party politics.

On the surface, the Democrats made the most radical attempt to reform their party within the old identity. Behind William Jen-

nings Bryan, the silverite, anti-administration Democracy made
the old machinery labor for a new western-based coalition. With
few experienced engineers to move the levers and practically no
money to lubricate the gears, the clanking and grinding reverber-
ated across the plains and the engine never reached the farms of
the Midwest and the cities of the East, where new fuel might be
located. The Republicans, on the other hand, found nothing but
pleasant surprises when they brought out the old engine for its
quadrennial journey. Massive shifts in voter preference offered unprecedented majorities in many areas; a frightened business community turned its financial support almost exclusively to the Republican candidate; local party politicians rushed to aid the national cause that promised campaign funds and electoral success.
It was still the old machine, but fresh fuel and oil had radically
improved its performance, preparing it to lumber on into the
twentieth century.

The 1896 campaign was the first clear test of the ability of an
amorphous national party system to absorb massive changes in
political demands without great structural alterations. For certainly
the Civil War had pointed ambiguous political lessons to the next
generation. Then, new demands had seemed to fracture the parties,
although in retrospect, one is impressed with how the party system continued unchanged despite the replacement of the Whigs
by the Republicans. The men of the nineties could not see that
this would happen again—and this time without a war or a new
party. They did not know whether the parties and the whole national system would metamorphize into some strange new form,
or if its evolution was to be brief but final, like the ganoid fish,
Pteraspis, which (along with the progress in Presidents from
Washington to Grant) had cost Henry Adams his belief in evolution.

Voters and Their Roots

The Politics of Rejection

by Paul Kleppner

For two Gilded Age decades the Republican and Democratic parties competed vigorously. Neither achieved national majority status, though the Republicans generally proved more successful. Presidential contests often turned on a few thousand votes; only in three Congresses did one party control both houses, and only in two did the party that controlled Congress also capture the presidency. This near-deadlock persisted despite the Republicans' apparent electoral advantage after 1865. Smeared with the brush of treason, Democrats had to overcome the bitter heritage of Civil War. Nevertheless, the party swiftly regained strength, aided by the collapse of Radical Reconstruction and resoration of "home" rule which brought the white South back into American politics as a solidly Democratic bloc.

While the South went Democratic, New England remained just as solidly Republican. In the rest of the country the two major parties fought on roughly equal terms. Voting patterns that had been forged in the heat of mid-nineteenth century sectional division and war persisted late into the century. Each party displayed strength among urban and rural voters, wealthy and poor, working class and middle class.

Striking differences in party preference stemmed from ethnocultural and religious backgrounds, however. Thus, Midwesterners of Southern ancestry tended to vote Democratic, while those of New England origin favored the Republicans. Among first- and second-generation immigrants, who were fast becoming a major element in the electorate, Protestants from Germany and Scandinavia tended to enter the Republican fold while Catholics from Ireland and Germany found their political home in the Democratic party. As a party born out of a crusade against the nation's cardinal sin, slavery, a crusade rooted in evangelical, Protestant efforts to purify public life, the Republicans attracted Northern Calvinists, both native and foreign-born, who were alarmed over the growing influence of immigrants with "strange" life styles and mores.

The Democratic party then, committed to negative government and states' rights, had a long history of collaboration with non-WASP ethnic groups. Since Protestants often attempted to use government to impose their standards on unwilling minorities, the Democracy seemed the safest bet for Catholics. On this basis, many of them joined Southern Protestants to form a powerful Democratic coalition. Thus two very distinct groups united in one national party to defend their distinct "gut" interests.

By the 1890's, therefore, the major parties represented coalitions of mixed, often contradictory elements. Political organization brought them together in a common cause and, in the process, provided much-needed cohesion to an otherwise fragmented, though consolidating, society. Americans traditionally divided along ethnocultural and sectional lines far more than they did along class lines, a fact which produced a sobering lesson for the class-oriented politicians of the Populist crusade and the Bryan campaign of 1896. Though the economic and social crises of the 1890's might well have been expected to topple the existing American political structure, and though many thought that the election of 1896 would end in revolution, once Bryan embraced free silver, and once the Populists endorsed him, the American business community closed ranks behind McKinley's candidacy.

Radical realignment failed to materialize, and the return of prosperity ended most talk of class war. Paul Kleppner analyzes the failure of Bryan's 1896 campaign, and points up the persistence of ethno-cultural voting patterns during the crises of 1890's.

✿ After three years of depression, political parties in 1896 were forced to offer an explanation of economic events and future prospects to the voters. The repudiation of the Democracy in the state and federal elections of 1893 through 1895 created a leadership vacuum within the Democratic party. The defeat of northern and midwestern Democrats in the 1894 congressional elections shifted the leadership roles to the southern and western representatives of the party. Political leaders from these sections, responding to constituency pressures, hoped to remake the image of the party. They hoped to create a political vehicle expressive of, and responsive to, the economic demands of the semicolonial depressed agricultural regions. Aware of this sectional discontent with the eastern party leadership, William Jennings Bryan assiduously cultivated the prospective delegates to the 1896 national convention from the southern and western states. His efforts were capped with the success he had worked for; he was nominated by the Chicago convention as the party's candidate for the presidency. That nomination and the platform that the convention adopted gave the Democratic party's answer to the depression: commodity price inflation.

The Republicans had less difficulty in formulating their explanation of the depression and selecting a candidate whose image was consonant with it. Republican rhetoric following the 1890 defeats had so closely linked William McKinley with the tariff that, when that question assumed new importance, large numbers of party leaders immediately saw him as the "logical" nominee. McKinley encountered opposition from the party's eastern leaders, who were suspicious of his stand on the silver question. But through skillful utilization of his extensive network of personal contacts, and aided by Mark Hanna's organizational techniques, the "Napoleon of Protection" was able to secure his party's nomination for the presidency.

The ensuing contest was a dramatic one. As Bryan toured the

From *The Cross of Culture: A Social Analysis of Midwestern Politics 1850–1900* (New York: The Free Press, 1970), pp. 279–80, 298–315, 369–75. Reprinted by permission.

country preaching the free silver gospel, McKinley waged an energetic "front porch" campaign for tariff protection and honest money. Both were concerned not just with the audience within earshot, but with the broader one that would be exposed to their rhetoric through the written reports of their comments. The Bryan strategy was both apparent and simple. He aimed at uniting the "toiling masses" against the vested interests who oppressed both farmer and laborer. Since, collectively, farmers and urban workers constituted the bulk of the electorate, the strategic aim was pre-eminently reasonable. The crucial question is how well he succeeded in implementing his strategy. . . .

Two dimensions of the failure of the "toiling masses" to cohere in the support of Bryan's Democracy deserve consideration. First, Bryan was not able to restore even the usual levels of Democratic support. Second, he failed to attract workers and farmers *as economic groups*, i.e., he failed to produce a class polarization of politics.

Once we realize that the political configuration that Bryan envisaged did not involve an extension of the old social bases of political action but the creation of an entirely new one, Bryan's lack of attraction for traditional Democrats becomes understandable. Democratic partisan loyalties were not rooted in economic class distinctions, but in religious value systems. In election contests prior to 1896, Democratic strategists had recognized the basis of these traditional attachments and designed their rhetoric *both* to reactivate latent loyalties and to reinforce the proclivity of such voters to support the Democracy.

Current studies of political behavior demonstrate the importance of these types of appeals in a political campaign. One such study offers this assessment of the over-all effects of the campaign on the vote intention: "This is what the campaign does: reinforcement 53%; activation 14%; reconversion 3%; partial conversion 6%; conversion 8%; no effect 16%." [1] The important point to observe

1. Paul F. Lazarsfeld, Bernard Berelson, and Hazel Gaudet, *The People's Choice: How the Voter Makes Up His Mind in a Presidential Campaign*

is that the first three categories, reinforcement, activation, and reconversion, involve a "return," in one sense or another, of the voter to his traditional partisan attachment. These data also indicate the disproportionately important role these effects play in shaping the final voting intention: they sum to 70.0%.

The most obvious fact about the 1896 rhetoric is the absence of reactivating appeals. The Bryanites did not greatly concern themselves with appeals to the underlying bases of traditional Democratic attachments. On the contrary, they explicitly argued that the old bases of political divisions were no longer relevant and that they welcomed support from "old Democrats" only when that arose from an agreement with the party's new program and ideology. We should not, of course, take seriously the claim by Bryan supporters that they sought only votes motivated by complete ideological concurrence. What is important here is not the validity of the claim, but the image being projected to traditional Democrats by the fact that the claim was being made and the fact that the party's rhetoric was devoid of the customary and expected types of reactivating appeals. In brief, that image was one of a *new* and *different* Democracy. It was *not* the image of the traditional Democratic party, the image of negative government and of maximum "personal liberty." [2]

Nor was it merely Bryan's enemies, Republican or Democratic, who were responsible for projecting such an image. Indeed, Democratic organs that opposed Bryan reiterated the theme that he did not represent the traditional Democracy. Their concern with this type of theme was a reflection of their awareness of the potency of party identifications in mobilizing voters. That anti-Bryan organs

(2nd ed.; New York, 1948), p. 103, and also see Table V, p. 102, for a more detailed breakdown of its effects by categories of "vote intention in May."

2. My description of the public image projected by Bryanites in 1896 is based upon a systematic content analysis of the relevant state and national platforms, Bryan speeches, numerous excerpts of which are in *The First Battle* (Chicago, 1896), and full texts of which are available in contemporary newspapers, and of more than 1,000 pro-Bryan newspaper editorials that appeared in September and October, 1896. . . .

projected such an image to Bryan's Democracy was less important than the fact that this was *by design* the image the Bryanites projected of themselves. Their concern was not with the reactivation of *old* loyalties, but with the creation of a *new* configuration of political forces. That involved *conversion*, not mere reactivation and reinforcement of old loyalties.

Late nineteenth-century midwestern partisan identifications were not rooted in economic class identifications. Voting behavior was not signficantly determined by differences in relative degrees of economic prosperity. Bryan's appeals were directed to class awareness and designed to polarize voters along economic lines. To produce such a configuration required that large numbers of voters not only accept a new set of priorities, ones that placed economic considerations above ethnic and religious ones, but that they structure entirely new political perspectives. Essentially, Bryan was asking Democrats to view their party not as a preserver of their religious value system, not in the way in which they had seen it since the 1850's, but as a vehicle through which they could implement class objectives. In formal terms, such rhetoric was *disruptive* rather than *reactivating*. That is, its objective was to orient traditional Democrats to a pattern of values and a basis of party identifications that was specifically in conflict with their time-honored political perspective and its attendant values and definitions.[3]

Since perception is a selective mechanism, and the nature of the selectivity has partisan overtones, numerous Democrats undoubtedly drew the candidate and his program closer to their own positions. But even this mechanism was relatively *less effective* in 1896 than in earlier elections. Misperception requires a certain degree of ambiguity in the objective situation being perceived. In 1896 the objective situation was less ambiguous than usual in

3. See Talcott Parsons, *Essays in Sociological Theory* (Free Press ed.; New York, 1964), ch. viii, "Propaganda and Social Control," pp. 142–76, and especially the distinctions given on pp. 171–72; also see James O. Whittaker, "Cognitive Dissonance and the Effectiveness of Persuasive Communications," *Public Opinion Quarterly*, XXVIII (Winter, 1964), 547–55.

presidential contests. This, coupled with the disruptive impact of Bryan's rhetoric, resulted in his failure to poll even the normal levels of Democratic support.

Conceivably, however, the free silver rhetoric could have served as a reinforcing type of appeal, i.e., it could have provided partisans with a series of arguments with which both to answer their own questions concerning the current economic situation and to counter the opposing Republican arguments. By design it was intended, of course, to do much more than this. It was intended to mobilize the bulk of the "toiling masses," regardless of previous partisan identifications, behind the Bryan candidacy. As the empirical data demonstrate, it achieved neither effect. We can understand this failure by examining that rhetoric in relationship to the social context in which the voter arrived at his partisan decision.

As an economic group urban workers, even those who had previously supported the Democrats, did not respond in a disproportionately favorable way to Bryan. Historians have often explained this on the grounds that the free silver argument offered little advantage to wage earners. There is a large measure of validity in such arguments, but they usually have been posited within a faulty conceptual framework. The implication is that the voter clearly perceived the relationship between the economic effects of free silver and his own class interests. The assumption, in short, is that free silver constituted a substantive "issue" and was rejected, after considerable ratiocination, by issue-oriented voters.[4] There is no factual basis for such assumptions. This does not mean that the free silver rhetoric played no role in Bryan's rejection by urban workers. It means that we have to analyze that

4. While varying in the particular mode of their treatments, the most recent studies of the 1896 contest share this type of framework; see Paul W. Glad, *McKinley, Bryan, and the People* (Philadelphia, 1964), pp. 203–4; Stanley L. Jones, *The Presidential Election of 1896* (Madison, 1964), pp. 332–50; and J. Rogers Hollingsworth, *The Whirligig of Politics* (Chicago, 1963), pp. 84–107. For a much different type of approach, see the perceptive suggestions offered by Hollingsworth in "The Historian, Presidential Elections, and 1896," *Mid-America*, XLV (July, 1963), 185–92, and in "Populism: The Problem of Rhetoric and Reality," *Agricultural History*, XXXIX (April, 1965), 81–85.

rejection within a more useful and realistic conceptual framework.

It is of little analytical value to consider free silver as a substantive issue. But is very meaningful to consider both the money question and the tariff as ideological instruments of voter mobilization and party combat. Both were intended by party strategists to provide voters with an explanation of the 1893 depression and the subsequent economic crisis. Both were designed to offer voters a structured response to their inquiries concerning future economic prospects. In this analytical context the question of whether the tariff or free silver was the major substantive issue in the 1896 election is an irrelevant one; "The important struggle during that campaign was not over two sides of an issue, but over whether or not one issue or the other should be the primary focus of attention. . . . Each [presidential candidate] tried to mobilize voters around explanatory ideological positions with which those voters could identify." [5]

Through the free silver ideology Bryan and his supporters tried to explain both the advent of "hard times" and the process through which prosperity would be restored. The explanations, however, were not consonant with either the experiences or the perceptions of urban workers. An examination of the three major themes of the ideology illustrates the point.

The Bryan rhetoric spoke of the "crime of 1873" and emphasized that "crime" as the underlying cause of all subsequent discontent. The demonetization of silver, the act of "a corrupt and corrupting set of abominable traitors," had "assassinated labor"; it had reduced the "toiling masses" to subservience to "the interest of avarice and greed." [6] The remonetization of silver would undo this great evil and free the "common people" from the yoke of oppression by restoring the pristine virtues and social relationships

5. Samuel P. Hays, "Political Parties and the Local–Cosmopolitan Continuum, 1865–1929" (unpublished paper delivered at Washington University Conference on Political Development, Spring, 1966), p. 13, and his discussion of the importance of conceiving such "proposals" as ideologies rather than substantive issues, pp. 12–14.

6. The quotations are from the *Milwaukee Advance*, October 31, 1896, and the *Monroe Sun Gazette*, September 4, 1896.

that had characterized the earlier era. This type of explanation hardly accorded with the experience of urban workers. They attributed their difficulties, not to a long-term price decline, but to the immediate and severe impact of unemployment and wage reductions that had begun in 1893. The story of twenty years of cumulating hardship hardly accounted for this experience. Nor did the promise of a return to the relationships of a simpler, less complex social system hold out much hope for the restoration of jobs and wages. Free silver, from this perspective, was not a forward-looking, adjustive ideology, not one attuned to the growing complexity of a modern industrial society, not one addressed to the immediate problems of urban workers.[7]

When Bryan and his supporters spoke in terms of immediate solutions they used a theme equally discordant to urban workers. Commodity price inflation was the solution offered to overcome the problems of "the producers of the nation's wealth." This type of explanation bore little relationship to urban workers' perceptions. The size of the job supply was probably more salient to them than that of the money supply, and wage increases more relevant than price increases. But more important was the fact that the explanation revealed the jarringly anachronistic perception the Bryanites held of the role that the wage earner played in the industrial system. To Bryan and his followers commodity price infla-

7. The concern here is with the public image of the free silver ideology, as that image can be reconstructed through a systematic content analysis of the relevant *public* sources. This is both conceptually and analytically a much different approach from that which Norman Pollack criticizes in *The Populist Response to Industrial America: Midwestern Populist Thought* (Cambridge, Mass., 1962), p. 6. Pollack inveighs against the line of reasoning that contends that "Populism did not adjust to industrialism" and was, therefore, "unrealistic." In my opinion the argument, regardless of which side one takes, is an ahistorical one. "Populism" is an abstraction and incapable of adjustment or nonadjustment. It is only through an illogical resort to reification that historians discuss it in such terms. It is more meaningful to speak of *particular* Populists, occupying *particular* positions in the social structure from which they derived *particular*, and often quite conflicting, perspectives. The homogenization of these differences, which is an integral part of Pollack's own research design and which he has combined with an *eclectic* use of both public and *private* qualitative sources, adds little to our understanding.

tion, a producer-oriented solution, was not inconsistent with the best interests of urban workers precisely because the latter *were* producers. Their vision of what the worker *should be*, a petty entrepreneur, was some forty years out of date. The urban laborer, who had accepted the wage system and sought pragmatic adjustments within its confines, saw the normative dictum of the free silver ideology in conflict with the reality he daily experienced.[8]

The third major theme of the free silver rhetoric also created a problem of cognitive dissonance for urban workers. The Bryanites emphasized the primacy of agriculture over industry. They concentrated on the agricultural producer and his role in the creation of the moral and just society. When they turned themselves to the welfare of the urban worker, they attempted to link that directly with the welfare of the farmer. The type of nexus they emphasized was significant. The economic recovery of the farmer had to precede that of the urban worker. Bryan was doing more than displaying his oratorical prowess when, in his address before the Democratic National Convention, he claimed that "the great cities rest upon *our* broad and fertile prairies. Burn down *your* cities and leave *our* farms, and *your* cities will spring up again as if by magic; but destroy *our* farms and the grass will grow in the streets of every city in the country.[9] He was giving verbal expression to his view of the world about him, and enunciating a central theme of the free silver ideology. The relationship between urban workers and farmers that ideology stressed was more than one of mutual interde-

8. Since the 1860's laboring groups had been skeptical of monetary solutions to their difficulties; see Irwin Unger, *The Greenback Era: A Social and Political History of American Finance, 1865–1879* (Princeton, 1964), pp. 94–114 and 181–90.

9. The quotation is from Bryan, *The First Battle*, p. 205, I have added the emphasis. The divergent perspectives that rural and urban "reformers" held created tensions even at the leadership level; see J. H. Berker, August 27, 1894, James P. Corse, September 3, 1894, and L. B. Howrey, September 7, 1894, all to T. C. Richmond, in Richmond MSS, State Historical Society of Wisconsin; Chester McArthur Destler, "Consummation of a Labor–Populist Alliance in Illinois, 1894," *Mississippi Valley Historical Review*, XXVII (March, 1941), 589–602; and William F. Zornow, "Bellamy Nationalism in Ohio, 1891 to 1896," *Ohio History*, LVIII (April, 1949), 162–70.

pendence, it was one in which the worker's concerns had to be subordinate to those of the farmer.

It is a mistake, of course, to suggest, or imply, that contemporary human actors separated one theme of the free silver ideology from another. Voter reactions were not based upon such analytical distinctions. These themes were not separated, but fused into an explanatory ideology through which Bryan hoped to mobilize supporters. That urban workers were not significantly responsive to these attempts was the result of the fact that the free silver ideology was *relatively less* consonant with their experiences and perceptions than the competing ideology offered by the opposition.

The Republican tariff ideology explained the "hard times" in terms that accorded with the urban worker's experiences. Its focus was not on distant causes, but on the very immediate ones that had converted the prosperity of 1892 into the depression of 1893. It addressed itself directly to the immediate problems of the urban worker: employment and wages. It did not propose to solve these problems by increasing prices, or by expanding the purchasing power of *farmers*, but by protecting the laborer's job and his wage levels. It was an ideology which the urban worker could translate into personally relevant terms.

Republican strategists were cognizant of the role played by the tariff ideology, by the "tariff as wage and job protection." Historians have often called attention to the fact that anti-Bryan sources emphasized the harm that would befall the worker whose wages were paid in fifty-cent dollars. To provide their supporters with arguments with which to answer the claims of free silverites. Republicans did use such rhetoric. What is more significant is that in addition to attacking the free silver solution, in urban areas the Republican party newspapers offered a counter-solution. For example, both the *Chicago Tribune* and the *Milwaukee Sentinel* devoted relatively more of their worker-directed symbolism to extolling the necessity of "restoring prosperity by restoring the tariff," than they did to attacks on "funny money."

Midwestern farmers were relatively more responsive to the

Bryan candidacy than urban workers, but as an economic group they failed to provide disproportionate support to his Democracy. Since the Bryanites were especially convinced of their strength among midwestern farmers, the failure is particularly significant. One analysis of the "farm vote" has attempted to explain Bryan's poor showing on the grounds that he was faced with the task of making inroads into a solidly Republican bloc of voters, "Bryan had to convert traditionally Republican farmers to the Democratic cause and convince them to forsake their regular party allegiance." [10] This hypothesis could serve as the basis for an extremely important explanation of the variations in the degree of rural receptivity to Bryan, were it not for the fact that it is in no way congruent with the empirical voting data. Midwestern farmers were not solidly Republican prior to 1896. As a group they had tended to divide rather evenly between the two major parties since at least 1876. Reacting negatively to the party of "hard times," they were more Republican than usual in 1894, but even then a *substantial* minority was anti-Republican. The hypothesis has two more crucial weaknesses. It cannot begin to explain his failure in Michigan and Wisconsin to capture even the normal *Democratic* rural percentage. Nor can it explain the fact that in all three states some of his most pronounced gains came in units that had been solidly and steadfastly Republican during every election in the preceding twenty years.

Bryan's failure to elicit a favorable response from rural voters involved more than farmers voting their traditional party identification. For present purposes, it is adequate to focus on one aspect of this analytical problem: Why didn't these midwestern rural producers, who had suffered from long-term price declines and the short-term impact of the depression, respond favorably to an ideology explicitly designed to attract rural support? No doubt the prospects of repaying their mortgage indebtedness in inflated cur-

10. Gilbert G. Fite, "Republican Strategy and the Farm Vote in the Presidential Campaign of 1896," *American Historical Review*, LXV (July, 1960), 804–5.

rency, and of rising commodity prices, were attractive to midwestern farmers. But the farmer did not approach the 1896 election without his own explanation of the ills that had befallen him during the previous two decades. He had his own perception of both the nature of his problems and the possible solutions available to him. That he found little congruence between these perceptions and the free silver ideology resulted in Bryan's failure to translate rural dissatisfaction into a favorable partisan voting intention.

Although they all had been squeezed between falling commodity prices and rising costs, farmers in the Midwest, the East, the trans-Missouri West, and the South, did not define their problems in the same way. Those definitions varied because the structure of agriculture and the impact of the "overproduction crisis" differed among regions. While no region was similar to any of the others, and none was internally homogeneous, it is adequate here to focus on the ways in which the midwestern farmer's perception of his problems diverged from those held by rural producers in the South and the West.[11]

Producers in the latter areas saw their difficulties arising from exploitation by the financial interests of the East. Capital and credit shortages required the importation of eastern money, at what western producers saw as ruinous interest rates. The absence of nearby large urban centers required the shipment of their products to eastern markets and made him highly vulnerable to changes in transportation costs. Involvement in an impersonal price and marketing system controlled by easterners merely intensified their sense of powerlessness. While these and other particulars could be endlessly extended, it suffices to observe that southern and western producers explained their problems to themselves in terms of exploitation by avaricious easterners. To them, "Wall Street" became a potent symbolic expression of what was wrong with their world.

11. Lee Benson's analysis of the reaction of New York farmers to Populism is unusually perceptive and served as the basis for the following reexamination of the reaction of midwestern farmers; see "The New York Farmers' Rejection of Populism: The Background" (unpublished M. A. thesis, Columbia University, 1948). The explanation here overtly follows Benson's model.

The solution that they envisaged involved wresting political and financial control from the exploiters. Bryan's free silver ideology was addressed to precisely such perspectives.

Midwestern farmers lived in a region that had a different set of structural relationships with the East. They tended to see their world, to define their problems in entirely different ways; they came, as a result, to propose different genera of solution.

When the midwestern farmer asked himself what was wrong with his world, why his prices were declining and his property depreciating in value, his response gave no consolation to his western counterpart. The principal problem was not exploitation by eastern capitalists, nor excessive railroad freight rates, but the "unfair" competition created by western production. The availability of cheap land frequently provided by the government, relatively lower taxes, and advantageous long-haul freight rates enabled the western producer to send his beef, hogs, corn, and wheat "to enter and compete in markets which by natural contact should belong to others." Midwestern farm leaders attributed the depression of agriculture to an oversupply of production, not to an undersupply of currency. The chief villain was not the eastern financier but the western farmer, who was responsible for the overproduction. The president of the Ohio Agricultural Society translated the causative sequence into directly and personally relevant terms when he claimed that, "It has been overproduction by the opening up of the great West . . . that has placed mortgages upon the farmers' homes of this state." [12]

The antagonism of interests that the midwestern farmer perceived between himself and his western brethren found expression in the frequent resolutions adopted by all types of agricultural organizations against continued government expenditures for western

12. The respective quotations are from *Annual Report of the Ohio Farmers' Institutes*, 1891–92, p. 47, and the *Annual Report of the Ohio State Board of Agriculture*, 1891, p. 58. These, and the other sentiments described here, recurred frequently in the relevant agricultural sources. For more detailed documentation of all these matters, see Paul Kleppner, "The Politics of Change in the Midwest: The 1890's in Historical and Behavioral Perspective" (unpublished Ph.D. dissertation, University of Pittsburgh, 1967), pp. 476–85.

irrigation and reclamation projects. In what they frequently described as "an age of competition," it made little sense to the embattled midwestern farmer for the federal government to appropriate public funds to aid his competitor. Midwestern farmers showed little sympathy for what they viewed as "a scheme to bring in competition with the farmer east of the Mississippi all these vast acres of land at the expense of the general government." [13]

The midwestern farmer was not content with a monistic explanation of his difficulties. He constructed a litany of troubles. But this shared little in common with the southern and western ejaculatory recitation. When the midwesterner railed against the railroads, he more often than not criticized them for the role they played in abetting the "unfair" western competition. His focus of complaint was not so much that his rates were too high, but that rates on western shipments were *too low*. He attributed some portion of his difficulty to the tax structure, and supported legislation to reduce the tax levels on real property and increase those on personal property. He sought to eliminate the "unfair" competition created by "fraudulent" products, oleo and filled-cheese, through legislative proposals at both state and national levels to outlaw or severely restrict the sale of such products. Such attempts involved farmers in conflict and combat with *local* Grocers and Retailers Associations. When the farmer directed his ire against financial manipulators, it was not eastern capitalists, not "Wall Street," that fell under fire, but "the *local* Boards of Trade" that speculated in futures, coerced local dealers, and depressed prices. Finally, he raised his voice against the tariff: not to oppose its principle, but to demand the extension of its protection to the products of the farm. Though midwestern farmers frequently complained that manufacturing interests received relatively too great a measure of tariff protection, and demanded a counterbalancing increase in the level of protection afforded their own products, they did not op-

13. The quotations are from the *Proceedings of the Annual Meeting of the Illinois State Dairymen's Association*, 1890, p. 29, and *Annual Report of the Ohio State Board of Agriculture*, 1890, p. 3–4.

pose the principle of tariff protection for industry. To the contrary, this protection guaranteed full employment in cities and a nearby, lucrative market for farm products. The farmers' objective was to "protect" that market both by continued high employment and by eliminating the "unfair" competition of western producers and "fake goods." [14]

When the midwestern producer sought relief, he turned to measures designed to combat *his* problems. He pressed for I.C.C. rulings to increase the freight rates on shipments from the West. He advocated legislation to eliminate the tax disparity between real and personal property. He favored legislative enactments to reduce the power of his *local* enemies, the Grocers and Retailers Associations and the Boards of Trade. But he did not confine himself to suggestions aimed only at changing the roles played by others. His own role, too, had to change.

Western and southern producers blamed their repressed condition on eastern exploiters, but rural opinion leaders in the Midwest allotted a major portion of the responsibility to the farmer himself. Success required farmers doing more than "going over the same routine of work that their fathers have laid out before them." If the farmer was not receiving a just share of society's profits, it

14. For examples of such sentiments, see *Annual Report of the Indiana State Board of Agriculture*, 1890–91, pp. 419–20, 1891–92, pp. 351–52, 1893–94, p. 349; *Proceedings of the Annual Meeting of the Illinois State Dairymen's Association*, 1890, pp. 497–98, 1891, p. 47, 1895, p. 272; *Prairie Farmer* (Chicago), September 30 and November 13, 1893, and April 21 and August 4, 1894; *Annual Report of the Michigan State Board of Agriculture*, 1890, p. 483; *Transactions of the Michigan Dairymen's Association*, 1895, pp. 29, 34–35, 56–66, and 114, 1896, p. 16–17, 27, 28–32, 96, and 159; *Annual Report of the Ohio State Board of Agriculture*, 1893, p. 223, 1894, pp. 192–94, 1895, pp. 278–81; *Proceedings of the Annual Session of the Ohio Dairymen's Association*, 1895, p. 564; *Ohio Farmer* (Cleveland), January 2 and 23, 1886, September 14, and October 12 and 26, 1889, August 22 and 29, 1891, February 1 and 8, March 1, April 19, June 14 and 28, 1894, January 2 and 23, February 13, March 5, 1896; *Annual Report of the Wisconsin Dairymen's Association*, 1894, pp. 190–91, 1895, pp. 35 and 170–72, 1896, pp. 50–51 and 193–95; *Transactions of the Wisconsin State Agricultural Society*, 1876, p. 164, 1889, pp. 281–82, 1892, pp. 237–42, 1895, pp. 260–76, 1896, pp. 123 and 139–43; and *Hoard's Dairyman* (Fort Atkinson), January 3, 1896.

was not enough for him to "settle down to the role of the chronic grumbler." Nor should he expect solutions to be bestowed upon him by either a kindly providence or a munificent government. The remedy lay in self-help:

How long O! Lord, how long will it take the average American farmer to learn that the Lord helps those who help themselves? . . . Go out of the ruts then ye grumblers. Go to work and do your full share in trying to remedy existing evils, and until you have done that, shut up, and let us hear no more of your unmanly grumbling.[15]

It was not a *general* self-help ideology that distinguished midwestern solutions from southern and western ones, but the *specific* approaches into which that ideology channeled rural energies. If the midwestern producer was squeezed between falling prices and rising costs, the solution was "to economize," to adopt improved production techniques and thus reduce his costs. When his products sell for less than usual, the practical farmer "does not waste his vitality in trying to raise prices by grumbling about the times, but immediately turns his attention to producing an article at less cost." Even at the height of the depression, some farmers were able to make a profit. These, the opinion leaders argued, were the farmers who had adopted and adapted the "new knowledge" to the practical task of farming; the ones who had emulated, rather than castigated, businessmen and their principles and practices. If all farmers would model themselves after these, if they would follow the much-admired methods of the business world, then "every farmer can make a living, no matter how low prices are." [16]

In the Midwest, rural opinion leaders used two themes to elaborate their self-help ideology. First, businessmen were not enemies

15. The quotations are from *Ohio Farmers' Institutes*, 1890–91, p. 117; *Prairie Farmer* (Chicago), February 15, 1890; and *Journal of Proceedings, Annual Session of the Illinois State Grange*, 1889, p. 22. Also see the responses of Wisconsin farmers to a question concerning the causes of agricultural distress, in *Seventh Biennial Report of the Bureau of Labor, Census and Industrial Statistics, State of Wisconsin*, 1895–1896 (Madison, 1896), pp. 112–23.
16. Quotations are from *Wisconsin Farmers' Institutes, Session of* 1889, p. 82, and *Ohio Farmer* (Cleveland), October 1, 1896.

to be fought, but exemplars to be followed. If the captains of industry enriched themselves in "the battle of life," if the number
of millionaires in the country was growing, this was not evil: "Let
us put ourselves in the places of the successful individuals . . .
and methinks we should have done as they have done and thought
it no crime, but an honor." The farmers could learn from these
men, they could learn how to be successful; they could learn the
efficient, business-like principles of management and operation
that they, too, had to adopt in order to "get out of the ruts worn
deep by the sluggish, slow motion of our fathers." Profitable farming required the producer to adopt such methods.[17]

The necessity of conducting the farm as a business operation
dovetailed with the second theme, the need for a higher level of
practical education among farmers. Rural opinion leaders of all
types preached the doctrine of scientific farming. The farmer who
did not take advantage of the "new knowledge" emanating from
the experiment stations and agricultural colleges was the *"hayseed,
long-haired, backwoods clod-hopper."* If he expected to convert his
farm into a practical and profitable business operation, the farmer
had to "keep step with the advancing progress of the age, [or] he
may as well throw up the sponge." [18]

Of course, not all midwestern farmers would have structured the
same rank-ordering of the sources of their economic difficulties.
Nor did they all, or even a majority, idolize businessmen and
revere the test tube as deeply as the plow. There was undoubtedly
considerable animosity toward local merchants and middlemen; and
probably the majority of farmers ridiculed "kid-glove" farming.
The opinions and attitudes expressed in the rural press, agricultural
journals, Grange meetings, the conventions of agricultural societies
and dairymen's associations, and the farmers' institutes were those
of a much more cosmopolitanly oriented group than the average

17. The quotations are from the *Journal of Proceedings, Annual Session of
the Illinois State Grange*, 1893, p. 10, and 1894, p. 18.
18. *Ibid.* 1896, p. 18, and *Transactions of the Wisconsin State Agricultural
Society*, 1891, p. 229.

"hayseed." Nor was there a one-to-one relationship between these attitudes and grass-roots sentiments.

But in the midst of a severe depression such attitudes served an important function to farmers who were not of the leadership strata. Reiterated over a twenty-year period, collectively they created a climate of opinion which conditioned the political response of midwestern farmers to the "hard times" of the 1890's. The severity of the depression created a set of conditions beyond the experience of most rural producers; it created a literally unstructured situation. Atempting to impart meaning to that situation, to explain it to himself, the farmer was more likely to turn first to those ideologies which struck familiar chords. "Practical, or scientific, farming," "business-like management," "the tariff"; these were explanations whose terms and implications he could understand; these were ideologies through which his support could be mobilized.[19]

When the depression struck, and more farmers *actively* concerned themselves with seeking solutions to their problems, these ideologies channeled their discontent. It was no coincidence that the worst years of the depression, 1894–96, saw marked increases in the popularity of the farmers' institutes and in the circulation of the bulletins of the agricultural experiment stations. By 1896 experiment stations bulletins were reaching 70.0% more readers in Indiana than they had in 1892, 125.0% more in Michigan, and over 300.0% more in Wisconsin. The average attendance at sessions of the farmers' institute more than doubled in every one of the five midwestern states during each year between 1893 and 1896, and the number of institutes held also increased. While even after 1896 the "farmer constituency anxious to bring science down out

19. For useful insights see David O. Arnold and David Gold, "The Facilitation Effect of Social Environment," *Public Opinion Quarterly*, XXVIII (Fall, 1963), 513–16; James G. March and J. S. Coleman, "Group Influences and Agricultural Innovations," *American Journal of Sociology*, LXI (May, 1956), 588–94; and S. E. Asch, "Effects of Group Pressure Upon the Modification and Distortion of Judgments," in Harold Guetzkow (ed.), *Groups, Leadership and Men* (Pittsburgh, 1951), pp. 177–90.

of the skies and hitch it to the plow" was probably still only a minority, those who *actively* sought solutions to the economic difficulties during the depression were relatively more responsive to familiar ideologies than they were to one that inveighed against unfamiliar enemies and promised its chief benefits to groups that midwestern farmers saw as competitors.[20]

Bryan's free silver ideology did not elicit a cohesive and favorable response from midwestern farmers precisely because they could see in it little that was consonant with their perceptions of either the nature of their problems or what constituted feasible solutions.

Although he preached the free silver gospel with the zeal of a Methodist circuit-rider, Bryan failed to polarize the vote of the "toiling masses" in his favor. But if he was unable to realign the social bases of partisan support along class lines, he did succeed in producing considerable political movement among other categories of social groups. . . .

The voter realignment of the mid-1890's shattered a twenty-year political stalemate. The "politics of equilibrium" gave way to those of Republican dominance. Thereafter, through the first decade of the new century, the "party of McKinley" commanded the allegiance of a majority of the electorate, nationally and in the Midwest. This new Republican majority was quite different socially from that which the party had mobilized in the 1850's. This was not the party of evangelical Protestantism, not the "party of piety," but the "party of prosperity."

The voter realignment of the 1850's had produced a new structural configuration of political allegiances. Old personal and intrastate sectional loyalties were broken down. Sharing a common commitment to pietistic religious values, "reform" elements united in the support of a political party through which they could use the

20. The quotation is from Vernon Carstensen, "The Genesis of an Agricultural Experiment Station," *Agricultural History*, XXIV (January, 1960), 20; the estimates of the increase in circulation of agricultural experiment station bulletins and attendance at farmers' institutes are based on data in the annual reports of the experiment stations for the years 1892–96 and in the reports of the institutes for the same years.

power of government to impose their own canons of behavior upon the broader society. Native and immigrant pietists sublimated ethnic animosities and translated a shared religious perspective into a politically salient identification. Through united action they hoped to purge society of "ungodly" acts of behavior; they hoped to eliminate the "sins" of intemperance and Sabbath desecration and, through the agency of their public schools, to socialize the children of the "sinners" into a "righteous" value system.

But the "sinners" resisted. They condemned the fulsome zeal of the pietists and their tendency to see "sin" where there was none. Viewing their world from a much different religious perspective, the ritualists distinguished spiritual from secular activities and did not view as sinful those social customs against which the pietists inveighed. Clinging to their religious values as ardently as the pietists, they sought, through their own school system, to preserve and perpetuate them. In defense of their religious values, they mobilized for combat against the encroachments of imperialistic pietism in the ranks of the party of "personal liberty."

The conflicts between pietists and ritualists, in the 1850's and thereafter, focused on substantive issues. Not being able to convert the "sinner," the pietist would at least control him. The pietist sought to "reform" the sinner through legislative enactment. He sought government edicts, of various forms, against the "saloon power," to prevent the "desecration" of the Sabbath, and, eventually, to undermine the parochial school system. In the 1870's and 1880's, conflicts at the local and state levels over specific "reform" proposals kept alive the animosities between the two groups and reinforced the commitment of each to its chosen political vehicle of expression.

These conflicts involved much more than "policy positions" taken by groups of voters. It was not merely a specific temperance proposal, nor a particular Sunday closing law, that was at stake. It was a conflict rooted in divergent and conflicting religious perspectives. When the pietist defended temperance, he defended more than a legislative measure. Quite literally, he was defending his religious value system. When the ritualist, the "reformee," resisted, he was doing more than acknowledging his subservience to the "saloon power," he was defending and trying to preserve a sanctified set of values.

The conflict was not "unreal," not some distraction from the human actor's "real," or class, values. The contemporary human actor did not see his world as one in which economic values were somehow the ultimate and transcendent reality. Instead, he concerned himself with those matters which were an integral part of his daily life and experiences. He did not react to protracted and complex debates in "far away" Washington over the intricacies of national tariff policy. It is unlikely that he even perceived the ways in which such policies impinged upon his daily life. But he could perceive, and without the benefit of external instruction, the ways in which his religious values were relevant. He could see, also, the ways in which those values were imperiled by the onslaughts of religious groups whose values were antithetical. It was these perceptions, rooted in familiar grounds, that prompted his action.

Contemporary political leaders were not unaware of the motive impulses which underlay the structure of partisanship. They were not unaware that cultural identifications were stronger than economic ones in mobilizing voter support. Strategically, their problem was to forge a link between the activities of national and state party leaders, on the one hand, and the concerns of grassroots voters, on the other. While they used the matter of current events as the subjects of their rhetorical appeals, they shaped the "style" component of that rhetoric to reflect their perceptions of their supporters' concern with cultural matters.

The national and regional majorities that the Republicans had mobilized in the 1850's dwindled throughout the 1870's and 1880's. But while the Democracy increased its strength somewhat, it did not emerge as the new majority party. Instead, elections became closely fought contests in which neither party commanded a majority of the electorate. The political stalemate grew from a combination of two factors. First, the Republicans suffered from the fact that those groups that were strongly Democratic were coming to cast an increasing share of the ballots. Second, the Republicans suffered from the rise of third parties, especially the Prohibitionists, who siphoned off support.

The two developments were not unrelated. As strongly Democratic groups grew in relative electoral size, some Republican political leaders saw the need to broaden their party's social base of support. This required appealing to the one Democratic group that could potentially be led to support of the Republican Party, the German Lutherans. It was not that the party sought to convert the old German Lutherans voters, but that particular leaders hoped to win support among the new generation of Lutheran voters and from those immigrants who had not shared the Know-Nothing trauma of the 1850's.

To appeal to German Lutheran voters required the Republican party to reshape its strategy. It required that the party de-emphasize those cultural factors that had alienated Lutherans voters, especially temperance and sabbatarian measures. These, however, were precisely the measures that the pietists espoused. The attempts to integrate German Lutheran voters into the party's coalition produced a sense of sociological alienation among its intensely pietistis supporters. No longer perceiving congruence between their political goals and the Republican party as a means of achieving them, these voters were susceptible to mobilization by other political organizations in which they could perceive that congruence.

The factionalism that characterized both major parties during the "era of stalemate" was largely an outgrowth of differential leadership responses to conflicting subcoalitional demands. In Ohio, the Foraker faction responded favorably to the demands of the pietists. Hayes, McKinley, and Sherman were much more concerned with adjusting the party to changing demographic realities. In Wisconsin, the pietistic faction, led by La Follette, Haugen, and Hoard, inveighed against the pragmatists with the normative epithets of "bossism" and "corruption." In Michigan, the urban-based leadership of the party contended against its pietistic rural wing.

The temporary Democratic resurgence from 1889 through 1892

was the product of another act in the half-century-long struggle between the adherents of conflicting religious values. Ohio's pietists saw their champion, Governor Foraker, act to enforce Sunday-closing in Cincinnati and threaten to extend his concern for morality to other "sinful" areas of the state. They also saw the German Lutherans abandon the Republicans and provide the margin of victory for a Democratic candidate in the 1889 gubernatorial election. In Wisconsin, the pietists staged an assault against the parochial school system and earned, for their efforts, the election of a Democratic governor. In Michigan, the urban, non-pietistic wing of the party dominated its 1890 state convention and nominated a "wet" as its gubernatorial candidate. Capitalizing on the aroused disaffection of rural pietists, the Democrats offered a rural "dry" and captured the state house.

Even by 1892 the Democrats had lost the major portion of these gains. In 1894 they lost more than that. The industrial depression, which began to be felt in the late spring of 1893, dominated the elections of that and the following year. Unemployment, underemployment, and reduced wages led voters of all social groups to turn away from the party of "hard times." Though the rate of movement away from the Democracy varied over space, and with the degree of the group's commitment to the party, the central tendency persisted. But this anti-Democratic movement did not always benefit the Republicans. Frequently, Democratic voters turned to third parties to express their dissatisfaction. In those contexts in which the Populists were culturally neutral they tended to benefit from this type of anti-Democratic movement. At the same time, in some localities, the Populists garnered voting support from the Prohibitionists. The movement of new voters into the Populist party in 1894 did not signify the acceptance by those voters of the Populist program and its goals. To a large number, especially to the defecting Democrats, it was simply a convenient and reasonably safe means of expressing their dissatisfaction with their own party's inability to come to terms with the "hard times."

The Bryan–McKinley contest in 1896 did not produce a continuing movement of voter groups along the lines congruent with past partisan loyalties. It did not produce increasing levels of urban–rural tension; nor did it unite the "poor" in political opposition to the "rich." But it did produce a unique movement of voter groups and a new political alignment.

Groups that had been staunchly Democratic and had been the most resistant to the 1894 movement away from the Democracy moved toward the "party of McKinley" in 1896. Bryan's Democracy was not the old Democracy to which they had pledged their fealty for fifty years; it was a new entity, with a new leadership, crusading in the name of evangelical Protestantism for the creation of a moral society. As they had resisted the encroachments of imperialistic pietism for over fifty years, when those came in Republican dress, so they resisted them in their new attire. The Republicans could not mobilize such voters as the party of "personal liberty," but they could, and did, sublimate potentially divisive cultural concerns to a shared concern with "prosperity." The party could, and did, use its tariff ideology to mobilize a new coalition of voting groups.

Conversely, anti-Democratic groups, especially native, Norwegian, and Swedish pietists, tended to give higher levels of support to the Democracy of Bryan than they had to any Democratic candidate since the 1850's. Alienated from McKinley's brand of Republicanism, and not interested in a party that sacrificed morality to the pragmatic concern of building a winning electoral coalition, these voters turned to the new "party of morality," to the party of William Jennings Bryan.

The relative responses of these groups were not born solely of the events of 1896. They occurred against a half-century background of religious–political conflict. The partisan identifications formed as a consequence of that strife were tenaciously held commitments. Men did not take lightly their party identifications, because they did not take lightly their religious values. It was precisely because the Bryan crusade did not reactivate and reinforce that commitment among religious ritualists that these voter groups rejected his candidacy. It was precisely because they had identified with the Democracy as the party of "personal liberty," the party of negative government, that they were unresponsive to his evangelical fervor. Pietistic groups responded favorably because they, for half a century, had sought the type of moral "reformation" Bryan promised.

The realignment of the 1890's meant that the major parties faced the new century as much different social entities than the ones that had done battle since the 1850's. The Republican party was no longer a narrowly based social vehicle in the hands of evangelical crusaders. It was a functioning integrative mechanism with a much-broadened social base of support. The Democracy of Bryan was not the party of "personal liberty," but an instrument in the hands of "reformers" who aimed at the creation of a moral social order. Its leaders did not seek to come to terms with the complexities of a modern social system, but to eliminate these by sublimating them to a centuries-old morality. As the Bible contained all that was sufficient for human knowledge, so the morality it envisioned was the only solution to all social maladies.

Progressives and the Issues

Social Tensions and the Origins of Progressivism

by David P. Thelen

The Progressives were expert not only at publicizing the needs of reform but at establishing a positive public image of their own activities. American historians who first dealt with the many reform movements of the early twentieth century tended to inherit and embellish the reformers' own self-portraits. Thus the notion of a unified movement of reformers, selflessly dedicated to curbing the abuses of runaway industrialism through stern regulation, while at the same time ministering to the victims of poverty and injustice, passed from reportage and memoirs into history. This favorable collective self-portrait painted the Progressives as humane fighters for the extension of American democracy against corruption and interest group politics, compassionate friends of the underprivileged, unselfish agitators for preservation of America's natural and human resources.

On most scales of historical measurement, the Progressive self-portrait has recently been toned down. Even during the 1920's and 1930's, critics pointed to the Progressives' inability to alter significantly their era's political, social, and economic patterns. Several leading liberal historians joined the attack on the Progressive self-image in the decade after World War II. George Mowry and Richard Hofstadter, in particular, took aim at the reformers' vaunted selflessness, depicting Progressives as socially distraught, psychologically anxious burghers, intent upon capturing government as an instrument with which to reverse the declining status of middle-class Americans in a society ruled by giant corporations and immigrant voting blocs. Class fears, not public interest, dictated the concerns of Progressive politics, according to Hofstadter and Mowry.

Their work heralded even more drastic historical re-evaluations (some might argue under-valuations) of America's turn-of-the-century reformers. Christopher Lasch in The New Radicalism in America, for example, viewed the reform impulse among certain leading Progressives as expressions of deep-seated psychological needs and suggested the utter failure of most twentieth-century American reformers (including that early generation) to translate their cultural grievances into successful political programs. On a different tack, Gabriel Kolko saw Progressivism even more starkly: he considered it a deliberate attempt by business and financial leaders to rationalize their economic practices and privileges through the use of regulatory agencies designed largely to fulfill the needs of giant corporations. Robert H. Wiebe and Kolko demonstrated the degree to which specific pieces of reform legislation enjoyed widespread support from segments of the business community, but Kolko held a more relentless vision of the Progressives as political puppets, manipulated by the directors of American capitalism. Wiebe's synthesis of the period, published as The Search for Order, described the ultimately unsuccessful Progressive effort to impose an orderly bureaucratic structure upon the chaotic social and economic environment in which they functioned.

Most recent studies of early twentieth-century political leadership have disclosed that Progressives and their conservative political opponents shared similar social characteristics. David P. Thelen not only demonstrates this similarity in the case of Wisconsin politicians, whether reformers or regulars, but seriously calls into question the general practice by some historians of dabbling unsystematically in such borrowings from the social sciences as "status loss." Thelen's view of Progressive origins leans heavily *on the traumatic effect of the depression of the 1890's on politicians from every class.*

🏛 Recent historians have explained the origins of the Progressive movement in several ways. They have represented progressivism, in turn, as a continuation of the western and southern farmers' revolt, as a desperate attempt by the urban gentry to regain status from the new robber barons, as a thrust from the depths of slum life, and as a campaign by businessmen to prevent workers from securing political power. Behind such seemingly conflicting theories, however, rests a single assumption about the origins of progressivism: the class and status conflicts of the late nineteenth century formed the driving forces that made men become reformers. Whether viewed by the historian as a farmer, worker, urban elitist, or businessman, the progressive was motivated primarily by his social position; and each scholar has painted a compelling picture of the insecurities and tensions felt by the group that he placed in the vanguard of progressivism. Pressures and threats from other social groups drove men to espouse reform. In these class and status conflicts can be found the roots of progressivism.

How adequately does this focus on social tensions and insecurities explain the origins of progressivism? Since some of these scholars have invoked concepts from social science to support their rejection of earlier approaches, the validity and application of some of the sociological and psychological assumptions which make up the conceptual framework for the idea that social tensions impelled the progressive require analysis. Is the focus on social classes relevant to the rise of political movements like progressivism? Is it useful to rely upon a narrow, untestable, and unproved conception of motivation when other approaches are available? How much of a concrete situation does an abstract model explain?

From *The Journal of American History*, LVI (September 1969), 323–41. Reprinted by permission; most footnotes omitted.

First, theories borrowed from one discipline are not designed to encompass the data of another. In questioning the application of models from physiology and physics to psychology, the noted personality theorist George A. Kelly explained: "We are skeptical about the value of copying ready-made theories which were designed for other foci of convenience"; and he urged his fellow psychologists to resist the temptation of "poking about in the neighbors' back yards for methodological windfalls." Just as physiology and physics encompass only part of the psychologist's realm, so psychology, sociology, and political science are concerned with only part of the historian's realm.

Those historians who have borrowed the idea that social stratification explains the rise of political movements like progressivism illustrate the dangers inherent in borrowing theories from other fields. Most sociologists and political scientists now doubt the relevance of social stratification to the emergence of political movements. Reinhard Bendix, for example, maintained that "the study of social stratification, whether or not it is adumbrated by psychological analysis, is not the proper approach to an understanding of the role of cumulative political experience." In their pleas for more pluralistic approaches to political power, such political scientists as Nelson W. Polsby and Robert A. Dahl have found that social stratification is largely irrelevant to the exercise of political power. So severe were these criticisms of the assumption that social class determined political power that one sociologist, reviewing the literature of the field in 1964, concluded that "the problem has simply been dropped."

But an even greater problem with placing emphasis on social tensions is that it is ahistorical. Even sociologists like Seymour M. Lipset and Bendix have complained about the "increasingly ahistorical" drift of the focus of this field. After analyzing the major models of social change, another sociologist concluded that the fundamental error of these models was their failure to incorporate the dimension of time. Few scholars would deny that social tensions exist at all times and in all societies. For at least twenty years before 1900, various business groups had tried to take political power away from workers and bosses. But to focus on the social class motivation of businessmen is to obscure the basic historical problem of why progressivism emerged *when* it did. Conflicts between businessmen and workers were hardly unique to the years around 1900. The emphasis on social tensions obscures chronology. When sociologists are disturbed about this problem, historians should be wary indeed.

The assumption that progressivism derived from social tensions is at least as vulnerable to attack by psychologists. If the kinds of questions historians generally ask about the origins of political and social movements are reduced to the psychological level, then the theories of class and status motivation would seem to be premised on very debatable assumptions about individual motivation. Most historians would want to know the conditions that existed before a change occurred, why the change happened, and what were the results of that change.

The first problem—the conditions before a change occurred—reduces in psychological terms to the way an individual perceives himself, his self-image. Psychologists have approached this question in many ways, but a theory of change which assumes that social tensions were the basic cause implicitly accepts only one of these approaches. It assumes that an individual defines himself primarily in terms of his particular social role, that his behavior is motivated mainly by his class and status role perceptions. Only about one out of every three psychologists, however, would accept this premise to any real extent. Even some sociologists and anthropologists, who have traditionally seen individual behavior as primarily determined by culture, have retreated from that position and now see a more symmetrical interaction in which personality also influences culture. An overwhelming majority of psychologists have rejected role theory as an adequate explanation for the way an individual who enlists in a reform movement forms his self-image.

The second problem—why the change happened—reduces in

psychological terms to the mechanism by which an individual feels impelled to join a political movement like progressivism. Here again those scholars who emphasize social tensions have implicitly chosen only one of several alternatives offered by psychologists. They assume that the threat from some other social group frustrated the would-be progressive who, in turn, reacted aggressively against that threat. Very few psychologists, however, would claim that social tensions are the main source of frustration. Furthermore, individuals are generally capable of reacting to new roles without experiencing any major frustrations. The different ways in which Theodore Roosevelt and Calvin Coolidge, for example, remade the role of the presidency to fit their own personalities suggest how flexible roles can be without deeply frustrating an individual. Furthermore, different members of the same social class will perceive social challenges in different ways; many will experience no frustration at all.

Even if historians concede that social stresses can frustrate an individual, does it follow that he will react aggressively toward the source of that frustration? The frustration-produces-aggression model is one of the most debated propositions in psychology. Extreme critics have called it "nonsensical." Others have shown that frustration more often produces anxiety, submission, dependence, or avoidance than aggression. Even presumably simpleminded creatures like rats and pigeons do not necessarily react aggressively when they are frustrated. If some psychologists have shown that aggression is only one possible result of frustration, others have shown that frustration is only one possible source of aggression. Indeed, prior to 1939 most psychologists accepted Sigmund Freud's *Beyond the Pleasure Principle*, which contended that aggression derived from the Death Wish. Others have found the source of aggression in neither frustration nor the Death Wish. The assumption that social tensions will frustrate an individual and drive him to react aggressively has been riddled by the artillery of a great many psychologists. For historians to continue to assume that men react primarily to social threats is to ignore an impressive body of psychological literature.

The third problem—what were the results of that change—reduces in psychological terms to the way an individual outwardly expresses the internal change. If an individual felt angry following threats from another social group, how would he express that anger? The idea that he will sublimate his aggressive propensities into cries for political reform is one which is endorsed by many Freudians who follow *Civilization and Its Discontents*. But even some psychoanalysts claim that Freud never adequately explained sublimation. Other personality theorists have asserted that "everyone recognizes . . . that at present we have no theory which really explains the dynamics" of sublimation. Many psychologists have seen sublimation as only one possible way of expressing aggressive proclivities. Political reform is only one of hundreds of directions an individual can channel hostile impulses. But most personality theorists are so unimpressed by the concept of sublimation that they simply ignore it in their own theories.

By assuming that social tensions produced progressivism, historians have approached the basic questions about social and political movements from a very narrow psychological viewpoint. Even more important, the psychological underpinnings of this assumption are either disproved, disputed, ignored, or "untestable" by modern psychologists.

Moreover, the whole psychological framework which includes these theories has recently come under attack. Both behaviorists and psychoanalysts had previously assumed that individuals were motivated by "a state of tenseness that leads us to seek equilibrium, rest, adjustment, satisfaction, or homeostasis. From this point of view, personality is nothing more than our habitual modes of reducing tension." Men become reformers to relieve tensions, perhaps impelled by class and status anxieties. Now, however, many psychologists contend that personality theorists too long overemphasized the irrational components in motivation. As

early as 1953 Gordon Allport reported that the trend in motivational theory was away from the tension reduction approach and
toward an emphasis on the rational and healthy side of individuals. By stressing the rationality of free choice, these psychologists have argued that a commitment to reform, for example, may
in fact be the ultimate expression of a mature personality and reflect a man who is capable of getting outside of his self-preoccupa-
tion. Indeed, Erich Fromm has said that the revolutionary leader
might well be the only "sane person in an insane world." The decision to embrace progressivism may simply represent a conscious
choice between alternative programs, not an attempt to reduce
tensions which grew out of a man's efforts to maintain his social
position.

There is another problem in borrowing models: the more inclusive the model, the farther it is removed from the reality it is
attempting to explain. The data must be squeezed and distorted
to make them conform to the model. Many social scientists themselves have revolted against the top-heavy and abstract models
which have prevailed in their fields. One student of social stratification, for example, concluded from a review of 333 studies that
his field suffered from "the disease of overconceptualization." Similarly, many psychologists have rejected the abstract personality
constructs used to explain motivation because they are too far removed from the reality of individual people. Arguing for a focus
on the "life style" of each person, Allport has attacked theories
which emphasize "the abstract motivation of an impersonal and
therefore non-existent mind-in-general," preferring "the concrete,
viable motives of each and every mind-in-particular." In a like
vein, Kelly has argued that most psychological constructs ignore
an individual's "private domain, within which his behavior aligns
itself within its own lawful system." These abstract constructs can
only account for the individual as "an inert object wafted about
in a public domain by external forces, or as a solitary datum sitting
on its own continuum." Allport even charged that psychologists
who build universal models to explain human motivation are

seeking a "scientific will of the wisp"; the " 'irreducible unlearned motives' of men" they are seeking cannot be found because they do not exist.

This is not a critique of any particular psychological theory or approach to behavior. Rather it is a plea to be aware of the dangers in building a conceptual approach to such a problem as progressivism upon so many rickety psychological foundations. Historians should recognize that psychologists are not that different; they are at least as divided in their interpretations as we are. For historians to accept the assumptions that underlie the idea that social tensions produced progressivism would be similar to a psychologist borrowing Frederick Jackson Turner's frontier hypothesis for his research. Many of us would complain that there are other explanations for the development of American history; and a great many psychologists, in effect, are shuddering at the weak psychological underpinnings of the assumption that their social backgrounds made men become reformers.

The real test for the soundness of any approach is not theoretical, of course, but empirical. In this case the inadequacy of the sociological and psychological ideas which inform the assumption that social tensions produced progressivism becomes obvious after an examination of the types of men who became progressives and conservatives. If social tensions were relevant to the rise of progressivism, then clearly the class and status experiences of progressives should have differed in some fundamental way from those of the conservatives.

How different, in fact, were the social origins of progressives and conservatives? Following George E. Mowry's publication in 1951 of *The California Progressives*, several scholars examined the external social class attributes of progressive leaders and concluded that the reformers were drawn from the young urban gentry. But because they neglected to sample a comparable group of conservatives, these studies failed to prove their contention that class and status experiences impelled the progressives. Subsequent profiles of both progressive and conservative leaders in the election of

1912 and the legislative sessions of 1911 in Washington and 1905 in Missouri showed that both groups came from nearly the same social background. Objective measures of their social origins failed to predict the programs and ideologies of political leaders.

Scholars may not accept this finding because they question whether the 1912 campaign reflected political ideologies so much as the personalities of leaders and the desire for office. The studies of legislatures in Washington and Missouri might be questioned because in a single session such extraneous pressures as the personality of a powerful governor or the use of bribes might have interfered with a legislator's expression of his natural preferences. Furthermore, neither Washington nor Missouri was ever noted as a banner progressive state. Perhaps the issues in these states were not as hotly contested—and hence did not reveal as sharp social tensions—as in the more radical states.

The following profile of Wisconsin legislators was designed to avoid some of the possible objections to the other studies. Since contemporaries and historians alike have agreed on the pivotal position of Wisconsin, it is an ideal state to test whether social tensions were important in the development of progressivism. This sample begins with the 1897 session because it was then, for the first time, that the Progressive Republicans identified in their speeches, platforms, and votes the issues which divided them from the stalwarts, and concludes with the 1903 session, when many of their programs were enacted. The index for "progressivism" was based on votes growing out of the campaigns for a more equitable distribution of the tax burden, for regulation of quasi-public corporations, and for purification of the electoral and legislative processes. These were the issues which gave the thrust and tone to Wisconsin progressivism and served as the dividing lines between the old guard and the insurgents.

During these four sessions there were 286 roll calls on these issues. A "progressive" legislator was defined as one who voted for more than 75 per cent of the progressive measures; a "moderate" favored between 50 and 75 per cent of the progressive measures;

and a "conservative" opposed more than half of the progressive measures. Of the 360 Republican legislators included in this profile, 40 per cent were progressives, 38 per cent were moderates, and 22 per cent were conservatives.[1]

If social conflicts were important to the emergence of progressivism, the variable which would be most likely to reveal that fact would be the occupations of legislators. Convincing generalizations from [Table 1] would need to be based upon large statistical differences, since the relatively small sample is divided so many ways. Occupation clearly made little difference in a legislator's vote on progressive measures.

Table 1

	Farmer	Merchant	Professional	Manufacturer	Financier	Worker
	%	%	%	%	%	%
Progressives	20	27	26	13	9	5
Moderates	22	24	29	6	13	6
Conservatives	12	27	32	16	10	3

The extent of a man's education helps to locate his social position. In Wisconsin neither progressives (22 per cent), moderates (24 per cent), nor conservatives (27 per cent) were dominated by college graduates. At a time and place where college degrees were rare, perhaps a better measure of educational aspirations would be the proportion of men who sought any kind of formal schooling— high school, business college, night school—beyond the level of the common school. Here again, however, the differences in achievement between progressives (58 per cent), moderates (60 per cent), and conservatives (66 per cent) are insignificant.

1. The handful of Democrats, who seldom comprised over one-tenth of the legislators, were excluded because they contributed no programs to the development of Wisconsin progressivism and because they used their meagre numbers primarily to embarrass the conflicting Republican factions. Because absences could be interpreted in many ways, those legislators who were absent for more than 20 per cent of the roll calls on these issues were also excluded from the sample.

The place of a man's birth also indicates his social background. But the nativity of Wisconsin's legislators failed to differentiate progressives from conservatives (see Table 2).

If the Wisconsin sample corresponds roughly to those of other states in the occupations, education, and nativity of political leaders, it differs from them in two other respects. Students of the 1912 election found the progressives to be considerably younger than the conservatives in both age and political experience, a fact which led them to see progressivism as a revolt of the young, would-be politicians. In Wisconsin, however, progressives and conservatives both had an average age of forty-eight, and the moderates averaged forty-six. The median ages of progressives (49),

Table 2

	Midwest	East and New England	Canada	Europe
	%	%	%	%
Progressives	47	29	6	18
Moderates	61	24	2	13
Conservatives	49	30	5	16

moderates (45), and conservatives (47) likewise fail to suggest the existence of any generational conflict between progressives and conservatives.

Nor were Wisconsin's progressives the most politically immature of the rival factions. While service in the legislature is only one measure of political experience, it does reveal the effectiveness of politicians in winning renomination from their local organizations. Although Wisconsin's conservatives had the longest tenure in the legislature, they contrasted not so much with the progressives as with the moderates. Table 3 indicates the number of previous sessions attended by legislators.

The social origins of Wisconsin legislators between 1897 and 1903 clearly suggest that no particular manner of man became a progressive. Such variables as occupation, education, nativity, age, and previous legislative experience fail to differentiate the average progressive from the average conservative. The theories that progressivism was motivated by status or class tensions felt by the urban gentry, the businessmen, the workers, the farmers, or the incipient politicians are challenged in Wisconsin by the fact that members of these groups were as likely to become conservatives as progressives. And the Wisconsin profile parallels other studies. To the extent that social class allegiance can be measured by such attributes as occupation, nativity, education, and age, social tensions were apparently irrelevant to the formation of progressivism since the "typical" progressive and conservative came from the same social background.

Table 3

	None	One	Two or more
	%	%	%
Progressives	52	28	20
Moderates	62	27	11
Conservatives	35	37	28

Collective statistical profiles can, however, obscure more than they reveal. The five more prominent early Wisconsin progressive leaders, the men who forged the issues which Robert M. La Follette subsequently adopted, were most noteworthy for their different social origins. The man contemporaries hailed as the "father of Wisconsin progressivism" was Albert R. Hall, a small dairy farmer in the western part of the state. Nephew of national Grange head Oliver Kelley, Hall was basically an agrarian radical who developed the reputation of a fearless enemy of the railroads and other large corporations. No less important was John A. Butler, the lengthened shadow of the powerful Milwaukee Municipal League. A sharper contrast to Hall could scarcely be found than this independently wealthy and highly educated Brahmin who seemed to spend more time in his villa than he did in his Milwaukee office. Milwaukee also contributed Julius E. Roehr, or-

ganized labor's leading champion in the legislature. Born in New
York City—the son of German immigrants—this hardworking
lawyer and dissident Republican politician would have been extremely uncomfortable with the smells of either Hall's farm or
Butler's villa. James H. Stout, the most respected of the early progressives in the legislature, was born and raised in Iowa and educated at the University of Chicago. A fabulously wealthy lumber
baron, Stout used his company town of Menomonie to pioneer in
vocational education and in welfare benefits for his workers. The
orator of these early legislative progressives was James J. McGilli-
vray, a self-made Canadian-born architect and manufacturer who
lived in Black River Falls and authored the state's antitrust acts.
It would seem almost pointless to hunt for a common social
"type" in these early progressives. A Brahmin man of leisure and
self-made manufacturer, an agrarian radical who knew no workers
and a lawyer who never lived outside a large city and was the
workers' champion, young men and old men, Yankees and immigrants, these were the leaders who made common cause in Wisconsin and developed the progressive program.

The widely scattered backgrounds of the most prominent early
leaders and the remarkable collective similarity between the average progressive and conservative confirm the weaknesses in the
sociological and psychological framework for the assumption that
progressivism was rooted in social tensions. The widespread emphasis on social tensions is unsound sociologically because it draws
upon only a narrow spectrum of personality theory, and those
models upon which it does draw are either unproved or unprov-
able. The statistical profiles from Wisconsin and elsewhere reveal
empirically that the origins of progressivism cannot be found by
studying the social backgrounds and tensions of progressive leaders. Remembering Kelly's injunction to avoid "poking about in
the neighbors' back yards for methodological windfalls," historians
must develop alternative approaches which encompass not only
the realm of sociology and psychology but also that of history.

Such an alternative approach should at least restore chronology, a major casualty in the repeated emphasis on men's class and status feelings, to a more prominent position. At this point it is possible to offer a tentative explanation for the origins of progressivism when that movement is placed in the context of the chronological evolution of both industrialism and reform.

When the Progressive era is put against the backdrop of the growth of industrialism in America, the remarkable fact about that period is its relative freedom from social tensions. If conflicts between city and farm, worker and boss, younger and older generations, native-born and immigrant are more or less natural results of industrialization, then the years between the late 1890's and the early 1910's stand as a period of social peace when contrasted with either the Gilded Age or the 1920's, when those conflicts were raw and ragged. Not competition but cooperation between different social groups—ministers, businessmen, workers, farmers, social workers, doctors, and politicians—was what distinguished progressivism from such earlier reform movements as Mugwumpery, Populism, the labor movement, and civil service reform. To the extent that men and groups were motivated by tensions deriving from their class and status perceptions, they would have been unable to cooperate with men from different backgrounds. In focusing on the broadly based progressive thrust, the real question is not what drove groups apart, but what drove them together? To answer this question, progressivism must be located in the development of reform in the late nineteenth century.

The roots of progressivism reach far back into the Gilded Age. Dozens of groups and individuals in the 1880's envisioned some change that would improve society. Reformers came forward to demand civil service reform, the eight hour day, scientific agriculture, woman suffrage, enforcement of vice laws, factory inspection, nonpartisan local elections, trust-busting, wildlife conservation, tax reform, abolition of child labor, businesslike local government, regulation of railway rates, less patronizing local charity, and hundreds of other causes which would subsequently be identified with progressivism. Younger social scientists, particularly economists, were not only beginning to lambast the formalism and conservatism in their fields and to advocate the ideas which would undergird progressivism but they were also seeking to force governments to accept their ideas. Richard T. Ely's work on the Maryland Tax Commission in the mid-1880's, for example, pioneered in the application of the new economics to government and generated many of the programs which future reformers and politicians would soon adopt.

But this fertility of reform in the Gilded Age did not conceal the basic fact that individuals and groups remained fragmented. There was no common program which could rally all groups, and the general prosperity tended to reassure people that industrialism might cure its own ills. As late as 1892 one editor, reflecting this optimistic frame of mind, could state that "the rich are growing richer, some of them, and the poor are growing richer, all of them." Men and groups seeking major changes, whether elitists or Populists, were generally stereotyped as cranks who were blind to the vast blessings and bright future of industrialism. Circumscribed by such problems and attitudes reformers were understandably fragmented in the Gilded Age.

The catastrophic depression of 1893–1897 radically altered this pattern of reform. It vividly dramatized the failures of industrialism. The widening chasm between the rich and the poor, which a few observers had earlier called a natural result of industrialism, could no longer be ignored. As several tattered bands of men known as Coxey's Army tramped from town to town in 1894, they drew attention to the plight of the millions of unemployed and vividly portrayed the striking contrasts between the way of life of the poor and the "conspicuous consumption" of the rich. Furthermore, as Thorstein Veblen observed, they showed that large numbers of Americans no longer cherished the old gospel of self-help, the very basis for mobility in a democratic society. As desperation mounted, businessmen and politicians tried the traditional ways of reversing the business cycle, but by 1895 they realized that the time-honored formulas of the tariff and the currency simply could not dispel the dark pall that hung over the land. Worse still, President Grover Cleveland seemed utterly incapable of comprehending, let alone relieving, the national crisis.

The collapse of prosperity and the failure of national partisan politicians to alleviate the crisis by the traditional methods generated an atmosphere of restless and profound questioning which few could escape. "On every corner stands a man whose fortune in these dull times has made him an ugly critic of everything and everybody," wrote one editor. A state university president warned his graduates in 1894 that "you will see everywhere in the country symptoms of social and political discontent. You will observe that these disquietudes do not result from the questions that arise in the ordinary course of political discussion . . . but that they spring out of questions that are connected with the very foundations of society and have to do with some of the most elemental principles of human liberty and modern civilization." Was the American dream of economic democracy and mobility impossible in an industrial society? Would the poor overthrow an unresponsive political and economic system? Such questions urgently demanded answers, and it was no longer either wise or safe to summarily dismiss as a crank anyone who had an answer. "The time is at hand," cried one editor, "when some of the great problems which the Nineteenth century civilization has encountered are crying for a solution. . . . Never before in the history of the world were people so willing to accept true teaching on any of these subjects and give to them a just and practical trial." A man's social origins were now less important than his proposals, and many men began to cooperate with people from different backgrounds to devise and implement solutions.

This depression-inspired search for answers sprouted hundreds of discussion groups at which men met, regardless of background, to propose remedies. These groups gave men the habit of ignoring previously firm class lines in the face of the national crisis. When Victor Berger urged the Milwaukee Liberal Club to adopt socialism as the answer, for example, his audience included wealthy

bankers, merchants, and lawyers. In the same city, at the Church
and Labor Social Union, banker John Johnston urged a "new
society" where "class privileges will be abolished because all will
belong to the human family," and the discussion was joined by
Populists and Socialists as well as clergymen and conservative editors. In this context, too, all types of people sought the wisdom
of the men who had made a career of studying the social and economic breakdown. No one was surprised when unions, Granges,
women's clubs, and other groups wanted University of Wisconsin
economists like Ely to address them. Maybe they had an answer.
The social unrest accompanying the depression weakened class
and status allegiances.

The direct political effects of the depression also broke down
the previous rigidity and fragmentation of reform. The depression
created a clear sense of priorities among the many causes which
Gilded Age reformers had advocated. It generated broadly based
new issues which all classes could unite behind. One such program
was the urgent necessity for tax reform. When the depression
struck, individuals and corporations were forced to devise ways of
economizing as property values, sales, and revenues declined pre-
cipitously. Caught between higher taxes to cover the rising costs
of local government and their own diminishing revenues, many
wealthy individuals and corporations began to hide their personal
assets from the assessors, to lobby tax relief through local governments, and even to refuse to pay any taxes. The progressive program was forged and received widespread popular support as a
response to these economies. Citizens who lacked the economic or
political resources to dodge their taxes mounted such a crusade
against these tax dodgers that former President Benjamin Harrison
warned the wealthiest leaders that unless they stopped concealing
their true wealth from the tax assessors they could expect a revolution led by enraged taxpayers. The programs for tax reform—
including inheritance, income, and ad valorem corporation taxes—
varied from place to place, but the important fact was that most
citizens had developed specific programs for tax reform and had

now agreed that certain individuals and corporations had evaded a primary responsibility of citizenship.

A second major area which proved capable of uniting men of different backgrounds was "corporate arrogance." Facing declining revenues, many corporations adopted economies which ranged from raising fares and rates to lobbying all manner of relief measures through city and state governments. Even more important, perhaps, they could not afford necessary improvements which elementary considerations of safety and health had led local governments to demand that they adopt. Corporate arrogance was no longer a doctrinaire cry of reformers. Now it was an unprotected railway crossing where children were killed as they came home from school or the refusal of an impoverished water company to make improvements needed to provide the healthful water which could stop the epidemics of typhoid fever. Such incidents made the corporation look like a killer. These specific threats united all classes: anyone's child might be careless at a railroad crossing, and typhoid fever was no respector of social origins.

From such new, direct, and immediate threats progressivism developed its thrust. The more corporations used their political influence to resist making the small improvements, the more communities developed increasingly radical economic programs like municipal ownership or consumer-owned utilities and fought to overthrow the machines that gave immunity to the corporations. Political reforms like the initiative, direct primary, and home rule became increasingly important in the early stages of progressivism because, as William Allen White said, men had first to get the gun before they could hit anything with it. But it was the failure of the political system to respond to the new and immediate threats of the depression that convinced people that more desperate programs were needed.

Perhaps there are, after all, times and places where issues cut across class lines. These are the times and places where men identify less with their occupational roles as producers and more with their roles as consumers—of death-dealing water, unsafe railway

crossings, polluted air, high streetcar rates, corrupt politicians—
which serve to unite them across social barriers. There are also
universal emotions—anger and fear—which possess all men regardless of their backgrounds. The importance of the depression of the
1890's was that it aroused those universal emotions, posed dramatic and desperate enough threats to lead men of all types to
agree that tax dodging and corporate arrogance had to be ended
and thereby served to unite many previously fragmented reformers
and to enlist the support of the majority that had earlier been
either silent or enthusiastic only about partisan issues like the tariff
or symbols like Abraham Lincoln. The conversion of the National
Municipal League showed how issues were becoming more important than backgrounds. Originally composed of elitists who favored such Mugwumpish concerns as civil service reform, the
League by 1898 had become so desperate with the domination
over political machines by utility companies that it devoted its
energies to municipal ownership and to political devices which
promised "more trust in the people, more democracy" than its
earlier elitism had permitted. The attitude of moral indignation,
such an obvious feature of the early stages of progressivism, was
not rooted in social tensions but in the universal emotion of anger.

Whether this emphasis on the results of the depression—unrest,
new threats and new issues, and cooperation among social groups
—has widespread relevance or validity remains to be seen, but it
does help to explain the roots of progressivism in Wisconsin. The
most important factor in producing the intensity of Wisconsin
progressivism was the cooperation between previously discrete and
fragmented social groups both in forging popular issues and getting reforms adopted. And the most important factor in defining
the popular issues was the arrogance of certain corporations. In
Milwaukee the traction and electricity monopoly between 1894
and 1896 alone, for reasons ranging from extreme overcapitaliza-
tion to confidence in its political powers, raised both its lighting
and streetcar fares, refused to arbitrate with its striking employees,

enjoined the city from enforcing ordinances lowering its fares, and used its political power—the company's chief manager was the state's leading Republican boss—to cut its tax bill in half, kill an ordinance which would have prevented it from polluting the air, and thwart generally popular attempts at regulation. Each time the monopoly refused to obey an order, lobbied special favors from the city or state, or prostituted the Republican party to the company, the progressive coalition grew. By the end of the depression, the coalition drew together both ends of the economic spectrum— the Merchants and Manufacturers Association and the Chamber of Commerce as well as several labor unions and the Federated Trades Council. Politically it included the country Republican Club, the Democratic Jefferson Club, and the Socialists and Populists. The Mugwumpish and upper-class Municipal League was joined by German social clubs like the Turnvereine. So defiant was the company—so desperate were the people—that the traction managers became the state's most hated men by 1899; and humorist-politician George Peck observed that Wisconsin's parents "frighten children when they are bad, by telling them that if they don't look out," the traction magnates "will get them." Four hundred miles away, in Superior, the story was remarkably similar. Angered by the repeated refusals of that city's water company to provide the city with healthful enough water to prevent the typhoid fever epidemics that killed dozens of people each year, and blaming the company's political power within both parties for the failure of regulation, labor unions and Populists cooperated with business and professional men and with dissident politicians to try to secure pure water and to overthrow the politicians owned by the company. In Superior, political debate had indeed narrowed, as an editor observed, to a fight of "the people against corporate insolence." The water company, like the traction monopoly at Milwaukee, stood isolated and alone, the enemy of men from all backgrounds. In Wisconsin, at least, the community's groups continued to perform their special functions; and, by the

end of the depression, they were all agreed that corporate arrogance had to be abolished. Their desperation made them willing
to speak, lobby, and work together.

If, as the Wisconsin experience suggests, cooperation was the
underpinning of progressivism, historians should focus on reformers not as victims of social tensions, but as reformers. At any given
time and place, hundreds of men and groups are seeking supporters for their plans to change society and government. The
basic problem for the reformer is to win mass support for his
program. In Wisconsin a reformer's effectiveness depended on
how well he manipulated acts of corporate and individual arrogance that infuriated everyone in order to demonstrate the plausibility of his program. Desperate events had made tax dodging, corporate defiance and control of politics the main political issues
and had allowed this program to swallow the older reformers at
the same time that they created a much broader constituency for
reform. The question then becomes: Why did some succeed while
others failed? North Dakota never developed a full-blown progressive movement because that state's progressives never demonstrated the plausibility of their programs. Wisconsin's early progressives did succeed in drawing together such diverse groups as
unions, businessmen, Populists, and dissident politicians because
they adapted their program and rhetoric to the menacing events
which angered everyone. Reformers operate in their hometowns
and not in some contrived social background which could as easily
apply to New York or Keokuk, and it is in their hometowns that
they should be studied. Historians should determine why they
succeeded or failed to rally the support of their communities to
their programs, for the most significant criterion for any reformer
is, in the end, his effectiveness.

When the progressive characteristically spoke of reform as a
fight of "the people" or the "public interest" against the "selfish
interests," he was speaking quite literally of his political coalition
because the important fact about progressivism, at least in Wisconsin, was the degree of cooperation between previously discrete

social groups now united under the banner of the "public interest." When the progressive politician denounced the arrogance of quasi-public corporations and tax-dodgers, he knew that experiences and events had made his attacks popular with voters from all backgrounds. Both conceptually and empirically it would seem safer and more productive to view reformers first as reformers and only secondarily as men who were trying to relieve class and status anxieties. The basic riddle in progressivism is not what drove groups apart, but what made them seek common cause.

A Giant Step Backward

The Negro and Disfranchisement

by Sheldon Hackney

The end of Radical Reconstruction in 1877 had not terminated all Negro voting in the South. Even under the Redeemer governments, blacks continued to vote, although in smaller numbers, depending on the degree of physical coercion or economic pressures brought to bear on them in different localities. Yet in state after state, even during the 1870's and 1880's, black voting declined significantly as white Redeemer politicians stuffed the ballot boxes, complicated voting procedures for Negroes, and, if necessary, sanctioned violence. Throughout the 1880's, however, Southern white politicians continued to play with the dwindling Negro vote in order to bolster their particular factions. It was mainly the minority of prosperous Southern blacks or Negro politicians who allied their supporters with local groups of Redeemer politicians and kept disfranchisement from becoming complete even without legal impediments.

But even this controlled and harmless exercise in voting by blacks soon became anathema to the mass of white voters, and demands for total disfranchisement began to grow, reaching their peak during the Progressive Era. Beginning in the 1890's the restraints on black voting in the South became imbedded in con-

stitutional law. The movement for complete disfranchisement arose during the height of the agrarian Populist crusade and continued during the following decade, largely under the leadership of Southern demagogues who were Progressives in other matters but also bitter-end racists, "anti-trust and anti-Negro." Almost every Southern state during the 1890's and 1900's revised its constitution, state laws, or local ordinances to require some combination of poll taxes, literacy tests, and property qualifications that could generally be applied at the discretion of local voting registrars. Seven states even introduced into their constitutions the so-called "grandfather clause," waiving all other requirements for lineal descendants of persons who could vote in 1867, a provision designed to permit those poor whites to vote who were unable to meet the other new qualifications.

In addition, Southern states also passed legislation during this period allowing the Democratic party, which completely dominated the region's politics, to set its own rules for membership and primary voting, in other words, permitting "whites only" voting in the primary elections. Starting with Mississippi in 1890 and ending with Georgia in 1908, the South effectively excluded the Negro from voting through patently unconstitutional but "legal" devices. In the following selection Sheldon Hackney describes this dismal process in Alabama.

❧ Emancipation Day was celebrated on January 1, 1901, in Negro communities throughout Alabama just as it had been for many years. Numerous Negro speakers enumerated and detailed the progress of Negroes since the Civil War: progress made in literacy, land ownership, business, the professions, and the aggregate of personal achievements that reflected material progress. Measured against the lowly status of Negroes 35 years before, these advances seemed spectacular. But measured against the promise of American life, they were not great enough to dissuade whites from their belief in the doctrine of Negro inferiority. Some people felt Ne-

From *Populism to Progressivism in Alabama* (Princeton: Princeton University Press, 1969), pp. 180–208. Reprinted by permission; footnotes omitted.

groes had failed their test as Americans and deserved to be proscribed. Others, such as those for whom Tom Heflin spoke, feared
that Negroes were succeeding too well. For whatever reason, most
white men in Alabama agreed on the necessity of disfranchisement. It was the biggest and most important downward readjustment in the long and bitter process of redefining the Negro's
place in Southern life.

The trend in race relations had been evident in the South ever
since Florida enacted the first Jim Crow law in 1887. The tendency was to replace informal, fluctuating, and nonuniform patterns with legal, static, and uniform methods of treating Negroes.
For example, Negroes could vote and participate in politics in
various ways in some places during the 1890's. In other places
countless stratagems of dubious morality were employed to neutralize or utilize their votes. The constitutional convention, said
James Weatherly, was called to replace "this revolutionary method
by legal machinery. . . ."

The revolutionary methods had grown out of the vague feeling
among many whites that there was something impermanent and
not right about existing relations between the races. As a friend
wrote to John W. DuBose, probably in 1902, "The Civil War
. . . did not settle the problem. It is still unsettled and must remain so until settled right." But with no model of "right," there
was no agreement on the spheres of life from which even the
deferential Negro should be excluded.

Consequently the pattern of race relations was highly fluid in
Alabama in the period 1890 to 1910. Inconsistency was the primary characteristic. The law in its various guises brought increasing order to the situation, and in doing so abolished both the
freedom and the insecurity that went with inconsistency. The
workings of the law could be seen in various fields. The city council of Montgomery passed an ordinance segregating the seating on
streetcars in 1900. A Negro boycott that year failed to reverse the
decision. Jim Crow did not come to the railroad stations until
January 6, 1902, when the Alabama Railroad Commission issued

an order to the railroads operating in the state to maintain comfortable waiting rooms for their passengers. The order also required railroads to furnish separate waiting rooms for the two
races. The last company of Negro state militia, the Capitol City
Guards, was not disbanded until 1905. Meanwhile Birmingham's
mayor announced that the new Birmingham jail, famed in folk
song and pamphlets of protest, would be segregated at last.

While recognizing the law's creative role in the structure of
segregation, the growing separation of the races did exist independent of the law. This separation was even extended to the
domain of death. A Negro newspaper noticed in 1900 that the
Mississippi legislature had ordered the removal of the remains of
the Honorable James Lynch from the white cemetery where they
rested since his death. Two years later a Birmingham paper reported that "Will Mathis has requested Judge Lowry to have his
hanging at a different hour from the time that the negro, Orlando
Lester, will be hanged, and also that he be hanged from a different
set of gallows."

Labor was a particularly sensitive area of race relations. The vice
president of the Alabama Federation of Labor in 1902 was J. H.
Beanes, a Negro, who was host for the organization's annual convention in Selma in that year. Community pressure was strong
for the meeting to be segregated, but there was resistance. A delegate from Typographical Union Local 104 in Birmingham stated
that "rather than see one accredited delegate, black or white,
thrown out of this convention I would go to the woods and hold
this meeting." Union locals were thoroughly segregated, but conventions and governing bodies admitted Negroes in order to protect unionism from an increasingly hostile Negro labor force.

Perhaps nothing better captures the flux of patterns of segregation in the South at the turn of the century than the case of a
Southerner with an impeccable pedigree, Mary Custis Lee, the
daughter of Robert E. Lee. In 1902 she was arrested on the Washington, Alexandria & Mt. Vernon Railroad for refusing to move
from the Negro section of the car where she had taken her seat.
She was not a freedom rider; she simply was not aware that there

was a law segregating the races on that railroad, and evidently was not used to such a practice being dictated by custom.

Pathological evidence of the disturbed state of race relations was available in the statistics on lynching. The ten-year period 1889 to 1899 witnessed the most dramatic rise and decline of lynch law. The peak years were 1891 and 1892; in each year 24 people were dispatched by mobs in Alabama. The low point of a mere four lynchings was reached in 1900. But in 1901, a year of prosperity and rising cotton prices, contrary to the notion that the frequency of lynchings fluctuated in response to deviations from the long-term trend in cotton prices, there were 16 mob murders. It was no accident that disfranchisement was the single most important public issue that year. This raises the question of the cause of the ebb and flow in this form of physical aggression. It is certainly true that "respectable" groups in society carried on campaigns to discourage people from resorting to rope and faggot. Thomas G. Jones went so far as to argue that the Thirteenth and Fourteenth Amendments gave federal courts jurisdiction in lynching cases against mob members who deprived Negro victims of equal protection and due process of law. Governor William Dorsey Jelks (1901–1906) was sincerely devoted to the prevention of lynching, for which he suffered some criticism. He was deeply disturbed by the fact that "human life is about as cheap in Alabama as it is anywhere. . . ." Yet he was unable to get lynchers convicted even when the evidence appeared overwhelming. In view of the continued immunity of lynchers it would seem that some factor other than social disapproval was responsible for the decline of lynching.

It is likely that the high rate of extralegal sanctions against Negroes in the 1890's was related to the fluidity and uncertainty in patterns of race relations. The potential for conflict was greater as long as patterns of permissible conduct were poorly defined and changing. At the end of the decade and after, as legal devices were used increasingly to define and make uniform the prescribed boundaries of the permissible in race relations, anxious whites felt less need to assert their superiority. The Negro leader and president of Alabama A. and M. College at Normal, W. H. Councill, sensed this when he told an Emancipation Day audience in 1901 "that the salvation of the negro in this country depends upon drawing the social lines tighter, tighter all the while, North and South. The moment they become slack the white man becomes brutal—the negro goes down forever."

Councill's statement also reflected the deepening disillusionment of Negroes in the face of their increasing proscription. This despair was expressed in the half-dozen extant Negro newspapers in Alabama. As the 1890's wore on, Negroes postponed their quest for full citizenship through political self-assertion and turned to the more traditional paths favored by Booker T. Washington and W. H. Councill. Accommodation, material self-improvement, and dependence on upper-class whites seemed to be the only choice short of emigration for Negroes. H. C. Binford, schoolteacher, city alderman, and newspaper editor, in 1899 told his readers: "there is nothing in politics for us, it makes no difference which side wins none of them want the Negro." A year later he glumly admitted that "we have gotten use to being slighted and have ceased to kick. What's the use?" Negro newspapers of all shades of opinion put increased emphasis on the need to acquire education and property.

Prospects were so gloomy that Washington thought that "before we [Negroes] can make much progress we must decide whether or not the Negro is to be a permanent part of the South." Not only was there a Negro emigration movement of unknown strength, and white propagandists of colonization like John Temple Graves, Thomas Pearce Bailey, and John Tyler Morgan, but newspapers were full of plans to replace the Negro labor force and population of the South with white immigrants. The atmosphere was so tense that W. H. Councill surrendered to pessimism. In a controversial article in *The Forum* in 1899 he arrived at the conclusion that everything the Negro had was at the sufferance of the whites and that there was no future for the Negro in America.

Councill's despair led to two patterns of thought. On the one

hand there was the policy of accommodation—and Councill was
an expert accommodator. In 1901, as always, he needed funds
from the state government, and applied to Governor Samford hat-
in-hand. His letter argued that the state was getting a good deal
because "all of this vast property is deeded to the State of Alabama. The State has donated money only for a normal school
which is putting into rural districts as well as the towns teachers
who are not only competent to teach, but who are in harmony
with the institutions and customs of the South." To complete
this example of the policy of accommodation, Councill's request
was endorsed by General William C. Oates who played the role
of upper-class paternalist. Oates wrote that he thought "Councill
a good man and fine manager of this school and politically all
right."

The other fork of Councill's two-pronged pessimism was the
assertion of a perennial American Negro myth, "repatriation." The
redemption of Africa from barbarism by American Negroes was a
satisfying dream for Negroes who were alienated from American
life and suffering from a poor self-image.

The progressive alienation of Negroes sprang from several
sources. One prime cause was the dwindling sphere of economic
opportunity. Negro newspapers in Alabama were aware, as was
Councill, of the Negro's weakening position in the job market.
But while the Negro is anxious to work," commented the *Southern Watchman*, "there are those who are using every effort to deprive him of the wherewithal to earn his daily bread."

But it was the total impact of adverse change that Negroes
experienced. One Negro newspaper reacted with bitterness, indignation, despair, bewilderment, and resignation:

The "Jim Crow" car law, which forces the respectable and the dis-
respectable Negro to travel in the same car is infamous enough, an
insult is being added to injury continually. Have those in power
forgotten that there is a God, and do they not know that every
seed of unjust discrimination sown will in some due time come up.
. . . The Negro is as docile as he can be . . . and day after day he

is reminded through the daily papers . . . that some additional
project is on foot, or is about to be promulgated to stand as a menace
to his development, or a curb to his ambitious manhood . . . and we
wonder what the harvest will be.

Leaders of the white community were as aware as Negroes were
of the deterioration in race relations, for the future of the Negro
was a popular topic of public discussion. One evidence of this
concern and interest was The Southern Society for the Promotion
of the Study of Race Conditions and Problems in the South.
Edgar Gardner Murphy conceived the idea and quickly enlisted
Hilary Herbert and a blue-ribbon membership. The result was a
widely publicized meeting in May 1900 in Montgomery. The conference aired a broad range of opinion, from John Temple
Graves's call for colonization of Negroes in Africa to William A.
MacCorkle's insistence that Negroes be treated as citizens. A Negro observer reported that there was no support for Graves's proposal nor for the argument of a North Carolina man that Southern states ought not to educate Negroes. Other speakers evidently
met significant opposition when they expressed their belief in the
inherent inferiority of Negroes, when they maintained that Negro
criminality was getting worse, and when they thought that Negro
religious life should be guided and controlled by whites. Everyone
was opposed to lynch law. According to Murphy, even the Northerners agreed that enfranchising Negroes was a mistake.

This is an important indication of the state of informed opinion
at the time of the Alabama Constitutional Convention. Booker T.
Washington himself was yielding before it. In November 1899 he
had tried unsuccessfully to rally Negro opposition to a disfranchising measure pending before the Georgia Assembly. At the same
time, however, he was talking of backing an educational qualification for suffrage as a means of ensuring that Negroes would be
judged on the same basis as whites. G. W. Atkinson of West Virginia questioned the wisdom of such a deal with white leaders.
Atkinson advised Washington that he thought the Democratic
leaders of the South were using Washington and that any voting

law would be administered so as to discriminate against Negroes.

As later events proved, it was naïve of Washington to think registrars would apply suffrage tests fairly to both races. Atkinson grasped the essential evil of the Southern system when he understood this. But Washington understood that he had very little choice; he was simply trying to use his contacts among white leaders to make the best deal possible under the circumstances.

The problem was, those bent on disfranchisement were no longer restrained by the federal government or by opposition from within the state. The small force of 14 Populists and Republicans in the 155-member convention could do little, though they stood fast against limiting suffrage. The sizable opposition to disfranchisement registered in the referendum, more interested in white votes than black, was not nearly sufficient to block the powerful coalition whose divergent interests happened to focus on disfranchisement. There was so little resistance of any kind that there was little need to camouflage the purpose and intent of the convention.

"And what is it that we want to do?" asked John B. Knox in his presidential address to the Constitutional Convention of Alabama as it opened its deliberations on May 22, 1901. "Why it is within the limits imposed by the Federal Constitution, to establish white supremacy in this State." The subordinate position of the Negro race was about to be written into the fundamental law. "Our purpose is plain," delegate Thomas Watts asserted some days later. "It is not denied by any man upon the floor of this Convention or in this State."

There was such a consensus on disfranchising Negroes that the main question facing the convention was not whether to do it but how to do it without violating the Federal Constitution on the one hand and the pledge not to disfranchise any white men on the other hand.

The committee of the convention in charge of the delicate task of drafting the suffrage article was the Committee on Suffrage and Elections, composed of 21 lawyers and including 9 members from the Black Belt. The chairman of the committee was Thomas W. Coleman from Eutaw in Greene County. Coleman was a graduate of Princeton and the University of Alabama Law School, a former Associate Justice of the Alabama Supreme Court, an officer in the Confederate army, a member of the Constitutional Convention of 1875, and the president of the Merchants and Farmers Bank of Eutaw. Of such stuff was the convention made.

While the rest of the convention settled down for an uncomfortably hot and contentious summer of parliamentary maneuvering . . . the Suffrage Committee met for the first time on May 29 and began its long and arduous task of shaping a suffrage article. It drew on the suffrage provisions of other Southern states, as well as many ordinances submitted by delegates, sent by constituents, and published by newspapers. Through the month of June the committee debated in private the sundry suggestions of how best to disfranchise the Negro. Even without diabolical registrars, the constitution could eliminate Negroes by applying tests that took advantage of differing social conditons. Property tests, literacy tests, residence requirements, the poll tax, and disqualification for conviction of certain crimes all fell into this category.

The central problem was how, or whether, to provide for the whites who would be disfranchised by the anti-Negro provisions unless some special loophole were created for them. There is no doubt that many people in the state envisaged the disfranchisement of poor whites as well as poor Negroes.

In his opening address President Knox provided a rationale for those wishing to disfranchise whites while not violating the pledge of the party. On the one hand there were 236,476 white males of voting age of whom 31,681 were illiterate but who were not to be disfranchised. On the other hand there were 181,345 Negro males of voting age of whom 107,946 were literate and who were to be disfranchised. "We are pledged," said Knox, " 'not to deprive any white man of the right to vote,' but this does not extend unless this Convention chooses to extend it beyond the right of voters now living."

The Committee on Suffrage and Elections accepted Knox's rationalization. When it finally made its recommendations on June 30, the majority report was a grotesquely complicated document that eventually became Article VIII of the new constitution with very few alterations.

Article VIII, as finally passed, contained two distinct "plans." The permanent plan contained the disfranchising provisions, the qualifications that were to be a permanent part of the organic law. The temporary plan consisted of the devices designed to permit those of the favored race (or party) who would not be able to qualify under the permanent rules to register under special provisions. The temporary plan expired on January 1, 1903.

The permanent plan set up a most elaborate maze through which one had to grope to claim the privilege of becoming an elector. The basic conditions for registration were that a person must be a male citizen, or alien who had declared his intention of becoming a citizen, twenty-one years of age who had resided in the state for two years, the county for one year, and the precinct for three months. The second requirement was the ability to read and write any article of the United States Constitution, unless physical disability caused the deficiency. Except for the physically disabled, the prospective elector also must have been engaged in some lawful employment for the greater part of the preceding twelve months. If this requirement could not be met there was the alternative property qualification of 40 acres of land on which the prospective elector lived, or the ownership of real or personal property assessed for taxes at a value of $300 and on which the taxes had been paid. There was, in addition, a long list of disqualifying crimes, including vagrancy. Having become an elector, the last cul-de-sac in the labyrinth was the cumulative poll tax of $1.50 per year that had to be paid on or before the first day of February preceding the election in which the elector offered to vote.

Those who could meet all but the literacy and property qualifications were provided with loopholes that were to be open, for only a few months. For this purpose Louisiana's famous "grandfather clause" was adapted by Alabama, indeed the only novelty of the suffrage article, so that it became the "Fighting Grandfather Clause." This device allowed those to register who had served honorably in the land or naval forces of the United States or Confederate States in any war from 1812 on, or who were descendants of such veterans. If this were not enough, there was the further provision to register "all persons who are of good character and who understand the duties and obligations of citizenship under a republican form of government."

From July 23 to August 3 the convention gave itself over to a remarkably frank debate on the suffrage article. The most significant attack on the article came from an important group of men who questioned the "Fighting Grandfather" clause. In their minority report, they pointed out that the clause set up an arbitrary standard which discriminated against citizens of the United States on the basis of race and was therefore a violation of the Federal Constitution. They also asserted that it was undemocratic, that it insulted white men by requiring less of them than of Negroes, that it was open to manipulation, fraud, and perjury. These men wanted suffrage requirements that applied to all alike.

William C. Oates, the chief spokesman of the minority of the Committee on Suffrage and Elections, received support on the floor from Thomas G. Jones who spoke in the tradition of patrician paternalism. George P. Harrison and Stanley H. Dent, prominent men who had been colleagues of Jones in the gold Democratic Party in 1896, also signed the minority report. Senators Morgan and Edmund W. Pettus made their opposition known in letters to the convention. The instructive thing about this opposition to the granfather clause was that it was not all of one coloration.

The fourth signer of the minority report was Frank S. White of Birmingham who doubled at the convention as the leader of Comer's crew of railroad regulators. J. L. M. Curry was also op-

posed to providing loopholes for ignorant white men, and Robert
J. Lowe of Birmingham, Chairman of the State Democratic
Executive Committee and a man with some Progressive leanings,
thought the grandfather clause was "the very repudiation of
fairness."

Evidently, the Big Mules and the Progressives shared a pessimism about human nature as well as a passion for social order.
Much of the discussion of the grandfather clause and white
suffrage was based on a belief in the existence of a large, powerful,
and dangerous portion of the population that was "ignorant and
vicious." The convention was dedicated to limiting the suffrage to
the "intelligent and virtuous." Samuel Blackwell, a Progressive
from Morgan County, expressed his desire to put the suffrage only
in the hands of competent men so as to ensure good government.
He affirmed his belief that "nature has marked the weak and incompetent to be protected by Government, rather than to be the
directors of the Government."

This outlook received support from Alabama's most famous
reformer, Edgar Gardner Murphy. The crusading rector of St.
John's Episcopal church in Montgomery wrote an "open letter" to
the constitutional convention, in which he voiced his opposition
to the grandfather clause. Then in the midst of a campaign to
free the state of the evil of child labor, Murphy expressed doubts
about the natural goodness of man. His social reforms were essentially aimed at putting institutional limits on human capacity
for evil. But he also believed in secular progress, in industrialization, and in improving the material and moral condition of man.
He wanted to release the creative energies of men who were
cramped and rendered inefficient by human institutions. An
aristocracy of the educated would achieve that progress, so limiting
suffrage to the "intelligent and virtuous" was a step in the right
direction.

It is quite likely that some of the opposition to the grandfather
clause was influenced by personal obligations to Booker T. Washington who was actively soliciting the aid of white businessmen

for a letter-writing campaign. Murphy and Oates, in particular, were on easy terms with him, and Thomas G. Jones was appointed to a federal district judgeship in October 1901 by his grace. Washington's most open move was a petition to the convention signed by fifteen prominent Negroes which humbly asked that Negroes be allowed to share in the choice of their rulers.

This "humble and unnecessary" petition was not well received in some quarters of the Negro community. The *Southern Watchman* stigmatized Washington as "the white man's ideal Negro" and entered an eloquent plea for racial justice. "Do not show us how to be men and then blame us for being men," wrote the *Watchman*, which claimed to be speaking for "every intelligent Negro in America" when it asserted "that they are not satisfied with the present condition of things in the South."

Neither protesting Negroes, with whatever tone of voice, nor sympathetic whites could budge the majority. Defending the suffrage article from attacks on the left as well as the right, the convention tabled the minority report by a vote of 109 to 23. The "no" votes were cast by the opponents of the grandfather clause, joined by Populists and Republicans who were against the whole idea of suffrage restriction in spite of the inducements offered by the temporary plan.

To Knox and Coleman and other prominent champions of the clause, the most beautiful thing about the temporary plan was that it was temporary. Delegates who represented poor-white voters, whose support for the new constituion the compromise was designed to secure, made several attempts to widen and lengthen the loophole. A minor irony is the fact that the principal doctrinal support for belief in the common (white) man, or in the "democratic myth," was white supremacy—the doctrine that "the white man was always qualified to vote. He inherits his qualities. . . . The meanest white man in the State is within the saving clause. . . ." The adherents of such a philosophy failed in their attempt to make the grandfather clause permanent, and the convention also defeated other attempts to postpone the terminal date of the temporary plan.

In order to move the convention in the other direction representatives from the Black Belt tried to raise the age at which a man became exempt from the poll tax from forty-five to sixty. This was in reality a fight over white disfranchisement. After a series of close votes that indicated the restrictionists had a slight majority, the issue was compromised by setting the age of exemption at forty-five, but providing that the legislature could raise it to sixty. Similarly, for fear of creating opposition to the new constitution in the ratifying referendum, the convention gave north Alabama its way by defeating the Black Belt's attempt to raise the property requirements for suffrage.

The only victory won by those who wanted to expand the electorate beyond the limits set by the majority of the Committee on Suffrage and Elections came in regard to aliens. The majority report had reversed existing practice by not providing for the registration of aliens who had declared their intention of becoming citizens. On the motion and initiative of C. P. Beddow, a spokesman for Birmingham labor, the convention changed the majority report so that "first paper" aliens could register and vote. Beddow won another victory by getting the wording of the article changed so that strikers would not be proscribed by the ban against persons who were not regularly employed.

The meager results of attempts to change the suffrage article might give the impression that the debates were dull. Nothing could be further from the truth.

Among other things, the debates disclosed the gnawing sense of guilt that permeated the convention. They bore witness to the recent suggestion of Professor C. Vann Woodward that the peculiarities of the Southern identity owe much to the un-American experiences of defeat, poverty, and guilt. Every time electoral fraud was mentioned, every time a delegate argued that the suffrage article did not violate the Fifteenth Amendment, every time the pledge not to disfranchise any white man was explained away, the uneasy conscience was briefly exposed. Dr. Russell M. Cunningham remarked in a revealing jest that he had often in his life wanted to be a lawyer. "This is one time," he said, "I am glad that I am not. If I were a lawyer I would not only be expected to have a conscience, but I would also be expected to have an opinion, and leave the conscience to rest. (Laughter)."

Mike Sollie could not ignore his conscience. A rather traditional thinker who nevertheless supported Comer's drive for railroad regulation, Sollie was oppressed by the thought that the South's "history records a grievous error. . . . It was contrary to the principles of freedom and liberty embedded deep in the American heart that slavery should exist in our midst." And Sollie feared that the South's present and future woes were growing out of this sin of the fathers. "Our prostrated and devastated South," he said, "our unequal opportunities in the race of progress and the graves of our dead heroes are all parts of the painful accounting we have thus far given for the sin committed."

The uncomfortable themes of sin and retribution were suffocated under the patchwork quilt of the orthodox view of the past. This popular view gained authority from repetition, and dissent became perilous. The best of the speeches evoked all of the proper and approved historical symbols: the pernicious Yankee Slave Trader, the hallowed Founding Fathers, the Happy Slave, the glorious Lost Cause, the Faithful Retainer, Black Reconstruction, the Depraved Negro, the Blessed Redemption, the Required Corruption to maintain White Supremacy, and the Necessary Purification of the Ballot. The past was marshaled to justify the present.

The present that needed justifying was a time of racial proscription. In the melange of opinion four varieties of racial attitudes can be isolated. They might be called: (a) Orthodox White Supremacy, (b) Paternalism, (c) Radicalism, and (d) race-bating Demagoguery. The orthodox white supremacy was based on what was taken to be the simple and demonstrable fact of the superiority of the white race and its inherited capacity to rule. This fact was supported by an evolutionary conception of history, but Providential rather than Darwinian evolution. In this view, "the records of history are largely narratives of man's advancement from barbarism to civilization. The great, dominant, white races of the earth have been thousands of years in reaching their present state of development." Meanwhile the Negro race had been completely stationary. The turn-of-the-century euphoria about western civilization, which did so much to abet the forces of uplift, in this case contributed to the contrast between the races which justified the conclusion that "the white race must dominate because it is the superior race. . . ."

The key concept in the orthodox outlook was that there should be little or no differentiation among Negroes. Every Negro should carry the value that was assigned to the race as a whole by the white community's stereotype.

By looking at Negroness in much the same way that they looked at membership in the lower class, paternalists were able to recognize differences among Negroes. They normally wanted to hold out hope to the Negro that in the future he might individually improve his status and attain some of the rights of citizenship of which he was being denuded. Where orthodox racism was based on a vague and erroneous genetics, paternalism was based on a more plastic social judgment. Some paternalists hoped that in the distant future, equal education and employment opportunities would enable the Negro to stand on his own as a full citizen.

But in 1901 the Negro was not a full citizen. In fact, it seemed as if he was being pushed entirely out of society. In this atmosphere the distinctive note of paternalism was its insistence that society was an organic whole of which the Negro was an integral, although subservient, part and that the white man was chaged with moral responsibility for his welfare. "The negro race is under us," argued ex-Governor Thomas G. Jones, ". . . we have shorn him of all political power. . . . In return for that, we should extend to him . . . all the civil rights that will fit him to be a decent and self-respecting, law-abiding and intelligent citizen of this state."

Even more feeble in 1901 was the idealistic hope of racial cooperation. This radical point of view, extraordinary for the time, found its spokesmen among the Republicans and Populists. There was, for instance, John H. Porter from Coosa County who had in turn been a Whig, a Populist, and a Republican. Porter was not afraid to dispute the orthodox view of the past or of the present. He stated that all the Negro asked for as a citizen of the state was "to choose between two or more the one he prefers to rule over him. This right," said Porter, "in my judgment, he should have."

The Republicans had been the original experimenters with biracial politics and still had obligations to their constituents. But it would be too much to say that the Populists had taken up where the Republicans left off. I. L. Brock chided O. D. Street, who was in the process of becoming a Republican, for his opposition to disfranchisement. "You know the populists always were willing and ready for the negro to be disfranchised if it could be done without disfranchising the white man, . . ." he wrote. But the fact is that the foremost champion of Negro suffrage at the convention was a Populist who was also in transit to the Republican party.

Newton B. Spears was a Tennesseean and the son of a Union general. These facts do not explain his radical views on race, but perhaps they help account for his antipathy toward the Democratic Party and his freedom from its mythology. Men who were still Populists in 1901 were likely to be more unorthodox in their views on race relations than was the mass of Populists when the party was at full strength in 1894–96. Only congenital "outsiders" would cling to such an obviously dead party. In addition to this, those Populist politicians who wanted to make the shift to Republicanism had to prove they were good Republicans at heart, and standing up for Negro suffrage was one way to do this in 1901, for the lily whites had not yet taken over the party.

Spears declared that Negroes could no longer be treated as slaves. They were citizens. He challenged any delegate to stand up and "contend that the ordinance we are now considering does not

abridge the privilege of voting . . ." of both black and white men.
He praised the Thirteenth, Fourteenth, and Fifteenth Amend-
ments, characterized the proposed voter registration system as
tyranny, lauded William Lloyd Garrison and Lincoln, swore by
Old Hickory Jackson, called the equalitarian Jefferson the greatest
Populist, and thoroughly antagonized the convention.

Spears's defiance of the convention extended to thinking that
Negroes should have the right to vote. He thought, in fact, that
they should have justice. As the convention recovered from that
idea, he asked it most prophetically if it wanted "to pursue a
course and a policy that will make the negro look to Washington
and not to Montgomery for protection?"

Another theme, and one not at all muted, was that of strident
and aggressive racism cast in terms of race conflict. This jarring
chord was struck by the budding demagogue, J. Thomas Heflin.
On the verge of a political career that would take him to the
United States Senate, Tom Heflin was a new type in Alabama. He
became famous as a storyteller and spokesman for the common
white man. But if his performance in the convention of 1901 is a
true indication, while he was talking for the poor whites he was
voting for the rich ones.

The tone of Heflin's depiction of race relations, even where he
was not diverging from the orthodox view, was aggressive and
antagonistic. The Negro was not merely subordinate to the white
race, but he was ordained by God to be the white man's servant.
And Heflin did not stop at this sort of revival of the old pro-
slavery argument. When, in order to rationalize its action on
suffrage, the convention resorted to the theory that the ballot was
not a right but a privilege, Heflin went one step further and maintained that it was a natural right for the white man but a privilege
for the Negro. He insisted that Negroes and whites should never
be required to compete on the same level. "If you want to make a
foot race," said Heflin, "let us make it with the descendants of
our own tribe." Tribalism and race conflict were basic to Heflin's
philosophy.

Heflin thought the impending conflict rendered it mere folly to educate or otherwise equip the Negro. Consequently he supported the move (which ended in a compromise) to provide for separate Negro and white school systems, each supported by the taxes paid directly by that race. In the first place, thought Heflin, "he doesn't need encouragement. . . . Why as soon as you elevate him you ruin him." But more importantly, it was dangerous. Heflin gave new clothes to the old antebellum fear of educating the slaves. "The negroes are being educated very rapidly," he told his fellow delegates who professed to think Negroes incapable of education, "and I say in the light of all the history of the past, some day when the two separate and distinct races are thrown together, some day the clash will come and the survival of the fittest, and I do not believe it is incumbent upon us to lift him up and educate him on an equal footing that he may be armed and equipped when the combat comes." Heflin spoke with the voice of twentieth-century frustrations.

The shrewdness of the authors of the suffrage article, in reconciling the aims of the various racial theories, was revealed when the debates and motions to amend had run their ineffective course. The vote to approve the entire article showed an overwhelming victory, 95–19. The minority consisted of those on the right who opposed the grandfather clause and those on the left who adhered to the principle of universal manhood suffrage. Eleven of the "no" votes came from the Republicans and Populists. All of the "yes" votes were Democratic. Disfranchisement was a reality after ten years of talk and agitation.

The differential in voting between the races was immediate and marked. In 1906 there were 205,278 whites registered in Alabama, 83 per cent of the male whites of voting age. Only 3,654 Negroes, 2 per cent of the adult men, were registered. That has been much the ratio until the campaign to increase Negro registration in the South in the 1960's.

The effect of the new constitution on white voting is more debatable. Governor Jelks was anxious to prove that the consti-

tution worked properly. One of the big fears of white-county
delegates was that the registrars would not register white men
whom they suspected of improper political leanings. Could Christ
and his Disciples register under the good character clause? "That
would depend entirely on which way he was going to vote," said
John W. A. Sanford. After the constitution was in effect, Senator
Morgan became quite worried about reports that registrars in the
Black Belt were registering "politically reliable" Negroes.

I think you are perhaps unnecessarily alarmed [responded Jelks].
The Board of Appointment spent thirty days selecting these Registrars
and in every instance we were assured positively that the appointees
would carry out the spirit of the Constitution, which looks to the
registration of all men not convicted of crime, and only a few
negroes. . . .
What is distressing me now is the general apathy on the subject of
the Payment of polls.

Whether or not it resulted from apathy or poverty, Governor
Jelks had cause for concern about the nonpayment of the poll tax.
However, the figures for registration and for poll tax receipts
might shed some light on a murky point of interpretation. Scholars
are in dispute about the reasons for the rapid decline in white
voting. Undoubtedly both apathy and disfranchisement played a
part. The question is, which should get the greater emphasis? The
crux of the problem is that there is no way to measure the number
of adult men who would have voted had they not been prohibited
by some legal barrier.

Perhaps some rough indication can be devised to measure the
effect of at least the poll tax requirement in Alabama. The separate
acts of registering *and* paying poll tax *both* had to be accomplished
to enable one to vote. Men over forty-five years of age were exempt
from the poll tax but still had to register. By assuming that everyone forty-five or older actually did register, it is possible to calculate
that there were at least 132,117 men registered in 1904 who were
required also to pay the poll tax. Only 79,151 polls were actually

paid. If we assume that registration was a declaration of interest in voting, then failure to pay poll tax was caused by something other than apathy. On such a basis, a minimum of 5 per cent of the native white males between the ages of twenty-one and forty-four years, or 23.6 per cent of the total white, male, voting-age population was disfranchised by the poll tax alone. The convention had done its job well: white voters declined, Negro voters practically ceased to exist.

The Urban Thrust

American Political Parties and the Rise of the City

by Carl N. Degler

The overwhelming majority of urban political machines today are Democratic, not Republican, and in nearly all presidential elections since 1928, most Northern industrial cities have gone Democratic. These facts, along with large doses of Democratic rhetoric, have reinforced the popular notion that one party, the Democratic, has throughout our history been identified with urban voters. "Artisans for Jefferson" somehow blended into "Mechanics for Jackson," and these, in turn, blended into "Immigrant Workers for Cleveland" and all his Democratic successors, on up to the present. Historians have known for some time that actually urban voting patterns have shifted more erratically from party to party, depending on such factors as the specific issues in a campaign (rational or emotional), the candidates' ethnic and religious backgrounds, regional variations among cities in different sections; and voting distinctions between cities with predominantly native-born or immigrant populations.

From time to time major shifts in the over-all party allegiance of urban voters have taken place, but never in any simplistic or total fashion, of course. During the Gilded Age both major parties competed for the nation's cities, and each party possessed its par-

*ticular urban strongholds. Yet during the congressional elections
of 1894 a dramatic surge toward the Republican party occurred
in most major metropolitan areas. This surge ushered in a period
of Republican domination of national, urban politics which lasted
until the equally significant election of 1928, when the loser, Al
Smith, began the process of regaining for his party Democratic
strength among urban voters, especially among immigrants and
their children. During the next decade, the 1930's, Democratic
control of the cities would become one of the most important
realities of American politics, and Franklin Roosevelt would cash
in the chips bought by Al Smith. Carl Degler highlights these
shifts, and explains urban voting patterns over the previous century, in the following article.*

⚜ The ending of Reconstruction in 1877 deprived both Republican and Democratic parties of the issues that had sustained their
rivalry for half a century. As a result, in the presidential elections
from 1876 to 1892, neither party won decisively; never before nor
since has popular political inertia been so noticeable. More important, this indecision of the voters obscured the significant fact
that the Republican party was popularly weak. For despite the
preponderance of Republican Presidents during these years, only
James A. Garfield secured a popular plurality and his was the
smallest in history. The party's weak popular base was even more
evident in the congressional elections between 1874 and 1892
when the Democrats captured sizable majorities in the House of
Representatives in eight out of ten Congresses. So serious was this
popular weakness of the party that Republican Presidents from
Rutherford B. Hayes to Benjamin Harrison, as both Vincent P.
De Santis and Stanley P. Hirshson has shown, worked in a variety
of ways to build up a stronger Republican party in the South, but
with very limited success.

Thus in the opening years of the 1890's the Republicans as a

From *The Journal of American History*, Vol. LI (June 1964), pp. 41–59.
Reprinted by permission; most footnotes omitted.

national party were in obvious trouble. The elections of 1890 and 1892 were disastrous for them as the Democrats swept into firm control of the House of Representatives and into the White House as well. Despite the party's proud association with the winning of the War for the Union, the Republicans were no more popularly based than at their founding forty years earlier; the majority of the nation's voters remained stubbornly Democratic. Moreover, with each passing election the political value of that vaunted association depreciated further as memories grew dimmer. The party seemed destined to recapitulate the history of the Whigs by serving only as a convenient alternative to the Democrats.

At that point, though, a complete reversal in party prospects took place. In the congressional election of 1894 the Republicans clearly emerged as the majority party, leaving the Democrats to wander in the political wilderness for a generation. The transfer of seats in the election of 1894 from the Democratic to the Republican side of the House was the largest in history. The Republicans gained a majority of 132, whereas in twenty-four states not a single Democrat was elected and in six others only one Democrat was returned in each. Moreover, prominent Democrats like William L. Wilson of West Virginia, William McK. Springer of Illinois, and Richard L. Bland of Missouri—men associated with important Democratic doctrines like low tariffs and free silver—lost their places. This overwhelming Republican congressional victory in 1894 was confirmed two years later by what for the Republicans was to be their first decisive presidential victory without benefit of federal protection of Negro voting in the South. Measured against the margins of defeat in previous elections, William Jennings Bryan's defeat was crushing; he ran farther behind the winner than any candidate of a major party since Ulysses S. Grant trounced Horace Greeley.

Dramatic as the Republican victories for 1894 and 1896 undoubtedly were, their enduring significance lies in the continuance of the trend they began. For the next sixteen years the Republicans, without interruption, commanded the majorities in the House and elected the Presidents. Thus in the middle of the 1890's the Republicans, for the first time, emerged as the majority party of the nation.

The question which arises is: why? At the outset one can reject the hypothesis of challenging new leadership, since the party enjoyed none in the 1890's. Furthermore, since the shift in votes took place when Grover Cleveland, an acknowledged conservative, was President, and continued when a radical Democrat, Bryan, was the party's candidate, the policies of the opposition party do not offer much help in explaining the change. The only place left to look is among the voters themselves. It is their attitudes that changed as the United States passed from an agricultural to an industrial economy.

In spite of all that has been written to emphasize that the 1890's was the period during which this agrarian to industrial transition occurred, there are valid reasons for placing this momentous shift in the preceding decade. It was, for example, during the 1880's that the production of manufactured goods surpassed farm goods in dollar value, and it was in this same decade that a majority of the nation's work force became engaged in non-agricultural rather than agricultural pursuits. Also during the 1880's railroad construction reached unprecedented heights, with more miles of track laid than in any other decade in American history. These were years of peak membership of the Knights of Labor, something over 700,000; the American Federation of Labor was formed, and the number of industrial strikes sharply increased. It was the decade of the frightening Haymarket riot in Chicago, which, in its nationwide notoriety, epitomized the arrival of the new world of the factory, the city, and the immigrant. In fact the number of immigrants who flooded into the country in that decade exceeded that of any other similar period in the century. Furthermore, those ten years were the seedtime of the city. According to a contemporary analysis of the census, the number of cities with 8,000 or more population jumped from 286 in 1880 to 443 in 1890.

Many cities doubled in size in the ten years, and some, like Chicago, had been already large at the beginning of the decade. A few made spectacular records of rapid growth. Minneapolis jumped from 47,000 to 165,000; Omaha reached 140,000 in 1890, though ten years before its population had been no more than 31,000; Denver nearly tripled its population.

During that decade of transition neither the political parties nor the people were prepared by previous experience for the problems and nature of the new industrial, urban age. Hence the politics of the 1880's were sterile, uninteresting, and often trivial, as the parties and the voters rehashed stale issues and only reluctantly faced the new. Then, in the early 1890's, it would seem, the decision was made; the commitment of the voters hardened. The question then remains: why did the Republican party, which thus far had been sectionally based and numerically weak, rather than the popular Democratic party, emerge from this period of indecision as the dominant party of the nation?

A part of the answer seems to lie in the public image of the two parties. The Republican party was more suited to the needs and character of the new urban, industrial world that was beginning to dominate America. In those years the Republicans were the party of energy and change. They inherited from their antebellum beginnings as well as from the experience of Reconstruction a tradition which looked to the national authority first and to the states second. The party and its leaders had not hesitated to use the national power in behalf of economic growth by sponsoring such measures as the Homestead Act, land grants and loans to railroad construction companies, and protective tariffs. During the Civil War the Republicans demonstrated their willingness to use income and inheritance taxes, and fiat money when the nation's survival had seemed to require such novel measures. In the 1880's, it was Republican Senator Henry W. Blair who sought to employ the federal revenues and power in behalf of aid to the public schools. In each of the four times that the Blair education

bill came before the Congress, Republican support always exceeded Democratic support.

This nationalistic tradition and these specific measures, of
course, also added up to a national image of the party that would
appeal to urban voters and immigrants. As the self-proclaimed
party of prosperity and economic growth, the Republicans could
expect to win support from those who managed the expanding
factories and crowded into the tenements of the burgeoning cities.
Certainly party spokesmen made appeals to the urban working
class. In 1892, for example, President Harrison told the Congress:
"I believe that the protective system, which has now for something more than thirty years continuously prevailed in our legislation, has been a mighty instrument for the development of our
national wealth and a most powerful agency in protecting the
homes of our workingmen from the invasion of want. I have felt
a most solicitous interest to preserve to our working people rates
of wages that would not only give daily bread, but supply a comfortable margin for those home attractions and family comforts
and enjoyments without which life is neither hopeful nor sweet."
Nor should such appeals be hastily brushed aside as empty rhetoric. Republican claims received substance, if not proof, from
the steady rise in real wages during the last three decades of the
century. Moreover, foreign observers, like Friedrich Engels, who
certainly could not be accused of being partial to Republican
propaganda, cited the tariff as one of the principal reasons why
American workingmen were better off than European. In 1893
Engels wrote to his friend Friedrich A. Sorge that "through the
protective tariff system and the steadily growing domestic market
the workers must have been exposed to a prosperity no trace of
which has been seen here in Europe for years now. . . ."

The Democratic party, to a greater extent than the Republican
party, was more a congeries of state organizations than a national
party. Certainly in the South and in a northern state like Illinois,
there were many Democrats in the 1890's who were far from

agreement with the national leadership. But even with these cautionary observations, of the two parties between 1880 and 1896, the Democrats undoubtedly presented the more conservative face to the electorate. The hallmark of the party under the dominance of Cleveland was economy, which in practice meant the paring down of government assistance to business, opposing veterans' pensions, hoarding the national resources, lowering the tariff, and, in general, stemming the Republican efforts to spur economic growth and to enhance the national power. Besides, the Democrats were ideologically unsuited to any ventures in the expansion of governmental activities. Still steeped in the Jeffersonian conception of the limited role of the federal government, the national Democrats were less likely than the Republicans to use federal powers in new ways to meet new problems. It was Cleveland, after all, who had vetoed a meager $10,000 relief appropriation for drought-stricken Texas farmers with the stern warning: "though the people support the Government the Government should not support the people."

The election results of the 1880's suggest that the Republicans were even then receiving returns from their bid for working-class support. Today it is axiomatic that the big cities of the country will vote Democratic, but in that period most of the large urban centers outside the South were more likely to be Republican than Democratic. It is true that cities like New York, Boston, and San Francisco were usually safely Democratic, but in the three presidential elections of the 1880's a majority of the nation's cities over 50,000 outside the South went Republican. In these three elections—even though in two of them Cleveland polled a larger vote than his Republican opponents—eastern and midwestern cities like Philadelphia, Chicago, Cleveland, Cincinnati, Buffalo, Providence, Milwaukee, Newark, Syracuse, Paterson, and Minneapolis invariably appeared in the Republican column. In the election of 1884, which was won by Democrats, the Republicans captured twenty of the thirty-three non-southern cities over 50,000.

In 1888 the Republicans took twenty-six of the forty-four largest non-southern cities listed in the census of 1890.[1]

Furthermore, many of these Republican cities contained substantial proportions of immigrants. The 1890 census showed thirty per cent or more of the population of Chicago, Milwaukee, Paterson, Cleveland, Buffalo, Pittsburgh, Providence, and Rochester to be foreign-born.[2] All of these cities voted consistently Republican in the three presidential elections of the 1880's.

But the tendency for Republicans to do better than Democrats in northern cities must not be exaggerated. The election of 1892, with its upsurge of Democratic strength in the cities, demonstrated that Republican popularity in the urban centers was neither so overwhelming nor so fixed that the popular Democracy might not reduce it. Clearly some other force, some other ingredient in the mixture, was operative. That additional factor appears to be the depression of 1893.

The depression of the 1890's was an earth-shaker. Not only did it last five years or more, but it was the first economic decline since the United States had made the transition to full-scale industrialism. As a consequence its effects were felt especially in the growing cities and among the working class. A recent historian of this depression has estimated that real earnings for the population

1. According to the *Tribune Almanac of 1881* there were thirty-six cities in 1880 with a population of 50,000 or more. The two southern cities of Richmond and New Orleans, and Washington, D.C., which did not possess a national vote, have been excluded from my count. In the tabulation for 1888, Memphis, Nashville, and Atlanta, as southern cities, have also been excluded in addition to the three excluded for 1880 and 1884. It might be noted for the benefit of those unfamiliar with the form of the statistics in Burnham's and Robinson's compilations of the presidential vote that the county is the smallest unit reported. Thus, my figures for the cities are actually the returns for the counties in which the cities are located and not strictly the cities themselves.

2. See table in *Eleventh Census: 1890, Population* (Washington, 1895), pt. 1, xcii. Strictly speaking, these figures are not comparable with those on voting since the immigration statistics are for the city only while the voting figures are for the county. Nevertheless, the city figures certainly suggest the importance of the immigrant in these Republican districts and that is all that is intended.

dropped 18 per cent between 1892 and 1894. The single year of 1894 witnessed Coxey's army as well as other less well-known armies of unemployed workers on the march, widespread labor unrest, and the violence of the Pullman and Chicago railroad strikes. More workers went out on strike in that year than in any other in the century. The number was not equalled again until 1902.

Since it is true that the Republicans for all their belief in the national power would not have taken any stronger anti-depression measures than the incumbent Democrats, the election upset of 1894 might be considered as nothing more than a case of blind, rather than calculated, reprisal against the incumbents. Furthermore, it might be said that the Republicans had been chastised in much the same fashion in 1874 when they chanced to be in power at the beginning of the depression of 1873. The objection is not as telling as it appears. In the election of 1894 there was a third party, and if simple dissent were operating, the Populists should have benefited as much from it as the Republicans. But this they did not do. Although the total Populist vote in 1894 was higher than in 1892, not a single state that year, John D. Hicks has observed, could any longer be called predominantly Populist. Four western states, Kansas, Colorado, North Dakota, and Idaho, all of which had voted Populist in 1892, went Republican in 1894. In a real sense, then, the election was a victory for the Republican party and not simply a defeat for the Democrats.

If the terrible impact of the depression polarized the voting in a new way, thereby helping to explain the massive shift to the Republicans, the activities of the Democrats in 1896 could only confirm the urban voters in their belief that the Republican party was the more responsive political instrument. In their convention of 1896 the Democrats hardly noticed the cities; they had ears only for the cries of the farmers demanding currency reform. Many Populists, it is true, stood for something more than free silver, but the money issue was certainly accepted by Bryan and the vast majority of Democrats as the principal issue of the cam-

paign. Free silver was at best uninteresting to the urban population and, at worst, anathema to them. The adoption of such a
monetary policy would be inflationary and therefore contrary to
the interests of all urban consumers, whether bankers, petty
clerks, or factory workers. Mark Hanna, McKinley's campaign
manager, sensed this defect in Bryan's appeal from the outset.
Early in the campaign he said about Bryan: "He's talking silver
all the time, and that's where we've got him."

And they did have him. The cities, where the industrial workers were concentrated, voted overwhelmingly Republican. Only
twelve of the eighty-two cities with a population of 45,000 or
more went for Bryan—and seven of the twelve were in the Democratic South while two others were located in silver-producing
states. Seven of the seventeen cities in the states that Bryan carried gave a majority to McKinley; on the other hand, only three
of the sixty-five cities in states going to McKinley provided a
majority for Bryan. Bryan was hopeless in the industrial East; he
did not carry a single county in all of New England, and only one
in New York, and eleven rural counties in Pennsylvania. He even
lost normally Democratic New York City.

Taken together, the elections of 1894 and 1896 mark the emergence of the Republican party as the party of the rising cities.
Even a cataclysmic event like the Civil War, in which the Democrats were on the losing side, had not been able to dislodge the
Democracy from its favored place in the voters' hearts. But the
impact of an industrial-urban society with its new outlook and
new electorate had done the trick. It is significant that several
cities like San Francisco, Detroit, Indianapolis, Columbus, and St.
Paul, which had been Democratic in the 1880's and early 1890's,
voted Republican in 1896 and remained Republican well into the
twentieth century. None of the large cities which had been Republican in the 1880's and early 1890's, on the other hand, changed
party affiliation in 1896 or for decades thereafter. Another indication of the continuity between the elections of 1894 and 1896 is
that the states which showed the greatest Republican congres-

sional gains in 1894 also showed increased Republican strength in the presidential election two years later. There were twelve states, each of which gave the Republicans four or more new seats in 1894; of these, eight were among the states which in 1896 showed the greatest number of new counties going to the Republicans. Significantly, they were mainly industrial-urban states like Illinois, New Jersey, New York, Ohio, and Pennsylvania.

It is commonplace for textbooks to depict the Republican party of the late nineteenth century as the political arm of the Standard Oil Trust, but if the election returns are to be given any weight at all, that is not the way the voters saw the party in the 1890's. Not only was it the party of respectability, wealth, and the Union; it was also the party of progress, prosperity, and national authority. As such it could and did enlist the support of industrial workers and immigrants as well as merchants and millionaires. As one analyst of the 1896 New England vote saw it, the Democrats may have obtained their most consistent support among the poor and the immigrants of the cities, but the Republicans gained strength there, too, "just as they did in the silk-stocking wards. . . . They were able to place the blame for unemployment upon the Democrats and to propagate successfully a doctrine that the Republican party was the party of prosperity and the 'full dinner pail.' "

Ideologically, it is true, the Republican party in the 1890's had a long way to travel before it would translate its conception of the national power into an instrument for social amelioration. But it is suggestive that Robert M. La Follette in Wisconsin and Theodore Roosevelt in Washington, who are the best known of the early Progressives, were also Republicans. It is these men, and others like them in the party, who carried on the political revolution of 1894, which had first announced the Republican party as the majority party in the new America of cities and factories.

The significance of that political revolution is that the pattern of party allegiance then established continued for many years to come. To be sure, in 1912, because of a split in the Republican party, Woodrow Wilson was able to break the succession of Republican Presidents. But it is also evident that the success of the Democrats in 1912 and 1916 should not be taken as a sign of a fundamental change in voter preferences. One reason for thinking so is that in 1916 Wilson was re-elected by the very close margin of 600,000 popular and twenty-three electoral votes and in 1920 the Republicans swept back into the White House on a landslide. Another reason is provided by the Democratic losses in the House of Representatives after 1912. That year the Democrats achieved a margin of 160 seats over the Republicans, one of the largest in congressional history, but by the mid-term elections the difference between the parties was down to 35; by 1916 it was less than 10. In 1918 the Democrats lost control of the House.

The most persuasive evidence for believing that the Republicans continued to be the majority party of the nation, despite the interruption of the Wilson administrations, is the history of elections during the 1920's. In 1920 Warren G. Harding received over 61 per cent of the votes cast, a proportion of the total not achieved since the advent of universal manhood suffrage and only equalled once thereafter. Although other Republican presidential victories in the 1920's did not reach the proportions of the Harding landslide, they were all substantial. Furthermore, at no time between 1920 and 1928 was the Republican margin of strength in the House of Representatives endangered; it never went below twenty seats. In fact, near the end of the decade, Republican strength in the House was reaching out for a new high; in 1928 it was one hundred seats greater than the Democratic proportion. In the presidential election that year Herbert Hoover's majority over Alfred E. Smith was more than six million votes. In short, by the end of the 1920's the Republicans were as much the majority party of the nation as they had been in 1894 when the tide of history first turned in their favor.

Within four years, though, another political revolution had been consummated, this time returning the Democrats to the position of the majority party of the nation. In 1932 the Democrats elected their second president in forty-two years and captured the House of Representatives with a majority of unprecedented size, something like 190 seats. The true measure of the reversal of political patterns, though, did not come until 1934 and 1936. For with their overwhelming victories in those two elections, the Democrats showed that 1932 was not simply another 1912, when a large Democratic victory had been quickly eroded away in subsequent elections. Instead, in 1934 the Democrats reversed the patterns of the preceding fifty years; rather than losing seats in the House, as was customary in off-year elections, they actually added ten more to their swollen total. And then in 1936 they succeeded in re-electing Franklin D. Roosevelt by an overwhelming majority, with a proportion of votes that came very near topping Harding's landslide of 1920.

Because the Roosevelt revolution in politics coincided with the onset of the Great Depression, it is tempting to argue that it was economic adversity in 1932, much as it had been in 1894, which accounts for the shift in the voters' preferences. Certainly the impact of the depression had much to do with the long-range change; it undoubtedly accounts for the overwhelming character of the shift. But there is also much evidence to suggest that the shift which first became evident in 1932 was already in progress four years before. Beneath the surface of Hoover's victory the forces which would consummate the Roosevelt revolution were already in motion in 1928 in behalf of Alfred E. Smith.

The most obvious comment to be made about Smith's vote was its large size. Smith's 15 million votes were 6.5 million more than John W. Davis had polled in 1924, when La Follette's Progressive candidacy had drawn away some Democratic votes, and 5 million more than James M. Cox and Roosevelt had been able to capture in 1920. With this enormous gain, if by nothing else, Smith showed himself to be the most popular Democratic candidate since Bryan in 1896.

But important as Smith's ability to attract votes may have been, his contribution to the turn to the Democrats lay in something more than mere numbers. After all, Hoover increased the Republican vote by some five million over Coolidge's total in 1924 and Harding's in 1920. What was significant was that Smith's unique combination of politically effective personal attributes was attracting a new class of voters to the Democratic party. Many years after the election, Hoover pointed out that in 1928 the candidates of both major parties had risen from small beginnings to become figures of national prominence. But if this was true of the origins of Smith and Hoover, by 1928 the two men were poles apart. Unlike Hoover, or any previous presidential candidate of either party, Smith was both of lower class social background and a native of a big city. As is well known, his life and his career in politics were closely associated with New York City and the Tammany political machine. It is true that his four terms as governor of New York showed him to be progressive in thought and action as well as honest and courageous, but his loyalty to Tammany was both well known and unshakeable. Furthermore, Smith was a Roman Catholic and, though he had no intention of making his religion a political issue, many Protestants did. In fact, in 1927, an article that gained national prominence challenged him to show that his religion would not interfere with his proper execution of the duties of president. Although Smith's parents were native New Yorkers, his religion, his mother's Irish background, and his close association with Irish-dominated Tammany Hall stamped him as a spokesman for the urban immigrants. In short, he was the first presidential candidate to exhibit the traits of a part of the population that had never before been represented by a candidate of a major party.

Smith's religion, which hurt him in the South and helped to explain why Hoover was able to capture four southern states, undoubtedly assisted him in the North. Massachusetts and Rhode Island, both heavily Catholic in population, went Democratic in 1928 for the first time since the Civil War. In fact, while Hoover was taking 200 southern counties from the Democrats, Smith took 122 northern counties that had been consistently Republican. Moreover, of these 122 counties, 77 were predominantly Roman

Catholic; most of these 77 counties remained in the Democratic column, it is worth emphasizing, in subsequent elections.

Since Roman Catholicism in America is an immigrant religion and its communicants are largely concentrated in the big cities, most of the new counties Smith gained were urban. Indeed, the striking thing about Smith's candidacy was that it attracted the big city vote away from the Republicans for the first time since the 1890's. In 1920 Harding had taken all of the twelve cities with a population over 500,000, but in 1928, among these twelve, New York, Cleveland, St. Louis, Milwaukee, and San Francisco went for Smith though their states did not. Moreover, Pittsburgh and Baltimore failed to give Smith a majority by fewer than 10,000 votes each. Of the twelve cities only Los Angeles was strongly for Hoover. If the votes of all twelve cities are added together, Smith secured 38,000 more votes than Hoover; in 1920 the Republicans had carried the same cities by 1,638,000 votes. In a broader sample, a recent student of the election has shown that in 1920 Harding carried all twenty-seven of the principal cities outside the South; in 1928, Smith captured eight, and made appreciable gains in the others. He ran behind Cox and Roosevelt in only three of the twenty-seven. Such a reversal was one sign that a socio-political revolution was under way.

Despite all that has been written about Smith's appeal to the voters of the big cities, the significant point, often overlooked, is that his appeal was not of equal force in all cities. For example, he ran badly in southern cities, the residents of which exhibited, when compared with other southerners, the weakest commitment to the historic party principles that had made the South a stronghold of the Democrats. In fact, Dallas and Houston in Texas, and Birmingham in Alabama went Republican in 1928. More important was Smith's strikingly uneven attraction for the cities of the North. His attractive power was considerably stronger in those cities in which immigrant stock predominated than in those in which it was in the minority. (Immigrant stock is defined here as foreign-born whites and native whites born of one or more foreign-born parents.) According to the census of 1930, the closest to the election of 1928, there were thirty-six cities with populations in excess of a quarter of a million. In nineteen of these cities, immigrants and children of immigrants constituted 50 per cent or more of the population. In the presidential election of 1920, all of these nineteen cities voted Republican; in the election of 1924 all but one voted Republican. In the election of 1928, though, seven of them turned Democratic.

On the other hand, in the seventeen cities out of the thirty-six in which the native-born whites of native-born white parents constituted a majority of the population in 1930, only four went Democratic in 1928, and three of them were located in the traditionally Democratic South (Atlanta, New Orleans, and Memphis). The fourth was St. Louis. In fact, Democratic strength in these "native-white" cities actually declined in 1928, for in the 1920 and 1924 elections six of the seventeen had gone Democratic. All six of them, it should be noted, were in the Democratic South. Thus in the election of 1928 among the cities in which native whites consituted a majority, there was actually a loss in Democratic strength. In short, Smith's appeal to urban voters was not simply that he was of urban origin but that his Catholicism and Irish background stamped him as a champion of immigrants and children of immigrants. At the same time, those cities in which the immigrant stock was in the minority retained their allegiance to the Republican party—an allegiance which had been first clearly established in the 1890's for the big cities as a whole.

Yet it might be said that Smith failed, after all, to carry even a majority of the cities with a preponderance of immigrant stock. He won only seven of the nineteen cities of immigrant stock. Does not this fact call into serious question the assertion that there was a relationship between the social character of these cities and Democratic voting?

Closer analysis suggests not. As inspection of Table 1 makes evident, in every one of the cities with 50 per cent or more immigrant stock, whether they were carried by Smith or not, the Demo-

cratic vote increased enormously in 1928 over 1920, when the
Republican majorities had been very large. In fact, in none of the
cities in which immigrant stock predominated was the Democratic
increase less than 100 per cent, and in many it was considerably
higher. In these same cities, on the other hand, the Republican
vote increased as much as 100 per cent in only one of the nineteen
cities and in only three did it go above 50 per cent (Oakland,
Pittsburgh, and Seattle). In several of the cities that Smith carried, the Republican vote actually fell from that of 1920.

Table 1

Cities with 50 Per Cent or More Immigrant Stock *

City	Democratic vote in nearest thousand		% Change	Republican vote in nearest thousand		% Change
	1920	1928		1920	1928	
Boston	68	205	202	108	99	−7.7
Buffalo	40	126	215	100	145	45.0
Chicago	197	716	266	635	812	27.8
Cleveland	71	166	132	149	195	30.7
Detroit	52	157	201	221	265	19.9
Jersey City	63	153	143	102	100	−1.9
Los Angeles	56	210	275	178	514	189.0
Milwaukee	25	111	344	73	82	12.2
Minneapolis	143	396	178	519	561	8.1
Newark	41	118	188	116	169	45.6
New York	345	1,168	239	786	715	−9.1
Oakland	21	61	190	73	119	63.2
Philadelphia	90	276	209	308	420	36.5
Pittsburgh	40	161	301	139	216	55.5
Providence	46	97	112	80	86	7.5
Rochester	29	74	156	74	100	35.2
St. Paul	21	57	171	40	53	32.5
San Francisco	33	97	195	96	96	0.0
Seattle	17	47	176	59	96	62.9

* Two cities in this list, Oakland and Seattle, counted 47.8 and 48.2 per cent,
respectively, of immigrant stock, but they have been included here rather than
in Table 2, because they also have less than 50 per cent of native white population. Their proportions of native white population are 46.4 and 47.7 per cent,
respectively. The missing proportions are accounted for by colored persons.

If one examines the Democratic performance in those cities in which the native-white population predominated, the conclusion that there was a close association between the increase in Democratic votes and immigrant stock is further strengthened. In none of these cities was there much of an increase in either the total vote or in the vote for the Democratic candidate. (See Table 2.)

Table 2

Cities with Less than 50 Per Cent of Immigrant Stock

Cities	Democratic vote in nearest thousand		% Change	Republican vote in nearest thousand		% Change
	1920	1928		1920	1928	
Akron	28	32	14.3	44	79	79.5
Atlanta	9	7	−22.5	3	6	100.0
Baltimore	87	126	44.8	126	135	7.3
Birmingham	25	17	−32.0	7	18	157.0
Cincinnati	78	110	41.0	113	148	31.0
Columbus	48	47	−2.3	60	92	53.2
Dallas	14	17	21.4	5	27	440.0
Denver	23	41	78.5	44	74	68.1
Houston	15	22	47.7	8	27	237.0
Indianapolis	61	73	19.7	80	110	37.4
Kansas City, Mo.	77	97	26.0	80	127	58.6
Louisville	56	64	14.3	68	98	44.3
Memphis	16	18	12.5	9	12	33.3
New Orleans	33	56	70.0	18	14	−22.2
Portland, Ore.	28	45	60.5	45	76	68.8
St. Louis	106	176	66.0	163	162	−0.68
Toledo	30	45	50.0	52	78	50.0

Only in Denver did the Democratic vote increase as much as 75 per cent; in no city did it reach as high as 100 per cent as it did in every one of the cities in Table 1. In five the increase was less than 25 per cent and in three there was actually a loss of Democratic votes. The median value is 26.0 per cent.

The Republican vote in Table 2 provides a revealing contrast with the Democratic vote in Table 1, for now it can be seen that the "native-white" cities produced no upsurge in voting for Republicans comparable to that in the cities of immigrant stock. Except for a marked—and what turned out to be temporary—upturn in Republican strength in the southern cities of Atlanta, Birmingham, Dallas, and Houston, the increase between 1920 and 1928 in none of these cities was as much as 100 per cent. The median value is 53.2 per cent.

From this examination of the variability in the response of the cities to Smith's candidacy it seems clear that Smith brought out the immigrant vote in unprecedented numbers. Some of these voters of immigrant stock had probably been voting Republican all along and now switched to the Democrats. But many more, it would seem, voted for the first time, for otherwise one cannot explain the enormous increase in Democratic votes in the short span of eight years without a commensurate decline in Republican votes. These same people, backed by even greater numbers, would come out in 1932 to vote for Franklin Roosevelt and consummate the Roosevelt Revolution in politics. But it was Smith, the Catholic and the recognized champion of the urban-based immigrant, who first made the Democratic party the party of the cities and the immigrant. This upsurge in immigrant voting in 1928 helps to explain, at least negatively, the apparent paradox of urban support for a Republican party in the 1920's that defended Prohibition and pushed for restrictions on immigration. Prior to the galvanizing appearance of Smith on the political landscape, most urban imigrants just did not vote at all and many probably did not even think of themselves as part of the body politic. And to those who did vote, the Democratic party offered no candidates, other than Wilson, to lure them away from the party of national power, Theodore Roosevelt, and prosperity. Samuel Lubell has suggested, further, that the broadening educational opportunities of the 1920's also help to explain the upsurge in immigrant political participation in 1928.

Despite familiarity with the connection between the cities and the Democratic party today, that connection was not forged, as far as the nation was concerned, until 1928–1932. Indeed it is the conclusion of this paper that it was the political activity of urban voters which raised the Republican party to a position of dominance in American politics for a third of a century, just as it has been the cities which have been largely responsible for the Democratic party's leading place in the nation's political life for the most recent third of this century. For Franklin Roosevelt after the landslide of 1936 continued to receive the support of the vast majority of the 37 principal cities of over 250,000 population, carrying 32 of them in 1940 and 30 in 1944.[3] Harry Truman in 1948 did about as well, even though the Dixiecrat candidate took three of the traditionally Democratic southern cities. Truman's score was 30 of the big cities against 4 for Thomas E. Dewey.

The real test of the Democratic power in the cities came in 1952 with the first campaign of Dwight D. Eisenhower, certainly the most popular Republican of the twentieth century. In that election and the next, Eisenhower made substantial inroads into the urban territory of the Democrats. In his first election, for example, he carried 21 of the 39 cities over 250,000 and in 1956 he did even better by taking 28 of them—almost as many as Franklin Roosevelt did in 1944.[4]

But there are two good reasons for seeing this resurgence of Republican strength in the cities as temporary and nothing more than a reflection of the special appeal of Eisenhower rather than as a basic shift in popular party allegiance. The first reason is that Eisenhower was able to carry a majority of the House of Representatives for his party in only the first of his four congressional

3. The cities are those listed in Tables 1 and 2 above, but with San Antonio added since it passed 250,000 population by 1940. Conclusions about urban strength of the parties have been derived from the county voting statistics compiled in Edgar Eugene Robinson, *They Voted for Roosevelt: The Presidential Vote, 1932–1944* (Stanford, 1947) and from those in *The Political Almanac, 1952* (New York, 1952).

4. The thirty-nine cities are those listed in Tables 1 and 2 but with Fort Worth, Omaha, San Antonio, and San Diego added because they reached the 250,000 population mark by 1950 and with Providence eliminated because it fell below that level. The conclusions on the urban strength of the parties and the results of the congressional elections have been derived from Richard M. Scammon, ed., *America Votes* (4 vols., New York, 1956–1962).

elections. Indeed, his own popular vote in 1956 was greater than
that of 1952, but he proved unable, nonetheless, to do what every
popular president since Zachary Taylor had been able to do: carry
a majority of his party into the House of Representatives.

In this failure the cities played a part since many of them that
voted for Eisenhower did not grant the same degree of support
to the Republican congressional candidates. This tendency was
most obvious in the southern cities, where he showed great
strength. In 1952 he carried six of the eight southern cities and in
1956 he captured all but Atlanta. Yet in the congressional races
in all of these cities, Democratic congressmen, because of the
South's one-party system, were almost invariably returned. More
important, the same tendency could be observed in cities outside
the South. For example, in the Ninth Ohio District (Toledo) a
Democratic congressman was returned in all four of Eisenhower's
congressional elections, though the General personally carried the
city in 1952 and 1956. Although Eisenhower won Cook County,
Illinois in 1956, eight of the twelve congressional districts of the
city of Chicago went Democratic. Newark and Denver, both of
which supported Eisenhower in 1952 and 1956, sent only Democratic congressmen to Washington throughout the Eisenhower
years. Eisenhower won Milwaukee in 1956, but the two congressmen elected from the city that year were Democrats.

The second reason for seeing Eisenhower's substantial victory
as more personal than partisan is that in the election of 1960
John F. Kennedy, despite his close victory in the national popular
vote, regained the cities for the Democrats. He carried 27 of the
39 cities, even though he did less well than Stevenson in 1952
among southern cities, capturing only New Orleans, San Antonio,
and ever-faithful Atlanta. A large part of the explanation for Kennedy's failure to regain southern big city support commensurate
with his general increase in urban backing is to be found, of
course, in southern dislike of the Democratic party's stand on civil
rights which began with Truman and which Kennedy went out of
his way to support and advance. Nevertheless, the defection also

calls attention to the quite different social character of southern, as compared with northern, big cities. There are very few Catholics or children of immigrants in southern cities, so that an Al Smith and a John F. Kennedy have no religious or social appeal there as they do in the North. That this difference was influential is suggested by the return to the Democratic fold in 1960 of San Antonio and New Orleans, the only two southern cities containing substantial numbers of Catholics and children of immigrants.

In short, as the congressional strength of the Democrats throughout the Eisenhower years had suggested, the election of 1960 showed that the Democrats still retained the long-term allegiance of the big city voters, whose support had first been evident thirty-two years before in another campaign by a Roman Catholic grandson of an Irish immigrant.

WASP America's Pyrrhic Victory

Folklore of the Campaign of 1928

by Paul A. Carter

Calvin Coolidge may have sensed the dangers that lay ahead before he announced that he would not run for re-election in 1928. Republicans then turned to Herbert Hoover, "the Great Engineer," a Coolidge cabinet officer who was not the professional politicians' choice but who seemed the best available Republican. Hoover rose meteorically before World War I as a mining engineer and self-made millionaire. He won international fame and admiration during the war itself, directing American relief efforts in Europe.

To millions of Americans, Hoover came to symbolize the Progressive businessman at his best, a man who had harnessed administrative and organizing talents to humane purposes. As Secretary of Commerce from 1921 to 1928 he had brought advanced business ideas to Washington. Hoover wanted to replace conflict between capital and labor with welfare capitalism; cutthroat competition with trade associations and business cooperation; and negative government with active encouragement to all economic sectors, promoting prosperity and social stability. One of the most effective exponents of a more responsible "American individualism," his countrymen regarded him as an impartial public servant rather than a professional, and presumably self-serving, politician. Hoover seemed blessed with the vision and the technical expertise required to lead a modern, industrial society.

In this sense, Hoover represented a shift in Republican leadership from figures like Harding and Coolidge, men whose appeal stemmed largely from their ability to evoke nostalgia for a simpler, bygone America. In contrast, Hoover thoroughly identified with the view that America had entered a new era created by the genius of American business and capable of producing unprecedented affluence. Four more years of Republican rule, Hoover and his party promised, would bring the country closer to the day when it would achieve final victory over poverty.

Hoover's Democratic opponent, Governor Alfred E. Smith of New York, ran despite several political handicaps. He was the first representative of the Newer Americans, the first Catholic, and the first poor boy from a big city to run for President. In 1924 Southern and Western rural Democrats had blocked Smith's nomination, apparently willing to lose an election rather than accept someone with Smith's cultural background. When Smith did win the nomination four years later, many rural Democrats crossed party lines. Political feelings ran so high in 1928 that Republicans cracked the Solid South for the first time since Reconstruction. Many of the bolters voted for Hoover to save America, they thought, from a Catholic orgy of rum and Romanism. Conflicts between the two cultures, urban and rural, dominated the 1928 campaign and had been nationally divisive throughout the decade. Yet it is doubtful that any Democrat, even a Methodist bishop, could have beaten Hoover in that prosperity year.

Hoover won impressively, yet the extent of his victory obscured for a time an awareness of important shifts in voting behavior which would have long-term consequences. Smith ran unusually well in the Republican farm belt (though he did not, of course, carry it), and this was a clear sign of rural discontent with the GOP. His strength lay in the cities with their large ethnic populations. Although his New York (Noo Yawk) accent and manners evoked laughter and derision among the native-born Protestants, the urban immigrants accepted Smith as one of their own. Newer Americans who had previously voted Republican or had not both-

*ered to vote trooped to the polls in 1928 to support Smith and
help swing most big cities into the Democratic column.*

*"The cities exist," catechized Walter Lippmann in 1927, "but
they are felt [by old-stock Americans] to be alien, and in this uncertainty as to what the cities might yield up, men turn to the
old scenes from which the leaders they always trusted have come.
. . . Here are the new people, clamoring to be admitted to America, and there are the older people defending their household
gods." Hoover, though a technocrat and a business enthusiast,
reflected this village sense of virtue far more strongly than his opponent did in 1928. Paul A. Carter comments below on the meaning of the election for both American politics and society.*

❧ At an early stage in the presidential campaign of 1960, Denis
Brogan, interpreting that campaign from a foreign perspective,
wrote: "American politicians live to an extraordinary degree by
historical shorthand, by the memory of past . . . episodes that
'prove' that this *must* happen or that this *cannot* happen. And
high on the list of such political rules of thumb is the belief that
'Al' Smith was defeated in 1928 because he was a Catholic."

Up until election night of 1960, and indeed in some worried
minds up until the meeting of the electoral college in December,
the conclusion commonly drawn from this rule of thumb was that
any Catholic American who sought the Presidency could expect
the same fate as Smith. But even before the nomination and election of John F. Kennedy as the first Catholic President of the
United States, the rule of thumb had begun to be challenged.
Richard Hofstadter, for example, said in an article published early
in 1960: "There was not a Democrat alive, Protestant or Catholic,
who could have beaten Hoover in 1928." John D. Hicks in a review in 1958 declared: "Had Smith been nominated in 1932, he
would almost certainly have won." And in 1952 Samuel Lubell,
in an arresting sentence which is already reshaping the historiog-

From *Wisconsin Magazine of History*, XLVI (Summer 1963), 263–72.
Reprinted by permission; footnotes omitted.

raphy of the 1920's, maintained that the 1928 election demonstrated, not the fatal weakness of a Catholic candidate for the
Presidency, but precisely the reverse: "Before the Roosevelt Revolution there was an Al Smith revolution."

Yet political folklore dies hard. As recently as 1956 . . . Edmund A. Moore examined the 1928 presidential campaign and
warned that the supposed "unwritten law" against Catholic Presidents might still be in effect; therefore, politicians who were
Catholics would be better advised to aim at the relatively modest
office of the Vice-Presidency as a more realistic personal and political goal. Two years later, in the *dénouement* of his lucid and
moving biography of Al Smith, Oscar Handlin wrote that at the
time Smith's death "no Catholic . . . could aspire to be President, whatever other avenues of advance might be open."

"Can a Catholic be President?" As early as 1924, at least one
American Catholic, Martin Conboy, put the question in such a
way as to imply the answer "yes." In that era, when Alfred E.
Smith was Governor of the nation's most populous state, there
had already been a number of Catholic Governors and Senators,
and two Chief Justices of the United States: "Short of the Presidency, Catholics have held every position of importance within
the gift of their fellow citizens"—therefore, Conboy reasoned, why
not the Presidency? The closing of the question in the affirmative
as of 1960 invites at least a re-examination of the question as of
1924 and especially as of 1928.

One of the discoveries of the 1960 election has been that when
Americans ask themselves the question "Can a Catholic be President of the United States?" it is necessary to specify what kind of
Catholic. During 1959 and 1960, the thought of John F. Kennedy
as a prospective President prompted all kinds of misgivings, among
both liberals and conservatives, which had nothing whatever to
do with religion. *Mutatis mutandis*, the same may be presumed of
Al Smith in his day—although the misgivings roused by the man
from Fulton Street would have been of a different sort from those
roused by the man from Hyannis Port. One of President Ken-

nedy's pre-election critics, for example, summed up his impression of the candidate in the title of an article: "The Cool Eye of John F. Kennedy." It is difficult to imagine anyone making precisely this assessment of Smith. Stock campaign jokes of 1960 about the Democratic candidate's Harvard accent and his father's millions —related no doubt to the "country squire" stereotype of Franklin Roosevelt still popular among aging Republicans—are a far cry indeed from the Al Smith portrayed in some of the more savage political cartoons of 1928: a bibulous, ungrammatical roughneck.

Professor Moore in his study of the 1928 campaign has shown that the anti-Smith feeling contained a considerable element of sheer social snobbery, connected perhaps with the traditional middle-class Republican image of the Opposition as shiftless good-for-nothings—the image classically set forth in 1896 in the editorial "What's the Matter with Kansas?" "Can you imagine Al Smith in the White House?" the Republican National Committee-woman for Texas asked a W.C.T.U. meeting in Houston, visualizing for them a President Smith committing *gaucheries* of grammar and etiquette; and, more to the point for that audience, "Can you imagine *Mrs.* Smith in the White House?" Those last words would have rather a different ring had they been said about the former Jacqueline Bouvier!

While Moore's point on the effect of snobbery in the 1928 election is well taken, mere snobbism can not fully account for the detestation of Smith on the part of many who, like Al, could claim a heritage from the wrong side of the tracks. The most militant of all the anti-Smith forces, the Klansmen, liked to think of themselves as plain and even poor people (which some of them were), "open to the charge of being 'hicks' and 'rubes' and 'drivers of second hand Fords.' " For such voters to concur with W. C. T. U. ladies from Houston, there had to be something more than simple social condescension to unite them. The common bond most frequently assumed has been anti-Catholicism. But the Woman's Christian Temperance Union had quite another primary concern, and the members of the Ku Klux Klan spent a part of their energies in destroying whisky stills. An inescapable political issue throughout the 1920's for any candidate, regardless of his church or his manners, was Prohibition.

Common causes which unite rather widely disparate kinds of Americans—anti-Masonry, Free Soil, free silver, world peace, and most recently anti-subversion—are of course an old chapter in the republic's history. When they have been comparatively short-lived, or when they have not seemed clearly related to issues which are alive for a later generation, the emotions which such movements can arouse have often seemed inexplicably intense. Robert Moats Miller has wisely noted: "Nothing is more difficult than for an individual indifferent to a certain issue to appreciate that to others it might be of transcendent importance." It can only be said again that Prohibition *was* deemed to be of transcendent importance by millions of Americans both "wet" and "dry"; the sheer bulk of serious public discussion of the issue during the 1920's is enough to document the point. Since the anti-liquor crusade of the twentieth century emerged from nineteenth-century conflicts which pitted Protestant against Protestant, it would be begging the question to insist that the prohibitionist case against Smith was nothing but a cover for anti-Catholicism. Hoover was "sound" on liquor; Smith was not. For many a voter the issue was as simple as that.

Edmund A. Moore, in the able study of the 1928 election previously referred to, up to a certain point makes this same judgment: "There can be no doubt that the enforcement, by statute, of the ban on alcoholic beverages was an issue of great importance in its own right." But he warns us that "Prohibition . . . was often made to play hide-and-seek with the religious issue," and suggests that the extensive debate on Prohibition may have been a sublimated version of a debate on Catholicism, frank discussion of which was "limited by a widespread sense of delicacy and shame."

But to speculate on what discussants *may* have meant—on the "latent" as opposed to the "manifest" content of their discussion,

so to speak—is to play a very dangerous historiographic game indeed. Having in mind some of the imputations of religious prejudice in the 1960 campaign, as for example the journalistic treatment of the West Virginia presidential primary, the historian of
the 1928 campaign ought perhaps to be less concerned with
searching out anti-Catholicism assumed to be masquerading as
something else than with avoiding the error of assuming what
might be called "anti-Catholicism by association." This effort,
which would now be superfluous in the case of John Kennedy, is
still necessary when discussing Al Smith.

And yet a further pitfall awaits the historian of Prohibition,
after he has disentangled it from anti-Catholicism: the temptation to construe such a question in terms of equivalent *political*
ideas, so that the Wets become "liberal" and the Drys become
"conservative." This reading of the question then becomes as-
similable to a liberal-versus-conservative reading of the Smith-
Hoover campaign more generally, especially when one notices that
four of the conservative "solid-South" states carried by Herbert
Hoover were subsequently to be twice carried by Dwight Eisenhower, and three of them again by Richard Nixon. But in the case
of Prohibition, as least, these "left"–"right" categories of political
ideology break down; the present writer has shown elsewhere that
a progressive, social-welfare, and even radical outlook pervaded
the anti-liquor movement at least in its incipient stages and to
some extent throughout its existence. So unquestionably liberal
a journal as the *Christian Century* justified supporting Hoover in
1928 on prohibitionist grounds; and one social radical in 1932,
finding the Democrats, the Republicans, and the Socialists either
insufficiently liberal, insufficiently "dry," or both, by process of
elimination voted Communist!

Conversely, there were "wet" conservatives. Senator Oscar Underwood, for example, in his later years condemned the Eighteenth
Amendment because it "challenged the integrity of the compact
between the States" and compelled men "to live their lives in the
mold prescribed by the power of government." The Alabama Sen-

ator argued, furthermore, that the Drys could no more force their interpretation of the Eighteenth Amendment on the Wets than the North could force its interpretation of the Fourteenth Amendment on the South. When one reflects that this same conservative Southern Senator had courageously denounced the Ku Klux Klan at the Democratic Convention of 1924 and thereby ruined his own chances of being a presidential nominee, the campaign of 1928 which followed becomes even harder to see in "liberal" versus "conservative" terms.

Yet Smith himself is persistently seen by his latter-day admirers as a "liberal" who became "conservative" only upon the failure of his "liberal" expectations. He was not always seen in this light, however, by his contemporaries; Walter Lippmann wrote in 1925: "[Smith] is really a perfectly conservative man about property. . . . He believes in the soundness of the established order. . . . He is what a conservative ought to be always if he knew his business." When one finds a *New York Times* story on June 27th, the second day of the 1928 Democratic National Convention, headlined "Stocks up in 'Smith Market' as Raskob tells business it need not fear, the governor," one begins to understand what Lippmann was talking about: "Market leaders such as General Motors, United States Steel, Anaconda Copper, Allied Chemical and New York Central, had a sharp run-up. . . . Buying orders poured in so rapidly . . . that Wall Street began talking of a 'Smith market.' Friends of the Governor were said to be actively in the market, prepared to demonstrate that the financial and business interests are not hostile to his candidacy."

One of these friends of the Governor was John J. Raskob, whose remarks, the *Times* noted apparently without irony, "frequently have stimulated buying enthusiasm in the stock market." Franklin Roosevelt, among others, had serious misgivings about Smith's choice of Raskob as Democratic national chairman, largely on account of this Wall Street taint—yet some of Smith's putative liberalism has rubbed off on the General Motors financier, who is described in Oscar Handlin's biography of Al Smith as "another

poor boy who had come up in the world." Raskob grew up, Handlin writes, in "the free-and-easy atmosphere of Detroit where
religious prejudice seemed altogether out of place." Remembering the notorious anti-Semitism of the then president of the leading competitor of General Motors, one is a little surprised at
hearing Detroit described as being a city altogether free of religious prejudice; here is another indication that a straight liberal/
conservative interpretation of the campaign of 1928 must be bur-
dened with more ideological freight than it can carry.

Moore, in contrast to Handlin, sees Raskob's role in the campaign in terms not of liberalism but of expediency: the Democrats
had to win some of the business community away from its prosperous love affair with Hoover Republicanism, and Raskob was
their instrument for this purpose. But had not the candidacies of
stanch "gold standard" advocate Alton B. Parker in 1904 and corporation counsel John W. Davis in 1924 demonstrated that
Democratic attempts to beat Republican conservatism at its own
game usually failed? Moore does note that Raskob's appointment
as national chairman "seemed like an insult to the dry, Protestant,
rural South"; was it not equally an insult to the Democratic Party's anti-corporate, anti-speculative Progressives and liberals?

If, then, the campaign of 1928 will not reduce to a campaign
between liberals and conservatives, snobs and plain people, or
Wets and Drys, are we then left with Protestant against Catholic
by process of elimination? Not necessarily. Let us return again to
the contemporary assessment of Smith by Walter Lippmann:
"The Governor's more hasty friends show an intolerance when
they believe that Al Smith is the victim of purely religious prejudice. . . . There is an opposition to Smith which is as authentic
and, it seems to me, as poignant as his support. It is inspired by
the feeling that the clamorous life of the city should not be acknowledged as the American ideal."

Closely allied to the image of the corner saloon in American
folklore has been the image of the Eastern city slicker. It is a

venerable one; dissipated urban vice in contrast to abstemious rural virtue are themes as old in history as are cities themselves. In America, as witness Jefferson's *Notes on Virginia* and Royall Tyler's play *The Contrast*, they antedate the Constitution. There is also a long-standing tradition of the South and the West perennially arrayed politically against the urban East, almost regardless of the specific political issues confronting America at any given moment. The anti-Smith country in the election of 1928 was, by and large, the old Bryan country—which suggests that the Prohibition issue, and the Klan issue, and possibly even the Catholic issue, were surface stirrings of animosities of another kind. It may be noted in passing that this same trans-Mississippi Bryan country of 1896, which had become Hoover country by 1928, was to become Nixon country in 1960 and Goldwater country in the maneuverings which followed; so perhaps President Kennedy and Governor Smith had more in common as actors of an American political role than simply their religion, or their status as (by definition) liberal Democrats.

"The principal obstacle in Smith's way," wrote a contemporary observer of the pre-convention maneuverings of 1928, "never becomes palpable. . . . It lies in the fact that to millions of Americans he . . . embodies something alien. Not something alien in race or religion, but something alien to themselves . . . something they do not understand and which they feel does not understand them. . . . Some of the perturbed Methodist clergymen in the South opposed to Smith's nomination unconsciously revealed what really moves them most profoundly . . . when they said he was 'New York minded.' "

Had these words been written by one of those same perturbed Methodist clergymen, or indeed by any other Protestant, or even by a secularist liberal such as Lippmann, they could be cited as merely an unusually tortuous rationalization for anti-Catholicism. But they were written *by a Catholic*, and were printed in the Catholic liberal weekly *Commonweal*. And, conscious that bogeymen are not slain by one magazine article, the writer, Charles Willis Thompson, returned to the fray some months later in the *Catholic World*, with a piece entitled "The Tammany Monster." This second article was a ringing defense of the "monster" against attacks by the kind of outlander (Thompson mentioned Iowa, Nebraska, Oklahoma, and Little Rock, Arkansas) who viewed the mysterious East and all its works as evil, saying: "Tammany and Wall Street are the same thing, aren't they?"

Smith's own managers and friends were aware of this widespread fear of the urban East in the American hinterland. Norman Hapgood and Henry Moskowitz, in their campaign biography of Smith in 1927 (significantly titled *Up From the City Streets*), faced the problem squarely. The story of Al Smith, they wrote, "suggests that in the future our vast cities may do better by humanity than we have feared." Specifically, the politics characteristic of great cities, abhorred by some as "machine" or "Tammany" politics, might have creative possibilities undreamed of in the Mississippi Valley. Smith, in particular, "has been a product of the machine and . . . has remained a member of it, and at the same time has become a leader of the most progressive thought of the United States." Corner saloon politics, these authors argued, were not in essence very different from country store politics. Far from regarding "the machine" as oppressive and corrupt, the urban poor among whom Al Smith had grown up "were convinced that Tammany Hall was kind to them." Pressing this interpretation perhaps a shade too far in their enthusiasm, Hapgood and Moskowitz defined machine politics as "neighborliness—which on election day is translated into votes."

For the rural voter, who on successive days during the spring of 1928 might have seen headlines such as "Chicago's Election Starts with Kidnapping" and "Deneen Ticket Leads; His Candidate Slain," such a concept of big-city neighborliness was rather hard to take. New York was, of course, not Chicago, especially in 1928 when the Capone organization was near its peak; but to the rural mind one big city was much like another. With this problem in mind, local leaders in some rural areas—not all of them Democrats—strove to bridge the chasm between their constituents' world and Al Smith's.

One of the most interesting of these attempts, particularly in the light of what happened later in the campaign, was made by the Republican editor of the Emporia *Gazette*, William Allen White. Writing to Franklin D. Roosevelt on February 11, 1928, on behalf of the Kansas State Editorial Association, White invited Al Smith to come out to Kansas, "the center of the world which Smith does not know and which does not know Smith." "Smith is supposed to have horns and a tail out west," he wrote, and a confrontation between the New York Governor and a bipartisan group of Western newspaper editors "would do more for him politically than any other one thing he might possibly do." Frank Freidel has noted that Roosevelt tried to persuade Smith to accept this invitation, but failed; in that failure may lie a subtle indication of one reason for the failure of Smith's entire campaign.

The aftermath of this friendly gesture was saddening and distasteful. Throughout his life, William Allen White was the kind of partisan who can be a man of good will toward the Opposition "three and a half years out of every four," as Franklin Roosevelt himself later put it. As the campaign grew hotter than it ever could have been in February, even in 1928, an organization man "regular" enough to have supported Harding and Coolidge when the time came could have been expected to be drawn into the fray against Smith, even though White credited Al with "one of the important brains now functioning in American politics." But, as Professor Moore has shown at length in his study of the campaign, White's attacks on Smith went far beyond the generally acceptable limits of campaign behavior. White wrote that Smith's record as governor showed the New Yorker to be "soft" not only on Prohibition but also on gambling and prostitution. Worse, when he realized the enormity of such a charge when unproven, his retraction was grudging and ambiguous. It was, Moore concludes, a shocking lapse in a theretofore conspicuously honorable political career.

Professor Moore conjoins William Allen White's charges against the Governor with those of the Fundamentalist Baptist leader in New York City, the Rev. John Roach Straton—a conjunction which strongly implies that White's and Straton's warfare with Smith comes down essentially to the same thing, namely, anti-Catholicism. White in this period of the campaign saw Al Smith as a threat to "the whole Puritan civilization which has built a sturdy, orderly nation"; and Moore comments: "Of course one important facet of the 'whole Puritan civilization' was its stanchly Protestant character." Moore finds this attitude of the Kansas editor particularly "confused and distressing" because White, in a book which was already in press while these attacks were going on, "was about to present Smith in an essentially favorable light."

A re-reading of *Masks in a Pageant,* the work referred to, leads the present writer to a conclusion somewhat different from Professor Moore's. References to "Puritanism" and "a Puritan civilization" occur throughout White's writings in contexts having little or nothing to do with Smith or Catholicism. His apt characterization of Calvin Coolidge as "a Puritan in Babylon," for example, loses all its bite if the most cautious of all of America's Presidents is made merely a *Protestant* in Babylon. And parenthetically it may be observed that President Kennedy has had some notoriously kind words to say about Puritanism. What worried White far more than Al Smith's religious affiliation, or even his "wet" sympathies, was the old Jeffersonian bugbear of the great city as an enemy of liberty. In *Masks in a Pageant,* White was trying not only to reassure his readers about Smith but also to reassure himself about Smith's background.

William Allen White was aware that great cities had brought forth American Presidents before, and he cited Theodore Roosevelt—whose faithful vassal he himself had been—and Chester A. Arthur. But neither of these two men "was purely urbanite" (recall Mark Hanna's "damn cowboy" epithet hurled at T.R., for example), whereas Al Smith was "urbanite with an urbanity unstrained . . . city born, city bred, 'city broke,' city minded, and city hearted." And, White's urban reader might well have asked, why not? The Kansas editor did his best to agree: "There is no reason why the back alley cannot produce as good moral, spiritual, mental, and physical timber for politics as the backwoods. . . . The streets educated [Smith] as the woods and fields educated Lincoln." And yet, backwoods and back alley were inevitably headed for conflict in the twentieth century; "industrial democracy" was destined to "struggle for supremacy with . . . rural democracy—the America of our past."

As a determined political progressive, White was intellectually on the side of the new order; as a product of the Kansas frontier he was emotionally drawn to the old. The most revealing fact about the Al Smith sketch in White's *Masks in a Pageant* is that the author grouped it at the end of the book in a section titled "The Young Princes of Democracy"—and his other young prince was Mayor William Hale "Big Bill" Thompson of Chicago. The Al Smith essay *was*, in the main, favorable to Smith; but Al and Big Bill were of the same species in White's mind. In the epigraph to that part of the book, White wrote: "When we have sloughed off our rural philosophy—our fundamental Puritanism—we shall crown the young princes. In the meantime the warning is plain: 'Put not your trust in princes!' "

With mistrust of White's sort rampant throughout the Bryan country, it is understandable that practicing Democrats in the spring of 1928 might have cast about for a candidate who could hold Al Smith's constituents without alienating Willam Allen White's; ideally, a Catholic who was not one of the young princes. Predictably, some of them found him, in a state even more rural than Kansas. On March 4, Senator Thomas J. Walsh of Montana tossed his hat into the ring. On May 1, he was knocked out of the running in the California presidential primary; but in the meantime he had posed a major obstacle for the hypothesis of an "unwritten law" governing Catholic candidates. What is one to make of the fact that, in Professor Moore's words, "The two leading candidates for the Democratic nomination in 1928 were Catholic [and] one of them was nominated"? If the Walsh candidacy was a stalking-horse to divide the Catholic vote, as has been suggested, clearly the effort was unsuccessful; and if it was a serious bid for the presidency, then the "unwritten law" was already well on the way to being a dead letter. In either case, conclusions about toleration in American life more optimistic than those which have been customarily drawn for the 1920's would seem to be in order.

FDR in the Saddle

The Roosevelt Reconstruction

by William E. Leuchtenburg

The Harding-Coolidge decade of relatively prosperous "normalcy" ended abruptly with the stock market crash of 1929, but few Americans sensed even then the length and severity of the economic and social crisis that lay ahead. The Great Depression of the 1930's, the worst such downturn in American history, ushered into power the nation's longest and most influential modern presidential administration. Franklin Delano Roosevelt's "New Deal" turned government energies toward a broad-gauged assault on the problems of relief, recovery, and reform, and committed the government in Washington to a degree of involvement in American economic and social processes which all subsequent Presidents, Republican and Democratic, have merely extended, reluctantly or willingly.

The situation FDR confronted upon taking office in 1933 left him little choice: the economy required extensive federal intervention, and an enormous bureaucracy had to be created to manage it. Gross national product (GNP) had fallen from $104 billion in 1929 to $74 billion by early 1933. During the same period, American exports had plummeted from over $4.5 billion to less than $1.5 billion, while national income declined by more than half. Most ominous, the legions of unemployed Americans had swollen during the Hoover administration (1929–33) from 3 million to near 15 million, with both public and private relief agencies hopelessly overwhelmed by the dimensions of the distress.

Governmental deference to the business community, the central theme of the earlier decade's "Republican era," would no longer determine American politics. In Roosevelt's inaugural he pledged his administration to an unprecedented peacetime mobilization of economic resources to cope with the national emergency. By the time the New Deal's first hundred days had ended, the country recognized that FDR's initial pledge "to wage a war against the emergency, as great . . . as if we were in fact invaded by a foreign foe" had been more than platform rhetoric. Fifteen major executive programs and a raft of subsidiary bills whizzed through a receptive Congress in little more than three months— an improbable record for speedy passage of controversial legislation that helped alter the economic patterns and social ground rules of American life.

The New Deal struggled for the remainder of the decade to stimulate economic recovery and sidetrack social unrest. In the end, despite its substantial failure to restore the economy to full prosperity, the presidential administration had achieved profound changes upon the attitudes, values, and structure of American society as no other had before. William Leuchtenburg here analyzes the complex and multifarious impact of the New Deal on American life in a synthesis of his larger study of the New Deal years.

In eight years, Roosevelt and the New Dealers had almost revolutionized the agenda of American politics. "Mr. Roosevelt may have given the wrong answers to many of his problems," concluded the editors of The Economist. "But he is at least the first President of modern America who has asked the right questions."

From Franklin D. Roosevelt and the New Deal, 1932–1940, by William E. Leuchtenburg. Copyright © 1963 by William E. Leuchtenburg. Reprinted by permission of Harper & Row, Publishers, Inc., footnotes omitted.

In 1932, men of acumen were absorbed to an astonishing degree with such questions as prohibition, war debts, and law enforcement. By 1936, they were debating social security, the Wagner Act, valley authorities, and public housing. The thirties witnessed a rebirth of issues politics, and parties split more sharply on ideological lines than they had in many years past. "I incline to think that for years up to the present juncture thinking Democrats and thinking Republicans had been divided by an imaginary line," reflected a Massachusetts congressman in 1934. "Now for the first time since the period before the Civil War we find vital principles at stake." Much of this change resulted simply from the depression trauma, but much too came from the force of Roosevelt's personality and his use of his office as both pulpit and lectern. "Of course you have fallen into some errors—that is human," former Supreme Court Justice John Clarke wrote the President, "but you have put a new face upon the social and political life of our country."

Franklin Roosevelt re-created the modern presidency. He took an office which had lost much of its prestige and power in the previous twelve years and gave it an importance which went well beyond what even Theodore Roosevelt and Woodrow Wilson had done. Clinton Rossiter has observed: "Only Washington, who made the office, and Jackson, who remade it, did more than [Roosevelt] to raise it to its present condition of strength, dignity, and independence." Under Roosevelt, the White House became the focus of all government—the fountainhead of ideas, the initiator of action, the representative of the national interest.

Roosevelt greatly expanded the President's legislative functions. In the nineteenth century, Congress had been jealous of its prerogatives as the lawmaking body, and resented any encroachment on its domain by the Chief Executive. Woodrow Wilson and Theodore Roosevelt had broken new ground in sending actual drafts of bills to Congress and in using devices like the caucus to win enactment of measures they favored. Franklin Roosevelt made such constant use of these tools that he came to assume a legisla-

tive role not unlike that of a prime minister. He sent special messages to Congress, accompanied them with drafts of legislation
prepared by his assistants, wrote letters to committee chairmen or
members of Congress to urge passage of the proposals, and authorized men like Corcoran to lobby as presidential spokesmen on
the Hill. By the end of Roosevelt's tenure in the White House,
Congress looked automatically to the Executive for guidance; it
expected the administration to have a "program" to present for
consideration.

Roosevelt's most important formal contribution was his creation
of the Executive Office of the President on September 8, 1939.
Executive Order 8248, a "nearly unnoticed but none the less
epoch-making event in the history of American institutions," set
up an Executive Office staffed with six administrative assistants
with a "passion for anonymity." In 1939, the President not only
placed obvious agencies like the White House Office in the Executive Office but made the crucial decision to shift the Bureau
of the Budget from the Treasury and put it under his wing. In
later years, such pivotal agencies as the Council of Economic Advisers, the National Security Council, and the Central Intelligence
Agency would be moved into the Executive Office of the President. Roosevelt's decision, Rossiter has concluded, "converts the
presidency into an instrument of twentieth-century government;
it gives the incumbent a sporting chance to stand the strain and
fulfill his constitutional mandate as a one-man branch of our
three-part government; it deflates even the most forceful arguments, which are still raised occasionally, for a plural executive; it
assures us that the Presidency will survive the advent of the positive state. Executive Order 8248 may yet be judged to have saved
the Presidency from paralysis and the Constitution from radical
amendment."

Roosevelt's friends have been too quick to concede that he was
a poor administrator. To be sure, he found it difficult to discharge
incompetent aides, he procrastinated about decisions, and he
ignored all the canons of sound administration by giving men

overlapping assignments and creating a myriad of agencies which had no clear relation to the regular departments of government. But if the test of good administration is not an impeccable organizational chart but creativity, then Roosevelt must be set down not merely as a good administrator but as a resourceful innovator. The new agencies he set·up gave a spirit of excitement to Washington that the routinized old-line departments could never have achieved. The President's refusal to proceed through channels, however vexing at times to his subordinates, resulted in a competition not only among men but among ideas, and encouraged men to feel that their own beliefs might win the day. "You would be surprised, Colonel, the remarkable ideas that have been turned loose just because men have felt that they can get a hearing," one senator confided. The President's "procrastination" was his own way both of arriving at a sense of national consensus and of reaching a decision by observing a trial by combat among rival theories. Periods of indecision—as in the spring of 1935 or the beginning of 1938—were inevitably followed by a fresh outburst of new proposals.

Most of all, Roosevelt was a successful administrator because he attracted to Washington thousands of devoted and highly skilled men. Men who had been fighting for years for lost causes were given a chance: John Collier, whom the President courageously named Indian Commissioner; Arthur Powell Davis, who had been ousted as chief engineer of the Department of the Interior at the demand of power interests; old conservationists like Harry Slattery, who had fought the naval oil interests in the Harding era. When Harold Ickes took office as Secretary of the Interior, he looked up Louis Glavis—he did not even know whether the "martyr" of the Ballinger-Pinchot affair was still alive—and appointed him to his staff.

The New Dealers displayed striking ingenuity in meeting problems of governing. They coaxed salmon to climb ladders at Bonneville; they sponsored a Young Choreographers Laboratory in the WPA's Dance Theatre; they gave the pioneer documentary film maker Pare Lorentz the opportunity to create his classic films *The*

Plow That Broke the Plains and *The River*. At the Composers Forum-Laboratory of the Federal Music Project, William Schuman received his first serious hearing. In Arizona, Father Berard Haile of St. Michael's Mission taught written Navajo to the Indians. Roosevelt, in the face of derision from professional foresters and prairie states' governors, persisted in a bold scheme to plant a mammoth "shelterbelt" of parallel rows of trees from the Dakotas to the Panhandle. In all, more than two hundred million trees were planted—cottonwood and willow, hackberry and cedar, Russian olive and Osage orange; within six years, the President's visionary windbreak had won over his former critics. The spirit behind such innovations generated a new excitement about the potentialities of government. "Once again," Roosevelt told a group of young Democrats in April, 1936, "the very air of America is exhilarating."

Roosevelt dominated the front pages of the newspapers as no other President before or since has done. "Frank Roosevelt and the NRA have taken the place of love nests," commented Joe Patterson, publisher of the tabloid New York *Daily News*. At his very first press conference, Roosevelt abolished the written question and told reporters they could interrogate him without warning. Skeptics predicted the free and easy exchange would soon be abandoned, but twice a week, year in and year out, he threw open the White House doors to as many as two hundred reporters, most of them representing hostile publishers, who would crowd right up to the President's desk to fire their questions. The President joshed them, traded wisecracks with them, called them by their first names; he charmed them by his good-humored ease and impressed them with his knowledge of detail. To a degree, Roosevelt's press conference introduced, as some observers claimed, a new institution like Britain's parliamentary questioning; more to the point, it was a device the President manipulated, disarmingly and adroitly, to win support for his program. It served too as a classroom to instruct the country in the new economics and the new politics.

Roosevelt was the first President to master the technique of reaching people directly over the radio. In his fireside chats, he talked like a father discussing public affairs with his family in the living room. As he spoke, he seemed unconscious of the fact that he was addressing millions. "His head would nod and his hands would move in simple, natural, comfortable gestures," Frances Perkins recalled. "His face would smile and light up as though he were actually sitting on the front porch or in the parlor with them." Eleanor Roosevelt later observed that after the President's death people would stop her on the street to say "they missed the way the President used to talk to them. They'd say 'He used to talk to me about my government.' There was a real dialogue between Franklin and the people," she reflected. "That dialogue seems to have disappeared from the government since he died."

For the first time for many Americans, the federal government became an institution that was directly experienced. More than state and local governments, it came to be *the* government, an agency directly concerned with their welfare. It was the source of their relief payments; it taxed them directly for old age pensions; it even gave their children hot lunches in school. As the role of the state changed from that of neutral arbiter to a "powerful promoter of society's welfare," people felt an interest in affairs in Washington they had never had before.

Franklin Roosevelt personified the state as protector. It became commonplace to say that people felt toward the President the kind of trust they would normally express for a warm and understanding father who comforted them in their grief or safeguarded them from harm. An insurance man reported: "My mother looks upon the President as someone so immediately concerned with her problems and difficulties that she would not be greatly surprised were he to come to her house some evening and stay to dinner." From his first hours in office, Roosevelt gave people the feeling that they could confide in him directly. As late as the presidency of Herbert Hoover, one man, Ira Smith, had sufficed to take care of all the mail the White House received. Under Roosevelt, Smith had to acquire a staff of fifty people to handle the thousands of

letters written to the President each week. Roosevelt gave people
a sense of membership in the national community. Justice Douglas has written: "He was in a very special sense the people's President, because he made them feel that with him in the White
House they shared the Presidency. The sense of sharing the Presidency gave even the most humble citizen a lively sense of be-
longing."

When Roosevelt took office, the country, to a very large degree,
responded to the will of a single element: the white, Anglo-Saxon,
Protestant property-holding class. Under the New Deal, new
groups took their place in the sun. It was not merely that they received benefits they had not had before but that they were "recognized" as having a place in the commonwealth. At the beginning
of the Roosevelt era, charity organizations ignored labor when
seeking "community" representation; at the end of the period, no
fund-raising committee was complete without a union representative. While Theodore Roosevelt had founded a lily-white Progressive party in the South and Woodrow Wilson had introduced
segregation into the federal government, Franklin Roosevelt had
quietly brought the Negro into the New Deal coalition. When
the distinguished Negro contralto Marian Anderson was denied a
concert hall in Washington, Secretary Ickes arranged for her to
perform from the steps of Lincoln Memorial. Equal representation for religious groups became so well accepted that, as one
priest wryly complained, one never saw a picture of a priest in a
newspaper unless he was flanked on either side by a minister and
a rabbi.

The devotion Roosevelt aroused owed much to the fact that the
New Deal assumed the responsibility for guaranteeing every American a minimum standard of subsistence. Its relief programs represented an advance over the barbaric predepression practices that
constituted a difference not in degree but in kind. One analyst
wrote: "During the ten years between 1929 and 1939 more progress was made in public welfare and relief than in the three
hundred years after this country was first settled." The Roosevelt

administration gave such assistance not as a matter of charity but of right. This system of social rights was written into the Social Security Act. Other New Deal legislation abolished child labor in interstate commerce and, by putting a floor under wages and a ceiling on hours, all but wiped out the sweatshop.

Roosevelt and his aides fashioned a government which consciously sought to make the industrial system more humane and to protect workers and their families from exploitation. In his acceptance speech in June, 1936, the President stated: "Governments can err, Presidents do make mistakes, but the immortal Dante tells us that divine justice weighs the sins of the cold-blooded and the sins of the warm-hearted in different scales.

"Better the occasional faults of a Government that lives in a spirit of charity than the constant omission of a Government frozen in the ice of its own indifference." Nearly everyone in the Roosevelt government was caught up to some degree by a sense of participation in something larger than themselves. A few days after he took office, one of the more conservative New Deal administrators wrote in his diary: "This should be a Gov't of humanity."

The federal government expanded enormously in the Roosevelt years. The crisis of the depression dissipated the distrust of the state inherited from the eighteenth century and reinforced in diverse ways by the Jeffersonians and the Spencerians. Roosevelt himself believed that liberty in America was imperiled more by the agglomerations of private business than by the state. The New Dealers were convinced that the depression was the result not simply of an economic breakdown but of a political collapse; hence, they sought new political instrumentalities. The reformers of the 1930's accepted almost unquestioningly the use of coercion by the state to achieve reforms. Even Republicans who protested that Roosevelt's policies were snuffing out liberty voted overwhelmingly in favor of coercive measures.

This elephantine growth of the federal government owed much to the fact that local and state governments had been tried in the crisis and found wanting. When one magazine wired state governors to ask their views, only one of the thirty-seven who replied announced that he was willing to have the states resume responsibility for relief. Every time there was a rumored cutback of federal spending for relief, Washington was besiged by delegations of mayors protesting that city governments did not have the resources to meet the needs of the unemployed.

Even more dramatic was the impotence of local governments in dealing with crime, a subject that captured the national imagination in a decade of kidnapings and bank holdups. In September, 1933, the notorious bank robber John Dillinger was arrested in Ohio. Three weeks later, his confederates released him from jail and killed the Lima, Ohio, sheriff. In January, 1934, after bank holdups at Racine, Wisconsin, and East Chicago, Indiana, Dillinger was apprehended in Tucson, Arizona, and returned to the "escape-proof" jail of Crown Point, Indiana, reputedly the strongest county prison in the country. A month later he broke out and drove off in the sheriff's car. While five thousand law officers pursued him, he stopped for a haircut in a barber shop, bought cars, and had a home-cooked Sunday dinner with his family in his home town. When he needed more arms, he raided the police station at Warsaw, Indiana.

Dillinger's exploits touched off a national outcry for federal action. State and local authorities could not cope with gangs which crossed and recrossed jurisdictional lines, which were equipped with Thompson submachine guns and high-powered cars, and which had a regional network of informers and fences in the Mississippi Valley. Detection and punishment of crime had always been a local function; now there seemed no choice but to call in the federal operatives. In July, 1934, federal agents shot down Dillinger outside a Chicago theater. In October, FBI men killed Pretty Boy Floyd near East Liverpool, Ohio; in November, they shot Baby Face Nelson, Public Enemy No. 1, near Niles Center, Illinois. By the end of 1934, the nation had a new kind of hero: the G-man Melvin Purvis and the chief of the Division of Investigation of the Department of Justice, J. Edgar Hoover. By the end of that year, too, Congress had stipulated that a long list of crimes would henceforth be regarded as federal offenses, including holding up a bank insured by the Federal Deposit Insurance Corporation. The family of a kidnaped victim could call in the federal police simply by phoning National 7117 in Washington.

Under the New Deal, the federal government greatly extended its power over the economy. By the end of the Roosevelt years, few questioned the right of the government to pay the farmer millions in subsidies not to grow crops, to enter plants to conduct union elections, to regulate business enterprises from utility companies to air lines, or even to compete directly with business by generating and distributing hydroelectric power. All of these powers had been ratified by the Supreme Court, which had even held that a man growing grain solely for his own use was affecting interstate commerce and hence subject to federal penalties. The President, too, was well on his way to becoming "the chief economic engineer," although this was not finally established until the Full Employment Act of 1946. In 1931, Hoover had hooted that some people thought "that by some legerdemain we can legislate ourselves out of a world-wide depression." In the Roosevelt era, the conviction that government both should and could act to forestall future breakdowns gained general acceptance. The New Deal left a large legacy of antidepression controls—securities regulation, banking reforms, unemployment compensation—even if it could not guarantee that a subsequent administration would use them.

In the 1930's, the financial center of the nation shifted from Wall Street to Washington. In May, 1934, a writer reported: "Financial news no longer originates in Wall Street." That same month, *Fortune* commented on a revolution in the credit system which was "one of the major historical events of the generation." "Mr. Roosevelt," it noted, "seized the Federal Reserve without firing a shot." The federal government had not only broken down the old separation of bank and state in the Reserve system but had

gone into the credit business itself in a wholesale fashion under
the aegis of the RFC, the Farm Credit Administration, and the
housing agencies. Legislation in 1933 and 1934 had established
federal regulation of Wall Street for the first time. No longer
could the New York Stock Exchange operate as a private club
free of national supervision. In 1935, Congress leveled the mammoth holding-company pyramids and centralized yet more authority over the banking system in the federal government. After a
tour of the United States in 1935, Sir Josiah Stamp wrote: "Just
as in 1929 the whole country was 'Wall Street-conscious' now it
is 'Washington-conscious.' "

Despite this encroachment of government on traditional business prerogatives, the New Deal could advance impressive claims
to being regarded as a "savior of capitalism." Roosevelt's sense of
the land, of family, and of the community marked him as a man
with deeply ingrained conservative traits. In the New Deal years,
the government sought deliberately, in Roosevelt's words, "to
energize private enterprise." The RFC financed business, housing
agencies underwrote home financing, and public works spending
aimed to revive the construction industry. Moreover, some of the
New Deal reforms were Janus-faced. The NYA, in aiding jobless
youth, also served as a safety valve to keep young people out of
the labor market. A New Deal congressman, in pushing for public
power projects, argued that the country should take advantage
of the sea of "cheap labor" on the relief rolls. Even the Wagner
Act and the movement for industrial unionism were motivated in
part by the desire to contain "unbalanced and radical" labor
groups. Yet such considerations should not obscure the more important point: that the New Deal, however conservative it was
in some respects and however much it owed to the past, marked
a radically new departure. As Carl Degler writes: "The conclusion
seems inescapable that, traditional as the words may have been in
which the New Deal expressed itself, in actuality it was a revolutionary response to a revolutionary situation."

Not all of the changes that were wrought were the result of

Roosevelt's own actions or of those of his government. Much of the force for change came from progressives in Congress, or from nongovernmental groups like the C.I.O., or simply from the impersonal agency of the depression itself. Yet, however much significance one assigns the "objective situation," it is difficult to gainsay the importance of Roosevelt. If, in Miami in February, 1933, an assassin's bullet had been true to its mark and John Garner rather than Roosevelt had entered the White House the next month, or if the Roosevelt lines had cracked at the Democratic convention in 1932 and Newton Baker had been the compromise choice, the history of America in the thirties would have been markedly different.

At a time when democracy was under attack elsewhere in the world, the achievements of the New Deal were especially significant. At the end of 1933, in an open letter to President Roosevelt, John Maynard Keynes had written: "You have made yourself the trustee for those in every country who seek to mend the evils of our condition by reasoned experiment within the framework of the existing social system. If you fail, rational change will be gravely prejudiced throughout the world, leaving orthodoxy and revolution to fight it out." In the next few years, teams of foreigners toured the TVA, Russians and Arabs came to study the shelterbelt, French writers taxed Léon Blum with importing "Rooseveltism" to France, and analysts characterized Paul Van Zeeland's program in Belgium as a "New Deal." Under Roosevelt, observed a Montevideo newspaper, the United States had become "as it was in the eighteenth century, the victorious emblem around which may rally the multitudes thirsting for social justice and human fraternity."

In their approach to reform, the New Dealers reflected the tough-minded, hard-boiled attitude that permeated much of America in the thirties. In 1931, the gangster film *Public Enemy* had given the country a new kind of hero in James Cagney: the aggressive, unsentimental tough guy who deliberately assaulted the romantic tradition. It was a type whose role in society could easily be manipulated; gangster hero Cagney of the early thirties was transformed into G-man hero Cagney of the later thirties. Even more representative was Humphrey Bogart, creator of the "private eye" hero, the man of action who masks his feelings in a calculated emotional neutrality. Bogart, who began as the cold desperado Duke Mantee of *Petrified Forest* and the frightening Black Legionnaire, soon turned up on the right side of anti-Fascist causes, although he never surrendered the pose of noninvolvement. This fear of open emotional commitment and this admiration of toughness ran through the vogue of the "Dead End Kids," films like *Nothing Sacred,* the popularity of the St. Louis Cardinals' spike-flying Gas House Gang, and the "hardboiled" fiction of writers like James Cain and Dashiell Hammett.

Unlike the earlier Progressive, the New Dealer shied away from being thought of as sentimental. Instead of justifying relief as a humanitarian measure, the New Dealers often insisted it was necessary to stimulate purchasing power or to stabilize the economy or to "conserve manpower." The justification for a better distribution of income was neither "social justice" nor a "healthier national life," wrote Adolf Berle. "It remained for the hard-boiled student to work out the simple equation that unless the national income was pretty widely diffused there were not enough customers to keep the plants going." The reformers of the thirties abandoned—or claimed they had abandoned—the old Emersonian hope of reforming man and sought only to change institutions. This meant that they did not seek to "uplift" the people they were helping but only to improve their economic position. "In other words," Tugwell stated bluntly, "the New Deal is attempting to do nothing to *people,* and does not seek at all to alter their way of life, their wants and desires."

Reform in the 1930's meant *economic* reform; it departed from the Methodist-parsonage morality of many of the earlier Progressives, in part because much of the New Deal support, and many of its leaders, derived from urban immigrant groups hostile to the old Sabbatarianism. While the progressive grieved over the fate

of the prostitute, the New Dealer would have placed Mrs. Warren's profession under a code authority. If the archetypical progressive was Jane Addams singing "Onward, Christian Soldiers," the
representative New Dealer was Harry Hopkins betting on the
horses at Laurel Race Track. When directing FERA in late 1933,
Hopkins announced: "I would like to provide orchestras for beer
gardens to encourage people to sit around drinking their beer and
enjoying themselves. It would be a great unemployment relief
measure." "I feel no call to remedy evils," Raymond Moley declared. "I have not the slightest urge to be a reformer. Social workers make me very weary. They have no sense of humor."

Despite Moley's disclaimer, many of the early New Dealers like
himself and Adolf Berle did, in fact, hope to achieve reform
through regeneration: the regeneration of the businessman. By
the end of 1935, the New Dealers were pursuing a quite different
course. Instead of attempting to evangelize the Right, they mobilized massive political power against the power of the corporation.
They relied not on converting industrial sinners but in using sufficient coercion. New Dealers like Thurman Arnold sought to
ignore "moral" considerations altogether; Arnold wished not to
punish wrongdoers but to achieve price flexibility. His "faith" lay
in the expectation that "fanatical alignments between opposing
political principles may disappear and a competent, practical, op-
portunisitic governing class may rise to power." With such expectations, the New Dealers frequently had little patience with legal
restraints that impeded action. "I want to assure you," Hopkins
told the NYA Advisory Committee, "that we are not afraid of
exploring anything within the law, and we have a lawyer who will
declare anything you want to do legal."

In the thirties, nineteenth-century individualism gave ground
to a new emphasis on social security and collective action. In the
twenties, America hailed Lindbergh as the Lone Eagle; in the
thirties, when word arrived that Amelia Earhart was lost at sea,
the *New Republic* asked the government to prohibit citizens from
engaging in such "useless" exploits. The NRA sought to drive news-

boys off the streets and took a Blue Eagle away from a company
in Huck Finn's old town of Hannibal, Missouri, because a fifteen-
year-old was found driving a truck for his father's business. Josef
Hofmann urged that fewer musicians become soloists, Hollywood
stars like Joan Crawford joined the Screen Actors Guild, and Leo-
pold Stokowski canceled a performance in Pittsburgh because
theater proprietors were violating a union contract. In New York
in 1933, after a series of meetings in Heywood Broun's penthouse
apartment, newspapermen organized the American Newspaper
Guild in rebellion against the dispiriting romanticism of Richard
Harding Davis. "We no longer care to develop the individual as
a unique contributor to a democratic form," wrote the mordant
Edgar Kemler. "In this movement each individual sub-man is important, not for his uniqueness, but for his ability to lose himself
in the mass,.through his fidelity to the trade union, or cooperative
organization, or political party."

The liberals of the thirties admired intellectual activity which
had a direct relation to concrete reality. Stuart Chase wrote of one
government report: "This book is live stuff—wheelbarrow, cement
mixer, steam dredge, generator, combine, power-line stuff; library
dust does not gather here." If the poet did not wish to risk the
suspicion that his loyalties were not to the historic necessities of
his generation, wrote Archibald MacLeish, he must "soak himself
not in books" but in the physical reality of "by what organization
of men and railroads and trucks and belts and book-entries the
materials of a single automobile are assembled." The New Dealers
were fascinated by "the total man days per year for timber stand
improvement," and Tugwell rejoiced in the "practical success" of
the Resettlement Administration demonstrated by "these healthy
collection figures." Under the Special Skills Division of the RA,
Greenbelt was presented with inspirational paintings like *Con-
structing Sewers, Concrete Mixer,* and *Shovel at Work.* On one
occasion, in attempting to mediate a literary controversy, the critic
Edmund Wilson wrote: "It should be possible to convince Marx-
ist critics of the importance of a work like 'Ulysses' by telling them

that it is a great piece of engineering—as it is." In this activist world of the New Dealers, the aesthete and the man who pursued a life of contemplation, especially the man whose interests centered in the past, were viewed with scorn. In Robert Sherwood's *The Petrified Forest*, Alan Squier, the ineffectual aesthete, meets his death in the desert and is buried in the petrified forest where the living turn to stone. He is an archaic type for whom the world has no place.

The new activism explicitly recognized its debt to Dewey's dictum of "learning by doing" and, like other of Dewey's ideas, was subject to exaggeration and perversion. The New Deal, which gave unprecedented authority to intellectuals in government, was, in certain important respects, anti-intellectual. Without the activist faith, perhaps not nearly so much would have been achieved. It was Lilienthal's conviction that "there is almost nothing, however fantastic, that (given competent organization) a team of engineers, scientists, and administrators cannot do today" that helped make possible the successes of TVA. Yet the liberal activists grasped only a part of the truth; they retreated from conceptions like "tragedy," "sin," "God," often had small patience with the force of tradition, and showed little understanding of what moved men to seek meanings outside of political experience. As sensitive a critic as the poet Horace Gregory could write, in a review of the works of D. H. Lawrence: "The world is moving away from Lawrence's need for personal salvation; his 'dark religion' is not a substitute for economic planning." This was not the mood of all men in the thirties—not of a William Faulkner, an Ellen Glasgow— and many of the New Dealers recognized that life was more complex than some of their statements would suggest. Yet the liberals, in their desire to free themselves from the tyranny of precedent and in their ardor for social achievement, sometimes walked the precipice of superficiality and philistinism.

The concentration of the New Dealers on public concerns made a deep mark on the sensibility of the 1930's. Private experience seemed self-indulgent compared to the demands of public life.

"Indeed the public world with us has *become* the private world, and the private world has become the public," wrote Archibald MacLeish. "We live, that is to say, in a revolutionary time in which the public life has washed in over the dikes of private existence as sea water breaks over into the fresh pools in the spring tides till everything is salt." In the thirties, the Edna St. Vincent Millay whose candle had burned at both ends wrote the polemical *Conversation at Midnight* and the bitter "Epitaph for the Race of Man" in *Wine From These Grapes*.

The emphasis on the public world implied a specific rejection of the values of the 1920's. Roosevelt dismissed the twenties as "a decade of debauch," Tugwell scored those years as "a decade of empty progress, devoid of contribution to a genuinely better future," Morris Cooke deplored the "gilded-chariot days" of 1929, and Alben Barkley saw the twenties as a "carnival" marred by "the putrid pestilence of financial debauchery." The depression was experienced as the punishment of a wrathful God visited on a nation that had strayed from the paths of righteousness. The fire that followed the Park Avenue party in Thomas Wolfe's *You Can't Go Home Again*, like the suicide of Eveline at the end of John Dos Passos's *The Big Money*, symbolized the holocaust that brought to an end a decade of hedonism. In an era of reconstruction, the attitudes of the twenties seemed alien, frivolous, or—the most cutting word the thirties could visit upon a man or institution—"escapist." When Morrie Ryskind and George Kaufman, authors of the popular *Of Thee I Sing*, lampooned the government again in *Let 'em Eat Cake* in the fall of 1933, the country was not amused. The New York *Post* applauded the decision of George Jean Nathan and his associates to discontinue the *American Spectator*: "Nihilism, dadaism, smartsetism—they are all gone, and this, too, is progress." One of H. L. Mencken's biographers has noted: "Many were at pains to write him at his new home, telling him he was a sophomore, and those writing in magazines attacked him with a fury that was suspect because of its very violence."

Commentators on the New Deal have frequently characterized it by that much-abused term "pragmatic." If one means by this that the New Dealers carefully tested the consequences of ideas, the term is clearly a misnomer. If one means that Roosevelt was exceptionally anti-ideological in his approach to politics, one may question whether he was, in fact, any more "pragmatic" in this sense than Van Buren or Polk or even "reform" Presidents like Jackson and Theodore Roosevelt. The "pragmatism" of the New Deal seemed remarkable only in a decade tortured by ideology, only in contrast to the rigidity of Hoover and of the Left.

The New Deal was pragmatic mainly in its skepticism about utopias and final solutions, its openness to experimentation, and its suspicion of the dogmas of the Establishment. Since the advice of economists had so often been wrong, the New Dealers distrusted the claims of orthodox theory—"All this is perfectly terrible because it is all pure theory, when you come down to it," the President said on one occasion—and they felt free to try new approaches. Roosevelt refused to be awed by the warnings of economists and financial experts that government interference with the "laws" of the economy was blasphemous. "We must lay hold of the fact that economic laws are not made by nature," the President stated. "They are made by human beings." The New Dealers denied that depressions were inevitable events that had to be borne stoically, most of the stoicism to be displayed by the most impoverished, and they were willing to explore novel ways to make the social order more stable and more humane. "I am for experimenting . . . in various parts of the country, trying out schemes which are supported by reasonable people and see if they work," Hopkins told a conference of social workers. "If they do not work, the world will not come to an end."

Hardheaded, "anti-utopian," the New Dealers nonetheless had their Heavenly City: the greenbelt town, clean, green, and white, with children playing in light, airy, spacious schools; the government project at Longview, Washington, with small houses, each of different design, colored roofs, and gardens of flowers and veg-

etables; the Mormon villages of Utah that M. L. Wilson kept
in his mind's eye—immaculate farmsteads on broad, rectangular
streets; most of all, the Tennessee Valley, with its model town of
Norris, the tall transmission towers, the white dams, the glistening
wire strands, the valley where "a vision of villages and clean small
factories has been growing into the minds of thoughtful men."
Scandinavia was their model abroad, not only because it summoned up images of the countryside of Denmark, the beauties of
Stockholm, not only for its experience with labor relations and
social insurance and currency reform, but because it represented
the "middle way" of happy accommodation of public and private
institutions the New Deal sought to achieve. "Why," inquired
Brandeis, "should anyone want to go to Russia when one can go
to Denmark?"

Yet the New Deal added up to more than all of this—more
than an experimental approach, more than the sum of its legislative achievements, more than an antiseptic utopia. It is true that
there was a certain erosion of values in the thirties, as well as a
narrowing of horizons, but the New Dealers inwardly recognized
that what they were doing had a deeply moral significance however much they eschewed ethical pretensions. Heirs of the Enlightenment, they felt themselves part of a broadly humanistic
movement to make man's life on earth more tolerable, a movement that might someday even achieve a co-operative commonwealth. Social insurance, Frances Perkins declared, was "a fundamental part of another great forward step in that liberation of
humanity which began with the Renaissance."

Franklin Roosevelt did not always have this sense as keenly as
some of the men around him, but his greatness as a President lies
in the remarkable degree to which he shared the vision. "The new
deal business to me is very much bigger than anyone yet has expressed it," observed Senator Elbert Thomas. Roosevelt "seems to
really have caught the spirit of what one of the Hebrew prophets
called the desire of the nations. If he were in India today they
would probably decide that he had become Mahatma—that is,

one in tune with the infinite." Both foes and friends made much of Roosevelt's skill as a political manipulator, and there is no doubt that up to a point he delighted in schemes and stratagems. As Donald Richberg later observed: "There would be times when he seemed to be a Chevalier Bayard, *sans peur et sans reproche,* and times in which he would seem to be the apotheosis of a prince who had absorbed and practiced all the teachings of Machiavelli." Yet essentially he was a moralist who wanted to achieve certain humane reforms and instruct the nation in the principles of government. On one occasion, he remarked: "I want to be a *preaching President*—like my cousin." His courtiers gleefully recounted his adroitness in trading and dealing for votes, his effectiveness on the stump, his wicked skill in cutting corners to win a point. But Roosevelt's importance lay not in his talents as a campaigner or a manipulator. It lay rather in his ability to arouse the country and, more specifically, the men who served under him, by his breezy encouragement of experimentation, by his hopefulness, and—a word that would have embarrassed some of his lieutenants—by his idealism.

The New Deal left many problems unsolved and even created some perplexing new ones. It never demonstrated that it could achieve prosperity in peacetime. As late as 1941, the unemployed still numbered six million, and not until the war year of 1943 did the army of the jobless finally disappear. It enhanced the power of interest groups who claimed to speak for millions, but sometimes represented only a small minority. It did not evolve a way to protect people who had no such spokesmen, nor an acceptable method for disciplining the interest groups. In 1946, President Truman would resort to a threat to draft railway workers into the Army to avert a strike. The New Deal achieved a more just society by recognizing groups which had been largely unrepresented— staple farmers, industrial workers, particular ethnic groups, and the new intellectual-administrative class. Yet this was still a half-way revolution; it swelled the ranks of the bourgeoisie but left many Americans—sharecroppers, slum dwellers, most Negroes— outside of the new equilibrium.

Some of these omissions were to be promptly remedied. Subsequent Congresses extended social security, authorized slum clearance projects, and raised minimum-wage standards to keep step with the rising price level. Other shortcomings are understandable. The havoc that had been done before Roosevelt took office was so great that even the unprecedented measures of the New Deal did not suffice to repair the damage. Moreover, much was still to be learned, and it was in the Roosevelt years that the country was schooled in how to avert another major depression. Although it was war which freed the government from the taboos of a balanced budget and revealed the potentialities of spending, it is conceivable that New Deal measures would have led the country into a new cycle of prosperity even if there had been no war. Marked gains had been made before the war spending had any appreciable effect. When recovery did come, it was much more soundly based because of the adoption of the New Deal program.

Roosevelt and the New Dealers understood, perhaps better than their critics, that they had come only part of the way. Henry Wallace remarked: "We are children of the transition—we have left Egypt but we have not yet arrived at the Promised Land." Only five years separated Roosevelt's inauguration in 1933 and the adoption of the last of the New Deal measures, the Fair Labor Standards Act, in 1938. The New Dealers perceived that they had done more in those years than had been done in any comparable period in American history, but they also saw that there was much still to be done, much, too, that continued to baffle them. "I believe in the things that have been done," Mrs. Roosevelt told the American Youth Congress in February, 1939. "They helped but they did not solve the fundamental problems. . . . I never believed the Federal government could solve the whole problem. It bought us time to think." She closed not with a solution but with a challenge: "Is it going to be worth while?"

"This generation of Americans is living in a tremendous moment of history," President Roosevelt stated in his final national address of the 1940 campaign.

"The surge of events abroad has made some few doubters among us ask: Is this the end of a story that has been told? Is the book of democracy now to be closed and placed away upon the dusty shelves of time?

"My answer is this: All we have known of the glories of democracy—its freedom, its efficiency as a mode of living, its ability to meet the aspirations of the common man—all these are merely an introduction to the greater story of a more glorious future.

"We Americans of today—all of us—we are characters in the living book of democracy.

"But we are also its author. It falls upon us now to say whether the chapters that are to come will tell a story of retreat or a story of continued advance."

From FDR to Truman

Congress and the Fair Deal

by Richard E. Neustadt

The French historian André Maurois once described Franklin Roosevelt as a presidential "Moses, [who] led his people through the desert of the depression and the trials of the war toward an awareness of their social and international responsibilities." Maurois shrewdly categorized Roosevelt's less polished successor, Harry S Truman, differently. "Truman's ambition," he observed, "was rather to be a Joshua, the faithful lieutenant who, after the prophet's meeting with his God and the proclamation of the Tables of the Law, undertook the application of them."

Essentially Maurois described Truman's desire, once he became President in 1945, to consolidate and complete "the Roosevelt revolution" in American domestic life. Truman's Fair Deal programs built generally on uncompleted aspects (some barely begun) of the New Deal agenda. Plagued from almost the beginning of his presidency by an uncooperative congressional coalition of Republicans and conservative Southern Democrats, Truman never enjoyed the initial period of harmony between executive and legislative branches that made Roosevelt's first term so spectacularly successful. Thus many of Truman's most cherished domestic programs, including a federally sponsored medical care plan and major civil rights legislation, failed to become law; and Truman's limited talents for congressional arm-twisting (despite some achievements on Capitol Hill), never matched Roosevelt's illustrious record.

Practically from the night he took office upon hearing word of Roosevelt's sudden death, a "night the moon, the stars and all the planets fell on me," Truman recalled, the new President found himself involved in controversy with Soviet Russia, one of America's World War II allies, over the nature of the postwar settlement. During the Truman presidency a Cold War between the world's two superpowers led the United States into forming a series of global alliances with the avowed aim of "containing" Russia. Much of the historiographic debate over the quality of Truman's presidency has pitted a generation of liberal anti-Communist historians who consider Truman's view of Soviet intentions reasonably accurate against a more recent wave of "New Left" revisionists who have placed equal or primary responsibility on Truman for provoking Russian hostility. It is doubtful that the latter group would sustain a 1964 poll among historians that judged Truman as a "near-great" President, but even today, many scholars admire Truman's adroit handling of American foreign policy, particularly considering the Missourian's lack of preparation for the massive presidential responsibilities he inherited.

The verdict on Truman's direction of domestic affairs remains mixed. Despite his passionate opposition to the rise of McCarthyism, recent scholars have demonstrated convincingly the role which the Truman administration's own sweeping investigations of the loyalty of government workers had in preparing the ground for professional Red-baiters such as Joe McCarthy. Truman's presidency, which had begun bright with hope for a peaceful postwar era, ended in cheap scandal, political mudslinging, a grinding and costly Cold War, and with an American army stalemated after a three years of inconclusive fighting in Korea. Yet even his severest critics are frank to acknowledge Truman's honest, candid, and feisty presidential leadership. Richard Neustadt evaluates the President's relationship with Congress in the article that follows, accentuating some of the advantages and drawbacks that affected Truman as FDR's successor.

✿ On September 6, 1945, three weeks after V–J Day, Harry S
Truman sent to Congress a twenty-one point program of domestic
legislation—his first comprehensive venture in home affairs since
Franklin Roosevelt's death five months before. This marked the
beginning of a long series of presidential proposals for congressional action in the fields of economic development and social
welfare; proposals which streamed out of the White House for
nearly seven years, from the first session of the 79th Congress
through the second session of the 82nd; a legislative program
which became each year more comprehensive, more organized,
more definite, receiving after 1948, the distinction of a label: The
Fair Deal.

Looking back upon this enterprise, this Fair Deal program and
its fortunes in those years, no less an observer than Elmer Davis
has ventured the following verdict:

All in all, in domestic affairs, Mr. Truman was an unsuccessful President. [He] presented . . . a liberal program which was coherent and
logical as the New Deal had never been. Congress, not being liberal,
refused to take it; yet every year he persisted in offering it all to them
again and they still wouldn't take it. . . . Truman kept asking for
all of it and getting none of it.

This retrospective vision of the President who never changed
his pace and of the Congress never altering in opposition is no
doubt widely shared these days. No doubt, there is an element
of reality behind it. Certainly, President Truman held out for
more than he could reasonably hope to gain; certainly his four
Congresses persisted in frustrating many of his aims.

Yet in its bold relief and simple black and white, this vision of
the Truman record misses much light and shadow in a very complex situation. And by virtue of its very sharpness and simplicity,
it becomes a stumbling block to understanding and appraisal.
Students of postwar politics and of the presidency, and Congress,

From *Public Policy*, V (1954), 351–81. Reprinted by permission; footnotes
omitted.

have need to start their march through Truman's years with a more elaborate guide to the terrain than this quick characterization can supply.

It is much too soon, of course, for the definitive appraisal of the Fair Deal legislative program, its fundamental emphasis and purposes, its ultimate success or failure. But it is not too soon to go behind neat generalizations and draw a balance on the record as it stood when Truman left the White House. What was attempted, what accomplished, what lost? And more important still, what seem now, at this reading, to have been the underlying motivations, the determinative circumstances? These are the questions to which this essay is addressed.

A General Note on Congress: 1945 to 1952

Before turning to the Fair Deal, as such, something need be said by way of background about the work load and the composition of the four Congresses which Truman faced as President.

These were the Congresses of post-war reconstruction and cold war and Korea. For seven successive years their sessions tackled and put through an extraordinary series of Administration measures in the fields of international cooperation, collective security and national defense; a series which for scope and scale and continuity has no precedent in our history.

On no previous occasion has American foreign policy required —much less received—comparable congressional participation for such a span of time. Rarely before, save at the onset of our greatest wars, has the Congress broken so much new and unfamiliar ground; rarely, if ever, has momentum been so long sustained.

One thinks of Franklin Roosevelt's first four years, and the legislative break-through into broad new areas of Federal action here at home. We look back on that as a revolution—a stunning departure from the traditional limitations of pre-depression years. So, too, were these postwar programs revolutionary—shattering all manner of shibboleths and precedents, in the international sphere untouchable right up to World War II. And what stands out historically is a record of immense accomplishment, in legislative terms, both for the Administration that framed the measures and for the Congresses that put them through.

The record becomes still more impressive when one recalls that President Truman never did command a "safe" working majority of the rank and file in either House of Congress. His "honeymoon" did not outlast the war. There was no bloc of "Truman men," sufficient for his purposes, on which he could rely to follow through, without cavail, whatever leads he gave. Rather, the thing was done through that extraordinary phenomenon, postwar "bipartisanship," a carefully conceived and executed coalition launched by Roosevelt, husbanded by Truman, actively furthered by effective leadership in the congressional power centers of both parties.

This enterprise was in its way as distinctive an achievement, for both President and Congress, as the roster of enactments which it helped to frame and legislate. Of course, the idyl of bipartisanship did not last forever. But even in 1952, the "internationalist" alignment, though reduced in strength by mass Republican defections—and some Democratic backsliding as well—remained a strong bi-factional, if not bipartisan reality, producing —in support of foreign policy—majorities, however bare, which could not have been mustered for a moment behind most Fair Deal domestic programs.

This raises a crucial point: the internationalist coalition, which supported Truman's foreign policy, existed, cheek by jowl, with a "conservative" coalition, which opposed Administration policies at home. What's more, the two most vital elements in the conservative alignment, were also chief participants in the internationalist bloc—the "moderates" of both parties; the Vandenberg Midwest Republicans and the Russell Southern Democrats.

These were the swing groups, joining the "Fair Dealers" to beat off the "extremists" of both parties in their raids on foreign programs; joining the extremists in opposition to most of the

Fair Dealers' pet proposals at home. Internationalism combined with conservatism was the formula which kept two coalitions going, side by side, through issue after issue, Congress after Congress.

A great deal happened after 1949, to sap the strength of the internationalist coalition. On the personality side, of course, came Vandenberg's illness and death, Connally's advancing age, Acheson's unpopularity. Deeper down were the accumulating frustrations of twenty Democratic years, capped with "Communism, Corruption, Korea"—and China; mercilessly exploited by congressional Republicans made desperate after 1948 and cured, thereby, of any faith in "high level" politics, or the "me-too" approach. In addition, after 1950, after Korea, came a development which threatened the whole basis of compatibility between internationalism and conservatism: the full cost of our commitments in the world—in dollars and in human terms as well—took on a new and frightening dimension. Conservatism and internationalism began to come unstuck, to war with one another. And if the Democratic "moderates"—taken as a whole—did not react as sharply or as soon as the Republicans who buried Vandenberg, this may be taken, partly, as a tribute to party loyalties and hopes for 1952.

Taking Truman's four Congresses together, in all these terms of workload and alignment, three further observations are in order. First, had no more been attempted or accomplished, by way of major, controversial, forward measures, than the great landmarks in the international and mobilization fields alone, we would still have to grant, in retrospect, that these were busy and productive years of legislation for the Congress—outstanding years, by prewar standards.

Moreover, whatever else might have been tried, on the domestic front, there was no time, from 1945 to 1952, when Truman's Administration—given its foreign policy and the international situation from year to year—could afford to trade a major objective in the foreign field for some advantage in the domestic. Consistently, it was, and had to be, the other way around.

Finally, considering the integral relationships between the

"internationalist" coalition which supported Truman and the
conservative coalition which opposed him, every major venture
in home affairs was bound to complicate the progress, endanger
the timetable of those all-important measures in his foreign policy.
From his first days in office, when he reaffirmed Roosevelt's arrangements for Republican participation in the San Francisco
Conference, Truman acknowledged his dependence, in the foreign
field, on elements of the anti-New Deal coalition—an enterprise
which, always potent after 1937, had spent the wartime "truce"
maturing its relations, building its lines and thwarting FDR on
secondary issues.

Why, then, did Truman press a host of "hot" Fair Deal domestic issues, sure to arouse the wrath of this entrenched conservative alignment? To this question there is no single, easy answer,
but rather a whole series, arising out of motivations and responses
which varied with circumstance, over the years. To get at these
we need now turn to straight, historical review, beginning with
the first Truman "inventory" of legislative needs in home affairs
—the twenty-one point program of 1945.

To Reaffirm the Roosevelt Purpose: 1945–46

The original "twenty-one point" program went to Congress by
special message on September 6, 1945. Then, within a ten-week
span, the President sent Congress six more special messages, each
adding a major new proposal to the September list. In January
1946, Truman again presented a "twenty-one point" program, in
a radio appeal to the country, reiterated three weeks later in his
annual message to the Congress. This second listing was somewhat
different from the first. Most of September's minor points had
been removed from the enumeration to make room, among the
twenty-one, for measures recommended in October and November. And in the annual message there was discussion of additional
proposals—over and above the list of twenty-one—which had
not previously been mentioned at all.

In summarizing the domestic program which Truman set forth

after V–J Day, it makes no sense at all to attach significance to order or to timing of particular proposals in this confusing sequence. Obviously some things were ready, came to mind, or got approval earlier than others. Obviously, also, these were the days of scatter-shot approach, when everything was put on record fast, in a sort of laundry-listing of postwar requirements with little indication of priority or emphasis.

What counts, here, is that between September 1945 and January 1946, Truman staked out for himself and his Administration a sweeping legislative program in the fields of social welfare and economic development, embracing, in essential outline if not in all details, the whole range of measures we now identify with the Fair Deal.

Nearly everything was there, though later formulations were to alter some specifics. Among September's numbered "points" were full employment legislation, expanded unemployment compensation, the permanent FEPC, an increased minimum wage, comprehensive housing legislation, a National Science Foundation, grants for hospital construction, permanent farm price supports, and—less specifically—protection and assistance for small business and expanded public works for resource conservation and development.

To these, the "points" of January's message added a comprehensive health program—including health insurance—nationalization of atomic energy and development of the St. Lawrence project. In addition, the message stressed, though it did not number, a "thorough-going reconsideration of our social security laws"; financial aid "to assist the states in assuring more nearly equal opportunities for . . . education"; an emergency veterans housing program "now under preparation"; and various kind words for statehood or self-government in the territories and insular possessions and the District of Columbia. Finally, of course, there were appropriate exhortations about extending price and rent controls.

This was the program Truman threw at Congress, the moment the war was won. Roosevelt had supplanted "Dr. New Deal" with

"Dr. Win-the-War." Why then did Truman hurry so to call the old physician in again?

Look back two years, to January 1944, and part of the answer becomes plain. Remember Roosevelt's "Economic Bill of Rights," with which he opened that election year, the year of hoped-for victory in Europe and feared postwar depression here at home:

> The right to a useful and remunerative job. . . .
> The right to earn enough. . . .
> The right of every farmer to . . . a decent living.
> The right of every businessman . . . to trade in . . . freedom from unfair competition. . . .
> The right of every family to a decent home.
> The right to adequate medical care. . . .
> The right to adequate protection from . . . fears of old age, sickness, accident and unemployment.
> The right to a good education.
> All these rights spell security. And after the war is won, we must be prepared to move forward in the implementation of these rights. . . .

Truman was thus reasserting Roosevelt's stated purpose; not in so many words, not necessarily in Roosevelt's way, or with his means, or his specifics—or his men—but consciously and definitely this was for Truman an affirmation of fidelity to the cause and the direction of liberal Democracy; rekindling the social outlook of the New Deal, if not, precisely, of the New Dealers.

The legislative program of 1945 was a reminder to the Democratic party, to the Congress, to the country, that there was continuity between the new national leadership and the old—and not merely in war policy, but in peace policy as well; not only overseas, but here at home.

Beyond this, the new President had a very personal stake in his September message: reaffirmation of his own philosophy, his own commitments, his own social outlook; denial of the complacent understandings, the comfortable assertions that now, with "That Man" gone, the White House would be "reasonable," "sound" and "safe." Harry Truman wanted, as he used to say, to separate the "men" from the "boys" among his summertime supporters. V–J Day brought him his first real chance to think or act in terms of home affairs, and he lost no time in straightening out the record on who he was and what he stood for.

Some of the New Dealers may not have been convinced; conservatives, however, were quick to understand that here, at least on paper, was a mortal challenge. Editors glowered; so did Congressmen. And one of the President's "soundest" advisors, who ornamented the Administration in that capacity from first to last, fought to the point of threatened resignation against sending that "socialistic" message to the Congress.

Here, then, is explanation for the character and over-all direction of Truman's program. But what of its specific scope and range? Granting all this, why was so much territory covered all at once; why so many points; why, in fields like health and housing, go "all out" in a single bite?

Most commentators have seen these things simply as errors in tactics and judgment, charging them off to personal idiosyncrasy, or inexperience. Other Presidents, it is said, would never have concocted so diverse a program, or asked, indiscriminately, for everything at once. But something more was operating here than just the human factor, however significant that may have been. We have no means of knowing what Roosevelt would have done, after the war. But we do know that he had made the "Economic Bill of Rights" an issue in the 1944 campaign—with Truman as his running mate. And in one of his last major campaign addresses, Roosevelt came out strongly, if in general terms, for most of the controversial measures Truman, a year later, urged on Congress.

We also know that in the postwar period, a Democratic President was bound to face a fundamentally different situation, a different set of popular alignments and demands than Roosevelt dealt with in the thirties. Then, the New Deal pioneered, releasing a flood of ideas and impulses for reform that had been dammed up since Wilson's time. And every effort in those years, each new program, every experiment, set into motion, a widening circle of needs and expectations for governmental action—and of organized interest groups to defend the gains and voice the new requirements.

The first Roosevelt Administration broke into virgin territory; the Truman Administration had to deal with the demand for its consolidation and development. Clearly, Roosevelt was aware of this in 1944. Clearly, Truman's sweeping program in 1945 was conceived as a response. And not alone in 1945; from first to last, the Fair Deal legislative program sought to express the vastly heightened expectations of those groups of Americans on which the liberal cause depended for support.

For all these reasons, then, the 79th Congress found itself encumbered with a great, diverse collection of proposals from the President. And what did Congress do? Not very much. This was the Congress elected with the Roosevelt–Truman ticket in 1944. But even before Roosevelt's death, it had shown little disposition to follow the White House lead in home affairs. At the very start of the first session, the conservative coalition got the bit between its teeth and almost overturned Henry Wallace's appointment as Secretary of Commerce. From then on, the coalition remained a power to be reckoned with, its temper not improved by Truman's exhortations, its influence culminating, finally, in emasculation of the price control extender, during the summer of 1946.

From the confusions, irritations and forebodings of defeat, which marked the whole course of its second session, the 79th Congress did produce a number of the major measures Truman had proposed—most notably the Employment Act, the Atomic Energy Act, the Hospital Construction Act and the Veterans Emergency Housing Act. The Congress was not ungenerous in authorizing and appropriating funds for reclamation, flood control, power and soil conservation; these also raised some landmarks on the Fair Deal road. But for the rest, at least in terms of final action, Congress stood still, or even "backslid" here and there—as with the Russell Amendment eliminating the wartime FEPC.

Perhaps, if experience over the months had not dispelled the spectre of postwar unemployment, much more might have been done with Truman's program of September, 1945. But as it was, this turned out to be the least of worries for most Congressmen and their constituents back home. Not job shortages, but strikes, not pay envelopes but price regulations bothered both. The country, like the Congress, far from rallying to presidential visions of a better future, reacted negatively against the irritations of the present, and punished Truman's party with its worst congressional defeat in eighteen years.

To Pillory the Opposition: 1947–48

To gauge the impact of the 1946 election on the attitude and outlook of the Truman Administration, one merely has to contrast the President's address to the incoming 80th Congress, with his wide-ranging message and radio appeal of the preceding year.

The change in tone was very marked. In the annual messages of 1947 domestic affairs were relatively played down; domestic recommendations limited to a few specifics and some gently-phrased, general remarks. In his State of the Union Message, Truman gave more emphasis to budget balancing (e.g., no tax relief) than to any "welfare" measure, save the comprehensive housing program—which had Senator Taft among its sponsors. He also did "urge" action on the balance of his 1945 health program, but not under the heading of "major policies requiring the attention of the Congress." And while brief mention was made of social security, minimum wages and resource development, it is clear from the context that these, too, were relegated to some secondary category.

This was the comparatively mild and qualified domestic program which the President presented to a supremely confident opposition Congress, where he was generally regarded—on both sides of the aisle—as an historical curiosity, a holdover, a mere chair warmer by accident of constitution, for two more years. The view was widely shared. Inside the Administration, many, perhaps most, of Truman's advisers were persuaded, if not that all was over, at least that the postwar reaffirmation of the liberal cause had been a crashing failure at the polls—out of fashion with the public, out of date for officeholders.

The counsels of caution and conservatism within the President's own entourage, muffled somewhat since the fall of 1945, were now heard everywhere, voiced by almost everybody. Whatever Truman's own views may have been, the course of his Administration through much of 1947 seemed to display real hesitancy, real indecisiveness about further assertion of the cause he had so vigorously espoused a year before.

It is true that as the spring wore on, the White House sent up certain special messages along reminiscent lines. In May, another health message repeated the proposals of 1945—but the tone was mild and the issue, then, by no means so inflammable as it was to become in later years. In June, the President vigorously protested inadequacies in the rent control extender and called again for a comprehensive housing program—but this included specific indorsement for Senator Taft's own bill.

Lump these reminders in with the rest, and Truman's domestic program in the spring of 1947 still remains a very conciliatory version of what had gone before. Under the initial impact of defeat, the Administration, clearly, had fallen way back to regroup. And with the Truman Doctrine to be implemented that same spring, by that same opposition Congress, it is no wonder there was hesitation and divided counsel about where to take a stand and when, if ever, to resume the forward march.

Yet, scarcely a year later, Harry Truman was back at the old stand, once again, raising old banners, rubbing salt in old wounds, firing broadsides at Congress more aggressively than ever. What happened here? Wherefore the change from the conciliatory tone of 1947 to the uncompromising challenge of 1948? Obviously, somewhere along the line, the President became convinced that his initial impulse had been correct, that he was right in 1945— that the New Deal tradition, brought up to date, remained good

policy—and good politics—despite the set back of 1946. In this
decision, Truman's temperament, his social outlook, all sorts of
subjective factors, no doubt played a part. But also, in the course
of 1947 there appeared some perfectly objective indications that
a renewed offensive would be not merely "natural" but rational.

Twice, in the early summer of 1947, Truman vetoed tax reductions voted by the Congress. Both times he charged that the reductions were inequitable and ill-timed; that they relieved only
upper income groups, and would add new burdens of inflation
for the rest to bear. Both times there was some stirring of approval
and response around the country—both times his veto was sustained.

In point of fact, these vetoes were no new departure. They had
been foreshadowed from the first by warnings in the annual messages. But the actuality of veto, and the words in which expressed,
did convey a fresh impression: the vision of a sturdy President—
courageous even in the face of lower taxes—defending the "national" interest and the "poor," against a heartless (Republican)
Congress mindful only of the "rich." This was a new note—and
it did not go badly.

Four days after his first tax veto, Truman vetoed the Taft-
Hartley Act. To the general public, the measure was chiefly notable, then and since, because it did something about work stop-
pages in "national emergency" disputes—an issue the President
himself had recognized in prior messages to Congress. But to the
spokesmen for organized labor the act was shot full of unwarrant-
able interferences with basic union rights which had been guaranteed, by law, for half a generation.

And when Truman struck out against these interferences—in
the strongest language he had yet addressed to the 80th Congress
—he evoked a warm response from a part of the public whose
apathy, in 1946, had prominently helped defeat his party and his
postwar cause. The quick congressional override of Truman's
veto merely heightened this response from those who felt themselves despoiled—and further dramatized, for them, the vision of

the presidential "tribune" standing up against the onslaughts of a rapacious (Republican) Congress.

Here, in the summer of 1947, were some straws in the wind. Their meaning was confirmed for the Administration, even enlarged upon, at the special session in the fall.

When Truman called the Congress back to Washington, the principal emergency was international—with the economies of Western Europe verging on collapse. But in his address to the special session, Truman asked not only for interim aid abroad— pending completion of the European Recovery Program—but also for a ten-point program against inflation, billed as an equal emergency at home. And the tenth point of this domestic plan was nothing less than selective restoration of price and wage controls.

This was the first occasion when Truman made an all-out public effort to revive and dramatize an issue which had failed him in 1946, capitalizing on a measure which—as everybody knew—was still anathema to the majority in Congress. This was the first occasion, too, since the election of 1946, when the President presumed to give so controversial a domestic issue equal billing with an essential aspect of his foreign policy.

The program for the 1947 special session was, no doubt, a trial run, in a sense. Had the result been very bad, the President might perhaps have stayed his hand in 1948. In the event, however, the majority in Congress found it expedient to enact something called an "anti-inflation" bill, a most limited measure but indicating that times—and prices—had changed since 1946. Moreover, despite the patent irritations which the price issue aroused, interim aid for Europe went through Congress without a hitch, and just before adjournment, the European Recovery Program was sent up and well received.

By January, 1948, the President had obviously read the signs and portents of the half-year before, and put out of mind the memory of defeat in 1946, with all the cautious counsels it provoked. Truman's address to the new session was confident and sharp, evoking all the liberal issues half suppressed a year before. His presentation was much more coherent than it had been in 1945 or 1946, the language tighter, the focus sharper, the follow-up firmer. But nothing was omitted from the original postwar program and in a number of respects Truman went beyond any earlier commitments.

This was the message which set forth goals for the decade ahead. This was the message which proposed a new, "anti-inflationary" tax program: credits for low income groups to offset the cost of living, with revenues to be recouped by increased levies on corporate profits.

The "tribune" of six months before, who had risen to protect the people against the acts of Congress, now sought their protection in demands on Congress for actions it could not, or would not, take. If the record of Congress could be turned against the opposition, then the President would make that record, not on performance, but on non-performance, not on the opposition's issues but on his issues—those liberal measures which, perhaps, had not gone out of fashion after all.

And as Truman began, so he continued through the spring, with "a message a week," to keep Congress off balance and the spotlight on. In this series there was but one great new formulation—the civil rights message of February, 1948. The legislative program it set forth incorporated most of the proposals of the President's Committee on Civil Rights, which had reported in December 1947. The resulting explosion is still echoing in Congress and the Democratic Party.

Of all Truman's proposals through eight years in office, these were, perhaps, the most controversial. That they loosed a lasting political storm, everyone knows; that they had special political significance in early 1948—appearing just as Henry Wallace made his break to the Progressive Party—is certainly no secret. But there was much more than politics in this. The Civil Rights Committee had originally been established out of genuine concern lest there be repeated in the postwar years, the rioting and retrogression which followed World War I. Congressional indifference had been made manifest in 1946—hence the turn to prominent outsiders. Once having set these people to their task, on problems so potentially explosive, it is hardly credible that Truman could have ignored their report, no matter what the politics of his own situation.

Nothing else, half so dramatic, was unveiled by the President in 1948. But all the older measures were furbished up and trotted out anew. And as the months wore on, Truman's tone to Congress grew steadily more vigorous. He began by lambasting in January, and ended by lampooning in July.

His last address to the 80th Congress was the nearest thing to an outright campaign speech that he—or probably any other President—ever made before the assembled Houses. Opening the post-convention special session, he first demanded action to stop inflation and start more houses—the ostensible purposes for which Congress had been recalled. He then proceeded to list nine other measures which he thought the Congress might be able to enact without delaying the two primary items. Finally he listed every other major proposal advanced since 1945, commenting: ". . . If this Congress finds time to act on any of them now, the country will greatly benefit. Certainly, the next Congress should take them up immediately."

Of course, that hapless session accomplished precisely nothing, in any of these categories. And Truman proceeded to pillory the 80th Congress at every whistle stop across the country, working his way to victory in the presidential election of 1948.

Toward a Liberal Majority: 1949–50

The legislative program Harry Truman presented in 1949, to the new Congress which had shared his victory, reflected all the Fair Deal commitments of the 1948 campaign. "Certainly, the next Congress should take them up immediately," he had proclaimed to the Republicans in July. And he could do no less in January

than spread them out—all of them—before his brand-new Democratic majorities.

All interest groups and sponsoring politicians understood the
"law of honeymoon"; none was prepared to stand aside, leaving
a pet proposal for some later, less naturally advantageous date.
All civil rights groups, and most politicians North and South,
knew very well that only the extra leverage of an early log jam
would suffice, in time, to shut off debate. All trade union spokesmen were agreed that there could be no compromise on Taft-
Hartley "repeal" and no delay on any part if it. And so it went,
group after group, issue after issue.

Both President and Congress were thus prisoners, in a sense, of
the election and the way it had been won. It was one thing to
throw a host of highly controversial measures at an opposition
Congress which could—and did—reject most of them out of hand.
It was quite another thing to throw the same load on a relatively
receptive Congress, prepared to make a try at action on them all.
Action is much harder than inaction; action on this scale, of this
variety, an almost intolerable burden on the complex machinery
of the legislative process—and on a President's capacity to focus
attention, to rally support.

Despite this handicap, the 81st Congress, be it said, turned out
more New Deal–Fair Deal measures than any of its predecessors
after 1938, or its successors either; becoming, on its record, the
most liberal Congress in the last fifteen years.

This was the Congress that enacted the comprehensive housing
program, providing generously for slum clearance, urban redevel-
opment and public housing; the Congress that put through the
major revision of social security, doubling insurance and assistance
benefits and greatly—though not universally—extending coverage.
This was the Congress that reformed the Displaced Persons Act,
increased the minimum wage, doubled the hospital construction
program, authorized the National Science Foundation and the
rural telephone program, suspended the "sliding scale" on price
supports, extended the soil conservation program, provided new

grants for planning state and local public works and plugged the long-standing merger loophole in the Clayton Act. And it was principally this Congress that financed Truman's last expansions of flood control, rural electrification, reclamation, public power and transmission lines.

But this record of domestic accomplishment was obscured for commentators, public, and Administration by a series of failures on the most dramatic and most dramatized of 1948's great expectations. In the first session of the 81st Congress—the last full session before Korea—aid to education, health insurance, FEPC and Taft-Hartley repeal were taken up, debated, fought over and either stalled or killed outright somewhere along the line.

General aid to education—that is, maintenance and operation funds for state school systems—had won Senate approval in 1948, in a form that represented careful compromise among religious interests and between the richer and the poorer states. Reintroduced in 1949, the same measure speedily received Senate approval once again. But as the year wore on, these compromises started to unravel; various groups and individuals took second looks, had second thoughts. The whole basis of agreement fell apart before the Senate bill had cleared the House Committee. There the bill remained, unreported at the session's end, eight months after Senate passage. There the second session found it—and left it.

The story on health is similar in some respects. The interest groups supporting Truman's health program and its congressional sponsors did not seriously hope for early victory on compulsory health insurance. But they—and the Administration—saw this issue as a stick with which to beat the Congress into passing other major aspects of the program—increased hospital construction and research, aid to medical education and grants to local public health units; all obvious and necessary preliminaries to effective operation of any general insurance scheme. In the Senate, all four of these secondary measures were approved by early fall of 1949. Hospital construction and research grants—both expansions of existing programs—also fared well in the House. But the medical education and local health bills never got to the House floor. They were smothered to death in committee by a resurgent opposition—medical and other—which seized the stick of health insurance and used it to inflict increasing punishment, not only on these bills, their sponsors and supporters, but on the whole Administration and the Democratic party.

In the case of civil rights, Truman's program was not merely stalled but buried during 1949. At the session's start, the interest groups—supported by the leadership in Congress and Administration—would stand for nothing but a test on the most controversial measure of them all: compulsory FEPC. The measure's proponents were perfectly aware they could not gain compulsion from the House, nor cloture from the Senate, without a major showing of Republican support. This was not forthcoming; the test proved that at any rate. It also helped Democrats, Southern as well as Northern, discharge some pressing obligations toward constituents. But the long filibuster of 1949 was all the Senate could endure. None of its leaders was prepared to face another bloodletting in 1950.

The Congressional failure on Taft-Hartley repeal was just as conclusive as that on civil rights and much more surprising to Administration, press and public. In 1949, the struggle in both Houses was intense, but save for the injunction in emergency disputes—the one feature opponents of repeal could press home to the general public—the advocates of a new law probably would have had their way. The interest groups could not, or would not give on this; the Administration could not, or would not impel them—so everything was lost; lost in 1949 and left, then, to await a new test in a new Congress. A decisive beating in the first session might be compromised in the second, but hardly reversed. And trade union leadership was in no mood for compromise.

Nor was the President. His response to each of these defeats in 1949—and other, lesser scars sustained that year—was a renewed recommendation in 1950. His January messages to the second session of the 81st Congress included virtually all proposals still outstanding, that he had listed to the first session in his moment of honeymoon a year before.

Clearly, there was little hope, in 1950, for much of what he asked. Yet the 81st Congress, as Truman was to say that spring, had "already reversed" its predecessor's backward "trend." And if the "trend" now ran the Fair Deal's way, perhaps what this Congress withheld, would be forthcoming from the next—the 82nd Congress to be elected in November.

Not since 1934, had the Democratic party increased its majorities in a mid-term election; breaking into new terrain in North and West. Yet that, and nothing less, was surely Truman's goal for 1950. "I hope," remarked the President, "that by next January, some of the obstructionists will be removed." And not content with pressing, once again, all the remaining issues of 1948, he urged on Congress three further measures each of which, if it appealed at all, would tap new sources of support, beyond the groups and areas where Democratic power was presumably entrenched.

One of these measures involved a new departure for the President on farm legislation. His 1950 State of the Union Message was the occasion for Truman's first formal use of the magic words connoting the "Brannan Plan." There he first attached the adjective "mandatory" to price supports, first urged "a system of production payments," first declared, "as a matter of national policy," that "safeguards must be maintained against slumps in farm prices," in order to support "farm income at fair levels."

To the uninitiated these words may look very little different from their counterparts in prior presidential messages. But in the language of farm bureaucrats and organizations, these were magic words indeed, fighting words, emphasizing finally and officially, a sharp turn in Truman's agriculture policy—a turn which had begun in 1948, progressively distinguishing Democratic from Republican farm programs, and bringing the Administration now to ground where the Republicans in Congress—not to speak of many Democrats—could not or would not follow.

By the time Truman spoke in January 1950, the more far-reaching measures his words implied had already been rebuffed at the preceding session of the Congress—and the "Brannan Plan" had already become a scare word, rivalling "socialized medicine" in the campaign arsenal the Republicans were readying. Yet by his endorsement Truman seemed to say that scare word or no, here was an issue to cement for Democrats the farm support which he had gained so providentially in 1948.

The second new measure to be proposed in the State of the Union message for 1950, concerned the housing shortage "for middle-income groups, especially in large metropolitan areas." The Housing Act of 1949 had granted more aids for private home financing which swelled the flood of relatively high priced houses. The Act also had promised more public housing, with subsidized rentals for people in the lowest income brackets. Between these two types of housing was a gap, affecting mainly urban and suburban "middle" groups of white collar and blue collar families; swing groups politically, as time would show. For them, in 1950, the President proposed "new legislation authorizing a vigorous program to help cooperatives and other non-profit groups build housing which these families could afford."

The third of 1950's new proposals was billed as a mere promissory note in the State of the Union message. "I hope," said Truman, "to transmit to the Congress a series of proposals to . . . assist small business and to encourage the growth of new enterprises." As such, this was no more concrete than the benign expressions in many earlier messages and party platforms. But in the spring of 1950, the President kept his promise and put meat on these old bones with a comprehensive small business program far more elaborate than anything advanced since the emergency legislation of the early thirties. The immediate reaction, in Congress and out, was very favorable. A leading spokesman for "big" business called the Truman message "tempered, reasoned, non-political." Small business groups expressed great interest; even some bankers had kind words to say.

The President's small business program went to Congress as he entrained for the Far West, on his "non-political" tour of May, 1950. The Fair Deal's prospects were then enticing numbers of Administration stalwarts to leave their safe House seats and campaign for the Senate. Many signs encouraged them. The country was prosperous, recession ending; the presidential program popular, to all appearances, attracting interest in useful quarters and stirring overt opposition only where most expected and least feared. Foreign policy was costly but not noticeably burdensome, defense pared down, the budget coming into balance.

Yet on the other side were signs of change, foretastes of things to come, making 1950 a very special year, a year of sharp transition, in retrospect a great divide. The preceding winter saw the last of Chinese Nationalist resistance on the Asian mainland. In January Alger Hiss was convicted in his second trial—and Secretary Acheson quoted from the Scriptures. In February, Senator McCarthy first shared with the public his discovery of Communism's menace here at home. In May, Senator Kefauver's committee began televised crime hearings, exposing criminal connections of political machines in some of the nation's largest cities —where, as it happened, the Democratic party had been long in control.

And on the twenty-fifth of June, the North Korean Communists invaded the Republic of Korea.

Korea: The Great Divide

In legislative terms, the initial impact of Korea on the Fair Deal is symbolized by the collapse of Truman's small business program. Senate hearings had just got under way when the fighting began. They terminated quickly in the first days of July. The Senate committee which had started down this track enthusiastically, turned off to tackle the Defense Production Act—controls for the new, part-way war economy.

All along the line, Fair Deal proposals were permanently shelved or set aside, as Congress worked on measures for defense. And on one of these measures, price controls, which had long been identified with the Fair Deal, not the President but Congress forced the issue—never again was Truman able to resurrect it as his own.

This calls for a short digression. In July, 1950, the President did not raise the price control issue, because he feared it might delay congressional response on other needed measures of control; fearing, moreover, lest opinion overseas might take his call for direct controls as indicating all-out preparation for the general war Korean intervention was intended to avert, not foster.

But Congress proceeded, on its initiative, to include discretionary price and wage controls among the economic powers in the Defense Production Act. The measure became law September 8, 1950. For a variety of reasons, no general application of direct controls was attempted until nearly five months later. Meanwhile the Chinese attack of November 27 set off new buying waves, with consequent sharp price increases. And by the time a general freeze was instituted, January 26, 1951, this sequence of events had thoroughly shaken confidence in the Administration's leadership on the inflation issue.

The fact that Truman subsequently fought for strengthened control legislation, while his congressional opponents shot holes in it at every opportunity, seems not to have restored the President's position in the public mind, nor recreated for the Democrats that popular response the issue had accorded them in 1948. The Republicans, if anyone, drew strength from popular discomfort with high prices, in subsequent elections.

Apart from price controls, the conflict in Korea drew congressional—and national—attention away from the traditional Fair Deal issues. As election time approached, in 1950, there was no back drop of recent, relevant congressional debate to liven up these issues, stressing their affirmative appeal. Instead, the opposition had a field day with the negative refrain of "socialism"— or worse—invoking spectres of the "Brannan Plan," "socialized medicine," and Alger Hiss, to unnerve a public preoccupied with sacrifices in a far-off peninsula, nervous over rumors about "Chinese volunteers."

In the first week of November, the electorate—far from increasing Democratic power—reduced to a bare minimum the Democratic party's lead in both Houses of Congress, abruptly closing the careers of some very senior Senators and some very staunch Administration Congressmen. And in the last week of November the full-scale Chinese intervention in Korea turned virtual victory into disastrous retreat, confronting the Administration and the country with a "new" war, a most uncertain future, and endless possibilities of worse to come.

Mobilization and Reluctant Retreat: 1951–52

On December 15, 1950, the President proclaimed a National Emergency. Three weeks later, in January, 1951, the 82nd Congress assembled to hear, in virtual silence, what Truman had to say.

His State of the Union Message was somewhat reminiscent, in its tight organization and sharp phrasing, of the fighting address of 1948. But in tone and content it was, by far, the most conciliatory annual message since 1947.

The entire address was devoted to events abroad and mobilization at home. Its ten-point legislative program was couched in emergency terms. Among the ten points only one Fair Deal item remained in its entirety—aid for medical education, now billed as a means of "increasing the supply of doctors . . . critically needed for defense. . . ." Two other pillars of the Fair Deal program were included in qualified form. General aid to education was requested, "to meet . . . most urgent needs . . . ," with the proviso that "some of our plans will have to be deferred. . . ." And while there was no specific mention of Taft-Hartley, or its repeal, the President did ask "improvement of our labor laws to help provide stable . . . relations and . . . steady production in this emergency."

Aside from a bland and wholly unspecific reference to "improvements in our agriculture laws," an opening for subsequent proposals never made, these were the only references to Fair Deal measures in the presidential list of "subjects on which legislation will be needed. . . ." They were almost the only references in the entire message; but not quite. After his ten-point numeration, Truman remarked "the government must give priority to activities that are urgent," and offered "power development" as an example. Then he added, "Many of the things we would normally do . . . must be curtailed or postponed . . ."; the door was finally closing, but—the Congress should give continuing attention ". . . to measures . . . for the long pull." There followed four brief and unelaborated but unmistakable references to increased unemployment and old age insurance, disability and health insurance and civil rights.

As in 1947, so in 1951, the President was shifting emphasis, relegating most welfare measures to some secondary order of priority, without quite ceasing to be their advocate. It was too subtle a performance for the press; the distinctions much too fine for headlines or wide public notice—though not, perhaps, for Congressmen to grasp. Yet in its way, this message represented Truman's recognition of the fundamental change in his circumstances and the Nation's; his nearest approach to Roosevelt's sharp, dramatic switch, a decade earlier, from "Dr. New Deal" to "Dr. Win-the-War."

And unlike 1947, this mild beginning, in January 1951, heralded a more conciliatory tone, an increased interest in negotiation, on some of the Fair Deal's most striking programs. As the year wore on, Truman gradually changed tactics on at least three fronts, seeking different ground from that staked out in pre-Korean years.

The first of these shifts came in the field of health. There the Administration was hopelessly on the defensive by 1951. The vocal presence of an aroused and potent medical opposition, victorious in trials of strength at 1950's elections, sufficed to make most Congressmen suspect and fear a taint of "socialized medicine" in any

Truman health measure, however limited its purpose or narrow its scope. The President had barely raised the health insurance issue in January, 1951, but its mere invocation was now enough to halt all legislation in the field. So far had the opposition come, from its days on the defensive, back in 1949.

Finally, Truman voiced his recognition of the situation: "I am not clinging to any particular plan," he told an audience in June. This was followed, six months later, by appointment of the President's Commission on the Health Needs of the Nation, charged with surveying, from the ground up, all problems and proposals in the field. In January 1952, addressing the second session of the 82nd Congress, the President remarked of health insurance, "So far I know it is still the best way. If there are . . . better answers I hope this Commission will find them."

A second change in tactics during 1951 came on the issue of Taft-Hartley. Senator Taft's triumphant re-election, the preceding autumn, had symbolized how futile were the hopes of 1949 for a renewal, in a "better" Congress, of that year's stalled attack. In Truman's January messages of 1951 there was no mention of "repeal." The following October, his first address at a trade-union affair, that year, was notable for subdued treatment of the issue. "We want a law . . . that will be fair . . . ," he said, "and . . . we will have that kind of law, in the long run . . ." and that was all. Two months later, the President enlarged upon this theme, telling the Congress, "we need . . . to improve our labor law . . . even the sponsors . . . admit it needs to be changed. . . ." The issue of "repeal" was dormant, so Truman seemed to say. Amendment, even perhaps piecemeal amendment—anathema in 1949—now measured the ambitions of his Administration.

The President's third shift in emphasis came on his agriculture program. Since the Korean outbreak, farm prices had soared, along with the demand for food and fibre. There was little in the current situation to promote wide interest in Brannan's innovations, or counteract the socialistic spectres that his "plan" invoked. In January 1951, the President had no specific comment on the ideas he had endorsed a year before. By January 1952, Truman was prepared with some specifics, but on much narrower ground. That year, his State of the Union message asked—and Congress shortly granted—renewed suspension of the "sliding scale" on price supports, which otherwise would have become effective at the end of 1952. For the rest, he simply remarked that there was "need to find . . . a less costly method for supporting perishable commodities than the law now provides"—a plug for "production payments," surely, but in a fashion that softpedalled the far-reaching overtones of 1950.

The year of 1951 turned out to be a hard and unrewarding time for the Administration; a year marked by MacArthur's firing, by strenuous debates on foreign policy and on controls, by blighted hopes for quick truce in Korea, by snowballing complaints of government corruption—and by prolonged Congressional indifference to the welfare measures on the trimmed-down Truman list.

The State of the Union message in January, 1952, was less incisive than its predecessor—so was the emergency—but hardly less moderate in its approach on home affairs. Besides the new departures on health insurance, labor laws and farm legislation, the President appealed again for aid to education and the supplementary health bills of a year before. Again he mentioned power needs. Again he raised, briefly and generally, the issues of civil rights. Otherwise, in only two respects did he go beyond specifics urged in 1951—asking cost-of-living increases for social security recipients and readjustment benefits for Korean veterans.

These two requests were granted rather promptly, giving Truman his last minor successes. But in the spring of 1952, the second session of the 82nd Congress was interested less in legislating than investigating; less concerned with pending measures than with Administration struggles over corruption—and the steel dispute; preoccupied above all else with the coming presidential nominations and the campaign to follow in the fall. The session's main contribution to the Fair Deal program was not positive, but negative, rousing one last Truman proposal in opposition to the McCarran Act; creating one more Fair Deal issue; liberalization of the immigration laws.

In this fashion, Truman's last Congress slowed to a close. And in Chicago, that July, appeared a final summary of Fair Deal business left undone—the Democratic platform of 1952.

What Truman had played down, in his last annual messages, the platform now set forth in some detail. It called for action on the civil rights program, avoiding retrogression by a hair; pledged still more improvement in the social insurance laws; promised more resource conservation and development, including public power; urged Federal help for schools, this time stressing construction along with "general" aid; called for a firm stand on public housing and revived the "middle income" issue of two years before; spoke feelingly of protection and assistance for small business, hinting at specifics unmentioned since Korea; adopted Truman's formula on health, with kind words for the President's Commission; followed him also on farm price supports, on immigration and on a host of lesser issues, long the stock-in-trade of Democratic documents.

At one point only did the platform diverge sharply from the President's more recent formulations. On Taft-Hartley it abandoned his new stand, reverting to the cliche of "repeal." The Democratic candidate was put to some trouble by this change, but it cannot be said to have much mattered to the voters.

It had been seven years since Harry Truman, reaffirming Roosevelt's purpose, first charted the Fair Deal in his twenty-one point program of 1945. Now it received its last expression in his party's platform for 1952. This remains the final statement. In January 1953, Truman and his party yielded office to the first Republican Administration in twenty years.

A *Fair Deal Balance Sheet*

Set the platform of 1952 alongside the program of 1945, allow for changing circumstances and particulars, then run a quick calculation on the Fair Deal legislative program. What did Truman gain in seven years from his four Congresses? What came of all the trials and tribulations recorded in this essay?

In the first place, it is clear that Truman managed to obtain from Congress means for modernizing, bringing up to date, a number of outstanding New Deal landmarks in social welfare and economic development among them: social security, minimum wages, public health and housing; farm price supports, rural electrification, soil conservation, reclamation, flood control and public power. Not all of these were strictly New Deal innovations, but all gained either life or impetus from Roosevelt in the thirties. And in the new circumstances of the postwar forties they were renewed, elaborated, enlarged upon, by legislative action urged in Truman's Fair Deal program; even their underlying rationale nailed down in law by the Employment Act of 1946.

This is significant, and not alone by virtue of particulars attained. A generation earlier, the very spirit of Wilsonian New Freedom had been buried deep in the debris of reaction following world war. Not so with the New Deal.

As a consolidator, as a builder on foundations, Truman left an impressive legislative record; the greater part achieved, of course, in less than two years' time, and by a single Congress. Moreover as protector, as defender, wielder of the veto against encroachments on the liberal preserve, Truman left a record of considerable success—an aspect of the Fair Deal not to be discounted. He could not always hold his ground, sustained some major losses, but in the process managed to inflict much punishment on his opponents.

The greater Truman vetoes pretty well define what might be called the legislative program of the conservative coalition in his time. On many of these measures he made his veto stick, as with the offshore oil bills in 1946 and 1952, or natural gas and basing points in 1950. On certain others—like the Gearhardt Resolution in 1948—what one Congress enacted over his veto, the next retracted at his demand. And on a few—especially the two already noted—Congress overrode him, and the ground once lost was not made up in Truman's time: the Taft-Hartley Act in 1947 and the McCarran Act in 1952.

Besides these, Truman asked of Congress four main things which were denied him: aid to education, health insurance, civil rights

and—for want of better shorthand—"Brannan Plan." On the outstanding features of these four, he got no satisfaction: no general
grants for all school systems; no national prepayment plan for
medical care; no FEPC, or anti-poll tax or anti-lynching laws; no
wholesale renovation of price supports to insure good returns from
general farm production. Here, if anywhere, does Elmer Davis'
refrain approach reality: "Truman kept asking for all of it and
getting none of it."

Why did he keep asking? From 1945 to 1950, one may concede
that year by year there always seemed to be good reason to press
on: reason to hope and plan for action, if not in one session then
the next, reason to believe the very chance for future action might
depend on present advocacy. But after 1950, after Korea, faced
with a dozen hard new issues, on the defensive all the way from
"Communism to corruption," what then explains the Truman
course? He must have known, his actions show awareness, that
there had come a real sea change in his affairs and in the country's.
Why move so slowly towards a bare minimum of reappraisal, readjustment?

Perhaps the answers lie, in part, in Truman's temperament;
partly in his concept of the presidency. Unquestionably he thought
these measures right for the country; hence proper for the President to advocate, regardless of their chances in the Congress. He
had assumed responsibility as keeper of the country's conscience
on these issues; as its awakener, as well, by virtue of stands taken
far ahead of the procession. For civil rights, especially, Truman
could claim—like Roosevelt after the court fight of 1937—that
while he may have lost a legislative battle, the forcing of the issue
helped to win a larger war. "There has been a great awakening of
the American conscience on the issue of civil rights," he was to
say in his farewell report to Congress, "all across the nation . . .
the barriers are coming down." This was happening; by his demands for legislation he conceived that he helped make it happen.
On that promise, he was bound not to abandon his position, no
matter what the legislative outcome, present or prospective.

Even in strictly legislative terms there was, perhaps, much to be gained by standing firm. Were not some of the fights that failed a vital stimulus to others that succeeded? Were not some votes against a measure such as health insurance, repaid by other votes in favor of reciprocal trade renewal, say? Was not a total presidential program basically advantaged if it overshot the limits of assured congressional response? There are no ready measurements providing certain answers to these questions. But Presidents must seek them all the same. And on his record there is little doubt what answers Truman found.

For Truman then, each of his great outstanding issues had value as a legislative stalking horse, if nothing more. But that is not to say he saw no more in them. On the contrary, had he not thought many things attainable, still actionable in the not too distant future—still meaningful, therefore, in rallying political support—he scarcely would have bothered, during 1951, to cleanse his farm and health programs—much less Taft-Hartley—of the worst taints absorbed in the campaign of 1950, thus rendering them useable for 1952.

Those changes in approach were hardly aimed at Congress—not, anyway, the current Congress. Rather, the President was preparing new positions for his party, shifting to ground on which it could afford to stand with him and to uphold, if in adjusted guise, the Fair Deal label and the Truman cause.

Right to the last, then, Truman was persuaded that those Fair Deal issues touched felt needs, roused real response among Americans; no longer viable objectives for his time in office, but crucial undertakings in his party's future.

The Politics of Stasis

A Word on Eisenhower

by Emmet John Hughes

*During the 1960's, for almost the same reasons that Harry Tru-
man's presidential leadership declined in reputation among some
historians, Dwight Eisenhower's has grown. Liberal historians,
writing during or immediately after Ike's presidency, had often
criticized Eisenhower for a failure to provide adequate leadership,
especially in domestic affairs, where they quipped "the bland were
leading the bland." Pressing national problems such as widespread
denials of civil rights and civil liberties, the "invisible" poverty of
one out of every five Americans, and the growing dangers of en-
vironmental pollution received almost no sustained attention from
the federal government. "Never has a popular leader who dominated so completely the national political scene," lamented historian Norman Graebner in a widely-shared 1960 appraisal, "affected so negligibly the essential historic processes of his time."*

*More recently, however, historians have begun detecting a sig-
nificant set of accomplishments beneath the bland surface of
Eisenhower's presidency. The single most influential element in
triggering recent reappraisals of American leadership has been
the Vietnamese nightmare. After continuous escalations toward
disaster in Vietnam by two activist Democratic presidents, John*

*Kennedy and Lyndon Johnson, many war-weary scholars and
students have begun looking back nostaligically at the comparative "normalcy" of Eisenhower's foreign policy. Such historians
now claim to find, underlying the apocalyptic world-saving rhetoric
of cold-warrior John Foster Dulles and other like-minded administration officials, a basic pattern of restraint in the actual use of
American power by Eisenhower himself. American interventions
during his presidency tended to be* covert, *as in the CIA-sponsored
Guatemalan coup of 1954, or small-scale, as in the role of U.S.
military advisers in selected "trouble spots," or limited, as in the
case of a short-lived 1958 Marine landing in Lebanon. Nuclear
Armageddon was avoided during the Hungarian and Suez crises
of 1956 in large measure due to American restraint, and Truman's
prolonged Korean "police action" ended swiftly by truce agreement early in Eisenhower's presidency.*

*If historical attitudes have changed somewhat on the quality
of Ike's statesmanship, however, there are few historians even today who will grant him high marks as a domestic political leader.
American professional soldiers who go on to the White House
have not proved to be strong Presidents, and Dwight Eisenhower
was no exception. His eight years in office provided an extended
breathing spell following the super-contentious Roosevelt–Truman years, and most Americans welcomed this caretaker regime
which put the presidency into a state of suspended animation. Ike
declared that he wanted "to take that straight road down the
middle."*

*Eisenhower was a genuinely modest man, perhaps too much
so, since awareness of his intellectual limitations tended to im-
mobilize him. He found details bothersome, and preferred to be
briefed in military staff fashion, with analyses of complex issues
boiled down to a single page. And he had a limited conception of
the role of government. He rejected the examples of a strong
presidency set by his two predecessors, regarding himself as a "presiding" officer and little more. In the following selection, a disil-
lusioned former member of Ike's White House staff, Emmet John
Hughes, ruminates over the sparse achievements and the many
failures of the Eisenhower presidency.*

"The human story does not always unfold like a mathematical calculation on the principle that two and two make four. Sometimes in life they make five or minus three; and sometimes the blackboard topples down in the middle of the sum and leaves the class in disorder and the pedagogue with a black eye."

Winston Churchill

❧ A free and prosperous people in the second half of the twentieth century, amply attended by all the time-saving marvels of modern technology and automation, enjoys far greater leisure than any generation of its ancestors. This historic dispensation extends to nearly all phases of a free nation's life. But there is one stunning exception. And this is the enterprise upon which the nation's survival may depend—the attainment of a wise and fair understanding of its own immediate past.

Here the very rhythm of revolutionary change, so generously favoring all other endeavors, harshly exacts its price. For it leaves to a free people—contemplating the sudden crisis or the instant challenge—less time, less chance for perception and reflection, than any other epoch of man. An age not long dead when the sound of musketry on Boston's Bunker Hill would take a fortnight to echo in London's House of Commons—and an age when the firing of an intercontinental missile from the far side of the globe might leave citizens of Detroit a quarter of an hour to prepare themselves for the blast—are two ages distant and distinct from each other by measure more profound than clock or calendar. For the newer of these ages does not challenge merely the speed of sound: it defies the speed of thought. It requires the processes of democratic decision to revolve and to react as fast as all the world in historic upheaval. And it prescribes a rate of obsolescence that dispenses as harshly with yesterday's ideas as with yesterday's weapons.

From Emmet John Hughes, *The Ordeal of Power: A Political Memoir of the Eisenhower Years.* Copyright © 1962, 1963 by Emmet John Hughes. Reprinted by permission of Atheneum Publishers.

Thus all witnesses to such an age are denied the chance to wait for those comforting prerogatives of the historian—dispassion and detachment. The witnesses must speak, instead, from the swiftest of glances and the briefest of visits. For the long-deliberated and delicately balanced judgment, finally pronounced after exhaustive examination of amassed archives, can emerge to the light only to peer around for the once-living, once-urgent dilemma—and squint in vain. The dilemma will be dead, beneath the rubble of accomplished facts.

And so, falteringly and presumptuously, one can only try to catch some glimpses of the fleet shapes of the men or the events . . . to touch with the senses some part of their meaning, before they vanish over the rim of remembrance and understanding . . . someday to be recovered for the learning, but too late for the living.

This much one must try to do, as the Eisenhower Years slip fast into the past. . . .

II

What happened to all those fine young people with stars in their eyes who sailed balloons and rang doorbells for us in 1952?
                        Dwight D. Eisenhower (to Sherman Adams), July 1960 *

Dwight David Eisenhower, the man of many paradoxes, left the office of the presidency as the most widely popular—and the most sharply criticized—citizen of his nation. By almost unanimous consensus of all political leaders of both parties, only the constitutional bar to a third term kept him from inflicting upon John Fitzgerald Kennedy an electoral rout as severe and complete as those twice suffered by Adlai Stevenson. By almost equally unanimous consensus of the national community of intellectuals and critics—journalists and academicians, pundits and prophets

* *First-hand Report*, p. 453.

—his conduct of the presidency was unskillful and his definition of it inaccurate. And these fiercely contradictory judgments inspired two images: the profile acidly etched by his detractors, the portrait warmly painted by his idolators.

The caricature was—as always—easier to draw.

Here, in this vignette, was a weak and irresolute man, surrounded by vastly stronger men, their vision small but their will powerful. To them, this man delegated the powers of the presidency slackly and carelessly. To the role of national leader, he came unequipped by experience, by knowledge, by temperament, or even by taste for politics. To the role of military responsibility, he brought the prejudices of a professional life that had effectively ended before the advent of nuclear weapons. To the role of world statesman, he brought a genial and gregarious disposition, undisciplined and unsophisticated, never holding promise of a diplomacy more profound than a rather maudlin kind of global sociability. On the world scene, he sought to check the power of Soviet Communism by complacent citation of the "spiritual" superiority of American life; and he thereby showed a blindness to national danger reminiscent of a Stanley Baldwin of the 1930's, assuring the people of Great Britain of their serene immunity to the menace of Nazi power. On the national scene, he persisted, too, in facile exhortations on "spiritual" and "moral" values—even while he practiced an aloof neutralism toward the struggle for civil rights that seemed, to many of his citizens, the most pure and urgent moral issue to confront his presidency. As a politician, he set forth to remake the blurred image of the Republican party, but he merely ended by suffering himself to be remade in *its* image. As an intellectual, he bestowed upon the games of golf and bridge all the enthusiasm and perseverance that he withheld from books and ideas. As a President, he sought to affirm the dignity of his high office by the simple device of reducing its complex functions to the circumspect discharge of its ceremonial obligations. As the leader of the world's greatest democracy—charting its flight through all the clouds and storms of the mid-twentieth century, on toward the mysteries and perils of the Age of Space—he elected to leave his nation to fly on automatic pilot.

The appreciative portrait was—as almost always—not so easy to draw.

Here, by this portrait, was a man of selfless and serious patriotism. Physically, he gave of himself unstintingly, in bearing the burden of the presidency, despite three illnesses that would have crippled weaker men. Morally, he gave uncompromising scorn to all temptations of expediency, despite knowing full well the easy accolades to be won at almost any instant—by publicly chastising a McCarthy, by blaming congressional leadership for failures, by wrathfully denouncing a Faubus, by combating recession with tax reduction or government deficit, by appeasing critics with the replacement of a Dulles or a Benson, or, most dramatically, by proclaiming himself the soldier-champion of gigantic military programs to assure American supremacy in the Age of Space. Whatever the crisis or the clamor, he stayed defiantly faithful to the policy—or to the man—as honest conviction decreed. As a national leader, he avoided, through the greater part of a perilous decade, his and his people's two greatest fears—war in the world and depression at home. As a partisan leader, he steered Republicanism toward new historic ground, far from its isolationist traditions; and, for all the conservatism of his economics, he left the policies of the New Deal and the Fair Deal intact and secure after eight years of a Republican Administration. Personally, he led his party to two successive and smashing national triumphs, after it had endured twenty years of failure and rebuff. He brought to the White House itself a personal sense of dignity and honor that could only elevate the office of the presidency in the eyes of his people. When he entered this office, the political air of the nation was sulphurous with bitterness, recrimination, and frustration. And when he left office, this air was clean of all such rancor, fresh with good will and good feeling.*

* Nine months after leaving the presidency, Eisenhower cited this as the first item, when asked to enumerate "your greatest achievements." In his

The two portraits of the man deny and taunt each other. It is easy and obvious to note—as I believe—that each contains some pieces and fractions of the whole truth. It is less easy—but more important—to discern that both suffer from the same flaws and tricks. Both confuse the plausible with the actual, the logical with the reality. Both ignore the capricious and the imponderable and the elusive in history. And so, by the neat fancy of fitting every event to some intent, they contrive the most seductive distortions: the happy occurrence confers credit, where none may be due, and the mourned occasion decrees guilt, where blame may be impossible.

A few instances may give warning. Thus, for example . . .

The hugeness of a President's popularity may be consoling or alarming, according to the viewer's prejudice, but it is of little relevance to a historian's judgment. Through the years, the upward graph of Eisenhower's popularity seemed a fact of formidable meaning. Yet almost immediately upon his departure from office, the significance of this fact seemed dramatically to depreciate, for his successor in the presidency—a man with a wholly different concept of the office and with a record of only mingled successes and reverses—scaled even higher peaks in the favor of opinion polls. The generosity of such popular tributes to both men suggests that these accolades may reveal not much about either of the men, but more about the temper of the nation. For the awareness of national peril seems inevitably to inspire an anxious sense of dependence upon the presidency, unbridled by the strict appraisal of logic or fact. And this sense—of both danger and dependence—may be greatly quickened, in fact, by a manifest lapse in presidential leadership. Thus the humiliation suffered by Eisenhower on his Far Eastern journey, in the summer of 1960, only brought

words: "When I came to the presidency the country was rather in an unhappy state. There was bitterness and there was quarreling . . . in Washington and around the country. I tried to create an atmosphere of greater serenity and mutual confidence, and I think that it . . . was noticeable over those eight years that that was brought about." ("Eisenhower on the Presidency," CBS telecast with Walter Cronkite, October 12, 1961.)

forth new signs of popular acclaim. At such moments of national stress, partisans cannot rejoice and critics cannot gloat—and a Chief Executive's political error or diplomatic defeat can acquire a weirdly self-nullifying quality. In a democracy—whose very life may depend upon the clarity and courage of its faculties for self-criticism—this could be an alarming sign of intellectual slackness. It cannot be confused, in any event, with a true estimate of the merit or the vigor of a President's leadership.

And the national political scene, quite as much as the world scene, carries its own warnings against the too simple and sweeping judgment. An indictment of Eisenhower, for example, for allowing himself to be a meek creature of traditional Republican conservatism, rather than a bold creator of a new Republican liberalism, must start from the premise that Eisenhower was not, in fact, a conservative. The passage of years proved this premise largely false. Initially, the reality was obscured by Eisenhower's *foreign* policies, for his stands on mutual security or reciprocal trade invited the label of "liberal," even as they invited the hostility of most Republican traditionalists. But Eisenhower, after leaving the presidency, candidly compared himself and Robert Taft: "I found him to be more liberal in his support of some policies even than I was. . . . I laughed at him one day, and I said, 'How did you ever happen to be known as a conservative and me as a liberal?' " The progress of his presidency brought a more and more heavily conservative accent to Eisenhower's policies and pronouncements. But this was not a matter of slow acquiescence to new political pressures: it meant a gradual reaffirmation of old political persuasions. And to appreciate this, one need only imagine the personal politics of a Dwight David Eisenhower from Abilene, Kansas, who never served in World War II; who passed no memorable years in Europe, there to become the comrade of a Churchill or a De Gaulle; and who became known to the political annals of the 1950's as the quite predictable congressman from the Fourth District of his native Kansas.

For like reasons, there is some unrealism in any tribute to

Eisenhower for ratifying or consolidating the social gains of New
Deal and Fair Deal. Eight years of a Republican Administraton did
leave intact all such laws and measures. Yet it is hardly accurate to
ascribe this to presidential statesmanship, liberalism, or even
choice. The Administration was not required to defend these
measures against challenge, but merely to accept their immuta-
bility, as a matter of political necessity. And even with this tacit
act of acceptance, the President himself held an antipathy toward
TVA—and at least a tolerance toward right-to-work-laws—scarcely
reminiscent of the basic social attitudes of the New Deal. There
was exceedingly little here, then, to suggest the labor of a President
who was *trying* to be a far-sighted consolidator of past social
legislation. And it is not easy to assign historic credit to a man for
achievements he never attempted.

All these cautions and qualifications bring some light to the
question of the final fate of one of the supreme objectives of the
Eisenhower presidency.

This purpose was the invigoration and the rejuvenation of the
Republican party.

This purpose ended in defeat.

The size of the defeat was easy to measure. The loss of Executive power in the 1960 elections, despite all advantages enjoyed by
the incumbent Administration, could not be ascribed, harshly or
entirely, to popular distaste for the personality of Richard Nixon.
For the signs of Republican weakness and ineptitude were visible
almost everywhere across the political landscape. The Republican
party that in 1930 claimed governorships in thirty states could
boast of merely sixteen in 1960. Of the nation's forty-one major
urban centers, the Democrats in 1960 swept a total of twenty-
seven. Through all the Eisenhower Years, in fact, the total polling
strength of the GOP had steadily declined despite the President's
personal electoral triumphs—from 49 per cent in 1950, to 47
per cent in 1954, finally to 43 per cent in 1958. In the Congress
convening as Eisenhower left the presidency, the GOP was out-
numbered three to two in the House of Representatives and two

to one in the Senate. Such a stark reckoning more than sufficed, in short, to justify Eisenhower's own unhappy query to Sherman Adams: "What happened . . . ?"

The answer clearly lay, in great part, with the man who asked the question. The very definition he imposed upon his roles as President and party leader approached a political philosophy of self-denial. Months after leaving office, for example, he was asked if he had "ever sort of turned the screw on Congress to get something done . . . saying you'll withhold an appointment or something like that." And with disarming accuracy, Eisenhower answered: "No, never. I took very seriously the matter of appointments and [their] qualifications. . . . Possibly I was not as shrewd and as clever in this matter as some of the others, but I never thought that any of these appointments should be used for bringing pressure upon the Congress." The President proudly forswearing the use of "pressure," of course, comes close to brusquely renouncing power itself. And such smothering of his own voice must have two inescapable consequences: the floundering of his legislative program in the halls of the Congress, and the blurring of his party's image in the eyes of the electorate.

As he treated the political present, so, too, Eisenhower faced the future: he served as a passive witness, rather than an aggressive judge, in the choice of leadership to follow him. It is reasonable to accept the sincerity of his belief—by 1960—that "experience" significantly qualified Richard Nixon for the presidency. It is no less certain, however, that—before 1960—Eisenhower constantly reviewed and privately discussed many alternatives to a successor whom he regarded as less than ideal. Along with such personal favorites as Robert Anderson or Alfred Gruenther, he faced—after the 1958 elections—the far more serious political possibility of a Nelson Rockefeller. Even if all calculations of simple political success were disregarded—including John Fitzgerald Kennedy's own calm judgment that his defeat could have been easy—the striking fact is that Eisenhower did nothing to encourage his party to weigh such alternatives, even while he pondered them within himself.

The conclusion must be that—for the Republican party under the leadership of Eisenhower—the 1950's essentially were a lost decade. Let the measure be the growth of the party in popular vote or popular confidence. Let it be the record of specific legislative achievements. Let it be the less specific but more meaningful matter of clear commitment to abiding principles or exhilarating purposes, relevant to an age of revolution. By all criteria, the judgment must be the same. And it darkly suggests no political truth more modern, perhaps, than the venerable warning of Edmund Burke: "The only thing necessary for the triumph of evil is for good men to do nothing."

And yet, there can be no just criticism of a political leader, obviously, without full reference to the political circumstances. And of the Republican party itself, the serious question must be asked: would some other kind of presidential leadership, more vigorous and more creative, have cleanly prevailed over this party's capacity to resist change? The chance of revitalizing a major political organization depends critically upon the nature of the material with which the work must begin. And, in this instance, the circumstances confronting Eisenhower might at least be called mitigating.

For the full half-century since the historic struggle of 1912 between Theodore Roosevelt and William Howard Taft, the Republican party has been known to the nation, of course, as the citadel of conservative orthodoxy. In this span of time, it summoned from its own ranks no President who could lay serious historic claim to greatness. It collectively offered no leadership that could be hailed, by a grateful nation, as imaginative, bold, or memorable. For thirty of those years, the party could not win a presidential election except under the leadership of a war hero. Over this same thirty-year period, it held control of the Congress for a meager total of four years. All this added up to a distinction of the most unwanted kind.

Yet, behind this near-barren half-century, there lies a Republican tradition of a vastly different fiber. This was, almost instantly upon birth, the party that abolished slavery. Throughout the

decades of frenetically expanding capitalism—and the lawless
acquisitiveness of "the robber barons"—this was the party that
conceived and wrote the national laws most vital to the public
good and welfare. These included: the first laws of civil service,
the anti-trust legislation, the control of the railways, the first
federal regulation of food and drugs, the first acts to conserve the
nation's natural resources. And throughout this full and rich
earlier life, the Republican party logically was both the home and
the hope—rather than the enemy and the despair—of the
American intellectual.

The third half-century of the story of the Republican party has
now just begun. The party, quite obviously, still does not know
which of its two selves to *be* in the years immediately ahead. And
Dwight David Eisenhower—by his own austere and negative pre-
scription for the role of party leader—could not help it to make up
its deeply divided mind.

I have witnessed closely some of this party's recent inner travail.
I confess to frequent and sharp dismay at the pettiness of its
calculations and the narrowness of its vision. And yet, I presume
to believe that the choice before it, as it faces its *third* half-century
of life, is as clear as it is historic.

It must, if it is to be a live and generous force in American politics, stir with the energy of enduring convictions, rather than
appeal for saving moments to the popularity of a new hero or
the plausibility of an ancient shibboleth. It must comprehend and
assimilate, in its own mind and spirit, some of the political and
intellectual qualities that have enabled British Conservatism to
hold power for a full decade and that have animated Christian
Democratic parties on the European continent ever since World
War II. It must honor, too, its own very origin as a party—by
conscientious leadership in the struggle for civil rights. It must
learn to use political power in some exercise other than the reflexes
of opposition and denunciation. It must forswear the charades of
hysterical duels with the imagined menaces of "socialism" and
"totalitarianism." It must learn to assess its own political worth
by some arithmetic more elevated than the facile addition of its

own congressional votes to those of southern Democrats, to contrive the frustration of a fairly impressive number of Executive
actions in any congressional session. It must attain a self-respecting
sense of identity—and sense of purpose—that can turn cold and
confident scorn upon the tawdry political temptations proffered
by a Senator Joseph McCarthy or a John Birch Society. And—with
these and a host of kindred acts—it might begin to celebrate each
political year, each session of the Congress in Washington, by
offering the nation a modest minimum of one proud sign of
imaginative political action, dedicated unabashedly to the common
weal.

To inspire and to lead—indeed, to *re-create*—such a Republican
party can only be, still, a patient and painful labor.

To this labor, there was, perhaps, not a great deal that such a
President as Eisenhower could bring. This was not only because
of the nature of the Republican party long before he encountered
it. It was also because of the nature of the man long before the
party encountered him. For he appeared upon the national scene as
the political father of a phenomenon called "modern Republicanism." Yet his economic and social views could not convincingly
be described as "modern." And his political behavior could not,
with rare exception, be described as militantly and passionately
"Republican." The fact is that the President who was supposed
to lead the Republican party toward new, high ground—both
"liberal" and "modern"—could not seriously be distinguished
from a conservative Democrat.

If this suggests some kind of political paradox about the man,
it suggests a more profound paradox about the system of political
parties by which America governs itself in the middle of the
twentieth century.

And it suggests the final reason why Dwight Eisenhower left
the Republican party—politically and intellectually—where first
he found it.

> Things are in the saddle,
> And ride mankind.
> *Ralph Waldo Emerson*

The second and the grander of the two high purposes pursued by the Eisenhower presidency was the quest of "peace with justice."

This, too, ended in frustration.

The President's own appraisal of himself as a peacemaker, as fully and finally spoken, sounds rather like a judgment at odds with itself. Thus—on the one side—he publicly recited, within a year of leaving the presidency, what he called "my greatest disappointments," and concluded: "I suppose the most important . . . is a lack of definite proof that we had made real progress toward achieving peace with justice." Yet—on the other side—he had proudly voiced, only a week before surrendering office, a quite different and less disparaging opinion in his final State of the Union Message to the Congress. According to this review of the eight years of his presidency, he professed to see "Communist imperialism held in check." And he invited the Congress to share the Chief Executive's pleasure in his conclusion: "We have carried America to unprecedented heights."

The two contrary appraisals were not as hard to reconcile as they might appear, even apart from the fact that one could not reasonably have expected Eisenhower's final address to the Congress to catalogue his personal disappointments. For the State of the Union message did not, in truth, presume even to suggest "definite proof" of "real progress." Instead, all the alleged achievements merely attested to the practice of a diplomacy of "containment," although its rewards were hailed—now—as "unprecedented heights."

The satisfying summits cited by the departing President were quite specific. They numbered seven in all. And they are worth quick scanning to appreciate the nature of the diplomatic terrain upon which he looked back. . . .

1. Whereas "when I took office, the United States was at war," the nation had "lived in peace" since the Korean Armistice of 1953. *But* . . . there seemed some irony in the fact that this list of eight years of diplomatic accomplishments should be headed by

the prudent acceptance, seven years earlier, of a military status quo whose toleration, even at the time, had elicited only frowns and doubts from the Secretary of State.

2. The United States had "strongly supported" the United Nations in the 1956 Suez Crisis, thus achieving "the ending of the hostilities in Egypt." *But* . . . the prologue to this crisis had entailed the chronic deterioration of Anglo-American relations—and the epilogue had consisted of the alarming expansion of Soviet influence throughout the Middle East.

3. "Again in 1958, peace was preserved in the Middle East"—by prompt American military action in Lebanon. *But* . . . while this action had been vitally required and efficiently executed, its very necessity implied rather critical comment on the political heritage from American Middle Eastern diplomacy two years earlier.

4. "Our support of the Republic of China . . . restrained the Communist Chinese from attempting to invade the offshore islands." *But* . . . the honoring of this defensive action as the major triumph of eight years of diplomacy in the Far East seemed oddly to mock the "initiative" of 1953—supposedly freeing Nationalist China to assume a more menacing military posture toward the Communist mainland.

5. As for Latin America, there was not much that could be said beyond this: "Although, unhappily, Communist penetration of Cuba is real and poses a serious threat, Communist-dominated regimes have been deposed in Guatemala and Iran." The fragile apologia could not even find sufficient supporting evidence in all the Western Hemisphere.

6. As for Europe—while the peripheral issues of an Austrian peace treaty and a Trieste settlement could be remembered from the first term with some justified satisfaction—there was no echo of the 1953 cries of "rollback" or "liberation," but the most modest of observations: "Despite constant threats to its integrity, West Berlin remained free."

7. Finally, there were alleged to be "important advances . . . in building mutual security arrangements." Thus: SEATO was

established in Southeast Asia and the CENTO Pact in the Middle
East, NATO was "militarily strengthened," and the Organization
of American States was "further developed." *But* . . . a number
of dispassionate critics would have felt compelled to note the
following: (a) the political or military value of SEATO was
highly questionable; (b) the birth of CENTO merely followed
the death of the Baghdad Pact when Baghdad itself severed this tie
to the West; (c) the political structure of NATO betrayed signs
of growing division rather than greater unity; and (d) the OAS
probably faced a graver crisis over Cuban Communism than it
had ever known in all its political life.

The President's own chosen list of historic events thus strikingly
revealed the limits and the lacks of eight years of American
diplomacy, and the nation might well ask—as the President himself occasionally must have wondered—why his pursuit of peace,
so ample in both motion and emotion, had yielded such meager
reward. A part of the answer, it is true, might cite sheer bad luck.
Only a glibly assured student of contemporary history could pro-
fess to know the course of East-West diplomacy in 1960, at least
in its appearances and its amenities, if there had been no disaster
with the U-2 flight. But one such mischance could not suffice to
explain the sum of nearly a decade of national policy.

The climactic global effort of Eisenhower's peace-making suggested a peacetime variation on a familiar wartime lament. This
was the case of—too much, too late. Through all the years ruled
by the taut doctrines of John Foster Dulles, the national policy
had decreed an almost religious kind of commitment to a moralistic definition of the relations between nations. By the terms of
this orthodoxy, the promise of salvation lay in a kind of political
excommunication of Soviet power. The means of grace, moreover,
were assured: the political weakness of Soviet power was ultimately
guaranteed by its moral wickedness. And the contaminating
stigma of sin therefore attached to all acts or gestures of diplomacy
that, by directly touching the unclean enemy, might give counte-
nance to the damning offenses of his tyranny at home and his

conquests abroad. It was as bad and unthinkable as selling indulgences.

Time and history, however, played a cruel trick. For the years when these strictures had been respected were precisely the years when the advantages of politics and power had rested with the United States. Militarily, American nuclear power then had stood beyond challenge. Politically, the Soviet Union had to suffer through all the complex conflicts wracking the Communist state after Stalin's death. But such factors were drastically changed by the time the clenched fist of Dulles came to be replaced, in the world of diplomacy, by the outstreched hand of Eisenhower. The Soviet power that Eisenhower now confronted was the new and ingenious pioneer of the Age of Space. The Soviet leadership that he faced, now no longer strife-torn, was personified by a Khrushchev politically more agile and skillful than a Stalin. Conversely, the American power that Eisenhower now commanded had passed under a cloud of world doubt. The American diplomacy that he directed was caught in a cross fire between colonialism and anti-colonialism, all through the very areas of Asia and Africa marked for political agression by new Soviet leadership. And the American leadership that Eisenhower himself personified now could boast—by the constitutional law of his nation—only a few more months to live.

There was a moral as well as political edge, moreover, to the sad incongruity of all this. The Soviet leadership so righteously shunned by the diplomacy of Dulles stood indicted—a little belatedly—for political crimes essentially rooted in World War II. The Soviet leadership so hopefully encountered by the diplomacy of Eisenhower came—quite freshly—from the savage suppression of Hungarian freedom. And so American policy of the 1950's fashioned its supreme irony: a host of decent intents, generous gestures, and dramatic acts of peace were scrupulously hoarded—through years proclaiming the need for them—to be lavishly spent only when the moral occasion was least appropriate and their political value was least impressive.

The confused timing of such major diplomatic acts had to be-
tray, too, some lack of substance, since the fully reasoned acts
would have borne the much earlier dates. And this fact gave to the
President's personal diplomacy its disconcerting overtones of im-
petuosity and improvisation. The reach of the leader was undeniably long, but his grasp did not seem firm; his manner was kind,
but uncertain; his words were benign, but unclear. And all this
explained why so many national capitals, warm as they felt in the
presence of the man, also sensed a little shiver of unreality as they
watched and listened. Even as he disarmed his critics, he dis-
quieted his friends. For they could not suppress a fear that perhaps
he had never understood the lesson recorded by one historian who
had personally witnessed the travail of peace-making, as long ago
as 1919: "It would be interesting to analyze how many false decisions, how many fatal misunderstandings, have arisen from such
pleasant qualities as shyness, consideration, affability, or ordinary
good manners."

The strivings of Eisenhower to conciliate the world of nations
thus markedly resembled his equally earnest attempts to conciliate
the Congress of the United States. Over the years, the tortuous
struggle to evolve Republican legislative programs with the help
of political leaders as unreconciled as William Knowland was no
more remarkable than the effort to evolve a foreign policy by
mingling, in equal measures, Eisenhower's views of the world and
those of John Foster Dulles. The truth was that all the public
allusions to a "Dulles-Eisenhower" foreign policy were no more
sensibly descriptive than some fantastic diplomacy proclaiming
itself "radical-reactionary" or "bellicose-pacific." And in the councils closest to Eisenhower, the deep conflict of premises found a
kind of analogy in a conflict of persons, also unadmitted by the
President. For in Eisenhower's Cabinet, through all the years, no
two men stood closer to him than Dulles and Humphrey. In the
same Cabinet, no two men clashed more fundamentally on national policy. And the President warmly respected them both—
equally.

A foreign policy beset by such inner contradictions inevitably could attain results of only one kind: the negative or the passive. Such results were not wholly to be scorned: they could include acts as important as countering the threatened chaos in Lebanon or the presidential veto upon military intervention in Indochina. But a national policy so nearly schizophrenic was powerless to create a positive political design.

In the deepest sense, it could neither conceive nor execute a truly *historic act*.

This was not because it lacked the courage to act.

This was because it could not decide upon a definition of history.

And so the years inscribed a record, not stained with the blots of many foolish or reckless acts, but all too immaculate. All the acts of omission signified a waste of something more than a briefly enjoyed military superiority. The great waste could be measured only by the vastness of the unused political resources at the command of the most powerful and popular leader of any free nation in the world. For Eisenhower had constantly enjoyed the freedom, so fantastically rare in a modern democracy, of the full and affectionate confidence of a people who would have followed him toward almost any conceivable military enterprise or diplomatic encounter.

The final reckoning upon such a period of singular opportunity truly revealed, in short, a "lack of definite proof" of the achievement of "real progress." At the end of his presidency and confronting his harshest critics, Eisenhower never had to suffer hearing criticism as biting as the accusation that Macaulay once hurled in the House of Commons at Sir Robert Peel: "There you sit, doing penance for the disingenuousness of years." But the chargeable offense might have been the exact opposite: the ingenuousness of years.

A last, small irony was reserved for his last months in office: The President then was fighting an increasingly bitter battle against critics who insistently warned of a faltering of American purpose and American power. While some of these critics focused their concern upon domestic issues—from the health of the aged to the education of the young—the majority saw the world scene as the sharpest cause for anxiety. Essentially, the sources of this anxiety were the multiplying signs of Soviet achievement, from progress of their missile power to education of *their* youth. The President found himself harassed by questions and laments upon a single theme: could not, should not, would not the federal government do more to spur comparable American achievement? Emphatically, then stubbornly, at last almost petulantly, Eisenhower insisted that such demands threatened an enlargement of federal authority that would "take our country and make it an armed camp and regiment it." And he went further—to contend angrily that such acknowledgment of Soviet power implied an almost unpatriotic disparagement of American life, as he gruffly admonished one press conference: "Our people ought to have greater faith in their own system." Thus—strangely—did an intensely patriotic President come finally to argue that the nature of American freedom, and the resourcefulness of the American people, were so limited that they could give retort to the challenge of Soviet Communism only by fractional sacrifice and rationed effort.

The distance in time and in spirit, from the First Inaugural, seemed—in these last days of the Eisenhower presidency—more than the meager sum of seven or eight years. . . . "We must be ready to dare all for our country. . . . The peace we seek . . . is nothing less than the practice and fulfillment of our whole faith. . . . It signifies much more than the stilling of guns, easing the sorrow, of war. More than an escape from death, it is a way of life. More than a haven for the weary, it is a hope for the brave."

The presidency that had followed upon these words had appeared only occasionally to be inspired by any such preachment about peace.

It had settled, instead, for the half-solace of a series of truces.

> O! it is excellent
> To have a giant's strength, but it is tyrannous
> To use it like a giant.
> *Measure for Measure*

The man who, for these several years, entered his office each morning to nod approvingly at the legend on his desk—"Gentle in manner, strong in deed"—would have commended Shakespeare's admonition on "a giant's strength" as an admirable definition of the proper use of power in the presidency of the United States. Because he so believed, he would be charged—quite justly —with refusal to give vigorous leadership even to cherished purposes. And he would also be condemned—not at all justly—for wholly lacking any concept of presidential leadership.

The Eisenhower who rose to fame in the 1940's, under the wartime presidency of Franklin Roosevelt, brought to the White House of the 1950's a view of the presidency so definite and so durable as to seem almost a studied retort and rebuke to a Roosevelt. Where Roosevelt had sought and coveted power, Eisenhower distrusted and discounted it: one man's appetite was the other man's distaste. Where Roosevelt had avidly grasped and adroitly manipulated the abundant authorities of the office, Eisenhower fingered them almost hesitantly and always respectfully—or generously dispersed them. Where Roosevelt had challenged Congress, Eisenhower courted it. Where Roosevelt had been an extravagant partisan, Eisenhower was a tepid partisan. Where Roosevelt had trusted no one and nothing so confidently as his own judgment and his own instinct, Eisenhower trusted and required a consensus of Cabinet or staff to shape the supreme judgments and determinations. Where Roosevelt had sought to goad and taunt and prod the processes of government toward the new and the untried, Eisenhower sought to be both guardian of old values and healer of old wounds.

The contrast was quite as blunt in the case of an earlier—and a Republican—Roosevelt. For the Eisenhower who so deeply disliked all struttings of power, all histrionics of politics, would have found the person and the presidency of Theodore Roosevelt almost intolerable. He would have applied to this Roosevelt, too, the homely phrase of derision that he reserved for politicians of such verve and vehemence: they were "the desk-pounders." Echoing

back across the decades would have come the lusty answer of
T.R.—exulting in the presidency as the "bully pulpit." And it is
hard to imagine a concept of the presidency more alien to Eisenhower: to preach and to yell.

A yet more exact and intimate insight into the Eisenhower
presidency was revealed by his particular tribute to the Abraham
Lincoln of his admiration. He was asked, on one occasion, to
describe this Lincoln. And he chose these adjectives: "dedicated,
selfless, so modest and humble." He made no mention or suggestion of such possible attributes as: imagination, tenacity, single-
mindedness, vision. Pressed gently by his interrogator as to whether
Lincoln were not something of a "desk-pounder," Eisenhower
denied such a notion and spontaneously related the one episode of
Lincoln's life that surged to the surface of memory . . .

Oh no. Lincoln was noted both for his modesty and his humility.
For example, one night he wanted to see General McClellan. He
walked over to General McClellan's house . . . but General McClellan was out. He . . . waited way late in the evening. But when the
general came in, he told an aide . . . he was tired and he was going
to bed, and he would see the President the next day. And when criticized later . . . someone told Mr. Lincoln he ought to have been
more arbitrary about this. He said: "I would hold General McClellan's
horse if he would just win the Union a victory."

The Eisenhower appreciation of Lincoln, in short, reflected one
sovereign attitude: all esteemed qualities of the founder of Republicanism were personal and individual, and not one was political
or historical. And if the logic of such an estimate were carried
coldly to its extreme, it would end in the unspoken implication
that the highest national office should be sought and occupied less
as an exercise of political power than as a test of personal virtue.
To excel in this test, the man would live not *with* the office but
within it—intact and independent, proudly uncontaminated by
power, essentially uninvolved with it. Rather than a political life,
this would be a life in politics. Its supreme symbol would be not
the sword of authority but the shield of rectitude.

While this self-conscious kind of idealism sprang from deep within the man who was Eisenhower, it found reinforcement—and rationalization—in his explicit theory of political leadership. This theory was profoundly felt and emphatically argued. It claimed even to bespeak a sense of responsibility more serious than the conventional shows of leadership. And no words of Eisenhower stated this theory more succinctly than these:

> I am not a . . . leader. I don't want you to follow me or anything else. If you are looking for a Moses to lead you out of the . . . wilderness, you will stay right where you are. I would not lead you into this promised land if I could, because if I could lead you in, someone else could lead you out.

These words might have been spoken by Dwight David Eisenhower—at almost any moment in the years from 1952 to 1960—to the Republican party or, indeed, to the American people at large. They were actually spoken, however, by one of the great leaders of American labor, Eugene V. Debs, more than a half a century earlier. And they are worthy of note here as simple evidence that, quite apart from all impulses of personal character, the political posture assumed by Eisenhower toward the challenge of national leadership could not, in fact, be curtly described as negligent, eccentric, or even entirely original.

This posture *was* Eisenhower—remarkably and unshakably—because it was prescribed for him by *both* the temper of the man and the tenets of his politics. In any President, or in any political leader, these two need not necessarily coincide: they may fiercely clash. A man of vigorous and aggressive spirit, restless with the urge for action and accomplishment, may fight frantically against the limits of a political role calling for calm, composure, and self-effacement. Or a man of easy and acquiescent temper, content to perform the minimal duties of his office, may strain pathetically and vainly to fill the vastness of a political role demanding force, boldness, and self-assurance. Eisenhower suffered neither kind of conflict. The definition of the office perfectly suited and matched the nature of the man. And neither critical argument nor anxious appeal could persuade him to question, much less to shed, an attire of leadership so appropriate, so form-fitting, so comfortable.

The want and the weakness in all this was not a mere matter of indecision. The man—and the President—was never more decisive than when he held to a steely resolve *not* to do something that he sincerely believed wrong in itself or alien to his office. The essential flaw, rather, was one that had been suggested a full half-century ago—when the outrageously assertive Theodore Roosevelt had occupied the White House—and Woodrow Wilson had then prophesied that "more and more" the presidency would demand *"the sort of action that makes for enlightenment."* The requisite for such action, however, is not merely a stout sense of responsibility, but an acute sense of history—a discerning, even intuitive, appreciation of the elusive and cumulative force of every presidential word and act, shaped and aimed to reach final goals, unglimpsed by all but a few. And as no such vision ever deeply inspired the Eisenhower presidency, there could be no true "enlightenment" to shine forth from its somber acts of prudence or of pride.

This is not to say that the record of the Administration wholly lacked zeal—of a kind. It is doubtful if the leadership of any great nation can endure for nearly a decade without at least the flickering of some flame of commitment. The man who came closest to a display of such fervor in these years, however, was not the President but his Secretary of State. This man possessed at least his own understanding of what Theodore Roosevelt meant when he spoke of a "pulpit." And yet, this particular ardor of John Foster Dulles could not be enough. For this kind of zeal was neither creative nor impassioned. It was austere, constrained, and cerebral. And in lieu of fire, it offered ice.

Ultimately, all that Eisenhower did, and refused to do, as a democratic leader was rigorously faithful to his understanding of democracy itself. When the record of his presidency was written and done, he could look back upon it and soberly reflect: "One definition of democracy that I like is merely the opportunity for self-discipline." He lived by this definition. And by all acts of eight years of his presidency, he urged its acceptance by the people of his nation.

The implications of this simple political credo could not instantly be dismissed as shallow. Forbearance and constraint, patience and discipline—those are not virtues for a democracy to deride. They can be fatefully relevant to the ways of free men.

And yet, by the year 1960, they did not seem to serve or to suffice, as full statement of either the nation's purpose or a President's policy.

What was so wrong or wanting in them?

Perhaps one might have caught some hint of the answer, if one were listening attentively, on Inauguration Day in 1961. The provocative moment came shortly before John Fitzgerald Kennedy took his oath of office. At this moment, there stood at the lectern of the Inaugural platform on Capitol Hill not a politician but a poet. His white hair was whipped by the chill January wind. His fingers fumbled clumsily with his text. He was eighty-six years of age—old enough to forget some of his own written lines. But the voice of Robert Frost was strong, and his meaning was clear . . .

> Something we were withholding left us weak
> Until we found it was ourselves
> We were withholding from our land of living
> And forthwith found salvation in surrender.

Reaffirming the Stalemate

Stability and Change in 1960

by Philip E. Converse, Angus Campbell,
Warren E. Miller, and Donald E. Stokes

*It became certain in 1960 that the presidential father-figure of
Dwight Eisenhower would be replaced by a much younger politician. Vice President Richard M. Nixon, then forty-six, easily
obtained the Republican nomination, while on the Democratic
side, John F. Kennedy, a forty-three-year-old senator from Massachusetts, had run a skillful and successful pre-election campaign.
His principal rival at the Democratic convention, Senator
Lyndon B. Johnson, a Texas conservative and one of the country's
most powerful politicians during the final years of the Eisenhower
administration, surprised the country by agreeing to run with
Kennedy.*

*Although Kennedy criticized the drift and lethargy of the Eisen-
hower years, his election strategy dictated the creation of a positive
image rather than merely assailing the record of a Republican
incumbent who remained personally popular. Kennedy promised
to accelerate the low rate of economic growth and to reduce the
comparatively high existing rate of unemployment; he also promised new and massive federal programs for support of public education and government-financed medical care for those over sixty-
five. "Vigor" became the key word in his appeal: Kennedy con-*

*tended that the nation had to "move ahead," and that it could
do so only with young, fresh, White House leadership. He also
touched bases with the scattered elements of the Democratic coalition, some of which had drifted away from the party during the
'fifties, matching familiar promises to organized labor and farmers with appeals to ethnic minorities and declarations of support
for civil rights and racial desegregation.*

*In contrast, Nixon, though of the same generation as Kennedy,
a generation which came to maturity during the Depression and
World War II, seemed old-fashioned. As Eisenhower's political
heir he dutifully defended the Republican administration's record, stressing the nation's general prosperity and adding a few
vague feints in the direction of reform and welfare legislation.
Essentially, however, Nixon appealed to those segments of the
electorate which were content with the accomplishments of the
1950's, especially those with an economic or psychological stake
in the status quo. He opposed, among other Democratic suggestions, federal aid to education and Medicare, charging that they
would lead to bureaucratic tyranny and socialized medicine.*

*Kennedy won in one of America's closest presidential contests,
but the result mainly confirmed the previous shift to the center,
the stalemate in domestic politics which Dwight Eisenhower's
victories had first symbolized and later consolidated. The Democrats kept their stranglehold on Congress, although the "conservative coalition" of Republicans and Southern Democrats remained
powerful. The Democrats' majority party status did not extend
automatically to the presidency, however. Kennedy won by a hair's
breadth: of nearly seventy million votes cast, he obtained only
113,000 more than Nixon, a margin of but 0.2 per cent. Kennedy
easily captured the personality contest between the two contend-
ers, but this advantage was nearly offset in November by Protestant defections to Nixon in the South's Bible Belt, where both
Kennedy's Catholicism and his support for Negro civil rights cost
him votes. Yet 1960 was not like 1928: most of the South stayed
Democratic, demonstrating Kennedy's short-term political fore-
sight in placing Johnson on the ticket.*

*The following article by Philip E. Converse and his associates
shows how the 1960 election reaffirmed the "normal" Democratic*

electoral majority while it failed to provide a new and effective governing majority. As the country was soon to learn, the Eisenhower Era's politics of stalemate left in its wake a legacy of congressional inaction that Kennedy and his New Frontiersmen had not bargained for. It would take the unifying symbolism of Kennedy's assassination and the additional shock of Lyndon Johnson's landslide victory in 1964 to break the legislative logjam, at least temporarily.

John F. Kennedy's narrow popular vote margin in 1960 has already insured this presidential election a classic position in the roll call of close American elections. Whatever more substantial judgments historical perspective may bring, we can be sure that the 1960 election will do heavy duty in demonstrations to a reluctant public that after all is said and done, every vote does count. And the margin translated into "votes per precinct" will become standard fare in exhortations to party workers that no stone be left unturned.

The 1960 election is a classic as well in the license it allows for "explanations" of the final outcome. Any event or campaign stratagem that might plausibly have changed the thinnest sprinkling of votes across the nation may, more persuasively than is usual, be called "critical." Viewed in this manner, the 1960 presidential election hung on such a manifold of factors that reasonable men might despair of cataloguing them.

Nevertheless, it is possible to put together an account of the election in terms of the broadest currents influencing the American electorate in 1960. We speak of the gross lines of motivation which gave the election its unique shape, motivations involving millions rather than thousand of votes. Analysis of these broad currents is not intended to explain the hairline differences in popular vote, state by state, which edged the balance in favor of Kennedy rather than Nixon. But it can indicate quite clearly the

From *The American Political Science Review*, LV (June. 1961), 269–80. Reprinted by permission; footnotes omitted.

broad forces which reduced the popular vote to a virtual stalemate, rather than any of the other reasonable outcomes between a 60–40 or a 40–60 vote division. And it can thereby help us to understand in parsimonious terms why a last feather thrown on the scales in November, 1960, could have spelled victory or defeat for either candidate.

1. Surface Characteristics of the Election

Any account of the election should not only be consistent with its obvious characteristics as they filtered clear from raw vote tallies in the days after the election, but should organize them into a coherent pattern of meaning as well. These characteristics are, of course, the ones that have nourished post-election speculation. In addition to the close partisan division of the popular vote, the following items deserve mention:

1 *The remarkably high level of turnout.* About 62.7 per cent of estimated adults over 21 voted in the 1952 election, a figure which had stood as the high-water mark of vote turnout in recent presidential elections. The comparable turnout proportion for the 1960 presidential election appears to have been 64.3 per cent.

2 *Upswing in turnout in the South.* The South appears to have contributed disproportionately to the high level in turnout. Outside the South, the increase in total presidential votes cast in 1960 relative to the 1956 election was about 7 per cent, a figure scarcely exceeding estimated population growth in this period. In the South, however, presidential ballots in 1960 increased by more than 25 per cent relative to 1956, an increase far outstripping population growth in this region.

3 *Stronger Republican voting at the presidential level.* On balance across the nation Nixon led Republican tickets, while Kennedy trailed behind many other Democratic candidates, especially outside of the Northeast. These discrepancies in the partisanship of presidential voting and ballots at other levels were not, of course, as striking as those in 1956. Nevertheless, their political significance

has an obvious bearing on the future expectations of the two youthful candidates, and therefore occasions special interest.

4 *The stamp of the religious factor in 1960 voting patterns.* While the Kennedy victory was initially taken as proof that religion had not been important in the election, all serious students of election statistics have since been impressed by the religious axis visible in the returns. Fenton, Scammon, Bean, Harris and others have commented upon the substantial correlation between aggregate voting patterns and the relative concentration of Catholics and Protestants from district to district.

Of these surface characteristics, probably the last has drawn most attention. Once it became clear that religion had not only played some part but, as these things go, a rather impressive part in presidential voting across the nation, discussions came to hinge on the nature of its role. It could safely be assumed that Kennedy as a Catholic had attracted some unusual Catholic votes, and had lost some normally Democratic Protestant votes. A clear question remained, however, as to the *net* effect. The *New York Times,* summarizing the discussion late in November, spoke of a "narrow consensus" among the experts that Kennedy had won more than he lost as a result of his Catholicism. These are questions, however, which aggregate vote statistics can but dimly illuminate, as the disputed history of Al Smith's 1928 defeat makes clear. Fortunately in 1960 the election was studied extensively by sample surveys, permitting more exact inferences to be drawn.

The national sample survey conducted by the Survey Research Center of The University of Michigan in the fall of 1960 had features which give an unparalleled opportunity to comment on the recent evolution of the American electorate. The fall surveys were part of a long-term "panel" study, in which respondents first interviewed at the time of the 1956 presidential election were reinterviewed. In the fall of 1956 a sample of 1763 adults, chosen by strict probability methods from all the adults living in private households in the United States, had been questioned just before and just after the presidential election. This initial sample was constituted as a panel of respondents and was interviewed again in 1958 and twice in connection with the 1960 presidential election. These materials permit the linking of 1960 and 1956 voting behavior with unusual reliability.

2. The Evolution of the Electorate, 1956–1960

The difference in presidential election outcome between 1956 and 1960 might depend upon either or both of two broad types of change in the electorate. The first includes shifts in the physical composition of the electorate over time due to non-political factors, *i.e.*, vital processes. Some adult citizens who voted in 1956 were no longer part of the eligible electorate in 1960, primarily because of death or institutionalization. On the other hand, a new cohort of voters who had been too young to vote in 1956 were eligible to participate in the 1960 election. Even in a four-year period, vital processes alone could acount for shifts in the vote. In addition, changes in the electoral vote, though not in the nationwide popular vote margin, might result from voters changing their residences without changing their minds.

Secondly, there are obviously genuine changes in the political choice of individuals eligible to vote in both elections. Such citizens may enter or leave the active electorate by choice, or may decide to change the partisanship of their presidential vote.

The contribution of these two types of change to the shift in votes from a 1956 Eisenhower landslide to a narrow 1960 Kennedy margin—a net shift toward the Democrats of almost 8 per cent—may be analyzed. Somewhat less than 10 per cent of the eligible 1956 electorate had become effectively ineligible by 1960, with death as the principal cause. Older people naturally bulk large in this category. The felt party affiliation or "party identification" expressed in 1956 by these "departing" respondents was somewhat Republican relative to the remainder of the sample. Nonetheless, these people cast a vote for president which was about 48 per cent Democratic, or 6 per cent *more Democratic* than the vote of the 1956 electorate as a whole. Although this appears to be a contradiction, it is actually nothing more than a logical consequence of existing theory. The high Republican vote in 1956 depended on a massive defection to Eisenhower by many people identified with the Democratic party. Since the strength of party attachments increases as a function of age, and since defections are inversely related to strength of party identification, it follows that 1956 defection rates were much higher among younger citizens than among older. The data make it clear that the group of older people voting for the last time in 1956 had cast a much straighter "party vote" than their juniors. Only about 5 per cent of these older Democrats had defected to Eisenhower, as opposed to about a quarter of all Democrats in the electorate as a whole. So both things are true: this departing cohort was more Republican than average in party identification but had voted more Democratic than average in 1956. If we remove them from the 1956 electorate, then, we arrive at a presidential vote of about 60 per cent for Eisenhower among those voters who were to have the option of voting again in 1960. Hence the elimination of this older group from consideration increases the amount of partisan change to be accounted for between 1956 and 1960, rather than decreasing it.

Comparable isolation of the new cohort of young voters in 1960 does very little to change the picture. Little more than one half of this new group of voters normally votes in the first election of eligibility; furthermore, in 1960 its two-party vote division differed only negligibly from that of the nation as a whole. As a result, its analytic removal leaves the vote among the remainder of the electorate nearly unchanged. By way of summary, then, differences in the 1956 and 1960 electorates arising from vital processes do not explain the 1956–1960 vote change; if anything, they extend the amount of change to be otherwise explained.

We may further narrow our focus by considering those people eligible in both 1956 and 1960, who failed to join the active electorate in 1960. A very large majority of these 1960 non-voters had not voted in 1956, and represent Negroes in the South as well as persistent non-voters of other types. Among those who *had* voted in 1956, however, the vote had been rather evenly divided between Eisenhower and Stevenson. As with the older voters, removal of this group leaves an active 1956–1960 electorate whose vote for Eisenhower now surpasses 60 per cent, broadening again the discrepancy between the two-party divisions in the 1956 and 1960 votes. The final fringe group which we may set aside analytically is constituted of those citizens eligible to have voted in 1956 who did not then participate, yet who joined the electorate in 1960. The fact that young voters often "sit out" their first presidential election or two indicates part of the composition of such a group. Once again, however, these newly active citizens divided their ballots in 1960 almost equally between the two major candidates, and the residual portion of the 1960 electorate changes little with their removal.

By this point we have eliminated all the fringe groupings whose entry or departure from the active electorate might have contributed to change in the national vote division between 1956 and 1960. We come to focus directly, then, on the individuals who cast a vote for Kennedy or Nixon in 1960 *and had voted for president in 1956* (Table 1). As we see, paring away the fringe group-ings has had the total effect of increasing the net shift in the vote division between the two years from 8 per cent to 11 per cent. If we can explain this shift it will be clear that we have dealt with those broad currents in the electorate which brought the 1960 election to a virtual stalemate.

Naturally, the most interesting features of Table 1 are the cells involving vote changers. In a sequence of elections such as the 1956–1960 series it is a temptation to assume that about 8 per cent of the Eisenhower voters of 1956 shifted to Kennedy in 1960, since this was the net observable change between the two years. Much analysis of aggregate election statistics is forced to proceed on this assumption within any given voting unit. However, we see that the net shift of 11 per cent in the vote of the active 1956–1960 electorate in fact derived from a gross shift of 23 per cent,

over half of which was rendered invisible in the national totals
because counter-movements cancelled themselves out.

A traditional analysis of these vote changers would specify their
membership in various population groupings such as age and occupation category, union membership, race and the like. However,
results of this sort in 1960 are so uniform across most of these
population groupings that they seem to reflect little more than
national trends, and change seems at best loosely connected with
location in various of these specific categories. If we took the fact

Table 1

1956–1960 Vote Change Within the Active
Core of the Electorate

1956 Vote for

1960 Vote for ↓	Stevenson %	Eisenhower %	Total %
Kennedy	33	17	50
Nixon	6	44	50
	39	61	100

Note: Since we usually think of vote shifts in terms of
proportions of the total electorate, percentages in this
table use the total vote as a base,.rather than row or
column totals.

in isolation, for example, we might be struck to note that union
members voted almost 8 per cent more Democratic in 1960 than
in 1956. However, such a figure loses much of its interest when
we remind ourselves that people who are not labor union members
also shifted their votes in the same direction and in about the
same degree between 1956 and 1960. Such uniform changes char-
acterize most of the standard sociological categories.

There is, of course, one dramatic exception. Vote change between 1956 and 1960 follows religious lines very closely. Within
the 6 per cent of the active 1956–1960 electorate who followed
a Stevenson-Nixon path (Table 1), 90 per cent are Protestant and
only 8 per cent are Catholic. Among the larger group of Eisen-

hower-Kennedy changers, however, only 40 per cent, are Protestant and close to 60 per cent are Catholic. In the total vote in 1956 and 1960, Protestants show almost no net partisan change. Eisenhower had won 64 per cent of the "Protestant vote" in 1956; Nixon won 63 per cent. Meanwhile, the Democratic proportion of the two-party vote among Catholics across the nation skyrocketed from a rough 50 per cent in the two Eisenhower elections to a vote of 80 per cent for Kennedy. These gross totals appear to substantiate the early claims of Kennedy backers that a Catholic candidate would draw back to the Democratic party sufficient Catholics to carry the 1960 election. Furthermore, it appears that Kennedy must have gained more votes than he lost by virtue of his religious affiliation, for relative to Stevenson in 1956, he lost no Protestant votes and attracted a very substantial bloc of Catholic votes.

The question of net gains or losses as a result of the Catholic issue is not, however, so simply laid to rest. The data cited above make a very strong case, as have the aggregate national statistics, that religion played a powerful role in the 1960 outcome. The vote polarized along religious lines in a degree which we have not seen in the course of previous sample survey studies. Moreover, the few interesting deviations in the 1960 vote of other population group-ings, to the degree that they are visible at all, seem with minor exceptions to reflect the central religious polarization. That is, where a group exceeded or fell below the magnitude of the national shift to the Democrats, it is usually true that the group is incidentally a more or less Catholic group. The central phenome-non therefore was religious; the question as to its net effect favor-ing or disfavoring Kennedy remains open.

In a strict sense, of course, the answers to this question can only be estimated. We know how the election came out, with Kennedy a Catholic. We cannot, without major additional assumptions, know what the election returns might have been if Kennedy were a Protestant and all other conditions remained unchanged. We can make an estimate, however, if we can assume some baseline, some vote that would have occurred under "normal" circumstances. A number of such baselines suggest themselves. We might work from the 1956 presidential vote, as we have done above (42 per cent Democratic); or from the more recent Congressional vote in 1958 (56 per cent Democratic); or from some general average of recent nation-wide votes. But it is obvious that the simple choice of baseline will go a long way toward determining the answer we propose to the question of net religious effect. If we choose the 1958 vote as a baseline, it is hard to argue that Kennedy could have made any net gains from his religion; if we choose the 1956 presidential vote, it is equally hard to argue that he lost ground on balance.

Indeed, the most cogent arguments documenting a net gain for Kennedy—those accounts which appear to express the majority opinion of election observers—use the 1956 presidential vote quite explicitly as a baseline. Yet the second Eisenhower vote seems the most bizarre choice for a baseline of any which might be suggested. The vote Eisenhower achieved in 1956 stands out as the most disproportionately Republican vote in the total series of nation-wide presidential and congressional elections stretching back to 1928. In what sense, then, is this extreme Republican swing plausible as a "normal vote?" Its sole claim seems to lie in the fact that it is the most recent presidential election. Yet other recent elections attest dramatically to the extreme abnormality of the 1956 Eisenhower vote. In the 1954 congressional elections the nation's Democrats, although they turned out less well than Republicans in minor elections, still fashioned a solid majority of votes cast. The fall of 1958 witnessed a Democratic landslide. Even in 1956, "underneath" Eisenhower's towering personal margin, a Democratic popular vote majority exceeding that which Kennedy won in 1960 appeared at other levels of the ticket. Finally, if 1956 is taken as a normal baseline and if it is true that Kennedy did score some relative personal success in 1960, how can we possibly explain the fact that other diverse Democrats on state tickets around the nation tended to win a greater proportion of popular votes than he attracted?

It seems more reasonable to suggest that Kennedy did not in any sense *exceed* the "normal" vote expectations of the generalized and anonymous Democratic candidate; rather, he fell visibly below these expectations, although nowhere nearly as far below them as Adlai Stevenson had fallen. This proposition is congruent not only with the general contours of election returns in the recent period, but with the great mass of sample survey data collected in the past decade as well. With this proposition we can draw into a coherent pattern the several surface characteristics which seemed intriguing from the simple 1960 vote totals. With it, we can locate the 1960 election more generally in the stream of American political history.

3. *The Basic Voting Strength of the Two Parties*

We have found it of great explanatory value to think of election results as reflecting the interplay of two sets of forces: stable, long-term partisan dispositions and short-term forces specific to the immediate election situation. The long-term partisan dispositions are very adequately represented by our measures of party identification. The stability of these dispositions over time is a matter of empirical record. Their partisan division over any period, as it may favor one party or the other, provides the point from which one must start to understand any specific election. This underlying division of loyalties lends itself admirably to the goal of indicating what a "normal" vote would be, aside from specific forces associated with the immediate election.

In these terms, the basic Democratic majority in the nation is scarcely subject to dispute. Year in and year out since 1952, national samples of the American electorate have indicated a preference for the Democratic party by a margin approaching 60–40. However, since no election in recent years has shown a Democratic margin of this magnitude, it would be as absurd to take a 60–40 Democratic majority for a baseline as it would be to work from the 1956 presidential vote. Actually there is little temptation to do so. Over the years large amounts of information have been accumulated on the behavior of people identifying with the two major parties, and it is clear that the realistic voting strength of the Democrats—and this is the sort of baseline which interests us—falls well short of a 60–40 majority. The fact that heavy Democratic majorities in the South are concealed by low voting turnout is but one factor which reduces realistic Democratic strength. Outside the South, as well, Democrats under the same conditions of short-term stimulation are less likely to vote than Republicans.

It is possible to manipulate the data in such a fashion as to take into account all of the significant discrepancies between nominal party identification and realistic voting strength. We thereby arrive at a picture of the vote division which could be expected in the normal presidential election, if short-term forces associated with the election favored neither party in particular, but stood at an equilibrium. In such circumstances, we would expect a Democratic proportion of the two-party popular vote to fall in the vicinity of 53–54 per cent. Outside of the South, such a vote would fall short of a 50–50 split with the Republicans; within the South there would be a strong Democratic majority exceeding a 2-to-1 division.

Short-term forces associated with a specific election may, according to their net partisan strength, send the actual vote in that election deviating to one side or the other of the equilibrium point. In 1952 and 1956 the popularity of Eisenhower constituted one such force, and this force was strongly pro-Republican. The distortions produced in the behaviors of party identifiers of different types have now become familiar. If the net partisan force is strong, as in 1956, identifiers of the favored party vote almost *en bloc*, without defection. The small group of "independents" who do not commit themselves to either party divide very disproportionately in favor of the advantaged party, instead of dividing their vote equally as in the equilibrium case. And members of the disfavored party defect in relatively large numbers, as Democrats did in 1956. A useful description of any specific election, then, is an account of the short-term forces which have introduced these strains across the distribution of party identification.

In such a description, the existing division of deeper party loyalties is taken for granted. Its current character is not to be explained by the immediate political situation. The point is made most clearly by the 1960 election. The fact that the Democrats enjoyed a standing majority was in no way a consequence of the personal duel between Kennedy and Nixon, for it was a majority created long before either candidate became salient as a national political figure, and long before most of the campaign "issues" of 1960 had taken shape. In this perspective, then, we can consider some of the forces which drew the 1960 vote away from its equilibrium state.

4. *Short-term Forces in the 1960 Election*

Popular vote tallies show that Kennedy received 49.8 per cent of the two-party vote outside of the South, and 51.2 per cent of the popular vote cast in the South. The vote outside the South is almost 1 per cent more Democratic than our equilibrium estimates for this part of the nation. In the South, however, the Democratic deficit relative to the same baseline approaches 17 per cent. Naturally, some short-term forces may balance out so that no net advantage accrues to either party. But the comparisons between our baselines and the 1960 vote suggest that we should find some short-term forces which gave a very slight net advantage to Kennedy outside of the South, and yet which penalized him heavily within the South.

As in all elections that attract a wide degree of public attention, a number of short-term forces were certainly at work in 1960. A comprehensive assessment of these must await further analysis. However, there can be little doubt that the religious issue was the strongest single factor overlaid on basic partisan loyalties in the 1960 election, and we have focused most of our initial analyses in this area. Fortunately we know a great deal about the "normal" voting behavior within different religious categories, and can use this knowledge to provide baselines which aid in estimating the net effect of Kennedy's Catholicism upon his candidacy.

The Catholic Vote. As we have observed, the vote division among Catholics soared from a 50–50 split in the two Eisenhower contests to an 80–20 majority in the 1960 presidential vote. However, it is hard to attribute all of this increment simply to the Kennedy candidacy. In the 1958 election, when there were mild short-term economic forces favoring the Democratic party, the vote among Catholics went well over 70 per cent in that direction. Even since our measurements of party identification began in 1952, only a small minority—less than 20 per cent—of Catholics in the nation have considered themselves as Republicans, although a fair portion have typically styled themselves as "Independents." Most of what attracted attention as a Republican trend among Catholics during the 1950's finds little support in our data, at least as a trend peculiar to Catholics. To be sure, many Democratic Catholics defected to vote for Eisenhower in 1952 and 1956. So did many Democratic Protestants. As a matter of fact, the defection rate among Democratic Catholics in 1952 was very slightly less than among Democratic Protestants, and in 1956 was very slightly more. In neither case do the differences exceed sampling error. There is some long-term evidence of a faint and slow erosion in the Catholic Democratic vote; but this has been proceeding at such a glacial pace that the 1956–1960 vote trends which we are treating here dwarf it completely. There is no reason to believe that the short-term personal "pull" exerted on Democrats generally by Eisenhower had a different strength for Catholics than for Protestants. The myths that have arisen to this effect seem to be primarily illusions stemming from the large proportion of Democrats who are Catholics. Their loss was painful in the two Eisenhower votes. But they were at the outset, and remained up to the first glimmer of the Kennedy candidacy, a strongly Democratic group.

We may specify this "normal" Democratic strength among Catholics by applying the same operations for Catholics alone that we have employed for the electorate as a whole. In the equilibrium case, it turns out that one would expect at least a 63 per cent Democratic margin among Catholics. The difference between 63 per cent and the 80 per cent which Kennedy achieved can provisionally be taken as an estimate of the increment in Democratic votes among Catholics above that which the normal, Protestant Democratic presidential candidate could have expected.

We can readily translate this 17 per cent vote gain into proportions of the total 1960 vote, taking into account levels of Catholic turnout and the like. On such grounds, it appears that Kennedy won a vote bonus from Catholics amounting to about 4 per cent of the national two-party popular vote. This increment is, of course, very unequally divided between the South and the rest of the nation, owing simply to the sparse Catholic population in the South. Within the 1960 non-Southern electorate, Kennedy's net gain from the Catholic increment amounts to better than 5 per cent of the two-party vote. The same rate of gain represents less than 1 per cent of the Southern popular vote.

The Anti-Catholic Vote. Respondents talked to our interviewers with remarkable freedom about the Catholic factor during the fall of 1960. This is not to say that all respondents referred to it as a problem. There were even signs that some Protestant respondents were struggling to avoid mention of it although it was a matter of concern. Nonetheless, nearly 40 per cent of the sample voluntarily introduced the subject before any direct probing on our part in the early stages of the pre-election questionnaire. Since this figure certainly understates the proportion of the population for whom religion was a salient concern in 1960, it testifies rather eloquently to the importance of the factor in conscious political motivations during the fall campaign.

These discussions of the Catholic question, volunteered by our respondents, will, in time, provide more incisive descriptions of the short-term anti-Catholic forces important in the election. Our interest here, however, is to estimate the magnitude of anti-Catholic voting in terms of otherwise Democratic votes which Kennedy lost. In such an enterprise, our material on the political backgrounds of our respondents is most useful.

We focus, therefore, upon the simple rates of defection to Nixon among Protestants who were identified in 1960 with the Democratic party. As Figure 1 shows, this defection rate is strongly correlated with regularity of attendance at a Protestant church. Protestant Democrats who, by self-description, never attend church, and hence are not likely to have much identification with it, defected to Nixon only at a rate of 6 per cent. This rate, incidentally, is just about the "normal" defection rate which we would predict for both parties in the equilibrium case: it represents the scattered defections which occur for entirely idiosyncratic reasons in any election. Therefore, for Democrats who were nominal Protestants but outside the psychological orbit of their church, the short-term religious force set up by a Catholic candidacy had no visible impact. However, as soon as there is some evidence of identification with a Protestant church, the defection rate rises rapidly.

Although Protestant Independents are not included in Figure 1, they show the same gradient at a different level of the two-party vote division. The few Protestant Independents not attending church split close to the theoretically-expected 50–50 point. Then the Nixon vote rises to 61 per cent in the "seldom" category; to 72 per cent for the "often" category; and to 83 per cent for the Protestant Independents attending church regularly. This increment of Republican votes above the "normal" 50–50 division for Independents matches remarkably the increment of Republican votes above the "normal" figure of 6 per cent in the case of the Democrats.

We customarily find in our data certain substantial correlations between church attendance and political behavior. The correlation between church attendance and vote among Protestant Democrats and Independents is not, however, one of these. The strong

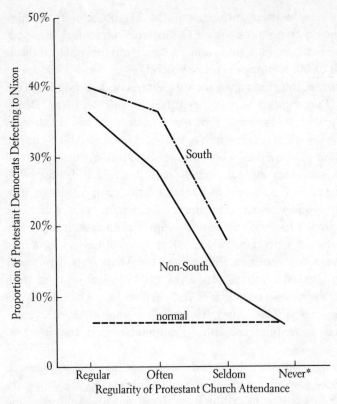

The number of Protestant Democrats who "never" attend church in the South is too small for inclusion.

Figure 1.
Defections to Nixon among Protestant
Democrats as a Function of Church Attendance.

associations seem linked in an obvious way to the 1960 election. We need not assume, of course, that each defection pictured here represents a sermon from the pulpit and an obedient member of the congregation. Social science theory assures us that whether through sermons, informal communication or a private sense of reserve toward Catholicism, the faithful Protestant would react more negatively to the presidential candidacy of a Catholic than would more indifferent Protestants. It remains notable, however, that Democrats who were at the same time regular Protestants defected to Nixon at rates far exceeding those which Eisenhower had attracted in 1952 or 1956.

We may use Figure 1, then, as a tool to estimate the magnitude of the anti-Catholic vote. It is easily argued that the area below the dotted line in Figure 1 represents "normal" defections within each category of church attendance, and that the votes represented by the triangle above the dotted line are votes which Kennedy lost on religious grounds. It is then a simple mechanical matter to convert this triangle into proportions of the popular vote for South and non-South.

On the surface, Figure 1 seems to say that the impact of the religious factor was very nearly the same, North and South, for the Southern gradient of defections is only slightly higher than the non-Southern gradient. If we think of the impact of short-term forces *on individuals* as a function of their party and religious loyalties, this conclusion is proper. Indeed, as we consider in later analyses the impact by different types of Protestantism, it may well be that the character of the impact will show no remaining regional difference whatever. However, to construe Figure 1 as suggesting that the *magnitude* of the anti-Catholic effect was about the same in votes cast in North and South is quite improper. The differences between the regions turn out to be substantial.

We must consider first that less than two-thirds of the active non-Southern electorate is Protestant, whereas within the South the electorate is almost completely (95 per cent) Protestant. Secondly, Protestants are more faithful church-goers in the South than outside it. Quite specifically, we find that over half of the Southern presidential vote is cast by Protestants who go to church regularly, whereas less than 20 per cent of the vote outside the South comes from regular, church-going Protestants. Finally, of the minority outside the South who are Protestant and attend church regularly, only a small proportion are Democratic identifiers: Republicans clearly predominate in this category. In the South, the situation is reversed, with regular Protestants being far more often than not Democratic identifiers.

This conjunction of regional differences means that the defecting votes represented in Figure 1 are of vastly different sizes, South and non-South. It turns out that outside the South regular, church-going Protestants who are Democrats cast only about 5 per cent of the total non-Southern vote. Within the South, however, regular church-going Protestants who are Democrats contributed over 35 per cent of the total Southern vote. Thus it is that the anti-Catholic impact in the South turns out to involve a much larger share of the votes than elsewhere. The anti-Catholic vote in the South fulfills our search for a short-term force of strong net Republican strength in that region.

Summing up these apparent anti-Catholic votes as proportions of the total vote in the South, the non-South, and the nation as a whole, we can compare them with our estimations of the bonuses received by Kennedy from Catholics. Table 2 shows the balance sheet.

There is every reason to believe that these preliminary estimates under-estimate the importance of religion in the 1960 vote and, in particular, under-estimate the magnitude of the anti-Catholic vote. We have at no point taken account, for example, of the possibility that certain Republican identifiers, exposed to short-term forces which would normally have produced defections to the Democrats, may have been inhibited from such defection by Kennedy's Catholicism. In the midwest there were signs of a "farm revolt" favoring the Democrats which failed to materialize in the presidential balloting. At lower levels on farm belt tickets one finds that major Democratic candidates consistently surpassed "normal" Democratic expectations. Yet Kennedy seems to have been peculiarly insulated from any of this profit-taking: in these areas he lagged behind other major Democrats by a rather consistent 5 per cent. It is difficult not to believe that at lower levels of office net short-term forces were favoring the Democrats, and

Republican identifiers were defecting at unusual rates. Analyses may show that religion was a primary force inhibiting such defections at the presidential level.

Other early glimpses of our data also suggest the estimates of anti-Catholicism in Table 2 are conservative. It is likely that a number of non-religious short-term forces generated by the campaign itself were favorable to Kennedy on balance. As a number of other surveys reported, Nixon held a substantial lead over Kennedy in the early stages. At the outset, Kennedy was little known to the public: he stood primarily as the Democratic candidate and a Catholic. As the campaign went on, other and non-religious aspects of the Kennedy image filled in, and the public

Table 2
Offsetting Effects of the Catholic Issue,
1960 Democratic Presidential Vote

Area	% of 2-party vote in area
Outside the South, Kennedy's "unexpected" . . .	
Gains from Catholics	5.2%
Losses from Protestant Democrats and Independents	−3.6
Net	+1.6%
Inside the South, Kennedy's "unexpected" . . .	
Gains from Catholics	0.7%
Losses from Protestant Democrats and Independents	−17.2
Net	−16.5%
For the nation as a whole, Kennedy's "unexpected" . . .	
Gains from Catholics	4.3%
Losses from Protestant Democrats and Independents	−6.5
Net	−2.2%

impression was usually positive. In this crucial shift in sentiment during the campaign, the television debates probably played an important role. Although there were Democrats who reacted warmly to Nixon's performance, our materials show quite strikingly that the net response to the debates favored Kennedy, as has been commonly supposed. In case studies, a reading of interviews has already turned up numerous Protestants of varying partisanship who were much more impressed by Kennedy as a candidate than by Nixon, yet who could not bring themselves to vote for a Catholic. In the measure that Kennedy's attractiveness as a candidate exceeded Nixon's and other short-term forces apart from religion were favoring the Democrats, the total popular vote should have been drawn to the Democratic side of the equilibrium point. The fact that it stayed instead on the Republican side may represent further damaging effects of religion for Kennedy.

Refined analyses at a later date will permit us to estimate more adequately the role which all the major motivational factors, including religion, played in the 1960 outcome. For the moment, however, it is impressive the degree to which the surface characteristics of the 1960 election become intelligible even when viewed simply as the result of an "ancient" and enduring division of partisan loyalties overlaid by a short-term cross-current of religious motivation.

Normally we would expect a national vote falling as close to its equilibrium point as the 1960 case to be a relatively low-turnout election. That is, a vote near the equilibrium point suggests either weak short-term forces or else a balance of stronger forces creating conflict in individuals and thereby lowering their motivation to vote. It is rare that forces strong enough to compel indifferent citizens to come out and vote do not also favor one party over the other quite categorically.

In 1960, however, the motivational picture underlying the vote was somewhat different, and can best be understood by separating the Protestant South from the rest of the nation. In the South, of course, a strong and unidirectional short-term force was reflected in a sharp departure from equilibrium and a surge in turnout, as fits normal expectations. What is abnormal is that this strong Republican short-term force raised motivation in a Democratic preserve, rather than diluting it through conflict. It is likely that conflict *was* created, especially where Democratic partisanship was strong. "Strong" Democrats in our sample made virtually no contribution to the 1960 rise in Southern turnout. The increase came from weaker Democrats, whose participation increased so radically over 1952 and 1956 that their turnout even surpassed that of strong Democrats in very exceptional fashion. For these voters, it seems likely that such forces as anti-Catholic feelings rapidly overcame relatively weak party loyalties and left strong motivation to turn out.

While turnout elsewhere did not show the same remarkable surge which appeared in the South, it remained at the fairly high level characteristic of the 1952 and 1956 elections, despite a partisan division of the vote near the regional equilibrium point. Strong balancing forces appear to have been in operation which did not create much conflict within individuals. The reason is clear: to the degree that religious motivations were engaged, forces were conflicting between groups rather than within individuals. Non-Southern Catholics, predominantly Democratic, were exposed to strong unidirectional short-term forces motivating them to get out and vote for Kennedy. Non-Southern Protestants, predominantly Republican, were exposed to contrary forces, at least where Protestant religious fidelity was strong. Thus the vote fell near the equilibrium point, but there was rather high turnout as well.

The other surface characteristics of the election are equally intelligible in these terms. Despite his position as majority candidate, Kennedy very nearly lost and tended to run behind his ticket. In the northeast, where concentrations of Catholics are greatest, his relation to the rest of the ticket was not generally unfavorable. The penalty he suffered becomes visible and consistent in the Midwest, where Catholics are fewer and Protestant church attendance is more regular. In the South, and for the same reasons, the dif-

ferences between the Kennedy vote and that of other Democrats
become large indeed. Everywhere, if one compares 1956 vote statistics with 1960 statistics, the course of political change is closely
associated with the religious composition of voting units.

There was some relief even outside the more committed Democratic circles when the Kennedy victory, slight though it was,
demonstrated that a Catholic was not in practice barred from
the White House. Yet it would be naive to suppose that a
Catholic candidate no longer suffers any initial disadvantage
before the American electorate as a result of his creed. Not only
did Kennedy possess a type of personal appeal which the television
debates permitted him to exploit in unusual measure, but he was
also the candidate of a party enjoying a fundamental majority in
the land. Even the combination of these circumstances was barely
sufficient to give him a popular vote victory. Lacking such a
strong underlying majority, which Al Smith most certainly lacked
in 1928, it is doubtful that the most attractive of Catholic presidential candidates in 1960 would have had much chance of
success. It remains to be seen how far the experience of a Catholic
president may diminish the disadvantage another time.

5. *The 1960 Election in Historical Perspective*

In a publication which appeared a few months prior to the 1960
elections we posed the question of "how long a party can hope to
hold the White House if it does not have a majority of the party-
identified electorate." We had identified the two Eisenhower
victories as "deviating elections," in which short-term forces had
brought about the defeat of the majority party. We had not
found any evidence in our 1952 or 1956 studies that these short-
term forces were producing any significant realignment in the
basic partisan commitments of the electorate. We felt that unless
such a realignment did occur, "the minority party [could] not hope
to continue its tenure in office over a very extended period."

We now know that the eight-year Eisenhower period ended

with no basic change in the proportions of the public who identify themselves as Republican, Democrat, or Independent. If there had been an opportunity in 1952 for the Republican party to re-win the majority status it had held prior to 1932, it failed to capitalize on it. The Democratic party remained the majority party and the 1960 election returned it to the presidency. It was, to extend the nomenclature of our earlier publication, a "rein-stating" election, one in which the party enjoying a majority of party identifiers returns to power. The 1960 election was remark-able not in the fact that the majority party was reinstated but that its return to power was accomplished by such a narrow margin. We had recognized the possibility that "the unfolding of national and international events and the appearance of new political figures" might swing the vote away from its natural equilibrium. We now see that such a deflection did occur and that it very nearly cost the majority party the election.

It may be argued that the deficit the Democratic presidential candidate suffered from his normal expectation did not derive from damaging circumstances which were specific to the 1960 election but from a progressive weakening in the willingness of some Democratic partisans to support their ticket at the presidential level. It has been suggested that some voters who consider themselves to be Democrats and customarily favor Democratic candidates at the lower levels of office may have come during the Eisenhower period to have a perverse interest in favoring Republican candidates for president, either because of notions of party balance in government, because of local considerations in their states, or simply out of admiration for Eisenhower.

Important differences no doubt exist between voting at the presidential level and voting for a congressman. Our studies have shown, for example, that the popular vote for lesser offices is a more party-determined vote than the vote for president and varies around the normal equilibrium vote figure within a much narrower range than does the presidential vote. However, the supposition that Kennedy failed to win a normal Democratic majority because of a cadre of Democrats who are covertly Republican in their presidential voting is not supported by our data.

Table 1 has already demonstrated that the over-all shift in partisanship of the vote between 1956 and 1960 cannot be explained as a simple unilateral movement of erstwhile Eisenhower Democrats. The election did not depend, as was often supposed, upon the number of Eisenhower Democrats whom Nixon could retain as "covert Republicans." Our panel materials show that if Nixon had been forced to depend only upon the Eisenhower Democrats whom he retained, he would have suffered a convincing 54–46 defeat, assuming that other Democrats had continued to vote for Kennedy. He did not suffer such a defeat because he drew a new stream of Democratic defections nearly sufficient to put him in the White House.

The patterns of short-term forces in the 1960 election were independent of those shaping the 1956 election, then, in the sense that they affected a new set of people, on new grounds. There were Democrats susceptible to Eisenhower in 1956; there were Democrats sensitive to religion in 1960: the two sets of people do not intersect much more than one would expect by chance. In short, there is little evidence that the two Eisenhower elections had created a set of Democrats peculiarly disposed to vote for a Republican presidential candidate.

Analysis of our 1960 data is not sufficiently complete to enable us to describe the entire pattern of forces to which the electorate was reacting on Election Day. We do not know, for example, what the partisan impact of international affairs, which had favored the Republican candidate so strongly in the preceding two elections, was in the 1960 election. We do not know the effect of the Negro discrimination issues. We do not know in detail as yet how the personal attributes of the major candidates, other than their religious affiliations, were evaluated by the public. We feel confident, however, that we will not find any short-term force which moved as large a fraction of the 1960 electorate as did the issue of a Catholic president. This was the major cause of the net departure of the vote totals from the division which the comparative underlying strength of the two parties in 1960 would have led us to expect. After two consecutive "deviating" elections won at a presidential level by the minority party, the 1960 election reinstated the Democratic party. But short-term forces generated by the immediate 1960 situation once again favored the Republicans on balance, and the difference in votes which separated this "reinstating election" from a third "deviating election" was slight indeed.

Lonesome Lyndon

The Wrong Man from the Wrong Place at the Wrong Time

by Eric F. Goldman

The White House years of Lyndon B. Johnson (1963–1969) be-
gan in national tragedy, shifted quickly to national euphoria, and
ended in national crisis. On the domestic front, Johnson's presi-
dency produced more significant federally sponsored change in
American society than any administration since Franklin Roose-
velt's.

Johnson had earned his political spurs as a young New Dealer
in the National Youth Administration, then as a pro-Roosevelt
Texas congressman. He entered the Senate during the Truman
administration, became its Democratic leader early in the Eisen-
hower years, and played a dominant and generally conservative
role in Senate policy-making throughout the 1950's. An unsuc-
cessful candidate for the 1960 Democratic nomination, he startled
the nation by agreeing to become John Kennedy's running-mate.
After the election Johnson chafed noticeably in the reduced role
of Vice President for nearly three years. Then Kennedy's assassi-
nation in November 1963 gave him the top job.

Johnson's first months as President were occupied necessarily
with the business of replacing Kennedy men with his own, and in
formulating presidential goals in foreign and domestic policy. The

Kennedy-Johnson transition, on balance, took place less rancorously and with more effective continuity that the shift to a Truman administration after FDR's death.

But mid-1964 a Kennedy faction, "Camelot"-in-exile, had resurfaced in Washington, rallying around the indeterminate yet high-level ambitions of Attorney-General Robert F. Kennedy. Johnson rejected Kennedy, however, and made Hubert H. Humphrey, a long-time Senate colleague, but a liberal, the vice-presidential candidate in 1964. LBJ criss-crossed the country denouncing Republican Barry Goldwater as a trigger-happy rightwinger who might stumble into an unrestricted land war in Vietnam and perhaps beyond that, into nuclear catastrophe. Bolstered by defections among prominent Republican liberals who recoiled from Goldwater, Johnson proposed major advances in health care for the aged, federal aid to education, civil rights legislation, and assistance to the nation's hard-pressed cities—a virtual "war on poverty" that he claimed would produce a "Great Society."

Johnson won the greatest electoral sweep in American history, defeating Goldwater by sixteen million votes, 43 million to 27 million. Goldwater, on his program of uncompromising, doctrinaire conservatism and opposition to civil rights legislation, carried only his home state of Arizona and five others, all in the Deep South. Even more significant than Johnson's 61.1 per cent of the major party vote was the extraordinary length of his presidential coattails; Democrats won two-to-one majorities in both houses of Congress.

Within two years, these congressional majorities passed substantial portions of the "Great Society" program. Before the 1966 congressional elections, Democrats, aided by liberal Republican votes, had passed a major health program for the aged (Medicare); a billion-dollar aid-to-education measure; an even larger antipoverty program; major public housing and public works legislation; a strong Civil Rights Act that finally provided federal registrars to protect Negro voters in the South; legislation prohibiting racial discrimination in public housing; rent supplements for low-income families; a "model cities" program appropriating federal funds for the nation's under-financed urban areas; and other significant pieces of reform legislation.

In 1966, however, a conservative mood set in, as voters sent 47 more Republicans to the House and 4 more to the Senate, making even the President's strongest congressional supporters leery of further social experiments. By that time riots in the black ghettoes of Northern and Western cities had carved inroads into public support for additional federal civil rights action, and American escalation in Vietnam had produced further bloodshed but no victory. Assailed with increasing ferocity by both conservatives and left-liberals, especially the latter, Johnson's dream of a liberal-moderate coalition supporting a "politics of consensus" evaporated. His once-unassailable popularity had plummeted by 1968. The President announced his decision not to run again in a dramatic March 1968 television speech. The bitter anti-administration primary fights between Eugene McCarthy and Robert Kennedy and Kennedy's June assassination were accompanied by George Wallace's third-party defection, and climaxed by massive demonstrations and police violence at the 1968 Chicago Democratic Convention.

The remnants of Johnson's "Great Society" coalition fought the ensuing campaign in a state of apathetic shock against Richard Nixon's well-organized, well-financed Republican drive. Nixon's victory with a plurality of popular votes over Hubert Humphrey and George Wallace's "American Independents" (a flag-waving label thinly disguising his anti-black party) sealed the demise of Lyndon Johnson's bitter tenure as a national leader. Never had a ruling political party's fortunes been brought so low so quickly and by so few. Eric Goldman, a historian of American reform, who spent several unhappy years as a Johnson adviser, analyzes below "the tragedy of Lyndon Johnson."

❦ Lyndon Johnson is about to leave the White House with every appearance of a thoroughly repudiated President. Since Herbert Hoover rode down Pennsylvania Avenue on a cold day

From the *New York Times Magazine*, January 5, 1969. Copyright © 1969 by Eric F. Goldman, adapted from the book *The Tragedy of Lyndon Johnson* published by Afred A. Knopf.

in 1933, no President has ended his tenure with so few hosannas and so widespread a sense of good riddance.

The story, it seems, is simple: the accident of Dallas made Lyndon Johnson President, and he failed to measure up. So it appears—but in the field of evaluating Presidents, appearances can be sharply deceiving. The cardinal rule for any historian venturing into it is to remember that he is a historian, not History, and that no powers of divination have been bestowed upon him by his profession or even by his abounding faith in his own judgment. Yet I think it should be suggested, and with emphasis, that after the furies of the sixties are laid to rest, Lyndon Johnson may well rank a good deal above where the national mood would now place him.

Certainly in past instances the public esteem of a President during his period in office has borne no particular relationship to future judgment. In 1962, the late historian Arthur M. Schlesinger, Sr., asked 75 well-known scholars of American history to rate the Chief Executives up to John Kennedy. The preponderant opinion called five Presidents "great" in this order: Abraham Lincoln, George Washington, Franklin Roosevelt, Woodrow Wilson and Thomas Jefferson. Again in order, it placed in the "near-great" category Andrew Jackson, Theodore Roosevelt, James Polk, Harry Truman, John Adams and Grover Cleveland. The historians categorized as failures Ulysses Grant and Warren Harding. Popular sentiment in 1962 probably would have gone along with most of these judgments. But of the 11 men called "great" or "near-great," five—Jefferson, Lincoln, T.R., F.D.R. and Truman—were subject to widespread and sustained abuse during their incumbencies. Woodrow Wilson was also roundly repudiated, first by the Senate and then by the voters, on the issue of his most cherished program, the League of Nations. Harry Truman, a man reviled during much of his Presidency, went through an almost identical withdrawal ceremony just 16 years before Lyndon Johnson. Then, while still living, he emerged a favorite of the historians and something of a folk hero. The two Chief Executives deemed failures by a later generation, Ulysses Grant and Warren Harding, were enormously popular during their Presidencies. It is rarely remembered that when the Harding funeral train crossed the United States, it called forth a grief, respect and affection fully equal to, if not exceeding, the public reaction to the death of Abraham Lincoln.

The question of a President's just place in history is complicated not only by shifts in opinion as time passes but by the inherent difficulties of the assessment process. Schlesinger included among the men to whom he sent his 1962 questionnaire a sometime historian, President John Kennedy. J.F.K. was interested, started to fill out the ballot then stopped. "How the hell can you tell?" he remarked. "Only the President himself can know what his real pressures and his real alternatives are. If you don't know that, how can you judge performance?" Historian-President John Kennedy's ultimate test seemed to be concrete achievements. This was an intriguing commentary on the problem of judging Presidents from a Chief Executive who, at least in domestic affairs during his short tenure, was far more notable as an opinion builder than as an achiever of specific legislation.

Of course, central to any long-range judgment of the Johnson Administration is the President's decision to commit American combat forces in the Vietnam war. I happen to be among those who became convinced that the action was a grave mistake; and if this assessment—which seems to be that of so many Americans in 1969—holds, the Vietnam war will certainly prove a heavy drag on the L.B.J. reputation. Just how heavy is quite a different matter. Other Presidents who are today called great or near-great made moves in foreign policy which are now considered serious errors. But with the passage of the years, the specific was submerged in the general memory of the man. If President Johnson or his successor can bring the Vietnam war to an end without much further damage, in time a kindly haze may obscure the pointless clomp of American soldiers across a defenseless civilization, what amounts to an American defeat, even napalm.

This is the more possible because the future might emphasize that, in a sense, L.B.J. inherited the Vietnam commitment. Three previous Chief Executives had ordered American noncombat involvement in the area. At least two of these Presidents, Eisenhower and Kennedy, believed that preventing South Vietnam from coming under Communist rule was important to American national security. None faced a situation in which the region appeared about to fall, and consequently none had to decide whether preventing a Communist takeover was important enough to justify United States entrance into the fighting war. Lyndon Johnson was forced to make that judgment, and another generation may decide that he committed an error prepared for by his predecessors and one which either President Eisenhower or President Kennedy might have made.

And always there is the possibility which many anti-L.B.J. commentators of the nineteen-sixties simply refuse to entertain: the Vietnam intervention might not have been a mistake at all. President Johnson could be right when he says, let the future decide. A Communist victory in South Vietnam, he was convinced, would be followed by a gradual fall of much of Asia to Communism, the domination of the huge region by a hostile and potentially powerful China and—because China had not been warned by a strong American stand—by ultimate war between China and the United States. If a successor to President Johnson should accept a compromise peace that was followed by such a chain of developments, Lyndon Johnson would be more than forgiven; he would emerge a figure of Churchillian stature, a wise, courageous voice crying out in a crowd of myopic and timid men.

L.B.J.'s place in the long sweep of American domestic affairs can be assessed with much more assurance. Three times in the twentieth century the United States has faced up to the harsh facts of an industrializing, urbanizing civilization—at the beginning of the century, under Theodore Roosevelt and Woodrow Wilson; after the crash of 1929, under Franklin Roosevelt; and then, slowly, in the period following World War II.

The thirties were *sui generis*. The urgency was unique; so too was the public mood. The situations in the early nineteen-hundreds and after World War II were much more alike. In both instances, there was little sense that the country was falling apart. National opinion, jabbed by a zealous left and troubled by the arguments of a dogged right, was gradually forming around the proposition that the general population was being given too little access to economic and social opportunity. More laws were needed; the President ought to lead Congress in getting them.

At the start of the century Theodore Roosevelt bounded into the White House, caught up the strands of dissidence, wove them into an attractive pattern. "Teddy," the journalist William Allen White observed, "was reform in a derby, the gayest, cockiest, most fashionable derby you ever saw." T.R. moved few bills through Congress, but he prepared the way for Woodrow Wilson, who, without derby or gaiety, had the roused public sentiment, the votes in Congress and the Covenanter certitudes to grind the bills through the House and the Senate.

After World War II, the process began all over again. The opinion kept building, the opposition kept fighting and another generation of leaders prepared the way for another wave of action. Harry Truman, his expletives and vetoes poised, fought off a Congress that yearned to turn back. Dwight Eisenhower, before he drifted into his second somnolent term, led the Republican party into some accommodation with the day. John Kennedy appeared, a second Theodore Roosevelt, associating social change with vigor and glamour and the mischievous cocked eye, legislating little but educating many. Then Lyndon Johnson, the cloakroom operator, reenacted the presbyter-professor Woodrow Wilson. He, too, seized the moment to execute the decade's needs—seized it so firmly and wrung it so hard that he built a monument to himself as big as all Texas in that 1965 Congress, which wrote into law just about everything that the public had decided was long past due.

And all the while, breaking out now and again, however explained or explained away, came the voice which spoke of something far removed from cloakroom chicanery, which caught the age-old American insistence that somehow, by some effort of hardheadedness and decency, ordinary men and women can be enabled to live in greater comfort and joy and to walk in the tonic air of self-respect. The voice was there. . . .

. . . when L.B.J., told by a visitor that he was rushing Congress, replied, "An old man on the Hill said to me a long time ago that there are some Administrations that do and some that don't. This one is gonna do";

. . . when he signed an education bill, a mist across his cratered face, and muttered: "Not enough, not nearly enough. But I'm proud, damned proud, to have got this much. Education—that's what's needed, and that's what every kid ought to get, as much of it as he can take, right up to his neck";

. . . when he told a group of corporation executives: "I have thought a great deal the last few days—I missed being an elevator boy by just about that much, when my mother reached up and made me go back to school after laying out for two years. When you're dealing with these [Negro] people, in your company, or in your firm, or in your business, just remember it's some daughter's father, or some boy's mother, or someone's sister, or somebody's brother that you are dealing with. And except for the grace of God, it might be you. And think how you would like it if you lived in a land where you could not go to school with your fellow Americans, where you could not work alongside of them, where you could travel from Texas to Washington, across many states, and not be able to go to the bathroom without hiding in a thicket or dodging behind a culvert. Ask yourself how you would feel";

. . . and when, addressing a White House Conference on Natural Beauty, he shoved aside his prepared text and spoke his memories of boyhood walks: ". . . those hills, and those fields, and the river were the only world that I really had in those years. . . . We were not a wealthy family, but this was my rich inheritance. All my life I have drawn strength, and something more,

from those Texas hills. Sometimes, in the highest councils of the
nation, in this house, I sit back and I can almost feel that rough,
unyielding, sticky clay soil between my toes, and it stirs memories
that often give me comfort and sometimes give me a pretty firm
purpose.

"But not all the boys in America had the privilege to grow up
in a wide and open country. We can give them something, and
we are going to. We can let each of them feel a little of what the
first settlers must have felt, as they stood there before the majesty
of our great land."

History has been generous, and should be, to Presidents who
have talked like that and taken action to turn the talk into laws.
Probably history will be generous—and it should be—to Lyndon
Johnson.

Probably—but all this is in the murky realm of speculation.
There remains a hard, clear fact. Lyndon Johnson has served his
whole five years in the White House with little genuine hold on
the thinking or on the emotions of the American people.

What went so wrong? Obviously, he has been an able, hardworking Chief Executive, eager to serve the interests of the mass
of the population, more than eager to win their camaraderie. He
tried desperately hard, and he delivered in important respects.
Lyndon Johnson not only put through a powerhouse program of
legislation. He had taken over the Presidency at a moment of
national emotional disarray and conducted a transition that is
considered by many experts the most skillful the United States
has ever known. He went on to preside over a country marked
by that condition which so often has been the prime test of the
public's attitude toward an Administration—an America that was
generally prosperous, in fact more prosperous than any society in
all of man's 5,000 years of recorded history.

White House aides kept telling President Johnson that the
whole source of the public's disaffection was what the aides called
his "courageous" stand on Vietnam. Well before I resigned from
the White House staff, I became accustomed to the litany. Any

war creates frustration and resentment, he was told, and discontent is always directed at the leader. Abraham Lincoln himself was assailed with unbridled vehemence. Modern limited wars, with their especially frustrating quality, exacerbate these public feelings.

Yet L.B.J.'s unpopularity cannot be so totally attributed to the Vietnam war. Actually, American wars have generally made of the Commander in Chief a rallying point for support and enthusiasm. Moreover, as early as 1965—before his foreign policy became a major divisive issue and when L.B.J. was at the height of his successes—a widespread distaste for him was plain. Many Americans have been snappish about Lyndon Johnson not so much because they were positive he was wrong on Vietnam but because they believed he was the kind of man who was quite capable of making a bad mistake and, having made it, of not admitting it or moving to correct it.

During the campaign of 1964, when the evidence indicated both that President Johnson would win easily and that the trend was as much anti-Goldwater as pro-Johnson, Lyndon Johnson would remark querulously to visitors, "Why don't people like me?" One guest, too old to be concerned about preferment by the White House and enough of a Washington character to get away with irreverence, answered the question. He said, "Because, Mr. President, you are not a very likable man." Bald as it was, this statement expressed a major part of L.B.J.'s problem with the American people. The fact that he was not a very likable man could not be concealed from the public despite all the arduous efforts of his friends and aides, myself included, who wanted so much to believe otherwise and who did their damnedest to present him in a way that would convince themselves and the country.

Lyndon Johnson may have risen from Johnson City to being the head of a family he cherished, a multimillionaire and the leader of the free world, but he had not risen above something nagging inside him. All the way to the top, and especially at the top, he was cumulatively, combatively insecure. Having started out as the apple of his mother's eye, overloved, overprotected and over-praised, he was thoroughly unprepared for a world that did not view him in such a glow. In his youth he was keenly sensitive to the fact that the Johnsons were not among the leading families of the area. He himself was gawky and no great charmer.

Maturing in an action-worshiping environment, it took him a long time to realize the high value of one resource he had in abundance: brains. By then, the asset was denigrated even in his own eyes by the low status of his schooling (a social abyss existed between his alma mater, Southwest Texas State Teachers College, and the University of Texas). And almost as soon as his career was really started, he had to function in large measure not amid the congenial ways of Texas but in the sharply different atmosphere of Washington.

Of course, the L.B.J. genes dictated that he would have had many of his personal characteristics if he had been born a graceful son of a Brahmin family. But a sense of insecurity was so thoroughly woven into the man by external circumstances that it brought to a high state of development his innate tendencies. Facing a world that he thought looked down on him, he sought constantly to prove, to himself and to it, that he could beat it. Dubious whether people liked him, he pleaded, clawed and maneuvered to have them love him. Desperately seeking proof of loyalty—from friends, aides and the public—he pushed his demand for loyalty close to the point where it meant obeisance. He was ready to give anything—his own driving efforts, sentiment, preferment for their wishes—to hold this loyalty, anything except what people wanted and what his lurking suspicion of them held back, the gift of his genuine self.

Toward the longtime members of his entourage, L.B.J. could be considerate and more than considerate. One aide who found himself overwhelmed by family medical expenses received a substantial financial gift from "a friend"; a person working with the President before a meal—be he a high official or a secretary who had been taking dictation—might be invited to eat with the family. But all the while Lyndon Johnson not only felt it necessary to keep testing the devotion of his most veteran assistants but to assert his mastery in scenes of demeaning tongue-lashing and by manipulating them with extremes of the carrot-and-stick technique. An aide would go along for some time, receiving extravagant praise. Then, for no particular reason, he was excommunicated, his work rejected almost *in toto* and the man himself scarcely spoken to. Just as suddenly, he would be reinstated, and someone else given the treatment.

The insecurity mounted in proportion as President Johnson was removed from familiar situations and types of people. In the spring of 1964, he approved a suggestion that he lunch with a group of writers who had distinguished themselves by their books on Presidents or the Presidency. L.B.J. was at a high point in his administration; his polls were soaring, his bills were rolling through Congress, he had just settled a labor-management deadlock in the railroad industry which two presidents, Congress, three Secretaries of Labor and endless committees and boards had failed to resolve. Yet this group, markedly different from his usual associates, roused all kinds of defenses. He treated the guests warily, almost like a hostile force, and he ended up smothering their efforts at conversation by a near-compulsive monologue. In between, he got onto a protective, complaining theme that he was not given a "fair shake as President because I am a Southerner." It was an intimation of a later Lyndon Johnson who would growl about criticism of the Vietnam war: "I'll never be given credit for anything I do in foreign policy because I didn't go to Harvard."

Always fighting off the devils of insecurity, Lyndon Johnson was vain, not proud; boomerish, not confident; to a considerable extent he was grandiose, not grand, in conceiving his programs and grandiloquent, not eloquent, in expressing them. Gnawed by his inner needs, he turned a Congressional career shot through with instincts for the national good into a feral pursuit of personal domination, and a Presidency marked by a broad streak of idealism into what so often appeared an exercise in self-interest.

Self-interest—here is the only-too-well-recognized part of the

L.B.J. story. As a student of history, I have read a great deal about men who are said to have been motivated merely by self-aggrandizement. I have never really believed the analyses. I think over the array of people I have known well, many of whom are not particularly noble, and they have never seemed totally dominated by self-interest. Neither was Lyndon Johnson—and perhaps Lyndon Johnson especially was not.

But President Johnson, lashed by his insecurity, fought his better angels harder than any man I have ever known. It was a hostile world out there, far removed from mother and Texas and his trusted buddies; you had to keep handling it. Most of the time he appeared afraid to rely on anything except the doctrine that life and politics and government are simply a conflict and confluence between the self-interest of various people and groups. He seemed driven to function as Machiavelli in a Stetson, part of which posture was to keep assuring everyone that rugged he-men in Stetsons would never be Machiavellis.

So lacking in confidence, so defensive and wary, those hard eyes always searching the room or across the country for enemies, he was determined that nobody and no circumstance would get the better of him by playing to his strong personal ideals and emotions. This attitude led to increasing justification for, and ever more extended practice of, his natural bent toward exorbitant secretiveness, labyrinthine maneuverings, a sanctimonious glossing over of reality, the plain withholding of truth which had no need of being withheld and the plain distortion of truth which, at least in part, was much better stated and done with.

The American public delights in ferreting out the shortcomings of its Chief Executives. A nation of President-watchers knew that Franklin Roosevelt was an incorrigible political gamesman, that Harry Truman could sound like the village calliope, that Dwight Eisenhower often tried to grin away massive problems, that John Kennedy had some of the frailties as well as the assets of the charmer. But endlessly critical, it has also shown itself remarkably indulgent, provided that the virtues of the President appear to outweigh his defects. In this balance, the critical weight is the judgment that at bottom the President is a "good man," fundamentally decent, putting the welfare of the nation first in all his really important considerations. Most Americans have believed this to be true of every president from the thirties through 1963. It was a fundamental difficulty of Lyndon Johnson that he did not leave such an impression.

His background of the Texas wheeler-dealers, his long years as a Congressional manipulator and the association with Bobby Baker, his family's accumulation of considerable wealth based on a Government-regulated television station, his very appearance and mannerisms which easily suggested the riverboat gambler—all had prepared the public for skepticism of his basic motives as soon as he entered the White House. Nothing happened to change that attitude. Even the two achievements that President Johnson considered irreproachable brought him no surcease from suspicion.

He felt that he had incontestably established his right to the national leadership by his landslide victory in the election of 1964. But millions came to feel that he had incontestably established that he was ready to double-talk about anything, including taking the country into a grisly war, in order to win votes. He believed that the great success of his legislative program after the election earned him the confidence and admiration of the nation. The great success of that drive was, among other things, his great undoing; it made more people more sure that he did everything only by political legerdemain and only for political advantage.

It was within this context that the charge of credibility gap cut so deeply. Other modern Chief Executives—widely popular ones like Theodore and Franklin Roosevelt, Dwight Eisenhower and John Kennedy—had been known to play fast and loose with the facts. President Johnson not only played faster and looser; he did it amid a widespread conviction that self-serving deceit was part of his essential make-up.

This distrust militated powerfully against his whole Presidential leadership. It went beyond stripping him of much of the credit for his domestic legislative achievements; with the credit blunted, it dulled public interest in helping him make the laws work. "Why don't people, especially young people," President Johnson once complained, "really jump into the poverty program, roll up their sleeves and get it roaring, like we did back in the New Deal?" None of the men in the room with the President had the heart to tell him.

In foreign policy, the pervasive suspicion meant that L.B.J. was given little benefit of the doubt. Worried citizens, facing World War I, World War II or the Korean War, had been inclined to hesitate before opposing the President. He was a good man doing his best, with greater knowledge of the situation than themselves; the odds were that he was right. Few worried citizens hesitated to oppose Lyndon Johnson's Vietnam policy, and once in opposition, their attacks came with special virulence.

There was President Lyndon Johnson, the human being, and then there was President Lyndon Johnson, the maker of and symbol of certain national policies.

Those policies were coming from a man of exceedingly high intelligence. Many times when I have remarked this, during and after my White House days, people have looked at me as if I were a sycophant of the President or as if, during my association with him, I had taken leave of my good sense. Of course, they were thinking of intelligence in terms of a well-educated mind or, I'm afraid, being stuffy and parochial and finding it impossible to associate brains with a man who looked like a polished cowboy and who drawled out so much buncombe and bawdiness. They were decidedly wrong. After years of meeting first-rate minds in and out of universities, I am sure I have never met a more intelligent person than Lyndon Johnson—intelligent in terms of sheer I.Q.— a clear, swift, penetrating mind, with an abundance of its own type of imagination and subtlety.

The point is that little had happened to fill or to stretch this mind. The high school Lyndon Johnson attended, Johnson City High School, was so bad it lacked accreditation even by the lax standards of its region. Southwest Texas State Teachers College taught a watery pedagogese. Almost nothing in such schooling suggested to Lyndon Johnson that, once out of college, he ought to read books, travel, seek out interesting people, try to keep up with new trends, shake himself out of Johnson City and into the later twentieth century. Uncomfortable in the bigger world, obsessed with his political career, he had no personal urge to do these things. The powerful mind was feeding on small fare. The grown man came to the White House with a grab-bag of facts and non-facts, conceptions and misconceptions, ways of thinking and ways to avoid thought which had been gathered largely from his early crabbed environment.

It was this mental matrix which explains why, in his basic policy attitudes, L.B.J. was a passé President all the while he crowded the daily television screens. A man out of a kind of boondocks liberalism that had marked one element in Texas politics, he was easily able to move into New Dealism and to take over much of the tone of the thirties, but for the most part he stopped there. The United States did not stop at all. Nations change not at a steady pace but in slow swings or in rampant rushes, and America had been rampaging between the thirties and the sixties. The alterations were so swift and so deep that the country was changing right out from under President Lyndon Johnson.

Like a good nineteen-thirties man, he expressed his authentic thinking during the campaign of 1964 when he would shout, "Remember Molly and the children," or "We Americans don't want much. We want decent food, housing and clothing." In the nineteen-sixties there were still plenty of Mollies with plenty of troubles. But the essential mass problem had shifted; it was less food, housing and clothing than how to live with a weirdly uneasy affluence, marked by maldistributions that a significant part of the population was no longer ready to accept and a mounting race problem that was only in part economic. Like F.D.R., President Johnson might think of domestic policy in terms of satisfying the economic and social urges of the grand political coalition which dominated the period before World War II—labor, the farmers, the cities, the minorities and the youthful voters. But now much of labor sounded like threatened burghers, and the farm vote was disappearing into technology. The uplifted white minorities had been lifted to a condition where their concern was less social legislation than assuaging their own status trauma. The cities meant more and more the Negroes; the Negroes were wondering how much they wanted to do with any white leadership. The youthful, whether moving left, right or careering down the middle, were inclined to think of bread-and-butter liberalism as quaint, if not downright camp.

Among all age groups, the idealism which had helped sweep along the F.D.R. program, and which L.B.J. kept trying to touch, now sought not simply better pay for teachers and more school buildings but a drastically altered educational atmosphere and curriculum; not simply Medicare but aid for the aged fitted into a whole social welfare structure that found a way of asserting human dignity; not simply civil rights laws but a society in which civil rights laws would not be necessary. A new era, a new pattern of social and political forces, a new agenda—President Johnson, acting upon the kind of consensus domestic policy that would merely codify and expand the programs of the thirties, was about as contemporary as padded shoulders, a night at the radio and Clark Gable.

Again in the mood of the thirties, President Johnson assumed that foreign policy was something you had, like measles, and got over with as quickly as possible. Suddenly forced to confront the world, he reached into the past and laid hold of an attic doctrine which included even apostrophes to the flag and international deeds of derring-do. At the farthest stretch of his modernity, he reached thinking that was substantially of cold war vintage.

In the nineteen-sixties, a considerable and influential part of the public simply would not go along with such a foreign policy. They assumed that international affairs were a constant high-priority subject. Contemptuous of talk of the flag and derring-do, they were alarmed by what they were sure were outmoded cold war attitudes of crusading against Communism and of joining with foreign regimes that sought to use military power to stop social change. Out of a sense of guilt over America's past role in world affairs, a sympathy with the aspirations of underdeveloped nations and fear of nuclear holocaust, they favored accommodation, compromise, political and economic rather than military moves.

Many of these critics were Metro-Americans, part of a group in the cities and even more in the suburbs which was steadily growing in numbers and in its influence in determining national opinion. Relative to the rest of the country, the Metro-American was youthful, well-educated, affluent, more likely to have some minority blood in his veins. His mind had been shaped by an environment which had been good to him. It was no less formed by an American scene of irritating big organizations, brassy media and grinding social dislocations, and by a world situation of wars and threats of still worse wars. His thinking and his attitudes were a tangle of ambivalence. The Metro-American was avidly on the make, economically and socially, but he shied away from the appearance of sheer money-making or sheer caste and preferred the manner of public-spiritedness and cultivation. He had ideals but was skeptical of other people's—and even, a bit, of his own. He was liberal but without ideology; tolerant but intolerant of dogoodism; flexible, pragmatic and a devotee of the ironic edge.

Metro-America was increasingly the focal point of the abrasion between President Johnson and his public. There the uneasiness with him as a human being was greatest; the dissatisfaction with his domestic and foreign policies, the strongest. There, too, was the chief gathering place for a disaffection that joined the criticisms of the man and of his programs and added a third—that one concerning "style"—which really had little to do with the other two but increased the virulence of both.

The Metro-American—whether living in New York, Chicago, San Francisco or Houston—tended to take his style of life from the successful classes of the Northeast; to him, everything else was darkest boorishness. Over the years Texas and Texas mores had become a cherished subject for the gibes of Metro-American cocktail parties. Mention almost any of the personal habits of Lyndon Johnson—whether the sentimentalists or the big white Continental on a roar down a Texas highway—and you brought up something that made Metro-America snicker.

And always there were the Kennedys. After his sweeping victory in 1964, President Johnson may have eliminated virtually all references to President Kennedy in his public remarks. He could not eliminate the fact that his predecessor was legend and that the legend was a restive, bitter, yearning element in the whole life of the generation, especially in Metro-America. Not only did the urge to be different from J.F.K. affect what L.B.J. did and did not do day after day; every difficulty of President Johnson with public opinion was magnified by the Kennedy legend, which made John Kennedy precisely the opposite of all the things that Americans, and especially Metro-Americans, thought were wrong with Lyndon Johnson.

Eight times American Vice Presidents become Presidents have had to cope with the memory of the men they succeeded. Only once has the new Chief Executive been faced not only with a memory but with its living embodiment in a large, talented, energetic, abundantly endowed family, most of whom considered Lyndon Johnson a temporary and unfortunate interruption of the Kennedy years and one of whom thought so from a powerful political base.

Senator Robert F. Kennedy was the looks, the voice, the long stabbing finger of the martyred President. He was youthfulness, celebritese, the Northeast, the new-mode family, canoeing into high rapids and then sitting quoting Aeschylus; the Metro-American's unabashed ambition and the Metro-American's delight in the throw-away manner. He was post-nineteen-thirties politics, talking the quality of American civilization, moving increasingly toward outright opposition to the Vietnam war, centering his domestic legislative program on the cities, probing for a voting coalition based not on the old economic lines but on the new sense of dislocation bringing together Negroes, young people, intellectuals and the suburbanites who had acquired money at the price of malaise.

Nine weeks after President Johnson's speech of withdrawal, more crazed bullets were fired in Los Angeles. An R.F.K. legend immediately started forming, an idealization of the younger brother that joined perfectly with the J.F.K. legend.

The Johnson years were clamped in grim parentheses of happenstance. Lyndon Johnson came into the White House to the caissons for John Kennedy and he was leaving it to the dirges for Robert Kennedy. He entered and he was departing with a Kennedy more central than he in the national thinking and emotions.

In the final months, President Johnson tried hard to appear, what did not come easily to him, philosophical and serene. Strange, complex man in strange, complex circumstances—the towering figure still stalking, endlessly stalking the Oval Office, too astute not to know how seriously things had gone wrong, too limited by background and by self to grasp what had really happened.

No one who worked in Lyndon Johnson's White House can fail to have been moved by the dedication, the abilities and the force he brought to the Presidency of the United States. It is equally difficult not to recall the lines from one of the copybook poems of his school days in Johnson City, John Greenleaf Whittier's "Maud Muller": "For of all sad words of tongue or pen,/The saddest are these: 'It might have been.' " The story of Lyndon Johnson's Presidency is a story of tragedy in the ancient haunting sense of the word, the strong man overwhelmed by forces from within and without.

Hurtled into the leadership of the United States and of the free world in the fiercely demanding nineteen-sixties, he was not ready for them. Seriously flawed in personal characteristics, his virtues could not transform him into an engaging public figure. Functioning in the shadow of a relentless legend, he was beset by a host of attitudes which that legend continuously fed.

Lyndon Johnson could win votes, enact laws, maneuver mountains. He could not acquire that something beyond, which cannot be won, enacted or maneuvered but must be freely given. He could not command that respect, affection and rapport which alone permit an American President genuinely to lead. In his periods of triumph and of downsweep, in peace as in war, he stood the tragic figure of an extraordinarily gifted President who was the wrong man from the wrong place at the wrong time in the wrong circumstances.

Intimations of Mortality

The End of American Party Politics

by Walter Dean Burnham

Upon entering the White House, Richard Nixon inherited a nation more divided, fearful, and embittered by class and generational hostilities than at any time since the Great Depression. Even the inflation-ridden affluence of the Kennedy-Johnson 1960's had failed to restrain the growing alienation of working-class and middle-income voters—traditional Republicans, white ethnics and suburbanites, "Middle Americans" all—repelled by a youthful drug culture, campus political protest and violence, black ghetto riots, and understandably frightened by a growing crime rate which has made life in American cities dangerous, sometimes hellish. Yet this widespread malaise cut two ways, and Nixon's critics began arguing immediately that "the young, the poor and the black" had little place in the new President's political calculations.

Nixon moved cautiously, both in domestic and foreign affairs, apparently choosing to accept most "Great Society" programs at reduced spending levels, rather than attempt a dismantling campaign, especially since Democrats still controlled Congress. Nixon presented only one major new piece of social legislation to his first Congress, a welfare reform bill designed to federalize the largely unsuccessful and financially bankrupting state and local welfare programs. Liberal critics of the idea pointed out that the welfare benefits it proposed were considerably lower than those already paid in most Northern, industrial states, while Nixon's supporters insisted that once the principle of presidential responsibility for handling the welfare mess had been established, payments could be increased in time. Congressional bickering prevented passage of the measure before the 1970 congressional elections, and whatever its ultimate legislative future, the plan's actual impact on the "poverty cycle" among the millions living on welfare remains in doubt.

Nixon also began a highly publicized and cautious policy of American troop withdrawal from Vietnam soon after taking office, reacting to public opinion polls showing that most Americans were sick of the war. American invasions of Cambodia and Laos—Washington preferred to call the comparatively limited moves "incursions"—provoked antiwar demonstrations in the United States even greater than those seen during the Johnson years. Most analysts agree, however, that Nixon appears intent on winding down the role of American ground troops in Vietnam before the 1972 elections to the lowest level compatible with the survival of South Vietnam's government. Whether this is possible will probably determine the administration's future.

Elsewhere, Nixon has pursued a conciliatory policy toward Communist China without abandoning his commitment to protect the Chinese Nationalists on Formosa, a series of moves pointing toward expanded trade and diplomatic contacts in 1970 and 1971 which culminated in China's invitation to Nixon to visit Peking for summit-level discussions. Thus a President who began politicking by accusing Roosevelt and Truman of having "sold out" China to the Communists has come full circle and now appears intent primarily on "buying in." Earlier, Nixon attempted to capitalize on Middle America's hurts in the 1970 congressional elections, but the Nixon–Agnew–Mitchell "law and order" campaign failed to dent liberal Democratic strength in Congress significantly.

America's political future in the early 1970's seems to resist prophecy, so confused and numerous are the complex cross-currents of national problems and prospects. "The nation seems to slouch

onward into its uncertain future like some huge inarticulate beast,"
historian Richard Hofstadter wrote shortly before his death in
1970, "too much attainted by wounds and ailments to be robust,
but too strong and resourceful to succumb." William Dean Burn-
ham ventures a provocative analysis of the American political fu-
ture in this concluding yet necessarily inconclusive article.

American politics has clearly been falling apart in the past
decade. We don't have to look hard for the evidence. Mr. Nixon
is having as much difficulty controlling his fellow party members
in Congress as any of his Democratic predecessors had in controlling theirs. John V. Lindsay, a year after he helped make Spiro
Agnew a household word, had to run for mayor as a Liberal and
an Independent with the aid of nationally prominent Democrats.
Chicago in July of 1968 showed that for large numbers of its
activists a major political party can become not just a disappoint-
ment, but positively repellant. Ticket-splitting has become widespread as never before, especially among the young; and George
C. Wallace, whose third-party movement is the largest in recent
American history, continues to demonstrate an unusually stable
measure of support.

Vietnam and racial polarization have played large roles in this
breakdown, to be sure; but the ultimate causes are rooted much
deeper in our history. For some time we have been saying that we
live in a "pluralist democracy." And no text on American politics
would be complete without a few key code words such as "consensus," "incrementalism," "bargaining" and "process." Behind it
all is a rather benign view of our politics, one that assumes that
the complex diversity of the American social structure is filtered
through the two major parties and buttressed by a consensus of
middle-class values which produces an electoral politics of low intensity and gradual change. The interplay of interest groups and

From *Trans-Action*, VII (December 1969), 12–23. Copyright © December
1969 by TRANS-Action, Inc., New Brunswick, New Jersey. Reprinted by
permission.

public officials determines policy in detail. The voter has some leverage on policy, but only in a most diffuse way; and, anyway, he tends to be a pretty apolitical animal, dominated either by familial or local tradition, on one hand, or by the charisma of attractive candidates on the other. All of this is a good thing, of course, since in an affluent time the politics of consensus rules out violence and polarization. It pulls together and supports the existing order of things.

There is no doubt that this description fits "politics as usual," in the United States, but to assume that it fits the whole of American electoral politics is a radical oversimplification. Yet even after these past years of turmoil, few efforts have been made to appraise the peculiar rhythms of American politics in a more realistic way. This article is an attempt to do so by focusing upon two very important and little celebrated aspects of the dynamics of our politics: the phenomena of critical realignments of the electorate and of decomposition of the party in our electoral politics.

As a whole and across time, the reality of American politics appears quite different from a simple vision of pluralist democracy. It is shot through with escalating tensions, periodic electoral convulsions and repeated redefinitions of the rules and general outcomes of the political game. It has also been marked repeatedly by redefinitions—by no means always broadening ones—of those who are permitted to play. And one other very basic characteristic of American party politics that emerges from an historical overview is the profound incapacity of established political leadership to adapt itself to the political demands produced by the losers in America's stormy socioeconomic life. As is well known, American political parties are not instruments of collective purpose, but of electoral success. One major implication of this is that, as organizations, parties are interested in control of offices but not of government in any larger sense. It follows that once successful routines are established or reestablished for office-winning, very little motivation exists among party leaders to disturb the routines of the game. These routines are periodically upset, to be sure, but

not by adaptive change within the party system. They are upset
by overwhelming external force.

It has been recognized, at least since the publication of
V. O. Key's "A Theory of Critical Elections" in 1955, that some
elections in our history have been far more important than most
in their long-range consequences for the political system. Such
elections seem to "decide" clusters of substantive issues in a more
clear-cut way than do most of the ordinary varieties. There is even
a consensus among historians as to when these turning points in
electoral politics took place. The first came in 1800 when Thomas
Jefferson overthrew the Federalist hegemony established by Washington, Adams and Hamilton. The second came in 1828 and in
the years afterward, with the election of Andrew Jackson and the
democratization of the presidency. The third, of course, was the
election of Abraham Lincoln in 1860, an election that culminated
a catastrophic polarization of the society as a whole and resulted
in civil war. The fourth critical election was that of William Mc-
Kinley in 1896; this brought to a close the "Civil War" party
system and inaugurated a political alignment congenial to the
dominance of industrial capitalism over the American political
economy. Created in the crucible of one massive depression, this
"System of 1896" endured until the collapse of the economy in a
second. The election of Franklin D. Roosevelt in 1932 came last
in this series, and brought a major realignment of electoral politics
and policy-making structures into the now familiar "welfare-
pluralist" mode.

Now that the country appears to have entered another period of
political upheaval, it seems particularly important not only to
identify the phenomena of periodic critical realignments in our
electoral politics, but to integrate them into a larger—if still very
modest—theory of stasis and movement in American politics. For
the realignments focus attention on the dark side of our politics,
those moments of tremendous stress and abrupt transformation
that remind us that "politics as usual" in the United States is not
politics as always, and that American political institutions and

leadership, once defined or redefined in a "normal phase" seem *themselves* to contribute to the building of conditions that threaten their overthrow.

To underscore the relevance of critical elections to our own day, one has only to recall that in the past, fundamental realignments in voting behavior have always been signalled by the rise of significant third parties: the Anti-Masons in the 1820's, the Free Soilers in the 1840's and 1850's, the Populists in the 1890's and the La Follette Progressives in the 1920's. We cannot know whether George Wallace's American Independent Party of 1968 fits into this series, but it is certain—as we shall see below—that the very foundations of American electoral politics have become quite suddenly fluid in the past few years, and that the mass base of our politics has become volatile to a degree unknown in the experience of all but the very oldest living Americans. The Wallace uprising is a major sign of this recent fluidity; but it hardly stands alone.

Third-party protests, perhaps by contrast with major-party bolts, point up the interplay in American politics between the inertia of "normal" established political routines and the pressures arising from the rapidity, unevenness and uncontrolled character of change in the country's dynamic socioeconomic system. All of the third parties prior to and including the 1968 Wallace movement constituted attacks by outsiders, who felt they were outsiders, against an elite frequently viewed in conspiratorial terms. The attacks were made under the banner of high moralistic universals against an established political structure seen as corrupt, undemocratic and manipulated by insiders for their own benefit and that of their supporters. All these parties were perceived by their activists as "movements" that would not only purify the corruption of the current political regime, but replace some of its most important parts. Moreover, they all telegraphed the basic clusters of issues that would dominate politics in the next electoral era: the completion of political democratization in the 1830's, slavery and sectionalism in the late 1840's and 1850's, the struggle between

the industrialized and the colonial regions in the 1890's, and welfare liberalism vs. laissez-faire in the 1920's and 1930's. One may
well view the American Independent Party in such a context.

The periodic recurrence of third-party forerunners of realignment—and realignments themselves, for that matter—are significantly related to dominant peculiarities of polity and society in
the United States. They point to an electorate especially vulnerable to breaking apart, and to a political system in which the sense
of common nationhood may be much more nearly skin-deep than
is usually appreciated. If there is any evolutionary scale of political
modernization at all, the persistence of deep fault lines in our
electoral politics suggests pretty strongly that the United States
remains a "new nation" to this day in some important political
respects. The periodic recurrence of these tensions may also imply
that—as dynamically developed as our economic system is—no
convincing evidence of *political* development in the United States
can be found after the 1860's.

Nationwide critical realignments can only take place around
clusters of issues of the most fundamental importance. The most
profound of these issues have been cast up in the course of the
transition of our Lockeian-liberal commonwealth from an agrarian
to an industrial state. The last two major realignments—those of
1893–96 and 1928–36—involved the two great transitional crises
of American industrial capitalism, the economic collapses of 1893
and 1929. The second of these modern realignments produced,
of course, the broad coalition on which the New Deal's welfarist-
pluralist policy was ultimately based. But the first is of immediate
concern to us here. For the 1896 adaptation of electoral politics
to the imperatives of industrial-capitalism involved a set of developments that stand in the sharpest possible contrast to those occurring elsewhere in the Western world at about the same time.
Moreover, they set in motion new patterns of behavior in electoral
politics that were never entirely overcome even during the New
Deal period, and which, as we shall see, have resumed their forward march during the past decade.

As a case in point, let me briefly sketch the political evolution of Pennsylvania—one of the most industrially developed areas on earth—during the 1890–1932 period. There was in this state a preexisting, indeed, preindustrial, pattern of two-party competition, one that had been forged in the Jacksonian era and decisively amended, though not abolished, during the Civil War. Then came the realignment of the 1890's, which, like those of earlier times, was an abrupt process. In the five annual elections from 1888 through November 1892, the Democrats' mean percentage of the total two-party vote was 46.7 per cent, while for the five elections beginning in February 1894 it dropped to a mean of 37.8 per cent. Moreover, the greatest and most permanent Republican gains during this depression decade occurred where they counted most, numerically: in the metropolitan areas of Philadelphia and Pittsburgh.

The cumulative effect of this realignment and its aftermath was to convert Pennsylvania into a thoroughly one-party state, in which conflict over the basic political issues were duly transferred to the Republican primary after it was established in 1908. By the 1920's this peculiar process had been completed and the Democratic party had become so weakened that, as often as not, the party's nominees for major office were selected by the Republican leadership. But whether so selected or not, their general-election prospects were dismal: of the 80 statewide contests held from 1894 through 1931, a candidate running with Democratic party endorsement won just one. Moreover, with the highly ephemeral exception of Theodore Roosevelt's bolt from the Republican party in 1912, no third parties emerged as general-election substitutes for the ruined Democrats.

The political simplicity which had thus emerged in this industrial heartland of the Northeast by the 1920's was the more extraordinary in that it occurred in an area whose socioeconomic division of labor was as complex and its level of development as high as any in the world. In most other regions of advanced industrialization the emergence of corporate capitalism was asso-

ciated with the development of mass political parties with high
structural cohesion and explicit collective purposes with respect
to the control of policy and government. These parties expressed
deep conflicts over the direction of public policy, but they also
brought about the democratic revolution of Europe, for electoral
participation tended to rise along with them. Precisely the opposite
occurred in Pennsylvania and, with marginal and short-lived exceptions, the nation. It is no exaggeration to say that the political
response to the collectivizing thrust of industrialism in this American state was the elimination of organized partisan combat, an
extremely severe decline in electoral participation, the emergence
of a Republican "coalition of the whole" and—by no means co-
incidentally—a highly efficient insulation of the controlling in-
dustrial-financial elite from effective or sustained countervailing
pressures.

Irrelevant Radicalism

The reasons for the increasing solidity of this "system of 1896" in
Pennsylvania are no doubt complex. Clearly, for example, the introduction of the direct primary as an alternative to the general
election, which was thereby emptied of any but ritualistic significance, helped to undermine the minority Democrats more and
more decisively by destroying their monopoly of opposition. But
nationally as well the Democratic party in and after the 1890's was
virtually invisible to Pennsylvania voters as a usable opposition.
For with the ascendency of the agrarian Populist William Jennings
Bryan, the Democratic party was transformed into a vehicle for
colonial, periphery-oriented dissent against the industrial-metropol-
itan center, leaving the Republicans as sole spokesmen for the
latter.

This is a paradox that pervades American political history, but
it was sharpest in the years around the turn of this century. The
United States was so vast that it had little need of economic colonies abroad; in fact it had two major colonial regions within its

own borders, the postbellum South and the West. The only kinds of attacks that could be made effective on a *nationwide* basis against the emergent industrialist hegemony—the only attacks that, given the ethnic heterogeneity and extremely rudimentary political socialization of much of the country's industrial working class, could come within striking distance of achieving a popular majority—came out of these colonial areas. Thus "radical" protest in major-party terms came to be associated with the neo-Jacksonian demands of agrarian smallholders and small-town society already confronted by obsolescence. The Democratic party from 1896 to 1932, and in many respects much later, was the national vehicle for these struggles.

The net effect of this was to produce a condition in which—especially, but not entirely on the presidential level—the more economically advanced a state was, the more heavy were its normal Republican majorities likely to be. The nostalgic agrarian-individualist appeals of the national Democratic leadership tended to present the voters of this industrial state with a choice that was not a choice: between an essentially backward-looking provincial party articulating interests in opposition to those of the industrial North and East as a whole, and a "modernizing" party whose doctrines included enthusiastic acceptance of and cooperation with the dominant economic interests of region and nation. Not only did this partitioning of the political universe entail normal and often huge Republican majorities in an economically advanced state like Pennsylvania; the survival of national two-party competition on such a basis helped to ensure that no local reorganization of electoral politics along class lines could effectively occur even within such a state. Such a voting universe had a tendency toward both enormous inbuilt stability and increasing entrenchment in the decades after its creation. Probably no force less overwhelming than the post-1929 collapse of the national economic system would have sufficed to dislodge it. Without such a shock, who can say how, or indeed whether, the "System of 1896" would have come to an end in Pennsylvania and the nation? To ask such a question is to raise yet another. For there is no doubt that in Pennsylvania, as elsewhere, the combination of trauma in 1929–33 and Roosevelt's creative leadership provided the means for overthrowing the old order and for reversing dramatically the depoliticization of electoral politics which had come close to perfection under it. Yet might it not be the case that the dominant pattern of political adaptation to industrialism in the United States has worked to eliminate, by one means or another, the links provided by political parties between voters and rulers? In other words, was the post-1929 reversal permanent or only a transitory phrase in our political evolution? And if transitory, what bearing would this fact have on the possible recurrence of critical realignments in the future?

Withering Away of the Parties

The question requires us to turn our attention to the second major dynamic of American electoral politics during this century: the phenomenon of electoral disaggregation, of the breakdown of party loyalty, which in many respects must be seen as the permanent legacy of the fourth party system of 1896–1932. One of the most conspicuous developments of this era, most notably during the 1900–1920 period, was a whole network of changes in the rules of the political game. This is not the place for a thorough treatment and documentation of these peculiarities. One can only mention here some major changes in the rules of the game, and note that one would have no difficulty in arguing that their primary latent function was to ease the transition from a preindustrial universe of competitive, highly organized mass politics to a depoliticized world marked by drastic shrinkage in participation or political leverage by the lower orders of the population. The major changes surely include the following:

The introduction of the Australian ballot, which was designed to purify elections but also eliminated a significant function of the older political machines, the printing and distribution of ballots, and eased a transition from party voting to candidate voting.

The introduction of the direct primary, which at once stripped the minority party of its monopoly of opposition and weakened the control of party leaders over nominating processes, and again hastened preoccupation of the electorate with candidates rather than parties.

The movement toward nonpartisan local elections, often accompanied by a drive to eliminate local bases of representation such as wards in favor of at-large elections, which produced—as Samuel Hays points out—a shift of political power from the grass roots to citywide cosmopolitan elites.

The expulsion of almost all blacks, and a very large part of the poor-white population as well, from the southern electorate by a series of legal and extralegal measures such as the poll tax.

The introduction of personal registration requirements the burden of which, in faithful compliance with dominant middle-class values, was placed on the individual rather than on public authority, but which effectively disenfranchised large numbers of the poor.

Breakdown of Party Loyalty

Associated with these and other changes in the rules of the game was a profound transformation in voting behavior. There was an impressive growth in the numbers of political independents and ticket-splitters, a growth accompanied by a sea-change among party elites from what Richard Jensen has termed the "militarist" (or ward boss) campaign style to the "mercantilist" (or advertising-packaging) style. Aside from noting that the transition was largely completed as early as 1916, and hence that the practice of "the selling of the president" goes back far earlier than we usually think, these changes too must be left for fuller exposition elsewhere.

Critical realignments, as we have argued, are an indispensable part of a stability-disruption dialectic which has the deepest roots in American political history. Realigning sequences are associated with all sorts of aberrations from the normal workings of American party politics, both in the events leading up to nominations, the nature and style of election campaigning and the final outcome at the polls. This is not surprising, since they arise out of the collision of profound transitional crisis in the socioeconomic system with the immobility of a nondeveloped political system.

At the same time, it seems clear that for realignment to fulfill some of its most essential tension-management functions, for it to be a forum by which the electorate can participate in durable "constitution making," it is essential that political parties not fall below a certain level of coherence and appeal in the electorate. It is obvious that the greater the electoral disaggregation the less effective will be "normal" party politics as an instrument of countervailing influence in an industrial order. Thus, a number of indices of disaggregation significantly declined during the 1930's as the Democratic Party remobilized parts of American society under the stimulus of the New Deal. In view of the fact that political parties during the 1930's and 1940's were once again called upon to assist in a redrawing of the map of American politics and policy-making, this regeneration of partisan voting in the 1932–52 era is hardly surprising. More than that, regeneration was necessary if even the limited collective purposes of the new majority coalition were to be realized.

Even so, the New Deal realignment was far more diffuse, protracted and incomplete than any of its predecessors, a fact of which the more advanced New Dealers were only too keenly aware. It is hard to avoid the impression that one contributing element in this peculiarity of our last realignment was the much higher level of electoral disaggregation in the 1930's and 1940's than had existed at any time prior to the realignment of the 1890's. If one assumes that the end result of a long-term trend toward electoral disaggregation is the complete elimination of political parties as foci that shape voting behavior, then the possibility of critical realignment

would, by definition, be eliminated as well. Every election would
be dominated by TV packaging, candidate charisma, real or manufactured, and short-term, ad hoc influences. Every election, therefore, would have become deviating or realigning by definition, and
American national politics would come to resemble the formless
gubernatorial primaries that V. O. Key described in his classic
Southern Politics.

The New Deal clearly arrested and reversed, to a degree, the
march toward electoral disaggregation. But it did so only for the
period in which the issues generated by economic scarcity remained central, and the generation traumatized by the collapse
of 1929 remained numerically preponderant in the electorate. Since
1952, electoral disaggregation has resumed, in many measurable
dimensions, and with redoubled force. The data on this point are
overwhelming. Let us examine a few of them.

A primary aspect of electoral disaggregation, of course, is the
"pulling apart" over time of the percentages for the same party
but at different levels of election: this is the phenomenon of split-
ticket voting. Recombining and reorganizing the data found in
two tables of Milton Cummings' excellent study *Congressmen and
the Electorate,* and extending the series back and forward in time,
we may examine the relationship between presidential and congressional elections during this century.

Such an array captures both the initial upward thrust of disaggregation in the second decade of this century, the peaking in the
middle to late 1920's, the recession beginning in 1932, and especially the post-1952 resumption of the upward trend.

Other evidence points precisely in the same direction. It has
generally been accepted in survey-research work that generalized
partisan identification shows far more stability over time than
does actual voting behavior, since the latter is subject to short-
term factors associated with each election. What is not so widely
understood is that this glacial measure of party identification has
suddenly become quite volatile during the 1960's, and particularly
during the last half of the decade. In the first place, as both Gal-

lup and Survey Research Center data confirm, the proportion of independents underwent a sudden shift upwards around 1966: while from 1940 to 1965 independents constituted about 20 per cent to 22 per cent of the electorate, they increased to 29 per cent in 1966. At the present time, they outnumber Republicans by 30 per cent to 28 per cent.

Second, there is a clear unbroken progression in the share that independents have of the total vote along age lines. The younger the age group, the larger the number of independents in it, so that among the 21–29 year olds, according to the most recent Gallup findings this year, 42 per cent are independent—an increase of about 10 per cent over the first half of the decade, and representing greater numbers of people than identify with either major party. When one reviews the June 1969 Gallup survey of college students, the share is larger still—44 per cent. Associated with this quantitative increase in independents seems to be a major qualitative change as well. Examining the data for the 1950's, the authors of *The American Voter* could well argue that independents tended to have lower political awareness and political involvement in general than did identifiers (particularly strong identifiers) of either major party. But the current concentration of independents in the population suggests that this may no longer be the case. They are clearly and disproportionately found not only among the young, and especially among the college young, but also among men, those adults with a college background, people in the professional-managerial strata and, of course, among those with higher incomes. Such groups tend to include those people whose sense of political involvement and efficacy is far higher than that of the population as a whole. Even in the case of the two most conspicuous exceptions to this—the pile-up of independent identifiers in the youngest age group and in the South—it can be persuasively argued that this distribution does not reflect low political awareness and involvement but the reverse: a sudden, in some instances almost violent, increase in both awareness and involvement among southerners and young adults, with the former being associated both with the heavy increase in southern turn-out in 1968 and the large Wallace vote polled there.

Third, one can turn to two sets of evidence found in the Survey Research Center's election studies. If the proportion of *strong* party identifiers over time is examined, the same pattern of long-term inertial stability and recent abrupt change can be seen. From 1952 through 1964, the proportion of strong Democratic and Republican party identifiers fluctuated in a narrow range between 36 per cent and 40 per cent, with a steep downward trend in strong Republican identifiers between 1960 and 1964 being matched by a moderate increase in strong Democratic identifiers. Then in 1966 the proportion of strong identifiers abruptly declines to 28 per cent, with the defectors overwhelmingly concentrated among former Democrats. This is almost certainly connected, as is the increase of independent identifiers, with the Vietnam fiasco. While we do not as yet have the 1968 SRC data, the distribution of identifications reported by Gallup suggests the strong probability that this abrupt decline in party loyalty has not been reversed very much since. It is enough here to observe that while the ratio between strong identifiers and independents prior to 1966 was pretty stably fixed at between 1.6 to 1 and 2 to 1 in favor of the former, it is now evidently less than 1 to 1. Both Chicago and Wallace last year were the acting out of these changes in the arena of "popular theater."

Finally, both survey and election data reveal a decline in two other major indices of the relevance of party to voting behavior: split-ticket voting and the choice of the same party's candidates for President across time.

It is evident that the 1960's have been an era of increasingly rapid liquidation of pre-existing party commitments by individual voters. There is no evidence anywhere to support Kevin Phillips' hypothesis regarding an emergent Republican majority—assuming that such a majority would involve increases in voter identification with the party. More than that, one might well ask whether, if this process of liquidation is indeed a preliminary to realignment, the latter may not take the form of a third-party movement of truly massive and durable proportions.

The evidence lends some credence to the view that American electoral politics is undergoing a long-term transition into routines designed only to fill offices and symbolically affirm "the American way." There also seem to be tendencies for our political parties gradually to evaporate as broad and active intermediaries between the people and their rulers, even as they may well continue to maintain enough organizational strength to screen out the unacceptable or the radical at the nominating stage. It is certain that the significance of party as link between government and the governed has now come once again into serious question. Bathed in the warm glow of diffused affluence, vexed in spirit but enriched economically by our imperial military and space commitments, confronted by the gradually unfolding consequences of social change as vast as it is unplanned, what need have Americans of political parties? More precisely, why do they need parties whose structures, processes and leadership cadres seem to grow more remote and irrelevant to each new crisis?

Future Politics

It seems evident enough that if this long-term trend toward a politics without parties continues, the policy consequences must be profound. One can put the matter with the utmost simplicity: political parties, with all their well-known human and structural shortcomings, are the only devices thus far invented by the wit of Western man that can, with some effectiveness, generate countervailing collective power on behalf of the many individually powerless against the relatively few who are individually or organizationally powerful. Their disappearance as active intermediaries, if not as preliminary screening devices, would only entail the unchallenged ascendancy of the already powerful, unless new structures of collective power were somehow developed to replace them, and unless conditions in America's social structure and political culture came to be such that they could be effectively used. Yet *neither* of these contingencies, despite recent publicity for the term "participatory democracy," is likely to occur under immediately conceivable circumstances in the United States. It is much more probable that the next chapter of our political history will resemble the metapolitical world of the 1920's.

But, it may be asked, may not a future realignment serve to recrystallize and revitalize political parties in the American system?

The present condition of America contains a number of what Marxists call "internal contradictions," some of which might provide the leverage for a future critical realignment if sufficiently sharp dislocations in everyday life should occur. One of the most important of these, surely, is the conversion—largely through technological change—of the American social stratification system from the older capitalist mixture of upper or "owning" classes, dependent white-collar middle classes and proletarians into a mixture described recently by David Apter: the technologically competent, the technologically obsolescent and the technologically superfluous. It is arguable, in fact, that the history of the Kennedy-Johnson Administrations on the domestic front could be written in terms of a coalition of the top and bottom of this Apter-ite mix against the middle, and the 1968 election as the first stage of a "counterrevolution" of these middle strata against the pressures from both of the other two. Yet the inchoate results of 1968 raise some doubts, to say the least, that it can yet be described as part of a realigning sequence: there was great volatility in this election, but also a remarkable and unexpectedly large element of continuity and voter stability.

It is not hard to find evidence of cumulative social disaster in our metropolitan areas. We went to war with Japan in 1941 over a destruction inflicted on us far less devastating in scope and intensity than that endured by any large America city today. But the destruction came suddenly, as a sharp blow, from a foreign power; while the urban destruction of today has matured as a result of our own internal social and political processes, and it has been unfolding gradually for decades. We have consequently learned somehow to adapt to it piecemeal, as best we can, without changing our lives or our values very greatly. Critical realignments, however, also seem to require sharp, sudden blows as a precondition for their emergence. If we think of realignment as arising from the spreading internal disarray in this country, we should also probably attempt to imagine what kinds of events could produce a sudden, sharp and general escalation in social tensions and threatened deprivations of property, status or values.

Conceivably, ghetto and student upheavals could prove enough in an age of mass communications to create a true critical realignment, but one may doubt it. Student and ghetto rebellions appear to be too narrowly defined socially to have a *direct* impact on the daily lives of the "vast middle," and thus produce transformations in voting behavior that would be both sweeping and permanent. For what happens in times of critical realignment is nothing less than an intense, if temporary, quasi revolutionizing of the vast middle class, a class normally content to be traditionalists or passive-participants in electoral politics.

Yet, even if students and ghetto blacks could do the trick, if they could even begin, with the aid of elements of the technological elite, a process of electoral realignment leftward, what would be the likely consequences? What would the quasi revolutionizing of an insecure, largely urban middle class caught in a brutal squeeze from the top and the bottom of the social system look like? There are already premonitory evidences: the Wallace vote in both southern and nonsouthern areas, as well as an unexpected durability in his *postelection* appeal; the mayoral elections in Los Angeles and Minneapolis this year, and not least, Lindsay's narrow squeak into a second term as mayor of New York City. To the extent that the "great middle" becomes politically mobilized and self-conscious, it moves toward what has been called "urban populism," a stance of organized hostility to blacks, student radicals and cosmopolitan liberal elites. The "great middle" remains, after all, the chief defender of the old-time Lockeian faith; both its material and cultural interests are bound up in this defense. If it should become at all mobilized as a major and cohesive political force in today's conditions, it would do so in the name of a restoration of the ancient truths by force if necessary. A realignment that directly involved this kind of mobilization —as it surely would, should it occur—would very likely have sinister overtones unprecedented in our political history.

Are we left, then, with a choice between the stagnation implicit in the disaggregative trends we have outlined here and convulsive disruption? Is there something basic to the American political system, and extending to its electoral politics, which rules out a middle ground between drift and mastery?

The fact that these questions were raised by Walter Lippmann more than half a century ago—and have indeed been raised in one form or other in every era of major transitional crisis over the past century—is alone enough to suggest an affirmative answer. The phenomena we have described here provide evidence of a partly quantitative sort which seems to point in the same direction. For electoral disaggregation is the negation of party. Further, it is—or rather, reffects—the negation of structural and behavioral conditions in politics under which linkages between the bottom, the middle and the top can exist and produce the effective carrying out of collective power. Critical realignments are evidence not of the presence of such linkages or conditions in the normal state of American electoral politics, but precisely of their absence. Correspondingly, they are not manifestations of democratic accountability, but infrequent and hazardous substitutes for it.

Taken together, both of these phenomena generate support for the inference that American politics in its normal state is the negation of the public order itself, as that term is understood in politically developed nations. We do not have government in our domestic affairs so much as "non-rule." We do not have political parties in the contemporary sense of that term as understood elsewhere in the Western world; we have antiparties instead.

Power centrifuges rather than power concentrators, they have been immensely important not as vehicles of social transformation but for its prevention through political means.

The entire setting of the critical realignment phenomenon bears witness to a deep-seated dialectic within the American political system. From the beginning, the American socioeconomic system has developed and transformed itself with an energy and thrust that has no parallel in modern history. The political system, from parties to policy structures, has seen no such development. Indeed it has shown astonishingly little substantive transformation over time in its methods of operation. In essence, the political system of this "fragment society" remains based today on the same Lockeian formulation that, as Louis Hartz points out, has dominated its entire history. It is predicated upon the maintenance of a high wall of separation between politics and government on one side and the socioeconomic system on the other. It depends for its effective working on the failure of anything approximating internal sovereignty in the European sense to emerge here.

The Lockeian cultural monolith, however, is based upon a social assumption that has come repeatedly into collision with reality. The assumption, of course, is not only that the autonomy of socioeconomic life from political direction is the prescribed fundamental law for the United States, but that this autonomous development will proceed with enough smoothness, uniformity and generally distributed benefits that it will be entirely compatible with the usual functioning of our antique political structures. Yet the high (though far from impermeable) wall of separation between politics and society is periodically threatened with inundations. As the socioeconomic system develops in the context of unchanging institutions of electoral politics and policy formation, dysfunctions become more and more visible. Whole classes, regions or other major sectors of the population are injured or faced with an imminent threat of injury. Finally the triggering event occurs, critical realignments follow, the universe of policy and of electoral coalitions is broadly redefined, and the tensions generated by the crisis receive some resolution. Thus it can be argued that critical realignment as a periodically recurring phenomenon is as centrally related to the workings of such a system as is the archaic and increasingly rudimentary structure of the major parties themselves.

Party vs. Survival

One is finally left with the sense that the twentieth-century decomposition of partisan links in our electoral system also corresponds closely with the contemporary survival needs of what Samuel P. Huntington has called the American "Tudor polity." Electoral disaggregation and the concentration of certain forms of power in the hands of economic, technological and administrative elites are functional for the short-term survival of nonrule in the United States. They may even somehow be related to the gradual emergence of internal sovereignty in this country—though to be sure under not very promising auspices for participatory democracy of any kind. Were such a development to occur, it would not necessarily entail the disappearance or complete suppression of sub-group tensions or violence in American social life, or of group bargaining and pluralism in the policy process. It might even be associated with increases in both. But it would, after all, reflect the ultimate sociopolitical consequences of the persistence of Lockeian individualism into an era of Big Organization: oligarchy at the top, inertia and spasms of self-defense in the middle, and fragmentation at the base. One may well doubt whether political parties or critical realignments need have much place in such a political universe.

A Selected Modern
Bibliography

General Works

Richard Hofstadter, *The American Political Tradition* . . . (New York, 1954)

Ralph H. Gabriel, *The Course of American Democratic Thought* . . . (New York, 1940)

Arthur A. Ekirch, Jr., *The American Democratic Tradition* . . . (New York, 1963)

Louis Hartz, *The Liberal Tradition in America* . . . (New York, 1955)

Arthur A. Ekirch, Jr., *The Decline of American Liberalism* (New York, 1955)

Clinton Rossiter, *Conservatism in America* . . . (2nd edition, New York, 1962)

Daniel J. Boorstin, *The Genius of American Politics* (Chicago, 1953)

Wilfred E. Binkley, *American Political Parties: Their Natural History* (4th edition, New York, 1962)

Herbert Agar, *The Price of Union* (Boston, 1950)

William Nisbet Chambers and Walter Dean Burnham (eds.), *The American Party Systems, Stages of Political Development* (New York, 1967)

Kirk H. Porter and Donald B. Johnson (eds.), *National Party Platforms, 1840–1956* (Urbana, Ill., 1956)

Pendleton Herring, *The Politics of Democracy: American Parties in Action* (New York, 1940)

Clinton Rossiter, *Parties and Politics in America* (Ithaca, N.Y., 1960)

Joseph LaPalombara and Myron Wiener (eds.), *Political Parties and Political Development* (Princeton, 1966)

V. O. Key, Jr., *Politics, Parties, and Pressure Groups* (5th edition, New York, 1964)

Hugh A. Bone, *Party Committees and National Politics* (Seattle, 1958)

Cornelius P. Cotter and Bernard C. Hennessy, *Politics Without Power: The National Party Committees* (New York, 1964)

Frank R. Kent, *The Democratic Party, a History* (New York, 1928)

Henry A. Minor, *The Story of the Democratic Party* (New York, 1928

Ralph M. Goldman, *The Democratic Party in American Politics* (New York, 1966)

Ronald F. Stinnett, *Democrats, Dinners and Dollars* (Ames, Iowa, 1967)

William T. Cash, *History of the Democratic Party in Florida* (Tallahassee, 1936)

George L. Willis, *Kentucky Democracy* (3 vols., Louisville, Ky., 1935)

Thomas E. Powell, *The Democratic Party of . . . Ohio* (Columbus, 1913)

Malcolm C. Moos, *The Republicans: A History . . .* (New York, 1956)

George H. Mayer, *The Republican Party, 1854–1966* (2nd edition, New York, 1967)

Francis Curtis, *The Republican Party . . . 1854–1904* (2 vols., New York, 1904)

Charles O. Jones, *The Republican Party . . .* (New York, 1965)

Milton Viorst, *Fall from Grace: The Republican Party and the Puritan Ethic* (New York, 1968)

Paul D. Casdorph, *A History of the Republican Party in Texas . . .* (Austin, 1965)

Eugene H. Roseboom, *A History of Presidential Elections* (New York, 1957)

James W. Davis, *Springboard to the White House: Presidential Primaries* . . . (New York, 1967)

William B. Brown, *The People's Choice: The Presidential . . . Campaign Biography* (Baton Rouge, 1960)

W. Dean Burnham (comp.), *Presidential Ballots, 1836–1892* (Baltimore, 1955)

V. O. Key, *The Responsible Electorate: Rationality in Presidential Voting, 1936–1960* (Cambridge, Mass., 1966)

Lucius Wilmerding, Jr., *The Electoral College* (New Brunswick, N.J., 1958)

Wallace S. Sayre and Judith H. Parris, *Voting for President: The Electoral College* . . . (Washington, D.C., 1971)

George F. Milton, *The Use of Presidential Power, 1789–1943* (Boston, 1944)

Edward S. Corwin, *The President: Office and Powers, 1787–1948* . . . (3rd edition, New York, 1948)

Morton Borden (ed.), *America's Ten Greatest Presidents* (Chicago, 1961)

Harold J. Laski, *The American Presidency* . . . (New York, 1940)

Sidney Hyman, *The American President* (New York, 1954)

Sidney Hyman (ed.), "The Office of the American Presidency," *Annals of the American Academy of Political and Social Science*, Vol. 307 (September 1956)

Clinton Rossiter, *The American Presidency* (2nd edition, New York, 1960)

Herman Finer, *The Presidency* . . . (Chicago, 1960)

Richard E. Neustadt, *Presidential Power* (New York, 1960)

Wilfred E. Binkley, *The Man in the White House: His Powers and Duties* (rev. edition, New York, 1964)

Carleton Jackson, *Presidential Vetoes, 1792–1945* (Athens, Ga., 1967)

James Hart, *The Ordinance Making Powers of the President* . . . (Baltimore, 1925)

Richard P. Longaker, *The Presidency and Individual Liberties* (Ithaca, N.Y., 1961)

James E. Pollard, *The Presidents and the Press* (New York, 1947)

Rexford G. Tugwell, *The Enlargement of the Presidency* (New York, 1960)

Mary L. Hinsdale, *A History of the President's Cabinet* (Ann Arbor, Mich., 1911)

Richard F. Fenno, Jr., *The President's Cabinet: . . . from Wilson to Eisenhower* (Cambridge, Mass., 1959)

Dorothy G. Fowler, *The Cabinet Politician: The Postmasters General, 1829–1909* (New York, 1943)

Carl Russell Fish, *The Civil Service and the Patronage* (New York, 1905)

Paul P. Van Riper, *History of the United States Civil Service* (Evanston, Ill., 1958)

W. Lloyd Warner *et al.*, *The American Federal Executive* . . . (New Haven, 1963)

Harold Seidman, *Politics, Position and Power: The Dynamics of Federal Organization* (New York, 1971)

Wilfred E. Binkley, *President and Congress* (3rd edition, New York, 1962)

Clinton Rossiter, *The Supreme Court and the Commander in Chief* (Ithaca, N.Y., 1951)

Glendon A. Schubert, Jr., *The Presidency in the Courts* (Minneapolis, 1957)

Ernest S. Griffith, *Congress: Its Contemporary Role* (3rd edition, New York, 1961)

Randall B. Ripley, *Majority Party Leadership in Congress* (Boston, 1969)

Charles O. Jones, *The Minority Party in Congress* (Boston, 1970)

Barbara Hinckley, *The Seniority System in Congress* (Bloomington, Ind., 1971)

Marshall E. Dimock, *Congressional Investigating Committees* (Baltimore, 1929)

Emmy E. Werner, "Women in Congress, 1917–1964," *Review of Politics*, XIX (March 1966)

George H. Haynes, *The Senate of the United States: Its History and Practice* (2 vols., Boston, 1938)

Joseph P. Harris, *The Advice and Consent of the Senate: . . . Confirmation of Appointments* . . . (Berkeley, 1953)

Donald R. Matthews, *U.S. Senators and Their World* (Chapel Hill, 1960)

George B. Galloway, *History of the House of Representatives* (New York, 1961)

H. B. Fuller, *The Speakers of the House* (Boston, 1909)

Robert G. McCloskey, *The American Supreme Court* (Chicago, 1960)

Leo Pfeffer, *This Honorable Court* . . . (Boston, 1965)

John R. Schmidhauser, *The Supreme Court, Its Politics, Personalities, and Procedures* (New York, 1960)

Carl B. Swisher, *The Supreme Court in Modern Role* (rev. edition, New York, 1965)

Conyers Read (ed.), *The Constitution Reconsidered* (New York, 1938)

Robert K. Carr, *The Supreme Court and Judicial Review* (New York, 1942)

Charles G. Haines, *The American Doctrine of Judicial Supremacy* (rev. edition, Berkeley, 1932)

William W. Crosskey, *Politics and the Constitution* . . . (2 vols., Chicago, 1953)

Martin Shapiro, *Law and Politics in the Supreme Court* . . . (Glencoe, Ill., 1964)

Richard Claude, *The Supreme Court and the Electoral Process* (Baltimore, 1970)

Horace B. Davis, "The Occupations of Massachusetts Legislators, 1790–1950," *New England Quarterly*, XXIV (March 1951)

DeAlva S. Alexander, *A Political History of the State of New York* (4 vols., New York, 1906–23)

V. O. Key, *Southern Politics in State and Nation* (New York, 1949)

Perry H. Howard, *Political Tendencies in Louisiana, 1812–1952* (Baton Rouge, 1957)

Jasper B. Shannon, *Presidential Politics in Kentucky, 1824–1948* (Lexington, Ky., 1950)

J. Stephen Turett, "The Vulnerability of American Governors, 1900–1969," *Midwest Journal of Political Science*, XV (February 1971)

Allan G. Bogue, "United States: The 'New' Political History," *Journal of Contemporary History*, III (January 1968)

George M. Belnap, "A Method for Analyzing Legislative Behavior," *Midwest Journal of Political Science*, II (November 1958)

Lee F. Anderson *et al.*, *Legislative Roll-Call Analysis* (Evanston, Ill., 1966)

Robert P. Swierenga, "Ethnocultural Political Analysis: A New Approach to American Ethnic Studies," *Journal of American Studies*, V (April 1971)

Charles A. McCoy and John Playford, *Apolitical Politics: A Critique of Behavioralism* (New York, 1967)

I *Colonial Politics, 1607–1776*

Jack P. Greene, "Changing Interpretations of Early American Politics," in Ray Allen Billington (ed.), *The Reinterpretation of Early American History* . . . (San Marino, Calif., 1966)

Wesley Frank Craven, *The Colonies in Transition, 1660–1713* (New York, 1968)

James M. Smith (ed.), *Seventeenth-Century America* . . . (Chapel Hill, 1959)

Oliver M. Dickerson, *American Colonial Government* . . . (Cleveland, 1912)

Bernard Bailyn, *Origins of American Politics* (New York, 1968)

Bernard Bailyn, "Political Experience and Enlightenment Ideas in Eighteenth-Century America," *American Historical Review*, LXVII (January 1962)

Michael Kammen, *Deputyes and Libertyes: The Origins of Representative Government in Colonial America* (New York, 1969)

Roy N. Lokken, "The Concept of Democracy in Colonial Political Thought," *William and Mary Quarterly*, XVI (October 1959)

Mary P. Clarke, *Parliamentary Privilege in the American Colonies* (New Haven, 1943)

Leonard W. Labaree, *Conservatism in Early American History* (New York, 1948)

William S. Carpenter, *The Development of American Political Thought* (Princeton, 1930)

Lawrence H. Leder, *Liberty and Authority: Early American Political Ideology, 1689–1763* (Chicago, 1968)

John B. Kirby, "Early American Politics—The Search for Ideology: An Historiographical Analysis . . . ," *Journal of Politics*, XXXII (November 1970)

T. H. Breen, *The Character of the Good Ruler: Puritan Political Ideas in New England, 1630–1730* (New Haven, 1970)

Richard S. Dunn, *Puritans and Yankees: The Winthrop Dynasty of New England* . . . (Princeton, 1962)

Michael Zuckerman, *Peaceable Kingdoms: New England Towns in the Eighteenth Century* (New York, 1970)

Thomas J. Wertenbaker, *The Puritan Oligarchy* (New York, 1947)

Edmund S. Morgan, *The Puritan Dilemma: The Story of John Winthrop* (Boston, 1958)

B. Katherine Brown, "Freemanship in Puritan Massachusetts," *American Historical Review*, LIX (July 1954)

Kenneth A. Lockridge and Alan Kreider, "The Evolution of Massachusetts Town Government, 1640 to 1740," *William and Mary Quarterly*, XXIII (October 1966)

Robert M. Zemsky, ". . . Leadership Patterns in the Massachusetts Assembly, 1740–1755," *William and Mary Quarterly*, XXVI (October 1969)

John A. Schutz, *William Shirley: King's Governor of Massachusetts* (Williamsburg, Va., 1961)

Alan Simpson, "How Democratic Was Roger Williams?" *William and Mary Quarterly*, XIII (January 1956)

Edmund S. Morgan, *Roger Williams: The Church and the State* (New York, 1967)

Charles S. Grant, *Democracy in the Connecticut Frontier Town of Kent* (New York, 1961)

Robert Sklar, "The Great Awakening and Colonial Politics: Connecticut's Revolution in the Minds of Men," *Connecticut Historical Society Bulletin*, XXVIII (July 1963)

Nicholas Varga, "Election Procedures and Practices in Colonial New York," *New York History*, XLI (July 1960)

Milton M. Klein, "Democracy and Politics in Colonial New York," *New York History*, XL (July 1959)

Milton M. Klein, "Politics and Personalities in Colonial New York," *New York History*, XLVII (January 1966)

Jerome R. Reich, *Leisler's Rebellion* . . . (New York, 1953)

Stanley N. Katz, *Newcastle's New York: Anglo-American Politics, 1732–1753* (Cambridge, Mass., 1968)

Lawrence H. Leder, *Robert Livingston . . . and the Politics of Colonial New York* (Chapel Hill, 1961)

Patricia U. Bonomi, "Political Patterns in Colonial New York City . . . ," *Political Science Quarterly*, LXXXI (September 1966)

Bruce M. Wilkenfeld, "The New York City Common Council, 1689–1800," *New York History*, LII (July 1971)

Jerome J. Nadelhaft, "Politics and the Judicial Tenure Fight in Colonial New Jersey," *William and Mary Quarterly*, XXVIII (January 1971)

Joseph E. Illick, *William Penn the Politician* . . . (Ithaca, N.Y., 1965)

Mary M. Dunn, *William Penn: Politics and Conscience* (Princeton, 1967)

Edwin B. Bronner, *William Penn's "Holy Experiment": The Founding of Pennsylvania, 1681–1701* (New York, 1962)

Gary B. Nash, *Quakers and Politics: Pennsylvania, 1681–1726* (Princeton, 1968)

Roy N. Lokken, *David Lloyd, Colonial Lawmaker* (Seattle, 1959)

Joan de Lourdes Leonard, "Elections in Colonial Pennsylvania," *William and Mary Quarterly*, XI (July 1954)

G. B. Warden, "The Proprietary Group in Pennsylvania, 1754–1764," *William and Mary Quarterly*, XXI (July 1964)

William S. Hanna, *Benjamin Franklin and Pennsylvania Politics* (Stanford, Calif., 1964)

Jack P. Greene, *The Quest for Power: The Lower Houses of Assembly in the Southern Royal Colonies* . . . (Chapel Hill, 1963)

Donald M. Owings, *His Lordship's Patronage: Offices of Profit in Colonial Maryland* (Baltimore, 1953)

Aubrey C. Land, *The Dulanys of Maryland* . . . (Baltimore, 1955)

Robert L. Morton, *Colonial Virginia* (2 vols., Chapel Hill, 1960)

Sigmund Diamond, "From Organization to Society: Virginia in the Seventeenth Century," *American Journal of Sociology*, LXIII (March 1958)

Thomas J. Wertenbaker, *Torchbearer of the American Revolution: The Story of Bacon's Rebellion* . . . (Princeton, 1940)

Wilcomb E. Washburn, *The Governor and the Rebel: A History of Bacon's Rebellion in Virginia* (Chapel Hill, 1957)

John C. Rainbolt, "The Alteration in the Relationship Between Leadership and Constituents in Virginia, 1660 to 1720," *William and Mary Quarterly*, XXVII (July 1970)

Leonidas Dodson, *Alexander Spotswood, Governor of Colonial Virginia, 1710–1722* (Philadelphia, 1932)

Carl Bridenbaugh, *Seat of Empire: The Political Role of Eighteenth-Century Williamsburg* (Williamsburg, Va., 1950)

Desmond Clarke, *Arthur Dobbs Esquire* . . . *Governor of North Carolina* (Chapel Hill, 1957)

M. Eugene Sirmans, *Colonial South Carolina: A Political History* . . . (Chapel Hill, 1966)

M. Eugene Sirmans, "The South Carolina Royal Council," *William and Mary Quarterly*, XVIII (July 1961)

Richard P. Sherman, *Robert Johnson, Proprietary & Royal Governor of South Carolina* (Columbia, S.C., 1966)

Robert L. Middlekauff, "The American Continental Colonies in the Empire," in Robin W. Winks (ed.), *The Historiography of the British Empire–Commonwealth* . . . (Durham, N.C., 1966)

Leonard W. Labaree, *Royal Government in America* . . . (New Haven, 1930)

Alison G. Olson and Richard Maxwell Brown (eds.), *Anglo-American Political Relations, 1675–1775* (New Brunswick, N.J., 1970)

Carl Ubbelohde, *The American Colonies and the British Empire* . . . (New York, 1968)

Michael Kammen, *Empire and Interest: The American Colonies and the Politics of Mercantilism* (Philadelphia, 1970)

Lawrence A. Harper, *The English Navigation Laws* . . . (New York, 1940)

I. K. Steele, *Politics of Colonial Policy: The Board of Trade* . . . *1696–1720* (New York, 1968)

Michael G. Hall, *Edward Randolph and the American Colonies, 1676–1703* (Chapel Hill, 1960)

Michael G. Kammen, *A Rope of Sand: The Colonial Agents, British Politics, and the American Revolution* (Ithaca, N.Y., 1968)

Jack M. Sosin, *Agents and Merchants: British Colonial Policy and the Origins of the American Revolution, 1763–1775* (Lincoln, Nebr., 1965)

Thomas C. Barrow, *Trade and Empire: The British Customs Service in Colonial America* . . . (Cambridge, Mass., 1967)

Louis B. Namier, *The Structure of Politics at the Accession of George III* (London, 1929)

Louis B. Namier, *England in the Age of the American Revolution* (London, 1930)

Herbert Butterfield, *George III and the Historians* (rev. edition, New York, 1959)

Max Savelle, *Seeds of Liberty: The Genesis of the American Mind* (New York, 1948)

Clinton Rossiter, *Seedtime of the Republic: The Origin of the American Tradition of Political Liberty* (New York, 1953)

Bernard Bailyn, *The Ideological Origins of the American Revolution* (Cambridge, Mass., 1967)

Edmund S. Morgan, *The Birth of the Republic, 1763–1789* (Chicago, 1956)

Bernhard Knollenberg, *Origin of the American Revolution* . . . (New York, 1960)

Lawrence Henry Gipson, *The Coming of the Revolution* . . . (New York, 1954)

Randolph G. Adams, *Political Ideas of the American Revolution* . . . (3rd edition, New York, 1958)

Charles M. Andrews, *Colonial Background of the American Revolution* (New Haven, 1924)

Robert C. Newbold, *The Albany Congress and Plan of Union* (New York, 1955)

Edmund S. and Helen M. Morgan, *The Stamp Act Crisis* . . . (Chapel Hill, 1953)

Robert J. Chaffin, "The Townshend Acts of 1767," *William and Mary Quarterly*, XXVII (January 1970)

Oliver M. Dickerson, *The Navigation Acts and the American Revolution* (Philadelphia, 1951)

R. Coupland, *The Quebec Act* . . . (Oxford, England, 1925)

Arthur M. Schlesinger, *Prelude to Independence: The Newspaper War on Britain, 1764–1776* (New York, 1957)

Ira D. Gruber, "The American Revolution as a Conspiracy: The British View," *William and Mary Quarterly*, XXVI (July 1969)

Carl L. Becker, *The Declaration of Independence* (New York, 1922)

John M. Head, *A Time to Rend: An Essay on the Decision for American Independence* (Madison, Wisc., 1968)

Jere R. Daniell, *Experiment in Republicanism: New Hampshire Politics and the American Revolution, 1741–1794* (Cambridge, Mass., 1970)

Richard D. Brown, *Revolutionary Politics in Massachusetts: The Boston Committee of Correspondence* . . . (Cambridge, Mass., 1970)

John C. Miller, *Sam Adams: Pioneer in Propaganda* (Boston, 1936)

Benjamin W. Labaree, *The Boston Tea Party* (New York, 1964)

Alan and Katherine Day, "Another Look at the Boston 'Caucus,'" *Journal of American Studies*, V (April 1971)

David S. Lovejoy, *Rhode Island Politics and the American Revolution* . . . (Providence, 1958)

Mack E. Thompson, "The Ward–Hopkins Controversy and the American Revolution in Rhode Island," *William and Mary Quarterly*, XVI (July 1959)

Oscar Zeichner, *Connecticut's Years of Controversy, 1750–1776* (Chapel Hill, 1949)

Carl L. Becker, *The History of Political Parties in the Province of New York, 1760–1776* (Madison, Wisc., 1909)

Bernard Mason, *The Road to Independence: The Revolutionary Movement in New York* . . . (Lexington, Ky., 1966)

Don R. Gerlach, *Philip Schuyler and the American Revolution in New York* (Lincoln, Nebr., 1964)

Roger Champagne, "New York's Radicals and the Coming of Independence," *Journal of American History*, LI (June 1964)

Bernard Friedman, "The Shaping of the Radical Consciousness in Provincial New York," *Journal of American History*, LVI (March 1970)

Donald L. Kemmerer, *Path to Freedom: The Struggle for Self-Government in Colonial New Jersey, 1703–1776* (Princeton, 1940)

Theodore Thayer, *Pennsylvania Politics and the Growth of Democracy, 1740–1776* (Harrisburg, Pa., 1953)

Dietmar Rothermund, *The Layman's Progress; Religious and Political Experience in Colonial Pennsylvania, 1740–1770* (Philadelphia, 1961)

Richard Bauman, *For the Reputation of Truth: Politics, Religion, and Conflict Among the Pennsylvania Quakers, 1750–1800* (New Haven, 1971)

David L. Jacobson, *John Dickinson and the Revolution in Pennsylvania, 1764–1776* (Berkeley, 1965)

Charles A. Barker, *The Background of the Revolution in Maryland* (New Haven, 1940)

James Haw, "Maryland Politics on the Eve of the Revolution . . . ," *Maryland Historical Magazine*, LXV (Summer 1970)

Lucille Griffith, *The Virginia House of Burgesses, 1750–1774* (rev. edition, University, Ala., 1970)

Thad W. Tate, "The Coming of the Revolution in Virginia . . . ,"
   William and Mary Quarterly, XIX (July 1962)
George E. Frakes, *Laboratory for Liberty: The South Carolina Legis-
   lative Committee System, 1719–1776* (Lexington, Ky., 1971)
Robert M. Weir, ". . . Pre-Revolutionary South Carolina Politics,"
   William and Mary Quarterly, XXVI (October 1969)
Richard Walsh, *Charleston's Sons of Liberty* . . . (Columbia, S.C.,
   1959)
Richard Maxwell Brown, *The South Carolina Regulators* . . . (Cam-
   bridge, Mass., 1963)
W. W. Abbott, *The Royal Governors of Georgia, 1754–1775* (Chapel
   Hill, 1959)

II *The Revolutionary Struggle, 1776–1789*

Jack P. Greene, "The Reappraisal of the American Revolution in
   Recent Historical Literature," in Greene (ed.), *The Reinter-
   pretation of the American Revolution* . . . (New York, 1968)
R. R. Palmer, *The Age of the Democratic Revolution: A Political
   History of Europe and America, 1760–1800* (2 vols., Prince-
   ton, 1959–64)
J. R. Pole, *Political Representation in England and the Origins of
   the American Republic* (London, 1966)
Forrest McDonald, *E Pluribus Unum: The Formation of the Ameri-
   can Republic 1776–1790* (Boston, 1965)
Gordon S. Wood, *The Creation of the American Republic, 1776–
   1787* (Chapel Hill, 1969)
Thad W. Tate, "The Social Contract in America, 1774–1787 . . . ,"
   William and Mary Quarterly, XXII (July 1965)
Merrill Jensen, "Democracy and the American Revolution," *Hunting-
   ton Library Quarterly*, XX (August 1957)
Cecilia M. Kenyon, "Republicanism and Radicalism in the American
   Revolution," *William and Mary Quarterly*, XIX (April 1962)
Richard Buel, Jr., "Democracy and the American Revolution . . . ,"
   William and Mary Quarterly, XXI (April 1964)
Elisha P. Douglass, *Rebels and Democrats: The Struggle for Equal
   Political Rights and Majority Rule* (Chapel Hill, 1961)
J. R. Pole, "Historians and the Problem of Early American Democ-
   racy," *American Historical Review*, LXVII (April 1962)
Philip Davidson, *Propaganda and the American Revolution* . . .
   (Chapel Hill, 1941)

A Selected Modern Bibliography

Edmund C. Burnett, *The Continental Congress* (New York, 1941)

Lynn Montross, *The Reluctant Rebels . . . the Continental Congress* (New York, 1950)

Jackson Turner Main, *The Upper House in Revolutionary America, 1763–1788* (Madison, Wisc., 1967)

Jackson Turner Main, "Government by the People: The American Revolution and the Democratization of the Legislatures," *William and Mary Quarterly*, XX (July 1966)

Allan Nevins, *The American States During and After the Revolution* (New York, 1924)

Richard Upton, *Revolutionary New Hampshire . . .* (Hanover, N.H., 1936)

Robert E. Brown, *Middle-Class Democracy and the Revolution in Massachusetts . . .* (Ithaca, N.Y., 1955)

David Syrett, "Town-Meeting Politics in Massachusetts, 1776–1786," *William and Mary Quarterly*, XXI (July 1964)

Ellen E. Brennan, *Plural Office-Holding in Massachusetts 1760–1780 . . .* (Chapel Hill, 1945)

Robert J. Taylor, *Western Massachusetts in the Revolution* (Providence, 1954)

Christopher Collier, *Roger Sherman's Connecticut: Yankee Politics and American Revolution* (Middletown, Conn., 1971)

Thomas J. Wertenbaker, *Father Knickerbocker Rebels: New York City During the Revolution* (New York, 1948)

J. Paul Selsam, *The Pennsylvania Constitution of 1776 . . .* Philadelphia, 1936)

Philip A. Crowl, *Maryland During and After the Revolution . . .* (Baltimore, 1942)

Robert E. and B. Katherine Brown, *Virginia, 1705–1786: Democracy or Aristocracy?* (East Lansing, 1964)

Robert L. Ganyard, "Radicals and Conservatives in Revolutionary North Carolina . . . ," *William and Mary Quarterly*, XXIV (October 1967)

Kenneth Coleman, *The American Revolution in Georgia . . .* (Athens, Ga., 1958)

C. H. Van Tyne, *Loyalists in the American Revolution* (New York, 1902)

William H. Nelson, *The American Tory* (Oxford, 1961)

Wallace Brown, *The King's Friends* (Providence, 1966)

North Callahan, *Flight from the Republic* . . . (Indianapolis, 1967)

Julian P. Boyd, *Anglo-American Union: Joseph Galloway's Plans To Preserve the British Empire* . . . (Philadelphia, 1941)

Lawrence Henry Gipson, *American Loyalist: Jared Ingersoll* (New Haven, 1920)

L. F. S. Upton, *The Loyal Whig: William Smith of New York and Quebec* (Toronto, 1969)

Robert O. DeMond, *Loyalists in North Carolina* . . . (Durham, N.C., 1940)

Richard B. Morris, "The Confederation Period and the American Historian," *William and Mary Quarterly*, XIII (April 1956)

Merrill Jensen, *The Articles of Confederation* . . . (Madison, Wisc., 1940)

Merrill Jensen, *The New Nation* . . . 1781–1789 (New York, 1950)

E. James Ferguson, *The Power of the Purse* . . . 1776–1790 (Chapel Hill, 1961)

Jackson Turner Main, *Political Parties Before the Constitution* (New York, 1971)

Irwin H. Polishook, *Rhode Island and the Union, 1774–1795* (Evanston, Ill., 1969)

Ernest W. Spaulding, *New York in the Critical Period* . . . (New York, 1932)

Richard P. McCormick, *Experiment in Independence: New Jersey in the Critical Period* . . . (New Brunswick, N.J., 1950)

Jackson Turner Main, "Sections and Politics in Virginia, 1781–1787," *William and Mary Quarterly*, XII (January 1955)

James R. Morrill, *The Practice and Politics of Fiat Finance: North Carolina in the Confederation* . . . (Chapel Hill, 1969)

W. W. Abbot, "The Structure of Politics in Georgia: 1782–1789," *William and Mary Quarterly*, XIV (January 1957)

Marian L. Starkey, *A Little Rebellion* [Shays'], (New York, 1955)

Robert A. Feer, "Shays' Rebellion and the Constitution: A Study in Causation," *New England Quarterly*, XLII (September 1969)

Stanley Elkins and Eric McKitrick, "The Founding Fathers: Young Men of the Revolution," *Political Science Quarterly*, LXXVI (June 1961)

Max Farrand, *The Framing of the Constitution* . . . (New Haven, 1913)

Charles Warren, *The Making of the Constitution* . . . (Boston, 1928)

Clinton Rossiter, *1787: The Grand Convention* (New York, 1966)

John P. Roche, "The Founding Fathers: A Reform Caucus in Action," *American Political Science Review*, LV (December 1961)

Edward M. Burns, *James Madison: Philosopher of the Constitution* (New Brunswick, N. J., 1938)

Arthur N. Holcombe, "The Role of Washington in the Framing of the Constitution," *Huntington Library Quarterly*, XIX (August 1956)

Staughton Lynd, "The Compromise of 1787," *Political Science Quarterly*, LXXXI (June 1966)

Paul Eidelberg, *The Philosophy of the American Constitution* . . . (New York, 1968)

Douglass Adair, ". . . David Hume, James Madison and the Tenth Federalist," *Huntington Library Quarterly*, XX (August 1957)

Charles A. Beard, *An Economic Interpretation of the Constitution* (new edition, New York, 1935)

Forrest McDonald, *We the People: The Economic Origins of the Constitution* (Chicago, 1958)

Gottfried Dietze, *The Federalist* . . . (Baltimore, 1960)

Charles W. Roll, Jr., "We, Some of the People: Apportionment in the Thirteen State Conventions Ratifying the Constitution," *Journal of American History*, LVI (June 1969)

Cecilia M. Kenyon, "Men of Little Faith: the Anti-Federalists . . . ," *William and Mary Quarterly*, XII (January 1955)

Jackson T. Main, *The Anti-Federalists* (Chapel Hill, 1961)

Hamilton M. Bishop, *Why Rhode Island Opposed the Federal Constitution* (Providence, 1950)

Linda Grant De Pauw, *The Eleventh Pillar: New York State and the Federal Constitution* (Ithaca, N.Y., 1966)

Staughton Lynd, *Anti-Federalism in Dutchess County, New York* . . . (Chicago, 1962)

Louise I. Trenholme, *Ratification* . . . *in North Carolina* (New York, 1932)

Robert A. Rutland, *The Birth of the Bill of Rights* . . . (Chapel Hill, 1955)

III *Foundations for a New Politics, 1789–1824*

James Hart, *The American Presidency in Action, 1789* (New York, 1948)

Ralph V. Harlow, *History of Legislative Methods . . . Before 1825* (New Haven, 1917)

Richard R. Beeman, "Unlimited Debate in the Senate: The First Phase," *Political Science Quarterly*, LXXXIII (September 1968)

Patrick J. Furlong, "The Origins of the House Committee of Ways and Means," *William and Mary Quarterly*, XXV (October 1968)

J. R. Saylor, "Creating the Federal Judiciary," *Baylor Law Review*, VIII (Summer 1956)

John C. Miller, *The Federalist Era . . .* (New York, 1960)

Jacob E. Cooke, "The Compromise of 1790," *William and Mary Quarterly*, XXVII (October 1970)

Leland D. Baldwin, *Whiskey Rebels: The Story of a Frontier Uprising* (Pittsburgh, 1939)

Stanley D. Rose, "Alexander Hamilton and the Historians," *Vanderbilt Law Review*, XI (June 1958)

Gerald Stourzh, *Alexander Hamilton and the Idea of Republican Government* (Stanford, Calif., 1970)

Edward Handler, *America and Europe in the Political Thought of John Adams* (Cambridge, Mass., 1964)

John R. Howe, Jr., *The Changing Political Thought of John Adams* (Princeton, 1966)

Stephen G. Kurtz, "The Political Science of John Adams . . . ," *William and Mary Quarterly*, XXV (October 1968)

Stephen G. Kurtz, *The Presidency of John Adams . . .* (Philadelphia, 1957)

Samuel F. Bemis, *Jay's Treaty . . .* (rev. edition, New Haven, 1962)

Jerald A. Combs, *The Jay Treaty: Political Battleground of the Founding Fathers* (Berkeley, 1970)

Alexander DeConde, *The Quasi-War: The Politics and Diplomacy of the Undeclared War with France, 1797–1801* (New York, 1966)

John A. Munroe, *Federalist Delaware, 1775–1815* (New Brunswick, N.J., 1954)

Charles S. Sydnor, *Gentlemen Freeholders: Political Practices in Washington's Virginia* (Chapel Hill, 1952)

Roy F. Nichols, *The Invention of the American Political Parties* (New York, 1967)

Joseph Charles, *The Origins of the American Party System* (Williamsburg, Va., 1956)

William N. Chambers, *Political Parties in a New Nation* . . . (New York, 1963)

Morton Borden, *Parties and Politics in the Early Republic* . . . (New York, 1967)

Harry Ammon, "The Genêt Mission and the Development of American Political Parties," *Journal of American History,* LII (March 1966)

Charles A. Beard, *Economic Origins of Jeffersonian Democracy* (New York, 1915)

Manning J. Dauer, *The Adams Federalists* (Baltimore, 1953)

David Hackett Fischer, *The Revolution of American Conservatism: The Federalist Party in the Era of Jeffersonian Democracy* (New York, 1965)

Linda K. Kerber, *Federalists in Dissent: Imagery and Ideology in Jeffersonian America* (Ithaca, N.Y., 1970)

Shaw Livermore, Jr., *The Twilight of Federalism: The Disintegration of the Federalist Party* . . . (Princeton, 1962)

Anson E. Morse, *The Federalist Party in Massachusetts to the Year 1800* (Princeton, 1909)

James M. Banner, Jr., *To the Hartford Convention: The Federalists and the Origins of Party Politics in Massachusetts, 1789–1815* (New York, 1969)

Robert Ernst, *Rufus King: American Federalist* (Chapel Hill, 1968)

Lisle A. Rose, *Prologue to Democracy: The Federalists in the South, 1789–1800* (Lexington, Ky., 1968)

Norman K. Risjord, "The Virginia Federalists," *Journal of Southern History,* XXXIII (November 1967)

U. B. Phillips, "The South Carolina Federalists," *American Historical Review,* XIV (April–July 1909)

John R. Howe, Jr., "Republican Thought and the Political Violence of the 1790's," *American Quarterly*, XIX (Summer 1967)

Leonard W. Levy, *Freedom of Speech and Press in Early American History* . . . (New York, 1963)

James Morton Smith, *Freedom's Fetters: The Alien and Sedition Laws* . . . (Ithaca, N.Y., 1956)

James Morton Smith, "Grass Roots Origins of the Kentucky Resolutions," *William and Mary Quarterly*, XXVII (April 1970)

Adrienne Koch and Harry Ammon, "The Virginia and Kentucky Resolutions . . . ," *William and Mary Quarterly*, V (April 1948)

Donald H. Stewart, *The Opposition Press of the Federalist Period* (Albany, 1969)

Marshall Smelser, *The Democratic Republic, 1801–1815* (New York, 1968)

Merrill D. Peterson, *Thomas Jefferson and the New Nation* (New York, 1970)

Dumas Malone, *Jefferson the President: First Term, 1801–1805* (Boston, 1970)

Charles O. Lerche, Jr., "Jefferson and the Election of 1800: A Case Study of the Political Smear," *William and Mary Quarterly*, V (October 1948)

Raymond Walters, Jr., *Albert Gallatin* . . . (New York, 1957)

Sidney H. Aronson, *Status and Kinship in the Higher Civil Service: Standards of Selection in the Administrations of John Adams, Thomas Jefferson, and Andrew Jackson* (Cambridge, Mass., 1964)

Carl E. Prince, "The Passing of the Aristocracy: Jefferson's Removal of the Federalists, 1801–1805," *Journal of American History*, LVII (December 1970)

Thomas P. Abernethy, *The Burr Conspiracy* (New York, 1954)

Adrienne Koch, *Jefferson and Madison: The Great Collaboration* (New York, 1950)

Irving Brant, *The Fourth President: A Life of James Madison* (Indianapolis, 1970)

Francis Harrold, "The Upper House in Jeffersonian Political Theory," *Virginia Magazine of History*, LXXVIII (July 1970)

Joseph Cooper, "Jeffersonian Attitudes Toward Executive Leadership and Committee Development in the House of Representatives," *Western Political Quarterly*, XVIII (March 1965)

Paul Goodman, "Social Status of Party Leadership: The House of

Representatives, 1797–1804," *William and Mary Quarterly*, XXV (July 1968)

James Sterling Young, *The Washington Community, 1800–1828* (New York, 1966)

Richard E. Ellis, *The Jeffersonian Crisis: Courts and Politics in the Young Republic* (New York, 1971)

Caleb P. Patterson, *The Constitutional Principles of Thomas Jefferson* (Austin, 1953)

Leonard W. Levy, *Jefferson and Civil Liberties . . .* (Cambridge, Mass., 1963)

Donald O. Dewey, *Marshall versus Jefferson: The Political Background of Marbury v. Madison* (New York, 1970)

C. Peter Magrath, *Yazoo: Law and Politics in the New Republic* (Providence, 1966)

Ronald F. Banks, *Maine Becomes a State: The Movement To Separate Maine from Massachusetts, 1785–1820* (Middletown, Conn., 1970)

Dixon Ryan Fox, *The Decline of Aristocracy in the Politics of New York, 1801–1840* (New York, 1919)

Alvin Kass, *Politics in New York State, 1800–1830* (Syracuse, N.Y. 1965)

Howard L. McBain, *DeWitt Clinton and the Origins of the Spoils System in New York* (New York, 1907)

Walter R. Fee, *The Transition from Aristocracy to Democracy in New Jersey . . .* (Somerville, N.J., 1933)

Stanford W. Higginbotham, *The Keystone in the Democratic Arch: Pennsylvania Politics, 1800–1816* (Harrisburg, Pa., 1952)

Willey E. Hodges, "The Theoretical Basis of Anti-Governmentalism in Virginia, 1789–1836," *Journal of Politics*, IX (August 1947)

Thomas P. Abernethy, *From Frontier to Plantation in Tennessee: A Study in Frontier Democracy* (Chapel Hill, 1932)

Alfred B. Sears, *Thomas Worthington: Father of Ohio Statehood* (Columbus, 1958)

Noble E. Cunningham, Jr., *The Jeffersonian Republicans . . .* (2 vols., Chapel Hill, 1957–63)

Leonard D. White, *The Jeffersonians: A Study in Administrative History* (New York, 1951)

W. A. Robinson, *Jeffersonian Democracy in New England* (New Haven, 1916)

Paul Goodman, *The Democratic-Republicans of Massachusetts . . .* (Cambridge, Mass., 1964)

Alfred F. Young, *The Democratic Republicans of New York: The Origins, 1763–1797* (Chapel Hill, 1967)

Ray W. Irwin, *Daniel D. Tompkins: Governor of New York and Vice-President of the United States* (New York, 1968)

Carl E. Prince, *New Jersey's Jeffersonian Republicans . . .* (Chapel Hill, 1967)

Norman K. Risjord, *The Old Republicans: Southern Conservatism in the Age of Jefferson* (New York, 1965)

Harry Ammon, "The Richmond Junto, 1800–1824," *Virginia Magazine of History . . .* , LXI (October 1953)

Delbert H. Gilpatrick, *Jeffersonian Democracy in North Carolina* (New York, 1931)

John H. Wolfe, *Jeffersonian Democracy in South Carolina* (Chapel Hill, 1940)

Lowell H. Harrison, *John Breckinridge, Jeffersonian Republican* (Louisville, Ky., 1969)

Louis M. Sears, *Jefferson and the Embargo* (Durham, N.C., 1927)

Norman K. Risjord, "1812: Conservatives, War Hawks, and the Nation's Honor," *William and Mary Quarterly*, XVIII (April 1961)

Reginald Horsman, *Causes of the War of 1812* (Philadelphia, 1962)

Roger H. Brown, *The Republic in Peril: 1812* (New York, 1964)

Victory A. Sapio, *Pennsylvania and the War of 1812* (Lexington, Ky., 1970)

Myron F. Wehtje, "Opposition in Virginia to the War of 1812," *Virginia Magazine of History*, LXXVIII (January 1970)

George Dangerfield, *The Era of Good Feelings* (New York, 1951)

Charles S. Sydnor, "The One-Party Period of American History," *American Historical Review*, LI (April 1946)

Harry Ammon, *James Monroe* (New York, 1971)

Norris W. Preyer, "Southern Support of the Tariff of 1816—a Reappraisal," *Journal of Southern History*, XXV (August 1959)

Vincent J. Capowski, "The Era of Good Feelings in New Hampshire . . . ," *Historical New Hampshire*, XXI (Winter 1966)

Philip S. Klein, *Pennsylvania Politics, 1817–1832: A Game Without Rules* (Philadelphia, 1940)

James A. Kehl, *Ill Feeling in the Era of Good Feeling: Western Pennsylvania Political Battles, 1815–1825* (Pittsburgh, 1956)

Thomas P. Abernethy, *The Formative Period in Alabama, 1815–1828* (Montgomery, 1922)

Lonnie J. White, *Politics on the Southwestern Frontier: Arkansas Territory, 1819–1836* (Memphis, 1964)

Lynn L. Marshall, "Genesis of Grass-Roots Democracy in Kentucky," *Mid-America*, XLVII (October 1965)

Edward S. Corwin, *John Marshall and the Constitution* (New Haven, 1920)

Robert K. Faulkner, *The Jurisprudence of John Marshall* (Princeton, 1968)

Gerald T. Dunne, *Justice Joseph Story* (New York, 1971)

Donald G. Morgan, *Justice William Johnson, the First Dissenter* (Columbia, S.C., 1954)

William G. North, "The Political Background of the Dartmouth College Case," *New England Quarterly*, XVIII (June 1945)

Harold J. Plous and Gordon E. Baker, "McCulloch *v.* Maryland . . . ," *Stanford Law Review*, IX (July 1957)

Maurice G. Baxter, *Daniel Webster and the Supreme Court* (Amherst, Mass., 1966)

Robert J. Steamer, "Congress and the Supreme Court During the Marshall Era," *Review of Politics*, XXVII (July 1965)

R. Kent Newmyer, *The Supreme Court Under Marshall and Taney* (New York, 1968)

IV *Jacksonian Politics in Action, 1824–1848*

Everett S. Brown, "The Presidential Election of 1824–1825," *Political Science Quarterly*, XL (September 1925)

Paul C. Nagel, "The Election of 1824 . . . ," *Journal of Southern History*, XXVI (August 1960)

Charles Sellers, "Jackson Men with Feet of Clay," *American Historical Review*, LXII (April 1957)

Samuel Flagg Bemis, *John Quincy Adams and the Union* (New York, 1956)

George A. Lipsky, *John Quincy Adams: His Theory and Ideas* (New York, 1950)

Robert V. Remini, *The Election of Andrew Jackson* (Philadelphia, 1963)

Chilton Williamson, *American Suffrage from Property to Democracy* . . . (Princeton, 1960)

Marchette Chute, *The First Liberty: A History of the Right To Vote* . . . (New York, 1969)

J. R. Pole, "The Suffrage in New Jersey, 1790–1807," *New Jersey History*, LXXI (January 1953)

J. R. Pole, "Representation and Authority in Virginia from the Revolution to Reform," *Journal of Southern History*, XXIV (February 1958)

George F. Taylor, "Suffrage in Early Kentucky," *Register of the Kentucky Historical Society*, LXI (January 1963)

George D. Luetscher, *Early Political Machinery in the United States* (Philadelphia, 1903)

William G. Morgan, ". . . the Congressional Nominating Caucus," *Proceedings of the American Philosophical Society*, CXIII (April 1969)

James S. Chase, "Jacksonian Democracy and the Rise of the Nominating Convention," *Mid-America*, XLV (October 1963)

Richard Hofstadter, *The Idea of a Party System: The Rise of Legitimate Opposition in the United States, 1780–1840* (Berkeley, 1969)

Michael Wallace, "Changing Concepts of Party in the United States: New York, 1815–1828," *American Historical Review*, LXXIV (December 1968)

David P. Peltier, "Party Development and Voter Participation in Delaware, 1792–1811," *Delaware History*, XIV (October 1970)

Homer C. Hockett, *Western Influences on Political Parties to 1825* (Columbus, 1917)

Richard P. McCormick, *The Second American Party System: Party Formation in the Jacksonian Period* (Chapel Hill, 1966)

Ronald P. Formisano, "Political Character, Antipartyism, and the Second Party System," *American Quarterly*, XXI (Winter 1969)

Brian G. Walton, "The Second Party System in Arkansas, 1836–1848," *Arkansas Historical Quarterly*, XXVIII (Spring 1969)

Ronald P. Formisano, "A Case Study of Party Formation: Michigan, 1835," *Mid-America*, L (April 1968)

Rodney O. Davis, ". . . Party Divisions in the Illinois Legislature, 1834–1841," in Robert P. Swierenga (ed.), *Quantification in American History* . . . (New York, 1970)

Charles Sellers, "Andrew Jackson versus the Historians," *Mississippi Valley Historical Review*, XLIV (March 1958)

Alfred A. Cave, *Jacksonian Democracy and the Historians* (Gainesville, Fla., 1964)

Frederick Jackson Turner, *The United States: 1830–1850* (New York, 1935)

Glyndon G. Van Deusen, *The Jacksonian Era, 1828–1848* (New York, 1959)

Arthur M. Schlesinger, Jr., *The Age of Jackson* (Boston, 1946)

Edward Pessen, *Jacksonian America: Society, Personality and Politics* (Homewood, Ill., 1969)

John William Ward, *Andrew Jackson: Symbol for an Age* (New York, 1955)

Robert V. Remini, *Andrew Jackson* (New York, 1966)

Erik M. Erikson, "The Federal Civil Service Under President Jackson," *Mississippi Valley Historical Review*, XIII (March 1927)

Norman A. Graebner, "James K. Polk: A Study in Federal Patronage," *Mississippi Valley Historical Review*, XXXVII (March 1952)

Richard P. McCormick, "New Perspectives on Jacksonian Politics," *American Historical Review*, LXV (January 1960)

Samuel R. Gammon, *The Presidential Campaign of 1832* (Baltimore, 1922)

Donald B. Cole, "The Presidential Election of 1832 in New Hampshire," *Historical New Hampshire*, XXI (Winter 1966)

Chauncey S. Boucher, *The Nullification Controversy* . . . (Chicago, 1916)

William W. Freehling, *Prelude to Civil War: The Nullification Controversy* (New York, 1966)

Charles M. Wiltse, *John C. Calhoun* . . . (3 vols., Indianapolis, 1944–51)

Gerald M. Capers, *John C. Calhoun, Opportunist* . . . (Gainesville, Fla., 1960)

Richard P. Longaker, "Andrew Jackson and the Judiciary," *Political Science Quarterly*, LXXI (September 1956)

William S. Hoffman, "Andrew Jackson, State Rightist: The Case of of the Georgia Indians," *Tennessee Historical Quarterly*, XI (December 1952)

Joseph C. Burke, "The Cherokee Cases: A Study in Law, Politics, and Morality," *Stanford Law Review*, XXI (February 1969)

Carl B. Swisher, *Roger B. Taney* (New York, 1935)

Stanley I. Kutler, *Privilege and Creative Destruction: The Charles River Bridge Case* (Philadelphia, 1971)

Michael A. Conron, "Law, Politics and Chief Justice Taney . . . ," *American Journal of Legal History*, XI (October 1967)

John P. Frank, *Justice [Peter V.] Daniel Dissenting . . .* (Cambridge, Mass., 1964)

Francis P. Weisenburger, *The Life of John McLean: A Politician on the . . . Supreme Court* (Columbus, 1937)

Bray Hammond, *Banks and Politics in America from the Revolution to the Civil War* (Princeton, 1957)

Ralph C. H. Catterall, *The Second Bank of the United States* (Chicago, 1903)

Thomas P. Govan, *Nicholas Biddle: Nationalist and Public Banker . . .* (Chicago, 1959)

Robert V. Remini, *Andrew Jackson and the Bank War* (New York, 1967)

Frank Otto Gatell, ". . . Van Buren, the Albany Regency, and the Wall Street Conspiracy," *Journal of American History*, LIII (June 1966)

Lynn L. Marshall, "The Authorship of Jackson's Bank Veto Message," *Mississippi Valley Historical Review*, L (December 1963)

Frank Otto Gatell, "Spoils of the Bank War: Political Bias in the Selection of Pet Banks," *American Historical Review*, LXX (October 1964)

John M. McFaul, *The Politics of Jacksonian Finance* (Ithaca, N.Y., 1972)

James Roger Sharp, *The Jacksonians versus the Banks: Politics in the States After the Panic of 1837* (New York, 1970)

Alden Whitman, *Labor Parties, 1827–1834* (New York, 1943)

Edward Pessen, "The Workingmen's Movement of the Jacksonian

Era," *Mississippi Valley Historical Review*, XLIII (December 1956)

Walter Hugins, *Jacksonian Democracy and the Working Class* . . . (Stanford, Calif., 1960)

Carl N. Degler, "The Loco-Focus: Urban 'Agrarians,'" *Journal of Economic History*, XVI (September 1956)

William A. Sullivan, "Did Labor Support Andrew Jackson?" *Political Science Quarterly*, LXII (December 1947)

Edward Pessen, *Most Uncommon Jacksonians: The Radical Leaders of the Early Labor Movement* (Albany, 1967)

Reginald C. McGrane, *The Panic of 1837* . . . (Chicago, 1924)

William G. Carleton, "Political Aspects of the Van Buren Era," *South Atlantic Quarterly*, L (April 1951)

William Trimble, "Diverging Tendencies in New York Democracy in the Period of the Locofocos," *American Historical Review*, XXIV (April 1919)

James C. Curtis, *The Fox at Bay: Martin Van Buren and the Presidency* . . . (Lexington, Ky., 1970)

Max M. Mintz, "The Political Ideas of Martin Van Buren," *New York History*, XXX (October 1949)

Robert G. Gunderson, *The Log-Cabin Campaign* [1840], (Lexington, Ky., 1957)

Arthur B. Darling, *Political Changes in Massachusetts, 1824–1848* . . . (New Haven, 1925)

Lee Benson, *The Concept of Jacksonian Democracy: New York as a Test Case* (Princeton, 1961)

Frank Otto Gatell, "Money and Party in Jacksonian America: A Quantitative Look at New York City's Men of Quality," *Political Science Quarterly*, LXXII (June 1967)

The Jacksonian Heritage, *Pennsylvania Politics, 1833–1848* (Harrisburg, Pa., 1958)

Howard Braverman, "The Economic and Political Background of the Conservative Revolt in Virginia," *Virginia Magazine of History*, LX (April 1952)

William S. Hoffman, *Andrew Jackson and North Carolina Politics* (Chapel Hill, 1958)

Robert V. Remini, *Martin Van Buren and the Making of the Democratic Party* (New York, 1959)

Leonard D. White, *The Jacksonians* . . . (New York, 1954)

Marvin Meyers, *The Jacksonian Persuasion: Politics and Belief* (Stanford, Calif., 1957)

Russel B. Nye, *George Bancroft, Brahmin Rebel* (New York, 1945)

John A. Garraty, *Silas Wright* (New York, 1949)

Charles H. Ambler, *Thomas Ritchie* (Richmond, 1913)

William N. Chambers, *Old Bullion [Thomas Hart] Benton* . . . (Boston, 1956)

Donald B. Cole, *Jacksonian Democracy in New Hampshire* . . . (Cambridge, Mass., 1970)

Arthur B. Darling, "Jacksonian Democracy in Massachusetts," *American Historical Review*, XXIX (January 1924)

Robert V. Remini, "The Albany Regency," *New York History*, XXXIX (October 1958)

Jerome Mushkat, *Tammany: The Evolution of a Political Machine*, 1789–1865 (Syracuse, N.Y., 1971)

Mark H. Haller, "The Rise of the Jackson Party in Maryland," *Journal of Southern History*, XXVII (August 1962)

W. Wayne Smith, "Jacksonian Democracy on the Chesapeake . . . ," *Maryland Historical Magazine*, LXII (December 1967), LXIII (March 1968)

Constance M. Green, "The Jacksonian 'Revolution' in the District of Columbia," *Mississippi Valley Historical Review*, XLV (March 1959)

Clarence C. Norton, *The Democratic Party in Ante-Bellum North Carolina* . . . (Chapel Hill, 1930)

Arthur W. Thompson, *Jacksonian Democracy on the Florida Frontier* (Gainesville, Fla., 1961)

Edwin A. Miles, *Jacksonian Democracy in Mississippi* (Chapel Hill, 1960)

Robert E. Shalhope, "Jacksonian Politics in Missouri . . . ," *Civil War History*, XV (September 1969)

Harry R. Stevens, *The Early Jackson Party in Ohio* (Durham, N.C., 1957)

E. Malcolm Carroll, *Origins of the Whig Party* (Durham, N.C., 1925)

Lynn L. Marshall, "The Strange Stillbirth of the Whig Party," *American Historical Review*, LXXII (January 1967)

Edwin A. Miles, "The Whig Party and the Menace of Caesar," *Tennessee Historical Quarterly*, XXVII (Winter 1968)

Glyndon G. Van Deusen, "Some Aspects of Whig Thought and The-
    ory in the Jacksonian Period," *American Historical Review*,
    LXIII (January 1958)
George R. Poage, *Henry Clay and the Whig Party* (Chapel Hill,
    1936)
Glyndon G. Van Deusen, . . . *Henry Clay* (Boston, 1937)
Clement Eaton, *Henry Clay* . . . (Boston, 1957)
Norman D. Brown, *Daniel Webster and the Politics of Availability*
    (Athens, Ga., 1969)
Albert D. Kirwan, *John J. Crittenden* . . . (Lexington, Ky., 1962)
Glyndon G. Van Deusen, *Thurlow Weed: Wizard of the Lobby* (Bos-
    ton, 1947)

Henry R. Mueller, *The Whig Party in Pennsylvania* (New York,
    1922)
Charles M. Thompson, *The Illinois Whigs* . . . (Urbana, Ill., 1915)

Arthur C. Cole, *The Whig Party in the South* (Washington, D.C.,
    1913)
Charles Sellers, "Who Were the Southern Whigs?" *American His-
    torical Review*, LIX (January 1954)
Henry H. Simms, *Rise of the Whigs in Virginia* . . . (Richmond,
    1929)
Max R. Williams, "The Foundations of the Whig Party in North
    Carolina . . ." *North Carolina Historical Review*, XLVII
    (April 1970)
Paul Murray, *The Whig Party in Georgia* . . . (Chapel Hill, 1948)
Herbert J. Doherty, Jr., *The Whigs of Florida* . . . (Gainesville,
    Fla., 1959)
Thomas B. Alexander *et al.*, "Who Were the Alabama Whigs?"
    Alabama Review, XVI (January 1963)
Randolph Campbell, "The Whig Party of Texas . . . ," *Southwest-
    ern Historical Quarterly*, LXXIII (July 1969)
John Vollmer Mering, *The Whig Party in Missouri* (Columbia, Mo.,
    1967)

V   *The Politics of Slavery, 1820–1860*

Glover Moore, *The Missouri Controversy, 1819–1821* (Lexington,
    Ky., 1953)
Philip F. Detweiler, "The Congressional Debate on Slavery . . .
    1819–1821," *American Historical Review*, LXIII (April 1958)

Richard M. Brown, "The Missouri Crisis, Slavery, and the Politics of Jacksonianism," *South Atlantic Quarterly*, LXV (Winter 1966)

Philip J. Staudenraus, *The African Colonization Movement* (New York, 1961)

Robert J. Clarke, *The Road from Monticello: . . . the Virginia Slavery Debate of 1832* (Durham, N.C., 1941)

Gerald S. Henig, "The Jacksonian Attitude Toward Abolitionists in the 1830's," *Tennessee Historical Quarterly*, XXVIII (Spring 1969)

Leonard L. Richards, *"Gentlemen of Property and Standing": Anti-Abolition Riots . . . in the 1830's* (New York, 1970)

James M. McPherson, "The Fight Against the Gag Rule . . . ," *Journal of Negro History*, XLVIII (July 1963)

Russel B. Nye, *Fettered Freedom: Civil Liberties and the Slavery Controversy . . .* (East Lansing, 1949)

Robert J. Morgan, *A Whig Embattled: The Presidency Under John Tyler* (Lincoln, Nebr., 1954)

James C. N. Paul, *Rift in the Democracy* (Philadelphia, 1951)

Charles Seller, *James K. Polk . . .* (2 vols., Princeton, 1957–66)

Charles A. McCoy, *Polk and the Presidency* (Austin, 1960)

James J. Horn, "Trends in Historical Interpretation: James K. Polk," *North Carolina Historical Review*, XLII (October 1965)

Norman A. Graebner, *Empire on the Pacific: A Study in American Continental Expansion* (New York, 1955)

John Hope Franklin, "The Southern Expansionists of 1846," *Journal of Southern History*, XXV (August 1959)

Chaplain W. Morrison, *Democratic Politics and Sectionalism: The Wilmot Proviso Controversy* (Chapel Hill, 1967)

Eric Foner, "The Wilmot Proviso Revisited," *Journal of American History*, LVI (September 1969)

Peter T. Harstad and Richard W. Resh, "The Causes of the Mexican War: A Note on Changing Interpretations," *Arizona and the West*, VI (Winter 1964)

Kinley J. Brauer, *Cotton versus Conscience: Massachusetts Whig Politics and Southwestern Expansion . . .* (Lexington, Ky., 1967)

Arthur M. Mowry, *The Dorr War: Or, the Constitutional Struggle in Rhode Island* (Providence, 1901)

H. D. A. Donovan, *The Barnburners . . .* (New York, 1925)

Edgar A. Holt, *Party Politics in Ohio, 1840–1850* (Columbus, Ohio, 1931)

Floyd B. Streeter, *Political Parties in Michigan, 1837–1860* . . . (Lansing, Mich., 1918)

Robert M. Ireland, "Aristocrats All: The Politics of County Government in Ante-Bellum Kentucky," *Review of Politics,* XXXII (July 1970)

Stanley Siegel, *A Political History of the Texas Republic, 1836–1845* (Austin, 1956)

Theodore C. Smith, *The Liberty and Free Soil Parties in the Northwest* (New York, 1897)

Betty Fladeland, *James Gillespie Birney* . . . (Ithaca, N.Y., 1955)

Ralph L. Morrow, "The Liberty Party in Vermont," *New England Quarterly,* II (April 1929)

Joseph G. Rayback, "The Liberty Party Leaders of Ohio . . . ," *Ohio Historical Quarterly,* LVII (April 1958)

Eric Foner, "Politics and Prejudice: The Free Soil Party and the Negro . . . ," *Journal of Negro History,* L (October 1965)

Edward C. Schriver, "Antislavery: Free Soil . . . in Maine . . . ," *New England Quarterly,* XLII (March 1969)

Richard H. Sewell, *John P. Hale and the Politics of Abolition* (Cambridge, Mass., 1965)

Frank Otto Gatell, *John Gorham Palfrey and the New England Conscience* (Cambridge, Mass., 1963)

Frederick J. Blue, "Ohio Free Soilers . . . ," *Ohio History,* LXXXVI (Winter 1967)

Allan Nevins, *Ordeal of the Union* . . . (2 vols., New York, 1947)

Jesse Macy, *Political Parties* . . . *1846–1861* (New York, 1900)

Deal L. Yarwood, "Legislative Persistence: A Comparison of the United States Senate in 1850 and 1860," *Midwest Journal of Political Science,* XI (May 1967)

Holman Hamilton, *Prologue to Conflict: The Crisis and Compromise of 1850* (Lexington, Ky., 1964)

Holman Hamilton, *Zachary Taylor* . . . (2 vols., Indianapolis, 1941–51)

Frank H. Hodder, "The Authorship of the Compromise of 1850," *Mississippi Valley Historical Review,* XXII (March 1936)

Major L. Wilson, ". . . Webster and His Critics in the Crisis of 1850," *Civil War History,* XIV (December 1968)

Robert R. Russel, "What Was the Compromise of 1850?" *Journal of Southern History*, XXII (August 1956)

Larry Gara, "The Fugitive Slave Law: A Double Paradox," *Civil War History*, X (September 1964)

Stanley W. Campbell, *The Slave Catchers: Enforcement of the Fugitive Slave Law* . . . (Chapel Hill, 1970)

Larry Gara, *The Liberty Line: The Legend of the Underground Railroad* (Lexington, Ky., 1961)

Horatio T. Strother, *The Underground Railroad in Connecticut* (Middletown, Conn., 1962)

Norman L. Rosenberg, "Personal Liberty Laws and Sectional Crisis . . ." *Civil War History*, XVII (March 1971)

Roy F. Nichols, "The Kansas-Nebraska Act: A Century of Historiography," *Mississippi Valley Historical Review*, XLIII (September 1956)

Robert R. Russel, "The Issues in the Congressional Struggle over the Kansas-Nebraska Bill," *Journal of Southern History*, XXIX (May 1963)

James C. Malin, *The Nebraska Question, 1852–1854* (Lawrence, Kans., 1953)

Alice Nichols, *Bleeding Kansas* (New York, 1954)

James A. Rawley, *Race and Politics: "Bleeding Kansas" and the Coming of the Civil War* (Philadelphia, 1969)

Samuel A. Johnson, *Battle Cry of Freedom: The New England Emigrant Aid Company in the Kansas Crusade* (Lawrence, Kans., 1954)

Ray A. Billington, *The Protestant Crusade, 1800–1860* (New York, 1938)

David Brion Davis, "Some Themes of Counter-Subversion: An Analysis of Anti-Masonic, Anti-Catholic, and Anti-Mormon Literature," *Mississippi Valley Historical Review*, XLVII (September 1960)

William G. Bean, "Puritan versus Celt, 1850–1860," *New England Quarterly*, VII (March 1934)

Larry A. Rand, "The Know-Nothing Party of Rhode Island . . . ," *Rhode Island History*, XXIII (October 1964)

Carroll J. Noonan, *Nativism in Connecticut, 1829–1860* (Washington, D.C., 1938)

Louis D. Scisco, *Political Nativism in New York State* (New York, 1901)

Warren F. Hewitt, "The Know-Nothing Party in Pennsylvania," *Pennsylvania History*, II (April 1935)

Evangeline Thomas, *Nativism in the Old Northwest* (Washington, D.C., 1936)

George M. Stephenson, "Nativism in . . . the Mississippi Valley," *Mississippi Valley Historical Review*, IX (December 1922)

W. Darrell Overdyke, *The Know-Nothing Party in the South* (Baton Rouge, 1950)

Mary S. McConville, *Political Nativism in . . . Maryland . . .* (Washington, D.C., 1928)

Leon C. Soulé, *The Know Nothing Party in New Orleans . . .* Baton Rouge, 1961)

Ralph A. Wooster, ". . . the Texas Know-Nothings," *Southwestern Historical Quarterly*, LXX (January 1967)

Wallace B. Turner, "The Know-Nothing Movement in Kentucky," *Filson Club Historical Quarterly*, XXVIII (July 1954)

Avery O. Craven, *The Growth of Southern Nationalism, 1848–1861* (Baton Rouge, 1953)

Douglas Bowers, "Ideology and Political Parties in Maryland, 1851–1856," *Maryland Historical Magazine*, LXIV (Fall 1969)

Avery O. Craven, *Edmund Ruffin, Southerner . . .* (New York, 1932)

J. G. DeRoulhac Hamilton, *Party Politics in North Carolina, 1835–1860* (Durham, N.C., 1916)

Ralph A. Wooster, *The People in Power: Courthouse and Statehouse in the Lower South, 1850–1860* (Knoxville, Tenn., 1969)

Harold S. Schultz, *Nationalism and Sectionalism in South Carolina, 1852–1860 . . .* (Durham, N.C., 1950)

Horace Montgomery, *Cracker Parties* (Baton Rouge, 1950)

Lewy Derman, *Party Politics in Alabama from 1850 to 1860* (Wetumpka, Ala., 1935)

Thomas B. Alexander *et al.*, "The Basis of Alabama's Ante-Bellum Two-Party System," *Alabama Review*, XIX (October 1966)

Donald M. Rawson, "Democratic Resurgence in Mississippi, 1852–1853," *Journal of Mississippi History*, XXVI (February 1964)

Ralph A. Wooster, "Membership in Early Texas Legislatures, 1850–1860," *Southwestern Historical Quarterly*, LXIX (October 1965)

Eugene H. Berwanger, *The Frontier Against Slavery: Western Anti-Negro Prejudice and the Slavery Extension Controversy* (Urbana, Ill., 1967)

Loomis M. Ganaway, *New Mexico and the Sectional Controversy* . . . (Albuquerque, 1944)

William H. Ellison, *A Self-Governing Dominion: California, 1849–1860* (Berkeley, 1950)

Robert W. Johannsen, *Frontier Politics and the Sectional Conflict: The Pacific Northwest* . . . (Seattle, 1956)

Roy F. Nichols, *The Democratic Machine, 1850–1854* (New York, 1923)

Joel H. Silbey, "The Southern National Democrats, 1845–1861," *Mid-America*, XLVII (July 1965)

Andrew W. Crandall, *Early History of the Republican Party* . . . (Boston, 1930)

Eric Foner, *Free Soil, Free Labor, Free Men: The Ideology of the Republican Party Before the Civil War* (New York, 1970)

Ruhl J. Bartlett, *John C. Fremont and the Republican Party* (Columbus, 1930)

Edward P. Brynn, "Vermont . . . and the Emergence of the Republican Party," *Vermont History*, XXXVIII (Spring 1970)

Martin B. Duberman, ". . . Beginnings of the Republican Party in Massachusetts," *New England Quarterly*, XXXIV (September 1961)

David Donald, *Charles Sumner and the Coming of the Civil War* (New York, 1960)

Jeter A. Isely, *Horace Greeley and the Republican Party* (Princeton, 1947)

Michael F. Holt, *Forging a Majority: The Formation of the Republican Party in Pittsburgh* . . . (New Haven, 1969)

Roger H. Van Bolt, "Rise of the Republican Party in Indiana . . . ," *Indiana Magazine of History*, LI (September 1955)

David S. Sparks, "Birth of the Republican Party in Iowa . . . ," *Iowa Journal of History*, LIV (January 1956)

Morton M. Rosenberg, "The First Republican Election Victory in Iowa," *Annals of Iowa*, XXXVI (Summer 1962)

Victor B. Howard, "Cassius M. Clay and the Origins of the Republican Party [in Kentucky]," *Filson Club Historical Magazine*, XLV (January 1971)

Roy F. Nichols, *Disruption of American Democracy* (New York, 1948)

Philip S. Klein, *President James Buchanan* . . . (University Park, Pa., 1962)

Vincent C. Hopkins, *Dred Scott's Case* (New York, 1951)

Robert W. Johannsen, "Stephen A. Douglas, Popular Sovereignty and the Territories," *The Historian*, XXII (August 1960)

Robert W. Johannsen, "Stephen A. Douglas and the South," *Journal of Southern History*, XXXIII (February 1967)

Kirk Jeffrey, Jr., "Stephen Arnold Douglas in American Historical Writing," *Illinois State Historical Society Journal*, LXI (Autumn 1968)

Harry V. Jaffa, *Crisis of the House Divided* . . . *the Lincoln–Douglas Debates* (Garden City, N.Y., 1959)

Allan Nevins, *The Emergence of Lincoln* . . . (2 vols., New York, 1950)

Don E. Fehrenbacher, *Prelude to Greatness: Lincoln in the 1850's* (Stanford, Calif., 1962)

Stephen B. Oates, *To Purge This Land with Blood: A Biography of John Brown* (New York, 1970)

Keith Sutherland, "The Structure of Congress as a Factor in the Legislative Crisis of 1860," *Mid-America*, LI (October 1969)

Thomas J. Pressly, *Americans Interpret Their Civil War* (Princeton, 1954)

Thomas N. Bonner, "Civil War Historians and the 'Needless War' Doctrine," *Journal of the History of Ideas*, XVII (April 1956)

John S. Rosenberg, "Toward a New Civil War Revisionism," *American Scholar*, XXXVIII (Spring 1969)

James G. Randall, "The Blundering Generation," *Mississippi Valley Historical Review*, XXVII (June 1940)

Avery Craven, *The Civil War in the Making* . . . (Baton Rouge, 1959)

David M. Potter, *The South and the Sectional Conflict* (Baton Rouge, 1968)

George H. Knoles (ed.), *The Crisis of the Union, 1860–1861* (Baton Rouge, 1965)

Norman A. Graebner (ed.), *Politics and the Crisis of 1860* (Urbana, Ill., 1961)

Reinhard D. Luthin, *The First Lincoln Campaign* (Cambridge, Mass., 1944)

Frederick C. Luebke (ed.), *Ethnic Voters and the Election of Lincoln* (Lincoln, Nebr., 1971)

Ollinger Crenshaw, *The Slave States in the Presidential Election of 1860* (Baltimore, 1945)

Seymour Martin Lipset, "The Emergence of the One Party South—The Election of 1860," in Lipset, *Political Man* . . . (New York, 1960)

Frank H. Heck, "John C. Breckinridge in the Crisis of 1860–1861," *Journal of Southern History*, XXI (August 1955)

Arthur C. Cole, "Lincoln's Election an Immediate Menace to Slavery . . . ?" *American Historical Review*, XXVI (July 1931)

VI   *Division and Forced Reunion, 1860–1877*

Ralph A. Wooster, "The Secession of the Lower South: . . . Changing Interpretations," *Civil War History*, VII (June 1961)

William J. Donnelly, ". . . the Historiography of the Support for Secession," *North Caroline Historical Review*, XLII (January 1965)

Dwight L. Dumond, *The Secession Movement* . . . (New York, 1931)

Ralph A. Wooster, *The Secession Conventions of the South* (Princeton, 1962)

Henry T. Shanks, *The Secession Movement in Virginia* . . . (Richmond, 1934)

Joseph C. Sitterson, *The Secession Movement in North Carolina* (Chapel Hill, 1939)

Stephen A. Channing, *Crisis of Fear: Secession in South Carolina* (New York, 1970)

Clarence P. Denman, *The Secession Movement in Alabama* (Montgomery, 1933)

Percy L. Rainwater, *Mississippi: Storm Center of Secession* . . . (Baton Rouge, 1938)

Charles B. Dew, "Who Won the Secession Election Louisiana?" *Journal of Southern History*, XXXVI (February 1970)

Wallace B. Turner, "The Secession Movement in Kentucky," *Register of the Kentucky Historical Society*, LXVI (July 1968)

Mary Scrugham, *The Peaceable Americans of 1861* (New York, 1921)

Robert G. Gunderson, *Old Gentlemen's Convention: The Washington Peace Conference of 1861* (Madison, Wisc., 1961)

Kenneth M. Stampp, *And the War Came: The North and the Secession Crisis* . . . (Baton Rouge, 1950)

John S. Tilley, *Lincoln Takes Command* (Chapel Hill, 1941)

David M. Potter, *Lincoln and His Party in the Secession Crisis* (New Haven, 1942)

Richard N. Current, *Lincoln and the First Shot* (Philadelphia, 1963)

Benjamin P. Thomas, *Portrait for Posterity: Lincoln and His Biographers* (New Brunswick, N.J., 1947)

David M. Potter, *The Lincoln Theme and American National Historiography* (Oxford, England, 1948)

James G. Randall, *Lincoln the President* (4 vols., New York, 1945–55)

Benjamin P. Thomas, *Abraham Lincoln* (New York, 1952)

Harry J. Carman and Reinhard Luthin, *Lincoln and the Patronage* (New York, 1943)

Benjamin Quarles, *Lincoln and the Negro* (New York, 1962)

John Hope Franklin, *The Emancipation Proclamation* (New York, 1963)

Mark M. Krug, "The Republican Party and the Emancipation Proclamation," *Journal of Negro History*, XLVIII (April 1963)

Forrest G. Wood, *Black Scare: The Racist Response to Emancipation and Reconstruction* (Berkeley, 1968)

Clarence E. Macartney, *Lincoln and His Cabinet* (New York, 1931)

Burton J. Hendrick, *Lincoln's War Cabinet* (Boston, 1946)

Glyndon G. Van Deusen, *William Henry Seward* (New York, 1967)

Benjamin P. Thomas and Harold M. Hyman, *Stanton: . . . Lincoln's Secretary of War* (New York, 1962)

Leonard P. Curry, *Blueprint for Modern America: Nonmilitary Legislation of the First Civil War Congress* (Nashville, Tenn., 1968)

Allan G. Bogue, "Bloc and Party in the United States Senate: 1861–1863," *Civil War History*, XIII (September 1967)

Hans L. Trefousse, "The Joint Committee on the Conduct of the War . . . ," *Civil War History*, X (March 1964)

David M. Silver, *Lincoln's Supreme Court* (Urbana, Ill., 1956)

James G. Randall, *Constitutional Problems Under Lincoln* (rev. edition, Urbana, Ill., 1951)

Frank L. Klement, *The Limits of Dissent: Clement L. Vallandigham and the Civil War* (Lexington, Ky., 1970)

Joseph G. Gambone, "Ex Parte Milligan . . . ," *Civil War History*,
    XVI (September 1970)

William F. Zernow, *Lincoln and the Party Divided* (Norman, Okla.,
    1954)
Sidney Kaplan, "The Miscegenation Issue in the Election of 1864,"
    Journal of Negro History, XXXIV (July 1949)
Grady McWhiney (ed.), *Grant, Lee, Lincoln and the Radicals*
    (Evanston, Ill., 1964)
T. Harry Williams, *Lincoln and the Radicals* (Madison, Wisc., 1941)

H. J. Eckenrode and Bryan Conrad, *George B. McClellan: The Man
    Who Saved the Union* (Chapel Hill, 1941)
Wood Gray, *The Hidden Civil War: The Story of the Copperheads*
    (New York, 1942)
Frank L. Klement, *The Copperheads in the Middle West* (Chicago,
    1960)

William B. Hesseltine, *Lincoln and the War Governors* (New York,
    1948)
Edith Ellen Ware, *Political Opinion in Massachusetts During Civil
    War and Reconstruction* (New York, 1916)
John Niven, *Connecticut for the Union* (New Haven, 1965)
Stewart Mitchell, *Horatio Seymour of New York* (Cambridge, Mass.,
    1938)
James A. Rawley, *Edwin D. Morgan* . . . (New York, 1955)
Erwin S. Bradley, *The Triumph of Militant Republicanism: . . .
    Pennsylvania and Presidential Politics, 1860–1872* (Philadel-
    phia, 1964)
William Dusinberre, *Civil War Issues in Philadelphia* . . . (Phila-
    delphia, 1965)
Harold Hancock, *Delaware During the Civil War* (Wilmington,
    1961)
Richard O. Curry, *A House Divided: A Study of Statehood Politics
    . . . in West Virginia* (Pittsburgh, 1964)
George H. Porter, *Ohio Politics During the Civil War* (New York,
    1911)
Kenneth M. Stampp, *Indiana Politics During the Civil War* (Indian-
    apolis, 1949)
William E. Parrish, *Turbulent Partnership: Missouri and the Union*
    (Columbia, Mo., 1963)

Charles R. Lee, Jr., *The Confederate Constitutions* (Chapel Hill, 1963)

Ralph Richardson, "The Choice of Jefferson Davis as Confederate President," *Journal of Mississippi History*, XVII (May 1955)

Hudson Strode, *Jefferson Davis* . . . (3 vols., New York, 1955–65)

Rudolph Von Abele, *Alexander H. Stephans* . . . (New York, 1946)

Robert W. Patrick, *Jefferson Davis and His Cabinet* (Baton Rouge, 1944)

Robert D. Meade, *Judah P. Benjamin* . . . (New York, 1943)

Ulrich B. Phillips, . . . *Robert Toombs* (New York, 1913)

Wilfred B. Yearns, *The Confederate Congress* (Athens, Ga., 1960)

Richard E. Beringer, "A Profile of the Members of the Confederate Congress," *Journal of Southern History*, XXXIII (November 1967)

Frank L. Owsley, *State Rights in the Confederacy* (Chicago, 1925)

Curtis A. Amlund, *Federalism in the Southern Confederacy* (Washington, D.C., 1966)

May S. Ringold, *The Role of the State Legislatures in the Confederacy* (Athens, Ga., 1966)

Bernard H. Nelson, "Legislative Control of the Southern Free Negro, 1861–1865," *Catholic Historical Review*, XXXII (April 1946)

David M. Potter, "Jefferson Davis and the Political Factors in Confederate Defeat," in David Donald (ed.), *Why the North Won the Civil War* (Baton Rouge, 1960)

Robert D. Little, "Southern Historians and the Downfall of the Confederacy," *Alabama Review*, IV (January 1951)

Herman Belz, *Reconstructing the Union: Theory and Policy During the Civil War* (Ithaca, N.Y., 1969)

William B. Hesseltine, *Lincoln's Plan for Reconstruction* (Chicago, 1967)

Wilbert H. Ahern, "The Cox Plan of Reconstruction: . . . Ideology and Race Relations," *Civil War History*, XVI (December 1970)

John G. Sproat, "Blueprint for Radical Reconstruction," *Journal of Southern History*, XLV (December 1958)

W. E. B. DuBois, *Black Reconstruction* . . . (New York, 1935)

John Hope Franklin, *Reconstruction* . . . (Chicago, 1961)

Kenneth M. Stampp, *The Era of Reconstruction* . . . (New York, 1965)

Rembert W. Patrick, *The Reconstruction of the Nation* (New York, 1967)

David Donald, *The Politics of Reconstruction . . .* (Baton Rouge, 1965)

Albert Castel, "Andrew Johnson: His Historiographical Rise and Fall," *Mid-America*, XLV (July 1963)

Eric L. McKitrick, *Andrew Johnson and Reconstruction* (Chicago, 1960)

LaWanda and John Cox, *Politics, Principle and Prejudice: . . . 1865–1866* (Glencoe, Ill., 1963)

W. R. Brock, *An American Crisis: Congress and Reconstruction, 1865–1867* (New York, 1963)

Michael Perman, "The South and Congress's Reconstruction Policy, 1866–1867," *Journal of American Studies*, IV (February 1971)

Theodore B. Wilson, *The Black Codes of the South* (University, Ala., 1965)

Joe M. Richardson, "The Florida Black Codes," *Florida Historical Quarterly*, XLVII (April 1969)

Martha M. Bigelow, "Public Opinion and . . . the Mississippi Black Codes," *Negro History Bulletin*, XXXIII (January 1970)

Larry Kincaid, "Victims of Circumstance: . . . Changing Attitudes Toward Republican Policy Makers and Reconstruction," *Journal of American History*, LVII (June 1970)

John G. Clark, "Historians and the Joint Committee on Reconstruction," *Historian*, XXIII (May 1961)

Richard N. Current, *Old Thad Stevens . . .* (Madison, Wisc., 1942)

Fawn M. Brodie, *Thaddeus Stevens . . .* (New York, 1959)

David Donald, *Charles Sumner and the Rights of Men* (New York, 1970)

Hans L. Trefousse, *The Radical Republicans . . .* (New York, 1968)

George R. Bentley, *A History of the Freedmen's Bureau* (Philadelphia, 1955)

William S. McFeeley, *Yankee Stepfather: General O. O. Howard and the Freedmen* (New Haven, 1968)

Jacobus TenBroek, *The Antislavery Origins of the Fourteenth Amendment* (Berkeley, 1951)

Joseph B. James, *The Framing of the Fourteenth Amendment* (Urbana, Ill., 1956)

George P. Smith, "Republican Reconstruction and Section Two of the Fourteenth Amendment," *Western Political Quarterly*, XXIII (December 1970)

Alfred H. Kelly, "The Congressional Controversy over School Segregation, 1867–1875," *American Historical Review*, LXIV (April 1959)

James E. Sefton, "The Impeachment of Johnson: A Century of Writing," *Civil War History*, XIV (June 1968)

Bertram Wyatt-Brown, "The Civil Rights Act of 1875," *Western Political Quarterly*, XVIII (December 1965)

Ronald B. Jager, "Charles Sumner . . . and the Civil Rights Act of 1875," *New England Quarterly*, XLII (September 1969)

J. David Hoeveler, Jr., "Reconstruction and the Federal Courts: The Civil Rights Act of 1875," *Historian*, XXXI (August 1969)

Charles O. Lerche, Jr., "Congressional Interpretations of the Guarantee of a Republican Form of Government . . . ," *Journal of Southern History*, XV (May 1949)

Stanley I. Kutler, *Judicial Power and Reconstruction Politics* (Chicago, 1968)

Harold M. Hyman, *Era of the Oath: Northern Loyalty Tests . . .* (Philadelphia, 1954)

David Montgomery, *Beyond Equality: Labor and the Radical Republicans . . .* (New York, 1967)

LaWanda and John H. Cox, "Negro Suffrage and Republican Politics: The Problem of Motivation in Reconstruction Historiography," *Journal of Southern History*, XXXIII (August 1967)

Charles H. Coleman, *The Election of 1868* (New York, 1933)

Leslie H. Fishel, Jr., "Northern Prejudice and Negro Suffrage, 1865–1870," *Journal of Negro History*, XXXIX (January 1954)

Glenn M. Linden, ". . . Negro Suffrage and Republican Politics," *Journal of Southern History*, XXXVI (August 1970)

Edgar A. Toppin, ". . . The Negro Suffrage Issue in Post-Bellum Ohio Politics," *Journal of Human Relations*, XI (Winter 1963)

G. Galin Berrier, "The Negro Suffrage Issue in Iowa . . . ," *Annals of Iowa*, XXXIX (Spring 1968)

Robert R. Dykstra and Harlan Hahn, "Northern Voters and Negro Suffrage: The Case of Iowa, 1868," *Public Opinion Quarterly*, XXXII (Summer 1968)

William Gilette, *The Right To Vote: Politics and the Passage of the Fifteenth Amendment* (Baltimore, 1965)

Everette Swinney, "Enforcing the Fifteenth Amendment . . . ,"
    Journal of Southern History, XXVIII (May 1962)

George R. Woolfolk, *The Cotton Regency: The Northern Merchants
    and Reconstruction . . .* (New York, 1958)
Frank B. Evans, *Pennsylvania Politics, 1872–1877 . . .* (Harrisburg,
    Pa., 1966)
Felice A. Bonadio, *North of Reconstruction: Ohio Politics, 1865–
    1870* (New York, 1970)
Richard O. Curry (ed.), *Radicalism, Racism, and Party Realign-
    ment: The Border States During Reconstruction* (Baltimore,
    1969)
Allen W. Trelease, "Who Were the Scalawags?" *Journal of Southern
    History*, XXIX (November 1963)
Jack P. Maddex, Jr., *The Virginia Conservatives, 1867–1879: A
    Study in Reconstruction Politics* (Chapel Hill, 1970)
W. McKee Evans, *Ballots and Fence Rails: Reconstruction on the
    Lower Cape Fear* (Chapel Hill, 1967)
Francis B. Simkins and Robert H. Woody, *South Carolina During
    Reconstruction* (Chapel Hill, 1947)
Olive H. Shadgett, *The Republican Party in Georgia, from Recon-
    struction through 1900* (Athens, Ga., 1964)
Elizabeth S. Nathans, *Losing the Peace: Georgia Republicans and
    Reconstruction . . .* (Baton Rouge, 1968)
David Donald, "The Scalawag in Mississippi Reconstruction," *Journal
    of Southern History*, X (November 1944)
William C. Harris, "A Reconsideration of the Mississippi Scalawag,"
    Journal of Mississippi History, XXXII (February 1970)
Howard A. White, *The Freedmen's Bureau in Louisiana* (Baton
    Rouge, 1970)
W. C. Nunn, *Texas Under the Carpetbaggers* (Austin, 1962)
Thomas B. Alexander, *Political Reconstruction in Tennessee* (Nash-
    ville, Tenn., 1950)

Robert Cruden, *The Negro in Reconstruction* (Englewood Cliffs,
    N.J., 1969)
Samuel D. Smith, *The Negro in Congress, 1870–1901* (Chapel Hill,
    1940)
Alrutheus A. Taylor, *The Negro in the Reconstruction of Virginia*
    (Washington, D.C., 1926)
Joel Williamson, *After Slavery: The Negro in South Carolina During
    Reconstruction . . .* (Chapel Hill, 1965)

Okon Edet Uya, *From Slavery to Public Service: Robert Smalls* . . .
(New York, 1971)

Edward F. Sweat, "Francis L. Cardozo: . . . Integrity in Reconstruction Politics," *Journal of Negro History*, XLVI (October 1961)

E. Merton Coulter, *Negro Legislators in Georgia During the Reconstruction Period* (Athens, Ga., 1968)

Joe M. Richardson, *The Negro in the Reconstruction of Florida* . . .
(Tallahassee, 1965)

Vernon L. Wharton, *The Negro in Mississippi, 1865–1877* (Chapel Hill, 1947)

Melvin I. Urofsky, "Blanche K. Bruce: United States Senator, 1875–1881," *Journal of Mississippi History*, XXIX (May 1967)

John Hope Franklin (ed.), . . . *The Autobiography of John Roy Lynch* (Chicago, 1970)

Charles Vincent, "Negro Leadership and Programs in the Louisiana Constitutional Convention of 1868," *Louisiana History*, X (Fall 1969)

Agnes S. Grosz, "The Political Career of P. B. S. Pinchback," *Louisiana Historical Quarterly* (April 1944)

Alrutheus A. Taylor, *The Negro in Tennessee, 1865–1880* (Washington, D.C., 1944)

William B. Hesseltine, "Economic Factors in the Abandonment of Reconstruction," *Mississippi Valley Historical Review*, XXII (September 1935)

Patrick W. Riddleberger, "The Radicals' Abandonment of the Negro During Reconstruction," *Journal of Negro History*, XLV (April 1960)

Alfred B. Williams, *Hampton and His Red Shirts: South Carolina's Deliverance in 1876* (Charleston, 1935)

Garnie W. McGinty, *Louisiana Redeemed: The Overthrow of Carpetbag Rule, 1876–1880* (New Orleans, 1941)

C. Vann Woodward, *Reunion and Reaction: The Compromise of 1877* . . . (2nd edition, Garden City, N.Y., 1956)

Vincent P. DeSantis, *Republicans Face the Southern Question* . . .
(Baltimore, 1959)

Stanley P. Hirshon, *Farewell to the Bloody Shirt: Northern Republicans and the Southern Negro* . . . (Bloomington, Ind., 1962)

II   *The Gilded Age, 1877–1892*

John A. Garraty, *The New Commonwealth, 1877–1890* (New York, 1968)

Robert H. Wiebe, *The Search for Order: 1877–1920* (New York, 1967)

Fred A. Shannon, *The Centennial Years* . . . (Garden City, N.Y., 1967)

Leonard D. White, *The Republican Era: 1869–1901* (New York, 1958)

H. Wayne Morgan, *From Hayes to McKinley* . . . (Syracuse, N.Y., 1969)

Matthew Josephson, *The Politicos: 1865–1896* (New York, 1938)

Albert V. House, "Republicans and Democrats Search for New Identities, 1870–1890," *Review of Politics*, XXXI (October 1969)

David J. Rothman, *Politics and Power: The United States Senate, 1869–1901* (Cambridge, Mass., 1966)

Irwin Unger, *The Greenback Era: A Social and Political History of American Finance, 1865–1879* (Princeton, 1964)

Allen Weinstein, *Prelude to Populism: Origins of the Silver Issue, 1867–1878* (New Haven, 1970)

Walter T. K. Nugent, *Money and American Society, 1865–1900* (New York, 1968)

F. W. Taussig, *The Tariff History of the United States* (8th edition, New York, 1931)

Mary R. Dearing, *Veterans in Politics: The Story of the G. A. R.* (Baton Rouge, 1952)

H. Wayne Morgan (ed.), *The Gilded Age* . . . (2nd edition, Syracuse, N.Y., 1968)

Paul Kleppner, *The Cross of Culture: A Social Analysis of Midwestern Politics, 1850–1900* (New York, 1970)

Richard Jensen, "The Religious and Occupational Roots of Party Identification: Illinois and Indiana in the 1870's," *Civil War History*, XVI (December 1970)

C. Vann Woodward, *Origins of the New South, 1877–1913* (Baton Rouge, 1951)

William I. Hair, *Bourbonism and Agrarian Protest: Louisiana Politics, 1877–1900* (Baton Rouge, 1969)

Joy J. Jackson, *New Orleans* . . . *Politics and Urban Progress, 1880–1896* (Baton Rouge, 1969)

Robert D. Marcus, *Grand Old Party: Political Structure in the Gilded Age* (New York, 1971)

Harry Barnard, *Rutherford B. Hayes and His America* (Indianapolis, 1964)

R. G. Caldwell, *James A. Garfield: Party Chieftain* (New York, 1931)

George F. Howe, *Chester A. Arthur* (New York, 1934)

Harry J. Sievers, *Benjamin Harrison* . . . (3 vols., Chicago and New York, 1952–68)

William G. Eidson, "Who Were the Stalwarts?" *Mid-America*, LII (October 1970)

L. L. Sage, *William Boyd Allison: A Leader in Practical Politics* (Iowa City, 1956)

David S. Muzzey, *James G. Blaine* . . . (New York, 1934)

Leon B. Richardson, *William E. Chandler, Republican* (New York, 1940)

David M. Jordan, *Roscoe Conkling of New York* . . . (Ithaca, N.Y., 1971)

J. W. Neilson, *Shelby M. Cullom: Prairie State Republican* (Urbana, Ill., 1962)

Richard E. Welch, Jr., *George Frisbie Hoar and the Half-Breed Republicans* (Cambridge, Mass., 1971)

Mark D. Hirsch, *William C. Whitney: Modern Warwick* (New York, 1948)

Allan Nevins, *Grover Cleveland: A Study in Courage* (New York, 1932)

Horace Samuel Merrill, *Bourbon Leader: Grover Cleveland* . . . (Boston, 1957)

Alexander C. Flick, *Samuel Jones Tilden* . . . (New York, 1939)

David Lindsey, *"Sunset" Cox: Irrepressible Democrat* (Detroit, 1959)

John R. Lambert, *Arthur Pue Gorman* (Baton Rouge, 1953)

Festus P. Summers, *William L. Wilson and Tariff Reform* (New Brunswick, N.J., 1953)

Geoffrey Blodgett, *The Gentle Reformers: Massachusetts Democracy in the Cleveland Era* (Cambridge, Mass., 1966)

Gerald W. McFarland, "The Breakdown of Deadlock: The Cleveland Democracy in Connecticut . . . ," *The Historian*, XXXI (May 1969)

Alexander B. Callow, Jr., *The Tweed Ring* (New York, 1966)

Horace Samuel Merrill, *Bourbon Democracy of the Middle West, 1865–1896* (Baton Rouge, 1953)

Joseph F. Wall, *Henry Watterson, Reconstructed Rebel* (New York, 1956)

Leslie E. Decker, *Railroads, Lands, and Politics* . . . (Providence, 1964)

Lee Benson, *Merchants, Farmers, and Railroads: Railroad Regulation and New York Politics, 1850–1887* (Cambridge, Mass., 1955)

Stanley P. Hirshon, *Grenville M. Dodge: Soldier, Politician, Railroad Pioneer* (Bloomington, Ind., 1967)

Joseph F. Wall, *Andrew Carnegie* (New York, 1970)

Robert G. McCloskey, *American Conservatism in the Age of Enterprise* (Cambridge, Mass., 1951)

Sidney Fine, *Laissez-Faire and the General Welfare State* . . . 1865–1901 (Ann Arbor, 1956)

Richard Hofstadter, *Social Darwinism in American Thought* (rev. edition, Boston, 1955)

John G Sproat, *"The Best Men": Liberal Reformers in the Gilded Age* (New York, 1968)

Karel D. Bicha, "A Further Reconsideration of American Populism," *Mid-America*, LII (January 1970)

George H. Knoles, "Populism and Socialism . . . 1892," *Pacific Historical Review*, XII (September 1943)

Jack Abramowitz, "The Negro in the Populist Movement," *Journal of Negro History*, XXXVIII (July 1953)

R. V. Scott, *The Agrarian Movement in Illinois* . . . (Urbana, Ill., 1962)

Martin Ridge, *Ignatius Donnelly* . . . (Chicago, 1962)

Frederick E. Haynes, *James Baird Weaver* (Iowa City, 1919)

Walter T. K. Nugent, *The Tolerant Populists: Kansas Populism and Nativism* (Chicago, 1963)

O. Gene Clanton, *Kansas Populism: Ideas and Men* (Lawrence, Kans., 1969)

David B. Griffiths, "Far Western Populism: The Case of Utah . . . ," *Utah Historical Quarterly*, XXXVII (Fall 1969)

Marion Harrington, *The Populist Movement in Oregon* (Eugene, Ore., 1940)

W. DuBose Sheldon, *Populism in the Old Dominion* (Princeton, 1935)

Stuart Noblin, *Leonidas F. Polk* . . . (Chapel Hill, 1949)

C. Vann Woodward, *Tom Watson: Agrarian Rebel* (New York, 1938)

William Warren Rogers, *The One-Gallused Rebellion: Agrarianism in Alabama, 1865–1896* (Baton Rouge, 1970)
Albert D. Kirwin, *Revolt of the Rednecks* (Lexington, Ky., 1951)
Roscoe C. Martin, *The People's Party in Texas . . .* (Austin, 1933)
Daniel M. Robison, *Bob Taylor and the Agrarian Revolt in Tennessee* (Chapel Hill, 1935)

Charlotte Erickson, *American Industry and European Immigration: 1860–1885* (Cambridge, Mass., 1957)
Thomas N. Brown, *Irish-American Nationalism, 1870–1890* (Philadelphia, 1966)
Frederick G. Leubke, *Immigrants and Politics: The Germans of Nebraska, 1880–1900* (Lincoln, Nebr., 1971)
John Higham, *Strangers in the Land: Patterns of American Nativism, 1860–1925* (rev. edition, New Brunswick, N.J., 1963)
Barbara M. Solomon, *Ancestors and Immigrants: A Changing New England Tradition* (Cambridge, Mass., 1956)
Ari Hoogenboom, *Outlawing the Spoils: . . . the Civil Service Reform Movement, 1865–1883* (Urbana, Ill., 1961)
F. W. Patton, *The Battle for Municipal Reform . . . 1875–1900* (Washington, D.C., 1940)
Arthur Mann, *Yankee Reformers in the Urban Age* (Cambridge, Mass., 1954)
Kermit Vanderbilt, *Charles Eliot Norton* (Cambridge, Mass., 1959)
Claude M. Fuess, *Carl Schurz, Reformer* (New York, 1932)
Charles A. Barker, *Henry George* (New York, 1955)

III *Ferment in the 'Nineties, 1892–1900*

Harold U. Faulkner, *Politics, Reform and Expansion: 1890–1900* (New York, 1959)
Ray Ginger, *Age of Excess . . . 1877–1914* (New York, 1965)
George H. Knoles, *The Presidential Campaign of 1892* (Stanford, Calif., 1942)

Earl W. Hayter, *The Troubled Farmer, 1850–1900* (DeKalb, Ill., 1970)
Fred A. Shannon, *The Farmer's Last Frontier . . .* (New York, 1945)
Paul W. Gates, "The Homestead Act in an Incongruous Land System," *American Historical Review*, XLI (July 1936)
Allan G. Bogue, *Money at Interest . . .* (Ithaca, N.Y., 1955)

Theodore Saloutos, "The Agricultural Problem and Nineteenth-Century Industrialism," *Agricultural History*, XXII (July 1948)

Gerald Prescott, "Wisconsin Farm Leaders . . . 1873–1900," *Agricultural History*, XLIV (April 1970)

Solon J. Buck, *The Granger Movement* (Cambridge, Mass., 1913)

John D. Hicks, *The Populist Revolt* (Minneapolis, 1931)

Norman Pollack, *The Populist Response to Industrial America . . .* (Cambridge, Mass., 1962)

C. Vann Woodward, "The Populist Heritage and the Intellectual," in *The Burden of Southern History* (Baton Rouge, 1960)

Oscar Handlin, "Reconsidering the Populists," *Agricultural History*, XXXIX (April 1965)

Theodore Saloutos, "The Professors and the Populists," *Agricultural History*, XL (October 1966)

Walter T. K. Nugent, "Some Parameters of Populism," *Agricultural History*, XL (October 1966)

Norman J. Ware, *The Labor Movement . . . 1860–1895* (New York, 1929)

Gerald N. Grob, *Workers and Utopia: . . . Ideological Conflict . . . 1865–1900* (Evanston, Ill., 1961)

Donald L. McMurry, *The Great Burlington Strike of 1888* (Cambridge, Mass., 1956)

Leon Wolff, *Lockout: . . . the Homestead Strike of 1892* (New York, 1965)

Almont Lindsey, *The Pullman Strike* (Chicago, 1942)

Gerald G. Eggert, *Railroad Labor Disputes: The Beginnings of Federal Strike Policy* (Ann Arbor, 1967)

Philip Taft, *The A.F. of L. in the Time of Gompers* (New York, 1957)

Chester M. Destler, *American Radicalism, 1865–1901* (Menasha, Wisc., 1946)

Charles Hoffman, "The Depression of the Nineties," *Journal of Economic History*, XVI (June 1956)

Samuel Reznick, "Unemployment, Unrest, and Relief . . . During the Depression of 1893–1897," *Journal of Political Economy*, LXI (August 1953)

Harry Bernard, *"Eagle Forgotten," The Life of John Peter Altgeld* (Indianapolis, 1938)

Benjamin R. Twiss, *Lawyers and the Constitution: How Laissez-Faire Came to the Supreme Court* (Princeton, 1942)

Arnold M. Paul, *Conservative Crisis and the Rule of Law . . .* (New

York, 1960)

Alan F. Westin, "The Supreme Court, The Populist Movement, and the Election of 1896," *Journal of Politics*, XV (February 1953)

J. Rogers Hollingsworth, *The Whirligig of Politics: The Democracy of Cleveland and Bryan* (Chicago, 1963)

Paolo Coletta, "Bryan Cleveland the Disrupted Democracy . . . ," *Nebraska History*, XLI (March 1960)

Robert F. Durden, *The Climax of Populism* (Lexington, Ky., 1965)

Paul W. Glad, *McKinley, Bryan and the People* (Philadelphia, 1964)

Stanley L. Jones, *The Presidential Election of 1896* (Madison, Wisc., 1964)

Gilbert C. Fite, "Republican Strategy in . . . 1896," *American Historical Review*, LXV (July 1960)

Herbert Croly, *Marcus Alonzo Hanna* (New York, 1912)

H. Wayne Morgan, *William McKinley and His America* (Syracuse, N.Y., 1963)

Paolo E. Coletta, *William Jennings Bryan* . . . Lincoln, Nebr., 1964)

James A. Barnes, "Myths of the Bryan Campaign," *Mississippi Valley Historical Review*, XXXIV (December 1947)

William Diamond, "Urban and Rural Voting in 1896," *American Historical Review*, XLVI (January 1941)

Walter LaFeber, *The New Empire* . . . *American Expansion, 1860–1898* (Ithaca, N.Y., 1963)

William A. Williams, *The Roots of the Modern American Empire* (New York, 1969)

Julius W. Pratt, *Expansionists of 1898* (Baltimore, 1936)

Margaret Leech, *In the Days of McKinley* (New York, 1959)

William A. Swanberg, *Citizen Hearst* (New York, 1961)

Robert L. Beisner, *Twelve Against Empire: The Anti-Imperialists* (New York, 1968)

David F. Healy, *The United States in Cuba, 1898–1902* (Madison Wisc., 1963)

Howard K. Beale, *Theodore Roosevelt and the Rise of America to World Power* (Baltimore, 1956)

IV   *Reforms and Repressions, 1900–1920*

Richard Hofstadter, *The Age of Reform* . . . (New York, 1955)

Samuel P. Hays, *The Response to Industrialism, 1885–1914* (Chicago, 1957)

Gabriel Kolko, *The Triumph of Conservatism . . . 1900–1916* (Glencoe, Ill., 1963)

Dewey W. Grantham, Jr., "Theodore Roosevelt in American Historical Writing . . . ," *Mid-America*, XLIII (January 1961)

George E. Mowry, *The Era of Theodore Roosevelt, 1900–1912* (New York, 1958)

Henry F. Pringle, *Theodore Roosevelt* (New York, 1931)

John M. Blum, *The Republican Roosevelt* (Cambridge, Mass., 1954)

Willard B. Gatewood, Jr., *Theodore Roosevelt and the Art of Controversy* (Baton Rouge, 1970)

Oscar Kraines, "The President versus Congress . . . 1905–1909," *Western Political Quarterly*, XXIII (March 1970)

Peter G. Filene, "An Obituary for 'The Progressive Movement,' " *American Quarterly*, XXII (Spring 1970)

Jack Tager, "Progressives, Conservatives and the Theory of the Status Revolution," *Mid-America*, XLVIII (July 1966)

David W. Noble, *The Paradox of Progressive Thought* (Minneapolis, 1958)

J. Joseph Huthmacher, "Urban Liberalism and the Age of Reform," *Mississippi Valley Historical Review*, XLIX (September 1962)

Samuel P. Hays, "The Social Analysis of American Political History, 1880–1920," *Political Science Quarterly*, LXXX (September 1965)

John D. Buenker, "Urban Liberalism and the Federal Income Tax Amendment," *Pennsylvania History*, XXXVI (April 1969)

Joseph F. Mahoney, "Women Suffrage and the Urban Masses," *New Jersey History*, LXXXVII (Autumn 1969)

Paul E. Isaac, *Prohibition and Politics: Turbulent Decades in Tennessee, 1885–1920* (Knoxville, Tenn., 1966)

Samuel P. Hays, *Conservation and the Gospel of Efficiency . . . 1890–1920* (Cambridge, Mass., 1959)

James Penick, Jr., *Progressive Politics and Conservation: The Ballinger–Pinchot Affair* (Chicago, 1968)

Oscar E. Anderson, *The Health of a Nation: Harvey W. Wiley and the Fight for Pure Food* (Chicago, 1958)

Gabriel Kolko, *Railroads and Regulation, 1877–1916* (Princeton, 1965)

Stanley P. Caine, *The Myth of a Progressive Reform: Railroad Regu-*

lation in Wisconsin, 1903–1910 (Madison, Wisc., 1970)

Robert H. Wiebe, *Businessmen and Reform: A Study of the Progressive Movement* (Cambridge, Mass., 1962)

C. C. Regier, *The Era of the Muckraker* (Chapel Hill, 1932)

David M. Chalmers, *Social and Political Ideas of the Muckrakers* (New York, 1964)

Harold S. Wilson, *McClure's Magazine and the Muckrakers* (Princeton, 1970)

Samuel P. Hays, "The Politics of Reform in Municipal Government in the Progressive Era," *Pacific Northwest Quarterly*, LV (October 1964)

Marguerite Green, *The National Civic Federation and the American Labor Movement, 1900–1925* (Washington, D.C., 1956)

Stephen B. Wood, *Constitutional Politics in the Progressive Era: Child Labor and the Law* (Chicago, 1968)

Walter I. Trattner, *Crusade for the Children: . . . the National Child Labor Committee . . .* (Chicago, 1970)

Jeremy P. Felt, *Hostages of Fortune: Child Labor Reform in New York State* (Syracuse, N.Y., 1965)

Robert H. Bremner, *From the Depths: The Discovery of Poverty . . .* (New York, 1956)

Roy Lubove, *The Progressives and the Slums . . . in New York City* (Pittsburgh, 1962)

Richard M. Abrams, *Conservatism in a Progressive Era: Massachusetts . . .* (Cambridge, Mass., 1964)

Richard B. Sherman, "The Status Revolution and Massachusetts Progressive Leadership," *Political Science Quarterly*, LXXVIII (March 1963)

Robert F. Wesser, *Charles Evans Hughes: Politics and Reform in New York, 1905–1910* (Ithaca, N.Y., 1967)

Arnold S. Rosenberg, "The New York Reformers of 1914: A Profile," *New York History*, L (April 1969)

Irwin Yellowitz, *Labor and the Progressive Movement in New York State* (New York, 1965)

Ransom E. Noble, Jr., *New Jersey Progressivism Before Wilson* (Princeton, 1946)

John D. Buenker, "Urban, New-Stock Liberalism and Progressive Reform in New Jersey," *New Jersey History*, LXXXVII (Summer 1969)

Russel B. Nye, *Midwestern Progressive Politics . . .* (East Lansing, 1951)

Hoyt L. Warner, *Progressivism in Ohio . . .* (Columbia, Ohio,

1964)

Zane L. Miller, *Boss Cox's Cincinnati: Urban Politics in the Progressive Era* (New York, 1968)

Robert M. Crunden, *A Hero in Spite of Himself: Brand Whitlock . . .* (New York, 1969)

Robert S. Maxwell, *La Follette and the Rise of the Progressives in Wisconsin* (Madison, Wisc., 1956)

David P. Thelen, "Social Tensions and the Origins of Progressivism," *Journal of American History*, LVI (September 1969)

E. Daniel Potts, "The Progressive Profile in Iowa," *Mid-America*, XLVII (October 1965)

Arthur S. Link, "The Progressive Movement in the South," *North Carolina Historical Review*, XXIII (April 1946)

Hugh C. Bailey, *Liberalism in the New South: Southern Social Reformers and the Progressive Movement* (Coral Gables, Fla., 1969)

James B. Crooks, *Politics and Progress: The Rise of Urban Progressivism in Baltimore . . .* (Baton Rouge, 1968)

William D. Miller, *Memphis During the Progressive Era . . .* (Memphis, 1957)

Sheldon Hackney, *Populism to Progressivism in Alabama* (Princeton, 1969)

William F. Holmes, *The White Chief: James Kimble Vardaman* (Baton Rouge, 1970)

George E. Mowry, *The California Progressives* (Berkeley, 1951)

John L. Shover, "The Progressives and the Working Class Vote in California," *Labor History*, X (Fall 1969)

Walton Bean, *Boss Reuf's San Francisco . . .* (Berkeley, 1952)

D. H. Leon, "Whatever Happened to an American Socialist Party? . . . the Spectrum of Interpretations," *American Quarterly*, XXIII (May 1971)

Donald Drew Egbert and Stow Persons (eds.), *Socialism and American Life* (2 vols., Princeton, 1952)

David A. Shannon, *The Socialist Party of America* (New York, 1955)

Howard H. Quint, *The Forging of American Socialism . . .* (Columbia, S.C., 1953)

Ira Kipnis, *The American Socialist Movement, 1897–1912* (New York, 1952)

Henry Bedford, *Socialism and the Workers in Massachusetts . . .* (Amherst, 1966)

Marvin Wachman, *History of the Social-Democratic Party of Mil-waukee* . . . (Urbana, Ill., 1945)

Ray Ginger, *The Bending Cross: A Biography of Eugene V. Debs* (New Brunswick, N.J., 1949)

August C. Bolino, "American Socialism's Flood and Ebb . . . ," *American Journal of Economics*, XXII (April 1963)

R. Laurence Moore, *European Socialists and the American Promised Land* (New York, 1970)

Daniel Bell, *Marxian Socialism in the United States* (Princeton, 1967)

James Weinstein, *The Decline of Socialism in America, 1912–1925* (New York, 1967)

John Laslett, *Labor and the Left* . . . *Socialist and Radical Influences* . . . (New York, 1970)

Melvyn Dubofsky, *We Shall Be All: . . . the Industrial Workers of the World* (Chicago, 1969)

Murray Seidler, *Norman Thomas, Respectable Rebel* (Syracuse, N.Y., 1961)

Horace Samuel Merrill and Marion Galbraith Merrill, *The Republican Command, 1897–1913* (Lexington, Ky., 1971)

Jerome M. Clubb and Howard W. Allen, "Party Loyalty in the Progressive Years: The Senate, 1909–1915," *Journal of Politics*, XXIX (August 1967)

Blair Bolles, *Tyrant from Illinois: Uncle Joe Cannon's Experiment with Personal Power* (New York, 1951)

William R. Gwinn, *Uncle Joe Cannon, Archfoe of Insurgency* (New York, 1957)

Kenneth W. Hechler, *Insurgency: Personalities and Policies of the Taft Era* (New York, 1940)

Laurence J. Holt, *Congressional Insurgency and the Party System, 1909–1916* (Cambridge, Mass., 1967)

Stanley D. Solvick, "William Howard Taft and the Payne-Aldrich Tariff," *Mississippi Valley Historical Review*, L (December 1963)

Claude E. Barfield, ". . . The Democratic Party, Cannonism, and the Payne-Aldrich Tariff," *Journal of American History*, LVII (September 1970)

Richard Lowitt, *George W. Norris: The Making of a Progressive* (Lexington, Ky., 1963)

George E. Mowry, *Theodore Roosevelt and the Progressive Move-*

ment (Madison, Wisc., 1947)

Norman M. Wilensky, *Conservatives in the Progressive Era: The Taft Republicans of 1912* (Gainesville, Fla., 1965)

Evans C. Johnson, "The Underwood Forces and the Democratic Nomination of 1912," *Historian*, XXXI (February 1969)

Charles Forcey, *The Crossroads of Liberalism* . . . (New York, 1961)

Arthur S. Link, *Woodrow Wilson and the Progressive Era, 1912–1917* (New York, 1954)

Richard L. Watson, Jr., "Woodrow Wilson and his Interpreters . . . ," *Mississippi Valley Historical Review*, XLIV (September 1957)

Arthur S. Link, *Wilson: The New Freedom* (Princeton, 1956)

John M. Blum, *Joe Tumulty and the Wilson Era* (Boston, 1951)

Richard M. Abrams, "Woodrow Wilson and the Southern Congressmen," *Journal of Southern History*, XXII (November 1956)

Burton I. Kaufman, "Virginia Politics and the Wilson Movement . . . ," *Virginia Magazine of History*, LXXVII (January 1969)

C. Vann Woodward, *The Strange Career of Jim Crow* (rev. edition, New York, 1964)

William A. Mabry, *Studies in the Disfranchisement of the Negro in the South* (Durham, N.C., 1933)

Margaret Law Callcott, *The Negro in Maryland Politics, 1870–1912* (Baltimore, 1969)

Charles E. Wynes, *Race Relations in Virginia, 1870–1902* (Charlottesville, 1961)

Dewey W. Grantham, "The Progressive Movement and the Negro," *South Atlantic Quarterly*, LIV (October 1955)

Seth Scheiner, "President Theodore Roosevelt and the Negro," *Journal of Negro History*, XLVII (July 1962)

Howard W. Allen *et al.*, "Political Reform and Negro Rights in the Senate, 1909–1915," *Journal of Southern History*, XXXVII (May 1971)

John B. Wiseman, "Racism in Democratic Politics, 1904–1912," *Mid-America*, LI (January 1969)

Willard H. Smith, "William Jennings Bryan and Racism," *Journal of Negro History*, LIV (April 1969)

Henry Blumenthal, "Woodrow Wilson and the Race Question," *Journal of Negro History*, XLVIII (January 1963)

Nancy J. Weiss, "The Negro and the New Freedom: Fighting Wilsonian Segregation," *Political Science Quarterly*, LXXXIV (March 1968)

Charles Flint Kellogg, *NAACP: A History of the National Association for the Advancement of Colored People*, Vol. I: 1909–1920 (Baltimore, 1967)

William E. Leuchtenberg, "Progressivism and Imperialism . . . ," *Mississippi Valley Historical Review*, XXXIX (December 1952)

Ernest R. May, *The World War and American Isolation* . . . (Cambridge, Mass., 1959)

John M. Cooper, Jr., *The Vanity of Power: American Isolationism* . . . 1914–1917 (Westport, Conn., 1969)

Howard W. Allen, "Republican Reformers and Foreign Policy, 1913–1917," *Mid-America*, XLIV (October 1962)

J. A. Thompson, "American Progressive Publicists and the First World War, 1914–1917," *Journal of American History*, LVIII (September 1971)

N. Gordon Levin, Jr., *Woodrow Wilson and World Politics* . . . (New York, 1968)

Seward W. Livermore, *Politics Is Adjourned: Woodrow Wilson and the War Congress, 1916–18* (Middletown, Conn., 1966)

Robert D. Cuff, "Woodrow Wilson and Business–Government Relations During World War I," *Review of Politics*, XXXI (July 1969)

H. C. Peterson and Gilbert Fite, *Opponents of War, 1917–18* (Seattle, 1957)

Harry N. Scheiber, *The Wilson Administration and Civil Liberties* (Ithaca, N.Y., 1960)

Donald D. Johnson, *The Challenge to American Freedoms: World War I and the . . . American Civil Liberties Union* (Lexington, Ky., 1963)

Carl Wittke, *German-Americans and the World War* (Columbus, 1936)

Arno J. Mayer, *Politics and Diplomacy of Peacemaking* . . . (New York, 1967)

Wolfgang J. Helbich, "American Liberals in the League of Nations Controversy," *Public Opinion Quarterly*, XXXI (Winter 1968)

Joseph P. O'Grady (ed.), *The Immigrants' Influence on Wilson's Peace Policies* (Lexington, Ky., 1967)

Thomas A. Bailey, *Woodrow Wilson and the Great Betrayal* (New York, 1945)

Ralph Stone, *The Irreconcilables: The Fight Against the League of Nations* (Lexington, Ky., 1970)

John A. Garraty, *Henry Cabot Lodge* . . . (New York, 1953)

Robert K. Murray, *Red Scare* . . . (Minneapolis, 1955)

Stanley Coben, "A Study in Nativism: The American Red Scare of 1919–1920," *Political Science Quarterly*, LXXIX (March 1964)

David Brody, *Labor in Crisis, The Steel Strike of 1919* (Philadelphia, 1965)

Robert L. Friedheim, *The Seattle General Strike* (Seattle, 1964)

Stanley Coben, *A Mitchell Palmer, Politician* (New York, 1963)

Fred D. Ragan, "Justice . . . Holmes . . . and the Clear and Present Danger Test . . . 1919," *Journal of American History*, LVIII (June 1971)

Zechariah Chafee, Jr., *Free Speech in the United States* (Cambridge, Mass., 1941)

Samuel J. Konefsky, *The Legacy of Holmes and Brandeis* . . . (New York, 1956)

V   *The Abnormal 'Twenties, 1920–1932*

Burl Noeggle, "The Twenties: A New Historigraphical Frontier," *Journal of American History*, LIII (September, 1966)

Henry May, "Shifting Perspectives on the 1920's," *Mississippi Valley Historical Review*, XLIII (December 1956)

Don S. Kirschner, "Conflicts and Politics in the 1920's: Historiography and Prospects," *Mid-America*, XLVIII (October 1966)

William E. Leuchtenberg, *The Perils of Prosperity* . . . (Chicago, 1958)

Karl Schriftgiesser, *This Was Normalcy:* . . . 1920–1932 (Boston, 1948)

John D. Hicks, *Republican Ascendancy* . . . (New York, 1960)

Wesley M. Bagby, *The Road to Normalcy* (Baltimore, 1962)

Gary W. Reichard, "The Aberration of 1920: An Analysis of Harding's Victory in Tennessee," *Journal of Southern History*, XXXVI (February 1970)

Donald C. Swain, *Federal Conservation Policy, 1921–1933* (Berkeley, 1963)

Burl Noggle, *Teapot Dome: Oil and Politics in the 1920's* (Baton

Rouge, 1962)

J. Leonard Bates, "The Teapot Dome Scandal and the Election of 1924," *American Historical Review*, LX (January 1955)

Kenneth C. MacKay, *The Progressive Movement in 1924* (New York, 1947)

James H. Shideler, "The La Follette Progressive Party Campaign of 1924," *Wisconsin Magazine of History*, XXXIII (June 1950)

Arthur S. Link, "What Happened to the Progressive Movement in the 1920's?" *American Historical Review*, XLIV (July 1959)

Edmund A. Moore, *A Catholic Runs for President . . . 1928* (New York, 1956)

Ruth C. Silva, *Rum, Religion, and Votes: 1928 Re-examined* (University Park, Pa., 1962)

Paul A. Carter, "The Campaign of 1928 Re-examined . . . ," *Wisconsin Magazine of History*, XLVI (Summer 1963)

Jerome M. Clubb and Howard W. Allen, "The Cities and the Election of 1928: Partisan Realignment?" *American Historical Review*, LXXIV (April 1969)

Andrew Sinclair, *The Available Man: The Life Behind the Masks of Warren G. Harding* (New York, 1965)

Robert K. Murray, *The Harding Era: Warren G. Harding and His Administration* (Minneapolis, 1969)

William A. White, *A Puritan in Babylon: The Story of Calvin Coolidge* (New York, 1939)

Donald R. McCoy, *Calvin Coolidge* (New York, 1967)

David Burner, *The Politics of Provincialism: The Democratic Party in Transition, 1918–1932* (New York, 1968)

Lawrence W. Levine, *Defender of the Faith, William Jennings Bryan . . . 1915–1925* (New York, 1965)

Lee N. Allen, "The McAdoo Campaign . . . in 1924," *Journal of Southern History*, XXIX (May 1963)

Oscar Handlin, *Al Smith and His America* (Boston, 1958)

Howard Zinn, *La Guardia in Congress* (Ithaca, N.Y., 1959)

Bernard Bellush, *Franklin D. Roosevelt as Governor of New York* (New York, 1955)

Alex Gottfried, *Boss Cermak of Chicago* (Seattle, 1962)

Elmer L. Puryear, *Democratic Party Dissension in North Carolina, 1928–1936* (Chapel Hill, 1962)

Franklin D. Mitchell, *Embattled Democracy: Missouri Democratic*

Politics, 1919–1932 (Columbia, Mo., 1968)

John W. Prothro, *Dollar Decade: Business Ideas in the 1920's* (Baton Rouge, 1954)

Otis Pease, *The Responsibilities of American Advertising . . . 1920–1940* (New Haven, 1958)

Keith Sward, *The Legend of Henry Ford* (New York, 1948)

Allan Nevins and Frank E. Hill, *Ford, The Times, The Man, The Company* (3 vols., New York, 1954–1963)

Joseph Brandes, *Herbert Hoover and Economic Diplomacy: Department of Commerce Policy, 1921–1928* (Pittsburgh, 1962)

Paul W. Glad, "Progressive and the Business Culture of the 1920's," *Journal of American History*, LIII (June 1966)

George B. Tindall, "Business Progressivism: Southern Politics in the Twenties," *South Atlantic Quarterly*, LXII (Winter 1963)

Theodore Saloutos and John D. Hicks, *Agricultural Discontent in the Middle West, 1900–1939* (Madison, Wisc., 1951)

James H. Shideler, *Farm Crisis, 1919–1923* (Berkeley, 1957)

Robert L. Morlan, *Political Prairie Fire: The Nonpartisan League, 1915–1922* (Minneapolis, 1955)

Donald L. Winters, *Henry Cantwell Wallace as Secretary of Agriculture, 1921–1924* (Urbana, Ill., 1970)

Gilbert C. Fite, *George N. Peek and the Fight for Farm Parity* (Norman, Okla., 1954)

William D. Rowley, *M. L. Wilson and the Campaign for Domestic Allotment* (Lincoln, Nebr., 1970)

Gilbert C. Fite, "The Agricultural Issue in . . . 1928," *Mississippi Valley Historical Review*, XXXVII (March 1951)

Don S. Kirschner, *City and County: Rural Responses to Urbanization in the 1920's* (Westport, Conn., 1970)

J. Joseph Huthmacher, *Massachusetts People and Politics, 1919–1933* (Cambridge, Mass., 1959)

John M. Allswang, *A House for All Peoples: Ethnic Politics in Chicago, 1890–1936* (Lexington, Ky., 1971)

Irving Bernstein, *The Lean Years: . . . the American Worker, 1920–1933* (Boston, 1960)

David Brody, *Steelworkers in America: The Nonunion Era* (Cambridge, Mass., 1960)

Robert H. Zieger, *Republicans and Labor, 1919–1929* (Lexington,

Ky., 1969)

Paul A. Carter, *The Twenties in America* (New York, 1968)
Norman F. Furniss, *The Fundamentalist Controversy, 1918–1931* (New Haven, 1954)
Paul A. Carter, *The Decline and Revival of the Social Gospel . . . 1920–1940* (Ithaca, N.Y., 1956)
Ray Ginger, *Six Days or Forever? Tennessee v. John Thomas Scopes* (Boston, 1958)
Charles Merz, *The Dry Decade* (Garden City, N.Y., 1931)
Andrew Sinclair, *Prohibition: The Era of Excess* (New York, 1962)
Anne Firor Scott, "After Suffrage: Southern Women in the Twenties," *Journal of Southern History*, XXX (August 1964)
Paul L. Murphy, "Sources and Nature of Intolerance in the 1920's," *Journal of American History*, LI (June 1964)
William Preston, Jr., *Aliens and Dissenters: Federal Suppression of Radicals, 1903–1933* (Cambridge, Mass., 1963)
Francis Russell, *Tragedy in Dedham: . . . the Sacco-Vanzetti Case* (New York, 1962)

David M. Chalmers, *Hooded Americanism: . . . the Ku Klux Klan* (rev. edition, Chicago, 1968)
Kenneth T. Jackson, *The Ku Klux Klan in the City,. 1915–1930* (New York, 1967)
Emerson Loucks, *The Ku Klux Klan in Pennsylvania* (Harrisburg, Pa., 1936)
Charles C. Alexander, *The Ku Klux Klan in the Southwest* (Lexington, Ky., 1965)
E. David Cronon, *Black Moses: The Story of Marcus Garvey . . .* (Madison, Wisc., 1955)
Richard B. Sherman, "The Harding Administration and the Negro . . . ," *Journal of Negro History*, XLIX (July 1964)
John L. Blair, ". . . The Negro During the Coolidge Years," *Journal of American Studies*, III (December 1969)

Dewey W. Granthtam, Jr., "Recent American History and the Great Depression," *Texas Quarterly*, VI (Winter 1963)
Harris Gaylord Warren, *Herbert Hoover and the Great Depression* (New York, 1959)
Albert U. Romasco, *The Poverty of Abundance: Hoover the Nation, the Depression* (New York, 1965)

Carl N. Degler, "The Ordeal of Herbert Hoover," *Yale Review*, LII (Summer 1963)

Jordan A. Schwartz, *The Interregnum of Despair: Hoover, Congress, and the Depression* (Urbana, Ill., 1970)

VI   *The New Deal, 1932–1945*

Otis L. Graham, Jr., "Historians and the New Deals . . . ," *Social Studies*, LIV (April 1963)

Richard S. Kirkendall, "The New Deal as Watershed: The Recent Literature," *Journal of American History*, LIV (March 1968)

Jerold S. Auerbach, "New Deal, Old Deal, or Raw Deal: Some Thoughts on New Left Historiography," *Journal of Southern History*, XXXV (February 1969)

Basil Rauch, *History of the New Deal* (New York, 1944)

Denis W. Brogan, *The Era of Franklin D. Roosevelt* . . . (New Haven, 1950)

Edgar E. Robinson, *The Roosevelt Leadership* . . . (Philadelphia, 1955)

Dexter Perkins, *The New Age of Franklin Roosevelt* . . . (Chicago, 1957)

Arthur M. Schlesinger, Jr., *The Age of Roosevelt* . . . (3 vols. to date, Boston, 1957–)

William E. Leuchtenberg, *Franklin D. Roosevelt and the New Deal* . . . (New York, 1963)

Paul Conkin, *The New Deal* (New York, 1967)

William E. Leuchtenberg, "The New Deal and the Analogue of War," in John Braeman (ed.), *Change and Continuity in 20th Century America* (Columbus, 1964)

Arthur A. Ekirch, Jr., *Ideologies and Utopias: The Impact of the New Deal on American Thought* (Chicago, 1969)

Clarke A. Chambers, "FDR, Pragmatist-Idealist: An Essay in Historiography," *Pacific Northwest Quarterly*, LII (April 1961)

Frank Freidel, *Franklin D. Roosevelt* . . . (3 vols. to date, Boston, 1952–)

James McGregor Burns, *Roosevelt: The Lion and the Fox* (New York, 1956)

Rexford G. Tugwell, *The Democratic Roosevelt* . . . (Garden City, N.Y., 1957)

Harold F. Gosnell, *Champion Campaigner: Franklin D. Roosevelt* (New York, 1952)

Alfred B. Rollins, Jr., *Roosevelt and Howe* (New York, 1962)

James A. Farley, *Jim Farley's Story* . . . (New York, 1948)

Rexford G. Tugwell, *The Brains Trust* (New York, 1968)

Raymond Moley, *The First New Deal* (New York, 1966)

Bernard Sternsher, *Rexford Tugwell and the New Deal* (New Brunswick, N.J., 1964)

Hugh S. Johnson, *The Blue Eagle—from Egg to Earth* [NRA] (Garden City, N.Y., 1935)

Sidney Fine, *The Automobile Under the Blue Eagle: Labor, Management and the Automobile Manufacturing Code* (Ann Arbor, 1963)

Thomas E. Vadney, *The Wayward Liberal: A Political Biography of Donald Richberg* (Lexington, Ky., 1970)

Cedric B. Cowing, *Populists, Plungers, and Progressives: . . . Stock and Commodity Speculation, 1890–1936* (Princeton, 1965)

Michael E. Parrish, *Securities Regulation and the New Deal* (New Haven, 1970)

Ralph F. DeBedts, *The New Deal's SEC . . .* (New York, 1964)

Ellis W. Hawley, *The New Deal and the Problem of Monopoly . . .* (Princeton, 1966)

C. Herman Pritchett, *The Tennessee Valley Authority . . .* (Chapel Hill, 1943)

Thomas K. McCraw, *TVA and the Power Fight, 1933–1939* (Chicago, 1971)

Charles O. Jackson, *Food and Drug Legislation in the New Deal* (Princeton, 1970)

Barry D. Karl, *Executive Reorganization and Reform in the New Deal* (Cambridge, Mass., 1963)

Josephine C. Brown, *Public Relief, 1929–1939* (New York, 1940)

Searle F. Charles, *Minister of Relief: Harry Hopkins and the Depression* (Syracuse, N.Y., 1963)

Roy Lubove, *The Struggle for Social Security, 1900–1935* (Cambridge, Mass., 1968)

Edwin E. Witte, *The Development of the Social Security Act* (Madison, Wisc., 1962)

Arthur J. Altmeyer, *The Formative Years of Social Security* (Madison, Wisc., 1966)

Paul K. Conkin, *Tomorrow a New World: The New Deal Community Program* (Ithaca, N.Y., 1959)

Jane DeHart Mathews, *The Federal Theatre, 1935–1939: Plays, Relief, and Politics* (Princeton, 1967)

Raymond Wolters, *Negroes and the Great Depression . . .* (Westport, Conn., 1970)

Leslie H. Fishel, Jr., "The Negro in the New Deal," *Wisconsin Magazine of History*, XLVIII (Winter 1964–65)

Rita Werner Gordon, "The Change in the Political Alignment of Chicago's Negroes During the New Deal," *Journal of American History*, LVI (December 1969)

Van L. Perkins, *Crisis in Agriculture: The AAA and the New Deal* (Berkeley, 1969)

Richard S. Kirkendall, *Social Scientists and Farm Politics in the Age of Roosevelt* (Columbia, Mo., 1966)

John A. Crampton, *The National Farmers Union: Ideology of a Pressure Group* (Lincoln, Nebr., 1965)

John L. Shover, *Cornbelt Rebellion: The Farmers' Holiday Association* (Urbana, Ill., 1965)

David E. Conrad, *Forgotten Farmers: . . . Sharecroppers and the New Deal* (Urbana, Ill., 1965)

Louis Cantor, *A Prologue to the Protest Movement: The Missouri Sharecropper Roadside Demonstration of 1939* (Durham, N.C., 1969)

Donald McCoy, *Angry Voices: Left-of-Center Politics in the New Deal Era* (Lawrence, Kans., 1958)

David H. Bennett, *Demagogues in the Depression* (New Brunswick, N.J., 1969)

Charles J. Tull, *Father Coughlin and the New Deal* (Syracuse, N.Y., 1965)

Abraham Holtzman, *The Townsend Movement: A Political Study* (New York, 1963)

T. Harry Williams, *Huey Long* (New York, 1970)

Frederick Rudolph, "The American Liberty League, 1934–1940," *American Historical Review*, LVI (October 1950)

George Wolfskill, *The Revolt of the Conservatives: . . . The American Liberty League . . .* (Boston, 1962)

Richard Polenberg, "The National Committee To Uphold Constitutional Government," *Journal of American History*, LII (December 1965)

Otis L. Graham, Jr., *An Encore for Reform: The Old Progressives and the New Deal* (New York, 1967)

James T. Patterson, *Congressional Conservatism and the New Deal . . .* (Lexington, Ky., 1967)

Robert H. Jackson, *The Struggle for Judicial Supremacy* . . . (New York, 1941)

Leonard Baker, *Back to Back: The Duel Between FDR and the Supreme Court* (New York, 1967)

William E. Leuchtenberg, "Roosevelt's Supreme Court 'Packing' Plan," in H. M. Hollingsworth (ed.) *Essays on the New Deal* (Austin, 1969)

Richard C. Cortner, *The Wagner Act Cases* (Knoxville, Tenn., 1964)

Richard C. Cortner, *The Jones and Laughlin Case* (New York, 1970)

Charles A. Leonard, *A Search for Judicial Philosophy: Mr. Justice Roberts and the Constitutional Revolution of 1937* (Port Washington, N.Y., 1971)

Samuel Hendel, *Charles Evans Hughes and the Supreme Court* (New York, 1951)

Alpheus T. Mason, *Harlan Fiske Stone* . . . (New York, 1956)

C. Herman Pritchett, *The Roosevelt Court* . . . *1937–1947* (New York, 1948)

Irving Bernstein, *Turbulent Years: the American Worker, 1933– 1941* (Boston, 1970)

J. O. Morris, *Conflict Within the AFL* . . . *1901–1936* (Ithaca, N.Y., 1958)

Walter Galenson, *The CIO Challenge to the AFL* . . . *1935–1941* (Cambridge, Mass., 1960)

Saul Alinsky, *John L. Lewis* (New York, 1949)

Matthew Josephson, *Sidney Hillman* . . . (Garden City, N.Y., 1952)

Milton Derber and Edwin Young (eds.), *Labor and the New Deal* (Madison, Wisc., 1957)

Irving Bernstein, *The New Deal Collective Bargaining Policy* (Berkeley, 1950)

Jerold S. Auerbach, *Labor and Liberty: The La Follette Committee and the New Deal* (Indianapolis, 1966)

Sidney Fine, *Sit-down: The General Motors Strike of 1936–37* (Ann Arbor, 1969)

Donald H. Grubbs, *Cry from the Cotton: The Southern Tenant Farmers' Union and the New Deal* (Chapel Hill, 1970)

James T. Patterson, *The New Deal and the States* . . . (Princeton, 1969)

J. Joseph Huthmacher, *Senator Robert F. Wagner* . . . (New York, 1968)

Allan Nevins, *Herbert H. Lehman . . .* (New York, 1963)

Frank Freidel, *F. D. R. and the South* (Baton Rouge, 1965)

Joseph L. Morrison, *Governor O. Max Gardner: A Power in North
    Carolina and New Deal Washington* (Chapel Hill, 1970)

Allan P. Sindler, *Huey Long's Louisiana: State Politics, 1920–1952*
    (Baltimore, 1956)

Richard B. Henderson, *Maury Maverick: A Political Biography* (Austin, 1970)

Leonard Arrington, "The New Deal in the West," *Pacific Historical
    Review*, XXXVIII (August 1969)

Michael P. Malone, *C. Ben Ross and the New Deal in Idaho* (Seattle,
    1970)

T. A. Larson, "The New Deal in Wyoming," *Pacific Historical Review*, XXXVIII (August 1969)

Robert E. Burke, *Olson's New Deal for California* (Berkeley, 1953)

Thomas Mathews, *Puerto Rican Politics and the New Deal* (Gainesville, Fla., 1960)

Arthur Mann, *La Guardia Comes to Power: 1933* (Philadelphia,
    1965)

William J. McKenna, "The Negro Vote in Philadelphia Elections,"
    Pennsylvania History, XXXII (October 1965)

Bruce M. Stave, *The New Deal and the Last Hurrah: Pittsburgh Machine Politics* (Pittsburgh, 1970)

Lloyd Wendt and Herman Kogan, *Big Bill of Chicago* (Indianapolis,
    1953)

Lyle W. Dorsett, *The Pendergast Machine* (New York, 1968)

A. Theodore Brown, *The Politics of Reform: Kansas City's Municipal
    Government, 1925–1950* (Kansas City, 1958)

Donald R. McCoy, *Landon of Kansas* (Lincoln, Nebr., 1966)

Milton Plesur, "The Republican Congressional Comeback of 1938,"
    Review of Politics, XXIV (October 1962)

Donald B. Johnson, *The Republican Party and Wendell Willkie*
    (Urbana, Ill., 1960)

Harry Barnard, *Independent Man: . . . Senator James Couzens* (New
    York, 1958)

Selig Adler, *The Isolationist Impulse* (New York, 1957)

Manfred Jonas, *Isolationism in America, 1935–1941* (Ithaca, N.Y.,
    1966)

John E. Wiltz, *In Search of Peace: The Senate Munitions Inquiry* . . . (Baton Rouge, 1963)

Wayne S. Cole, *America First: The Battle Against Intervention* . . . (Madison, Wisc., 1953)

Richard W. Steele, "Preparing the Public for War: Efforts To Establish a National Propaganda Agency, 1940–41," *American Historical Review*, LXXV (October 1970)

Mark Chadwin, *Hawks of World War II* (Chapel Hill, 1968)

James M. Burns, *Roosevelt: The Soldier of Freedom* (New York, 1970)

Robert E. Sherwood, *Roosevelt and Hopkins* . . . (New York, 1948)

H. Bradford Westerfield, *Foreign Policy and Party Politics: Pearl Harbor to Korea* (New Haven, 1955)

Edward S. Corwin, *Total War and the Constitution* (New York, 1947)

Eugene V. Rostow, "The Japanese American Cases—A Disaster," *Yale Law Journal*, LIV (June 1945)

Morton Grodzins, *Americans Betrayed: Politics and the Japanese Evacuation* (Chicago, 1949)

Jacobus tenBroek *et al.*, *Prejudice, War, and the Constitution* . . . (Berkeley, 1954)

Joel Seidman, *American Labor from Defense to Reconversion* (Chicago, 1953)

Alonzo L. Hambly, "Sixty Million Jobs . . . : The Liberals, The New Deal, and World War II," *Historian*, XXX (August 1968)

Davis R. B. Ross, *Preparing for Ulysses: Politics and Veterans During World War II* (New York, 1969)

Elias Huzar, *The Purse and the Sword: Control of the Army by Congress* . . . 1933–1950 (Ithaca, N.Y., 1950)

Donald H. Riddle, *The Truman Committee* . . . (New Brunswick, N.J., 1964)

Roland Young, *Congressional Politics in the Second World War* (New York, 1956)

John R. Moore, "The Conservative Coalition in the United States Senate, 1942–1945," *Journal of Southern History*, XXXIII (August 1967)

Donald R. McCoy, "Republican Opposition During Wartime . . . ," *Mid-America*, XLIX (July 1967)

VII   *The Search for Equilibrium, 1945–1960*

Cabell Phillips, *The Truman Presidency* . . . (New York, 1966)

Barton J. Bernstein (ed.), *Politics and Policies of the Truman Administration* (Chicago, 1970)

Alfred Steinberg, *The Man from Missouri* (New York, 1962)

Allen J. Matusow, *Farm Policies and Politics in the Truman Years* (Cambridge, Mass., 1967)

Richard O. Davies, *Housing Reform During the Truman Administration* (Columbia, Mo., 1966)

Richard E. Neustadt, "Congress and the Fair Deal . . . ," *Public Policy*, V (1954)

Susan M. Hartmann, *Truman and the 80th Congress* (Columbia, Mo., 1971)

Clifton Brock, *Americans for Democratic Action: Its Role in National Politics* (Washington, D.C., 1962)

William C. Berman, *The Politics of Civil Rights in the Truman Administration* (Columbus, 1970)

Richard M. Dalfiume, *Desegregation of the U.S. Armed Forces* . . . (Columbia, Mo., 1969)

Louis Ruchames, *Race, Jobs, and Politics: The Story of FEPC* (New York, 1953)

Robert A. Garson, "The Alienation of the South: A Crisis for Harry S Truman . . . ," *Missouri Historical Review*, LXIV (July 1970)

John M. Redding, *Inside the Democratic Party* (Indianapolis, 1958)

Irwin Ross, *The Lonliest Campaign* . . . (New York, 1968)

Karl Schmidt, *Henry A. Wallace, Quixotic Crusade, 1948* (Syracuse, N.Y., 1960)

Athan G. Theoharis, *The Yalta Myths: An Issue in U.S. Politics, 1945–1955* (Columbia, Mo., 1969)

Harold L. Hitchens, "Influences on the Congressional Decision To Pass the Marshall Plan," *Western Political Quarterly*, XXI (March 1968)

Annette B. Fox, "NATO and Congress," *Political Science Quarterly*, LXXX (September 1965)

Earl Latham, *The Communist Controversy in Washington* (Cambridge, Mass., 1966)

A Selected Modern Bibliography

Walter Goodman, *The Committee: . . . the House Committee on Un-American Activities* (New York, 1964)

Eleanor Bontecou, *The Federal Loyalty-Security Program* (Ithaca, N.Y., 1953)

Alan D. Harper, *The Politics of Loyalty: The White House and the Communist Issue, 1946–1952* (Westport, Conn., 1969)

C. Herman Pritchett, *Civil Liberties and the Vinson Court* (Chicago, 1954)

Alan Schaffer, *Vito Marcantonio, Radical in Congress* (Syracuse, N.Y., 1966)

Ronald J. Caridi, *The Korean War and American Politics* (Philadelphia, 1968)

Richard H. Rovere, *Senator Joe McCarthy* (New York, 1959)

Robert Griffith, *The Politics of Fear: Joseph R. McCarthy and the Senate* (Lexington, Ky., 1970)

Michael Paul Rogin, *The Intellectuals and McCarthy . . .* (Cambridge, Mass., 1967)

Richard H. Rovere, *Affairs of State: The Eisenhower Years* (New York, 1956)

Emmet John Hughes, *The Ordeal of Power: A Political Memoir of the Eisenhower Years* (New York, 1963)

Arthur Larson, *Eisenhower: The President Nobody Knows* (New York, 1968)

David A. Frier, *Conflict of Interest in the Eisenhower Administration* (Ames, Iowa, 1969)

Seymour E. Harris, *The Economics of Political Parties, with Special Reference to Presidents Eisenhower and Kennedy* (New York, 1962)

Louis Harris, *Is There a Republican Majority?* (New York, 1954)

Samuel Lubell, *Revolt of the Moderates* (New York, 1956)

Heinz Eulau, *Class and Party in the Eisenhower Years* (Stanford, Calif., 1962)

Stuart Gerry Brown, *Conscience in Politics: Adlai E. Stevenson in the 1950's* (Syracuse, N.Y., 1961)

Herbert J. Muller, *Adlai Stevenson* (New York, 1967)

James Q. Wilson, *The Amateur Democrat: Club Politics in Three Cities* (Chicago, 1962)

Jay S. Goodman, *The Democrats and Labor in Rhode Island, 1952–1962* (Providence, 1967)

Robert W. Anderson, *Party Politics in Puerto Rico* (Stanford, Calif., 1965)

Henry Lee Moon, *Balance of Power: The Negro Vote* (Garden City, N.Y., 1948)

Oscar Glantz, "The Negro Voter in Northern Industrial Cities," *Western Political Quarterly*, XIII (December 1960)

Hanes Walton, Jr., *Black Political Parties* . . . (New York, 1969)

James Q. Wilson, *Negro Politics: The Search for Leadership* (Glencoe, Ill., 1960)

Everett Carl Ladd, Jr., *Negro Political Leadership in the South* (Ithaca, N.Y., 1966)

Donald R. Matthews and James W. Prothro, *Negroes and the New Southern Politics* (New York, 1966)

Albert P. Blaustein and Clarence C. Ferguson, Jr., *Desegregation and the Law* . . . (2nd edition, New Brunswick, N.J., 1962)

Loren Miller, *The Petitioners: . . . the Supreme Court . . . and the Negro* (New York, 1966)

Numan V. Bartley, *The Rise of Massive Resistance: Race and Politics in the South During the 1950's* (Baton Rouge, 1969)

Anthony Lewis, *Portrait of a Decade: The Second American Revolution* (New York, 1964)

Alpheus T. Mason, "Understanding the Warren Court . . . ," *Political Science Quarterly*, LXXXI (December 1966)

Archibald Cox, *The Warren Court* . . . (Cambridge, Mass., 1968)

Lee Katcher, *Earl Warren: A Political Biography* (New York, 1967)

Richard C. Cortner, *The Apportionment Cases* (Knoxville, Tenn., 1971)

James A. Gazell, "One Man, One Vote: Its Long Germination," *Review of Politics*, XXIII (September 1970)

Clifford M. Lytle, *The Warren Court and Its Critics* (Tucson, 1968)

Walter F. Murphy, *Congress and the Court* [1954–59] (Chicago, 1962)

Adam C. Breckenridge, *Congress Against the Court* [1958–68] (Lincoln, Nebr., 1970)

VIII   *The Modern Distemper*, 1960

James M. Burns, *John Kennedy* (New York, 1960)

Theodore H. White, *The Making of the President, 1960* (New York, 1961)

Philip E. Converse *et al.*, "Stability and Change in 1960 . . . ,"
    American Political Science Review, LV (June 1961)

Lucy S. Dawidowicz and Leon J. Goldstein, *Politics in a Pluralist
    Democracy: A Study of Voting in the 1960 Election* (New
    York, 1963)

V. O. Key, Jr., *The Responsible Electorate: Rationality in Presidential
    Voting, 1936–1960* (Cambridge, Mass., 1966)

Hugh Sidey, *John F. Kennedy, President* (New York, 1964)

Richard E. Neustadt, "Kennedy in the Presidency . . . ," *Political
    Science Quarterly*, LXXIX (September 1964)

Amitai Etzioni, "The Kennedy Experiment," *Western Political
    Quarterly,.XX* (June 1967)

Theodore C. Sorensen, *Kennedy* (New York, 1965)

Arthur M. Schlesinger, Jr., *A Thousand Days* (Boston, 1965)

Pierre Salinger, *With Kennedy* (New York, 1966)

Edward Jay Epstein, *Inquest: The Warren Commission* . . . (New
    York, 1966)

Theodore H. White, *The Making of the President, 1964* (New York,
    1965)

Robert D. Novak, *The Agony of the G.O.P. 1964* (New York, 1965)

George F. Gilder and Bruce K. Chapman, *The Party That Lost Its
    Head* (New York, 1966)

John H. Kessel, *The Goldwater Coalition* . . . (Indianapolis, 1968)

Stephen Hess, *The Republican Establishment* (New York, 1967)

William S. White, *The Professional: Lyndon B. Johnson* (New York,
    1964)

Alfred Steinberg, *Sam Johnson's Boy* . . . (New York, 1968)

Eric F. Goldman, *The Tragedy of Lyndon Johnson* (New York,
    1969)

Edward C. Banfield, *The Unheavenly City* . . . *Our Urban Crisis*
    (Boston, 1970)

Gilbert Y. Steiner, *Social Insecurity: The Politics of Welfare* (Chi-
    cago, 1966)

Nathan Wright, *Black Power and Urban Unrest* (New York, 1967)

Benjamin Muse, *The American Negro Revolt* . . . *1963–1967*
    (Bloomington, Ind., 1968)

Jerome H. Skolnick, *The Politics of Protest* (New York, 1969)

Philip L. Geyelin, *Lyndon B. Johnson and the World* (New York, 1966)

George M. Kahin and John W. Lewis, *The United States in Vietnam* (New York, 1967)

Theodore H. White, *The Making of the President, 1968* (New York, 1969)

H. G. Nicholas, "The 1968 Presidential Elections," *Journal of American Studies*, III (July 1969)

George Christian, *The President Steps Down* . . . (New York, 1970)

Jack Newfield, *Robert Kennedy* . . . (New York, 1969)

Norman Mailer, *Miami and the Siege of Chicago* (New York, 1968)

Joe McGinnis, *The Selling of the President, 1968* (New York, 1969)

Gottfried Dietze, *America's Political Dilemma* (Baltimore, 1968)

Walter Dean Burnham, "The End of American Party Politics," *Trans-Action*, VII (December 1969)

Samuel Lubell, *The Hidden Crisis in American Politics* (New York, 1970)

Andrew Hacker, *The End of the American Era* (New York, 1970)